P9-APA-017

PUBLIC ADMINISTRATION
IN A DEMOCRATIC SOCIETY

PUBLIC
ADMINISTRATION
IN A DEMOCRATIC
SOCIETY

BY W. BROOKE GRAVES

LEGISLATIVE REFERENCE SERVICE, LIBRARY OF CONGRESS

015421

GREENWOOD PRESS, PUBLISHERS
WESTPORT, CONNECTICUT

The Library of Congress has catalogued this publication as follows:

Library of Congress Cataloging in Publication Data

Graves, William Brooke, 1899–
    Public administration in a democratic society.

    Includes bibliographies.
    1. U. S.--Politics and government. 2. Public
administration. 3. U. S.--Executive departments
--Management.
[JK421.G74 1972]   350   77-148635
ISBN 0-8371-6003-0

Copyright 1950 by D. C. Heath & Company

All rights reserved

Originally published in 1950
by D. C. Heath & Company, Boston

Reprinted with the permission
of D. C. Heath & Company

First Greenwood Reprinting 1972

Library of Congress Catalogue Card Number 77-148635

ISBN 0-8371-6003-0

Printed in the United States of America

To My Wife

HAZEL WALLACE GRAVES

PREVAILING CUSTOM seems to dictate that the author of a new book explain to his professional colleagues how he came to write it and why he felt impelled to inflict upon them another weighty tome. In deference to this custom, it may here be recorded that this book represents a culmination of approximately twenty-five years of study and experience in the field of public administration. Interest in the subject was stimulated originally at a series of round tables conducted at the Annual Meetings of the American Political Science Association by Dr. W. F. Willoughby. It is interesting now to recall that in those early days, only a dozen or so were sufficiently interested to attend. In the intervening years, interest has grown tremendously. Public administration has found an accepted place in our universities and colleges. It has acquired something of a professional status and boasts an active national society of its own with many active chapters and many hundreds of members.

The early years of my own experience were largely at the state and local level, and largely on the financial side. Later years brought an opportunity for extensive contact with administration at the Federal level, particularly with regard to personnel but involving also questions of management in many offices and installations in the field establishments of different departments and agencies. The last three years have been spent in writing and research, and to some extent in administration, in the Library of Congress, in the congenial atmosphere which that institution provides for the members of its professional staff. The work of the Senior Specialists in the Legislative Reference Services gives them varied and unusual opportunities to inform themselves on many problems in the field of Federal administration.

On the basis of this long-time interest in public administration, it seemed natural enough to attempt to present a comprehensive and well integrated view of the whole field. This involved giving specific attention to a number of different considerations — in the first place, recognition of the basic concept of administration as concerned with the transaction of *all* of the public business, whether legislative, executive, or judicial; whether international, national, state, or local. It necessitated giving greater emphasis than has been given heretofore to the coordination of organization, personnel, and fiscal operations in the actual processes of management, as has been done in Part IV. Regarding the individual department or agency as the center of the administrative process, it necessitated a clearer differentiation between the problems of internal management (Part IV) and the problems of sanctions and external relations (Part V). The effort has been made throughout to be realistic in the discussion of the problems of management, presenting sufficient detail to show what the problems really are without becoming involved in the kind of technicalities that properly belong in a procedures manual rather than in a general treatise.

It called for a steady emphasis upon the fact that these problems in administration are essentially the same, regardless of governmental level — national, state, or local. The effort has been made to achieve this emphasis through the selection of illustrative materials, now from one level, now from another. And in a day in which all believers in the democratic way of life are striving for a more effective realization of its basic principles in practice, this consideration has been emphasized, not only in the subtitle of the volume but by giving special attention throughout the book to the problem of adapting democratic principles to the determination of administrative policies and procedures. Whether these aims have been realized and, if they have, whether that realization achieves the basic purpose of clarifying our thinking regarding public administration, it is for others to judge.

The literature in the field has grown to enormous proportions, and its volume is steadily increasing. Extensive use has been made of the writings of others in the fields of their specialization. To a great many of these authors, I am deeply indebted for analysis and for illustrative material. Footnote acknowledgments have been made, it is believed, in each instance. Limitations of space have made necessary the curtailment of the lists of Selected References which appear at the end of each chapter; in the course of the work, however, very extensive lists of both books and articles were developed. These are being made available for general distribution in a new Bibliography on Public Administration, issued by the Library of Congress.

The book has been written by one who, though deeply interested in the problems of administration, still regards himself primarily as a political scientist; by one who believes that public administration is no more separable from basic political science than are the problems of political parties and elections, comparative government, or political theory. He has tried to write of the problems of public administration as a political scientist sees them, describing and discussing them in simple and understandable language and with a minimum resort to that jargon which some students and practitioners of administration have seemed to think essential to the establishment of a professional status.

As must invariably be the case in such an undertaking, the author is indebted to a great many persons, not all of whom can be listed here. Among a large number of professional colleagues, I am most indebted to Willoughby, White, Pfiffner, Walker, and Marx — all of whom have done yeoman service in their attempts to organize and open up a new field of knowledge. Public officials have continued to respond generously to my numerous inquiries, and to supply copies of official documents and reports. Particularly, however, I desire to record my indebtedness to Milon L. Brown, a close associate during several years in the Third Regional Office of the United States Civil Service Commission; Frederick P. Gruenberg, Secretary, The Fels Foundation, Philadelphia; Ernest S. Griffith, Director, Legislative Reference Service, Library of Congress; and above all, to my wife, Hazel Wallace Graves, to whom this volume is dedicated.

Many years ago, Phillimore in the Preface to his *International Law* wrote that he was "anxious to express a sincere hope that others of his fellow countrymen, profiting by what may be useful, avoiding what may be erroneous, supplying what may be defective in his labors, may be by them stimulated to undertake and execute a better treatise upon the same subject." I can only hope that this volume may, in similar manner, contribute something to an understanding of public administration — a relatively new and tremendously important aspect of the study of political science.

W. BROOKE GRAVES

The Library of Congress
Washington, D.C.

TABLE OF CONTENTS

015421

PART II. PERSONNEL MANAGEMENT

PART I

ADMINISTRATIVE STRUCTURE
AND ORGANIZATION

THE EXISTING
ADMINISTRATIVE STRUCTURE

THE administrative organization of the executive branch of the Federal government began simply enough. By degrees, at first almost imperceptible, it grew in size and complexity from a very small number of administrative departments headed by secretaries with cabinet rank, until it became the tremendously large and intricate mechanism it is today. As time passed, independent commissions and establishments were also created. Finally, to the administrations, agencies, offices, and boards established during the depression and the two world wars, there were added a considerable number of government corporations until, as one writer has suggested, the Federal administrative structure came to resemble an old-fashioned farm property upon which the original homestead and barn had been supplemented by a miscellaneous assortment of structures, shacks, sheds, and lean-tos for a variety of purposes.[1]

In the states essentially the same thing happened on a smaller scale. The original state governments were composed of a limited number of constitutional departments, the heads of which were chosen by popular election. As the number and scope of state functions increased during the latter half of the nineteenth century and the first half of the twentieth, not only did the number of departments increase but the method of selecting the heads was changed from election to appointment. Large numbers of independent boards and commissions appeared, not to mention government corporations and authorities. In both the Federal government and the states, and in the local units as well, there has been for many years an urgent need for administrative reorganization to bring some semblance of order out of a chaotic situation. Progress has been made in this direction but much remains to be done.

---

[1] The number of nondepartmental agencies, as reported by the Bureau of the Budget at intervals during the past quarter of a century, has been as follows:

June 30, 1923	24
June 30, 1929	30
June 30, 1934	40
June 30, 1940	32
September 18, 1947	40

Federal Departments and Independent Establishments

The 1st Congress of the United States created in 1789 the first four executive departments in the Federal government — State, Treasury, War, and Justice. To these were added the Navy Department in 1798, the Post Office Department in 1829, the Interior Department in 1849, the Department of Agriculture in 1889, and finally the Department of Commerce and Labor in 1903. The latter was separated in 1913 into the Department of Commerce and the Department of Labor.[2] The general nature of the duties in each instance is indicated by the name. In 1947 the War and Navy Departments were united, with a new Department of the Air Force, in the National Defense Establishment, the name of which was changed in 1949 to the Department of National Defense.

The beginning of the movement for independent establishments occurred in 1887 with the Interstate Commerce Act. The commission type of organization illustrated a certain distrust of centralized authority and at the same time a recognition of a new need. Conditions in the railroad business were intolerable: service was poor, rates were high, and every type of discriminatory practice existed in the treatment both of individual shippers and of territorial areas. In this era of cutthroat competition there were actually instances in which one road conspired to cause wrecks on a competing line in order to gain an advantage. Clearly the time had come when something had to be done.[3]

Congress was hesitant about entrusting such an assignment to a single individual because the duties cut across the lines of all three branches of the government. They were primarily executive, but they were also judicial or partly judicial (called quasi-judicial) and they were legislative or partly legislative (called quasi-legislative). On the theory that there was greater wisdom in several heads than in one, Congress provided for a seven-member commission which was entrusted with wide discretionary powers in rate making and in the regulation of service and facilities.[4]

In its early years the new Commission had a difficult time. It had no precedents. The validity of its powers was attacked in the courts at every turn, and the courts were none too friendly or sympathetic. In fact, most of the decisions were adverse and made it necessary to amend the act repeatedly in order to guarantee to the Commission powers that

---

[2] The trick word, "St. Wanpiac/l," which suggests the first letter in the name of each department, will enable one to remember the original departments in the order of their creation.

[3] The facts are fully revealed in the report of the Senate Committee on Interstate Commerce, commonly referred to as the Collom Committee (Senate Reports, 49th Cong., 1st Sess., No. 46, in two parts).

[4] See Sharfman, *The Interstate Commerce Commission*.

Congress had originally intended to give it. Ultimately these amendments succeeded in firmly establishing the powers of the Commission. The record made by this body, once its authority was established, demonstrated that this form of organization could be made to function effectively in regulatory work.

After a long interval the need for this type of control became evident in many other phases of business activity. In 1914, for instance, as part of the Wilson program, the Federal Trade Commission was established with five members for the purpose of promoting fair competition in trade and commerce by preventing the misbranding and misrepresentation of articles offered for sale in interstate commerce, unlawful price fixing or price discriminatory agreements among distributors of goods or services, or other agreements among producers or distributors of goods or services not in the public interest. It was also given the duty of preventing fraudulent or deceptive advertising of merchandise.[5]

Other regulatory commissions came in rapid succession. After years of effort and repeated recommendations from members of the cabinet, Congress established the Federal Power Commission in 1920. This body issues licenses for the construction of works to develop hydroelectric power and to improve navigation at nationally owned power sites and on navigable waters. It also determines rates for electric power generated and transmitted interstate and for natural gas transported and sold interstate, controls the issuance of securities by companies engaged in such activity, and in general supplements and strengthens the regulation of utilities furnishing electric power and natural gas, as carried on by the several state utility commissions.[6]

The Federal Communications Commission provides an interesting illustration of the evolution of an agency of this type. When radio first appeared and while it was passing through the gadget stage, such regulation as existed was carried on by the states. When it became apparent that here was an important new medium of interstate commerce, the Department of Commerce attempted to regulate it. Then in 1927, as a result of some dissatisfaction and public controversy, Congress created the Federal Radio Commission. In 1934 this agency was abolished, and the new Federal Communications Commission was established in its place but with the provision that, in addition to licensing radio stations

---

[5] See Blaisdell, Thomas C., Jr., *The Federal Trade Commission* (Columbia University Press, 1932), and Henderson, Gerard C., *The Federal Trade Commission* (Yale University Press, 1925).

[6] See Baum, Robert D., *The Federal Power Commission and State Utility Regulation* (American Council on Public Affairs, Washington, 1942), and Elsbree, Hugh L., *Interstate Transmisson of Electric Power: A Study in the Conflict of Federal and State Jurisdictions* (Harvard University Press, 1931).

and operators and assigning wave lengths, it would regulate interstate and foreign communications by telephone, telegraph, and cable. The latter functions had previously been performed by the Interstate Commerce Commission.

Nearly all the independent regulatory commissions are concerned with commerce and mostly with utility regulation. Another of this type is the Securities and Exchange Commission, established in 1934. It is a five-member body with overlapping terms, charged originally with the regulation of stock prospectuses and of stock market practices and transactions. By subsequent legislation it has been given power to dissolve corporate structures among public utility holding companies and to scrutinize their dividend payments to stockholders. It is responsible for registering and regulating all kinds of investment trusts and companies.[7]

New Types of Federal Agencies

In the last twenty-five years an amazing number of new types of administrative organization have made their appearance on the Federal scene. These include administrations, agencies, offices, services, corporations, and boards — not to mention a variety of miscellaneous establishments. Some have been the temporary creatures of emergency; others appear to be relatively permanent. Some are large, others are small. Some are charged with responsibilities of major importance, while others have minor functions. The name applied in any particular case gives little or no indication of the size of the agency or the importance of the service it renders. On either basis a good many of these new agencies would equal or outrank older cabinet positions, although none of them carry cabinet status for their administrative heads.

Administrations. The use of the term "administration" as a designation for an operating unit in the Federal government seems to have originated during World War I, when the Food and Fuel Administration was established. The term has often been applied to units with a single major purpose which is regarded at the time as being more or less temporary in character. During the depression period a large number of units of this type appeared — National Recovery Administration, Agricultural Adjustment Administration, Public Works Administration, Rural Electrification Administration, and many more. During World

---

[7] The best titles on the independent commissions are by Cushman and Fesler; see also the former's "Problem of the Independent Regulatory Commissions," in President's Committee on Administrative Management, *Report with Special Studies*, pp. 207-243 (Washington, 1937).

War II the Office of Price Administration and Civilian Supply was established by Executive Order in 1941, the name being shortened a few months later when the supply function was transferred to the Civilian Allocation Division of the War Production Board. Among other administrations may be mentioned the War Food Administration, War Shipping Administration, Petroleum Administration for War, and Foreign Economic Administration, all of which were war-duration agencies.

Agencies. Late in the Roosevelt regime a number of administrative units were formally designated as agencies. These were large, multipurpose units of relatively permanent character, any one of which on the basis of size and importance of function would have rated cabinet status. As of 1946 there were four of these — Federal Security Agency, National Housing Agency, Federal Works Agency, and Federal Loan Agency — all of them resulting from efforts to reorganize the Federal administrative structure. The heterogeneous character of these agencies is clearly shown by their composition, which includes offices, services, boards, administrations, authorities, and councils, each of which has the usual breakdown into divisions, bureaus, sections, and units.

The functions of the Federal Security Agency embrace the whole field of public health and welfare. In setting up this agency, a considerable number of related but previously scattered functions were pulled together into one administrative organization under the general direction of an administrator, as follows:

Office of the Administrator
Office of Education (transferred from the Department of the Interior)
United States Public Health Service (transferred from the Treasury Department)
Social Security Board (formerly independent)
Office of Vocational Rehabilitation (replacing the independent Federal Board of
    Vocational Rehabilitation)
Food and Drug Administration (transferred from the Department of Agriculture)

The component parts of the National Housing Agency were less numerous and all of recent origin. It represented an attempt to pull together a group of related but previously independent and uncoordinated units in the housing field — the Office of the Administrator (including Homes Use Service), Federal Home Loan Bank Administration, Federal Housing Administration, and Federal Public Housing Authority.

The Federal Works Agency was composed of the Public Roads Administration, transferred after a great many years in the Department of Agriculture, and renamed; the Public Buildings Administration, in which construction, space procurement, and maintenance activities were collected from many different departments and agencies; the Public Works Administration, at the time in process of liquidation; the Federal Fire Council; and the War Public Works and Services Programs.

The Federal Loan Agency brought together many previously independent and scattered units, mostly corporations, engaged in lending operations for a variety of purposes. Most important was the Reconstruction Finance Corporation, created by act of Congress in 1932; but there were in addition the Defense Plant Corporation, the Defense Supply Corporation, the Metals Reserve Company, the Rubber Reserve Company, the RFC Mortgage Company, the Federal National Mortgage Association, the Disaster Loan Corporation, and the War Damage Corporation. Obviously many of these activities could not long outlive the war, but it is safe to assume that as they disappear, their places will be taken at least in part by new agencies of similar purpose designed to meet peacetime needs. The Loan Agency was abolished by law in 1947, at which time all of its property and records were transferred to the Reconstruction Finance Corporation.

Offices. Until World War II no very extensive use was made of the term "office" as an official designation of an administrative unit. The Office of the Alien Property Custodian had, to be sure, functioned during World War I and in the years following. The title of the old Bureau of Education was changed to "the Office of Education." As a result of recommendations in the report of the President's Committee on Administrative Management, an Office of Emergency Management was set up as part of the Executive Office of the President. There had been occasional instances in which subdivisions of an agency had been referred to as offices, but it was not until World War II that this particular device came into its own. The list below, which makes no pretense of being complete, will suggest something of the number and scope of these agencies, practically all of which were obviously created for the duration:

> Office of Censorship
> Office of War Information
> Office of Defense Transportation
> Office of Civilian Defense
> Office of Economic Stabilization
> Office of War Mobilization
> Office of Strategic Services
> Office of Lend-Lease Administration
> Office of the Alien Property Custodian

Office of the Coordinator of Inter-American Affairs
Office of Scientific Research and Development
Office of Defense, Health and Welfare Services
Office of the Solid Fuels Coordinator for War

Boards. There have been boards and commissions ever since there was government — at least in the modern sense. The term "commission" seems to be used when the body is charged with important regulatory duties relating to public utility enterprises. Where the duties are primarily administrative or where, if regulatory in character, they relate to matters other than public utilities, the term "board" is in general use. During the Wilson era the Federal Reserve Board and the Federal Land Bank Board were created. The depression period yielded the Social Security Board, first independent and later brought under the Federal Security Agency, and the National Labor Relations Board, created by the Wagner Act and completely independent of the Department of Labor. World War II brought a number of important boards, including the War Production Board (later rechristened the Civilian Requirements Board); the National War Labor Board, a war agency that was too hastily abolished in the scramble to return to peacetime operations; the Board of Economic Warfare; the Board of War Communications; and various others.

Services. A number of the older and better established functions have been designated as "services," among them the Immigration and Naturalization Service, the United States Public Health Service, the Soil Conservation Service, and the Forest Service. The Central Administrative Services, operating under the Office for Emergency Management during World War II, was a short-lived experiment in centralizing procurement and service functions for a whole group of operating agencies. The theory was good, but it seems not to have been too successful in operation.

Corporations. The corporate form of organization is not new in government by any means, but only in recent years has extensive use been made of it. The first Bank of the United States was chartered in 1796. The charter was renewed in 1816 and would have been still further renewed had it not been for the determined opposition of President Jackson. After the National Banking Act of 1863 and the Federal Reserve Act of 1913, the creation of banking corporations under Federal authority again became possible. In 1933 there were twelve Federal corporations; by 1946 the number was up to thirty-six, having in the interval been considerably higher.[8]

---

[8] For the recent story at two-year intervals, see: *Government Corporations: No Man's Land of Federal Finance* (Citizens National Committee, Washington, 1943); *Reference*

The corporate form has been used for a variety of purposes, such as government lending, public works, and the conduct of business enterprises. In the first category one finds the Reconstruction Finance Corporation, the largest government corporation of modern times, and such others as the Commodity Credit Corporation and the Export-Import Bank, not to mention many smaller ones.[9] Frequent use has been made of it in the foreign field, the most recent illustration being the discussion of it in connection with emergency aid to Europe in 1947 and 1948.[10] Both the Federal government and the states have used it extensively in the housing field; the states have used it more for actual public works, as for example the Pennsylvania Turnpike Commission. Both have used it for the conduct of business enterprises. In this area the Federal government has the Tennessee Valley Authority, the states their liquor monopoly systems, Nebraska its public power system, and so on.[11]

The urge to establish government corporations has been strongest in emergency periods of depression and war. This has meant, as the Bureau of the Budget has observed,[12] that

> One of the immediate reasons for their establishment has really been the desire to achieve speed and flexibility of operation. This has meant, somewhat more specifically, freedom from standard financial and personnel controls. Another explanation of the creation of corporations is that when the Federal government undertook to perform business-type activities, it seemed more appropriate to use a business form of organization than the customary departmental and bureau system.

Regardless of its apparent advantages under certain circumstances, the use of this form of organization has raised difficult legal problems,[13]

Manual of Government Corporations as of June 30, 1945 (79th Cong., 1st Sess., Senate Document No. 86); *Assets of Wholly Owned Federal Government Corporations, Fiscal Year, 1947* (80th Cong., 1st Sess., Senate Committee Print).

[9] One Section of the report of the Byrd Committee in 1937 dealt with government lending agencies. The most recent study is by Galloway, George B., *Major Government Lending Agencies* (Legislative Reference Service, Library of Congress, Washington, 1947).

[10] See Mann, Fritz K., "The Government Corporation as a Tool of Foreign Policy," *Public Administration Review*, Summer, 1943, pp. 194–204.

[11] On the use of this device in the states, see Harris, Mark, "The Government Corporation in Kentucky," *Kentucky Law Journal*, March, 1941, pp. 297–300; King, Judson, "Nebraska, the Public Power State," *Public Utilities Fortnightly*, March 13 and 27, and April 10, 1947; McDiarmid, John, "California Uses the Government Corporation," *American Political Science Review*, April, 1940, pp. 300–304. For discussion of the propriety of its use. see Lilienthal, David E., and Marquis, R. H., "The Conduct of Business Enterprises by the Federal Government," *Harvard Law Review*, February, 1941, pp. 567–601, and Trimble, E. G., "Constitutionality of Government Competition with Business," *Temple Law Quarterly*, February, 1939, pp. 201–215.

[12] "Trends in the Development of Executive Branch Organization," a memorandum prepared for the Hoover Commission in 1947; for another statement of the advantages of the corporate form, see Pritchett, *The Tennessee Valley Authority*, pp. 23–25.

[13] See Pinney, Harvey, "The Legal Status of Federal Corporations," *California Law Review*, September, 1939, pp. 712–736, and Schnell, Robert H., "Federally Owned Cor-

and has occasioned strenuous and sometimes bitter debate. As a result, Congress passed in 1945 the Government Corporations Control Act, extending to these agencies application of the principle of the executive budget and of Congressional supervision over their affairs. Their budgets must be submitted to Congress by the President as a part of his annual budget message, and at the same time they are required to submit to commercial-type audits by the Comptroller General, with reports thereon to be submitted to the Congress.[14]

Authorities. Closely related to the corporate form of organization is the "authority," the first example of which was the Port of New York Authority established in 1921. An authority has been defined by Luther Gulick [15] as "a governmental business corporation set up outside the normal structure of traditional government so that it can give continuity, business efficiency, and elastic management to the construction or operation of a self-supporting or revenue-producing public enterprise." The British have made extensive use of this device. In this country authorities have been much more common in the smaller units of government [16] than in the larger, but examples are not wanting at the Federal level, as for instance the National Housing Authority and the Tennessee Valley Authority. This type of organization has the advantage of being able to incur debt and to issue bonds without reference to any existing debt limitations and without pledging the full faith and credit of the government, as is the rule in ordinary government borrowing.

Miscellaneous Agencies. The creators of new governmental agencies have shown a disturbing ingenuity in finding or discovering new names by which to designate newly established agencies. One finds corporations, agencies, offices, commissions, committees, systems, and authorities — some temporary, others of a relatively permanent nature. The Civilian Conservation Corps was a child of the depression, one which might well, because of the valuable character of the work it accomplished, have been retained in skeleton form even in prosperous times. The War Manpower Commission undertook, through the operation of its priorities system, the rationing of available man power among em-

porations and Their Legal Problems," *North Carolina Law Review*, I, April, 1936, pp. 238–273; II, June, 1936, pp. 337–366.
[14] See Pritchett, C. Herman, "The Government Corporation Control Act of 1945," *American Political Science Review*, June, 1946, pp. 495–509.
[15] " 'Authorities' and How to Use Them," *Tax Review*, November, 1947, entire issue.
[16] Under a law passed in 1935, Pennsylvania has made extensive use of authorities for local purposes. As of January 1, 1948, there were sixty-nine in actual operation: *Water:* original construction, nine; and acquisition, forty-three; *Sewage:* ten; *Miscellaneous:* seven. Altogether, 128 had been created under the law, some still being in the planning rather than the operating stage. See *Bulletin* of the Department of Internal Affairs, March, and September, 1947, and Edelstein, Mortimer S., "The Authority Plan–Tool of Modern Government," *Cornell Law Quarterly*, January, 1943, pp. 177–191.

ployers during the war. Then there were committees — the President's Committee on Fair Employment Practices, the Committee on Congested Production Areas, and many more. There was the Selective Service System, which might quite as properly have been designated as an administration. All these agencies were created to fill a temporary or emergency need; even so, from an administrative point of view they had a tendency to complicate still further an already intricate and confused administrative structure. There is urgent need for the development of a standard terminology to be used in the designation of executive agencies.

State Administrative Organization

Administrative organization in the states has passed through a series of changes not unlike those which have taken place in the Federal government. In the early days the number of state functions was small, the standards of administrative service low. A deep distrust of the executive had carried over from Revolutionary days, with the result that the governor was largely a figurehead, supposed to make speeches and preside on ceremonial occasions, but not to possess any significant powers. He was elected for a short term, often annually. He had neither a veto power over legislation nor any adequate powers of appointment and removal. Most of the heads of executive departments were, like himself, chosen by popular vote, unless perchance the administration of the function was directed by a board or commission. In this case, the members were either elected for overlapping terms or appointed by the governor, subject to senate confirmation, likewise for overlapping terms. In some cases heads of executive departments and agencies were selected by the legislature.

In any event, from an administrative point of view the result was unsatisfactory. The governor was held responsible for the conduct of an administration that he had no power to lead or to control. The elective heads of agencies could ignore his wishes with impunity, for they received their authority from the same source as he — directly from the people. Furthermore, they were little disposed to cooperate with him lest by so doing they contribute to his political influence and prestige. In the case of the multiple-headed agencies the overlapping term device operated very effectively to make executive leadership of the administration a practical impossibility. Under these circumstances the executive branch of the government had no policy and no program. Departments might proceed simultaneously in all directions, in the absence of any unifying or coordinating influence.

Out of this background have grown the two major types of administrative organization existing in the states at the present time. One is a continuation of the original form, with some modifications but still with a weak governor; the other is the strong executive type, found in those states where administrative codes have been adopted. While each of these will be briefly considered, it seems appropriate to note that the differentiation between the two is not always definite and clear-cut. In general, in nearly all the states there are two distinct classes among the heads of the executive departments.

The first includes the original constitutional offices, such as secretary of state, attorney general, treasurer, auditor, and superintendent of education, who are almost without exception elected officers. The second includes the multitude of newer service functions such as agriculture, conservation, health, highways, labor, and welfare, nearly all of which have been created by statute. In a large percentage of cases, the heads of these agencies are appointed by the governor, subject, however, to confirmation by the senate.

Weak Governor–Administrative Board Type. Those states in which the old type of organization still prevails are characterized by a weak governor and a multiplicity of executive agencies, many of them in the form of independent boards and commissions. The governor's powers of appointment and removal are severely restricted, his powers over the budget likewise. This situation is, as has been pointed out many times, grossly unfair to the governor, since the people tend to hold him responsible for the conduct of an administration over which, actually, he has no control. Illustrations may be found in Georgia, New Jersey before 1948, and Wisconsin.

Georgia, having had provision for a strong executive and having had unhappy experiences with some recent governors, moved toward weakening of the executive power under provisions adopted in the constitutional revision of 1945. New Jersey, on the other hand, prior to the adoption of its new constitution in 1947, might be presented as exhibiting simultaneously one of the best illustrations of this type of organization and one of the worst administrative structures in the country. Wisconsin is an interesting illustration because, in spite of its organization, it has the reputation of being a well-governed state. This has been possible because its administrative boards have employed executive secretaries who have been given broad powers to administer the agency program, under the supervision of the board, in a manner somewhat analogous to the position of a cabinet secretary in a code state in his relation to the governor. The critical difference between the two forms, and the major defect in this one, is to be found in the fact that, while it may produce efficient administration *within* an agency, it provides no central coordinating influence *between* agencies.

Administrative Code States. Approximately half of the states of the Union function under administrative codes, although most of the remaining states have been influenced to a greater or lesser degree by the code movement. Under this plan the governor is given powers adequate for the discharge of the responsibilities placed upon him. An effort is made to reduce to manageable proportions the number of executive agencies operating under his supervision and reporting to him. He is given responsibility for the appointment and removal of the heads of departments; such boards and commissions as are retained at all are restricted to an advisory function. The governor is made responsible for the planning and the execution of the state's fiscal program.

These are some of the basic principles upon which the code system is based; unfortunately, it is not often possible, as a practical matter, to realize them fully. Some agencies may have been established by constitutional provision and are thus beyond reach of the legislature. Theoretically the required changes might be made in the constitution; but again, in practice, amendment of the constitution is difficult if not impossible in many states. Other agencies acquire a preferred status which makes them politically untouchable. The result is that complete realization of the ideals of the code system is seldom achieved.

In this connection the Commonwealth of Pennsylvania may be taken as an illustration. Under the Administrative Code of 1929, as amended, there are in this state no less than five different types of agencies. Those created by the Constitution make up the executive department — the Governor, Lieutenant Governor, Secretary of the Commonwealth, Attorney General, Auditor General, State Treasurer, Secretary of Internal Affairs, Superintendent of Public Instruction, the Executive Board, and the Pennsylvania State Police. Then there are the administrative departments created by the Code — nineteen of them.[17] There are three independent boards and commissions, dealing with fish, game, and public utilities, respectively. There are the departmental administrative boards, commissions, and offices, and finally a wide variety of advisory boards and commissions attached to the various executive departments and agencies. This multitude of agencies may be grouped in broad categories, according to the type of service rendered, as fol-

---

[17] These are: Agriculture, Auditor General, Banking, Forests and Waters, Health, Highways, Internal Affairs, Insurance, Justice, Labor and Industry, Military Affairs, Mines, Property and Supplies, Public Assistance, Public Instruction, Revenue, State, Treasury, and Welfare.

lows: general government, finance, control over business and industry, conservation and development of natural resources, transportation, public health and welfare, and education.[18]

Local Government Organization

The units of local government in the United States are so vast in number and so diverse in their characteristics that any easy generalizations regarding them are impossible. Of more than 150,000 such units now existing, approximately 3000 are counties; 19,000, towns and townships; 16,000, municipalities — large and small, urban and rural; over 108,000, school districts; and over 8000, special districts of various types. Since this discussion is not primarily concerned with the pattern of local government in the various parts of the country and since limitations of space preclude analysis of the executive organization in the many forms that exist, attention will here be confined to the two most important units of local government — the counties and the municipalities.

County Government Organization. The form of county government organization was imported into this country from England in the days of colonization and has been retained in substantially its original form ever since. To be sure, there are a few exceptions, but the number still represents an insignificant percentage of the total, and such changes as have been made are furthermore of recent origin. While there are minor differences in the structure of county government in the several states, the major characteristics have been much alike.

The prevailing forms of county government — and there are several — may all be described from the point of view of their administrative structure as a headless congeries of miscellaneous agencies and functions. There is, to begin with, the long list of elective "row offices," including the sheriff, the coroner, county clerk, district or prosecuting attorney, and a veritable multitude of others. In some states the list is the same for all counties; in others it varies according to their classification. The sheriff once was in fact, and still is in theory, the chief law-enforcing officer; but he has never exercised any general executive authority comparable to that of a president, a governor, or a mayor. The over-all executive responsibility as well as the legislative power is combined in a body variously designated as the county board, the board of county commissioners, or the county board of supervisors. The county boards of the south and west and the Board of County Commissioners in Pennsylvania normally consist of three or five elected

---

[18] United States Bureau of the Census classification, as modified by the author; see his *American State Government*, Third Edition, Chapter 11 (Heath, Boston, 1946).

members, while the county boards of supervisors in New York and Michigan are much larger bodies, composed of at least one representative (the town supervisor) from each town in the county.

The Municipal Executive. At the present time there are two major forms (mayor and council, and council-manager types) and one minor form (commission government) used in the organization of municipal government in this country.

The widespread distrust of the executive, which was originally responsible for the effort to curtail so drastically the powers of the governors, had a like effect upon the office of the mayor. At the turn of the century the prevailing weak mayor and bicameral municipal council began to give way to other forms. Where the community desired to retain the mayor and council type of government in preference to one of the newer ones, it adopted a charter providing for a strong mayor, and a small, compact, unicameral council. This vast improvement over the earlier form has now won acceptance wherever mayor and council government is still retained.

Under this plan the mayor serves as the executive head of his administration, appointing the heads of the city departments, who serve as members of his cabinet. As chief executive of the city he is responsible for the administration of the various municipal services and for the formulation and enforcement of the city's fiscal program. The position of the mayor may be roughly compared to that of the governor in a code state. An effort has been made to give him powers commensurate with the duties and responsibilities imposed upon him.

The council-manager plan, often referred to as the city manager plan, has won acceptance in the period of one generation in more than eight hundred municipalities, large and small, throughout the country. This rapid progress indicates a growing realization of the need for professionalization of the public service. Under the manager plan there is a small unicameral council elected by the voters. This council performs two important functions in relation to the administration. (1) It elects a mayor from among its own membership; he presides at its sessions and performs other public duties as representative of the city government. This position carries with it a certain prestige value, but actually the mayor has no greater power than any other member of the council. (2) It selects and hires a city manager to serve as the chief executive officer of the city and to direct its business and financial operations.

The manager is — or should be — a man of ability and integrity, with professional training in public administration and previous experience in the field sufficient to warrant the assumption that he will be able to handle the position for which he is selected. While he is selected by and serves at the pleasure of the council, the city manager profession has built up standards of ethics applicable to its own members, and standards governing their appointment and dismissal which give members some protection from dismissals based upon political pressures or personal animosity.

The commission form of city government, which was developed and quite widely adopted during the early part of the century, has steadily lost ground in recent years. This plan calls for a popularly elected commission of five or seven members, who undertake to function jointly in the capacity of a city council and individually as the executive heads of the various departments of the city government. One member is elected as mayor, to preside at the commission meetings and to represent the city on public occasions. The plan demonstrated two major defects: (1) the lack of a centralized responsibility for the conduct of the executive functions of government made it difficult to ascertain who was at fault if the administration did not function satisfactorily; (2) there was a pronounced tendency for commissioners to seek the direction of the more important departments without regard to the nature of their own personal qualifications.

SELECTED REFERENCES

FEDERAL

Cushman, Robert E., *The Independent Regulatory Commissions* (Oxford University Press, New York, 1941). The standard treatise on regulatory commissions at the Federal level.

Gaus, John M., and Wolcott, Leon O., *Public Administration and the United States Department of Agriculture* (Public Administration Service, Chicago, 1940). An excellent analysis of the administrative operations of a Federal department long recognized as outstanding in its field.

McDiarmid, John, *Government Corporations and Federal Funds* (University of Chicago Press, 1938). Analysis of a significant aspect of a form of organization that has been constantly increasing in importance.

Millspaugh, Arthur C., *Democracy, Efficiency, Stability: An Appraisal of American Government*, and *Toward Efficient Democracy: The Question of Governmental Organization* (Brookings Institution, Washington, 1939 and 1949, respectively). Recent discussions of organization and reorganization.

Pritchett, C. Herman, *The Tennessee Valley Authority* (University of North Carolina Press, 1943). A thorough and readable account of an extremely interesting and important experiment in governmental organization and administration.

Sharfman, Isaiah L., *The Interstate Commerce Commission*, 4 vols. (Commonwealth Fund, New York, 1931–1937). The most exhaustive of many studies of individual Federal commissions.

Short, Lloyd M., *The Development of National Administrative Organization in the United States* (Johns Hopkins Press, 1923). A standard treatise on the historical development of administrative organization down to the date of publication.

Tompkins, Dorothy C., *Materials for the Study of the Federal Government* (Public Administration Service, Chicago, 1948). Annotated bibliographical aids, arranged largely on a functional basis.

Wallace, Schuyler C., *Federal Departmentalization* (Columbia University Press, 1941). Subtitle: a critique of theories of organization.

White, Leonard D., *Trends in Public Administration* (McGraw-Hill, New York, 1933). An able analysis of major lines of development.

Wooddy, Carroll H., *The Growth of the Federal Government, 1915–1933* (McGraw-Hill, New York, 1934). A study of the rapid expansion of governmental services during a significant period.

STATE

Buck, Arthur E., *The Reorganization of State Governments in the United States* (Columbia University Press, 1938). Standard treatise covering fully developments in all states down to date of publication.

Fesler, James W., *The Independence of State Regulatory Agencies* (Public Administration Service, Chicago, 1942). An excellent analysis of the operation of these agencies at the state level.

Hurt, Elsey, *California State Government: An Outline of Its Administrative Organization from 1850 to 1936* (State Printing Office, Sacramento, 1937–1939). A thorough study of the historical development of administrative organization in an important state over a period of nearly a century.

Lipson, Leslie, *The American Governor: From Figurehead to Leader* (University of Chicago Press, 1939). The only authoritative study of the evolution of the governorship.

Mathews, John M., *Principles of American State Administration* (Appleton, New York, 1917). An old but still useful study in a much neglected field.

New Jersey Legislative Reference Section, *State Organization and Reorganization: A Bibliography* (State Library, Trenton, January, 1948).

New York State Constitutional Convention Commission, *Problems Relating to Executive Administration and Powers* (Albany, 1938). A very useful volume in the series prepared for the last New York convention.

Porter, Kirk H., *State Administration* (Crofts, New York, 1939). The most recent treatise on administrative problems at the state level.

Weintraub, Ruth G., *Government Corporations and State Law* (Columbia University Press, 1939). An excellent analysis of the use of the corporate form at the state level.

LOCAL

For the historical development of administrative organization in two representative cities, see: Cincinnati Municipal Reference Bureau; *Cincinnati: The March of City Government, 1802–1936* (Cincinnati, 1937), and Upson, Lent D., *The Growth of a City Government* (Detroit Bureau of Governmental Research, 1922, 1931, and 1942).

Standard works on municipal organization and procedure include: MacCorkle, Stuart A., *Municipal Administration* (Prentice-Hall, New York, 1942). Pfiffner, John M., *Municipal Administration* (Ronald Press, New York, 1940). Reed, Thomas H., *Municipal Management* (McGraw-Hill, New York, 1941).

Little has been written on county administrative organization; for one study dealing with a single state, see Tharp, Claude R., *A Manual of County Administrative Organization in Michigan* (University of Michigan Press, 1944).

2

EFFORTS AT
ADMINISTRATIVE REORGANIZATION

For more than a century, but particularly since 1900, there have been periodic complaints concerning overlapping and duplication, and a general lack of coordination in the services of all three levels of government. These complaints have led to repeated investigations by legislative committees and by others and to the publication of many reports. Very often these complaints have not been without justification; the various administrative structures, through "piecemeal growth in response to immediate needs," had become a rambling and more or less ramshackle affair. Nobody planned it that way. Like Topsy, they just grew. The efforts at reorganization have met with only limited success because the same influences that tended to produce the unsatisfactory organization tended to perpetuate it. Each pressure group wanted — and still wants — the service it is interested in maintained independently and administered in accordance with its own desires.

Federal Administrative Reorganization

Early Attempts at Reorganization. As early as 1854 criticism was voiced in Congress of the deplorable condition of the public service, and a committee was appointed to find ways and means of improving it. Nothing happened as a result of this study nor in the long interlude of controversy, war, and reconstruction which followed. Four important commissions of varied origin and composition functioned in the quarter century beginning in 1887.

The Cockrell Commission of 1887–1888, created by Senate resolution, was composed of five Senators. The Dockery-Cockrell Commission of 1893–1895 was a joint commission of three members from the Senate and three from the House of Representatives. The Keep Commission of 1905–1909 consisted of four representatives of the executive departments, appointed by President Roosevelt without Congressional authorization. Then from 1910 to 1913 there was the President's Commission on Economy and Efficiency, created by President Taft but authorized by Congress, which appropriated altogether $260,000 for the Commission's expenses.[1]

Administrative Changes After World War I. This almost continuous agitation for reform, which appeared to accomplish nothing, finally began to bear fruit. In 1917 Congress passed a budget act, which President Wilson vetoed because he objected to certain features of it. In 1921, however, the present Budget and Accounting Act was passed and signed. Shortly thereafter the Classification Act of 1923 was adopted. The Retirement Act, passed originally in 1920, was revised and amended in 1926 and 1948. So eventually progress was made in the improvement of administrative procedure in the fields of finance and personnel.

Immediately after World War I great interest was shown for a few years in structural reorganization, and several plans were developed by both public and private groups. The nature of these proposals is shown in the table which appears on page 22. Analysis of these changes indicates a desire to modify the existing cabinet structure by giving recognition to new services without at the same time making any important change in the size of the cabinet. Perhaps because none of these proposals were put into effect, efforts at reorganization during the Roosevelt era adopted the expedient of developing these functions outside the cabinet framework. The idea of activity grouping in accordance with major purpose dominated in most of the new plans.

Nevertheless the demand for administrative reorganization continued. In the Presidential campaign of 1928 Governor Smith, the Democratic candidate, coming fresh from a successful reorganization of the government of New York, sought to make Federal reorganization a campaign issue. The Republicans, while refusing to accept the issue, carried on the fight during the Hoover administration. Mr. Hoover requested Congressional authorization during the latter part of his term to carry on an extensive reorganization of the Federal machinery, but a Democratic majority in Congress refused to approve the necessary legislation.

Reorganization Under Roosevelt. As shown in the table on page 22, President Roosevelt attempted on three different occasions to make important changes in the administrative structure of the Federal government — in 1933–1934, 1937, and 1939–1940. The first effort began,

---

[1] For a comprehensive treatment of the history of the reorganization movement, see the author's compilation of *Basic Information on the Reorganization of the Executive Branch, 1912–1948* (Public Affairs Bulletin No. 66, Legislative Reference Service, Library of Congress, Washington, 1949); and a series of memoranda by the Bureau of the Budget, also prepared for the Hoover Commission.

Investigating Commissions on the Subject
of Federal Administrative Reorganization, 1887 to Date

NAME OF COMMISSION	DATE	MAJOR REPORTS
Select Committee on Methods of Business in the Executive Departments (Cockrell Committee)	1887–1889	*Report of the Select Committee of the United States Senate*, 3 vol. (Senate Report No. 507, 50th Cong., 1st Sess.)
Joint Commission on Executive Departments, Organization, Etc. (Dockery-Cockrell Commission)	1893–1895	*Reference to Laws Organizing Executive Departments and Other Government Establishments at the National Capital* (House Reports Nos. 41 and 49, 53rd Cong., 1st Sess.)
Committee on Department Methods (Keep Committee)	1905–1909	
President's Commission on Economy and Efficiency	1910–1913	*Message of the President of the United States Submitting for the Consideration of Congress a Budget* (Sen. Doc. No. 1113, 62nd Cong., 1st Sess., and other reports)
National Budget Committee of New York City	1920	*A Proposal for Government Reorganization* (National Budget Committee, New York, 1921)
Joint Committee on the Reorganization of Government Departments	1923	*Reorganization of the Executive Departments* (Sen. Doc. No. 302, 67th Cong., 4th Sess.)
Brookings Institution	1923	Willoughby, W. F., *The Reorganization of the Administrative Branch of the National Government* (Johns Hopkins Press, 1923)
The Select Committee to Investigate the Executive Agencies of the Government (Byrd Committee)	1937	A series of fourteen reports, prepared by the Brookings Institution (Senate Committee Prints, 75th Cong., 1st Sess.)
President's Committee on Administrative Management	1937	*Report with Special Studies* (Government Printing Office, Washington, 1937)
Commission on Organization of the Executive Branch of the Government (Hoover Commission)	1947–1949	Series of eighteen reports and a Concluding Report together with eighteen published task force reports (Government Printing Office, Washington, 1949)

soon after he took office, with a renewal of President Hoover's request for authority to reshuffle the Federal agencies. Temporary authority was granted in 1933 and renewed in 1934. While some improvements resulted, the situation as a whole remained as bad as before because of the creation of a large number of new "alphabetical agencies" born out of the depression emergency. Reference has already been made to these administrations, agencies, offices, and other forms.

In 1937 the President initiated his second attempt at reorganization

Plans for Departmental Organization
Proposed for the Federal Government, 1921–1947

ORGANIZATION EXISTING	NATIONAL BUDGET COMMITTEE	BROOKINGS INSTITUTION	JOINT COMMITTEE ON REORGANIZATION	HOOVER PLAN	FIRST ROOSEVELT PLAN	SECOND ROOSEVELT PLAN	SENATE SELECT COMMITTEE	THIRD ROOSEVELT PLAN	JOINT COMMITTEE ON THE ORGANIZATION OF CONGRESS	TRUMAN PLAN	ORGANIZATION EXISTING
1913 to 1947	1921	1923	1923	1932	1933–1934	1937	1937	1939–1940	1945	1946	1947–
State	X	X	X	X	X	X	X	X	X	X	State
Treasury	X	X	X	X	X	X	X	X	X	X	Treasury
War	X			X	X	X	X	X			
Justice	X	X	X	X	X	X	X	X	X	X	Justice
Navy	X			X	X	X	X	X			
Post Office	X	X		X	X	X	X	X		X	Post Office
Interior			X	X	X		X	X		X	Interior
Agriculture	X	X	X	X	X	X	X	X	X	X	Agriculture
Commerce	X	X	X	X	X	X	X	X	X	X	Commerce
Labor	X	X	X	X	X	X	X	X	X	X	Labor
Education and Health	X										
and Science		X									
and Welfare			X								
Public Works	X					X			X	X	
and Public Domain		X									
National Defense		X	X						X	X	National Defense
Public Health		X									
Communications			X								
Conservation						X					
and Natural Resources									X		
Social Welfare						X	X		X	X	
Transportation							X				
and Communications									X		
Civil Services									X		
10	11	11	10	10	10	12	12	10	12	11	9

by appointing his Committee on Administrative Management,[2] composed of three outstanding authorities in public administration —

[2] This move was prompted by the Senate's authorization of the Select Committee to Investigate the Executive Agencies, commonly known as the Byrd Committee. Mr. Roosevelt apparently decided to tackle the job himself, promptly and effectively. That he did so is evident from the fact that the report of his Committee was published first and that it far overshadowed in significance the report of the Senate Committee.

Charles E. Merriam, Louis Brownlow, and Luther Gulick. These men, with the aid of a staff of specialists in particular fields, produced the notable report of the President's Committee, which contained the most authoritative analysis of the problems involved that had ever been prepared. Some of the recommendations had far-reaching effects. Unfortunately the proposals came before the Congress at the same time that the court reorganization plan was under consideration; the effort to turn administrative reorganization also into a partisan political issue was made with sufficient success to defeat much of the plan.

A couple of years later the administration and the Congress returned to a further consideration of the problem, and the Reorganization Act of 1939 was enacted. Under its terms no change was to be made in the number of departments, and fifteen leading independent establishments were wholly exempted. Provision for the extension of the merit system was omitted. The President was given authority, however, until January 20, 1941, to "reduce, coordinate, consolidate, and reorganize" the various agencies of government according to proposed "plans," which were to become effective sixty days after being transmitted to Congress unless in the meantime disapproved in their entirety by concurrent resolution of the two Houses. These plans were, therefore, clearly to be distinguished from Executive Orders.

The aims were the usual ones in reorganization efforts, namely, to reduce expenditures, reduce the number of agencies, increase efficiency, group agencies according to major purposes, and eliminate overlapping and duplication of effort. Under the provisions of this act, the President submitted Reorganization Plan No. 1 on April 25, 1939, and forwarded four additional plans during 1939 and 1940. Some opposition to particular proposals was expressed both in and out of Congress, but none of them were defeated. Several different types of change resulted from these plans, which may be summarized as follows:

1. By activity grouping according to major purpose, large numbers of establishments previously independent were placed in one or another of the ten executive departments.

2. Large numbers of others, while not placed in departments, were grouped in coordinated agencies, each under an administrator and constituting a new level (as previously described) in the general administrative setup.

3. A series of related and previously scattered coordinative and management agencies was brought together in the Executive Office of the President.

4. Several agencies were abolished outright and their functions transferred elsewhere.

5. Some units were transferred from one department to another to secure better departmental integration. Some units appearing under new names represented in whole or in part an integration of units previously scattered, whether in departments or otherwise.

Postwar Developments. Shortly before his death President Roosevelt requested new authority from Congress to make necessary shifts and changes in the Federal administrative structure. Congress failed to act on this recommendation, and in the pressure of events as the war drew to a close Mr. Roosevelt did not urge approval. Soon after he assumed office, President Truman made a request for practically identical authority. At first ignored by Congress, it was later granted.

The President in the meantime proceeded to accomplish some changes for which he already had requisite authorization. When he appointed a new Secretary of Labor, he brought together by Executive Order, under the Department of Labor, the numerous scattered organizations and agencies previously functioning independently in that field. Included were the National War Labor Board (later abolished and replaced by the Wage Stabilization Board), the Committee on Fair Employment Practices (later discontinued by failure of Congress to appropriate for it), and one or two other agencies. He was unable to include the National Labor Relations Board because this agency was established by law under the terms of the Wagner Act of 1936. It was also reported that extension of the authority of the Liaison Office for Personnel Management was planned, in the interests of a more comprehensive and better administered personnel program for the Federal government.

The 80th Congress was responsible for the enactment in 1947 of a measure for the merger of the armed services into the National Defense Establishment, under a Secretary of Defense of cabinet rank and with three subsidiary departments — Army, Navy, and Air Force — each headed by a Secretary. This proposal had been under consideration in one form or another ever since World War I. It had been recommended by the Brookings Institution and by the Joint Committee on Reorganization, both in 1923, and by the Joint Committee on the Organization of Congress and by President Truman, both in 1945. Oswald Garrison Villard had said in 1937 that "the most disappointing feature of the President's plan for a reorganization of the government is his failure to combine the army and navy under one head." [3]

---

[3] *Nation,* February 6, 1937, p. 155; for discussions of the problems involved, see Mr. Truman's special message to the Congress, December 19, 1945; *Editorial Research Reports,* "Army-Navy Consolidation," October 6, 1945; Elsbree, Hugh L., *Unification of the Armed Services* (Legislative Reference Service, Library of Congress, Washington, 1947); Connery, Robert H., "Unification of the Armed Services — The First Year," *American Political Science Review,* February, 1949, pp. 38–52. Both the army and the navy prepared elaborate reports on the subject: *Unification of the War and Navy Departments and Postwar Organization for National Security* (Senate Committee on Naval Affairs, Senate Committee Print, 79th Cong., 1st Sess.); *The Navy Plan for National Security* (Washington, March, 1946).

The need for this long overdue change was demonstrated anew during World War II, when both of the existing departments displayed jealousy of each other and each operated its own air service. It was possible to establish a unified command abroad, but the best that could be done at home was to attempt, by the use of coordinating committees, to bring some semblance of consistency into the operations of the nation's organization for defense. Because of serious defects in the legislation as adopted, the desired unity was not achieved. The service departments were still separate, and the Secretary of National Defense, who was supposed to coordinate their activities, was prohibited by law from developing a staff of his own. The result was that stories of bickering between the services continued to appear in the press during 1948 as the new defense program was launched.

In 1947 the 80th Congress established the Commission on Organization of the Executive Branch of the Government, charged with making a thorough study of the problem of executive organization and reorganization and with the submission of its report and recommendations to the Congress in January, 1949. In composition this was a mixed commission of twelve members, appointed as follows:

Four members appointed by the Speaker of the House of Representatives, two of whom should be members of the House, two private citizens

Four members appointed by the President of the Senate, two of whom should be members of the Senate, two private citizens

Four members appointed by the President of the United States, two of whom should be members of the administration, two private citizens

At its organization meeting in September, 1947, the Commission elected former President Herbert Hoover as its chairman. Plans were made for extensive inquiries in such fields as the organization of the President's office, the cabinet and its place in the administration, the independent agencies, Federal relations with other units of government, personnel management, and other questions of similar importance. "Task forces," as Mr. Hoover called them, were set up in each of these areas under a plan by which the necessary research would be done under contract by established organizations in the field of governmental research.[4] While this Commission was still in process of organization, the President in his annual message in 1948 set forth a number of important proposals for reorganization of executive agencies. After eighteen months of diligent effort, the Commission's series of reports was submitted during the early months of 1949.

---

[4] See Heady, Ferrel, "A New Approach to Federal Executive Reorganization," *American Political Science Review*, December, 1947, pp. 1118–1126.

State Administrative Reorganization

The movement for the improvement of administrative organization and procedure in the states began at the turn of the century and has developed more or less simultaneously since that time along four lines:

Personnel administration: beginning 1905
Fiscal administration: beginning 1911
Organizational structure: beginning 1917
Administrative procedure: beginning 1937

In connection with this analysis, attention is called to the fact that, in the past, discussions of administrative reorganization in the states have been largely confined to the structural aspects of the problem. In the light of current thinking in the field of administration, this represents a very narrow approach.

Many factors contributed to the awakening of interest in state problems, among them the increase in the number and scope of governmental functions [5] and the public's demand not only for more service but for improvement in the quality of public service. The gradual evolution of a science of administration and its application in business and industry has had its effect upon government. The early changes were usually made within the limits of the existing constitutional framework, although recent trends show an increasing tendency to incorporate some of them in the fundamental law either through amendment or through general revision. One of the most important characteristics of this period has been the transformation of the governorship.[6]

1. *Personnel Administration.* The spoils system developed a firm hold upon the states in the late eighteenth and early nineteenth centuries, spreading its influence into the Federal government at the beginning of the Jacksonian era. For half a century it held undisputed sway at all levels. Then in 1883 Congress passed the Pendleton Act. In that same year, New York passed the first state civil service law, and Wisconsin followed in 1884. For twenty years thereafter no additions to the list were made. The real movement for the improvement of personnel administration at the state level began early in the twentieth century. From 1905 on, when Illinois adopted a civil service law, one state after

---

[5] See Chatters, Carl H., and Hoover, Marjorie L., *An Inventory of Governmental Activities in the United States* (Municipal Finance Officers Association, Chicago, 1947), and two articles by John M. Pierce in *Tax Digest*: "Functional Growth of California State Government," January, 1933, pp. 5–10, and "420 State Activities: California Government Continues to Expand," August, 1936, pp. 260–261, 281–286.

[6] See Lipson, and the author's *American State Government,* Third Edition, Chapter 9 (Heath, Boston, 1946).

another has been added to the list, until now approximately half the states have state-wide coverage. The remaining states have partial coverage in those departments and agencies responsible for the administration of Federally aided programs, especially in the field of social security.[7]

2. *Fiscal Administration.* For generations Americans, living in a land of plenty, were notoriously lax in the management of the financial aspects of public business. The budget movement, which had made notable progress in governments abroad and in business and industry in this country, obtained its first recognition governmentally when in 1911 California and Wisconsin adopted state budgetary legislation. The subject was being widely discussed at the time in connection with President Taft's Commission on Economy and Efficiency. The time was ripe, and the movement spread with amazing rapidity until by 1926 all states had adopted some kind of budgetary legislation. Not all of it was good, but it represented at least a recognition of basic principles. Much of it has since been rewritten, for there has in fact been steady progress over the years in the development and improvement of budgetary procedures.

3. *Organizational Structure.* The weaknesses of the prevailing type of state organization were long recognized. The administrative reorganization movement appears to have begun in Oregon in 1909 or 1910 with a proposal of the Peoples' Power League to concentrate "executive power in the hands of the governor, checked only by an independent auditor, and to establish vital connections between the governor and the legislature." [8] Charles E. Hughes, in his inaugural address as Governor of New York in 1910 and later in an address at Yale University, likewise urged a concentration of responsibility, with fewer offices and short ballots. The movement was given further impetus by the report of President Taft's Economy and Efficiency Commission in 1912. Then in 1917 the first code was enacted in Illinois under the leadership of Governor Frank O. Lowden, and a movement that was to hold a position of primary importance in the state field for the next twenty years was inaugurated.

Under the Illinois plan, adopted subsequently in Massachusetts, New York, and Virginia by constitutional amendment and in twenty-two other states by statutory provisions, all or most of the existing agencies were abolished by law. The duties they performed were then

---

[7] For a recent tabulation, see *Book of the States, 1948–1949*, pp. 200–201.

[8] White, *Trends in Public Administration*, pp. 176–180, traces the various events and published studies which provided the groundwork upon which the Illinois and later reorganizations were based. See also Buck, and Bollens.

carefully classified under a limited number of headings, care being taken to group related services and to eliminate overlapping and duplication of functions. Each group of activities was then assigned to a newly created department, the head of which was appointed by the governor. It thus became possible for the governor to establish a direct line of responsibility through the department heads, bureau chiefs, and the heads of sections or divisions down to the minor employees of each department. The governor now became responsible in fact and not merely in theory for the conduct of his administration.

Characteristics of the Reorganization Movement. Arthur E. Buck has listed the following standards or principles of reorganization as applied to the executive department of the state governments:

1. Concentration of authority and responsibility
2. Departmentalization, or functional integration
3. Undesirability of boards for purely administrative work
4. Coordination of the staff services of administration
5. Provision for an independent audit
6. Recognition of a governor's cabinet

The application of these principles has made possible a number of important advantages, such as the financial savings which result from the elimination of overlapping, waste, inefficiency, and duplication of services. While it is possible to operate a system of budgetary control without reorganization, this plan provides a much more satisfactory basis for such a system. Adoption of the plan inevitably results in progress toward a short ballot; it is, in fact, impossible to have any satisfactory reorganization and still retain a large number of elective state officers. Centralization of administrative responsibility is impossible under the old-fashioned long ballot. While elective offices provided for by the constitution could be changed only by constitutional amendment, all others could be made appointive, and even those which remained elective could be stripped of important policy-determining functions.

Geographically there has been nothing either sectional or regional about the interest in the administrative reorganization movement. Approximately half of the states have adopted codes, and all of the states have been affected in some degree by the code movement. This has consistently recognized the desirability of having the states meet their own problems in their own way — a situation which has resulted, as Buck points out, in four distinct types of reorganization: (1) the integrated, which is recommended by the *Model State Constitution;* (2) the partially integrated, which is the usual type when reorganization is accomplished by statute; (3) the fiscal control type; and (4) the commission or plural executive type. It is thus clear that no attempt has been made to force all states into precisely the same mold. This point is further illustrated by the considerable variation in the departmental patterns created in the several states, and in the terminology applied to them. It would, in fact, have been preferable if some uniform standards could have been developed with regard to these matters.

4. *Administrative Procedure.* With the steadily increasing number of regulatory bodies at all levels of government, there has been a growing concern about observance of the basic requirements of due process in dealing with the rights of citizens. This has been occasioned partly by laxity in the publication of rules and regulations, resulting in ignorance of their requirements, and partly by arbitrary procedures, sometimes real, sometimes alleged. Legislation has been passed in many states designed to correct one or both of these situations. South Carolina in 1937 was the first state to adopt legislation requiring publication of rules and regulations. Fifteen other states have since — most of them in 1941 — adopted such measures, patterned largely on the Federal act of 1935 providing for the establishment of the *Federal Register.* On the procedural side, a uniform administrative procedures act has been drafted, and California, Pennsylvania, and a number of other states have adopted either this or acts similar to the Federal law passed in 1946.

The preceding section of this chapter closed with reference to the so-called Hoover Commission established by the Congress in 1947 to study the administrative structure of the Federal government and to develop plans and recommendations for its reorganization. Parallel with this action by the Congress was a resolution adopted by the Governors' Conference at Salt Lake City in July of that year, requesting the Council of State Governments

to make a comprehensive survey and investigation of the over-all organization and administration of state government, including the organization and operation of the governor's office, operation of the state departments and agencies, budget administration, personnel administration, planning and development, interim commissions and relationships between the executive and legislative branches; and to recommend to the governor a program for strengthening and improving the over-all organization and administration of state government.

Local Government Reorganization

Strengthening the Municipal Executive. The movement to strengthen the executive so that he would be able to perform the duties expected of him has been in evidence at all levels of government — national, state, and local. At the municipal level it has made itself felt in a number of ways: first, by the substitution of the strong mayor-and-council form for the weak form. This change corresponds quite closely to developments in the states, although different terminology has been used to describe them. There has been a definite tendency toward strengthening the powers of the mayor, so that he can actually control his administration. The number of independent and overlapping boards and commissions has been reduced and the operations of the city governments departmentalized. A cabinet composed of the heads of these departments provides an advisory body for the mayor and a mechanism for the coordination of the various functions performed by the city government.

The adoption of the city manager form in more than eight hundred municipalities throughout the country is evidence of the desire both to strengthen the executive and to separate the executive functions from the public and political ones, so that the manager could concentrate his attention on the one, the mayor on the other. Under the manager plan, the city manager appoints the heads of departments and supervises their work. He is responsible for implementing and carrying out the programs and policies adopted by the council. The tendency to strengthen the municipal executive is still further illustrated by the slow but steady decline in the number of commission-governed cities, most of which have now turned to city manager government.

Reorganization of County Government. There have been a large number of proposals for the reorganization of county government, which has long been regarded as "the dark continent of American politics." It is conceivable, of course, that by diligent effort it might be possible to make the existing system work better, and in some counties this has been done. In the opinion of most students, however, conditions require something more. The various proposals for structural change include the county president form, the county executive form, and the county manager plan, to say nothing of the possibilities of economy and greater efficiency through county consolidation.

The various plans for county government reorganization all provide for some kind of executive; they differ chiefly in the extent to which they confer real supervisory powers upon that official. The county president or county executive might be elected by the people or chosen by the county board; in either case, the plan is not likely to be very effective unless there is an accompanying reconstruction of the machinery of county government. These hybrid forms have, however, found considerable acceptance in some states, particularly in the south.

The county manager plan does for the county very nearly what the city manager plan has done for the haphazard organization and procedures of many city governments. He is selected by the county board and definitely charged with administrative responsibility. As in the municipal counterpart, the manager selects and supervises the work of the heads of the various departments. The plan substitutes a qualified administrator for a local political leader and makes possible the introduction of accepted methods of administration into the conduct of the county's business. So far, however, progress in securing adoption of the plan has been slow and uncertain. In 1945 eleven counties in six states had adopted it, and in 1948 four new counties were added to the list. The success of the plan where it has been used and the urgent need for county reform should stimulate more rapid progress in this field in the years ahead.[9]

Requirements for Effective Reorganization

The determination of the proper administrative structure for a governmental unit is one of those problems which are never solved, for no attempted solution is ever entirely satisfactory at the time of its adoption or ever suitable for a prolonged period of time. So true is this that it seems desirable to attempt some generalizations with regard to the nature and scope of the reorganization movement.

In the first place, the processes of change in the administrative structure move very slowly. The governmental tradition of the American people is that they dislike rapid change. Stability in itself is a good thing, but too much stability in a rapidly changing world may become an obstacle to progress. Furthermore, the established departments and agencies, which are often influential with members of the legislature, resist innovations either because they prefer the known to the unknown or because they fear the personal insecurity that might result from a shifting of duties, functions, responsibilities, and personnel. As a result the changes that are accomplished never quite catch up with the need.

In the second place, no ideal solution of the problem is possible and even if it were, the solution would not long remain ideal. The relative importance of one administrative function or agency as compared with another, depends to a considerable extent upon one's interests and one's point of view. It depends also upon time and place and circumstance. What seems of vital importance to one is a relatively minor matter to another; and what seems important at one time, under certain conditions, may not seem significant at all under other circumstances.

Furthermore, no organization is possible in which there are not con-

---

[9] See the author's *American State Government*, Chapter 20, and "Readjusting Governmental Areas and Functions," *Annals*, January, 1940, pp. 203–209.

flicts and some overlapping. Administrative problems are neither simple nor separable into neat compartments; on the contrary, they are complex and possess such a never-ending variety of interrelationships as to defy the ingenuity of the classifier. No matter how the work is divided, that of each department impinges upon that of several others. The department of education must concern itself with child health, and most departmental programs, regardless of the nature of their subject matter, must concern themselves with education. The result is that, rightly or wrongly, such administrative changes as are adopted are usually the result of compromise between conflicting pressures in the legislature, in the administration, and among special interest groups.

Perhaps one illustration of the complexity of these problems will suffice. During the war there was at one point a shortage of foundry workers. Paul V. McNutt, Chairman of the War Manpower Commission, was asked to do something about it. He wrote to James F. Byrnes, Director of War Mobilization, making six requests with regard to matters over which he had no control yet with regard to which action was necessary if the problem was to be solved.[10]

To avoid the risk of Congressional deadlock or inaction it has become standard Federal practice in recent years to follow a precedent established by the Overman Act in 1918, whereby the President is given

---

[10] It has been decided to exclude other than incidental mention of the problems of wartime organization and administration, which require extended treatment if discussed at all. The following are among the more important titles: Emmerich, Herbert, "Some Notes on Wartime Federal Administration," *Public Administration Review*, Winter, 1945, pp. 55-61; Gulick, Luther, *Administrative Reflections from World War II* (University of Alabama Press, 1948), and "War Organization of the Federal Government," *American Political Science Review*, December, 1944, pp. 1166-1179; Hoslett, Schuyler D., "Some Problems of Army Depot Administration," *Public Administration Review*, Summer, 1945, pp. 233-239; Millett, John D., "The Organizational Structure of the Army Service Forces," *ibid.*, Autumn, 1944, pp. 268-278; Nelson, Otto L., Jr., "The General Staff and the Future," *Infantry Journal*, January, 1946, pp. 8-27 (from his book, *National Security and the General Staff*), and "Wartime Developments in War Department Organization and Administration," *Public Administration Review*, Winter, 1945, pp. 1-15; Peak, George W., "The War Department Manpower Board," *American Political Science Review*, February, 1946, pp. 1-20; "Administrative Management in the Army Service Forces," a symposium, *Public Administration Review*, Autumn, 1944, pp. 255-308. For comment on the contribution of the states in the war effort, see Chapter 24 of the author's *American State Government*. The Civilian Production Administration published an extensive series of volumes on the work of the emergency war agencies — Office of Price Administration, War Production Board, etc. Several volumes dealing with wartime administration were published: Boutwell, William D., and others, *America Prepares for Tomorrow* (Harpers, New York, 1941); Crum, William L., and others, *Fiscal Planning for Total War* (National Bureau of Economic Research, New York, 1942); Herring, E. Pendleton, *The Impact of War* (Farrar & Rinehart, New York, 1941); *America Organizes to Win the War, A Symposium* (Harcourt, Brace, New York, 1942). The following are also of interest: Howard, Vaughn L., and Bone, Hugh A., *Current American Government*, Chapter 3 (Appleton-Century, New York, 1943); *Administrative Management in the Army Service Forces*, a symposium (Public Administration Service, Chicago, 1944); Hoslett, Schuyler D., *Aspects of Army Depot Administration* (American Historical Company, New York, 1945).

authority, ordinarily for a limited period of time, to make such changes as might seem to be in the best interest of the service, subject to Congressional disapproval within sixty or ninety days. This arrangement, by a simple shift of emphasis, tends to increase the chances of having recommendations of survey commissions become effective. Instead of requiring legislative approval, the recommendations take effect in the absence of positive action on the part of the legislature. This reduces the opportunities for defeating such proposals by pressure group influence, by use of obstructive tactics, or by sheer inaction.

Changing Character of the Reorganization Movement. Over the years there has been a notable change in emphasis. The early commissions, generally speaking, concerned themselves with the minutiae of internal organization and management, while later bodies correctly assumed that these were questions for management itself to deal with and that their concern should be with over-all problems of organizational structure and management. This has expressed itself in the effort to group activities according to major purpose and to improve and strengthen the coordinative and management agencies now grouped in the Executive Office of the President.

Experience with reorganization surveys — both Federal and state — has clearly demonstrated some other things. The initiation of surveys is primarily a legislative responsibility, while the carrying out of survey recommendations should be primarily the responsibility of the executive. The legislatures have been quite willing to provide the necessary authorization for surveys; but when the surveys have been completed, it has been well nigh impossible to secure favorable legislative action on their recommendations. This has been true in one administration after another, without regard to party, in one jurisdiction after another.

Reorganization as a Continuous Process. Because reorganization moves slowly and ideal solutions are so rarely obtainable, it follows that in a society where change is constant, the pressure for corollary administrative changes must also be constant. Reorganization, therefore, becomes a task that is always in process of fulfillment. The pressure for action may be stronger and more insistent at some times than at others, but as long as governmental services continue to increase in number and to change in character, the urge must ever be present to adapt better the machinery of government to the current needs of the people. The recently enlarged knowledge of administration and increased interest in the subject may help expedite the process.

It is a mistake to assume that a proper administrative organization can be maintained at any level by periodic upheavals of the governmental machinery. Adaptation of structure to function is — or should be — continuous. The President should be vested with authority, on a continuing basis, to make such changes as the needs of the service require. This would involve extension, without a time limit, of the same type of authority that Congress has often given him for a limited period of time. Organization and reorganization are essentially executive in character, not legislative. Congress has not been able to accomplish much in this field because of the conflict of political and pressure group interests and of pressure exerted by the agencies affected. The grant of power would be adequately safeguarded by provision for the type of review contained in recent reorganization acts, under which the Congress has been relieved of the burden of doing the job without relinquishing its authority.

Keeping a Reorganized Government Reorganized. The problem is pretty much the same at all levels. In the state and local units, as at the Federal level, there has been a pronounced tendency toward the multiplication of agencies as new functions have been authorized. Since older functions and agencies are rarely discontinued or consolidated, there results a steady growth in the number of agencies and a sprawling and haphazard governmental structure. Such a development is difficult to prevent, but it can be at least partially controlled. The problem of keeping a reorganized government reorganized is about as difficult as getting it reorganized in the first place.

New York has evolved the best solution yet adopted and in actual operation and has established a pattern which has been followed in Missouri and New Jersey. The principle employed seeks to compel continuous scrutiny of the executive organization by putting a ceiling on the number of departments that may be established. This plan is set forth in the following language in the *Model State Constitution* drawn up by the Committee on State Government of the National Municipal League:

Section 507. *Administrative Departments.* There shall be such administrative departments, not to exceed twenty in number, as may be established by law, with such powers and duties as may be prescribed by law. Subject to the limitations contained in this constitution, the legislature may from time to time assign by law new powers and functions to departments, offices, and agencies, and it may increase, modify, or diminish the powers and functions of such departments, offices, or agencies. All new powers or functions shall be assigned to departments, offices, or agencies in such manner as will tend to maintain an orderly arrangement in the administrative pattern of the state government. The legislature may create temporary commissions for special purposes or reduce the number of departments by consolidation or otherwise.

The initial survey comes easily enough, but the reorganization which follows is tremendously difficult to achieve because so many states cling to an archaic organization, while in others progress is not sustained. There is always danger in a state that elects a "bad" governor that an effort will be made to weaken the powers of the executive for the future rather than to elect governors who will use wisely the powers necessary to do the job properly. There are obstacles to reorganization also in some states in the form of constitutional barriers as well as in the influence of the economy bloc, which is often more interested in keeping down taxes than in obtaining good government.

These difficulties can be overcome and real reorganization achieved on a more or less permanent basis only if there is some official constantly on the job, charged with this specific responsibility. Budget officers have been provided for in the Federal government and in the states and municipalities to handle fiscal affairs. A central personnel agency runs the merit system in the Federal government, in approximately half of the states, and in a great many municipalities. There is need, certainly in all the larger units, for a similar staff officer whose responsibility is organization and management — an officer vested with sufficient power and authority to keep a reorganized government reorganized.

Recognition of the fact that day-to-day responsibility for administrative organization is primarily an executive responsibility is now receiving general acceptance. When the Reorganization Act of 1945 expired, President Truman requested several times that its provisions be renewed on a permanent basis. Similar recommendations contained in studies made for the Hoover Commission resulted in the submission of this specific proposal by the Commission to the Congress in its very first report in January, 1949. The nearest approaches to a realization of this plan at the state level are found in the Minnesota Division of Administrative Management and in the similar organization authorized by the Michigan act of 1948.

SELECTED REFERENCES

FEDERAL

Extensive bibliographies on Federal administrative organization and reorganization will be found in Graves, cited below, and in Bureau of the Budget, *Reorganization of the Executive Branch of the Federal Government: An Annotated Bibliography* (Washington, 1947), and Tompkins, Dorothy C., *Materials for the Study of the Federal Government* (Public Administration Service, Chicago, 1948).

Commission on the Organization of the Executive Branch of Government, *Report* (Washington, 1949). This is the report of the so-called Hoover Commission, and is the most extensive study of the type ever undertaken.

Graves, W. Brooke, *Basic Information on the Reorganization of the Executive Branch, 1912–1948* (Public Affairs Bulletin No. 66, Legislative Reference Service, Library of Congress, 1949). A documentary history of reorganization during an important thirty-five year period.

Meriam, Lewis, and Schmeckebier, Lawrence F., *Reorganization of the National Government* (Brookings Institution, Washington, 1939). Attempts to answer the question: what does it involve?

President's Committee on Administrative Management, *Report with Special Studies* (Washington, 1937). The most significant report on reorganization up to the 1949 Report of the Hoover Commission.

Wallace, Schuyler C., *Federal Departmentalization* (Columbia University Press, 1941). Subtitle: a critique of theories of organization.

White, Leonard D., *Trends in Public Administration* (McGraw-Hill, New York, 1933). An able analysis of major lines of development.

Willoughby, W. F., *The Reorganization of the Administrative Branch of the National Government* (Johns Hopkins Press, 1926). One of numerous works on the subject by one of the founders of the scientific study of administration in America.

STATE

An exhaustive state-by-state bibliography will be found in Buck, cited below. For more recent titles, see New Jersey Legislative Reference Section, *State Organization and Reorganization: A Bibliography* (State Library, Trenton, January, 1948), and Weiner, Grace, *Administrative Reorganization of State Governments: A Bibliography* (Joint Reference Library, Chicago, 1941). This item is brought down to date by Yates, Marianne, and Gilchrist, Martha, *Administrative Reorganization of State Governments, A Bibliography* (Council of State Governments, Chicago, August, 1948). Excellent administrative manuals are available in many states.

Bollens, John C., *Administrative Reorganization in the States Since 1939* (Bureau of Public Administration, University of California, 1947). Supplements Buck, bringing the story down to 1947.

Buck, Arthur E., *The Reorganization of State Governments in the United States* (Columbia University Press, 1938). Standard treatise covering fully developments in all states down to date of publication.

Lipson, Leslie, *The American Governor: From Figurehead to Leader* (University of Chicago Press, 1939). The only authoritative study of the evolution of the governorship.

3

THE OVER-ALL
ADMINISTRATIVE HIERARCHY

THE evolution of administrative organization in the United States, out-lined in the preceding chapters, is now to be followed by a considera-tion in some detail of the organization within a single governmental unit, i.e., the Federal government, a state, or a municipality. This organ-ization is both vertical and horizontal. Among the problems involved are departmentalization, types of agencies, establishment of lines of au-thority, and those human aspects of administration which may be con-sidered under the general heading of "bureaucracy."

Organization of the Administrative Hierarchy

Vertical Organization. The organization as a whole is copied from the military and is largely hierarchical. At the base, as Professor Corry has said, "are the great mass of private soldiers whose duty is to obey, and at each succeeding level wider and wider powers of command are lodged until the commander in chief with over-all authority is reached." [1] Stated in the terms of a specific governmental unit, the service as a whole is divided into a number of departments or agencies, each with its administrative head — a cabinet officer or administrator, with his dep-uties and assistants.

Each agency is divided into a number of bureaus, and these in turn are broken down into divisions, sections, units, and so on. The purpose of this division is partly to decentralize the bulk of decisions which have to be made in any large organization and partly to obtain the advan-tages of specialization which are vital to the success of any large under-taking. The subordinate units are subject to the same type of problem that arises from conflict of authority and overlapping of functions that occurs at the higher level between departments and agencies.

The assignment of services to the departments and to the bureaus within the departments should be based on a grouping of related func-tions. While the total number of units to be supervised must be held at

---

[1] See Corry, J. A., *Elements of Democratic Government*, Chapter 12 (Oxford Univer-sity Press, New York, 1947).

a minimum, it is just as bad to group unrelated services into the same department as it is to leave related services functioning independently or assigned to different departments. The number and complexity of the interrelations between functions is so great that it becomes exceedingly difficult to make and even more difficult to maintain an orderly pattern of administrative organization.[2]

The lines of authority in an over-all organization are indicated in the table on page 39, which shows the nature of the administrative hierarchy at the various levels of government — national, state, and local. All of these, it will be observed, have certain elements in common. In each of them one notes the employer, represented by top management; the employee, represented by the organization for production; and the supervisory group. The nature of this organizational structure is clearly indicated in the chart which appears on page 40.

Top management includes the head of the agency or unit and his immediate staff. These persons are the administration — the small group at the top of the pyramid who are responsible for the work of others, who make the decisions on questions both of policy and of practice, and who exercise authority in seeing that decisions are carried out.[3] Their duties include

1. Determination of organizational objectives within the limitations of legislative and executive authority
2. Recognition, knowledge of, and clarification of agency objectives, both long term and short term, formulated by others
3. Determination of administrative policy (general plans of carrying out predetermined organizational objectives)
4. Delineation, analysis, and solution of problems of organization and management
5. Responsibility for organization planning
6. Translation of over-all objectives and policies, for persons both inside and outside of the organization
7. Interpretation of agency objectives and policies, for persons both inside and outside of the organization
8. Delegation of authority and fixing of responsibility
9. Establishing, developing, and maintaining an effective staff: appraising and measuring organizational, administrative, executive, and supervisory competency
10. Developing joint participation of associate administrators on top and lower levels

---

[2] For a discussion of the different theories that have been applied to the solution of this problem, see Wallace, Schuyler C., *Federal Departmentalization* (Columbia University Press, 1941).

[3] Cleeton, Glen U., and Mason, Charles W., *Executive Ability, Its Discovery and Development*, Revised Edition, p. 8 (Antioch Press, Yellow Springs, 1946).

Lines of Authority in Administration

	FEDERAL	STATE	COUNTY	MUNICIPAL	AGENCY, INSTALLATION, OR ESTABLISHMENT
According to Level	President	Governor	Commissioners or Manager	Mayor or City Manager	Regional Director or Commanding Officer
TOP MANAGEMENT	Cabinet Secretary Commissioner Administrator Board of Directors	Cabinet Secretary Head of Independent Establishment	Elected Head of Department	Cabinet Director or Secretary Head of Independent Establishment	Executive Officer

According to Type of Agency	DEPARTMENT	INDEPENDENT ESTABLISHMENT	ADMINISTRATION	AGENCY	CORPORATION
	Cabinet Secretary	Commission; Chairman of Commission	Administrator	Administrator	Board of Directors; General Manager

(The Employer)

Middle Management SUPERVISION	Division Chiefs Bureau Chiefs
First-line Supervisors (The Supervisor)	Section Heads Unit Heads

PRODUCTION

INDIVIDUAL EMPLOYEES

(The Employee)

11. Keeping open direct channels of communication: horizontal, vertical, and diagonal

12. Responsibility for the exercise of discretion. "The fine art of executive decision consists in not deciding questions that are not now pertinent, in not deciding prematurely, in not making decisions that cannot be made effective, and in not making decisions that others should make." [4]

13. Responsibility for the leadership and motivation of the staff

14. Coordination of the organization. Perhaps this is the most important function of all; the more the advantages of specialization are sought, the more pressing becomes the task of integration, settling disputes between departments, and insuring that they do not frustrate one another by working at cross-purposes. The hierarchical organization gives the unity of ultimate command necessary for this purpose.

Under the heading of supervision may be included all those persons in the organization who are responsible for the work of others. They

[4] Barnard, Chester I., *The Functions of the Executive*, p. 194 (Harvard University Press, 1945).

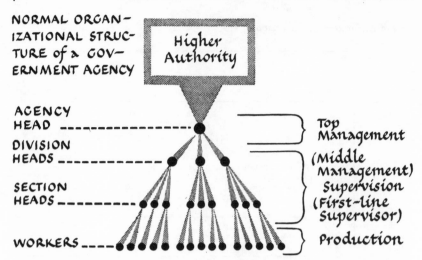

NORMAL ORGAN-
IZATIONAL STRUC-
TURE of a GOV-
ERNMENT AGENCY

Higher
Authority

AGENCY
HEAD ----------------

DIVISION
HEADS ------------

SECTION
HEADS ---------

WORKERS ----

Top
Management

(Middle
Management)
Supervision
(First-line
Supervisor)

Production

are the liaison between top management and the workers. Some may devote their full time to supervision; others may be "working supervisors," persons whose supervisory responsibilities do not require their full time and who in addition to performing some supervisory duties themselves engage in productive effort. It is the responsibility of the supervisor to plan the work of the unit on the basis of instructions received from the next higher echelon of authority or management, to parcel it out to the workers on the basis of their particular skills and abilities, and to keep a constant check on the progress of the work.

The term "supervision" includes management at all levels — top management, middle management, and first-line supervision. The nature of top management has already been indicated. Middle management — a very descriptive term coined by Mary C. H. Niles — refers to those persons in the line of authority between top management on the one hand and first-line supervisors on the other. They are high enough in the line of authority to be tagged with the stigma of management — if stigma it be — yet far enough down the line to be free from responsibility for making important policy decisions. The first-line supervisor is the person who supervises the work of the individual employees; it is said that approximately 85 per cent of the employees in the Federal government work under such unit supervisors. The spread of the administrative function in an agency is shown in the chart on page 41; the place of the supervisor in public administration, in another chart on page 43.

Lines of authority lead up through this administrative hierarchy; authority passes down from the top, through successive levels of management, to the first-line supervisor, while information and reports pass up

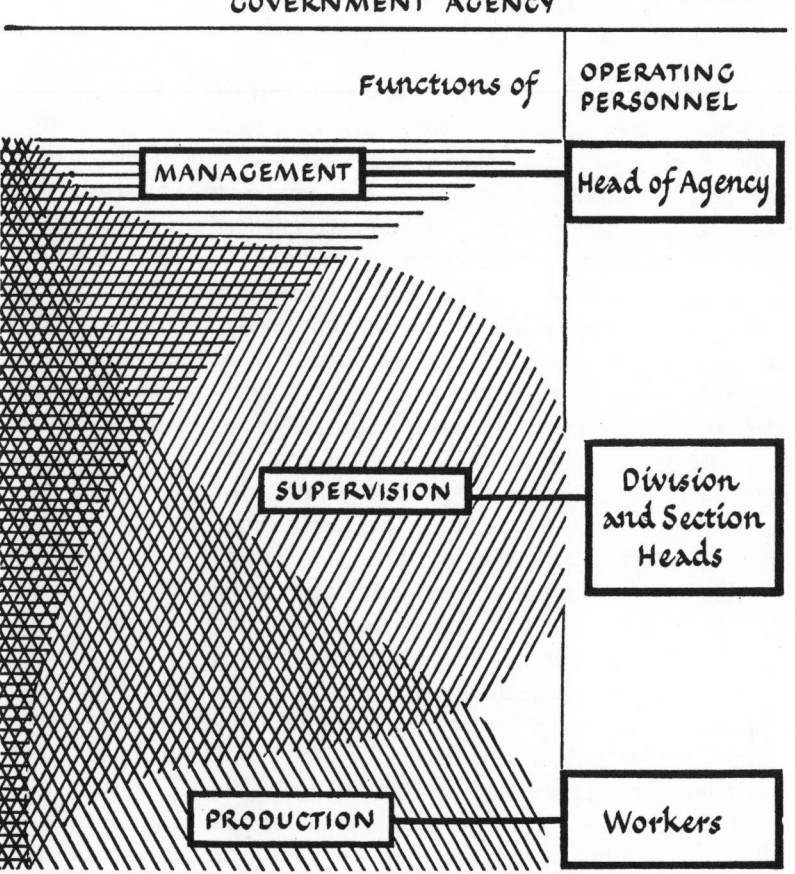

SPREAD of ADMINISTRATIVE FUNCTIONS in a
GOVERNMENT AGENCY

Functions of	OPERATING PERSONNEL
MANAGEMENT	Head of Agency
SUPERVISION	Division and Section Heads
PRODUCTION	Workers

through the same channels from the first-line supervisor to the top. In a
military organization authority passes down from the general, through
the lieutenant generals and major generals, the colonels, majors, cap-
tains, and lieutenants, to the noncommissioned officers — the lowest
level in the line of authority. A comparable situation exists in civilian
organizations; the names are different but the principle is the same.

The existence of this line of authority raises questions concerning
delegation of power and span of control, both of which will be considered in the following chapter. Important as is the element of supervision, the employees themselves are the unit cells in the production system, whether the product be letters typed, stencils cut, cases handled or
processed, or bearings turned out on a machine. Good management is
essential in any smoothly working organization, but without efficient
employees high production standards are impossible. Good manage-

ment magnifies the importance of the individual worker, seeking in various ways to impress upon each the value of his contribution and his effort in the program as a whole.

Line and Staff. Administrative departments and agencies may be classified in still another way — horizontally, as it were — according to the type of activity in which they are engaged in their particular unit. For this purpose the terms "line" and "staff" have now achieved universal acceptance, although their significance has changed somewhat over the years. Willoughby, whose *Principles of Public Administration* stood for many years as the standard systematic treatment of the subject, defined staff services as those which were necessary for the servicing of the line or operating agencies. He separated them (i.e., staff services) into two groups, housekeeping and regulatory, the first including activities such as personnel and finance whose effective functioning is a prerequisite to the performance of the duties of either the regulatory services such as public utility regulation or of such operating services as agriculture, health, or welfare. This classification, though no longer generally used, had much in its favor.

The classification now commonly accepted has been described by Gulick, White, and others. In their terminology the line services, often spoken of as the operating services, are those which come in close contact with the people, including activities of a regulatory character and those which furnish service or information. The control of plant and animal diseases and the enforcement of food and drug regulations, blue sky laws, public utility laws, and laws requiring the examination and licensing of practitioners of learned professions and technical trades are all examples of line or regulatory services. So too are the activities of the service type, called by some writers primary services, which include the farm marketing service, those phases of the plant and animal industry service which aid producers in getting a greater output at a minimum investment, public health service, free library programs, vocational and adult educational programs, and the like.

The auxiliary services — the term which White applies to the "housekeeping" services of Willoughby — are concerned with the routine activities of government: the collection and disbursement of revenues; the custody and budgeting of revenues and the supervision of their expenditure; the purchase and maintenance of property, supplies, and equipment; and the hiring, dismissal, promotion, and retirement of personnel. These services are of little direct benefit to the people, yet it would be utterly impossible for the line services to function if the auxiliary services were not regularly and efficiently maintained. They re-

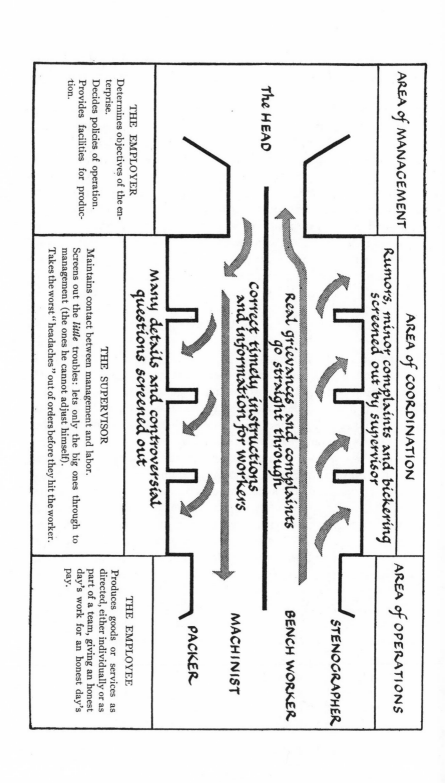

AREA of MANAGEMENT

AREA of COORDINATION

AREA of OPERATIONS

The HEAD

THE EMPLOYER
Determines objectives of the enterprise.
Decides policies of operation.
Provides facilities for production.

Rumors, minor complaints and bickering screened out by supervisor

Real grievances and complaints go straight through

Correct timely instructions and information for workers

Many details and controversial questions screened out

THE SUPERVISOR
Maintains contact between management and labor.
Screens out the *little* troubles: lets only the big ones through to management (the ones he cannot adjust himself).
Takes the worst "headaches" out of orders before they hit the worker.

STENOGRAPHER

BENCH WORKER

MACHINIST

PACKER

THE EMPLOYEE
Produces goods or services as directed, either individually or as part of a team, giving an honest day's work for an honest day's pay.

late in the main to functions of general government provided for in the Executive Office of the President in the Federal government and in the original constitutional offices in the states.

The staff services have been defined as the research and planning arm of the executive branch of government. They differ from the auxiliary services in that the latter are operating agencies concerned with the maintenance of the existing organizations and activities but not with major policies. The staff agency is a nonoperating agency concerned with thinking, research, and advisory work and with the revision of organization and procedures as new needs may arise. It is concerned with the formation of major policy decisions, although some agencies are obliged to perform duties in both categories.

The central personnel agency, for instance, is a staff agency for the government as a whole and an auxiliary agency so far as it is charged with the actual administration of the personnel function. The United States Bureau of the Budget provides an excellent illustration. It is responsible for financial supervision and control, but it is also the unit in the executive branch primarily responsible for planning and developing improved methods of administrative organization and procedure. There has, in fact, been serious question as to the propriety of placing in the same agency the responsibility for two such separate and distinct functions. The need for staff services in government is an acute need, but surprisingly little has been done in developing proper machinery to provide them.

The main functions of these agencies are to control and coordinate certain aspects of internal management of all other departments. Just as, in the army, the commander in chief is supported by a staff engaged in thinking and planning rather than in actual field command, so in government this plan has already been worked out in the fields of finance and personnel and is in process of development with regard to over-all planning. The budget office, by its control over departmental estimates and over expenditures under the budget, maintains a powerful check on the departments and agencies. The accounting office can indicate ways and means of stopping wasteful or inefficient practices. The central personnel office, with its responsibility for classification, inevitably becomes involved in problems of organization and coordination. Any of these offices may become a sort of efficiency expert for the chief executive, performing for him a great many of the tasks of coordination.

The relatively recent recognition of this important function of government has led to the development of specialists in administrative management, often referred to as administrative analysts. An administrative analyst has been defined as one whose major function is that of problem analysis, data collection, sorting, tabulating, testing, comparison, and interpretation, and whose objective is to furnish responsible officials with such summaries of pertinent findings and recommendations as will enable them to formulate intelligent decisions on policies, methods, and procedures of organization and management. This activity includes such specific functions as the following:

1. Exercising wide latitude in formulating methods and procedures of compiling and presenting material
2. Carrying on special studies and receiving direct assignments from the chief of the division regarding procedural and organizational matters
3. Making special investigations as to the effectiveness of a special procedure or related forms
4. Serving as principal assistant to the consultant on regulations and substituting for the consultant on occasion
5. Assisting the chief of the service section in developing standards for office management procedures in the regional and state offices
6. Conducting field investigations regarding all phases of emergency work; preparing monthly reports of such investigations and recommending changes affecting both production and personnel
7. Reviewing present or existing orders, instructions, and regulations for the purpose of detecting inconsistencies and apparent cause for duplication or overlapping of functions, and redrafting or recommending remedial measures
8. Making studies of problems of organization common to all or several agencies or of a particular agency; studying, analyzing, and reporting on problems of administrative procedure common to all agencies — such as duplication and reproduction facilities
9. Advising the coordinator as to the needs of individual bureaus, boards, and offices, and rendering technical assistance and advice in the coordination of requirements and standardization of all office equipment for the organization

Such devices make organization still more complex and are an aid to efficiency and coordination only if the administrative skill necessary to operate them is available. Rivalry between departments, for instance, may lead to efforts to sabotage the staff agency. Only by developing its controls and selling them to departments or a service basis can a staff agency expect to achieve a large measure of success. As long as it functions mainly as a policeman, it can expect at best only a grudging compliance with its regulations and its program.

It has been said times without number that the Presidency imposes an impossible job upon an individual. The President stands at the apex of authority and responsibility with nine cabinet members who manage their respective departments and are supposed to keep the President in touch with administration. But there are in addition not less than fifty or sixty heads of other executive agencies [5] outside of the departments and not under the supervision of any member of the cabinet. In addition to coordinating the nine departments, the President has some responsibility for supervising the work of each of these agencies. The job of the chief executive at all levels becomes more and more one of coordinating and influencing departmental policy. The number of departments and agencies and their multitudinous interrelationships make coordination of policy at once one of the most difficult and most vital problems in public administration. During World War II some effort was made to coordinate departmental policy below the level of the chief executive through the use of coordinating committees. Some solution of this problem is most urgently needed.

Realizing the impossibility of any one individual's effectively supervising and coordinating the work of all the departments and independent establishments, both the President's Committee on Administrative Management and the Hoover Commission recommended in 1937 and 1949, respectively, that the staff services of the chief executive be enlarged and improved.[6] The former proposed that the administrative aspects of the work of these independent establishments be brought under the supervision of the appropriately related departments; discussion of this most reasonable proposal unfortunately took a political turn, so that no action was taken.[7] The Hoover Commission proposed to meet this problem by vesting all administrative responsibility in the chairman of the commission and, among other things, delegating routine, preliminary, and less important work to members of the staffs under their supervision, thereby freeing the time and energies of the commissioners for more important tasks.

---

[5] A tabulation made by the Citizens National Committee in 1944 (a war year) showed a total of 428 functional units in the Federal government, 374 of them in the Executive Branch. Of these, 242 were created by statute and 58 by Executive Order. See *Federal Agencies* (Washington, 1944). The Hoover Commission and the Bureau of the Budget in 1948 agreed to a list of seventy-four, including the departments and the regulatory agencies; see their report, *General Management of the Executive Branch* (Washington, 1949).

[6] Failure to provide staff services in the past caused Presidents to create an enormous number of special advisory and special investigating committees and commissions to do for them, in many cases, what their own staff agencies should have been equipped to do. For the best discussions of this problem, see the Committee's *Report with Special Studies;* the Commission's *General Management of the Executive Branch;* Marx, *The President and His Staff Services;* and Price, Don K., "Staffing the Presidency," *American Political Science Review,* December, 1946, pp. 1154–1168.

[7] This thesis is developed in Cushman, Robert E., *The Independent Regulatory Commissions* (Oxford University Press, New York, 1941). On the duties of the chief executive as general manager, see Porter, Kirk H., *State Administration,* Chapter 2 (Crofts, New York, 1938), and White, Leonard D., *Introduction to the Study of Public Administration,* Third Edition, Chapter 4 (Macmillan, New York, 1948).

Some Essential Elements in Administration

Because the scientific study of public administration began so recently, there has been little standardization of subject matter. Each text previously published — not to mention the present one — has included discussion of some matters and excluded or minimized others according to the author's individual judgment. Gulick and Urwick have contributed perhaps more than any other writers to a standardization of subject matter; their summary of basic content, as represented in the coined word POSDCORB, has been generally accepted and widely quoted.

The letters in POSDCORB are intended to direct attention to the various functional elements in the work of an executive; these are

PLANNING: working out in broad outline the things that need to be done and the method for doing them in order to accomplish the purpose set for the enterprise. (Part IV)

ORGANIZING: the establishment of the formal structure of authority through which work subdivisions are arranged, defined, and coordinated for the defined objective. (Parts I and IV)

STAFFING: the whole personnel function of bringing in and training the staff and maintaining favorable conditions of work. (Part II)

DIRECTING: the continuous task of making decisions and embodying them in specialized and general orders and instructions and serving as leader of the enterprise. (Part IV)

COORDINATING: the all-important duty of interrelating the various parts of the work. (Part IV)

REPORTING: keeping those to whom the executive is responsible informed as to what is going on, which thus includes keeping himself and his subordinates informed through records, research, and inspection. (Parts III and V)

BUDGETING: with all that goes with budgeting in the form of fiscal planning, accounting, and control. (Part III)

These items are the subject matter of public administration. All of them will be discussed at some length later in this volume, in the Parts indicated. Important as they are, no one should assume that they are all of the essential elements of good administration; among others one might stress, for instance, the importance of specialization and of leadership.

With regard to specialization, one writer has pointed out that the clerks in a country store are generally able to serve at any counter, but in a large city department store there is a separate sales staff for each department. In much the same way governments find it necessary to set up separate departments or agencies and to employ persons possessing special knowledges and skills within those agencies, in order to supply all the different types of service demanded of modern government. Frequently also, specialization or particularization may be employed to emphasize the importance of a new activity, which after becoming established may be absorbed in some related department already existing.

Although a chapter in Part IV is devoted primarily to the subject of leadership, the subject is of such vital importance that it seems appropriate to point out here that no organization can function for long — certainly it cannot function well — without leadership. The tone of an organization is set by the quality of its leadership. The manner in which all the activities represented in the POSDCORB formula are performed is to a large extent dependent upon the ability of management in any given case to select and direct the supervisory personnel of the organization. Leadership in a democratic government presents peculiar problems and difficulties, in that — with the exception of city managers — practically all top governmental executives are selected for one task on the basis of their ability successfully to perform another, which is largely unrelated to the first. The solution of this problem has usually been thought to be a permanent professional career service of administrators who would be responsible through one administration after another, regardless of changes in political control, for the carrying out of policies determined by elected representatives of the people and by their popularly chosen executives.[8]

The Problem of Bureaucracy

In a consideration of the administrative hierarchy, it seems appropriate to inquire into the reasons for the growth of the so-called bureaucracy, about which so much has been written and spoken, and to examine both the nature and the merit of the objections that have been raised to it. A starting point is to be found in the changed position of the executive. Whereas the executive branch was formerly supposed to be something of an automaton carrying out the dictates of legislatures and of courts, it now does a great deal of legislating and legal interpretation in the course of administration. It is a powerful influence in the determination of legislative policy, and it has encroached to a certain extent upon the judiciary. Its power has been so expanded that it is changed beyond all recognition and is of a radically different character from its original form. Its size and the scope of its operations have created new problems of internal management. How is the President to coordinate and direct the activities of approximately two million Federal employees, the governors of the larger states, and the mayors of the larger cities?

The first requirement of sober analysis is to eliminate, so far as pos-

---

[8] Some of our most successful political executives have been fully aware of the desirability of divorcing the political or policy-determining activities of government from the managerial aspects; see, for instance, Smith, Alfred E., "How We Ruin Our Governors," *National Municipal Review*, May, 1921, pp. 277–280.

sible, the emotional content of the word "bureaucracy," a symbolic word commonly applied as an epithet to arouse mass prejudice. The denunciation of all governmental activity as bureaucracy, of all government employees as "tax-eaters" feeding at the public trough — whether in America or elsewhere — is a fine example of the name-calling technique so familiar in propaganda efforts in many fields.[9] The significant growth in the scope of governmental operations has been more appropriately christened by Paul Appleby as "Big Democracy." [10]

Growth of Governmental Activity. The tremendous growth of governmental activity not only in the United States but elsewhere in the last three quarters of a century has been one of the striking aspects of modern history. The gradual transformation from a predominantly agricultural to a predominantly industrial civilization created an almost infinite number of new governmental problems. The advances of science, the industrial revolution with the advent of the factory system, the consequent urbanization of populations, all tended to emphasize the need for new and more extensive governmental services. When 90 per cent of the population lived on farms and only 10 per cent in towns, only the most elementary functions were demanded of government.

The startling growth of cities and the rapid expansion of industry, particularly after the Civil War, brought demands for housing, water supply, paved and lighted streets, health services, public schools, fire and police protection, waste disposal, parks and playgrounds, and numerous other services. Although these demands were largely at the municipal level, the states were also faced with new responsibilities — the regulation of hours and conditions of work, women and children in industry, rates of pay, highway construction and maintenance, traffic control, and so on. As early as 1887 the first regulatory body was created by act of Congress, the Interstate Commerce Commission, "the granddaddy of Washington bureaucracies." This was followed by a host of others, as was indicated in an earlier chapter. All these activities — service and regulatory alike — required funds and personnel. This

---

[9] It is interesting to note that this epithet is commonly reserved for Federal employees, while the even more opprobrious term of "drones" is applied to local civil servants. In one Philadelphia campaign a candidate for the mayoralty asserted that it was not the drones that he objected to, it was the assistant drones. For comment on "Public Attitudes Toward Public Personnel," see a series of four articles in *Personnel Administration*, January, 1947, pp. 15-26, dealing with the popular views of bureaucrats here and abroad. See also Myrdal, Gunnar, *An American Dilemma* (Harpers, New York, 1944), and De Nike, J. Harold, "Notes of a Neophyte Bureaucrat," *Harvard Business Review*, Summer, 1944.
[10] See his volume under that title, and for a list of twelve characteristics of bureaucracy, Dimock, Marshall E., "Bureaucracy Self-Examined," *Public Administration Review*, Summer, 1944, pp. 197-207.

meant a continuing growth in the number and scope of governmental activities, a growth in the much maligned bureaucracy.

In very great measure these new frontiers reflected social and economic developments. Typical of the activities at the state level are such items as workmen's compensation; regulation of working conditions in factories, especially where women and children are employed; supervision of housing, particularly in the establishment of agencies for tenement supervision. Then in some jurisdictions the social conscience called for more adequate and humane treatment of offenders and for enlarged and better staffed agencies for probation and parole. Many of these services are still far below the requirements indicated by the body of existing knowledge, but new standards call for services vastly more extensive and more expensive to operate than those of yesteryear.

Nor were the states inactive in a number of regulatory fields. Long before the establishment of the Securities and Exchange Commission blue-sky laws to prevent the sale of fraudulent securities called for boards or commissions of a quasi-judicial nature. Insurance, long regarded as a business affected with a public interest, has been regulated by the states for many years, and in spite of a Supreme Court decision in 1945 it continues to be so regulated. Just as the Federal government has since 1863 exercised supervision over national banks, so the states have long examined and regulated state banks, trust companies, and, more recently, private bankers — banking being another field of private enterprise pretty universally regarded as affected with a public interest. The court reports for years back are studded with other cases involving borderline questions in this area: the manufacture of ice, the retail sale of milk, the sale of theater tickets, the regulation of the rates charged by employment agencies, to mention only a few.[11]

Is "Big Government" Inevitable? Certain it is that as government undertakes more activities and attempts to render more and better service in fields where it has long been accustomed to operate, it is going to spend more money and employ more people. In this sense "big government" is inevitable; new agencies are bound to be set up and old ones to increase in size. In another sense "big government" is not inevitable. Expansion does not have to mean a still further centralization of power in state and nation; that is, if state and local governments and the people who live under their jurisdiction are willing to assume the responsibility for performing those functions which it is possible to perform

---

[11] For an account of fifteen years of experience and observation in Michigan, see Brown, Vernon J., "The Growth of State Government," *State Government*, February, 1944, pp. 276–277, 283.

locally on an efficient basis. In this endeavor the local units and the people have a large responsibility which they cannot dodge; but the larger units can help in at least two ways: by lending assistance and encouragement to local effort and by restraining the grasp for more power and more responsibility which so often characterizes the efforts of governmental agencies.[12]

The Critics of Bureaucracy. Many critics of big government, not necessarily hostile to governmental activity as such, seem to forget that the great service and regulatory apparatus that characterizes the administrative arm of government is probably an inevitable concomitant of the positive or service state. It is found in big business as well as in big government. Most people approve of some of these new functions of government, but they often proceed to castigate the "bureaucracy" associated with those activities of which they disapprove. In this they are anything but consistent: they overlook the alleged faults of bureaucracy when the new service state is doing something that benefits them; when it is doing something that benefits someone else, governmental activity suddenly becomes bureaucracy in its most pernicious and objectionable form. Many of these critics must speak with tongue in cheek.

Another phase of the opposition to bureaucracy arises out of what might be termed natural causes. When for any reason people cannot get what they want or do what they want, they invariably blame the government — whether or not the condition is one within government control. If there was a shortage of meat or sugar, it was more convenient to blame the Office of Price Administration than to take the trouble to ascertain that there just was not enough of either to supply the total demand at home and the needs abroad. If there was a shortage of fuel, what could be more natural than to blame the Fuel Administrator or the Petroleum Administrator? This is not a criticism of the public's reaction but a simple observation of fact in the controversy over bureaucracy.

Nor should it be overlooked that government people themselves by their own conduct sometimes invite the very criticism under which they suffer. By an unreasoning insistence upon forms and procedures which seem reasonable enough to them but not to the citizens whom

---

[12] See, for instance, Lilienthal, David E., "Big Government Not Inevitable," *National Municipal Review*, February, 1947, pp. 65–71, 88 — which develops the thesis that the TVA has succeeded in carrying out national policy by cooperation with state and local agencies. Leonard D. White and others have of late been suggesting the return to the states of such functions as they might perform efficiently; with its new responsibilities in the international field and in national security, the Federal government would still have plenty to do.

they serve, they perpetuate the popular notion that all government operations are bogged down by "red tape." By an excess of zeal in the promotion of what is honestly believed to be in the public interest, they sometimes invite unfavorable reactions on the part of legislators or the public. Where seasoned employees seem unwilling to act at all lest they subject themselves to criticism, others seem unduly anxious to exercise discretion and expand the scope of executive power and influence. These persons often provoke criticism which reflects upon the entire government service.

One of the main charges leveled against government agencies, as a matter of fact, grows out of the exercise of discretionary power. The charge is that it is used in an uncertain and unpredictable manner, that as between individuals similarly situated it is used unfairly. In reply one can only remind the critics that laws do not enforce themselves; they have to be interpreted and applied — by men. Unless these men are qualified and proceed with fairness and understanding, there may well be grounds for exactly this type of unfavorable judgment.

Another stock argument is that governmental activity leads to regimentation, which in turn means a loss of individual liberty. The seriousness of this charge is often overemphasized. Persons are not being regimented when, as a result of measures adopted by the elected representatives of the people, each individual is required to do certain things according to his own situation. One can scarcely enter a valid claim of regimentation when he is required to act in accordance with a policy adopted by the people because they believe — rightly or wrongly — that it is in accordance with the principle of the greatest good to the greatest number.[13]

The Challenge to Better Management.[14] The crusade against what is called bureaucracy is carried on relentlessly, in season and out, sometimes because of a lack of appreciation of the problems involved, sometimes for selfish reasons. To point this out, however, is not enough; government is faced with a responsibility and a challenge. The responsibility is to the public it serves; the challenge is to provide the most service and the most efficient service at minimum cost. This requires constant and persistent effort to improve administrative organization and procedures.

It is easy enough to say these things, but how shall they be done? One obvious method is to simplify procedures, to cut the red tape which often characterizes government procedures as indeed it does

---

[13] For an excellent discussion of this matter, see Bendix, Reinhard, "Bureaucracy and the Problem of Power," *Public Administration Review*, Summer, 1945, pp. 194–209.
[14] See especially volumes by Appleby and Juran.

those of any large organization. But this is not easy. Every additional review of a set of papers, every seemingly unnecessary check was prescribed because of the knowledge that someone had or the fear that someone would do something improper. Sufficient checks to insure reasonable regularity in procedures are essential, but common sense must be relied upon to eliminate those checks whose irritating effect from the standpoint of public relations far outweighs their value in protecting the agency against possible irregularities. The agency which manages to maintain the middle course is much more likely to put its program across; the one which aims absolutely to prevent errors is apt to become so involved in its own procedures that little actual work will be accomplished.

SELECTED REFERENCES

Appleby, Paul H., *Big Democracy* (Knopf, New York, 1945). Discusses the challenge to big government to be efficient, and the ways in which it may become so.

Beck, James M., *Our Wonderland of Bureaucracy* (Macmillan, New York, 1933). Forerunner of the huge crop of current criticisms and tirades against bureaucracy.

Commission on Organization of the Executive Branch of the Government, *Regulatory Commissions* (Washington, March, 1949). Presents a plan for improving the administration of the so-called independent commissions.

Corwin, Edward S., *The President: Office and Powers* (New York University Press, 1940). Analysis emphasizing constitutional aspects of presidential power, by a distinguished authority in the field.

Herring, E. Pendleton, *Federal Commissioners* (Harvard University Press, 1936). Deals with Federal regulatory commissions from the point of view of the experience, qualifications, characteristics, etc., of the commissioners themselves.

——, *Public Administration and the Public Interest* (McGraw-Hill, New York, 1936). Analyzes influences of pressure groups and lobbies, not on legislation but on administration.

Juran, Joseph M., *Bureaucracy* (Harpers, New York, 1944). Able presentation of "a challenge to better management."

Macmahon, Arthur W., and Millett, John D., *Federal Administrators* (Columbia University Press, 1939). Does for other types of Federal administrators what Herring does for commissioners.

Marx, Fritz M., *The President and His Staff Services* (Public Administration Service, Chicago, 1947). A good current discussion, originally prepared to explain our system to a foreign audience.

Milton, George F., *The Use of Presidential Power* (Little, Brown, Boston, 1944). An able and sympathetic analysis of the growth and development of presidential power.

Niles, Mary C. H., *Middle Management: The Job of the Junior Executive*, Revised Edition (Harpers, New York, 1948). Pioneer study of the place and importance of the junior executive in the administrative hierarchy.

Smith, Merriman, *A President Is Many Men* (Harpers, New York, 1948). Fascinating story of the presidential office as seen by an experienced Washington correspondent.

Wallace, Schuyler C., *Federal Departmentalization* (Columbia University Press, 1941). An analysis of the different theories of departmental organization.

Whitlock, Brand, *Forty Years of It*, Revised Edition (Appleton, New York, 1925). An able and colorful personality describes his experiences as mayor of a medium-sized city in trying to apply now-recognized principles of good administration.

4

DEPARTMENT AND AGENCY

ORGANIZATION

In the preceding chapters a description of the over-all administrative organization, including the administrative hierarchy, has been attempted. One may now assume the existence of the normal setup of departments, administrations, commissions, corporations, and so on. The next consideration involves a description of the internal organization of the individual departments and agencies. Organization, at all levels of government, centers around the concept of authority, its organization, its extent, its decentralization, communications, and coordination. These are in the main the subject matter of public administration; even though most of them are dealt with at some length in later chapters, it seems necessary to discuss them briefly at this point.

Organization of Authority

Organization of authority is a basic consideration at all levels of government; the principles and problems involved are much the same wherever they are encountered, but they are discussed here particularly from the point of view of the operating department or agency. The discussion is, furthermore, concerned primarily with what has been referred to earlier as the vertical organization; the problems pertaining to the furnishing of staff services — personnel, finance, management — are to be considered later in Parts II, III, and IV, respectively.

Consideration of the appropriate organs of departmental management should be preceded by a discussion of the objectives to which it is addressed. This was pointed out a decade ago by the President's Committee on Administrative Management, which summarized these objectives as follows: [1]

1. To enable the department head to deal effectively with questions of policy, both in point of formulation and in point of execution
2. To promote coordination both within the department and without
3. To liberate the energies of the operating units

[1] Macmahon, Arthur W., *Problems of Administrative Management,* p. 5 (Washington, 1937).

How may these objectives best be accomplished? To begin with, agency functions to be performed must be classified on some rational basis — just as in the determination of the over-all organization of departments and agencies — according to one or another of the following generally accepted principles: [2]

1. According to *Purpose*, e.g., furnishing water, conducting education
2. According to *Process* or technical skill, such as engineering or accounting
3. According to the *Place* where performed
4. According to *Clientele* and persons served, such as immigrants, veterans, Indians
5. According to *Knowledge Available*, that is, the store of available information gathered in the course of administrative operations

Because governmental functions differ so greatly in purpose and character, it may sometimes be necessary to utilize a combination of principles in the same department or agency. The Department of Justice, for instance, is conceived primarily upon the basis of legal process and specialized knowledge of the law, but it includes the Bureau of Prisons, established on the basis of the major purpose of caring for and disciplining prisoners, and the Immigration and Naturalization Service, set up to serve a particular clientele.

This illustration, which is only one of many which might be cited, serves to show how complicated is the problem of classifying and assigning functions either on an over-all basis or within a department. If the task has been well done at the top level, then the departmental task is relatively simple, for it may then be assumed that the functions assigned are related one to another and are of a comparatively homogeneous character. But in each case the department or agency has to find a way of organizing whatever functions are assigned to it, and unfortunately the list usually includes some miscellaneous items that do not properly belong to it but that would be even more difficult to deal with in any other department to which they might have been assigned.

The basis of classification having been prescribed by law or having been otherwise determined, it is possible to proceed with the task of planning the administrative structure of the agency. This must be done in conformity with accepted principles of scientific management. These would require that so far as possible the principle of unity of command

---

[2] Numerous writers — Davis, Gulick, Hopf, Sheldon, Taylor — have attempted to classify types of administrative organization. This list follows Gulick, and Benson, George C. S., "Internal Administrative Organization," *Public Administration Review*, Autumn, 1941, pp. 472–484. The Commission on the Organization of the Executive Branch of the Government presents a very clear statement of the principle of grouping according to major purposes; see its report, *General Management of the Executive Branch*, Part III (Washington, 1949).

be observed; the span of control, or number of subordinates, of each supervising officer should be kept small; individuals should be clearly informed of their organizational location; and individuals, especially staff officers to whom authority is delegated, should be carefully informed of the limits of that authority.

Agencies With a Single Head. In the organization of every department or agency there is an executive head — a secretary of cabinet rank, a commissioner, director, administrator, or what not. He is normally appointed by the chief executive, although in the states and local units he may be elected by the people. His job is management, and management involves working with other people to achieve predetermined objectives. This in turn involves human relations and organization. "Management," said Lawrence A. Appley on one occasion, "is the responsibility of getting other people to do things, and even though they do not do it as well as you can, your job is to get them to do it better. This is the proper concept of management," the two basic elements of which are planning and control. Both of these may be in large measure achieved through proper organization.

To assist him in the performance of his duties, the department or agency head must have many assistants. The Hoover Commission stresses the fact that there must be an undersecretary to assume responsibility for the general management of the agency and to assume the duties of the department head in his absence. Then in addition there should be such a number of assistant secretaries as may be necessary in relation to the major functions assigned to the agency. These important policy officials, appointed by the chief executive subject to confirmation, are responsible for the actual administration of the work of the agency.

The personal staff of the head of the agency may include an executive officer, an administrative assistant, and secretarial aides, the size and character of this staff depending somewhat upon the work habits of the executive and the size and character of the agency. He must have a flexible corps of staff aides, free from the routine responsibilities which properly belong to his bureau chiefs. The Hoover Commission in 1949 recommended the following list, to be used uniformly in Federal departments and agencies, and emphasized the importance of the work in management research and review: [3]

> General Counsel
> Financial Officer (accounting, budgeting, and disbursements)
> Personnel Officer

---

[3] Hoover Commission report; also the Commission's Task Force Report on *Departmental Management* [Appendix E] (Washington, 1949).

Supply Officer
Management Research Officer
Information and Publications Officer
Congressional Liaison Officer

These staff services are essential in all agencies, whether organized with a single head or with a multiple head as in the case of the administrative boards and commissions.

Agencies With a Plural Head. The board or commission type of organization, still so common, seems to have originated in the states with a public-lands board set up in California in 1851; the first Federal board was the Interstate Commerce Commission, established in 1887. As the number has multiplied, the argument as to the merits of this plan of organization has gone on without interruption. Students of administration have been in substantial agreement that, for purely administrative work, it is far less satisfactory than a single executive head. It opens the way for division of authority, for lack of administrative responsibility, and for postponement and delay.

There are, of course, many instances in which this internal handicap has been largely overcome by the employment of an executive secretary or executive officer who functions under board decisions and instructions in very much the same manner as the top executive in a single-headed unit. Examples of this type of organization are found in a number of boards and commissions functioning in the state of Wisconsin as well as in numerous Hydra-headed agencies of the Federal government. The solution of the problem in internal organization does not, however, remove the other objection, which relates to lack of coordination and control at the top level. The board or commission can, in other words, efficiently perform most of its duties and still be obstreperous and noncooperative in its relations with the President, the governor, or the mayor, with regard to general over-all policies of the administration.[4]

Second-Line Supervision. The next level in the organization of authority involves the determination of the number and the character of the administrative subdivisions of the agency — the bureaus, offices, and divisions. It is obvious that this determination can be made only after careful study of the statutes under which the agency functions. It is

[4] For a discussion of this problem at the state level, see Mathews, John M., "State Administrative Reorganization," *American Political Science Review,* August, 1922, pp. 387-398; for an excellent treatment of central administrative controls by a plural executive in Michigan, see Benson, George C. S., and Litchfield, Edward H., *The State Administrative Board in Michigan* (University of Michigan Press, 1938); and in Minnesota, Short, Lloyd M., and Tiller, Carl W., *The Minnesota Commission on Administration and Finance, 1925-1939* (University of Minnesota Press, 1942).

preferable that the statutes should not be too specific on details of organization, that the department head should receive from the legislature authority to organize his department and control its administration, yet any directive contained in the statutes becomes a first requirement in setting up the organizational plan. The importance of the positions held by officials at this level can hardly be exaggerated, as Professor Macmahon pointed out many years ago.[5]

> The bureau chiefs are the key figures in national administration. The units that they direct are inclusive enough to lend themselves to the purposes of supervision and coordination and to bring their heads in touch with the machinery of budget making and legislation, but sufficiently focused to preserve for them a saving contact with details and technique.

The bureau chief is primarily concerned with the formulation and execution of basic policies; with carrying out the functions of the bureau prescribed by Congress and by the head of the department; with relations between the bureau and the public. His job has been compared by one writer to that of an operating vice-president in a privately owned business. He is responsible, says this writer, "for keeping the internal machinery of the bureau operating smoothly and for conducting government business with maximum efficiency and minimum friction." The departments have grown to such tremendous size, and the bureaus themselves have become so large that it has been suggested that some of them be separated from the departments in which they are now located.[6]

The regional director in charge of a major field office occupies a position comparing favorably in prestige and responsibility with that of a bureau chief. His is a small-scale reproduction of the central office. Whereas the work of a bureau chief is to a considerable extent professionalized (as in mines, labor statistics, agricultural marketing) and specialized, that of the regional director is so general as to include all phases of the agency's program. The job therefore becomes, within the limits of the authority delegated to the field, a replica of that of the head of the agency. Exceptions are to be noted in some especially large bureaus, as in the Department of Agriculture, which have field offices under bureau control rather than under the direct control of the Department.

[5] See Macmahon, Arthur W., "Selection and Tenure of Bureau Chiefs in the National Administration of the United States," *American Political Science Review*, I, August, 1926, pp. 548–582; II, November, 1926, pp. 770–806.
[6] This is diametrically opposed to the point of view of the Hoover Commission, which urged a two thirds reduction in the sixty-five independent departments and agencies existing in 1948. See their report, and Melton, Presley H., "Administration in a Federal Government Bureau," *American Political Science Review*, October, 1939, pp. 835–840, and Brecht, Arnold, "Smaller Departments," *Public Administration Review*, Summer, 1941, pp. 363–373.

Lower Levels of Supervision. At this point attention is directed to the lower levels of management, the group which Mary C. H. Niles has called "middle management," [7] and the first-line supervisors. Organizationally, middle management stands between top management and the second-line supervisor or bureau chiefs on the one hand and the first-line supervisors on the other. These minor executives preside over sections or other subdivisions of the bureaus or major operating units. The first-line supervisors preside over units or small sections, where they represent management in the daily contacts with employees. The farther down one goes in the hierarchy of authority, the fewer the occasions for contact with the upper levels of management and the larger the number of contacts with the individual employees, who have been called the unit-cells in the production system.

It is important to emphasize the fact that whatever form of organization is set up, it must be regarded as subject to such changes and modifications as the needs of the service may require. When necessary, additional subdivisions may be established at any level of supervision or existing ones abolished in order to turn out the work with a minimum of annoyance and inconvenience to the public and with a minimum of lost motion and internal friction within the agency.

Extent of Authority

Determination of the nature and scope of authority is a first major responsibility of top management. The sources of authority are set forth, for any given agency, in the following documents and publications:

THE CONSTITUTION: There is relatively little in the Federal Constitution applicable in such instances, but in the constitutions of some states this is a very important source, especially for certain regulatory agencies.

THE STATUTES: The legislature provides by law for the establishment of an executive agency, indicating in fairly general terms, and sometimes in specific terms, the nature and scope of its powers.

DIRECTIVES FROM TOP MANAGEMENT: These directives, applicable to all departments and agencies, come in the form of Executive Orders, decisions of the budget office or of the central personnel agency, rulings of the attorney general, comptroller general, or auditor general. They contribute to the legal framework within which the agency must function.

THE AGENCY'S OWN RULES AND REGULATIONS: Subject to such directives and restrictions as may emanate from the above sources, the agency itself may formulate rules and regulations which, when properly approved and published, add still further to the legal framework governing the agency. These rules may be procedural, directive, or explanatory, setting forth, respectively, the manner in which individual cases will be filed and processed, the manner in which persons subject to the authority of the agency may comply with its regulations, or rules

---

[7] See her book under this title.

which attempt merely to explain or amplify the meaning of certain portions of the statutes.

COURT DECISIONS: To all these sources of legal authority must be added the decisions of the courts, which from time to time interpret provisions of general law or provisions of the agency's own statutes, or pass upon, either affirmatively or negatively, some aspect of its procedure. To the extent that such decisions are applicable to the agency and its work they are, of course, binding.

Having thus determined the extent of authority of the agency, top management is next confronted with the problems of delegation of authority and of span of control, each of which is closely related to the other. Delegation of authority is essential in order to accomplish anything. No executive can possibly do everything himself. If he tries, he will merely succeed in making his office a bottleneck which ties up the work of the entire organization and prevents its proper functioning. The larger the organization, the truer this statement becomes. The delegation of responsibility *with adequate authority* is at the same time one of the most essential and one of the most difficult problems facing an administrator. Unless it is adequately solved, no effective administration is possible.

The problem of delegation creates almost inevitably the problem of span of control, as more and more people are assigned the responsibility for the doing of more and more specific things. Unless the administrator is careful, he soon finds himself confronted with what is, administratively, an impossible situation. There are so many people reporting to him regarding so many different things that he is unable to give proper attention to any of them. His supervisors cannot see him when they need to do so. The solution lies in the actual delegation of some of his authority to his subordinates, so that he will not be obliged to concern himself directly with so many different activities. He may also increase the distance from the apex to the base of the organizational pyramid by establishing an additional level of supervision. This may, of course, slow down operations and cause delays.

Much has been written about the limitations imposed by the concept of span of control. No one knows exactly what those limitations are. It is probable that no definite rule can be established and that the span will vary in any given case according to the ability and experience of the supervisor, the nature of the work being done, and the character and ability of the members of the staff. Experience has shown that there is a strict limit to the number of individuals an executive can effectively supervise. Probably the number should not exceed ten.

Delegation of authority in turn creates a problem of coordination. The fact that there is unity of command does not necessarily insure coordination. For one thing, interrelationships increase in geometric progression with the number of operating units supervised. Not only does the number of personal contacts become too great for the top executive, but the number of interrelationships becomes too great for the mind to grasp and retain. For this reason large departments with expanding programs provide for more levels for the decentralization of authority within them than are found in smaller departments. This raises the question of the subdelegation of authority, by which is meant the further distribution of administrative authority within the organizational hierarchy by the administrative officials to whom it had been initially delegated through legislative enactment.[8]

An examination of this question reveals a wide variety of possibilities. Not only is authority delegated by the chief executive to heads of departments and agencies, but it may in turn be delegated by them to assistant, under, and/or acting secretaries, to assistants to the secretary, and to subordinate administrative officers as well. Subdelegation as between such officers leads to sub-subdelegation. The necessity for this technique needs no laboring, but as one authority has noted, "the theories upon which the process rests and the limitations which hedge about its exercise are still in need of definition." The increase of the distance from apex to base has a tendency to slow up action and decision; this implies that there may be a point at which a huge, highly centralized organization will break down because of sheer size. Nevertheless, although present-day governmental organization imposes heavy demands on skill and ingenuity in organization and management, one may well conclude on the basis of experience that this danger is more theoretical than real.

Decentralization

Authority in any large organization must, then, be decentralized. The present tendency seems to be toward recognition of this fact. There are two major patterns in accordance with which decentralization may be achieved, one based on the principle of geographical distribution, the other on the principle of functional distribution. In large organizations administering programs of broad application, both principles may be employed.

Geographical Distribution. Geographical decentralization is necessary in the performance of functions like tax collection that involve a tre-

---

[8] For an excellent discussion, see Grundstein, Nathan D., "Subdelegation of Administrative Authority," *George Washington Law Review,* February, 1945, pp. 144–196. Although the executive may delegate responsibility administratively for the performance of a particular assignment, he cannot delegate his legal responsibility for seeing that the work is properly carried on.

mendous volume of work and functions which affect so substantial a portion of the population that accessibility for citizens is a primary consideration. It involves the establishment of field offices, usually regional or district. As applied to the agency's major purpose, however, it defeats itself unless the field offices are given a wide range of discretion in the determination of problems presented to them. If this is done, the field office becomes in reality a small-scale reproduction of the central office, under whose general instructions and supervision it operates in the handling of business on the spot. If there is no adequate delegation of authority, the field office becomes simply an office for the filing of cases and for passing out the decisions made in the central office. This problem of interrelationships within and without a given organization is discussed at some length in the chapter which follows.

The situation is somewhat different where the principle is applied to the so-called housekeeping services. An excellent illustration is the United States Public Health Service, which has recently resumed the decentralization of its work — a task which was started several years before the war. So far as possible, its several field offices are being given responsibility for personnel, budget, procurement, training, and other staff functions formerly handled in Washington. The Department of Agriculture and other agencies have made notable progress in the same direction.

The problem of geographic distribution is not simple. There is, to begin with, a conflict between this principle and that of functional distribution — a conflict which has been characterized by Herbert Emmerich as "the most difficult problem in administration, public or private, Federal, state, or local." [9] But this is not all, as experience during the war clearly demonstrated. There was, for instance, the impact of concentric programs upon the community, programs which were not too well coordinated at the top and which had to be coordinated at the local level if the local officials were to function with any degree of effectiveness. Mr. Emmerich concluded that in the reconversion era Federal action might spell ruin for localities unless concentric programs were planned with consideration for their impact upon the community.

Functional Decentralization. The principle of functional decentralization is based upon the application of the same techniques that should be used in determining the departmental structure: the analysis of the total picture and the grouping of like or related activities in the same operating unit. No wholly satisfactory solution is obtainable here any

---

[9] In his article, "Some Notes on Wartime Federal Administration," *Public Administration Review*, Winter, 1945, pp. 55–61.

more than it is in the process of departmentalization, for activities are seldom so clear cut as to be completely isolated or so self-sufficient in character as to be operated independently of other parts of the organization. Hence one finds on a smaller scale within an organization the same type of problems of interrelationship and the same need for coordination that exist in organization at the top level.

Every large organization has a more or less constant problem with regard to the placement and management of the necessary staff and auxiliary services. Personnel, finance, planning — often spoken of as "the arms of management" — are regularly centralized, that is, located under the immediate supervision of the top executive. Such services, on the other hand, as secretarial assistance, provision for duplicating service, the maintenance of files, and the distribution of supplies, may be either centralized or decentralized.

Should each member of the higher supervisory and/or professional staff have his own secretary, or should there be a stenographic and typing pool upon which staff members may call for assistance as required? Should there be a central departmental duplicating service, or should each major unit maintain its own? Should there be a central file, or should each unit maintain its own files? Should supplies be distributed upon requisition from a central stockroom or from a series of small supply rooms maintained within the various units?

These questions are examples of the type to which there is no right answer. Whatever solution is adopted, is likely to be a compromise between two conflicting points of view, and it is likely also to be not more than partially satisfactory. The arguments for centralization are efficiency and the greater economy resulting from quantity production and specialization. The arguments against such a policy are familiar to every person who has ever been in immediate need of assistance or of supplies and has had to wait his turn for hours or even days in a central service unit whose facilities were by no means adequate.

The Age-Old Argument: Centralization v. Decentralization. Experience has clearly demonstrated that a governmental unit operating within the framework provided by the concept of a service state cannot adequately meet the needs of its citizens with either a highly centralized or a highly decentralized organization. The nation is, as David E. Lilienthal has expressed it, faced with a dilemma, the need for strong central power on the one hand and the ineffectiveness of overcentralized administration on the other.[10] In order to serve the people the

---

[10] See his article, "Administrative Decentralization of Federal Functions," *Advanced Management*, January–March, 1940, pp. 3–9.

agency must operate where the people are, that is, in the field. That means that a field establishment must be set up, but it does not mean that every important administrative decision can or should still be made in the central office.

For some years the Tennessee Valley Authority has made "a constant effort to push its administration farther down into the 'grass roots.' " After adopting many methods used by other public and private agencies and doing some pioneering work of its own, it was able to determine three goals which it regards as essential characteristics of a decentralized administration of Federal functions: (1) the greatest possible number of decisions should be made in the field; (2) so far as possible, the active participation of the people themselves must be developed; (3) the work of state and local governments, aiming toward common objectives, must be coordinated with the field work of the Federal agency.

One must hasten to add, however, that the problem is not so simple as might at first appear. To decentralize any of the old-line agencies means a sharp break with long-established tradition and requires extensive and difficult readjustments within the agency. It creates problems of coordination, both within the agency and in its relations with other jurisdictions. The field offices must be able to receive and dispose of most of the types of business which come to the agency, or else there is no use in having them. But they must also be constrained to apply the same rules in substantially the same manner, for citizens similarly situated have a right to expect the same or similar treatment. There are problems of staffing, for the tradition of a responsible field service is not yet well established, and retention of the necessarily high-grade supervisory personnel increases costs of administration. There are problems, too, of determining the geographical limits of the administrative regions or districts to be established.[11]

Theoretically, these regions or districts ought to be uniform with those established for other purposes; practically, for a variety of reasons this solution often appears unworkable. New arguments emphasizing the urgency of finding some solution of the problem continue to appear. In June, 1947, Senator Wiley of Wisconsin urged that at least part of the Federal government be moved from Washington to the

[11] For discussion of these points, see Truman, David B., *Administrative Decentralization*, which deals with the Department of Agriculture in the Chicago area (University of Chicago Press, 1940), and the following articles: Fesler, James W., "Federal Use of Administrative Areas," *Annals*, January, 1940, pp. 111–115; Latham, Earl G., "Executive Management and the Federal Field Service," *Public Administration Review*, Winter, 1945, pp. 16–27; and the author's "Federal Administrative Areas: An Historical Record of Confusion and a Suggested Program of Action," *Western Political Quarterly*, March, 1948, pp. 54–70.

grassroots to protect it in the event of an atomic war. If an atomic bomb fell on Washington, it could destroy the nerve center of the nation. His proposal — that the major divisions of the Department of Agriculture be moved to the appropriate sections of the country where their particular commodities were produced — involved not only geographical decentralization but functional decentralization as well.[12]

Communications

A vital element in the organization of any agency is the machinery established for dissemination of instructions. This is a many-sided problem. The agency staff has to receive information essential to daily operations — rules and regulations, procedures and changes of procedures — as well as general information regarding individual employees, the latter disseminated largely for morale-building purposes. In the case of a staff agency it is essential that instructions be formulated and presented to the operating departments and agencies so that they may conform to the prescribed policies and procedures. The public, furthermore, must be given information essential to its understanding and observance of the agency's rules and regulations. Each of these problems of communication calls for a different approach and for skill both in preparing and presenting material.

The present concern is largely with informing and instructing employees regarding agency organization and policy. For this purpose, organization charts of the agency and flow charts indicating the steps in normal operations and the order in which they occur, are valuable. A manual of operations is another valuable tool. Such a manual will normally describe the organization of the agency and explain its program, aims, and objectives. This general material will be followed by a detailed analysis of operations in the agency or some unit of it, describing exactly what is done, why it is done, how it is done, and who does it. Such information enables the employee to gain some perspective of the agency as a whole and to understand better his own contribution to the entire program. This is essential to good employee morale.

Another device in common use is the staff memorandum or circular letter. If there is a manual of procedures, such circular letters usually contain new and supplementary information. This may be issued in such form as to be inserted in a loose-leaf manual. The wording is a matter requiring careful attention. Administrators, like other professional groups, have tended to develop a jargon of their own which may be meaningful to them but not to their employees or to the public.

---

[12] *Washington Post*, June 30, 1947.

Maury Maverick dubbed this type of official communication "gob-beldy-gook."

Finally, in this process of informing and instructing there must be provision for employee participation. There are many types of questions regarding which staff should be consulted before decisions are made. When new regulations or instructions are issued, opportunity should be given for staff questions and discussion. Such participation is a vital part of modern democratic administrative procedures. It involves establishing and keeping open what has been called a two-way channel of communication, whose purpose is to facilitate the passing of instructions from the top down, and the free movement of ideas, questions, and suggestions from individual employees and from the lower levels of supervision in the direction of top management.

Central Office–Field Office Relationships. Decisions regarding policy and procedures must be communicated by the central office to the field in the form of directives, manuals of instructions, or otherwise. Conferences of field office employees with representatives of the central office may be held for explaining and interpreting the instructions and for developing agreement with regard to their application and meaning; and subsequently reports may be required from the field so that the central office may be able to judge the effectiveness of the policies. The United States Civil Service Commission, for instance, inaugurated in 1944 a systematic plan to provide for a continuing survey of operating methods, policies, and procedures every ninety days.[13] Certain it is that if cooperation and understanding are to prevail between the central office and the field, the lines of communication must be kept open *both ways.*[14]

Coordination

Many of the problems of organization and management are difficult; nearly any one of them is sufficiently difficult so that it may, according to one's point of view, be regarded as the most difficult of all. Certainly coordination is no exception. Everybody wants coordination, at least on paper, but nobody wants to be coordinated in practice. Every agency wants to go its own way and have other agencies build around their own program. Unless there is strong leadership at the top, leader-

---

[13] Circular Letter No. 4033, Supplement No. 4, June 29, 1944.

[14] These same principles apply, regardless of the size of the central office and of the field units concerned. See, for instance, Ward, Erwin S., "Radio Speeds the Day's Work," *Better Roads,* April, 1943, pp. 19-21, which describes a two-way communications system used in the Highway Department of Kandiyohi County, Minnesota. Fourteen mobile units are kept constantly in touch with headquarters, thereby helping to provide modern highway service for the county.

ship with ability to induce different departments or units to work as a team, then in all probability these units will be proceeding simultaneously in all directions.

In times of emergency coordination is more important on jurisdictional and policy questions than in detailed operations. Contradictions and inconsistencies between programs must be ironed out somewhere along the line. Presumably it would be preferable to start the process of coordination at the top; but, as earlier indicated, if it is not done effectively at that level, it must be done at the lower levels. It has even been argued that it is better that operations should be coordinated at the ultimate field level.[15]

SELECTED REFERENCES

Fesler, James W., "Executive Management and the Federal Field Service," in President's Committee on Administrative Management, *Report with Special Studies*, pp. 275–294 (Washington, 1937). An early discussion of an increasingly important aspect of agency organization.

Gaus, John M., and Wolcott, Leon O., *Public Administration and the United States Department of Agriculture* (Public Administration Service, Chicago, 1940). A case study of a conspicuously effective Federal department.

Graves, W. Brooke, Ed., "Intergovernmental Relations in the United States," *Annals*, January, 1940, entire volume. Twenty-five contributors cooperate in presenting a comprehensive survey of the field, including numerous administrative aspects.

Institute for Training in Municipal Administration, *The Technique of Municipal Administration*, Second Edition (International City Managers Association, Chicago, 1945). A training manual designed to tell municipal officers how to perform their duties.

Macmahon, Arthur W., "Departmental Management," in President's Committee on Administrative Management, *Report with Special Studies*, pp. 249–270 (Washington, 1937). A distinguished authority considers the specific problems of departmental and agency organization.

Martin, Roscoe C., Ed., *New Horizons in Public Administration* (University of Alabama Press, 1945). Includes Donald Stone's discussion of the governmental executive, his role, and his methods.

Marx, Fritz M., Ed., *Elements of Public Administration* (Prentice-Hall, New York, 1947). Selected contributors deal with various aspects of agency organization.

Stone, Donald C., *The Management of Municipal Public Works* (Public Administration Service, Chicago, 1939). Discussion of problems of organization and management as presented in relation to a major municipal function.

Studenski, Paul, and Mort, Paul R., *Centralization and Decentralization in Relation to Democracy* (Teachers College, Columbia University, 1941). Analysis of a vital aspect of agency organization as it affects the field of education.

Wallace, Schuyler C., *Federal Departmentalization, A Critique of Methods of Organization* (Columbia University Press, 1941). Principles applied to departmentalization at the top level may also apply to problems arising in the organization of a department or agency.

---

[15] Emmerich, *op. cit.*

5

COOPERATIVE FEDERALISM:

INTERJURISDICTIONAL RELATIONS

PRACTICALLY every major administrative program in America today involves a network of interrelationships not only between the different levels of government but between different departments and agencies within the same unit. In days of old, when government was simple in structure and in functioning, one unit could perform all the duties relating to a particular function without giving any consideration to the impact of its program upon other units. Such a situation no longer exists; changing conditions and new governmental programs have caused the development of a new brand of cooperative federalism. Within the existing constitutional framework, units at all three levels have developed a pattern of cooperative relationships which are not only desirable but necessary for the efficient accomplishment of their objectives.

This general field involves four distinct classes of interrelations: Federal-state, interstate, state-local, and Federal-local. Many of these grow out of legislative provisions, especially in the case of those programs which operate on the basis of grants-in-aid, such as highways or social security. Others develop purely out of practical situations encountered in the normal processes of administration — situations in which the exchange of information and cooperative efforts along other lines seem to be the only method by which any of the units can effectively discharge the duties assigned to them.

It is the purpose of this chapter to explain how this system operates. The discussion includes, in addition, a brief statement of the methods by which standards are set by the larger units and enforced upon the smaller, especially where grants-in-aid are present, and a few specific illustrations of interlevel relations in fields where the techniques of cooperation have long been employed and are highly developed.

Intergovernmental Administrative Relations

Interlevel relations may involve two levels of government, as Federal-state or state-local, or all three at the same time. Since the organization of this chapter is centered somewhat around the Federal government, whose relations with the states are illustrated in relation to particular functional fields, no specific discussion of Federal-state relationships is presented at this point. Where all three are included, as in the field of tax administration, an effort has been made for a number of years to eliminate by this means those annoying and often unfair situations which result from overlapping and duplicating taxes. This was done in the case of the estate taxes by the 80-20 agreement, and in the case of income taxes through cooperation in devising forms, requiring computation of both Federal and state taxes on the basis of the same data, synchronizing filing dates, making adjustments in rates, and in other ways.[1] Where the political control at both levels rests in the hands of the same party, the development of cooperation is usually facilitated.

While administrative cooperation of this character commonly occurs in specific fields and will be discussed in a later section of this chapter, mention should be made of the extent to which the resources of all agencies of government, at all levels, were coordinated in the war effort [2] and were coordinated in peacetime on the West Coast by the Pacific Coast Board of Intergovernmental Relations. This Board was organized in 1945 on an experimental basis for a three-year period by representatives of California, Oregon, and Washington. A grant was obtained from one of the foundations for a small staff and incidental expenses. Its purposes were stated as follows:

> This Board is created purely on a voluntary cooperative basis for the purpose of mutual discussion and cooperation in administrative efforts to solve problems affecting people, and most especially such problems as are the responsibility of governments during the postwar readjustment period. Such mutual discussion and cooperation will strive for the elimination of duplication in the execution of local, state, and Federal laws and regulations, the pooling of facts regarding economic and social conditions, especially those due to industrialization, and the planning by local, state, and Federal governments for dealing with these matters constructively.

Membership was confined to representatives of local, state, and Federal governments, as follows:

> From each state the membership shall be the Governor of the state, the Chairman of the State Commission on Interstate Cooperation, an official representative of the League or Association of Cities or Municipalities, and an official representative of the State Association of County Supervisors or Commissioners;
> From the Federal government membership shall be Field Chiefs of Federal agencies, as selected by the Pacific Coast Federal Regional Council, and shall be less in number than the combined total of representatives of the other jurisdictions.

---

[1] See Martin, James W., "Functions of Intergovernmental Administrative Cooperation in Taxation," *State Government*, May, 1944, pp. 327–332, 340.
[2] See Gill, Corrington, "Federal-State-City Cooperation in Congested Production Areas," *Public Administration Review*, Winter, 1945, pp. 28–33.

Meetings of the Board were held quarterly, alternating between Washington and Oregon and California. The Governor of the state in which the meeting was held served as general chairman of the session. Although the conclusions of the Board were purely advisory, participants reported that in these meetings ways and means were developed for cutting through red tape and getting difficult assignments done through cooperative efforts of all levels of government.[3]

Interstate Relations. In the field of interstate relations there are a number of different types of cooperative effort. One of these involves use of the interstate compact clause of the Federal Constitution. While such compacts have been reasonably numerous, they have ordinarily been confined to such matters as the settlement of disputed boundary lines between adjoining states, allocation of surface waters and water supplies from adjacent streams, fishing rights, and the like. Although efforts were made a decade or more ago to utilize them in the handling of common problems of social and economic legislation, these efforts were not very successful.

The states of a region may be brought together either by use of the compact clause of the Federal Constitution, as in the case of the Colorado River Compact, or by act of Congress, as in the case of the Tennessee Valley Authority. One method is a kind of voluntary regionalism; the other might be called a compulsory regionalism. Both, however, have worked well, and both have been or are likely to be extended into other areas. The voluntary plan has been promoted by the Council of State Governments for the purpose of developing an organization capable of handling problems arising in whole river valleys and involving the interests of a number of different states. Notable examples include the Interstate Commission on the Delaware River Basin, the Interstate Commission on the Ohio River Basin, and the Interstate Commission on the Potomac River Basin, known respectively as Incodel, Incohio, and Incopot. These organizations do not have the resources to carry on a great power development program like that of the TVA, but they have accomplished much in clearing up stream pollution, developing the resources of their respective areas, allocating water supplies, and bringing about a solution of other related problems.[4]

One of the earliest movements in the field of interstate relations was

---

[3] The Board had a "Principles of Organization" and issued regularly a mimeographed report of its proceedings. The author is indebted to Mr. J. W. Rupley, Chief Field Representative, United States Bureau of the Budget, and Professor Samuel C. May, University of California, for information about this interesting development.

[4] All these problems in the field of interstate relations are discussed in the author's *American State Government*, Chapter 22, and in his *Uniform State Action, A Possible Substitute for Centralization*, as well as in the January 1940 volume of the *Annals*, on "Intergovernmental Relations in the United States."

that for uniform state laws. The National Conference of Commissioners on Uniform State Laws was organized in 1889 under the leadership of the American Bar Association, and it still maintains a close working relationship with that organization. While it drafted model laws relating to many subjects, its efforts in the realm of commercial law were by far the most successful. In later years, many other organizations have proposed model laws relating to subjects within their field of interest.

Fortunately for the present purposes some of the most productive effort in interstate relations has occurred within the province of administration. In some cases for more than three quarters of a century state administrators in specialized fields have been meeting annually to discuss common problems and to develop cooperative and often uniform and/or reciprocal arrangements. Such organizations exist in agriculture, banking and insurance, conservation, education, health and welfare, and labor. While their effectiveness may have been retarded by rapid rotation in membership, they have accomplished a great deal. In recent years their efforts have been supplemented by national organizations of professional persons engaged in administrative work in these several fields on a career basis. Many of these organizations maintain permanent headquarters in a building constructed for that purpose on the campus of the University of Chicago.[5]

Even so brief a sketch of interstate relations would be incomplete without some mention of the state commissions on interstate cooperation. These commissions, in fact, form the basis of participation in the Council of State Governments, the first one having been established in New Jersey in 1935. Each commission is composed of fifteen members: five senators, five representatives, and five persons representing the administrative branch of the state government. These members are appointed respectively by the president of the Senate, the speaker of the House, and the governor of the state. All matters within the field of intergovernmental relations, whether Federal-state or interstate in character, whether legislative or administrative, fall within their province. They have made an enormous contribution to the solution of interstate conflicts, especially in those jurisdictions which have made adequate financial provision for their work.

Federal-Local Relations. Relations between the Federal government and the local units, prior to 1933, were for the most part both indirect and more or less accidental. It was true that many Federal departments

---

[5] At 1313 East 60th Street, Chicago 37. Examples include, in addition to the Council of State Governments, the Civil Service Assembly of the United States and Canada, the American Public Welfare Association, the National Association of Housing Officials, the Federation of Tax Administrators, etc.

and bureaus carried on activities and informational services of which many local communities were glad to avail themselves, but no one had thought of developing, extending, and systematizing these relationships. After 1933 many new ones were created. In connection with emergency relief, public works, and housing programs, direct grants of funds were given to municipalities and other local units. In the effort to save time and to speed the recovery program, the time-honored practice by which any Federal relations with local units were channeled through the states was discontinued. The states were by-passed, much to their chagrin but to the great satisfaction of the local units, which thus attained a degree of recognition previously denied them.

The centralizing effect of these developments, which were continued and expanded during the war years, should not be overlooked. Not only through the operation of the grant-in-aid system but in other ways the Federal government has been able to exert a powerful influence on some phases of local administration. For instance, overcrowding in the Federal prisons was met by farming out prisoners in the county jails if — and only if — these jails were able to conform to rather rigid Federal standards with regard to facilities, maintenance, and operation. Where it was possible for them to do so, county authorities were glad to meet these standards in order to obtain the financial assistance which could be derived from the boarding of Federal prisoners. After the war, direct Federal-local relations were provided for in the Airport Construction Act which, in practice, has worked out rather badly.

State-Local Relations. The relations of the states with their local political subdivisions are both cooperative and supervisory. They cooperate in the administration of many important, jointly supported activities such as education, health, highways, and welfare. There are supervisory relationships in these fields also, especially in connection with the expenditure of state-aid moneys. Possibly the one field in which state supervision has been most extensive has been that of finance; in this area the extension of state control has not by any means been determined by the presence or absence of state aid.

With regard to many different aspects of the fiscal problem, the states have imposed supervisory controls because of negligence on the part of local officials, sheer incompetence, or worse. Such controls have been generally instituted throughout the country in the following areas: assessments, tax rates, tax collection, budgets, indebtedness, accounting procedures, auditing, financial reporting, and the selection of personnel engaged in fiscal work. Prior to such supervision, assessments were made by rule of thumb; decisions were colored by personal or political favoritism, with consequent inequities as between individuals and governmental units. Recklessness in the incurring of debt and repeated instances of ineptitude in debt administration required intervention in this field as in the various others mentioned.[6]

Cooperation of Local Units. In recent years local units have been abandoning ancient prejudices against cooperation and have been discovering that by this means they can obtain more in goods and services and give better service to the public. Probably the most extensive cooperation has been developed in the Los Angeles metropolitan area. In this area the county and its communities are attempting to solve common problems by contracts and agreements, exchange of personnel, and similar devices.[7]

But such developments are by no means restricted to California; they are now found in many states. In Pennsylvania cooperative purchasing is authorized by law and is being more and more relied upon to insure top quality at lowest cost. Adjoining or adjacent units are entering into cooperative arrangements with regard to the use as well as the purchase of expensive machinery and facilities, such as road machinery, sewage disposal plants, and incineration plants. There is no reason why, if the county governments were generally reorganized and modernized as they should be, they could not either individually or in cooperation with other counties or with the state purchase cooperatively all standard items required by the local units within their borders.

To facilitate this type of cooperation and develop means by which it may be more effectively carried out, the Federal Council on Intergovernmental Relations was set up in 1943. It was composed of a small group of public administrators and representatives of Federal departments with whom were associated state and local officials in various states, including California, Georgia, Indiana, and Minnesota. State councils were appointed by the governors, and local councils represented the public officials and interested laymen in the counties undertaking the experimental demonstrations. The following statement of objectives was agreed upon by all the cooperating groups: "To devise administrative procedures and mechanism for blending more harmoni-

---

[6] For a full discussion of these various types of control, see the author's *American State Government*, Third Edition, Chapter 21, and references therein cited (Heath, Boston, 1946).

[7] See Jamison volume, and her "Neighboring Areas Join Hands," *National Municipal Review*, March, 1946, pp. 111–114; also Stewart, Frank K., and Ketcham, Ronald M., "Intergovernmental Contracts in California," *Public Administration Review*, Spring, 1941, pp. 242–248.

ously the powers and interests of the Federal, state, and local governments in the execution of their common purposes."

Projects were set up on a purely cooperative basis. There were no legal compulsions. The assumption was that the mutual good will and confidence which might cause a local council to attempt the formulation and testing of a plan would find a similar response from state and Federal administrators. The Federal Council felt "that the unique feature of this proposal [was] the emphasis on a locally developed and tested plan of action. There [was] no pattern of administration or government to pass along already made. In this program the plan of action [was] formulated and tested by local councils with such assistance from state and Federal officials as [might] be requested by local councils." Experiments were carried on in Santa Clara County, California, Henry County, Indiana, and Blue Earth County, Minnesota.[8]

Standard Setting and Enforcement

From the administrative point of view the most important aspect of these interlevel relations is the extension of control by the larger unit over the smaller through standard setting and enforcement. The techniques are much the same whether the problem is considered at the Federal-state level, or at the state-local level and regardless of the nature of the function to which they are applied — highways, education, social security, housing, or any one of a dozen others. Furthermore, the effects are much the same, all of them contributing to the concentration of power in the larger unit. The more important of these techniques are standard setting, supervision and inspection, control over personnel, financial controls, the exertion of superior authority, and cooperative effort.[9] While each may be used separately, they may also be used in varying combinations.

1. *Standard Setting.* The larger unit may determine the minimum standards of quality of service to be observed by the smaller unit. If the service is supported in part by grants-in-aid from the larger unit, the problem of control is greatly simplified. If the standards are not observed — a fact which may be determined by a central review or by other means — the financial aid may be withheld. For instance, the Federal government in effect compels the states to maintain specified standards in the construction of highways included in the Federal aid pro-

---

[8] Each of the local councils has published one or more reports. A very good one is *A Practical Basis for Developing Better Intergovernmental Relations* (Santa Clara Council on Intergovernmental Relations, San Jose, 1947).

[9] A much longer list is presented in White, Leonard D., *Introduction to the Study of Public Administration*, Third Edition, pp. 164–167 (Macmillan, New York, 1948).

gram; and for another example, the states which contribute heavily to the support of the public schools may specify the minimum qualifications of teachers, the length of the school term, and other matters essential to the maintenance of minimum standards of public instruction.

2. *Supervision and Inspection.* It does little good to set standards unless the larger unit is equipped to see that they are observed and unless the smaller units know definitely that they will be held strictly to account. Inspections must therefore be made and records examined at frequent but preferably irregular intervals. When inspections are made, information and advice may be given to the officials in charge. Effective supervision may become rather complicated, involving many aspects of the work in a large general field. In the case of local finance the areas of supervision have been broken down functionally, along lines already indicated. All of this occurs in an area of general government, where grants-in-aid do not enter into the picture.

3. *Control over Personnel.* One of the most effective means of exerting administrative control is to select or to have something to say about the selection and/or removal of personnel. Like most powers, of course, this can be used for the good of the service or for the securing of personal or political advantage. In the former case, the larger unit may actually select key personnel in charge of administration of the service in the smaller unit or may reserve a veto power over such selections as may be desired by the smaller unit. Thus in the social security program the Federal government pays the expenses of administration in the states when they meet certain prescribed conditions.

The Social Security Board early decided that one of these conditions should be selection and appointment of personnel engaged in the administration of any program under the Board's jurisdiction on the basis of merit. If it should appear that in any given state this requirement was not being complied with, the funds allocated to and otherwise due the state might be withheld. Similarly, funds may be withheld when personnel engaged in activities supported in whole or in part by Federal funds are found to have violated the provisions of the Hatch Act.

An interesting illustration in the field of state-local relations is to be found in the method of selecting county health officers in Maryland. The Board of County Commissioners also serves as the county Board of Health; in the latter capacity, it is required by law to appoint a county health officer. The state law also requires the state Department of Health to appoint a deputy in each senatorial district, i.e., each one of the thirty-three counties of the state. In practice, the head of the state

Department goes to each county board and agrees on a candidate with proper training and qualifications, who is then appointed by both the county and the state to the position.

4. *Financial Controls*. Financial controls are in themselves an effective instrument for control of administrative activity within the limits prescribed. The mere threat to exercise the power to withhold or withdraw funds already allocated or about to be allocated — whether or not that power is actually used — is normally sufficient. But this is not the only means of exerting financial pressure. The smaller units may be limited in their powers to raise revenue or in the rates of the taxes they may impose or in the use which they may make of the revenues collected. In 1934 under the provisions of the Hayden-Cartwright Act states participating in the grant-in-aid program for highways were restrained from diverting more than a specified small percentage of their motor license and gasoline tax revenues to purposes other than highway construction and maintenance, and similar provisions have been continued in subsequent legislation providing for highway grants. The states have imposed similar restrictions upon the freedom of their political subdivisions to use funds collected in connection with activities for which grants-in-aid were given.

5. *Resort to Superior Authority*. Controls based upon the existence of superior power in the hands of the larger unit may be effective but they may also be dangerous. The Federal government can, where a use of the treaty power is involved, compel states to accept controls and invasions of their accustomed prerogatives growing out of its exercise.[10] In the states the organization and powers of the various units of local government are in most cases provided for by statute. Powers which the legislature had the authority to confer, it has also the authority to modify or withdraw. The use of this power may stir up trouble or may not be politically wise or expedient. But there can be no question regarding the right of the legislature to do so with or without a specific request from the administrative authorities concerned.

Cooperation in Illustrative Fields

In the preceding sections, the broad outlines of the various types of interlevel and interjurisdictional relationships that arise in a complicated federal system like our own have been indicated. A more detailed consideration of illustrative types of interlevel cooperation may now be attempted, in such fields as planning, agriculture, and food and drug administration. These illustrations clearly indicate the truth of the state-

10 See Missouri v. Holland, U. S. Game Warden, 252 U.S. 416, 1920.

ment that many functions of government today are no longer the exclusive concern of any one level but may involve cooperative relationships between two or more different levels. Furthermore, cooperative arrangements may be entered into between adjoining or adjacent local units for such purposes as purchasing, sewage treatment, incineration, and the like, as pointed out earlier in this chapter.

The Planning Movement. Accomplishments in the field of planning constitute an excellent example of what can be done through interlevel cooperation. There had long been planning commissions in the larger cities, but prior to 1930 modern planning techniques were virtually unknown in the national and state fields. In 1929 the President's Committee on Social Trends recommended the establishment of some kind of national planning board. Such a board was established by President Roosevelt by Executive Order and with the use of emergency funds. In the decade of its existence it went through numerous reorganizations and changes of name, until finally in 1944 Congress in an erring moment killed it off by failure to appropriate funds for its continued operation. Its early program included research projects of its own as well as efforts to assist the states in establishing individual planning commissions. Within a remarkably short time all but two or three states had some kind of planning agency, some established by the governor by Executive Order, others by legislative action. By 1944 some of these state boards had already disappeared. The significant thing is, however, that a great many of them still remain and are now established on a sound and permanent basis. They are not only carrying on research studies in population problems, natural resources, manufacturing potentialities, development of parks and recreational facilities, and so on, but they are working in close cooperation with the planning agencies in the political subdivisions of their respective states and are assisting them in the development of local planning work. The result is that planning efforts in communities where boards had long existed have been improved and that such programs have been set up in large numbers of other communities. The state board is able to lend the services of technically trained personnel which the local boards could not afford to hire. In many cases they are able to avoid duplication of effort by supplying information that has already been assembled and analyzed. They are able to save time, money, and effort by furnishing the know-how to get local programs organized and under way.

During the war another interesting but short-lived experiment was undertaken. The Congress provided a relatively small sum to support a postwar planning program, with the idea that projects which had been developed in states and in local communities should be studied to determine costs, priorities, and other factors and that the plans for public works should be in readiness to go ahead when needed to take up the slack of unemployment expected when the armed forces were demobilized. Congress, however, in an effort at economy, disapproved the small appropriation necessary for the continuance of the agency, and the project was abandoned just at the point when it was beginning to show results and when if it was needed at all — as it most certainly was — it was needed most.

Agriculture. The United States Department of Agriculture, because of its age, its administrative experience, and its generally intelligent leadership, has come to be regarded as an example of good administrative organization. In some of its programs it has long had intimate relationships with state departments and agencies. In recent years new programs have brought it also into contact with counties, newly established soil conservation districts, etc. In this way the effort to aid agriculture has been for all practical purposes molded into one great program in which all units of government from the largest to the smallest cooperate, each performing its part to the end that the whole job may be done.

As Miss Baker clearly showed, the administrative unit for much of this work is the county, the administrative officer being the county agent who works for and, in certain respects, is subject to the control of all three levels of government. The Federal government may, through its Extension Office, disapprove his appointment and may withhold funds from the state if it disapproves the work plans in the state service-extension budget. The Federal Regional Agent examines his reports. The state government has direct control over him through its own staff of field supervisors, who approve his work plans and money allotments (both Federal and state). The control of the county is based upon state laws under which appropriations are made for extension work and is generally operated on some cooperative basis with the state Extension Office.[11]

There has been no uniform system of selecting these agents. In many cases they are appointed by the county governing boards; in others the farm bureaus appoint them and pay part of the salary. They are generally young men, usually in their thirties, who have been active farmers, and they are preferably college graduates. Their average salary before the war was $2677, with no set system of raises and promotions. The average term of service was about six years. Beginning in the early years by furnishing information to farmers on farm crops, plant and

---

[11] See Baker, Gladys, *The County Agent* (University of Chicago Press, 1939).

animal industry, and related subjects, they functioned from 1914 on as demonstration agents. After World War I, during the depression era, they turned their attention to farm economics and to the promotion of farm marketing and cooperatives. In spite of reduced allotments they were able to render really useful service.

Their functions and the staff were both greatly enlarged under the AAA program during the Roosevelt administration. The county agent now not only assumed responsibility for explaining and interpreting the act and the administrative rules sent out from Washington, but he also served as one of the committeemen in the corn, hog, and wheat program in the North, and the cotton, tobacco, and peanut program in the South. Before the present soil conservation program was set up, he assisted in agricultural conservation work. He organized and conducted discussion groups among the farmers with a view to helping them make intelligent decisions regarding agricultural policies and assume an active part in directing them. Other programs included the Resettlement Administration, the Farm Security Administration, and the Farm Credit Administration.

Where the counties are used as administrative units, an elaborate series of instructions may be prepared in connection with each major program, indicating the methods of organization and the procedures to be followed. Thus in 1941 the Federal Crop Insurance Corporation, which functioned within the framework of the Department of Agriculture, issued a twenty-eight page pamphlet setting forth a procedure for wheat crop insurance for the 1942 program. At the beginning of this publication it was stated:

The county agricultural conservation committee is responsible to the state agricultural conservation committee for the administration of all phases of the crop insurance program. The county committee, under the direction of the state committee, shall develop plans for presenting the crop insurance program to all wheat growers in the county in sufficient time for growers to present their applications for crop insurance on or before the final date established by the Corporation for the receipt of applications in the county office. The county committee shall also make careful plans in conformity with this procedure for the handling of problems of administration and operation within the county so that the interests of both the wheat growers and the Corporation will be protected at all times. The county committee shall coordinate its activities in presenting this program, giving due consideration to timeliness, effectiveness, and economy of operation, in order to present the crop insurance program as a part of the general farm program being administered by the United States Department of Agriculture.

Under the soil conservation program each state sets up a soil conservation commission or board. Then in turn, when the farmers in a county or in adjoining counties desire to avail themselves of the benefits of this program, they organize a soil conservation district, as provided under both the Federal and the state laws.[12] This agreement, when finally approved by the county commissioners and the appropriate Federal and state authorities, provides for cooperation between the state commission, the district board, and the Soil Conservation Service of the United States Department of Agriculture. When the state commission approves such applications, it decides at the same time what agricultural associations within the area affected shall be eligible to send delegates to a meeting to nominate district board members. The whole setup is planned to insure democratic control by the persons and groups affected.

Food and Drug Administration. For many years the administration of the food and drug laws has provided an outstanding example of interjurisdictional cooperation. The Federal Food and Drug Administration, formerly in the Department of Agriculture and now under the Federal Security Agency, has jurisdiction under the Federal law over food and drug shipments in interstate commerce. The states, whose laws generally provide a close parallel to the Federal act, have jurisdiction over products produced and sold locally. Finally, the health departments of the municipalities have a definite interest in ascertaining that poisonous or deleterious substances are not retailed to the public in food and drug products.[13]

No one of these agencies has any authority outside its own jurisdiction. The nature of crookedness being what it is, the purveyors of objectionable products could easily find ways of evading the authorities if those in each jurisdiction worked independently or regarded their associates in other units with suspicion and distrust. Fortunately they do not. In fact, it has been the practice for many years to hold regular conferences of enforcement officers at all three levels in each of the larger cities. In these conferences the representatives of each enforcement agency or governmental unit bring up any difficult problems confronting them or describe any new situations that have come to their attention. After some discussion it is usually possible to develop a method of procedure that will be effective in controlling the situation.

SELECTED REFERENCES

In a voluminous literature from which the making of selections is often difficult, a limited number of related titles have been grouped together under appropriate subject-matter headings.

---

12 See Walker, Herman, Jr., and Parks, W. Robert, "Soil Conservation Districts: Local Democracy in a National Program," *Journal of Politics*, November, 1946, pp. 538–549.
13 See Conover, Milton, "National, State and Local Cooperation in Food and Drug Control," *American Political Science Review*, November, 1928, pp. 910–928.

RESEARCH

Anderson, William, *Federalism and Intergovernmental Relations: A Budget of Suggestions for Research* (Public Administration Service, Chicago, 1946).

GENERAL INTERLEVEL COOPERATION

Baker, Gladys, *The County Agent* (University of Chicago Press, 1939). The cooperation of all three levels of government in the agricultural program is discussed with special reference to the work done at the county level.

Committee on Expenditures in the Executive Departments, *Joint Hearings* on the establishment of a National Commission on Intergovernmental Relations (81st Cong., 1st Sess., 1949).

Graves, W. Brooke, Ed., "Intergovernmental Relations in the United States," *Annals* of the American Academy of Political and Social Science, January, 1940, entire volume. Comprehensive survey of the field, with some attention to administrative problems.

Pritchett, C. Herman, *The Tennessee Valley Authority* (University of North Carolina Press, 1943). Analysis of a significant administrative program whose guiding principle has been cooperation with state, county, and municipal authorities.

GRANT-IN-AID SYSTEMS

Clark, Jane P., *The Rise of a New Federalism* (Columbia University Press, 1938). Primarily concerned with new relationships arising from the social security program.

Key, V. O., Jr., *The Administration of Federal Grants to States* (Public Administration Service, Chicago, 1937). Comparative study of the administration of various types of Federal grants.

Macmahon, Arthur W., Millett, John D., and Ogden, Gladys, *The Administration of Federal Work Relief* (Public Administration Service, Chicago, 1941), and Williams, J. Kerwin, *Grants-in-Aid under the Public Works Administration* (Columbia University Press, 1939) — both are case studies of grant-in-aid administration in emergency agencies of the depression period.

For citation of numerous studies of state grant-in-aid systems, see the author's *American State Government*, Third Edition, pp. 896–900 (Heath, Boston, 1946).

INTERSTATE RELATIONS

Graves, W. Brooke, *Uniform State Action* (University of North Carolina Press, 1934). A comprehensive study of all phases of interstate relations, now somewhat out of date, but emphasizing the importance of administrative cooperation as a possible substitute for centralization.

Stone, Clifford H., Ed., *Interstate Compacts* (Colorado Water Conservation Board, Denver, 1946). A valuable compilation of articles from widely scattered sources, some of which deal with administrative aspects of the problem.

STATE AND LOCAL INTERRELATIONS

Hinderaker, Ivan H., *The Administrative Districts and Field Offices of the Minnesota State Government* (University of Minnesota Press, 1943). The only study available of zone administration in a particular state.

Jamison, Judith N., *Intergovernmental Cooperation in Public Administration in the Los Angeles Area* (Bureau of Governmental Research, University of California at Los Angeles, 1944). An important survey of cooperative practices in an area in which such practices are becoming numerous and highly developed.

6

INTERAGENCY AND INTRA-AGENCY
RELATIONSHIPS

THE previous chapter has been concerned with the general pattern of intergovernmental relations; it is now appropriate to examine some of the interrelations within a given department or agency and between departments. These involve the basic question of centralization or decentralization of authority; the relations between the central or departmental office of the agency on the one hand and its regional, district, zone, or field offices on the other; and the coordination of the field offices. At the same time interagency relations arise, for every agency is obliged to carry on normal contacts with other departments and agencies at its own level. Some agencies — like budget and personnel — have many more such contacts than others, but all agencies have some. Problems of this character present themselves at all levels of administration, state and local as well as Federal.

The proper formula for the distribution of authority between the central office and the field is the subject of never-ending controversy. Much of it, centering as it does on the meaning and application of terms, is quite pointless. "Centralization" and "decentralization," for instance, are much like some of the words in *Alice in Wonderland,* which mean what the people who use them want them to mean. They may refer to concentration of power in the hands of the Federal government and to the continuing absorption by the Federal government of powers presumably belonging to the states; or, in the case of the state-local relationship, absorption by the states of powers belonging to the local units. Or they may be applied to the concentration of departmental service in Washington as opposed to the wartime practice of moving departmental offices out into the hinterland.[1] Yet again, these terms may be applied to so much centering of power in the departmental office of an agency that field offices have little or no discretion but are obliged to refer all except routine questions to the central office for decision. In the field of municipal government these terms are used in

---

[1] See Senate Committee Report No. 1554, 77th Cong., 2nd Sess., 1942, and the hearings of the House Subcommittee on Public Buildings and Grounds on H. Res. 209, in the same Congress.

a still different sense and refer to the substitution of suburban and satellite communities for the heretofore customary concentration of population and business in the central city.[2]

The Field Establishment

For many years the Federal government has used administrative areas of various sorts for a wide variety of purposes. Very often, as a matter of convenience, it has utilized state boundary lines, which are generally familiar. In other cases, where these were or were thought to be unsuitable, new regions, districts, or zones have been set up without much regard for state boundaries. While in a few cases legitimate bases for such differences may exist, it is well known that the results of this policy have been unfortunate in that it has produced a high degree of confusion in interagency relationships in the field. Few people realize the extent to which the tendency toward this type of decentralization has progressed.[3]

A survey made by the Legislative Reference Service of the Library of Congress in 1943 contains the most recent information on the subject; since this survey was made, the situation has changed considerably in detail but not in principle. At that time there were thought to be 143 operating agencies in the Federal government with some kind of field organization, and one year later it was reported by the Civil Service Commission that the field forces of the Federal agencies constituted 92 per cent of the total number of Federal employees. The distribution of these among the various departments and agencies is indicated in the table which appears on page 84. The following more detailed information for the Department of the Army is typical:

---

[2] This question is discussed in most of the textbooks in municipal government; that the problem is not merely theoretical may be seen from such a report as *Decentralization, A Problem in Cleveland's Future* (Cleveland Chamber of Commerce, 1941).

[3] The National Resources Committee in 1935 made a pioneer study of this problem, with suggestions for the establishment of standard zones. They found that the regional headquarters for thirty-three of the largest Federal agencies were located in forty-five different cities. The ten most frequently selected are Chicago, New York, San Francisco, Atlanta, Boston, Kansas City, Dallas, Cleveland, Philadelphia, and Denver, but there is very little indication of a pattern among the remaining thirty-five. See Fesler, James W., "Federal Administrative Regions," *American Political Science Review*, April, 1936, pp. 257–268, and "Standardizing Federal Administrative Regions," *Social Forces*, October, 1936, pp. 12–21, and other articles by the same author; Latham, Earl G., "Executive Management and the Federal Field Service," *Public Administration Review*, Winter, 1945, pp. 16–27; and the author's "Federal Administrative Areas: An Historical Record of Confusion and a Suggested Program of Action," *Western Political Quarterly*, March, 1948, pp. 54–70. *Federal Field Offices* (Legislative Reference Service, Library of Congress, 1943) deals specifically with the question as to when regions should be established and when the states should be used. Kurt Wilk's *Decentralizing Governmental Work* (Institute of Public Administration, New York, 1942) deals with the numbers, types, and layers of administrative units and with the size of area and the allocation of functions.

Zone Administration in the Department of the Army

1. Bureau of Ordnance – procurement districts
2. Chemical Warfare Service – procurement districts
3. Military districts and Army areas
4. Engineer Department
   a. Division and district engineer offices
   b. Procurement districts
5. Finance Department
6. Medical Department – procurement districts
7. Office of the Quartermaster General
   a. Construction zones
   b. Procurement and regional depots
   c. Remount districts
8. Signal Corps – procurement districts

This problem may be further illustrated by reference to the Department of Agriculture. A *Directory of Organization and Field Activities* of this Department, published in 1947, required 264 pages merely to present a full picture of the organization and supervisory personnel of the Department in Washington and in the field. There were forty-nine bureaus and offices of the Department having field activities. The geographical directory showing these activities, listed by cities and towns at which employees are located, consumed 154 double column pages in fine print, more than twice the space required for the same purpose in an earlier edition in 1941.

Field Organization in the Federal Government

DEPARTMENT OR AGENCY	NUMBER OF BUREAUS WITH FIELD ORGANIZATION	TOTAL NUMBER OF FIELD ORGANIZATIONS
Department of Agriculture*	15	20
Department of Commerce	4	4
Department of the Interior	9	11
Department of Justice	3	3
Department of Labor	4	7
Department of the Navy	7	7
Post Office Department	3	3
Treasury Department	8	21
Department of the Army	9	12
Federal Loan Agency	6	6
Federal Security Agency	6	13
General Services Administration	7	8
Executive Office of the President	7	8
Agencies Showing Only One Map**	9	9
Interstate Commerce Commission	6	9
Veterans Administration	2	2
Totals	105	143

* Difference between figures in this table and in the text is accounted for by different dates of the source material, during a period of rapid expansion of field services.
** Includes the following group of independent establishments: Civil Service Commission, Employees Compensation Commission, Federal Communications Commission, Federal Deposit Insurance Corporation, Federal Power Commission, Federal Reserve System, National Labor Relations Board, Railroad Retirement Board, and the Securities and Exchange Commission. Nomenclature takes account of changes made through 81st Cong., 1st Sess.

About the same time the author made a tabulation of the number of field offices of various types in the first six states, from the *United States Government Manual,* noting the total number of such offices in each state, the number of cities in which they were located, and the number of such offices located in the capital city of the state. The results of this analysis are shown in the table on this page; a complete tabulation of this type for all the states would serve only further to emphasize the diversity that is here apparent.

Distribution of Field Offices in a Selected Group of States — 1948

	OFFICES			TYPES OF OFFICES							
STATES	TOTAL NUMBER	NUMBER OF CITIES IN WHICH LOCATED	NUMBER LOCATED IN CAPITAL CITY	FIELD	REGIONAL	BRANCH	DISTRICT	STATE	ATTORNEYS AND MARSHALS	VETERANS HOSPITALS	MISCELLANEOUS
Alabama	22	5	8	7	1	0	2	0	6	3	3
Arizona	14	3	9	3	1	0	1	0	2	3	4
Arkansas	12	4	8	2	1	0	1	0	4	2	2
California	80	14	1	24	17	2	12	0	4	7	14
Colorado	35	4	31	10	5	1	7	0	2	2	8
Connecticut	12	5	6	4	1	0	2	0	2	1	2

The establishment of a field organization presupposes a decision to decentralize the work of the agency, to some extent at least. This may be done along functional lines or along territorial lines. In the former case, while certain functions may be retained in the central office, responsibility for certain others is transferred to the field. In a territorial decentralization all the actual operations of the agency are put out into the field, the central office retaining only the functions of determining agency policy and important procedures and of exercising its powers of coordination and control. These functions, of course, are highly important — in fact, indispensable in any administrative unit carrying on its work through field offices.

Central Office–Field Office Relationships

In the organization of field offices certain fundamental principles should be observed. Conflict immediately arises between a desire for uniformity on the one hand and the necessity for recognizing local conditions and local needs on the other. The guiding principle, which it is much easier to state than to work out in practice, calls for such a degree of uniformity as may be essential to provide coordination, while at the same time the system provides flexibility sufficient to enable the field offices to meet their individual needs without violating either the law or their instructions. Within this general framework variations as to the type of intra-agency field organization may exist, resulting either in a functional centralization of field activities in the regional office or in a complete centralization of all agency activities in the regional offices.

Quite as important as the two considerations just discussed, is the nature of the organization at headquarters to serve the field. Neither level can function without the other, and the arrangements established to govern their relationships should facilitate rather than obstruct co-operative effort between them. Lines of communication — "channels" — may call for direct communication between the chief executive of the agency and the regional director. In this case matters involving other than routine business (which may usually, with the consent of the main line of command, be handled between the corresponding divisions of the central and the field offices) move up to the head of the agency and are transmitted by him to the regional directors (or the regional director concerned) who in turn pass the matter on down to the individual in their own organization responsible for handling such problems.

An alternative type of organization provides for a field division, the head of which serves as an intermediary between the central office and the regional directors. Although this arrangement introduces one more level of top management and requires one more handling of papers, it provides an opportunity for a general supervision and coordination of field work which in the opinion of many qualified persons justifies its existence. The circumstances surrounding the adoption of this type of organization in the National Labor Relations Board are well stated in an article appearing in one of the law reviews: [4]

First, the Board is establishing a new relationship with its regional officers. A new section has been set up, under a formal regional director, to head the Board's administrative relationships with its field staff. The Board's Secretary who previously performed this function has been relieved of it. The step is not merely a reorganization and an effort to relieve the field staff of the feeling that they have been "isolated and more or less neglected." It is, rather, the result of a realization of the extreme importance of the field staff and is an effort to improve administration at its major activity. As Chairman Millis wrote in his announcement of the change:

"The Board feels strongly that the regional offices are of major importance in its operations. There the cases are investigated and the great majority disposed of. There the cases not settled locally are prepared for further necessary proce-

---

[4] See Shulman, Harry, "Reforming Procedures of the National Labor Relations Board," *George Washington Law Review*, November, 1941, pp. 1–14.

dures. The whole future of a case depends upon the most careful investigation at the start. Moreover, it can be truthfully said that attitudes of labor, employers, and public toward the Board and the Act depend quite as much upon the work and demeanor of the regional staffs as upon all other things taken together, including Board decisions."

Finally, it is possible to permit, as a general policy, direct communication between functional units in the field and the corresponding functional units in the central office, depending upon top management for coordination in the field work as in other aspects of the agency's program. Whatever the form of organization decided upon, "the real job of the Washington staff is to help the field staff do its job, not to do the field job itself."

Regardless of the type of organization decided upon at each of these levels, there must be a definite understanding with regard to the nature and scope of the authority and responsibility to be exercised by each. Unless this is established, nobody will know either in the central office or in the field what he is supposed to do or what he is permitted to do. So far as the field is concerned, these powers must be ample to permit doing the job that needs to be done. The development of the principles governing such definition is not the responsibility of the central office alone. It may properly initiate and carry on the work of formulating such principles, but the determination should be the result of the joint counsel and effort of the central office and the field. In this way the central office may avoid serious blunders, while the field people will be reasonably satisfied that they have been consulted and that their views have been considered. From the point of view of morale this is extremely important.[5]

The field offices cannot function well unless they have proper working tools in the form of personnel, financial support, and material equipment. This they will not have if the central office tries to retain all the high-grade positions. Mention has already been made of the fact that decentralization necessarily involves greater expenditures for qualified supervisory personnel. It is also important that the responsible personnel of both the central office and the field be personally acquainted with the problems arising at the other level. This can be accomplished by rotation in assignments, giving personnel from each level an oppor-

---

[5] On this point, compare the judgment of Donald Stone, *op. cit.*, p. 18 (italics mine): "Let me repeat — and it needs continuous reiteration — under programs which are essentially of a field service character, the job of Washington staff is to formulate the programs, establish policy, develop standards and some of the principal procedures, and to create a field organization which is competent to administer and permitted to administer the programs. *These things cannot be done remotely by the Washington staff; field staff must participate all along the line.* Policy, programs, and procedures must be developed and constantly revalued in terms of operating and administrative experience, and, with a few exceptions, this experience is taking place in the field."

tunity for considerable tours of duty at the other level. In no other way can central office and field office personnel understand each other's problems and avoid the frictions which have so often in the past marred such relationships. Donald Stone and others have strongly urged this type of rotation as a means of overcoming many of the difficulties heretofore existing in central-field office relationships.[6]

On the financial side, control of field operations is essential, of course, but ways must be found to accomplish it without a rigidity which leaves the field offices no "latitude for independent judgment." Best results will be achieved if there is joint participation in the formulation of the budget and if, after allocations have been finally agreed upon, it is understood that modifications may be made in the field when necessary, within the maximum over-all limitations prescribed. In substance the same principle applies to the procurement of services and supplies. There should be a sufficient amount of centralization to promote economy, and a decentralization sufficient to permit speed and efficiency. It is difficult to specify a precise point with regard to this matter; it is likely to vary somewhat according to the character of the organization and the functions of the agency. Mr. Stone's comments on this general subject also are significant: [7]

> I should like to emphasize the need for providing field offices with the necessary management tools to carry on their responsibilities. The manager of a large field office must engage in budgetary planning and follow-up, personnel management, and program planning, and he must have staff to assist him in the general task of direction and coordination of operations. He cannot rely on budget and personnel staffs in Washington to perform his management job, as seems too often to be the prevailing view in Washington. They may help, they may set policies and procedures, they may give him other kinds of direct aid, but if he is to be manager he must have his kit of management tools within arm's reach for use on all parts of his working organization. The common disposition to bind regional operations by rigid procedures through such attempts to provide all of the staff resources from Washington must be resisted if effective field administration is to result.

The results of field service operations will vary, of course, according to the nature and function of the agency. Such operations in the Bureau of the Budget may yield, as Mr. Latham suggests they have yielded, elimination of duplicating surveys, coordination of space controls, and intergovernmental advice and coordination with state and lo-

---

[6] The nature of some of the common "gripes" that arise from both points of view is very interestingly illustrated in Donald C. Stone's contribution to *Washington-Field Relationships in the Federal Service* (Graduate School, United States Department of Agriculture, 1942). The knowledge of employees in the field may also be broadened by rotation among the field officials.

[7] *Ibid.*, p. 16.

cal activities. In some other agency they may produce results quite different. They will not produce worth-while results, however, in any agency unless the field organization is set up in accordance with such sound principles of organization as have here been suggested. Perhaps, in conclusion, it would be well to summarize these, as Martha Chickering has done on the basis of a number of years of experience in public welfare administration: [8]

Some Suggested Principles in the Organization and Direction
of a Field Staff

1. The field staff should be headed up by one person, especially (a) if the agency has a complex program and a large territory and (b) if it is desired to have the program development reasonably uniform throughout the territory.

2. The person directing the field operations should report to the administrative head of the agency and to no one else (unless the administrator has a deputy who genuinely acts for him across a large part of the agency operation).

3. Lines of communication must be kept freely open between the head of the field staff and all the bureau heads in the agency whose programs are carried out through the integrated field staff.

4. Policies must be consistently followed which develop a strong field staff.

5. If the field staff is expected to show initiative out in the territory covered by the agency, provision must be made in the agency for close check on what the field staff does.

6. When the headquarters officials go into the field, they should go under the direction of the chief field officer for that territory, however humble his rank.

The Problem at the State and Local Level. The problem of decentralization and field services is just as important in the states as in the Federal government. The administrative problems are fundamentally the same, although the areas are smaller and normally there are fewer districts. Even in the counties and in some of the larger cities the same problems arise. Reference has already been made to the use of highway districts in one Minnesota county, and numerous cities have found it necessary to decentralize not only police and fire services but tax collections as well. The conduct of elections is always carried on through voting districts, divisions, or precincts, and provision may be made for some decentralization in the administration of registration.

So far as the states are concerned, aside from districts established for tax collection practically all the decentralized functions are those associated with the concept of the service state, such as agriculture, conservation, health, highways, labor, and welfare. A few examples from a selected group of states are listed on the following page.

[8] See Latham, Earl G., "Executive Management and the Federal Field Service," *Public Administration Review,* Winter, 1945, pp. 16–27, and Chickering, Martha A., "Some Suggested Principles in the Organization and Direction of a Field Staff," *Public Welfare,* July, 1944, pp. 138–140.

CONNECTICUT — *Department of Forestry: Farm Forest Districts*

Four districts have been set up, each with a farm forester, whose job it is to help landowners, whether farmers or not, to get more value from their woodlands.[9]

INDIANA — *State Board of Health: Branch Office Administration*

A plan for the decentralization of the activities of the State Board of Health through the establishment of five branch offices has been set up as a means of getting closer to the work in the field. Governor Gates has given his full approval to the plan as being in harmony with his idea that the State House should be taken to the people. Each branch office will render service to approximately eighteen counties, thereby giving coverage to all ninety-two counties of the state.[10]

INDIANA — *Department of Conservation: Wildlife Habitat Improvement Program*

Indiana has been divided into six districts to carry on the wildlife habitat program sponsored by the Department of Conservation and to be carried out, under approval of the Pittman-Robertson Federal aid, by the Division of Fish and Game. There will be a district supervisor in each of the six districts. The project is to be a habitat development with the purpose of increasing game and fur.[11]

OREGON — *People's Utility Districts*

As the term "district" implies, the territory encompassed in a utility district is some part of the state less than the whole. The statute may prescribe that the boundaries of the district must follow those of some existing political unit, such as the county, or it may, as in Oregon, allow the boundaries to be determined by the sponsors of the district without reference to existing political subdivisions. Procedure for organizing utility districts varies considerably. However, most of the statutes provide for an expression of opinion by the electorate of the district at some point in the proceedings, either by petition or by popular vote, or both. Most of the statutes provide for some technically skilled administrative body to pass judgment upon the feasibility of the proposed district at some state of the formal proceedings.[12]

PENNSYLVANIA — *Department of Revenue: Collection Districts*

The primary function of the Field Investigation and Collection Section of the Bureau of Delinquent Accounts is to perform the field work and investigation necessary to the collection of delinquent accounts and to determine whether or not accounts are collectible. For this purpose, the territory of the Commonwealth has been divided into eight zones or districts, each with a central office. Through these various field offices, the Section receives all delinquent accounts

9 "Farm Forestry Districts," *The Wooden Nutmeg*, January, 1944.
10 "Plan for Decentralization of the State Board of Health," *Monthly Bulletin*, January, 1946.
11 "State Districts Made to Carry Out Wildlife Habitat Improvement Program," *Outdoor Indiana*, April, 1941.
12 Brown, Betty L., "People's Utility Districts in Oregon," *Oregon Law Review*, December, 1940, pp. 3-72; note that such districts, called by slightly different names, are authorized by law in ten states: Alabama, California, Mississippi, Nebraska, Nevada, Oregon, South Dakota, Tennessee, Washington, and Wisconsin.

which the several bureaus in the Department have been unable to collect by direct correspondence. By personal contact through the field investigators in each office, strenuous efforts are made to collect all overdue accounts. If these efforts are of no avail, a report must be prepared showing the reason why the account cannot be collected and furnishing such information as will enable the Bureau to submit the account with all the facts to the Department of Justice for final action.[13]

PENNSYLVANIA — *Department of Highways: Highway Districts*
The territory of the Commonwealth has been blocked out into divisions and districts for the administration of construction and maintenance work on the state highway system. The total mileage of the system has been so divided as to make the divisions as nearly equal in size as possible. The mileage in the individual counties varies widely, but with two exceptions each county constitutes a maintenance district. Under this plan there are six divisions, twelve districts, and sixty-five county maintenance districts.[14]

In states large enough in area or in population or in both to warrant an extensive use of field organizations, the same problems of uniformity (or lack of it) arise as in the Federal government. While there is a tendency to centralize field offices in the large communities, there is no assurance that different agencies having different functions to perform will select the same ones. New York has perhaps done better in this respect than most other states. It has a state office building in New York City, but as far back as 1931 it erected a "Junior Capitol" in the heart of Buffalo to house the local offices of the state government.[15]

Interagency Relations

Problems in the relations of one agency to another arise, of course, at all levels — in the departmental service in Washington, in the field service, and in the state and local units. It has often been said that a man cannot live unto himself alone. Neither can a government agency, which like an individual soon discovers that in order to do its own work assignment well, it must have the sympathetic understanding and perhaps the active cooperation of other agencies of government at its own and other levels.

Such of these problems as require no more than a little cooperation, which can be worked out at a conference, in the central office or in the field as the case may be, present no special difficulty. Very often, how-

[13] Joint Legislative Committee on Finances, *Survey of the Government of Pennsylvania*, pp. 375–376 (Harrisburg, 1934).
[14] *Ibid.*, pp. 492–494.
[15] For comments on the situation in several other states, see: Minnesota, Hinderaker; New York, "Task of Albany Office (Labor) Made Simpler by Contacts, Able Administrative Personnel," *Industrial Bulletin*, November, 1946, pp. 34–37; Virginia, Uhl, Raymond, "Administrative Regions in Virginia," *Public Administration Review*, Winter, 1942, pp. 30–33.

ever, so far as the field service is concerned, the problems grow out of conflicting policies or purposes arising from instructions which each agency has received from its central office. These obviously must be sent up to the central office with a suggestion that some solution be agreed upon at that level.

In this type of interrelationship as in others the nature and extent of an agency's relations with other agencies — one Federal agency with others, one state agency with others — will depend largely upon the nature of its major duties and responsibilities. A staff agency like budget or personnel will ordinarily find that the bulk of its work can be done only on the basis of close and almost continuous contacts with each of the operating agencies functioning in its area, central office or field as the case may be. Line agencies, on the other hand, will have some of their most frequent contacts with the staff agencies which provide administrative services, but each line agency will also have contacts with other line agencies engaged in work having some relation to its own.

Interagency Relations in the Departmental Service. Perhaps the best way to visualize the problems of interagency relations is to examine the experience of a particular agency, keeping constantly in mind the fact that no two agencies will present the same pattern of interrelations. Many of the problems in this area can be handled by regular procedures of the agencies involved, while others may require more than this.

So important were these relations conceived to be that in the summer of 1941, in the midst of the defense period, the Office of Government Reports compiled *A Guide for Federal Executives to Inter-Agency Service Functions, Contacts and Procedures.* This booklet of approximately one hundred pages presented in detail a description of the service functions performed by each staff agency in the departmental service, with supplementary information as to the authority for such service, whom to contact in order to secure it, and how to initiate the procedure. The Federal Personnel Council, which has been functioning now for more than a decade, and the field councils have been extremely valuable instruments for working out procedures for handling interagency problems in the personnel field, some of them long range, some of them immediate.

When problems are specific and require immediate settlement, a more or less permanent coordinating committee may be established, in which all the agencies involved are represented. This device was used during World War II with notable success in a number of different areas. The State-War-Navy Coordinating Committee (SWNCC), for instance, was set up to eliminate the causes of criticism that had become fairly widespread. The authority of this Committee was defined and formalized in a memorandum signed by the Secretaries of the three departments "as the agency to reconcile and coordinate the action to be taken by the State, War, and Navy Departments on matters of common interest and, under the guidance of the Secretaries of State, War, and Navy, establish policies on politicomilitary questions referred to it." [16]

Interagency Relations at the Field Level. Governmental agencies, not only at the departmental level but in the field, have a tendency to proceed each in its own way. This tendency is strengthened in the field by the conflict between the two principles of functional and territorial organization. As James W. Fesler has expressed it, "It is apparent that there is a flaw in a system of national administration that never pulls departmental operations together except at the Presidential level, and that seldom pulls bureau operations together except in the department head's office at Washington." [17] He continues:

The test of successful Federal administration is not, after all, simply to be found in statistical totals or averages for the nation as a whole. At some point in our Federal administration there must be a realization that the effect on one man's farm, on one community, or on one county of all the Federal programs operating simultaneously is the real test of the success of Federal administration. The aggregate of Federal programs must produce a pattern of effects that is as sound in terms of a few square miles occupied by some ordinary community as it is in terms of the "grand policy" of the top executives in Washington.

My thesis about interdepartmental relations in the field is very simple. It consists of the following propositions: (1) the basic organization of Federal administrative authority follows the functional principle. (2) Therefore, barring a drastic reorientation of the American government, the territorial principle of organizing Federal administrative authority must be regarded as secondary, and so must be abandoned whenever it conflicts directly with the functional principle. That is, you cannot organize on both principles. You can have one supplement the other, but you can't use both as the central principle. One or the other has to have the ascendency. And finally, as a recognition of the importance and desirability of working both together, (3) every effort should be made to utilize the territorial principle as a basis for energizing, informing, and integrating the work of officials in the functional hierarchy.

It may be well to consider at this point, in more specific terms, the methods to be employed and the advantages to be gained from devel-

---

[16] See Moseley, Harold W., and others, "The State-War-Navy Coordinating Committee," *Department of State Bulletin*, November 11, 1946, pp. 745-747.

[17] "Interdepartmental Relations in the Field Service of the Federal Government," in *Washington-Field Relationships in the Federal Service*, p. 52. See also Dobbs, John M., "Interagency Communication at the Regional Level," *Public Administration Review*, Winter, 1944, pp. 64-67.

oping such cooperative relations between independent operating units. As in all cooperative relations, each party to the arrangement gains something that it would not otherwise have had. Personnel may be loaned or exchanged, joint administrative efforts may be undertaken, uniform policies may be worked out and adopted, and cooperation on matters of common interest may be developed among a large number of agencies. Such efforts may result in economy and greater efficiency in operations, in improved public relations, or in the coordination of agencies in program planning or in operational matters or in both.

In one case involving the loan of personnel, a large field office had lost an able personnel officer through the operation of Selective Service. Being at the time unable to locate a replacement they thought suitable, they borrowed the assistant director of personnel from the departmental office of another agency in the same city. The man who was loaned gained experience in an agency other than his own, and both of the agencies benefited.

In a good many instances the antagonism that had formerly existed between the Civil Service Commission and the operating agencies was reduced if not eliminated during the war period by agreements for joint efforts in recruiting. The Civil Service Commission, specializing in recruiting techniques as it does, feels that it is best qualified, that it has the know-how to find the right type of person for any particular job. The operating agency, on the other hand, thinks it could do better, that its specialized knowledge of and contacts in the field should enable it to know what kind of person to look for and where to find him. By joint efforts, induced largely by the scarcity of man power, it was found that the job could be done as well if not better and to the greater satisfaction of the operating agency. The use of this principle has been continued in the postwar period by the establishment of boards in each agency, operating with the approval and under the general supervision of the Commission.

Everyone knows that when separate operating agencies adopt divergent policies with regard to the same subject, public relations are bad from the point of view of the government as a whole. It appears that the left hand knoweth not what the right hand doeth. The effect of divergent policies and procedures is no less detrimental to employee morale when occurring within the governmental family. When in a given city each agency interprets the leave regulations — let it be assumed — in its own way, employees working for different agencies compare notes and many are dissatisfied. In such a case a uniform interpretation of the leave regulations is obviously needed; but how is it to be obtained?

Here again the war experience provided an answer, or perhaps several answers. If the problem involves only a few agencies, representatives of those agencies can meet and work out a solution; but if the problem affects all agencies, the situation requires an opportunity for representatives of all agencies to discuss the problem. Such opportunities are now presented in every large city once or twice a month through the field councils of personnel administration, whose principal contribution has been the development of agreement, understanding, cooperation, and common policies with regard to matters of general interest to all agencies. The same kind of cooperation in the finance field is exemplified in Chicago and other cities through the organization of the Federal finance conferences.

The city of Philadelphia, for example, was paralyzed by a general transportation strike in the late summer of 1944. Large numbers of employees in every Federal agency were either absent from duty or were reporting in for work late, through no fault of their own. Many had to leave work early in order to reach home at night. In the old days field offices would have been madly writing and telephoning to their central offices in Washington for instructions handling tardiness and leave. In this instance a special meeting of the Council of Personnel Administration was called. After a general discussion a committee was appointed to draft a statement of policy, the outlines of which would be in conformity both with the realities of the situation and with the published rules and regulations governing leave. In agency after agency this statement, when approved by the Council, was put out by top management as the official statement of policy. Nobody had to consult Washington. The problem was handled promptly and effectively, and a uniform policy was in effect throughout the metropolitan area affected by the strike.

Essential Factors in Coordination. In his discussion of the problems of interdepartmental coordination in the field, Mr. Fesler suggests a number of factors whose presence seems to assist rather than impede coordination. These would seem to be quite as applicable in the departmental service as in the field. The first is familiarity with the work of other agencies, a familiarity which may be attained in a number of ways: through wide distribution and reading of the *United States Government Manual*,[18] the *Congressional Directory*, and similar publications, and through training programs for agency personnel. These should — but frequently do not — include material relating to the functions of

---

[18] Publication temporarily discontinued in 1948 on grounds of economy, and later resumed on an annual basis.

agencies other than the one sponsoring the training program.[19] A third source of information is the annual reports of those agencies whose work is most closely related to our own — whatever that may happen to be.

A second factor facilitating interagency coordination is informal acquaintance. Years ago the establishment of the Federal Business Associations was authorized by law; while some of these groups are still in existence, they have been of scant use in achieving the purposes for which they were established.[20] The United States Department of Agriculture clubs in many areas have been extremely useful, of course within the confines of a single large department.[21] More important are the councils of personnel administration, including in their membership personnel officers from all agencies, in Washington and in the field, and the new Federal finance conferences. The contribution of these organizations is by no means limited to their meetings, committee reports, and so on. The personal acquaintances they facilitate inspire countless luncheon and telephone conversations, productive of a vast amount of cooperation which never appears in the official record.

In the third place, since physical proximity is obviously a factor in interagency cooperation and coordination, the desirability of centering field offices in the same cities and if possible in the same or in adjacent buildings should not be overlooked.

A fourth basis for coordination is a specific objective. There is, as Mr. Fesler truthfully observes, "no such thing as coordination in general. You don't just coordinate. You coordinate about some specific problem limited to some particular subject-matter field."

A fifth factor involves the desirability of a limited number — preferably a small number — of participants, and these of as nearly equal status as possible. Agreement among them will be facilitated if they "have equal status in terms of discretionary authority to speak for and commit" their respective agencies and if they are equal in terms of the area represented.

---

[19] In the fall and winter of 1942, the author organized a fifteen-weeks course for the employees of the Third United States Civil Service Region, aimed at the specific purpose of informing them regarding the organization and functions of the operating agencies for which they were recruiting personnel. The first hour of each evening session was utilized by the author for presenting the historical background of the major problem connected with a given agency, and its social, economic, and political implications; the second hour by the head of the agency under consideration, whose function it was to explain their existing organization, purposes, and procedures, and to comment on the various types of personnel required by the agency.

[20] For a discussion of these organizations, see Truman, *op. cit.*, Chapters 7 and 8, and Fesler, James W., in the President's Committee on Administrative Management, *Report with Special Studies*, pp. 33–34 (Washington, 1937).

[21] See Hendrickson, Roy F., "Achieving Unity Through USDA Clubs," *Personnel Administration*, November, 1940, pp. 1–5.

SELECTED REFERENCES

In a voluminous literature from which the making of selections is often difficult, a limited number of related titles have been grouped together under appropriate subject-matter headings.

RESEARCH

Anderson, William, *Federalism and Intergovernmental Relations; A Budget of Suggestions for Research,* and Latham, Earl G., *The Federal Field Service: An Analysis with Suggestions for Research* (Both, Public Administration Service, Chicago, 1946).

FEDERAL INTERAGENCY RELATIONS

Executive Office of the President, *A Guide for Federal Executives to Interagency Service Functions, Contacts, and Procedures* (Office of Government Reports, United States Information Service, 1941).

Reynolds, Mary T., *Interdepartmental Commissions in the National Administration* (Columbia University Press, 1939). Only published study of an important technique for interagency coordination.

FEDERAL FIELD ESTABLISHMENTS

The National Resources Committee made the original survey of field establishments (*Regional Factors in National Planning and Development,* Washington, 1935), outlining also alternative proposals for a system of uniform administrative areas. This was followed, eight years later, by another survey showing the effects of the defense program and war mobilization on Federal field services: Legislative Reference Service, Library of Congress, *Federal Field Offices,* A Letter from the Director to Senator Carl Hayden (78th Cong., 1st Sess., Senate Document No. 22, 1943). Other significant studies include:

Fesler, James W., *Area and Administration* (University of Alabama Press, 1949). Discussion of problems of government in terms of their geographical setting, including the conflict between area and function, between specialization and generalization, between centralization and local autonomy.

Redford, Emmette S., *Field Administration of Wartime Rationing* (Office of Temporary Controls, Washington, 1947). Monograph on OPA experience by an active participant who served both in the central office and in the field.

Stone, Donald C., and others, *Washington-Field Relationships in the Federal Service* (United States Department of Agriculture, Graduate School, Washington, 1942). A valuable series of papers on the subject indicated.

Truman, David B., *Administrative Decentralization* (University of Chicago Press, 1940). Subtitle: a study of the Chicago field offices of the United States Department of Agriculture.

Wilk, Kurt, *Decentralizing Governmental Work* (Institute for Public Administration, New York, 1942). A valuable over-all analysis presenting conclusions from a comparative study of administrative areas.

STATE AND LOCAL INTERRELATIONS

Hinderaker, Ivan H., *The Administrative Districts and Field Offices of the Minnesota State Government* (University of Minnesota Press, 1943). The only thorough study available of zone administration in a particular state.

Jamison, Judith N., *Intergovernmental Cooperation in Public Administration in the Los Angeles Area* (Bureau of Governmental Research, University of California at Los Angeles, 1944). An important survey of cooperative practices in an area in which such practices are numerous and are highly developed.

PART II

PERSONNEL MANAGEMENT

7

EMPLOYMENT AND PLACEMENT

MODERN government is concerned with finding the best qualified personnel obtainable and keeping them after they have been appointed. This concept is quite different from that of the early civil service reformers, whose primary concern was to "keep the rascals out." It is highly important that every effort be made to interest in the public service persons of fine character, training, and experience, persons with ability and initiative who can, if properly placed and retrained from time to time for more responsible positions, make a real contribution to the service.

Employment and placement involve six different steps:

RECRUITING: devising techniques for attracting applicants and finding the right person for the position

EXAMINING: determining eligibility through tests designed to reveal intelligence level, achievement, and aptitude

CERTIFICATION: authorizing the appointment of the best qualified

APPOINTMENT: selection, and observation during probationary period

PLACEMENT: putting the new appointee to work in the right place

ORIENTATION: induction into the agency; training for particular job assigned

The first three of these steps are the responsibility of the central personnel agency, commonly designated as the Civil Service Commission; the last three are that of the operating agency! Each function will be considered individually in the sections which follow.

Recruiting

Mark Graves, for many years Chairman of the New York State Tax Commission, once observed that civil service does not guarantee that government will secure the best employees; it merely gives assurance that it will not get the worst. The old methods were reasonably effective in keeping out those who were least qualified, but they contributed very little indeed to obtaining the services of the exceptionally well qualified. They failed because their procedures were wrong. It was customary to issue examination announcements, which were sent to all first- and second-class post offices, where they were placed on bulletin boards for public inspection. In most cases they were also sent to newspapers, though they received little publicity from this source. The Commission then sifted out the best of whatever happened to apply, leaving the determination of quality largely to chance.

These processes would not work in either war or peace. It is obvious that high-grade business, administrative, and professional people, if perchance out of employment, do not commonly seek a position by browsing through a motley assortment of examination announcements on a post-office bulletin board. The method, bad in peacetime, was even worse in wartime, when practically every employable person was either serving in the armed forces or engaged in some phase of the war effort. Recruitment is by no means a simple problem; but unless it is solved, there is slight possibility of carrying on successfully the other essential phases of a personnel program. Capable people cannot be appointed unless they make application and qualify by taking such tests as may be required. No system of personnel administration can make dull and incompetent people bright and efficient. The difficulties in securing the right kind of people are attributable partly to the low prestige value of the public service [1] and partly to the desire of many potentially suitable applicants to try for larger financial returns than are available for most civil employees.

Recruiting, as that term is now understood, represents a relatively new technique, the purpose of which is to find the right person to fill a specified vacancy or type of vacancy. Before any action can be taken by the Commission, the operating agency must file a requisition which indicates the nature of the position to be filled, the duties, the qualifications, the salary, and the number of vacancies. This information must be studied carefully. If there are discrepancies, they should be worked out in conference with the agency before efforts at recruiting are undertaken.

The urgency of the war situation caused a great and rapid development both in types and in techniques of recruiting.[2] In the Federal service there were four main types: positive, direct, joint, and advance. In positive recruiting the effort was made to secure applications from qualified individuals and to submit them to the agencies. In direct recruiting, used chiefly in filling lower-grade jobs, an agreement was en-

---

[1] See White, Leonard D., *The Prestige Value of Public Employment* (University of Chicago Press, 1929 and 1932).

[2] The new methods of recruiting had much of permanent value: Unsigned, "War Places Heavy Strain on Civil Service," *National Municipal Review*, November, 1943, pp. 547–549; United States Civil Service Commission, *Manual of Recruiting Ideas* (Circular Letter, Inter-Regional Recruiting Series No. 48, November 23, 1944): *Getting a Job in the Federal Service* (Washington, 1941); and *Civilian War Service Opportunities for College and University Students* (Washington, 1943).

tered into between the operating agency and the Commission, by which the latter was authorized to recruit, examine, and appoint individuals judged to be qualified. Under this plan recruits were definitely assured of appointment on the spot; it saved time and prevented the loss of many who might have obtained employment elsewhere.[3] Joint recruiting was also undertaken by agreement between the Commission and the operating agency. Joint efforts were planned, joint interviews held, and appointments made on the spot. In some instances advance recruiting was undertaken to build up a reserve supply of applicants in categories where a heavy demand was anticipated.

Immediate Sources of Supply. The next step involves a thorough search of immediate sources of supply. One of these is the promotion registers if such exist. During the war a great many positions were filled by the promotion or transfer of persons already in the service; this became, in fact, the source of a great deal of criticism, some of it quite justified. The basic theory, however, was sound. Government has its own ways of doing business; many of them necessarily differ from those of private business. It was believed that persons already familiar with government organization and procedures would be more quickly useful in the development of new agencies and the expansion of old ones than persons lacking this background.

Applicant supply files[4] constitute another immediate source which should be exhausted before any new program is undertaken. If there are in the files any applications from individuals who appear to be qualified, these should first be carefully considered. Careful attention must be given to the maintenance of this file if it is to be of any real use. The applications must be numbered and coded according to the highest skills possessed by the applicants. Unless this work is done by high-grade employees who have an understanding of the requirements for widely varied types of employment and have the capacity to evaluate the work experience of applicants, the file is apt to be worse than useless. Constant effort is necessary to weed out names of persons no longer interested in government employment.

Recruiting Publicity. After the recruiter has the minimum qualifications for the position firmly fixed in his own mind and has satisfied himself that there are no suitable and available candidates in the imme-

---

[3] In 1942, the United States Civil Service Commission prepared "Direct Recruiting for Civil Service: Selected Bibliography."

[4] These files are built up from (1) individuals who file applications for consideration in connection with future vacancies; (2) individuals who file for specific positions for which examinations have been announced and for which they do not qualify; (3) individuals who, though qualified for the position for which they filed, did not rate high enough to be certified; (4) persons who were certified but not selected.

diate sources of supply, he is ready to consider where he may find the specific type of individual required.

As part of any such program the personnel agency must develop an effective plan for disseminating information regarding the positions to be filled. This may be done by the widespread distribution of examination announcements; by issuing periodically lists of employment opportunities; by the publication of notices regarding vacancies in various newspapers; and by the use of radio spot announcements. The purpose is to inform interested and qualified citizens about the nature of vacancies, job qualifications, compensation, and other details.

These devices are useful chiefly in meeting immediate needs. A properly functioning central personnel agency must think also in terms of a long-range program of public relations as well. This involves the appearance of top officials before various business, civic, religious, and other groups; the preparation of articles presenting a clear picture of the opportunities of the public service; participation in radio programs — in short, the use of all the common techniques of carrying on a publicity and public relations program.

Individual Recruiting. When a candidate is sought for a higher-grade position, the work must be done on a highly individualized basis, usually with a minimum of publicity. In such recruiting, publicity in the usual sense is not only unnecessary but may be an actual obstacle to accomplishing a good job. It brings in a crowd of hopeful souls who are attracted by a salary higher than they have ever earned but who have no discernible qualifications for the vacancy. Interviewing such applicants merely consumes time which the staff might employ to much better advantage.

Good recruiting calls for careful investigation of all possible sources of supply. The recruiter should analyze specifically the most likely sources for individuals possessing the exact type of training and experience the job requires. For this purpose it is helpful if he possesses an intimate knowledge of and a wide acquaintance in the business and professional, educational and civic life of the community. This will give him access to whatever sources of supply his analysis may seem to indicate.[5]

In recruiting for higher-grade positions, meeting immediate needs as they arise may be made infinitely easier by long-range planning. During the war the United States Civil Service Commission had its Committee on Administrative Personnel which in an advisory capacity

---

[5] See Graves, W. Brooke, and Herring, James M., "Recruiting Administrative Personnel in the Field," *Public Personnel Review*, Autumn, 1942, pp. 302–311.

sought to assist the Commission in accomplishing this specific objective. Later, in line with the Commission's policy of decentralization, regional committees were set up for the same purpose in the field. In somewhat revised form they are being continued. Such a program is based upon the sound assumption that the most desirable types of individuals can be obtained only with the assistance of influential citizens and organizations.[6]

One of the most important developments in this type of recruiting occurred during the war in the form of the National Roster of Scientific and Specialized Personnel. The primary objective was to record the names, qualifications, and competencies of the members of the highly specialized scientific and professional groups throughout the country, to the end that their skills might be evaluated and classified and the maximum use made of them in connection with the war effort. The Roster proved so successful in filling critical vacancies that it is being maintained now for use in peace or in any future emergency.[7]

Interviewing. Whatever recruiting techniques are employed and whether the applicants are many or few, some interviews will have to be conducted. The manner in which they are conducted is of vital concern both to the success of the recruiting effort and to the public relations of the personnel agency. None but experienced interviewers can do the job. It is essential not only that all applicants be treated courteously and sympathetically but that the interviewers know what they are looking for and that they possess skill in extracting information that will enable them to judge with some degree of accuracy whether or not the individual is qualified for the type of position to be filled.

Interviews should be conducted with some degree of privacy. The interviewer should answer questions and supply information, but it is important that the applicant be induced to do most of the talking. Applicants will often talk themselves out of a job, demonstrating beyond the slightest doubt their unfitness for the position for which they have

[6] On these developments, see Pollock, Ross, "The Joint College-Federal Service Councils: a New Recruiting Team," *Personnel Administration,* July, 1947, pp. 14–18, and Torpey, William G., "University Job Clinics for the Federal Service," *Personnel Administration,* September, 1947, pp. 27–29; also his "Problems in Recruiting Scientific and Technical Personnel," *Public Personnel Review,* January, 1948, pp. 11–17.
[7] For full description of this project, see the Roster's *Report* (Washington, June, 1942); Hattery, Lowell H., *Practices in the Collection and Maintenance of Information on Highly Trained and Specialized Personnel in the United States* (National Research Council, Washington, 1947), and the following articles: Burton, Arthur, "Recruiting Psychologists and Psychiatrists for the Public Service," *Public Personnel Review,* October, 1944, pp. 215–220; Gallup, George H., "Drafting the Nation's Brain Power," *National Municipal Review,* January, 1942, pp. 11–17; Rogers, William C., "Recruiting Administrative and Professional Personnel," *Public Personnel Review,* October, 1945, pp. 213–218.

applied. The length of the interview will depend partly upon the skill of the interviewer and partly upon the character of the work to be done.[8] For higher-grade positions a hurried interview is usually of little value.

Mass Recruiting. When on the other hand there are numerous lower-grade positions to be filled, mass recruiting techniques not only can but must be used. These include press releases, radio spot announcements, and all the miscellaneous devices available for attracting attention — show windows, exhibits, billboards, handbills, and booths in department stores or places where large numbers of people congregate. They may even include dropping leaflets from an airplane on a crowd at a football game.[9]

Specialized lists may be most helpful. State examining boards may be called upon to furnish lists of accountants, nurses, engineers, and architects, while membership lists may be obtained from business and professional groups such as engineers, pharmacists, comptrollers, personnel associations, and wholesalers in particular lines. The classified section of the telephone book or Thomas's *Directory of Industrial Firms* may be used on occasion. Chamber of Commerce lists of commercial and industrial establishments may be helpful in reaching persons with specialized experience.

In the early days of the war, schools and colleges were a fruitful source of recruiting. When enrollments were rapidly diminishing, many highly trained persons were drawn into the Federal service from college faculties. The employment services maintained by such institutions produced the names and addresses of many well trained individuals who were interested in changing their employment. Graduating classes in schools of engineering and in physics and chemistry were addressed by members of the Commission's recruiting staff. Graduates of secretarial schools and schools of comptometry and business machine operation were regularly contacted to draw as many graduates as possible into the government service. Similarly, vocational schools were relied upon as a source for workers in many types of manual operations.

---

[8] The standard treatise on interviewing is by Bingham, Walter V., and Moore, Victor S., *How to Interview*, Third Edition (Harpers, New York, 1941); see also Sixth Service Command, *The Employment Interview: A Training Workbook for Interviewers* (Chicago, 1944); United States Civil Service Commission, *Interviewing: A Selected List of References* (Washington, 1945); and Freeman, G. L., "Using the Interview to Test Stability and Poise," *Public Personnel Review*, April, 1944, pp. 89–94.

[9] See Bratton, Barbara L., "Exhibits as a Medium for Public Reporting and Positive Recruiting," *Public Personnel Review*, May, 1942, pp. 120–124; Wood, Albert J., and Blankenship, Albert B., "Getting Women Workers," *Public Opinion Quarterly*, Spring, 1944, pp. 100–103.

In addition to the press and radio and other usual channels of communication, a wide variety of appeals was used, including the distribution of printed material and oral announcements to large audiences such as church groups and service clubs. These methods brought the message to numbers of persons who might never actively seek government employment or who, for that matter, might not have considered obtaining employment at all. Bulletin boards, visual aids, bands, parades, sound trucks, caravans, displays in the entrances to office buildings and department stores, and window displays were used. Even house to house canvassing was resorted to when urgency justified such a procedure.

Examination announcements were used as an aid whenever it appeared that in spite of a tight labor market they might help produce qualified applicants. In normal times their use is required as a regular procedure. In any event they represent an additional and useful means of disseminating information regarding vacancies. Their limitations are that they consume time and that so-called normal distribution will probably never reach many of the right persons unless distributing announcements, especially for higher-grade positions, is handled on an individual basis.

In many cases recruiters found that opposition to Federal employment had to be overcome. Various devices were used for this purpose, such as letters from former recruits describing the satisfaction they found in contributing to the war effort through their new jobs. Interviews were arranged with former employees who had enjoyed their period of government service. Private employers were taken on conducted tours through government installations, and advance contacts were made with civic and professional groups. In some cases where the services of qualified individuals could not be obtained on a full-time basis, agreements were made with local firms to obtain their services for part time. Significant also is the fact that as the supply of qualified personnel in some fields became exhausted, job analyses made possible breakdowns which in turn led to hiring and training wholly inexperienced people to perform the simpler operations resulting from these breakdowns.

Review of Applications. Applications for positions in the government service may usually be filed either in person or by mail. When the Commission was operating solely under the Civil Service act and rules, applications were carefully scrutinized for acceptability. Under War Service regulations the examination was less exacting, since nearly all the applicants would be used in some way or other. Even under these conditions it was necessary to give a hurried preliminary examination to determine whether or not all the questions on the application form had been answered. In late 1942 standard Application Form No. 57 was adopted for universal use in the Federal service.

Examining

Examinations of some appropriate character are necessary under a merit system in order to determine the eligibility and suitability of the applicants. It is customary to give examinations simultaneously at various points throughout the country or the state, except those for a few higher-grade positions, which may be given at the capital only. This procedure enables the applicant to take examinations with the least expense and loss of time.

The first step is a careful scrutiny of the applications to determine which meet the minimum requirements set forth in the announcement. There is no purpose in spending time on those which do not; these may be promptly and automatically ruled out as ineligible.

Types of Examinations. The character of the examinations varies according to the nature of the position to be filled. Some are assembled, some unassembled, some competitive, some noncompetitive, some oral, some written. An assembled examination is used when there is a large number of applicants whose eligibility can be determined by a written test; such examinations are usually competitive. Experiments have been made in the use of oral examinations of groups of applicants.[10] The unassembled test, which may be either competitive or noncompetitive, is used where the number of qualified applicants is small and the position is in the higher grades. Such an examination consists not in writing answers to stated questions but in evaluating the education, experience, and qualifications of the applicants in relation to the requirements of the specific job.[11]

Competitive tests are normally used for such positions as stenographers, typists, and filing clerks. Noncompetitive or qualifying examinations are used for positions involving administrative work at the higher levels, for research positions, and for other positions requiring a high degree of specialized training. They may be oral or written, or partly

[10] See, for instance, Mandell, Milton M., "The Group Oral Performance Test," *Public Personnel Review,* October, 1946, pp. 209–212, and Morse, Daniel, and Hawthorne, Joseph W., "Some Notes on Oral Examinations," *ibid.,* January, 1946, pp. 15–18.

[11] See McCoy, W. A., "Improving the Rating of Training and Experience," *Public Personnel Review,* April, 1947, pp. 73–78; Pockrass, Jack H., "Rating Training and Experience in Merit System Selection," *ibid.,* July, 1941, pp. 211–222; and Beers, Fred S., and others, symposium on evaluation of education and experience, *Personnel Administration,* May, 1947, pp. 1–12.

oral and partly written; they may include tests of intelligence, common sense, academic information, general education, special education, character, and experience.[12] A personal interview is regularly required, but for the more important positions this interview may be of such a character as to justify its carrying considerable weight in determining the applicant's suitability.

The oral type of examination is usually unassembled; the written, assembled. The latter may also be either long form or short answer. The long form or essay type results in the usual kind of answer to examination questions; the short form answers are objective — true or false, matching, completion, and multiple choice. Performance tests may be used where physical skill or strength is required. Typists and stenographers may be given skill tests; [13] laborers may be given some form of strength test such as weight lifting, to determine whether or not they are physically capable of performing manual labor.[14]

For certain types of position, tests of general intelligence and aptitude may be used. Such tests are unnecessary where the educational background establishes beyond doubt the applicant's intelligence; but they are useful in determining whether or not the applicant has the ability to perform specialized duties.[15]

Tests of Character and Suitability. Tests of character and suitability are most difficult of all. In the lower-grade jobs, the investigation may be limited to what is called "vouchering" the references and previous employers whose names are listed by the applicant. A form is sent to a selected group of these, asking certain questions regarding the applicant's character, habits, and personal integrity. In normal times vouchering is completed before the names are entered on the registers; during the

[12] For a brief discussion of these types, see Wilmerding, Lucius, Jr., *Government by Merit*, pp. 104-112 (McGraw-Hill, New York, 1935).

[13] See Cozad, Lyman H., "The Use of Performance Tests by the Los Angeles City Civil Service Commission," *Public Personnel Review*, October, 1941, pp. 281-289; and Gallas, Nesta M., "Cooperative Performance Tests for Clerical Classes," *American Political Science Review*, July, 1944, pp. 156-163.

[14] See Adkins, Dorothy C., "Test Construction in Public Administration," *Educational and Psychological Measurement*, Summer, 1944, pp. 141-160; Babcock, James O., "Experts Examine," *Personnel Administration*, November, 1946, pp. 13-16; Dunford, Ralph E., and Hultquist, Katherine B., "Personnel Testing in the TVA," *Public Personnel Review*, July, 1944, pp. 133-139; Feder, D. D., "An Approach to Test Analysis for Public Personnel Agencies," *ibid.*, July, 1946, pp. 126-131; McConnell, Ira E., "The Application of Item Test Analysis," *ibid.*, October, 1947, pp. 205-210; Mandell, Milton M., "Testing for Administrative and Supervisory Positions," *Educational and Psychological Measurement*, Summer, 1945, pp. 217-228 and "Testing for the Public Service," *Personnel Administration*, June, 1946, pp. 8-10; and Sims, Lewis B., "The Social Science Analyst Examinations," *American Political Science Review*, June, 1939, pp. 441-450.

[15] See Thurstone, Louis L., "Testing Intelligence and Aptitudes," *Public Personnel Review*, January, 1945, pp. 22-27.

war most appointments were made subject to voucher inquiry, the appointments becoming valid only after the receipt of satisfactory replies to inquiries.

In higher-grade jobs involving special requirements of character and integrity, a more thorough investigation is obviously necessary. These are the key supervisory, personnel, and budgetary positions and law enforcement work. Investigation should be completed before the individual is appointed and entered on duty. Here also many appointments were made during the war subject to a satisfactory report of investigation. As a matter of procedure the investigators personally contact previous places of employment to ascertain whether or not the applicant's relations with the company, institution, or agency were satisfactory. They talk not only with the applicant's former supervisor and company officials but with fellow workmen at his own level of employment. They check his credit rating, his police record, and the Federal Bureau of Investigation fingerprint files. They check his claims with regard to education and degrees. They visit the neighborhood in which he resides and make random inquiries among the neighbors to gather any information which might affect his suitability as a government employee.

Record is made of the results of all these inquiries, and a transcript is furnished to the Recruitment and Placement Division of the Commission, together with a summary prepared by the investigator and indicating his general impressions of the applicant's suitability. These records are highly confidential. Where the results of the investigation are derogatory and the applicant's shortcomings are sufficiently serious, he may be barred from Federal employment for a period up to three years.[16]

Under normal procedures a medical certificate is required for all probational and permanent appointments. Although physical requirements were relaxed during the war, a medical certificate was still required for all but temporary appointments. If there was any evidence of infectious disease or any physical condition which would make the applicant a hazard to himself, to others, or to the agency (from the point of view of excessive sick leave), the Medical Division was asked for an advisory opinion. In those agencies which maintain a medical officer of their own, pre-appointment physical examinations are made by him. Where no medical service is available in the agency, the applicant must bring in a medical certificate executed by his personal physician.

---

[16] See Lippett, Lawrence, "The Personal Investigation in the Selection of Employees," *Personnel Administration*, September, 1946, pp. 23–28.

A complete physical examination should be made of each employee before appointment becomes effective. Such examinations protect the government from the employment of sick persons. They guard co-workers from close association with an individual having some contagious or infectious disease. They disclose to the applicant himself some condition requiring medical attention or prevent him from assuming duties he is not physically able to carry. The Medical Division has also performed a signal service in making an analysis of many positions in many agencies to determine the physical requirements which must be met by the individuals filling them. This information is important because it makes possible the full utilization of the skills of persons with certain physical disabilities.

The Process of Rating. The process of rating or, as it is called in educational work, of grading examinations, requires special knowledge and a high degree of skill in evaluating the educational background and experience of the applicant. This is not so true of the assembled tests for clerical and stenographic positions, which are in some cases scored by machine, as it is in rating for higher-grade positions. With written examinations, especially of the short answer variety, a key sheet is prepared, and rating becomes largely mechanical. The number of incorrect answers is determined and a grade assigned, in a process which is both simple and familiar.

The rating of unassembled examinations, either competitive or non-competitive or qualifying, is not so simple. This requires judgment and professional skill. When an examination for a higher-grade position is announced, it is customary to establish a rating board, the members of which are designated by the Chief of the Recruitment and Placement Division, to serve as required. This constitutes a protection both to the applicant and to the Commission. The applicant is protected from possible error in judgment in the evaluation of experience, and on the other hand the Commission can defend its position, should question arise, by the fact that the rating represents the judgment not of one but of several qualified individuals.

The first step in rating is the construction of a schedule. This should be done by careful study of the job requirements before the papers are opened. It involves determination of the values of different types of training and experience in relation to the requirements of the position. These types may be classified as A, B, C, or as 1, 2, 3, credits or units being allowed for each full year of acceptable experience. The schedule may assign credit for college or university training. Previous examination specifications are used if available. It is important that these standards be first established and agreed upon in order that there shall be a minimum of opportunity for favoritism in the final ratings in case any of the applicants should be personally known to those responsible for the rating.[17]

The board may then proceed to the analysis of the individual applications, noting for each so many years of experience of "A-grade" (highest level) in the most recent position, so many years of experience of A-grade in the previous position, so many years of C-grade experience in a preceding job, so many years of B-experience in another position, and so on. These evaluations are recorded on a rating sheet, upon the basis of which a rating clerk determines the numerical grade of the applicant. This analysis is continued with each period of employment reported by each applicant. When it is completed, the applications are arranged in the order of their numerical grades, and a number are referred to the Investigations Division to ascertain whether those who rank highest are eligible from the point of view of character and suitability. If there are physical requirements attached to the position, it may also be necessary to secure approval of the Medical Division.

When these reports are returned to the Recruitment and Placement Division, the Commission is in a position to determine final ratings. The board which made the preliminary ratings reviews them in the light of the additional information in the reports of the Investigations Division. Some of the individuals rated eligible in the preliminary rating may now be declared ineligible, or the relative positions of individuals may be changed.

Certification

The next step is certification, which involves two operations — establishing a register and issuing authorization to the appointing officer to fill the vacancy by the selection of one or more of the individuals whose names appear on the certificate. After the results of all the tests are available, they must be assembled and evaluated to determine the standing of the applicants. The central personnel agency is then able to certify to the departments and agencies the names of those eligible for appointment.[18] Under no circumstances are names certified to an appointing officer except upon his request. Before certification is issued, the availability of the persons named must also be ascertained. It may be found that some have died, some have moved away, some have taken other employment, and some are no longer interested.

---

[17] See McCoy, *op. cit.*

[18] See Adams, C. R., and Smeltzer, Clarence H., "Placing New Eligibles on Open Eligible Registers," *Public Personnel Review*, May, 1942, pp. 133–137; Mueller, Ralph, and Warren, George A., "The Use of Open Eligible Registers in Public Service Selection," *ibid.*, pp. 125–132.

Setting up a register is a highly technical process, involving the interpretation and application of numerous rules, not to mention the specific qualifications for the position for which the register is being established. Technicalities may make it possible for persons whose names appear on the re-employment list to come ahead of those not on the list even though the newcomer may have a higher examination rating. Similarly the names of qualified applicants in the service and eligible for transfer may be placed ahead of outsiders. Such practices have been established as part of the plan to develop a career service in government and are probably justified on that basis.

Qualifying Provisions. Certain qualifying provisions are enforced upon all appointees to government service practically without exception and without regard to the jurisdiction involved. These relate primarily to citizenship and residence. A natural-born citizen may be required to furnish a birth certificate, while a naturalized citizen may be asked to produce his certificate of naturalization. During the war persons whose national origins were in enemy countries were looked upon with suspicion if not actually barred from service. In the Federal government, however, departmental appropriations often carry a modest item for the salaries of a small number of noncitizens whose appointment must be justified on the ground that they possess particular knowledge or skills not available, so far as can be determined, in any American citizens.

The residence requirement usually appears in one form or another. In the Federal government it is provided that in normal times appointments to the departmental service must be distributed among the states in proportion to population, the purpose being to prevent the appointment of an excessive proportion of citizens of adjacent or nearby states, perhaps to the exclusion of others. In the state services residence in the state is normally sufficient, although exceptions may be made in the requirements for important professional positions. New York State has taken a very liberal attitude in this matter, trying to obtain the services of the best qualified individual regardless of residence. Most cities, on the other hand, have done the opposite. Many of them even refuse to hire nonresident teachers.

Restrictive Provisions. A good many restrictive provisions operate on occasion to keep off the registers and out of the service individuals who possess adequate job qualifications and who might be good public servants. One of these is the restriction on the number of members of a family eligible to Federal employment. Another is the exclusion of persons with criminal records. Naturally persons who possess some mental or physical disability which would make it impossible for them to perform their duties are excluded. Alcoholics and drug addicts are also excluded.

Veterans' Preference. The most difficult problem, of course, is that created by veteran-preference laws, which were adopted in some cases in the heat of patriotic fervor during the war years on the theory that "nothing is too good for the boys" and in other cases under the pressure of veterans' organizations after "the boys" had returned home. Strong pressure for veteran preference develops after every war. It is possible to make such preference effective either by weighting in favor of those who have performed military service or by selecting those with records of military service from the list of eligibles. The principle is generally accepted and acted upon that the government owes an obligation to those who have risked their lives in the service of their country, and to their dependents; but it is the unanimous opinion of students of personnel administration — and incidentally of some veterans — that giving concessions in favor of veterans in the administration of a civil service system is certainly not the proper way to discharge that responsibility.

One of the worst of these provisions was written into the Constitution of New York State by an amendment adopted in 1945. In effect it all but closes the state and municipal public services for a period of years to any applicants except veterans. It provides that if veterans compete for any position or promotion, their names must appear at the head of the list regardless of their standing. Disabled veterans are placed ahead of those not disabled and enjoy preference for an unlimited period of time. The veteran not disabled retains his right to a preferred position only for five years after discharge from the armed forces.[19]

Actually the problem involves, as the National Civil Service League has pointed out, three major aspects: (1) assisting war veterans to establish themselves in civil life; (2) the status of the younger generation, some members of which may desire a career in the public service; (3) the position of persons already in the public employ on a career basis, many of them veterans of earlier wars. Believing that any plan for exclusive or practically exclusive appointment of veterans is contrary to the nature and meaning of our democracy and that it would be detrimental to the effectiveness of the public service, as well as unnecessary and dangerous, the League recommended in 1945 the following nine-point program: [20]

---

[19] See Weintraub, Ruth G., and Touch, Rosalind, "Veterans Preferred, Unlimited," *National Municipal Review,* October, 1945, pp. 437–439, 444.
[20] *Veteran Preference in the Civil Service* (New York, 1945). For a good statement of the problem at the Federal level, see *Veterans Preferred* (United States Civil Service

1. The public interest makes imperative the maintenance of at least the present standards for entrance to the public service.

2. Veterans' preference should not apply beyond a period of five years after cessation of hostilities or five years after discharge of the veteran, whichever is later.

3. Experience gained in military service and training and education received through military agencies should be properly evaluated and recognized in determining eligibility and in rating education and experience.

4. Preference should be confined to original entrance and not applied to promotions within the service.

5. Regardless of the extent of privileges accorded, all veterans should be required to obtain at least a passing mark in competitive tests before being entitled to any preferred status.

6. Preference should be granted in the form of credits to be added to earned ratings in examinations, with disabled veterans receiving no more than ten points and other veterans no more than five points to be added to their earned ratings.

7. A disabled veteran should be defined as one who has been accorded a disability rating of at least 10 per cent and is receiving compensation payments therefor at the time of his application for appointment.

8. Retention in the service in case of reduction in force or abolition of positions should be based for all employees solely on relative seniority and efficiency, regardless of veteran status.

9. Civil service employees who, while in good standing in the civil service, left to engage in military service should be given credit for seniority purposes for time served in the military service. Those among them who became disabled in military service to such an extent that they may be unable to perform their previous duties should wherever possible be transferred to other positions in the service for which they may be fitted.

In order that the reader may compare theory with practice there are listed below the various types of preference benefits to which veterans are entitled in the Federal service under the provisions of the Veterans' Preference Act of 1944. The following are selected from a list of more than two score items appearing in the *Federal Personnel Manual*, as of 1948:

Preference Benefits in the Federal Service

Addition of points in examinations

Restriction of certain examinations to persons entitled to preference

Commission, Washington, 1944). The following are among the better recent articles: Anderson, Charles R., "The Veteran in Public Service," *Personnel Administration*, May, 1947, pp. 19–20; Donovan, Jeremiah H., "Reinstating Our Returning Veterans," *Public Management*, July, 1945, pp. 194–197; Moore, Dan S., "Reinstating Public Employees After Military Service," *Public Personnel Review*, January, 1944, pp. 14–18; Ordway, Samuel H., Jr., "The Veteran in the Civil Service," *Annals*, March, 1945, pp. 133–139; Sublette, Donald J., "The Returning Veteran," *Public Personnel Review*, July, 1945, pp. 147–153; Tyler, Ralph W., and Detchen, Lily, "Evaluation of Educational Growth During Military Service," *ibid.*, April, 1944, pp. 95–100; and White, Leonard D., "Veteran's Preference – a Challenge and an Opportunity," *State Government*, December, 1941, pp. 459–461, 469–472.

Experience credits in examinations for military or naval service
Experience credits for uncompensated service
Waiver of age, height, and weight requirements
Waiver of physical requirements
Waiver of members-of-family requirement
Waiver of apportionment requirement
Precedence on registers
Review by Civil Service Commission of agency's reasons for passing over veteran and selecting nonveteran from certificate
Reopening of examinations
Credit in reduction-in-force for active service in armed forces

Rule of Three. The law in most jurisdictions provides for what is known as "the rule of three." Where a single appointment is to be made, the three names highest on the eligible list are certified. Where a probationary period is provided for, as it usually is, it would be preferable to have only one name certified for one vacancy. Where several positions are to be filled, more names must of course be certified — five for two, seven for three, and so on. The rule has been clearly stated by Wilmerding, as follows: [21]

> For the first vacancy the appointing officer must select one of three names; for the second vacancy he must choose one of the two rejected or the fourth name on the list; and so on, selecting always from among the three highest names remaining on the list. One exception may be noted, namely, that names which have been rejected three times by the same appointing officer are not certified to him for subsequent vacancies.

In spite of its widespread use, the rule of three has often been severely criticized as an unwarranted compromise between merit and spoils, as an unjustifiable concession to those who put partisan considerations above merit in the selection of employees. It is argued also that the rule defeats the avowed purpose of the merit system to obtain the most competent and to keep out of the service persons with a background of activity in partisan affairs. It is claimed that any party organization can find some henchman with sufficient education and ability to merit a place on the register. During the war the practice of authorizing the appointment of particular individuals by issuing letters of authority to appointing officers was widely used in the Federal government and in some other jurisdictions.

The Hoover Commission in 1949 proposed abandonment of the rule of three and drew upon the wartime experience in developing the outlines of a new selection procedure under which applicants would be grouped into such categories as "outstanding," "well qualified," "qualified," and "unqualified." Appointing officers would be directed

---

[21] Wilmerding, *op. cit.,* p. 132.

to fill vacancies from the top listing, in which all disabled veterans who had been rated as "qualified" would be placed. Responsibility for the operation of the system would be transferred to the agencies; as a safeguard against favoritism or politics, all appointing officers would be subject to dismissal where misuse of authority was uncovered. A provision similar to this has been in operation in the Tennessee Valley Authority for some time.

Appointment

As matters now stand, the process of obtaining new employees shifts at this point from the central personnel agency to the operating agency. The actual selection from the names on the certificate is normally made by the immediate supervisor or by him in cooperation with his supervisor, but the processing of the appointment is carried on through the personnel office of the agency, and the appointment is made by the authority of the head of the agency. The normal procedure is for the personnel office to call in for interview the persons whose names appear on the certificate. The percentage of the new employees who succeed is a measure of the efficiency of the hiring methods employed.[22]

Entry on Duty. When the selection has been made, the personnel office of the agency is notified by the section or division in which the new employee will work. The personnel office notifies the candidate that he has been selected and informs him of his position and salary and when and where to report for duty. It must also return the certificate to the central personnel agency with notice of action taken. When the new appointee reports for duty, he takes his oath of office or, as it is often expressed, he is sworn in. He probably spends a part of the first morning in filling out what always seem like innumerable forms — an additional copy or copies of his application, the declaration of appointee, a form assigning retirement benefits, declaration of number of dependents for income tax purposes, form for savings-plan deductions, medical form, and fingerprint chart. The personnel office gives him such identification as he needs in the form of cards, badges, and the like.

Types of Appointments. There are many types of appointments that may be made — permanent, temporary, indefinite, term, provisional, probationary, and so on. In most merit systems operating officials are

---

[22] The subject is covered in the *Federal Personnel Manual;* see also Hawthorne, Joseph W., "Progress in Methods of Personnel Selection," *Public Administration,* January, 1942, pp. 11–19; Olson, Emery E., and Pollock, Ross, "Staffing and Training for Administrative Competence in the Federal Service," *Personnel Administration,* September, 1945, pp. 8–14; and for New York, "Appointments to State Service," *State Personnel News,* September, 1947, pp. 1–3.

permitted to make temporary appointments for a period of thirty, sixty, or ninety days, as required; these appointments create no particular problem unless through excessive renewals the incumbents are permitted to become virtually permanent employees. Term appointments may be made for stated periods for special projects authorized by law.

Very few appointments are made initially on a permanent basis because the agency wants to know — and it is entitled to know — whether the appointee can do the job. During the war, while the Federal War Service regulations were in effect, appointments were made on an indefinite basis with tenure presumed to be good for not more than one year after the official announcement of the termination of the war. This actually meant very little, for when hostilities ceased, drastic reductions of personnel began almost immediately — much faster in many cases than was advisable for the good of the service. Furthermore, the announcement of the termination of the war was itself long delayed.

Probationary Appointments. The probationary period usually lasts six months, although for higher-grade positions this is scarcely long enough to determine the competence of the appointee on the job. Most appointments are made subject to such a probationary period, which is intended to serve the twofold purpose of providing the appointee an opportunity to adjust himself, and the agency an opportunity to decide whether he can do the work and whether he is a suitable person to be retained on a permanent basis.

The proper use of this probationary period is extremely important; it is designed to protect the agency from being saddled permanently with undesirable employees. The difficulty is that supervisors often fail to avail themselves of the opportunity to terminate the appointments of unsuitable or incompetent probationers or, because they lack the courage to drop them, resort to the subterfuge of transferring them to some other part of the organization, thereby doing a long-time injury to the service. It is relatively easy to terminate them as probationers, but their removal may be difficult after the probationary period has expired. Then the employee has acquired "status" as a permanent employee, and charges must be preferred against him.[23]

Provisional Appointments. In many jurisdictions appointing officers are authorized to make provisional appointments under certain conditions, such as the absence of an eligible list. While a provisional appointment is justified in a real emergency, it should be avoided when-

---

[23] See the Civil Service Assembly's *Placement and Probation in the Public Service,* Part II. Oliver C. Short was chairman of the committee that prepared this report; see also an article which he wrote with Dow, E. F., "Dropping Duds During Probation," *Personnel Journal,* November, 1938, pp. 168–174.

ever possible because it opens the door to violations of the spirit if not the letter of the merit-system law.

In jurisdictions where, the administration has not been distinguished for its devotion to the merit system, this type of thing may develop into a racket. The situation in Philadelphia, for instance, would probably be much worse than it has been except for the constant watchfulness of the Bureau of Municipal Research. In October, 1946, the Bureau reported that from 1920 to 1940 provisional appointments showed a downward trend and that from then until 1944 the ratio of provisional to permanent appointments was kept consistently low. In 1945 there was a sharp upturn in the proportion to 27 per cent, compared to 19 per cent in 1944, 21 per cent in 1943, and 16 per cent in 1942. In this jurisdiction the rules provide that a civil service examination is required within three months and that the provisional appointee can win a permanent appointment only by placing first or second on the list.

Placement

The central personnel agency and the operating agency are both concerned with the problem of placement, but they approach it from different angles. Both are concerned with initial placements. Internal placement is primarily a responsibility of the operating agency, but in this instance responsibility may be divided between the personnel office of the agency, which can exert influence if not authority, and the line supervisor, who has authority but often lacks administrative capacity. Such personnel actions as transfer, promotion, and demotion all have placement aspects, but they will be considered in a later chapter dealing with changes in status of employees already a permanent part of the organization. In the placement problem there are three groups of individuals involved: the central personnel agency, the personnel office of the operating agency, and management in the operating unit.

The responsibility of the central personnel office is rather limited. In so-called normal times, when referral is made by certificate only, the commission certifies the three highest names ôn the register whenever a requisition is received for which that register is appropriate. The eligible, when contacted, may eliminate himself by stating that he is not interested or available or that he will wait for a vacancy in some other agency in which he desires to work. In a period of governmental expansion, however, and in a tight labor market members of the recruiting staff are constantly called upon to make placement decisions. Working under pressure as they are, they size up individuals from their applications and as a result of interview, deciding that this man would probably "fit in" in one agency, that one in another.

Making the Initial Placement. When the term "placement" is used, it usually refers to the problem of internal placement within the operating agency. Here are, in turn, the problems of initial placement and those of adjustments made later on the basis of experience. Some new employees are placed almost automatically. This is usually the case when only one position is being filled, and most frequently it occurs in the higher grades where appointees are selected on an individual basis with particular qualifications for filling specific vacancies. They need simply to be directed to their post of duty and set to work.

In other cases, where additions are being made to large groups of typists, clerks, or mechanical workers, the problem of making the best possible initial placement becomes vitally important. In a large organization the new employee might be assigned to any one of a number of different operating units. In any one of them he will perform the general type of work for which he was hired, but there may be reasons why he will be more contented and do better work in one place than in another.

There has been some misunderstanding regarding placement testing carried on by the agency after certification and selection. Some overzealous supporters of civil service have interpreted it as a reflection upon the testing methods of the commission in determining eligibility. It is nothing of the sort. The decision of the commission on eligibility has been accepted by the agency; the individual certified for appointment has been selected and has entered on duty. The question before the placement section is one of determining where the qualifications and experience of this particular appointee can be used to the best advantage of the agency and of the appointee. Determination of this question may involve extensive interviews and a whole battery of aptitude and attitude tests chosen with specific reference to the job to be done and designed to give the placement group as much information as possible about the personal characteristics of the appointee. Many war agencies carried on such programs, as, for example, the Philadelphia Quartermaster Depot and the San Bernardino Air Technical Service Command.[24] The facts so disclosed are weighed in the light of information regarding the units in the organization in which the new appointee might be placed — the characteristics of the supervisor, the presence or absence of work under pressure to meet deadlines, the hours of duty (if they are other than standard), the location of the job in relation to the

---

[24] See Lefever, D. Welty, and others, "Relation of Test Scores to Age and Education of Adult Workers," *Educational and Psychological Measurement*, Autumn, 1946, pp. 351–360. It is reported that workers under twenty and over fifty are at something of a disadvantage and that schooling does not appear to be a critical factor in determining job information test scores except for those with less than sixth grade education.

appointee's place of residence, and many other things. Such a procedure is necessarily time consuming, but in the long run it saves much more than it costs. The sole purpose is to make the best placements possible and to eliminate in advance the known causes of friction and dissatisfaction which produce unrest and impair efficiency.

Such procedures may be useful also with well-educated appointees on entry into the service at the lower grades such as junior administrative assistants. There are many places in the service where individuals with a natural science background may be useful, and there are also many places within a single department where such persons may be assigned. Similarly in the social science field, financial analysts and expert accountants are required in all departments. Economists, political scientists, statisticians, and many other types are needed in many agencies. The more the placement service knows about the individual appointee and the better it relates this information to the requirements of particular operating units, the better the placement job that will result.[25]

Making Placement Adjustments. Bad placements are expensive; they may result in low morale and poor production records. Correction of them is a joint responsibility of the agency's personnel office and of the line supervisor. In this relationship the personnel office may have influence but no authority, while the supervisor has the authority to make reassignments and to recommend transfers or removals but often regards as unwarranted interference any attempt on the part of the personnel office to help him solve his problems. The typical reaction of the supervisor on discovering that one of his employees is unsatisfactory is to blame personnel for sending him another "lemon" and either to demand the employee's transfer or removal or to "wall him off," giving him no attention, no supervision, and few if any assignments.

His unsatisfactory performance may be due simply to poor management. He may have too many bosses, conflicting assignments, or insufficient access to his superior, or he may lack authority adequate for the job assigned. Whatever the cause, the agency personnel office has a responsibility. In an excellent article on "Placement Programs in the Federal Government," Kenneth B. Atkinson points out that the original placement *service* of the personnel office must be supplemented by *influence*, often exercised through contacts with supervisors, the occasion for which has been carefully and deliberately planned or manu-

[25] See, for instance, Gregory, Wilber S., "Data Regarding the Reliability and Validity of the Academic Interest Inventory," *Educational and Psychological Measurement*, Autumn, 1946, pp. 375–390. The author reported that all but one of the twenty-eight scales in this inventory "yielded significantly high test-retest coefficients of correlation."

factured. On the basis of two years of study as chairman of a committee of the Council of Personnel Administration, he submits that there are five specific points in such a program: [26]

1. Making surveys to locate employees who have had no promotions for a long period of time to discover the cause — employee has reached his ceiling, is in the wrong job, or has been overlooked
2. Finding out what skills employees have that they are not using in their present jobs, i.e., personnel utilization
3. Studying employees who have low efficiency ratings to learn the cause — lack of ability, lack of application, need of training, etc.
4. Conducting follow-up interviews to check the adequacy of initial placements
5. Discussing with supervisors those employees who will shortly complete their probation or trial period to determine whether they would be better in another type of work, should be terminated, or should acquire permanent status

Orientation

Orientation involves induction into the agency — perhaps even a certain amount of indoctrination — and job instruction regarding the particular work assigned. This process, which is often regarded as properly within the province of the training division, is tremendously important both to the agency and to the new employee. A major part of the responsibility for proper induction must rest with the operating unit to which the new employee is assigned. Without such a program the new appointee, especially in a large organization, is likely to flounder around and be totally ignorant of what to do or how to do it. Without it the agency cannot properly expect any useful results to come from his efforts for a considerable period of time.

Agency Responsibility. The new appointee should in the first place be given some kind of over-all picture of the agency, its organization, its purposes and objectives, and its methods of operation. Top management can provide a number of things that will contribute to the accomplishment of this purpose: inspection tours, explanation of personnel practices, employee manuals and handbooks.

Inspection tours are useful, especially in a large organization carrying on a many-sided program. To be most beneficial they should be carefully planned in advance; new employees should be taken around in small groups so that the *modus operandi* can be explained to them and questions asked and answered on the spot. Organization charts and explanations of each unit and their relation to the whole should accompany such tours. Personal contacts with a few key officials should be

[26] See also Atkinson, Kenneth B., "But Is the Job Right?" *Personnel Administration,* May, 1947, pp. 13–15, 31, and the report of the Civil Service Assembly's committee.

arranged; they have a highly beneficial effect in stimulating the new employee's interest and loyalty and in boosting his morale.

It is important that the new employee be familiarized with the personnel practices of the agency. It is a good plan for the personnel office to set aside some time or times each week for the purpose of meeting with new employees taken on during the week, to explain the rules and regulations on such matters as leave, salary increments, promotions, grievances, and suggestions. While these are fairly uniform throughout a given service, there are often minor variations peculiar to a given agency.

Most large organizations, public and private alike, have found it desirable to compile and reissue from time to time employee manuals or handbooks, convenient in form and setting forth in simple language essential information relating to the organization and work of the agency. These handbooks, as the report of the Civil Service Assembly's Committee points out, "should contain information concerning the nature, organization, and functioning of the agency, civil service rules and regulations, internal personnel policies, employee services and organizations, and building regulations and facilities; they should be given to the employee at the time of the induction interview." [27]

Responsibility of the Operating Unit. Only part of the induction process can be handled by the agency's personnel office — only those parts, as a matter of fact, which are general in their application. On-the-job instruction with regard to specific tasks must be undertaken in the operating unit; the amount of time required will vary considerably according to the difficulty and complexity of the tasks. The principal methods available for this purpose are group training, individual training, and procedures manuals.

In cooperation with the training division, courses of instruction may be organized to train a number of persons simultaneously in the techniques and procedures relating to a particular job. Induction pools may be set up in clerical and stenographic units, combining training during part of the day with regular work under close supervision during the remainder.

While much can be accomplished by group methods, a good deal of the induction process has to be carried on individually. For part of this the immediate superior is responsible. He should make the new employee feel welcome, show him where he is to work, introduce him to

---

[27] *Placement and Probation in the Public Service,* p. 184, and Dominick, William B., "Orientation Programs for New Employees," *Public Personnel Review,* October, 1942, pp. 280–287.

the people he is to work with, and show him where his working tools and supplies are kept and the physical layout of the office or shop. He should also take time to explain the work to him and to show him how it is to be done.

In all probability the supervisor, however good his intentions, will not always be available to answer the many questions a new recruit is bound to ask. In this connection a sort of tutorial system is especially useful. (This is sometimes called a probationer-sponsor system.) There are usually a number of older employees available, some one of whom can be assigned to give more or less constant supervision and instruction to the new employee for a limited period of time until he becomes familiar with the work and is in a position to perform his duties without anything more than normal supervision. Such older employees, incidentally, often feel highly honored by such an assignment.

In most organizations there are definitely established procedures for handling the work. Where such procedures are varied and complicated, they should be written out and made available to all employees for reference. This is especially important for new employees. The most convenient means of presenting such information is a procedures manual set up in loose-leaf form so that as existing procedures are changed or modified, the manual may be kept up-to-date with replacement sheets. In clerical units, a style manual is effective.[28] The preparation of such a manual serves, incidentally, to accomplish another highly useful purpose: it causes management, in the process of trying to reduce its procedures to writing, to make a careful analysis of them and do some hard thinking about their logic, their adequacy, and their effectiveness.

SELECTED REFERENCES

The titles here listed are restricted to practices in public agencies. Here and in succeeding chapters much useful information may be obtained from the extensive literature relating to the same topics in private business and industry.

Adkins, Dorothy C., and others, *Construction and Analysis of Achievement Tests, the Development of Written and Performance Tests of Achievement for Predicting Job Performance of Public Personnel* (Government Printing Office, Washington, 1947). This significant title – the only one of its type – is a virtually complete textbook on an all-important aspect of the placement problem.

Bingham, Walter V., and Moore, Victor B., *How to Interview*, Third Edition (Harpers, New York, 1941). The standard title on the difficult art of effective interview techniques and procedures. See also: War Department, *The Placement Interview* (Civilian Personnel Pamphlet No. 15, Washington, 1945), and for bibliography, United States Civil Service Commission, *Interviewing: A Selected List of References* (Washington, 1945).

Carter, Harold D., *Vocational Interests and Job Orientation* (Stanford University Press, 1944). A ten-year review of developments in this aspect of effective placement.

[28] See Neuner, John J., and Haynes, Benjamin R., *Office Management and Practices*, pp. 470–491, on office manuals (Southwestern Publishing Company, Cincinnati, 1941).

Civil Service Assembly of the United States and Canada, *Oral Tests in Public Personnel Placement* (Chicago, 1943). The only treatise available on the subject, and a very good one.

——, *Placement and Probation in the Public Service* (Chicago, 1946). Another standard title from an Assembly committee.

Kingsley, J. Donald, *Recruiting Applicants for the Public Service* (Civil Service Assembly of the United States and Canada, Chicago, 1942). An authority in the personnel field discusses a long neglected phase of personnel work, including developments during the early part of World War II.

Mosher, William E., and Kingsley, J. Donald, *Public Personnel Administration*, Revised Edition (Harpers, New York, 1941). The only general text including consideration of all important phases of the subject.

Start, Dewey B., Ed., *Personnel Research and Test Development in the Bureau of Naval Personnel* (Princeton University Press, 1948). Record of experience in the Navy Department during World War II.

Tinkleman, Sherman, *Difficulty Prediction of Test Items* (Teachers College, Columbia University, 1947). Provides assistance in dealing with a very difficult aspect of testing.

Wagner, Tobias, *Selective Job Placement* (National Conservation Bureau, New York, 1946). A recent analysis of good placement procedures; for bibliography, see United States Civil Service Commission, *Employment Procedures: Selection, Recruitment, Placement – A Selected List of References* (Washington, 1945).

War Department, Army Service Forces, *Civilian Personnel Officer's Placement Manual* (Manual No. M213, Washington, 1945). A procedures manual for staff instruction.

8

POSITION CLASSIFICATION
AND COMPENSATION

BEFORE modern personnel administration was developed, each employee was hired separately, and the amount of his pay was determined by his personal or political influence. The result was a chaotic situation. Individuals performing work of the same character in different departments, bureaus, or even within the same office, received widely varying rates of pay. This situation, together with lack of tenure, was productive of widespread discontent and poor morale within the service. Modern classification and salary standardization have brought much improvement.

There were, as a matter of fact, numerous reasons for establishing a coordinated program of position classification and salary schedules. Through a single test it became possible to recruit a number of people to do like work. It enabled management to estimate budget needs accurately on the basis of a common denominator, to realize the principle of equal pay for work of equal difficulty, and at the same time to establish clearly recognized lines of promotion and transfer.[1] The classification and compensation plans cover four equally important divisions: [2]

1. Standard classification and grade specifications
2. Standard salary schedules for the respective grades
3. Allocation of existing positions to the classification and compensation plans
4. Regulations for effective administration of the classification and compensation plans after their adoption

Position Classification

Classification of positions in the Federal service dates back to the founding of the Republic. The problem was viewed largely from the standpoint of equal pay for equal work, but until recently the tools

---

[1] From *Classification: Can Supervisors Find Answers to It?* pp. 2-3 (United States Civil Service Commission, Washington, 1944).

[2] Civil Service Commission, *Classification and Compensation Plans of the Personal Service in the Executive Departments,* p. 9 (Philadelphia, 1930).

necessary for reaching that goal were not provided. Legislation relating to the subject was passed in 1789, in 1837, and in 1871. An Executive Order of 1921 called for a classification of employees as a means to establish salary standards. Two years later came the Classification Act of 1923, which with amendments and supplementary legislation is the basis for the present system. The modifications include the Welch Act of 1928, providing for a survey of field positions; the Brookhart Act of 1930, which directed field rates to be paid according to the schedules in the Act of 1923; the Ramspeck Act of 1940, which gave the President authority to extend the Classification Act by Executive Order to any position or group of positions and to grant exemptions from the pay schedules when advisable; the Mead-Ramspeck Act of 1941, providing for a uniform, one-step-within-grade salary advancement for employees with satisfactory records, and for meritorious increases; and finally the Custodial Act of 1942, which increased the salaries of the lower custodial and subprofessional grades.

Classification may be defined as the orderly sorting and ranking of jobs in a progressive sequence according to comparative difficulty and responsibility. It is a difficult task, based on job analysis. It is impersonal, concerned not with people but with the jobs the people hold. They do various kinds of work and perform tasks involving varying degrees of knowledge, skill, difficulty, and responsibility. The purpose of classification is to analyze what they do and to arrange the positions in some logical manner on the basis of this analysis. The first essential therefore is to obtain as complete information as possible about each position to be classified.

The term "position" has been variously defined. According to one writer it is a group of duties and responsibilities which normally require the full time and attention of one employee during regular working hours. Another regards it as a work-assignment composed of all the duties, tasks, and responsibilities one employee is assigned to perform; it covers his full working schedule. Positions come into being through the action of administrators or supervisors, acting of course within the prescribed limits of their authority, which may be either statutory or delegated from a higher supervisory level. Positions may be changed — and frequently are — in the same manner in which they were created, as a result of changes in work program, organization structure, or method of doing work, or as a result of a supervisor's observation of the abilities and performance of employees working under his direction.[3]

---

[3] *Position Classification as an Aid to Supervision*, p. 2 (United States Civil Service Commission, Washington, 1945).

Job Analysis. Job analysis, as applied to a position, is a description of the duties and responsibilities of the work-assignment and the qualifications necessary for the adequate performance of it. Precise information is essential. When a new position is involved, it is customary to compare it to existing positions as to the nature of the proposed duties and responsibilities and the special knowledge, equipment, and forms required. When a resurvey of an existing position is involved, the current instructions must be studied, and the duties or responsibilities added or removed must be analyzed.

Complete information about a position includes data with regard to the flow of work to and from the incumbent; the operations he performs, including procedures followed, plans or actions initiated, and decisions reached; nonsupervisory responsibilities, including the extent to which he reviews the work of others, the effect of his recommendations, his custody of money, and requirements with respect to accuracy; supervisory and administrative responsibilities, including types of supervision, the amount of supervision exercised, and the extent to which the incumbent is permitted to exercise initiative and independent judgment; and finally the size of the unit supervised, although this element is less important than the degree of supervision and the quality of work involved. For classification purposes the variety of functions and the complexity of the work are of vital importance.

This information may be obtained in any one of three ways: from the supervisor, from the employee, or by the personnel office through investigation and desk audit.[4]

(1) When the position is established, or "set up," as it is often expressed, the supervisor may attempt to write out in specific terms his concept of the job, describing the nature of the work, the extent of the responsibility, the amount of supervision, and other pertinent characteristics. Such a description is often preliminary in character, depending upon planning which has yet to be tested by work experience. In preparing it the supervisor will be guided by his knowledge of parallels between positions already classified and the new one under consideration. In addition he will take into account the nature of the proposed duties and responsibilities, the type of equipment needed, and the special knowledge required. In any event the draft of the new job-descrip-

---

[4] See Civil Service Assembly's *Position Classification in the Public Service,* Chapter 5, and Epperson, Lawrence L., "Getting the Most Out of Position Analysis," *Personnel Administration,* March, 1947, pp. 31–35, 43; Gallagher, Charles, and Coogan, Marguerite, "The Navy Classification Program in Retrospect," *ibid.,* July, 1947, pp. 26–30, 48; McDonald, William T., "The Navy's Method of Position Evaluation," *Public Personnel Review,* April, 1947, pp. 89–95; Monahan, James F., and Seversmith, Herbert F., "The Evaluation of Scientific Research Positions," *Personnel Administration,* November, 1947, pp. 14–17.

tion should be clear, complete, concise, and free from such vague and ambiguous phrases as "handle," "assist," "manage," and "with wide latitude for the exercise of independent judgment." [5]

(2) After the appointee has had some work experience in the new position, there may be some question as to the accuracy of the classification, for it often happens that in a new project things do not work out exactly as was anticipated. In such a case the employee may be asked to keep for a specified period — perhaps a couple of weeks — an exact record of the nature of the work performed, on the basis of the nearest hour or half hour devoted to a particular type of activity. Such a record may seem to require so much time that there is none left to work, but if conscientiously kept, it will give the classification officer a pretty clear idea of the nature of the duties performed. The principal weakness of this procedure — and one of which any classification officer is well aware — is the tendency to build up the job for all it is worth, to make it seem tremendously important, in order to obtain a high grade classification.

(3) When the classification officer has talked with the supervisor and with the employee and is still in doubt about the character of the position, there yet remains the possibility of a desk audit. In this procedure the classifier places himself by the desk or duty station of the incumbent for a period of time, asks questions, and makes observations of the duties performed and the amount of time consumed on each. Both management and the employee must be brought to realize that this work is not an inspection or a check on the efficiency of the department or agency.

From an analysis of these three methods of procedure, it is evident that correct classification is entirely dependent upon adequate factual data as to the nature of the position. Once all the facts are assembled, the classifier is ready to make a more detailed study and analysis, both horizontally on the basis of occupational groups (that is, the kind and character of the work irrespective of level) and vertically on the basis of the relative degree of difficulty and responsibility. As the analysis by occupational groups proceeds, similarities and divergencies will begin to appear. Having once determined what classes of positions — horizontally by kind and vertically by level — are necessary for effective operations, the classifier should get a description of each class down on paper. This is the class specification. It includes the title, general state-

[5] See Pollock, Ross, "Word Usage in Position Classification," *Public Personnel Review,* October, 1943, pp. 266–273, and on other phases of the problem, Kennedy, John J., and Waldenfels, Frank J., "The Responsibility Distribution Chart: A Classification and Administrative Tool," *ibid.,* pp. 254–259; Pennebaker, Kenneth C., "Eliminating Minimum Qualifications from Class Specifications," *ibid.,* January, 1942, pp. 25–28.

ment of duties, description of the distinguishing features of the class, examples of work, a statement of the knowledges, skills, and abilities required in order to perform the work in any position in the class, and finally a statement of the experience and training required to perform the duties of the class efficiently.

The Classification Process. What, then, is the classification process? It is simply arranging positions in groups according to the character and difficulty of the work and according to the nature of the training, skill, and experience required for its proper performance, subject to certain limitations imposed by the provisions of the Classification Act. Occupations are first grouped very roughly into major divisions called services according to obvious differences in the character of the duties performed. The Federal service includes four major services as defined in the Classification Act of 1923, as amended; in New York State, there are thirteen occupational services, with a varying number of grades in each. The framework of both systems is shown in the table below.

Occupational Services: Federal and State

FEDERAL GOVERNMENT

DESIGNATION	SERVICE	GRADES	SALARY RANGE
CPC	Crafts, Protective, and Custodial	1 to 10	$1410–$4730
SP	Subprofessional	1 to 8	2020– 4479
CAF	Clerical, Administrative, and Fiscal	1 to 15	2086–10330
P	Professional	1 to 8	2974–10330

NEW YORK STATE GOVERNMENT

DESIGNATION	SERVICE	GRADES	SALARY RANGE
1	Custodian and Domestic	2aa to 7	$1200–$3400
2	Junior Professional	1b to 7	1200– 5100
3	Clerical, Stenographic and Office Administration	1b to 6	1200– 4000
4	Agriculture and Conservation	1b to 8	1200– 7000
5	Welfare	1a to 7	1200– 5250
6	Workmen's Compensation	1 to 8	1400– 7300
7	Professional Service*	1 to 8	1800–11000
8	Business Administration Budget Examining Group**	1 to 8	1800–10500
9	Mechanical and Construction Public Safety and Service Operation***	1a to 7	1500– 5500
10	Accounting and Statistical Insurance Examining Group****	1 to 6	2700– 9000
11	General Administration	1 to 7	1500– 7500
12	Prison Safety	1a to 7	1300– 6000
13	Labor Group	1 to 5	1200– 1620

    * For full schedule of professional salaries, see page 146.
    ** Other groups on printing and publicity, purchase and stores, traffic and transportation.
    *** Another group on general construction.
    **** Other groups on bank examining, accounting and fiscal, taxation, statistical and actuarial.

The state and municipal systems seem generally to have adopted the policy of establishing an excessive number of services. A comparable state plan, recommended in the Griffenhagen report for the Virginia service in 1937, likewise provided for thirteen, as against four in the Federal service; but the situation in the cities is much worse. Philadelphia, operating under the Jacobs plan adopted in 1930, has sixteen, San Francisco twenty-two, and New York forty-seven. In favor of the former plan, it may at least be said that it has some basis in logic. It does not, like New York, include both a miscellaneous service and a menagerie service nor three or four separate services concerned with the same functional problem.[6]

After the initial examination of the position to determine the service — which is ordinarily quite easy — the next step is to establish the class. A class is a group of positions sufficiently alike in duties and responsibilities to justify common treatment in selection, pay, and other personnel processes. In the Federal service, where these classes are grouped in series of positions, the Civil Service Commission is now establishing standards to guide classification officers in their work and to insure uniformity in standards and the application of standards.[7] A given position will be in the librarian series, the statistical series, the public relations series, or some other, depending upon the essential character of the training and experience required and the work to be done.

The next step involves the determination of the grade, a term relating to a group of positions where the duties are substantially similar in respect to the authority, responsibility, and character of the work. This is by all odds the most difficult part of the process. Each service and each class provides for a series of grades, the number of which, and the upper and lower limits of which, depend upon the nature of the work. The number of grades in each of the Federal services is indicated in the table above. The following list from the New York State service shows the breakdown for the business administration field:

18 — 000	Purchasing and Stores
19 — 000	Institution Business Management
20 — 000	Budget Examining
21 — 000	Transportation and Traffic

[6] See Civil Service Commission, *Classification and Compensation Plans of the Personal Service in the Executive Departments* (Philadelphia, 1930); Civil Service Commission, *Classification of the Civil Service Commission of the City of New York* (New York, 1944); Civil Service Commission, *Classification of Duties and Salary Schedules of Positions in the Municipal Service* (San Francisco, 1940); and for the Virginia state service, Griffenhagen and Associates, *Report on Classification and Compensation of Positions* (Richmond, 1937).

[7] See Biren, Robert L., "Developing Adequate Class Specifications," *Public Personnel Review*, January, 1944, pp. 27-31, and the items listed in Selected References, especially the Civil Service Assembly report, Chapter 9, and entries under United States Civil Service Commission.

22 – 000	Printing and Publicity
23 – 000	Public Service
23 – 500	Real Estate Appraisal
24 – 000	Personnel Administration
24 – 500	Economic Research

Each series is then broken down again to show the exact names of the positions to be included within that particular group together with the proposed scales of pay, minimum and maximum, and the increments for each position and for each grade established within any given series.[8]

In the Federal service the Classification Act itself divides each of the occupational services horizontally into a series of grades, which are defined by law in terms of the difficulty and complexity of the work, the degree of responsibility, and the qualifications required to do the work. Grades should not be regarded as salary ranges but as zones or levels of difficulty and responsibility of work. The beginner usually rates a grade 1 or grade 2; the top grade of the series may but will not necessarily warrant the top grade in the service – P or CAF, as may be appropriate. The effort is made to determine a reasonable number of steps between the lowest grade and the highest to provide for a proper gradation of work. The difficulty arises in deciding what is grade 3 work, let us assume, and what is grade 4. The duties assigned to a given position are not always clear cut from the point of view of classification; usually, in fact, they are not. Some duties may clearly belong in one grade according to accepted classification standards, some in another. The classifier must weigh the facts and make his decision on the basis of the proportion of the employee's time spent on each of the various types of work assigned to him.[9]

Procedure in Classification Work. Classification means simply a grouping of similar things together. Just as a hardware merchant sorts nails or bolts into different bins according to their size, or an agricultural economist classifies farms as general, truck, dairy, or poultry, so a personnel technician classifies jobs. Whereas, as Griffenhagen pointed out more than a decade ago, "it would be impossible to fix fair rates indi-

---

[8] Full information is given here regarding the Federal plan; for an interesting state case, see Marsh, Harry W., and Powell, Norman J., "A Classification and Pay Plan for the State of New Hampshire," *Public Personnel Review*, April, 1945, pp. 109–113.

[9] On proposals for modification of the Federal system, see Hale, L. DeWitt, "Let's Rewrite the Classification Act," *Personnel Administration*, June, 1946, pp. 13–23; Hendrickson, Roy F., "If I Could Remake the Classification System," *ibid.*, June, 1942, 10–12; Pruefer, C. H., "Classification in the Federal Service and the Emergency," *American Political Science Review*, June, 1941, pp. 506–510; Clegg, Reed L., and others, symposium on progress in position classification, *ibid.*, July, 1947, pp. 26–48.

vidually for all positions, by comparing each one with every other one and determining the exact differences in value among them all it is relatively simple to compare kinds or classes of positions as to their relative value." [10] The report continues:

When positions of the same kind are grouped into one class, the question of determining the proper compensation rates is changed from one of considering each one of perhaps thousands of positions in its relations to thousands of others, to one of considering the particular kind of work involved in the class and what such work is worth. And since all other positions likewise are grouped into their appropriate classes, it is easy to compare the kinds of work involved in the several classes and to see that the relationships in positions as between related classes are right. When rates have been established for classes, they apply automatically to all positions in the respective classes.

In practice the classification process begins in the operating unit. The supervisor writes up the initial job-description and submits it through channels to the personnel office of the agency, where it is turned over to the classification section for action. The classification section studies the job-description and makes such inquiries of the supervisor and employee as in its judgment may be required to clarify its conception of the position. Its recommendation then goes to the personnel officer and perhaps to the head of the agency before it is submitted to the central personnel agency for approval. When this approval is given, the classification of this particular position becomes final and official.

Appeals and Reclassifications. If the central personnel agency fails to approve the agency recommendation, an appeal may be filed. Such action is likely to involve a complete restudy of the job all along the line. The supervisor, anxious to have the original recommendation sustained in order to retain an employee who is doing satisfactory work, tries to see how the assignment of duties can be modified to strengthen the position from a classification point of view. His decisions may be guided largely by the central personnel agency's objections to the original recommendation. A complete new job-description, drawn up on new lines, is likely to result, after which the whole process of review in the agency personnel office and the central personnel agency is re-enacted.

On other occasions new duties and responsibilities have been added over a period of time to a long-established position. The situation in the agency may not warrant a recommendation for promotion. There may be no suitable vacancy for which the incumbent is qualified, or it may be desired to hold an experienced employee in the job he is do-

---

[10] Griffenhagen report, p. 37.

ing. Under such circumstances a request is made for reallocation of the job or, as is often said, for a reclassification. A new job-description is drawn up, emphasizing the new duties and responsibilities and supporting the contention of management that the position is at present under-classified and underpaid. The process of review in the personnel offices of the operating agency and the central personnel agency are essentially the same as in the case of a new position.

There is a certain amount of difference in point of view with regard to classification matters — if not actual conflict — between the personnel office of the agency and the central personnel office. Both are bound by the same rules and regulations but the approach is different. The central personnel agency is responsible for helping the operating agencies in personnel matters; under its primary responsibility for enforcement of the law it has the final say as to what the law means. The operating agency, on the other hand, is interested in getting a job done. It is not necessarily hostile to the rules and regulations but its regard for them is at best secondary. The agency personnel office can and should, so far as it can within reason, stand ready to fight the battles of its operating officials. Sometimes, however, neither the central personnel agency nor the personnel office of the operating agency shows very much regard for the point of view of the other.

Question has also been raised as to the proper relation of position classification to budgeting.[11] It has even been suggested that the two should be combined, but there is little logic in such a proposal. True, the use of classification has important budgetary and fiscal implications, but the fact remains that it is not only essentially a personnel job but the very basis of a large part of the personnel program. There are few major concerns in any field that do not have such dual relationships, but it is not customary to proceed to misclassify them simply because of such complicating factors.

Uses of Position Classification

Position classification has many uses in the field of management in general and of personnel administration in particular. It is, in fact, the foundation for practically all other types of personnel activities. Many large corporations have adopted classification plans and salary schedules for precisely the same reasons that have led to their adoption in public agencies. Such a system provides a structural basis for the fair and objective handling of a variety of questions which otherwise would cause no end of trouble. Just before the end of the war the

---

[11] See McKean, H. Alan, "Should Position Classification and Budgeting Be Combined?" *Personnel Administration*, September, 1947, pp. 33-38.

United States Civil Service Commission put out a small pamphlet on the subject, *Position Classification as an Aid to Supervision*. In this discussion four types of aid are considered.

Setting Up Positions. The requirement that positions ultimately be classified may be of considerable assistance to a supervisor in planning his operations. His responsibility is to see that the total work in his organization is done effectively. He begins by breaking his activity down into its various component parts. In a statistical operation, for instance, he might have a professional unit, a tabulating unit, and a typing unit. Right at that point three supervisory work-assignments have been established. Each of these supervisors must in turn plan a series of work-assignments for individual employees by identifying certain groups of related tasks, each of which groups requires the full working time of one or more employees. Such planning tends to prevent the assignment of miscellaneous and unrelated duties to any employee. These work-assignments become positions which can be described, compared, and classified in the manner already described.

Writing Position Descriptions. If they served no other purpose, the requirement that supervisors must prepare position descriptions of the work-assignments of the employees under their direction could be justified on the basis that it compels them to do some careful and accurate thinking. In daily administration and supervision, however, these descriptions may be useful in a variety of ways, but they must be constantly revised and kept up-to-date.[12] There are many important uses from the point of view of the supervisor, who is responsible for knowing

1. The purpose of each work-assignment under his supervision
2. What he as a supervisor expects each employee to do
3. What he as a supervisor expects the relation to be among the employees with respect to scope of work and degree of responsibility
4. The performance requirements of each work-assignment
5. What each employee's work performance is in relation to the requirements of his particular work-assignment
6. What each employee's needs are for special instruction or training

In still another way position descriptions may aid the supervisor. In the induction of a new employee a careful reading and discussion of the contents of the job-description is a quick and thorough means of acquainting him with the broad outlines of his job. Such statements may be used by the personnel office for information that will aid in secur-

[12] *Position Classification*, pp. 2–3; see Civil Service Assembly's *Position Classification in the Public Service*, Chapter 4, for other uses and advantages.

ing the right type of personnel when vacancies are to be filled. They may serve as the basis for agreement on necessary qualifications, for internal comparisons to disclose overlapping and duplication of effort, and for better personnel utilization.

Fixing Compensation. Position classification is an important tool of management for establishing the principle of equal pay for equal work. It tends to minimize discrimination, favoritism, and guesswork in determining rates of pay for particular positions, inasmuch as the emphasis is on the job and the character of the work it requires rather than on the individual filling it at the time. In the absence of such classification, jobs with the same duties may be given widely different titles and paid at substantially different rates, or conversely jobs with highly different duties and degrees of responsibility may be lumped under the same title and given the same salary. Classification seeks to accomplish on as impersonal and objective a basis as possible the determination of questions which were formerly decided on a purely subjective and personal basis.

One of the criteria of a sound pay plan is the provision it makes for rewarding length of service. A constantly recurring problem in the field of management is the promotion of employees on the basis of quality of work and length of service. The classification plan, when coupled with a provision for automatic within-grade pay increases for employees whose efficiency rating is good or better (Ramspeck raises), helps to provide a satisfactory solution. By arranging positions in a logical order in accordance with the nature of the work performed and the responsibilities imposed, it provides an equitable basis for the promotion policy of the agency. This involves, in other words, not merely a within-grade increase but an actual promotion from one grade to another within the same series. Such changes are never automatic but depend upon the recommendation of the supervisor, which in turn is based upon his estimate of the work performance of the employee.

Allocating Positions. The classification system and the position descriptions which play so vital a part in its operation provide the basis — and the only proper basis — for the allocation of positions. The important question here is what the employee's work-assignment actually is and how it compares with the standards established for that particular position or group of comparable positions. It is difficult to eliminate from consideration questions relating to pay, but this should be done so far as humanly possible. When the grade classification has been set, the pay will be determined automatically by the salary schedule.

Development of Pay Policy

In the beginning all was chaos. Each individual employee, regardless of the nature of the duties, made the best arrangements he or she could on the basis of personal or political influence or even by "turning on the charm." The result was that there was no uniformity in rates of pay in any department or agency at any level of government, to say nothing of uniformity between departments or agencies at the same level. As the number of government employees continued to increase, it became more and more obvious that some attention would have to be given to this problem. After World War I provision was made for orderly pay plans in many jurisdictions; of these the Federal government was one of the first.

Factors Influencing Government Pay Scales. Certain determining factors regarding government pay plans are generally recognized as pertinent. An employee should be paid according to what he does, according to how well he does it, and, to a certain extent also, according to his length of service. Certain general economic factors should also be considered, such as recent changes in the cost of living, how much is necessary to permit the employee to maintain a socially desirable standard of living, what private employers pay for the same type of work, and what final pay decisions for all employees will cost the government or, more accurately, the taxpayers.[13] With many individuals the character of the compensation plan is a determining factor. Other critical factors include the esteem in which the public service is held, the extent to which equal pay is provided for equal work, and finally the possibility of the influence of collective bargaining in determining rates of pay, at least for certain types of employment.

One of the most important of these factors is the esteem in which the public service is held by the public and by the public's elected representatives. Americans have long been accustomed to hold it in scant regard; but at the same time they have been quite willing to pay well for anything that at the moment they regard as important, such as football coaches, baseball players, movie actors, business executives. If government service is not adequately compensated, it may be safely assumed that generally speaking it is not held in high regard, is not

---

[13] *Position Classification, op. cit.,* pp. 6–7; there is a good deal of literature on the subject of salary determination: Ells, Ralph W., *Salary and Wage Administration* (McGraw-Hill, New York, 1945), Riegel, John W., *Salary Determination* (Bureau of Industrial Research, University of Michigan, 1940); Litchfield, Edward H., "Theory and Practice in Public Service Salary Determination," *Public Personnel Review,* April, 1945, pp. 77–84; and Richey, Carl L., "Determining Pay Policy," *ibid.,* January, 1942, pp. 20–24.

thought to be sufficiently important to justify the expenditures necessary to secure and retain the highest grade of talent and ability.

Another factor is the nature and effectiveness of the position classification plan, as has been indicated earlier. One of the reasons why it is
necessary to classify jobs is to establish standards under which the principle of equal pay for equal work may be made effective.[14] Nothing is
more disrupting to the morale of an organization than to have two people engaged in the same or similar duties, paid at widely different rates.

Not only must the plan provide for equal pay for equal work, but
it must be so constructed that the rates offered for different types of
work bear a reasonable relationship one to another and to the time and
expense involved in preparation. The levels of compensation should be
so set as to show a proper regard for the education and experience required for the work. Although in most jurisdictions it is believed necessary to be very "hush-hush" about formal educational requirements,
it is nevertheless true that the amount of formal training usually necessary for the proper performance of a job constitutes at least one reasonable index of the level of compensation that should be offered for it.

Another important consideration is the compensation offered in private employment for the same type or similar types of work. Using this
as a criterion, a number of generalizations may be made. In the Federal
service, compensation in the middle and upper grades is low, while in
the lower grades it is high. In the larger states exactly the opposite is
true: compensation in the upper grades is high, while in the lower
grades it is extremely low. In the smaller states it is low at all grades.
The situation in the cities is about the same as in the states: the larger
cities pay quite well in the upper grades, but the smaller ones are low
at all grades. In the counties — except for a few in metropolitan areas —
and the smaller local units, the rates of compensation are all low.

Finally, mention has been made of the possible influence of collective bargaining in the determination of rates of pay. In the Federal
service there is little opportunity for the exercise of collective bargaining techniques, since the compensation for all positions in the classified
service is set by statute. The statute indicates what the government is
authorized to pay, and those who are or might be interested can take it
or leave it. In many of the state and local units, collective bargaining
might exercise a wholesome influence in raising prevailing rates, but
even at these levels the unionization of government employees has made
relatively little progress. Here also there are large numbers of cases in

---

[14] See Crowley, John C., "Job Evaluation Methods in Salary Analysis," *Public Personnel Review,* October, 1946, pp. 184–189.

which full scales of pay at the various levels have been established by statute or ordinance.

The Federal Service: Classified. In 1923 Congress passed the original Classification Act, which combined position classification with salary schedules for all positions in the classified service. At the time the rates were reasonably satisfactory. The act represented a vast improvement over previous arrangements. Through periods of prosperity and depression the rates remained substantially unchanged until in 1942, in the midst of war, provision was made for overtime pay. It was not real overtime: the act provided straight time for overtime, and even this provision had full application only for employees receiving $2900 or less. Above that, regardless of grade and salary, the maximum allowance was $628, with the result that higher-grade employees were actually paid less for overtime than those in lower grades and less for overtime than for regular time.

Effect of Recent Federal Employees Pay Legislation

POSITION	ORIGINAL BASIC PAY ACT OF 1923	OVERTIME PAY ACT OF 1942	BASIC PAY UNDER 1945 ACT	BASIC PAY UNDER 1946 ACT	PAY INCREASE ACT OF 1948
CAF-4	$1800	$360–$2160	$2100	$2394	$2724
CAF-7	2900	628– 3528	3310	3797	4127
CAF-10	3500	628– 4128	3970	4525	4855
CAF-12	4600	628– 5228	5180	5905	6235
CAF-14	6500	628– 7128	7175	8179	8509

A Federal Employees Pay Act was passed in 1945. Its passage was made imperative by the approaching end of the war and the expiration of the Overtime Pay Act of 1942. The Civil Service Commission had proposed a cost of living increase of 15 per cent in basic rates, straight across the board, in keeping with the terms of the Little Steel Formula then imposed on private industry. In Congressional committees this fair and reasonable proposal was so changed that to the basic rates for each grade an amount was added which was substantially the same as the overtime allowance under the 1942 Act. The formula provided for 15 per cent on the first $1200 — up to $1200; [15] 10 per cent on the

[15] For discussion of these developments, see articles by Ismar Baruch: "Federal Holiday Pay Policies," *Personnel Administration*, November, 1945, pp. 15–18; "Pay for Stand-by Duty," *ibid.*, January, 1947, pp. 27–31; "Basic Aspects of Position Classification," *Public Personnel Review*, October, 1940, pp. 1–17; "The Federal Employee Pay Act of 1945," *ibid.*, October, 1945, pp. 201–212; "The Structure of a Pay Scale," *ibid.*, July, 1946, pp. 141–147; "The Wartime Salary Problem," *ibid.*, April, 1944, pp. 77–88.

next $3400 — from $1200 to $4600; 5 per cent on all above $4600 — $4600 and above. The effect on a selected group of CAF positions is shown in the table on page 139. The act, it should be said, was not regarded at the time as permanent legislation; it was passed to meet a pressing current need with the avowed intention of continuing consideration of the questions involved in order to develop a new basic plan.

The second important aspect of the 1945 Pay Act was the revision of the provisions for overtime pay. Now for the first time full time and a half was allowed for overtime, but the provision of the earlier act limiting applicability to positions carrying a salary of $2900 or less was carried over. An act passed in 1946 increased the rates of compensation in the classified service by 14 per cent or $250 a year, whichever was the greater, except that no such rate might be increased more than 25 per cent. An increase of $330 across the board was authorized in 1948. The automatic within-grade increases provided for under the terms of the Ramspeck Act were operative during this period; the Hoover Commission recommended that in future such increases should be allowed only on written certification of the supervisor that the increase was warranted.

The advantages of the recent legislation were to a considerable extent nullified by its critical defects, which tended to accentuate previously existing faults in the Federal pay plan. Under the original schedules, with the overtime provided during the war, there was a serious discrepancy between Federal government and private rates of pay in higher-grade jobs. During the war it was possible to recruit high-grade personnel because the patriotic urge was strong and because such persons often found it better to be employed and earning something than to be idle while war restrictions prevented their following their usual occupations. With the coming of peace both of these advantages to the government were suddenly eliminated.

Plans for permanent pay legislation were introduced in every session of Congress since 1946 but failed of adoption. Lower-grade positions were overpaid during the war, and even more so afterward when across-the-board increases were made. The Hoover Commission reported that groups earning less than $5000 a year had had increases ranging from 38 to 56 per cent since 1939, while those earning above that amount had been advanced a maximum of 15 per cent and, in some cases, not at all. Commissioner Flemming, in his testimony before the House Committee on the Civil Service in February, 1946, asked for a 20 per cent increase in basic rates of compensation, plus the addition of two new grades to the salary schedules of the Classification Act of

1923, with a view to raising the ceiling for professional, scientific, administrative, and technical jobs from $9800 (now $10,330) to $15,000. This recommendation was accompanied by proposed increases for heads and assistant heads of executive departments, members of Congress, and judges of the United States Courts. The Legislative Reorganization Act did, of course, provide for an increase in the pay of members.[16]

In the fall of 1947 the author made an exhaustive study of salary arrangements in top-grade positions in government, in industry, and in the professions.[17] The discrepancy between rates paid for comparable knowledge, experience, and ability in public and in private employment is astounding. The effects are two: first, top-level people cannot as a rule be induced to accept public employment in normal times, and if they do accept, they do not long remain. They are unwilling to impose upon themselves and their families the financial sacrifices that such employment entails. The effect is seen, in the second place, at the second level of supervision, among the division heads, bureau chiefs, and scientific and professional personnel. Their salaries, too, suffer greatly by comparison with those paid for similar skills outside of government. They cannot be raised until the top salaries for key personnel are raised. The result is that the government is losing at an alarming rate trained, qualified, and experienced personnel in all the upper levels. The turnover is terrific.

The Federal Service: Unclassified. There are in the Federal service, as elsewhere, a large number of positions for which no particular requirements of education or skill can be established — laborer and helper positions which can be adequately filled by individuals with "a strong back and a weak mind." Such positions are not included in the classified service and are not therefore compensated on an annual salary basis. The hourly rates of pay are determined locally by wage boards in the light of local conditions of labor supply and prevailing rates. They are known, consequently, as wage-board positions. The rates are uniform locally within any given wage area but may differ considerably from one area to another and from one section of the country to another.

State Salaries. Developments in the state and local units paralleled fairly closely the effect of the war on pay rates in the Federal service. The pressure for higher salaries did not cease at any level of government when hostilities came to an end; in fact the pressure increased with the

---

[16] Hearings before the Committee on the Civil Service, House of Representatives, 79th Cong., 2nd Sess., *Salary and Wage Administration in the Federal Service*, pp. 2–3.
[17] *Salaries in Top Level Positions — in Government, in Industry, and in the Professions* (Legislative Reference Service, Library of Congress, Washington, 1947).

upward trends in prices that accompanied relaxation of wartime controls. In spite of valiant efforts to hold down price increases during the war, the cost of living did go up — not suddenly and drastically as during World War I, but slowly. Government employees, like other elements in the population, found themselves faced with rising living costs. Although efforts were being made to "hold the line" on wages as well as on prices, concessions had to be made. Government employees demanded at least as much relief as was accorded employees in private industry under the Little Steel Formula, which for a long time served as a pattern for industry.

This gave rise to a wave of so-called cost-of-living increases. In most jurisdictions these were assumed to be purely temporary. There was no recognition that there was anything wrong with existing wage scales, although many of them were notoriously low and inadequate. The increases were handed out, usually under pressure, as a concession and with the definite understanding that they did not constitute a precedent. They represented a more or less makeshift arrangement.[18] As time went on, two facts became quite clear. One was that prices were not going down and that these increases would have to be continued indefinitely. Thus a temporary measure of relief turned into an established policy. The second fact was that these increases brought about a significant increase in the cost of government at all levels. With many fewer employees on the payrolls because of war conditions, the total salary costs exceeded any previous figure in peacetime. States and cities had no choice; their personnel was already reduced to an absolute minimum if not below that point. They had to meet the increased costs or face the certainty of further losses to war industry and to the Federal government — losses which would cripple services already cut to the bone.

The New York Law of 1946 provides an excellent illustration of this type of emergency legislation. Its life was specifically limited to the year ending March 31, 1947, although it was later extended for another year. It provided for increases on the basis indicated in the table

---

[18] On this point see: California State Employees' Association, *Data Supporting Request for Adjustment of Salaries of State Employees* (Sacramento, 1945); Council of State Governments, *Wartime Pay Adjustments for State Employees;* Hearings before a Subcommittee of the Committee on Civil Service, House of Representatives, 78th Cong., 1st Sess., *Temporary Additional Compensation for Civilian Employees for the Duration of the War;* Karlen, Harvey M., "Wage Trends and State Employment, 1929–1944," *State Government,* November, 1945, pp. 217–218; Leonard, John M., and Mohaupt, Rosina, *Cost-of-Living Salary Adjustment Plans* (Detroit Bureau of Governmental Research, 1944); Snyder, Eleanor M., "Cost-of-Living Adjustment of State and Municipal Wages," *Monthly Labor Review,* November, 1943.

below.[19] In 1948 a further increase was made on the basis of a new formula, the nature of which is also indicated in the table.

Emergency Pay Legislation in New York State

1946 FORMULA	1948 FORMULA
0% on less than $1500 per annum	15% on the first $3000 of compensation
6% on more than $1500, but less than $2000 per annum	10% on the fourth and fifth $1000 of compensation
2% on more than $2000, but less than $3000 per annum	5% on that portion of compensation exceeding $5000 per annum
8% on more than $3000, but less than $4000 per annum	No employee shall receive an increase of more than $900.
4% on $4000 or more per annum	

Statutory Salaries? Serious question has been raised regarding the wisdom of establishing salary arrangements by constitutional or statutory enactment. Many states have set official salaries by constitutional provision; for many years, Kentucky was prohibited from paying any salary in excess of $5000. The Federal government and the states have set salaries in classified position by statutory provisions. These procedures establish a rigid system which makes adjustment difficult even when economic conditions urgently indicate the need for it. The system used for unclassified positions in the Federal service recognizes this need for elasticity.

Actually the need for elasticity is no more urgent in unclassified positions than in those which are classified; it is merely more obvious. Uniformity is desirable, but it makes recruiting difficult for higher-grade positions in many areas. A top salary that seems bountiful in a rural state may be wholly inadequate in a large city. The Hoover Commission recommended the adoption of a realistic pay policy under which the central personnel agency would fix rates of pay, subject to annual review, giving due regard to differential factors, and that Congress should limit its participation in the process to the establishment of maximum and minimum rates within which all general salary adjustments would be made. Authority for all other phases of pay administration would be delegated to the executive branch.

One significant factor which has facilitated adjustments of pay scales even by legislative action has been the fact that the public generally, and even on occasion the taxpayers' associations, have come to the rescue, realizing that it was impossible to obtain high-grade personnel at existing rates in many jurisdictions. It is news when taxpayers'

---

[19] Laws of New York, 1946, Chap. 222, reprinted in *Ninth Report* of the Salary Standardization Board, pp. 31–34 (Albany, 1946); 1948 data from *Watertown Times*, January 27, 1948.

groups come out for salary increases, although this very thing has hap
pened a number of times when leadership has recognized that cheap
help may be poor help and that in the long run good and efficient and
intelligent help is not only cheaper for the taxpayer but will provide
better service.

Guaranteed Annual Wages. For a long time economists have struggled
with the idea of stabilizing the purchasing power of the dollar. Empha
sis at present looks toward doing so by controlling the fluctuations in
the business cycle. In both private industry and in government effort
are now being made to solve the problem so far as particular groups of
workers are concerned by a guaranteed annual wage, in which upward
and downward adjustments are made in accordance with the trend in
dicated by the BLS consumers' price (cost of living) index or by other
similar indices.[20]

The plan began in the city of St. Paul in 1922. Later the Minnesota
State Highway Department and some county highway departments in
Michigan provided for both a guaranteed annual wage on a sliding-scale
arrangement and the stabilization of employment. Under the St. Paul
plan an annual adjustment of wages is made in accordance with changes
in the cost of living as revealed by standard indices; this assures both
civil employees and taxpayers a fair deal. Under the old system pay in
creases very belatedly follow increases in living costs and respond
rather promptly to decreases in living costs. Under the Minnesota plan
the time lag is largely eliminated.[21]

New converts to the plan have been reported regularly since 1940.
In the fall of 1946, five governments in the Milwaukee area were re
ported as having adopted the plan, "after playing hide-and-seek with
the business cycle for many years." At the end of 1947, seventeen cities
(including St. Paul and Milwaukee) were reported to have based pay
boosts on the price index. Included in the list were such widely sepa
rated communities as:

---

[20] In some lines of private industry, the problem of continuous employment presents
a complicating factor not generally present in government. In an article published in
April, 1947, *Fortune* took the position that "imposed on all industry, it would serve no
one; adopted by some businesses, it might benefit all." See American Management As
sociation, Research Report No. 8, *Annual Wages and Employment Stabilization Tech
niques.*
[21] See Leonard and Mohaupt, *op. cit.;* Pennebaker, Kenneth C., and Hart, Robert M.,
"Guaranteed Income and Employment Stabilization Plan for State Highway Employ
ees," *Public Administration Review*, July, 1942, pp. 177–189; Koronski, George W.,
"We Like Our Annual Salary Plan," *Better Roads*, October, 1945, pp. 40–42, and De
cember, 1945, pp. 29–30; Stover, Robert D., "The Minnesota Cost-of-Living Pay Plan,"
Public Personnel Review, July, 1948, pp. 133–137; Turner, Samuel E., Jr., "St. Paul
Adjustable Salary Scale for City Employees," *National Municipal Review*, December
1938, pp. 583–587.

Portland, Oregon
Duluth, Minnesota
Phoenix, Arizona
Brookline, Massachusetts
Sherwood, Wisconsin

Colorado Springs, Colorado
Jackson, Michigan
Madison, Wisconsin
Whitefish Bay, Wisconsin

Adjustments apply generally to the first $1200 to $1500 of salary, and they are made every three months. Columbus, Ohio, and San Diego, California, discontinued such plans during the war. In May, 1948, General Motors adopted such a plan, thereby becoming the first large corporation to accept such terms in a union contract.

The use of the plan in St. Paul over a considerable period of time affords perhaps the only indication of what the effects of deflation may be. Observing cost-of-living index decreases, St. Paul reduced municipal salaries 17 per cent between 1931 and 1933. It is significant that the price index dropped 26 per cent during the depression, indicating that the pay-adjustment plan appears to operate more accurately during inflation than during deflation. With returning prosperity St. Paul's salaries have been increased 41 per cent since 1940. The percentage increase applies to the first $100 of monthly salary.[22]

Salary and Wage Administration

It may now be assumed that the positions in the service have been classified and appropriate rates of pay determined. The rates should be set up in the form of a salary schedule or pay scale, two illustrations of which are included here. The first is the current pay scale under the Federal civil service system, the second an illustration from New York — the salary grades and minimum salaries for the professional service in that state. The basic principles were clearly stated a number of years ago in the Indiana survey report prepared by the Public Administration Service: [23]

1. Corresponding salary levels for corresponding classes in all organizational subdivisions in the same jurisdiction
2. Equal pay for the same type and quality of work
3. Pay which is comparable to that prevailing in the region and at least adequate to maintain a decent standard of living
4. Provision for revision of salary ranges as often as necessary to reflect changes in the general economic situation
5. Machinery for adjustment of salary rates within ranges to recognize increase or decrease in quality of work and for long and distinguished service

[22] "Cities Base Pay Boosts on Price Index," *Virginia Municipal Review*, February, 1947, p. 37; also Christopherson, Richard, "Milwaukee Seeks Pay Justice," *National Municipal Review*, September, 1946, pp. 408–412.
[23] *Personnel Administration and Procedure*, for the Indiana Department of Public Welfare, p. 10 (Chicago, 1938).

The Professional Service:*

Schedule of Annual Salary Rates by Grade

THE FEDERAL SERVICE (as of July 1, 1948)

GRADE	MINIMUM	INTERMEDIATE					MAXIMUM
1	$2974	$3100	$3225	$3351	$3476	$3601	$3727
2	3727	3852	3978	4103	4228	4354	4479
3	4479	4605	4730	4855	4981	5106	5232
4	5232		5482	5733	5984		6235
5	6235		6474	6714	6953		7192
6	7232		7671	7911	8150		8389
7	8509		8808	9108	9407		9706
8	10305		10330	10330	10330		10330

NEW YORK STATE CIVIL SERVICE

RATES OF COMPENSATION

GRADE	MINIMUM ANNUAL SALARY	MAXIMUM ANNUAL SALARY	ANNUAL INCRE-MENT	FIRST YEAR	SECOND YEAR	THIRD YEAR	FOURTH YEAR	FIFTH YEAR	SIXTH YEAR
1	$1800	$2300	$100	$1800	$1900	$2000	$2100	$2200	$2300
2	2400	3000	120	2400	2520	2640	2760	2880	3000
2a	2760	3360	120	2760	2880	3000	3120	3240	3360
3	3120	3870	150	3120	3270	3420	3570	3720	3870
3a	3600	4350	150	3600	3750	3900	4050	4200	4350
4	4000	5000	200	4000	4200	4400	4600	4800	5000
4a	4500	5500	200	4500	4700	4900	5100	5300	5500
4b	5000	6000	200	5000	5200	5400	5600	5800	6000
5	5200	6450	250	5200	5450	5700	5950	6200	6450
5a	5500	6750	250	5500	5750	6000	6250	6500	6750
5b	6200	7700	300	6200	6500	6800	7100	7400	7700
6	6700	8200	300	6700	7000	7300	7600	7900	8200
6a	7000	8500	300	7000	7300	7600	7900	8200	8500
6b	7500	9000	300	7500	7800	8100	8400	8700	9000
6c	8000	10000	400	8000	8400	8800	9200	9600	10000
7	8500	10500	400	8500	8900	9300	9700	10000	10500
7a	9000	11000	400	9000	9400	9800	10200	10600	11000
8	10000								

* Includes positions requiring training in law, science, medicine, health, graduate nursing, educational administration and supervision, library administration and supervision, veterinary science, forestry, civil service, engineering, architecture, and other recognized professions.

Such a schedule serves many purposes. It contributes greatly to the morale of the service. It gives specific and official answer to employees who are wondering about their own pay rate and how it compares with that of other employees. Administratively it provides an answer to many other questions presented by employees. More important still, it establishes a sound basis for budget estimates; once it is settled and agreed upon, the administrator can compute with a fair degree of accuracy the salary item in his budget.

The actual administration of such a plan calls for many specific steps. The list which follows is taken from a War Department manual issued in 1943; procedures in other departments or agencies would vary in detail but not in substance.[24]

Detailed Responsibilities of Certifying Officers. The prompt payment of employees is an integral part of a personnel program, and no responsibilities will be assigned to any payroll office which will interfere with the current operations of the office. The detailed operating responsibilities of a certifying officer, wherever located, are as follows:

1. Maintenance of pay roll records, including authorizations, attendance records, current schedules of authorized salary or wage rates, computations of gross earnings and of deductions therefrom . . . for each civilian employee, covering all deductions required by law or authorized by the employee with detail thereof, and net payment

2. Preparation, certification, and forwarding through the fiscal officer to the disbursing officer of pay rolls showing net amount paid for civilian personnel, compiled on the basis of the gross earnings less deductions

3. Preparation, certification, and forwarding to the bond issuing officer of the Treasury Department information for the issuance of war bonds on the basis of records maintained by the certifying officer for war bond deductions from pay of civilian employees

4. Preparation, certification, and forwarding to the District Collector of Internal Revenue of required reports for deductions made from the earnings of civilian employees for Federal withholding taxes and preparation of such reports and receipts in respect thereto as may be required by law to be issued to the employees. Certifying officers are designated as withholding agents under the Regulations of the Bureau of Internal Revenue.

5. Preparation, certification, and forwarding to the appropriate office of such reports and information as may be required in respect to the earnings and retirement deductions from earnings of civilian employees

6. Certification of the accuracy, legality, and completeness of the information furnished the Army Regional Accounting Office for audit by the General Accounting Office, together with such other data as may be required in support of certified civilian personnel pay rolls paid by the disbursing officer

7. Financial accountability for the correctness of amounts certified to the disbursing officer for payment and disposition of deductions, and to the bond issuing officer for issuance of bonds

8. Report through the fiscal officer to the disbursing office of the distribution of deductions from gross earnings for all pay roll adjustments — that is, check cancellations, refunds, errors, et cetera, so that correction of accounts may be made

9. Distribution of pay roll checks and War Bonds to civilian employees

10. Furnishing the commanding officer for approval and transmittal to the disbursing officer of an authenticated specimen of the certifying or deputy certifying officers' signatures

---

[24] *Payment of Civilian Personnel*, Civilian Personnel Regulation No. 120 (Washington, 1943).

There has been a good deal of discussion of late as to where in the organizational structure responsibility for salary and wage administration should rest. Recent practice tends to regard this as a financial and accounting problem rather than a responsibility of the personnel office. Regardless of who does the work, the task has come to be a most complicated one, in connection with which a great many problems arise. It has been complicated by the withholding tax, by bond deductions, and by deductions for hospitalization, welfare fund, or other purposes authorized by the employee, as well as by some requirements in the personnel regulations themselves relating, for instance, to such matters as overtime pay, meritorious increases, and within-grade promotions.[25] Among the special problems are to be noted such matters as the means of compelling contractors to comply with the provisions of the Walsh-Healey Act, wage administration for ungraded civilian jobs, and the payment of without-compensation and dollar-a-year personnel.[26]

SELECTED REFERENCES

Baruch, Ismar, *Position Classification in the United States* (Civil Service Assembly of the United States and Canada, Chicago, 1941). The foremost authority on position classification reports as chairman of a CSA committee.

Chernick, Jack, and Hellickson, George C., *Guaranteed Annual Wages* (University of Minnesota Press, 1945). Analysis of a new wage plan prepared in the state and city of its origin; for bibliography, see Thompson, Laura A., *The Guaranteed Annual Wage and Other Proposals for Steadying the Worker's Income: Selected References* (United States Department of Labor, Washington, 1945).

Citizens Budget Commission, Inc., *Compensation, Conditions of Employment and Retirement Benefits of Policemen and Firemen in New York City and 292 Other Cities in the United States* (New York, 1938). Valuable report on prewar conditions in the cities.

Council of State Governments, *Maintenance of Institutional Employees: Summary of Values Established in the Various States* (Chicago, 1942). Survey of practices relating to a large segment of state employees whose problems present peculiar difficulties; see also Crowley, John C., *Institutional Employee Maintenance* (Public Administration Service, Chicago, 1947).

Graves, W. Brooke, *Salaries in Top Level Positions in Government, in Industry, and in the Professions* (Legislative Reference Service, Library of Congress, 1947). Extensive report prepared for Senate Civil Service Committee, documents great discrepancy between top salaries in public and private employment.

---

[25] On these matters, see United States Civil Service Commission, *Salary and Wage Administration in the Public Service: A Selected List of References* (Washington, 1946); Martucci, Nicholas L. A., "Wage and Salary Administration," *Modern Management*, October, 1945, pp. 11–13, 30; Sisk, Katherine A., and Sheldrup, Gudrun, "Counting Service for Periodic Within-Grade Salary Advancements," *Personnel Administration*, November, 1946, pp. 34–36; and the discussion of record keeping in Chapter 12 following.

[26] See Civilian Production Administration, *Dollar-a-Year and Without-Compensation Personnel Policies of the War Production Board and Predecessor Agencies, 1939–1945* (Washington, 1947); War Department, Army Service Forces, *Wage Administration for the Ungraded Civilian Jobs*, Manual M202 (Washington, 1944); and Vietheer, George C., "How Uncle Sam Governs Personnel Administration by Its Contractors," *Personnel Administration*, May, 1947, pp. 5–8, 16.

Leonard, John M., and Mohaupt, Rosina, *Cost of Living Salary Adjustment Plans* (Detroit Bureau of Governmental Research, 1944). Study of efforts made in different jurisdictions to meet situation created by high prices in wartime, and high wage rates in defense industries.

New York State Salary Standardization Board, annual reports. These give the most nearly current and most valuable information on the subject at the state level.

Public Administration Service, *Merit System Installation* (Chicago, 1941). Manual of procedures shows clearly the necessity for sound classification and salary plans as a basis for merit system operations.

Stead, William H., and Masincup, W. Earl, *The Occupational Research Program of the United States Employment Service* (Public Administration Service, Chicago, 1942). Full information on occupations is essential to any sound classification plan.

The Library of the United States Civil Service Commission maintains reference lists, revised from time to time, on most aspects of personnel administration; as pertinent to the present discussion, see *Position Classification: A Selected List of References* (Washington, 1945), and *Salary and Wage Administration in the Public Service: A Selected List of References* (Washington, 1946). Important Commission publications dealing with these subjects include:

Class Specifications and Statements of Allocation Standards. . . . (Washington, 1943–).
Handbook of Occupational Groups and Series of Classes Established Under the Federal Position-Classification Plan (Washington, 1945).
Pay Structure of the Federal Civil Service, 1947 (Washington, 1948).
Position-Classification as an Aid to Supervision (Washington, 1945).

9

EDUCATION AND TRAINING
FOR THE PUBLIC SERVICE

BASIC education and training for the public service is no different from that required for any other professional career service. There is no substitute for a broad general education, and there are no short cuts by which an education may be obtained. The program should include basic courses in public administration, but these do not — certainly they should not — descend to the level of mere vocational training, which concentrates on telling how and ignoring the why. But education, even of the proper sort, is not enough; it does not fit a new appointee to sit down at a desk and do a good administrative job any more than graduation from a law school automatically makes a man a good trial lawyer. Skill comes in time as a result of experience and possibly further professional training.

Education for the Public Service
The universities and colleges were literally forced into training for the public service. They have usually been somewhat reluctant because boards of trustees, drawn largely from private industry and prominent alumni, have not been anxious to see their institutions enter this field nor have professional politicians demonstrated any unseemly haste in admitting the need for training or in utilizing its product. But training came because it had to come; government had grown so complex that it was increasingly difficult to carry on without training.

In the early stages, before specialization developed in the field of administration itself, educational institutions were inclined to use the courses and faculty they already had. Many of the efforts began with a survey of existing facilities, with a view to utilizing whatever could be used.[1] In time it came to be recognized that in training men for public administration the universities had a double function: to help the student build an intellectual foundation and to help him build mental

---

[1] This process has been repeated in many institutions; a good example is found in the proceedings of a conference held at the University of Minnesota in 1931: *University Training for the National Service* (University of Minnesota Press, 1932).

habits and skills. The first is met by a general education, which may be obtained in any good liberal arts college; the second, by specialized professional training at the graduate level, which may be obtained in only a relatively small number of institutions that have taken the trouble to analyze the problem and to attempt some suitable means of meeting it.[2]

The difficulties in developing such a program are both internal and external. The former involve preparing new courses based on an analysis of the needs of the public service, and finding qualified persons to teach them. This is not as simple as it sounds, for as Professor Graham has observed, government is complicated, and its problems are complicated. In addition, universities have — largely as a matter of administrative convenience — become highly departmentalized. Since the problems of government are not departmentalized according to the same pattern, the universities face a difficult problem of integration and of interdepartmental relationships.

The external problems include, first of all, the development of such cooperative relationships with government officials as will enable the institution to strengthen its program and at the same time do a reasonably effective placement job. There is little justification for spending time, money, and effort in training young men and women for public service if the individuals responsible for the administration of that service are unwilling to utilize them. At frequent intervals the Committee on Public Administration of the Social Science Research Council has published pamphlets listing the institutions offering special training in public administration. The programs vary greatly both in merit and in scope. The following institutions offer some of the older and more significant programs:

Bureau of Public Administration, University of Michigan
Maxwell School of Citizenship and Public Affairs, Syracuse University
The Woodrow Wilson School, Princeton University
Cooperative Training Program for Public Service, University of Cincinnati
Bureau of Public Administration, University of California
National Institute of Public Affairs, Washington, D.C.
Public Administration Training Center, University of Minnesota
Graduate School of Public Administration, Harvard University
Graduate Division for Training in Public Service, New York University
Southern Regional Internship Training Program, University of Alabama and
    other cooperating institutions
National Training School for Public Service, Wayne University

And there are many more. Some institutions like the University of Southern California, American University, Wayne University, New York University, and the Southern Regional Training Program empha-

---

[2] The best analysis of these programs will be found in Graham.

size in-service training carried on in cooperation with public or semi-public agencies.[3] Others, such as the University of Chicago and the University of Wisconsin, train a great many students for public service without any formally organized program. Some programs are designed to train "bureaucrats"; others seek to turn out civic secretaries and researchers for civic organizations. Clearly, there is no definite pattern as to either method or objective.[4]

The Need for Training

The need for training is constant. The personnel of any large organization is always shifting through deaths, resignations, retirement, dismissals, promotion, demotion, reductions in force, and new appointments. Every change means a new employee to be trained. If the change comes as a result of transfer or promotion, there may be a whole line of promotions underneath, and each of the individuals affected requires training. It may be assumed that the appointee has the native intelligence, the educational background, and the necessary experience or he would not have been appointed; but since he does not know the specific job, he needs training. The amount and character of training depend upon a number of variables: the nature and complexity of the job, the appointee's ability to "catch on," and other things.

When single individuals are involved, the problem can be handled adequately by the supervisor in more or less frequent personal consultation with the employee. When numerous employees, similarly situated, are involved, a formal procedure may be necessary. Top management must understand these simple facts, for no training program of any size or significance can be successful without support. Without it the program is likely to be sabotaged by middle management and first-line supervisors, who generally take their cue from the top and who may regard the man-hours consumed in training as just so much time lost from production. As in many other worth-while cases, success is

---

[3] The University of California has also done some very interesting cooperative work with the State Personnel Board; see Kroeger, Louis J., *Training for Public Personnel Administration in California*, and *Preliminary Report of the Committee on Training of Personnel Workers* (Civil Service Assembly of the United States and Canada, Chicago, 1936, and 1939); see also Hersey, Rexford, "Cooperative Training — Dare Management Try It?" *Advanced Management*, December, 1945, pp. 146-154.

[4] A number of them are discussed in Graham, *op. cit.*; for other recent comments, see Odegard, Peter H., "A School for Statecraft — a Modest Proposal," *Oregon Law Review*, December, 1945, pp. 1-9; Ronan, William J., "Public Service Training at New York University," *Personnel Administration*, November, 1941, pp. 17-19; Seidman, Harold, "City Hall Looks at the Colleges," *National Municipal Review*, February, 1944, pp. 70-74, 108; Walker, Robert A., "The University and the Public Service," *American Political Science Review*, October, 1945, pp. 926-933; and White, Leonard D., "Training for Public Service: University of Chicago," *National Municipal Review*, August, 1939, pp. 570-572.

dependent upon the support both of officials and of the rank and file, and this is obtainable only by selling the program before any actual training is undertaken.

Training programs frequently have tough going not only because of the difficulty of selling them to top management but because of external difficulties. The "pet peeves" of many legislators are training, public relations, and planning. If budgetary cuts are made, these activities are among the first to be affected. Another obstacle to training at the Federal level is the hostile attitude of the Comptroller General.[5] These difficulties simply indicate that training is new and that so far as laymen in the personnel field are concerned, it is very little understood. Until they understand that it is an integral and essential part of the personnel program, and until Congress adopts a clear statement of government policy on civilian training programs, as the Hoover Commission recommends, it will continue to have to battle against successive attacks.[6]

Why Training Is Needed. Training is essential for the induction of the new employee; unless he is given essential information about the organization and purposes of the agency and about his own work, it will be some time before he will be able to make any real contribution. Failure to give orientation training to speed the process of induction is inexcusable, unfair alike to the agency and to the new employee. Another less obvious indication of the need for training among employees who can no longer be classified as "new," may arise from the discovery of below-standard efficiency, from analysis of production records, and from comparisons with the records of similar undertakings. Granting that there may be many reasons for inefficient operation, one very common one is the lack of proper training. In such cases a remedial training program can be devised.

Other training needs develop in connection with promotion plans and reassignments of changes in organization and procedure. When the promotion of an employee is contemplated, he should be informed as soon as a definite decision is made in order that he may cooperate with management in his preparation for the new assignment. This may involve an understudy arrangement for a period of time, or some other form of training. Where employees are reassigned to positions involv-

---

[5] See Murphy, Lionel V., "The Comptroller General and Training," *Personnel Administration*, June, 1940, pp. 16-22.

[6] On training needs at the Federal and municipal levels, see Seckler-Hudson, Catheryn, "Training Needs in the Federal Service," *Personnel Administration*, June, 1946, pp. 4-7, and Morales, M. F., "An Approach to Municipal Employee Training," *Public Personnel Review*, April, 1947, pp. 79-82.

ing unfamiliar duties or when changes in organization or procedure modify existing procedures and work relationships, training is essential. Such changes may be highly desirable, but the employees affected are entitled to any necessary instruction. Furthermore, management is cheating itself if it fails to provide it.

Ascertaining the Need for Training. Any unsatisfactory condition in the operation of an agency presents an immediate responsibility for management to determine the cause, after which proper remedial action may be determined. Training is not necessarily the answer to all difficulties, but in a great many cases it is at least part of the answer. If production is not up to par or if there is reason to believe that it could be increased, or if there are too many errors or too great a spoilage of materials, training will help. If employee morale is at a low ebb, it may be partly due to the fact that employees do not fully understand the program of the agency and the importance of their own contribution to it. In this situation, again, training will very definitely help.

One hastens to add a word of caution, for outrageous sins have been committed in the name of training. During the war training ran riot in some establishments. Nearly all employees were given "training" whether they needed it or not, and training staffs were built up to unreasonable proportions. There is just as much waste in the abuse of this function as there is in failure to use it where needed. Training in most cases takes the employee away from his post of duty; it is justified only when it will so increase his efficiency as to help him more than make up for the time spent.

Checking the Value of a Training Program. Comparable only to the waste of using training without justification and careful planning is the waste resulting from failure to check carefully on what the program has accomplished. One way of doing this is to study the effect on both the quality and the quantity of production. This involves, one might say, a comparison of the condition of the patient before and after treatment; it implies systematic follow-up, without which the lessons are soon forgotten. This was demonstrated during the war in many plants, both public and private, in connection with the TWI program.[7]

In 1944 the Training Committee of the Philadelphia Federal Council on Personnel Administration put out a series of suggested criteria for the evaluation of a training unit and its program. This Committee suggested five major bases of evaluation: the organization of the unit,

---

[7] Much literature was published on this program; for an excellent brief description, see Dooley, R. R., "Training Within Industry in the United States," *International Labor Review*, September–October, 1946, pp. 159–178.

its administration, its supervision of training, its instructional methods, and its attempt to determine the results of its own efforts. Under this last heading, emphasis was laid upon such items as reduction in labor turnover, reduction in number of errors, reduction in waste, increase in production, improvement of safety record, more efficient use of man power, elimination or reduction of backlogs. These tests all involve objective evidences of the success or failure of the program; there is a yes or a no answer to each of them. In addition there are various more or less subjective indices of results, such as effect upon morale, increase of job knowledge, development of skills in productive processes, and wholesome attitudes toward the problems of the organization. These are the types of improvement that one has a right to expect of a training program.[8]

Types of Training

There is an almost bewildering variety of types of training activity. Some can be arranged in natural pairs, as pre-entry and post-entry or on-the-job and off-the-job training. Most types may be given to individuals or to groups. The in-service types are obviously a major consideration, affecting potentially all or most of the employees in any given establishment regardless of their position in the organization. Such types may be given either on the job or off the job. Most in-service training is off the job and may be conducted either by informational methods or by the conference method. The most important characteristics of each type will be briefly considered.

The various types may be viewed, from the standpoint of the individual employee, as a cycle: pre-entry training relates to what happened to him before he entered on duty; orientation training is given him when he enters on duty; any of the various types of in-service training may be given him during the course of his employment. Normally, if it is given on the job, the instruction will be given individually; if off the job, he will receive it as a member of a group. While he is employed, he may undertake some work in the form of post-entry education. If so, this will be chiefly on his own initiative, on his own time, and at his own expense.

Pre-Entry Training. Pre-entry training means, as the name suggests, all training and experience acquired prior to actual entry on duty, whether the individual is or is not on the payroll. University or college training is pre-entry training, but ordinarily the individual or his family must meet the expenses. In an internship program — a common form of pre-

---

[8] See Civil Service Assembly's *Employee Training in the Public Service*, Chapter 6.

entry training — the agency may assume part of the cost or pay the trainee a nominal wage. Such programs have become popular in recent years both in the universities and in the government itself.[9] One of them is the National Institute of Public Affairs, which has carried on such a program in Washington for well over a decade with a marked degree of success.[10] Another is the Southern Internship Training Program, which centers at the University of Alabama and involves the coopera-tion of a number of southern state universities as well as the Tennessee Valley Authority.[11] There are many institutions in which assignments of several months of actual work in an agency are part of the degree requirements in public administration.

Internship or trainee programs have also been successfully con-ducted by government agencies themselves. Late in 1942 the United States Civil Service Commission inaugurated such a program. The num-ber of trainees is limited to twenty-five or thirty each year, selected partly from the departmental service, partly from the field. Agencies are requested well in advance to submit nominations. All nominees are interviewed and their records studied; they are given a battery of tests before being selected. The course is intensive. It is designed to qualify for appointment to positions involving minor administrative responsi-

---

[9] See Bellows, R. J., "An Appraisal of the Internship Program," *Personnel Administra-tion*, March, 1940, pp. 8-12; Coman, Jean, "Internship Program for Federal Employees," *ibid.*, February, 1944, pp. 3-8; Mathewson, Daniel O., "Internship From a Worm's Eye View," *ibid.*, May, 1947, pp. 41-43; Reining, Henry, Jr., "The First Federal In-Service Internship Program," *ibid.*, December, 1944, pp. 8-20; Reining, and Stromson, Karl E., "An Approach to Public Service Training: Government Internship," *Public Personnel Review*, July, 1942, pp. 190-199; Roberts, Samuel M., and McCabe, Willis R., "Training Municipal Employees on the Job," *Public Management*, February, 1945, pp. 40-43.
[10] An analysis of the records of 397 "externs" of the first ten college groups, made late in 1946, showed that government and closely related public service employment was the occupation of a majority. Major groups were as follows:

Federal service	148
International, and other administrative work	20
Full-time teachers	14
Journalists, reporting public affairs	7
Practicing law	6
Taking full-time graduate work	65
Engaged in private business	45

Of the 159 women, 53 were devoting their time to housework and the rearing of their families, but of this group a considerable number reported their interest and part-time activity in community and political affairs. Most members of the group had responsi-bilities far larger than those usually given to their age group. "The rapid rate at which the interns have advanced to positions of responsibility is testimony not only to their ability and training but also to the need for administrative personnel." In 1947, it was announced that this program would in future be tied in with the Junior Professional Assistant examination offered by the United States Civil Service Commission.
[11] For excellent discussions of this program, see Greene, Lee S., "Regional Research and Training in Public Administration," *Public Administration Review*, Autumn, 1947, pp. 245-253, and White, Howard, "The Southern Regional Training Program in Public Administration," *Journal of Politics*, February, 1946, pp. 74-85.

bilities those who successfully complete the five months' work. The eighth program began September 7, 1948, and ended February 4, 1949.

The time required for pre-entry training varies according to its nature and purpose. During the war both public and private establishments paid full wages to hundreds and thousands of persons who never went near the plant for weeks or months after they were hired. Meantime at some vocational school they were given 30, 60, 90, or 120 hour courses in technical work. Every agency had its share of these 60 hour or 90 hour wonders who thought, whether anyone else did or not, that they were real mechanics.

Orientation Training. Most orientation or induction training requires relatively little time and is given after employment and, at least in part, before placement. The new employee may be given general orientation training, indoctrination, or pre-assignment training. In any case he is on the pay roll of the agency. Orientation training is really part of the induction process and has been considered in an earlier chapter under that heading.

In-Service Training: On-the-Job. No common term connected with training has been so much misused as "on-the-job training." Actually it may be properly applied only to in-service training that takes place during working hours at the duty station of the employee. It is individual instruction at the place where he works, not group instruction either in the plant or elsewhere. Usually it is given by the supervisor, though it may be combined with group instruction as in the case of an induction pool of typists and stenographers, where part of the day is devoted to class instruction and the remainder to closely supervised work under regular working conditions.[12]

The normal process of on-the-job instruction or work-methods training may be described as telling and showing, explaining and demonstrating, and then watching and assisting the new employee until he is able to perform the operation accurately without assistance or close supervision. Illustrative materials may of course be used where they

---

[12] See Miller, Frank E., and Harris, Martha J., "A Unit Plan for Training in Clerical Skills," *Personnel Administration*, March, 1947, pp. 34–35. Lieutenant Commander Paul B. Crudden, Vocational Training Officer, Philadelphia Navy Yard during the war, pointed out in an address before the Philadelphia Federal Council of Personnel Administration, three different types of on-the-job training: (1) where the individual is placed with a skilled mechanic; if the trainee has ability, he will learn to the extent that the mechanic will allow him to perform some of his highest skill duties; (2) where several employees are assigned to an instructor who is responsible for their upgrading; (3) where a person works independently on a given project under the guidance of a supervisor, the latter holding the trainee responsible for accomplishment. During the war the opportunities for upgrading provided the incentive which contributed greatly to the success of this and similar programs elsewhere.

have been developed and are known to be helpful. The initial period of telling and showing may be followed by one of supervised practice until the new employee gains confidence in his ability to do the work. Even then the supervisor should systematically follow up to make sure that the new man is making satisfactory progress.[13]

Job Instruction Training

A substantial part of the supervisor's time is spent on personnel matters; of these, training is one of the most important. The training of one person for each job is not enough; the good supervisor has two or more people trained to do most jobs so that in case of death, resignation, or absence, production will not be interrupted. This may be accomplished by the development of understudies or by rotation of assignments. The latter has the further advantage of freeing the employee from the monotony of remaining constantly at a single type of work. In a typing and clerical unit, for instance, all the girls may have identical job descriptions, although each one may have primary responsibility for the performance of some particular duty. This plan imposes an additional burden upon the supervisor, but it has many compensating advantages.

Apprentice training is one form of on-the-job training; it is similar to but should not be confused with internship training. The latter primarily describes the work of students who are being given work experience as part of their training; they may not become government employees, although most interns do. On the other hand, the apprentice has already been selected for employment and is subsequently being trained in the hope of making a more valuable employee out of him. In establishments like the Philadelphia Navy Yard which have for years operated apprenticeship programs, there is a long-range program covering from two to four years for those who are qualified, and a short-range program for less important assignments. Hundreds of employees are involved. A significant apprentice training program was also established by law in Wisconsin in 1937 and has been functioning successfully ever since.

---

[13] During the war, these techniques were used on a wide scale, first in industry, and later in government, in the so-called "J" programs:

> JIT — Job Instruction Training
> JMT — Job Methods Training
> JRT — Job Relations Training

Each had a small vest-pocket instruction card, which presented in simplest possible form the essentials of the ten-hour course. Of the three, JIT was most widely used and was most successful. For a description of the program, see article by Dooley, *op. cit.*, and for a state program, Farrington, Robert P., "New Work Training Program for State Employees," *Public Personnel Review*, October, 1945, pp. 236–239.

In-Service Training: Off-the-Job. Off-the-job training is usually conducted on a group basis, either by informational methods or by conference methods. In the former, lectures play a prominent part. They may be used alone or with follow-up reading, quizzes, or conferences. Textbooks, reports, outlines, or syllabi may also be used. The following program, organized in 1947 on a six weeks basis for new employees of the Legislative Reference Service in the Library of Congress, is illustrative:

1. Purpose and Functions of the Legislative Reference Service
2. Organization and Publications of the Legislative Reference Service
3. The Preparation of Reports
4. Personnel Policies: The Library of Congress
5. Personnel Policies: The Legislative Reference Service
6. General Reference and Bibliography Division
7. The Public and the Union Catalogues
8. Library of Congress Rules and Regulations

Administrators in a number of jurisdictions have been experimenting with "courtesy clinics" to teach their employees how to serve taxpayers in a more friendly and helpful manner. Municipal public relations programs have been tried in Jackson, Michigan; Pasadena, California; Kansas City, Missouri; and other cities. In Jackson, the program was made up of ten weekly two-hour sessions, conducted by the city personnel director. Although the training was voluntary, fifty employees registered for the first course. During the series different aspects of public relations were studied and dramatized including politeness, employee appearance, interpreting different kinds of information for the public, handling complaints, good speech habits, the necessity for employees to know the functions of their government in their own departments and in others, and telephone courtesy.[14]

The number of such training programs of one type or another is legion. The New Jersey program for the training of health officials is old and well established; it shows what can be accomplished by proper training methods: [15]

---

[14] For descriptions of such programs, see "Training Municipal Employees in Public Relations," *Public Management*, February, 1947, pp. 47–50, and Elliott, Clarence H., "Training Employees in Public Relations," *ibid.*, August, 1947, pp. 225–228.

[15] Blanchard, Cecil K., "Training Courses for New Jersey Health Officers," *New Jersey Public Health News*, 1946, pp. 137–140; for descriptions of other similar programs, see "The Sanitarian Returns to the Classroom," *The Sanitarian*, November–December, 1946, pp. 137–138; "Training Program Plan for Foresters," Oregon *Forest Log*, January, 1947; Harrison, Earl G., "Function and Possibilities of In-Service Training," Pennsylvania Department of Internal Affairs *Bulletin*, September, 1945, pp. 3–8; and Hearne, Camon C., "Extension Personnel Training," *Personnel Administration*, November, 1947, pp. 30–33.

Each Tuesday and Thursday for six weeks this autumn, forty-one future health officials spend the day at Rutgers University learning what to do and why and when to do it. After six hours in classroom, laboratory, or on a field trip, they have a day or more for this mental meal to digest and, if already employed in a health department, to practice some of their lessons

This special course in public health administration has been conducted annually by Rutgers in cooperation with the State Department of Health since 1926. During the twenty years, 342 students have enrolled in the course and 203 received the Rutgers certificate in Public Health Administration for successful completion of the 144 hours of instruction. Many of these graduates are now health officers of small cities and large towns, others are sanitarians in city health departments, some are public health nurses who supplemented their specialized training with this broader course in health administration, a few have been school teachers and several were physicians who required training in public health in order to qualify for health officer positions.

The conference method of instruction is a fairly recent and very important development; it has been defined as a "series of discussion meetings in which a number of experienced individuals guided by a conference leader pool their experience, knowledge, and thinking to reach better solutions of their problems than they would be likely to reach as individuals." [16] The effectiveness of this device involving, as it does, free discussion and the use of democratic procedures, has been shown by experience to be greater than is usually true of the older informational techniques. Its usefulness does not extend to new subject matter (which can best be covered by lecture or demonstration) nor to inexperienced groups. The most frequent techniques include the presentation and analysis of cases, a direct statement by the leader followed by questions and discussion, group discussion, and analysis of jobs by the group.

Post-Entry Education. Post-entry education, or training taken off the job, is primarily an individual matter. Such programs, which increase the potential usefulness of employees to the government, are normally pursued by employees subsequent to appointment, primarily for their own benefit and outside of working hours. The training may be ar-

---

[16] There is an enormous number of handbooks and manuals on the conference technique; one of the best is *Conference Method Training in Management* (International City Managers Association, Chicago, 1946), which discusses briefly the problem of organization of a conference, procedure, the leader's job, checking progress and results. For standard treatises see Cooper, Alfred M., *How to Conduct Conferences* (McGraw-Hill, New York, 1942); Cushman, Frank, *Training Procedures* (Wiley, New York, 1940); Hannaford, Earle S., *Conference Leadership in Business and Industry* (McGraw-Hill, New York, 1945); Perkins, John A., "The Conference Method of In-Service Training," *Public Management*, May, 1945, pp. 137–140; and Slocombe, Charles S., "Tragic Mistakes in Conferences," *Personnel Journal*, March, 1946, pp. 348–359.

ranged either at the place of employment or outside. The devices include correspondence courses, supervised reading and research, reading clubs, and evening courses which are held either at the agency or at local educational institutions. Such training is more general in character than on-the-job training and usually relates less specifically to the particular job to be done. A program of this character has been in operation for years in the Graduate School of the United States Department of Agriculture. Courses are offered for both graduates and undergraduates not only in government and administration but in most of the usual liberal arts subjects. An interesting program was inaugurated in New York in the fall of 1947, and an extensive curriculum in public administration at the graduate level was set up in Albany through the cooperation of the Graduate Division for Training in Public Service at New York University and the Maxwell School of Citizenship and Public Affairs at Syracuse University. For the first year 108 students were enrolled in four courses. A number of one-year internships have been set up, paying a minimum of $2000; additional compensation is awarded on the basis of each intern's experience and qualifications and on the basis of the regular salary for the job for which he is in training.[17]

Much training work for local officers and employees is carried on in short-term institutes conducted by state leagues of municipalities or by state training institutes organized under the George-Deen Act. The Institute for Training in Municipal Administration in Chicago offers a group of ten practical correspondence courses for municipal administrators — courses in finance, fire, personnel, planning, police, public works, recreation, welfare, the American city and its government, and the techniques of municipal administration. Mention will be made in a later chapter of the university scholarships awarded annually under the auspices of the Philadelphia Federal Council of Personnel Administration.

Planning the Training Program

Formulating the Program. The first task of the training officer is that of diagnostician. If a job analysis has already been made, he uses it; if not, he prepares one himself. Then he obtains standards of performance for it if they have been determined; otherwise he attempts to establish standards for himself. The chances are that by comparing present performance with the standards he will be able to determine rather exactly the nature of the difficulty. Having thus discovered what the employee

---

[17] "Special Training Provided," *State Personnel News,* August, 1947, p. 4.

knows and what he needs to know in order to do the job properly, he is now in a position to write a prescription to provide the help required.[18]

Such a prescription will at first be stated in general terms. In analyzing the production of a typing unit, for instance, it is relatively easy to prescribe training for speed or accuracy or both, where these qualities are at fault, or for spelling lessons where errors are due to ignorance of words. The exact content of the training should be determined, not by the training officer alone, but by him in conference with employees and supervisors. If spelling lessons are to be given, the words should be selected by word-frequency tests applied to the kind of material typed — legal, scientific, or technical. Similarly, the speed exercises given to a correspondence pool will be quite different from those suitable for a statistical unit in which many tables of figures have to be typed.

Others who may be called upon for assistance in determining course content include procedures analysts and specialists in the subject matter. While there are training materials available for many standard uses, analyses of needs indicate that a great many of them are not "standard." Their requirements deviate from the standards in varying degrees, depending upon the nature of the situation. In each instance the course and materials should be tailor made, so to speak, in accordance with the needs of the group.[19]

The essential steps in establishing a training program were summarized as follows in a directive which was issued by the Secretary of War in 1941: [20]

1. *Clearly define the jobs to be done,* by positions. There is a definite list outlining what an individual has to do or, in other words, what he has to be trained to do.

2. *Establish standards of performance* (degree of skill or attainment) required for jobs to be done.

3. *Designate actual training required* to develop the above performance. This calls for definite reference to subjects or established courses. For each established course, outlines are to be made which describe the subject material; list and explain the media used, such as texts, visual aids, equipment, et cetera; specify the most advisable type of instruction to be used (foreman, full-time

[18] See Hogan, Ralph M., and Davis, Wallace M., "Finding Training Materials for the Hard-to-Fill Job," *Personnel Administration,* March, 1943, and reissued by the United States Civil Service Commission under the title: "Developing Training Material through Job Analysis" (Washington, 1945).
[19] See Hausrath, Alfred H., Jr., "Guiding Principles of Training in the Federal Service," *Personnel Administration,* May, 1946, pp. 1-2; Miller and Harris, *op. cit.;* Seckler-Hudson, *op. cit.*
[20] See Kushnick, William H., "Civilian Training in the War Department," *Personnel Administration,* June, 1942, pp. 1-6, and for a somewhat parallel list, Moore, *op. cit.* See also War Department, *Handbook for the Director of Civilian Training,* and Hausrath, *op. cit.*

Department instructors, or outside instruction); indicate how much of the instruction is on-the-job and how much is in the classroom.

4. *Select sources of training to be used.* There are a number of alternatives, such as the shop during production, the shop outside of production hours, special classrooms and laboratories on the premises, or classrooms and laboratories located elsewhere. It should be determined, regardless of where the instruction is done, what part of it should be done by the War Department itself, and what part by other agencies.

5. *Determine training time required* to enable an employee to accomplish performance standards. This time factor is to be indicated in terms of hours, days, or weeks.

6. *Maintain progress reports* (individual performance analyses) of all civilian personnel. These reports should indicate measurement of performance and personal characteristics at various stages while in training and at work. The making of such reports should be a continuous process, indicating retraining or refresher training required.

The application of these principles will result in a pattern of training activity depending upon the major purpose of the organization and its particular problems. A good example may be seen in the following list of courses developed by the Pennsylvania Division of Unemployment Compensation, which has for years carried on an extensive training program:

> Introduction to Unemployment Compensation Service
> Training of Stenographic-Clerical Personnel in District and Local Offices
> Training Program for Managers of Local Offices
> Training for Reporting Personnel
> Training on Benefit Payment Procedures in the Local Office
> Induction Training for Interviewers
> Training for Receptionists
> Occupational Information
> Training for Employer Visiting
> Training Program for Field Accountants
> Letter Writing Program
> Introduction to Bookkeeping and Accounting

In addition to these more or less formal courses, which may be given from time to time as required, the Division has organized numerous conferences dealing with special problems such as the training of supervisors, state field training advisers, administrative policy and control (for supervisory personnel), reports and statistics, and methods of teaching.

Preparing Subject Matter for Presentation. If the philosophy of training here presented is adhered to, new decisions will have to be made in each case on a variety of questions such as form, emphasis, and order of topics. The form of the materials will depend upon the training method to be used — lectures, conferences, or demonstrations. A definite schedule should be prepared, indicating topics to be covered and the length of time allotted to each. The emphasis on any given topic will be indicated in general by the amount of time allotted to it. The difficulties in the organization of material will depend partly on the nature of the subject matter and partly on the characteristics of the trainees, their background and experience, and their ability to comprehend and absorb.

Where the demonstration method of presentation is to be used, it will be necessary (1) to find a suitable place and (2) to assemble materials, equipment, and supplies. Equipment should be limited to essentials in order to keep the demonstration as simple as possible, but any apparatus that is required should be set up in working order in advance. This will avoid wasting the time of the trainees and, as well, awkward periods of waiting while the trainer tinkers with the equipment.

Types of Training Materials. There is a wide variety of materials for training purposes. Each of the more common types listed below has its particular uses; no attempt will be made here to discuss the details pertaining to each item.

Production manuals	Handbooks [21]
Job instruction	Case studies
Outlines	Work problems
Texts	Question and answer training
Glossaries	materials
Correspondence courses	Tests
Records	Playlets
Miscellaneous visual aids — charts,	Motion pictures [22]
maps, etc.[22]	Sound slide films [22]

Putting the Training Program in Operation

In considering the problems involved in giving instruction, i.e., putting the training program into operation, one may almost resort to the use of the reporter's familiar: who, which, what, when, where, and why?

[21] For particularly good examples, see *Manual for Public Health Nurses* (Maine State Bureau of Health, Augusta, 1946) and Federal Security Agency, *A Manual for Executives and Personnel Officers* (Washington, 1944). The table of contents of the Maine manual is divided into five parts, dealing respectively with administration, family health, communicable disease control, group activities, and the community. Employee handbooks may also be very useful for other purposes than training.

[22] Industry has made extensive use of visual aids for training purposes, and government made some progress in this field during World War II; see Petrie, Frank A., "The Training Film in Our War Effort," *Personnel Administration*, June, 1942, pp. 13–15. The Philadelphia Council compiled in 1944 an extensive list of visual aids available on loan within the area, while the Philadelphia Signal Depot issued a leaflet on the use of training films.

Who is to be trained? What kind of training is to be given? Where is the training to be done? Who is going to do it? How is it going to be done?

Who Is to Be Trained? The secret of efficient training is to be able to give suitable instruction to the minimum number of the right persons for the minimum period of time necessary to accomplish the desired results. A decision must be made in each case as to who the right persons are. Can the problem be solved best by training supervisors or by employees, or must both be trained? Or is it a problem involving management training? Any one of these may properly be undertaken, but it is important that the problem be thought through in advance so that effort is not wasted in trying to train members of the wrong group.

Management Training Conferences. During World War II the United States Civil Service Commission instituted management-training conferences, based upon a plan used by a commercial oil company. Under this arrangement each supervisor attended two conferences each week — one presided over by his supervisor; and one of his own supervisors, over which he himself presided. The conferences at the various levels were designated by the letters A, B, C, D, the first including the top layer of supervision, such as division chiefs; the second, heads of sections; and so on. Every single employee in the organization was a member of and was required to attend a training conference weekly. These conferences were to provide a two-way track for the flow of information and instruction from the top down and for the flow of suggestions and information from the lower levels up.[23]

The plan may have had theoretical advantages but so far as actual operation was concerned, it was not successful. The conferences, plus all the other details that were necessary to conduct the operations of the agency, kept supervisors in conferences for an excessive number of hours each week. The disease of "conferencitis" became so serious at one time that supervisors setting out to attend one conference met themselves coming back from the previous one. The whole program made it quite clear that the conference technique, like most other things, was subject to abuse. There was virtually no planning for the actual conduct of these conferences, which consumed vast numbers of man-hours that might have been devoted to some much more useful purpose.

Supervisory Training. A more workable plan was developed at the Philadelphia Signal Depot by William J. Eisenberg, at the time head of the

---

[23] United States Civil Service Commission, *Management Training Conferences Handbook* (Washington, 1943).

Training Section and later Personnel Officer. His plan called for weekly conferences over a period of nine weeks, with monthly or semimonthly conferences thereafter as required. A depot committee representing all divisions was set up to work with the head of the training section in selecting topics and in planning the conferences. The methods of carrying out the plans so agreed upon were developed by the training staff, the members of which led the conference groups. Every supervisory employee of the depot was assigned to a conference group, each of which was limited to twenty-five persons. Assignments were made deliberately to cut across division lines, so that each group was representative of the depot as a whole.

For each supervisor a loose-leaf folder was prepared. It contained his conference assignments and an outline of the conference organization and procedure. Additional material could be inserted at each meeting. Although the major subject of each conference was selected by the depot committee, the training staff made it a point to include discussion of any changes in rules and regulations which should be known and understood by supervisors and passed on to employees. For a number of reasons this plan proved extremely helpful in the operation of the depot. Top management gave that full cooperation without which success in such a program is impossible. Conferences were limited in number; after the initial series they were scheduled for once a month, unless additional meetings were really needed. Finally, the agenda were carefully planned, and the conferences themselves were conducted by trained leaders, not by supervisors with no skill whatever in the art of conference leadership.

The Philadelphia Navy Yard with its huge Industrial Department approached the problem of supervisory training from another angle, establishing three different types of courses. The first, called presupervisory or instructor training, is built on the premise that one of the principal duties of a supervisor is to know how to give instruction on the job to the employee who needs it. The course goes into job analysis and methods of instruction. The trainee has to go into a shop and teach specific operations to someone foreign to that particular trade. When he successfully completes this assignment, he is regarded as qualified for the second type of training — the use of the conference method and the actual handling of human beings. The conferences deal with the development of leadership, safety-mindedness, morale, and the cooperative spirit among employees. The third aspect of the program involves advanced training in conference leadership. Twenty key supervisors, two from each of the principal shops, are put in training for two months;

upon completion of the course, they start out with about twenty supervisors to discuss mutual shop problems.

During the war approximately four hundred supervisors were in training, all of them in groups conducted by one of their own colleagues. The purposes of the program included not only the training and development of supervisors but the solving of some of the problems that exist in every large organization. Sometimes these problems remain buried because management does not know about them; at other times, because management does not know what to do about them. The conferences were designed to bring the problems to light and to develop suitable solutions for them upon the basis of democratic discussion.[24]

Where Is the Training to Be Done? The answer to the question as to where the training shall be done depends to a large extent upon the size and resources of the agency and upon the type of training required. If the problem involves the training of employees on the job, the chances are that the supervisors should be instructed first so that either alone or in cooperation with the members of the training staff they can in turn instruct the employees.

If group instruction off the job is to be undertaken, other questions present themselves. Will the instruction be given in the agency or outside? If the former, will members of the agency staff do the instructing or will instructors be brought in from outside? In a large agency it is probable that it will be done in the agency itself because it is less difficult to move an instructor from place to place than a whole group of trainees. Very often when instructors are to be brought in from outside, it is possible to secure faculty members from local educational institutions, and the course may become a part of the extension or off-campus program of the university. On the other hand, some qualified member of the staff may be called upon to give similar instruction outside the agency. In such a case certain employees may be advised or perhaps required to take the course.

By Whom Is the Training to Be Done? The question of the proper location of the training function is a matter on which there is much difference of opinion. There are several alternatives. Responsibility may be divided, as it must necessarily be in the case of orientation training. It may be centered in the supervisor. It may be made the principal responsibility of a central training unit which organizationally is either a part of or separate from the personnel office of the agency. Or again,

[24] See Whitelaw, John B., "An Approach to Supervisory Training," *Personnel Administration*, September, 1947, pp. 39–42, 46.

the agency may rely mainly upon local educational institutions — vocational schools, evening and extension schools, and local universities and colleges. Each of these solutions has its place, depending largely on the needs of the agency and the exigencies of the local situation.

Most important, perhaps, is the question of centralization, concerning which there are two principal viewpoints: one, that centralization is desirable; the other, that training, to be effective, cannot be delegated but must be the responsibility of the supervisor. In favor of the first it is pointed out that administrators know too much about their jobs and as a result are inclined to swamp the employee with details. Seldom do they possess a knowledge of educational psychology, which is essential to effective instruction. Again, the supervisor is often too busy to give proper attention to his training responsibility and delegates this important function to a subordinate who, in addition to being less interested in the project, may often regard the new employee as a competitor. If similar or identical training is needed in several of the offices in a large and far-flung organization, it is wasteful to have the projects planned and prepared by each separate unit.

On the other hand, there are definite advantages in decentralized training — training by the operating supervisor — that cannot be gained under any other plan. It quickly establishes the supervisor-employee relationship. It gives the supervisor an opportunity to learn the employee's strength and weakness. It gives the employee the advantage of learning his supervisor's attitude toward work requirements and the organization's policies and procedures. Only the operating supervisor, it is claimed, can give to the training the atmosphere of essential instruction rather than that of schoolroom theory. He alone intimately knows what the employee needs for success.

John E. Moore, in reporting a discussion of this problem held in Washington a few years ago, notes that a successful program may be a compromise between these two points of view. "There are areas of training for both the supervisor and the central training division. The staff-training man must be the moving spirit in the organization, sometimes working in the dark until the spark catches and some interested executive 'gets religion.' Under any circumstances, training must deal with real problems." [25]

How Is the Training to Be Done? No magic formula can be presented for determining the manner in which training should be done in any given instance. There are a great many possible methods, each of which has its proper uses, alone or in combination with others, depending

[25] Moore, *op. cit.*

upon the needs of the agency and the type of persons being trained. The list follows, with some brief comment indicating the particular usefulness of each method.

Course Instruction. This is useful when an agency has a group of persons performing some particular function, the basic concepts of which can be presented in a formal course; a course, for instance, in elementary or advanced statistics or in the underlying principles of the social security program.

Lectures. Lectures may be an integral part of the course technique. The author on one occasion used a series of lecturers from the war agencies in combination with a question and answer period at the conclusion of the lectures, for giving the group some idea of the powers and duties and program of the several agencies for which their recruiting efforts were being carried on. The basic theory was that the recruiters could do a better job if they knew what the people they recruited were expected to do.

Inspection Tours and Field Trips. Inspection tours are especially useful in connection with orientation programs where the purpose is to give new employees a quick over-all view of the operations of the establishment. An inspection tour is confined to the agency itself; a field trip includes other agencies engaged in the performance of the same or similar functions. Such trips give experienced employees an opportunity to compare methods and results. If hastily planned, they may be little more than sight-seeing expeditions; if properly planned, they may be very valuable to the employees and to the agency.

Demonstrations. A demonstration is the process of showing how something is done or how it works. This may be a very useful device, especially in the case of newer employees.

Simulated Situations. Simulated situations involve the creation of training situations that are identical in all essential respects with actual working conditions. This device is a practical one with any group of employees but is especially useful with new employees who are not particularly familiar with the working conditions in the establishment.

The Laboratory. The use of a laboratory usually involves research techniques. For employees engaged in such pursuits, the use of laboratory methods may be the most valuable means of instruction.

Conferences and Discussions. These techniques have already been discussed. Their use is based upon the assumption that the process of a group considering the facts and arriving at a given conclusion constitutes a more valuable and a more impressive experience than is obtained by the lecture method. In other words, it is more effective to have a group discover the truth or a fact than it is to have them told about it.

Institutes and Short Courses. The institute is usually a short and intensive course of study to which the student devotes his full working time. It covers a clearly defined field of knowledge which has been carefully outlined in advance by the instructor. When the attempt is made to cover a broad range of subject matter, such courses may be characterized as "quickie courses."

Seminars. The seminar is an old and well-established educational technique in which, under trained and presumably skillful leadership, the students try over a considerable period of time to make a careful and intensive study of the particular problem before them. It is extremely useful with mature students but may be a waste of time for the uninitiated.

Over-all Programs of Training for the Public Service

Training, like other phases of the personnel program, must be carried on primarily at the operating level under the supervision and leadership of the agency's personnel office. There is, however, a great deal that can be done by law and by administrative action at the top level to stimulate training activity in departments and agencies at all levels of administration.

Responsibility of the Central Personnel Agency. Under Executive Order No. 7916 of June 24, 1938, the Federal departments and agencies were authorized and directed to establish training facilities. The Civil Service Commission interpreted this directive to mean that such courses could be made available in three ways: (1) within and under the direction of the separate departments and agencies for the benefit of their own employees; (2) by the coordination of the activities of different agencies and institutions whenever cooperative action is necessary or advisable; (3) by the initiation and direction of certain types of training courses by the Commission itself.

In addition to providing leadership and guidance in the development of training programs, the Commission through its Consulting Service was able to provide the assistance of specialists in training methods, to aid line supervisors in planning, conducting, and appraising such instruction, and to organize and direct courses which cross lines of supervisional jurisdiction. As a central clearinghouse for information on training matters, the Commission also made available information regarding training programs in all Federal departments and agencies.[26]

Training Programs for Local Officials. The responsibilities of the central personnel agency in the states with state-wide merit-system legislation is parallel to that of the Federal Commission. The need for developing training programs for municipal and other local officials was originally recognized by their own organizations, but since 1936, under the impetus of Federal legislation, it has been taken over by the state departments of education. The development in New York may be taken as illustrative. Training schools for policemen and firemen were established by the New York State Conference of Mayors in 1928. By 193 the Conference had expanded its training programs to include twent groups of municipal employees. By 1935 the Regents recognized th soundness of the program by granting an educational corporate chart

---

[26] On these points, see *The United States Civil Service Commission's Part in Fede Training,* and *Training Programs in the Federal Service.* The latter describes the p grams in thirty-four Federal departments and agencies.

for the operation of the schools. This corporation, the Municipal Training Institute of New York State, was the first educational institution of its kind in the country.[27]

Attendance of city and village employees at training schools in the ten-year period from 1928 to 1938 totaled 62,568. Of these, 42,708 were firemen; 14,565 were policemen; the remainder was made up of such groups as assessors, city and village clerks, financial officers and employees, milk and dairy inspectors, sewage-works operators, and commissioners and employees of parks, public welfare, and public works. During a period of less than three years prior to our entry into World War II nearly 8000 county and town officers, justices of the peace, and town highway superintendents attended similar training programs.

Federal Aid for Training of Local Officials. The Federal government entered the picture in an important way — through the passage of the George-Deen Act in 1936, for the further development of vocational education. It stated specifically that "such moneys as are provided under authority of this act for trade and industrial subjects, and public and other service occupations, may be expended. . . ." This legislation led to a great and sudden expansion of training activity for local government officials. In state after state, public service institutes patterned after the one in New York were set up; with the aid of local educational institutions, state leagues of municipalities, and such national organizations as the American Municipal Association and the International City Managers Association, much progress was made in a short time. While these activities were to some extent suspended during the war, their resumption since that time has been evident in many jurisdictions.[28]

SELECTED REFERENCES

The literature in this field is voluminous, particularly so in relation to private employment. For a general list of references down to the war period, see Benton, Mildred, and Buckardt, Henry L., *Personnel Administration and Personnel Training: A Selected List of References* (Department of Agriculture, Soil Conservation Service, Washington, 1940).

Civil Service Assembly of the United States and Canada, *Employee Training in the Public Service* (Chicago, 1941). Another CSA committee provides an excellent summary of basic principles and procedures in the training field.

---

[27] University of the State of New York, *Training in the Public Service in New York State: Program and Policies*, pp. 8–9 (Albany, 1938), and Hunter, Robert L., "The Illinois State In-Service Training Program," *Public Personnel Review*, July, 1947, pp. 138–143.

[28] For the early stages of this development, see Hawke, Jerry R., *Training for Public Service Occupations* (United States Office of Education, Washington, 1938).

Furia, John J., and Winson, Harold A., *Spending Money to Save Money: In-Service Training in New York City* (Bureau of Training, New York City Civil Service Commission, 1940). A good discussion of the use of an important type of training in our largest city.

Hall, Milton, *Training Your Employees* (Society for Personnel Administration, Washington, 1940). A competent Federal administrator gives suggestions to executives and supervisors.

Hogan, Ralph M., and Hull, Fern L., *Training Employees to Apply Regulations and Written Instructions* (United States Civil Service Commission, Washington, 1943). Two Federal people deal with training as a solution for a very difficult and important problem in supervision.

International City Managers Association, *Conference Method Training in Management* (Chicago, 1946). A manual on the use of one of the newer training techniques at the municipal level.

Lambie, Morris B., Ed., *University Training for the National Service* (University of Minnesota Press, 1932). The original survey, covering early efforts in this field; for the current standard treatise on university training for the public service, with analysis of the programs in operation in selected institutions, see Graham, George A., *Education for Public Administration* (Public Administration Service, Chicago, 1941).

McLean, Joseph E., Ed., *The Public Service and University Education* (Princeton University Press, 1949). Symposium on how to find, train, and retrain talented individuals for the public service.

From the United States Civil Service Commission:
The United States Civil Service Commission's Part in Federal Training (Washington, 1939).
Training Programs in the Federal Service (Washington, 1942).
Procedures in Developing a Training Project (Washington, 1942).

From the United States Department of Agriculture, Office of Personnel:
Training Your Employees (Washington, 1941).
Suggestions to Supervisors for Quickly and Effectively Training New Employees and Developing Understudies (Washington, 1941).
Training for Personnel Replacements in Wartime (Washington, 1943).

From the United States Department of Labor, Apprentice-Training Service:
The National Apprenticeship Program (Washington, 1947).
Report on the Apprentice Training Program of the Tennessee Valley Authority (Washington, 1947).

From the War Department, Quartermaster General:
Handbook for the Director of Civilian Training (Washington, 1943).

10

EMPLOYEE RELATIONS
AND EMPLOYEE SERVICES

THE field of employee relations, which was extensively developed in private industry before World War II, first attained recognition in government during the war and then chiefly in some of the larger industrial establishments. It embodies a number of problems, each subsidiary to the basic one of developing and maintaining good morale. The subsidiary problems include, on the one hand, relations with employee unions if such exist — a kind of trouble-shooting responsibility of management in its relations with its employees. On the other hand, there are the personal and general advisory services which counselors render to employees in the solution of their individual problems. The benefits of these services both to management and employees are very great.

A broad program of employee health and welfare services bolsters morale (and production) by eliminating those causes of dissatisfaction which develop into issues and cause strife between management and labor. Such a program is fundamentally sound from the point of view of both groups, and it is as important in public as in private agencies.

The Problem of Morale

Morale is a fundamental problem in any organization. It is primarily the developing and maintaining of good human relations. Some unfortunate attempts to belittle morale-building programs have been based upon a misconception of their purpose, which is not to develop a Pollyanna attitude but rather to foster in the mind of the employee a firm conviction, based upon fact and experience, that "this is a good place to work" and that the undertaking in which he is engaged is worth while. Such a conviction results only from a sincere interest in the worker's problems and from a real but not ostentatious concern for his welfare. When such a conviction is achieved, when workers generally believe that every reasonable effort is being made to give them a fair deal, the superficial aspects of good working relations will to a large extent take care of themselves.

It would be difficult to overemphasize the importance of good morale in any organization. Its presence is reflected in the efficiency of the whole organization, in its productive capacity, in a minimum labor turnover above what is always to be expected from natural causes, and in the growth and development of individual employees. The maintenance of good morale is more difficult today than formerly, mainly because organizations are larger and life itself is infinitely more complicated. In the past the problem did not arise in the small organizations then existing or else, because of its small proportions, it was unrecognized. In large organizations the growth of minor differences into major issues and the multiplication of these issues create general dissatisfaction and distrust and promote industrial strife.

Factors Sustaining and Undermining Morale. One of the factors that tend to undermine morale is the highly impersonal relationship between management and labor which results from sheer bigness. The worker loses his identity as a person and becomes a mere cog in a huge organization. The fact that his absence may scarcely be noted wounds his pride. If differences arise, he as an individual is powerless to adjust them.

The first need, therefore, is to find some way of re-establishing the individual relationships which existed when units were small. One way is to establish an "open-door" policy. This means that management and supervisors generally make every reasonable effort to be accessible to individual employees who desire an opportunity to discuss their work or the problems of the organization. Management may have other things to do besides talking to Joe Doaks about work methods or assignments in the assembly unit, but these things are important to Joe. And perhaps management has, from the point of view of keeping a smoothly working organization, few more important tasks. The very fact that employees know they *can* drop in to talk with the boss is important, whether they actually do it very often or not. When they know they can do so, many will hesitate to impose upon his time.

A second requirement in sustaining morale, as pointed out by Fowler McCormick in an address before the American Management Association,[1] is to study human-relations technique in management. In view of the size and importance of the problem, it is amazing that efforts to solve it are so recent and so relatively meager in extent. Research is essential in the whole field of knowledge of human beings as individuals and as members of groups.

A third requirement, platitudinous though it may sound, is to make practical application of the Golden Rule. Good morale is an achieve-

---

[1] News report in *New York Times*, February 26, 1947.

ment. In most instances it is the result of a consciously developed program. One cannot moralize it into existence or gain it by wagging his finger at people, "jawing" them, or urging proper methods of conduct.

A Five Point Program. (1) The Adequacy of the Supervisor. The supervisor is of key importance in establishing the emotional tone of an organization. The opportunities he has to make or break morale or to provide incentive are innumerable. The way he gives orders, the way he makes job assignments, the manner in which he offers disciplinary correction, his care and patience in instructing subordinates — these are but a few typical situations in which his understanding of human nature and his ability to cope with the peculiarities of individual psychologies set the foundation for management by consent.

(2) Nonfinancial Incentives. In government, where financial incentives are difficult to obtain, nonfinancial incentives should be fully utilized. The validity of this approach has long been recognized in private industry. This incentive is a formal device which appeals to the various intrinsic drives, other than the acquisitive instinct, that motivate people. It uses symbols, rewards, and recognition to achieve a desired end. It appeals to interest in work, curiosity, the competitive spirit, the desire to excel, the creative impulse, and similar drives. Competition, public recognition, prizes, awards of one kind or another symbolize the individual's accomplishment. The fullest use of these methods has usually not been achieved because the layman supervisor seldom possesses the knowledge of a trained psychologist as to what makes human beings "tick."

(3) Financial Incentives. This plan recognizes extra production by financial remuneration. The form varies from a simple piece rate to the more intricate patterns of efficiency plans and even the Bedeaux plan. Extensive use was made of these devices in war plants. Because of statutory limitations on government pay plans, special legislation was necessary to extend the arrangements to government establishments. Providing greater incentive toward maximum production far outweighs any compensation aspect of this plan.[2]

(4) Interpretation of the Job. Of fundamental importance in developing an interested, alert force of employees is the need for giving meaning and significance to their jobs. The number who understand

[2] See Baker, John C., *Executive Salaries and Bonus Plans* (McGraw-Hill, New York, 1938); Gantt, Henry L., *Work, Wages and Profits* (Engineering Magazine Company, New York, 1919); Louden, J. K., *Wage Incentives* (Wiley, New York, 1944); Lytle, Charles W., *Wage Incentive Methods*, Revised Edition (Ronald Press, New York, 1942); and War Production Board, Management Consultant Division, *A Handbook on Wage Incentive Plans* (Washington, 1945).

not only the importance of their jobs but their relation to each other and to the work of the organization as a whole is disappointingly small. This situation is the responsibility of and a challenge to management. Bulletin boards, company organs, training, departmental meetings, intelligent instruction, departmental tours are but a few of the ways in which meaning can be given to the humblest job.

(5) Employee-Attitude Survey. In shaping a program most executives and personnel men consult only the experience of other executives or such sources of information as books and professional journals. But one of the best ways to find out how a program is going over is to consult the employees who are affected by it. This is the essence of the employee-attitude survey; it means literally that the uninfluenced reactions of the employees are sought. Of the wide variety of techniques that have been tried, the best emphasizes candor.[3] The survey must be conducted by an impartial group in whom employees have the utmost confidence.

Employee Participation in Management. If participation of employees in management finds an obstacle in the size of modern organizations, it finds assistance and support in other ways. For one thing it is aided by a definite change in attitude in the field of management-labor relations. Many old-line employers were tough; they would tell those "blankety-blank so-and-sos" what to do. There was contempt on the part of management for workers, fear and hate on the part of workers toward management. This has largely given way to a philosophy of teamwork and partnership. The "I will show you who is running this place" attitude has been largely replaced by a "we will run this place together" attitude. The question then becomes one of finding ways by which the employees can resolve their own differences and crystallize their views in such manner as to present them and have them considered by management before, not after, decisions are made.

Management can and should help to develop such teamwork, which will pay dividends in greater understanding and support of the policies so adopted. Means of securing active employee participation must not only be developed but be used when developed. One means that has proved useful is the employee suggestion system, which will be discussed later in this chapter. Another is the recognition of particularly meritorious service by means of salary increases, bonuses, promotions, or otherwise.[4]

[3] Brecht, Robert B., "Morale and Incentives," an address before the Philadelphia Federal Council of Personnel Administration, May 3, 1944, and Cole, Remsen J., "A Survey of Employee Attitudes," *Public Opinion Quarterly*, September, 1940, pp. 497–506.
[4] See Webb, James E., "Main Factors in Administrative Morale," *Personnel Administration*, March, 1947, pp. 3–6.

Employee participation in administration is dependent upon and indicative of the degree of the employee's understanding of the total problem of the organization. Developing such understanding is but another method of reinforcing the employee's sense of belonging. Early in 1947 the Library of Congress adopted an interesting program designed in part to achieve this objective.[5] The Library had long had a Professional Forum with a program determined by the Librarian in consultation with a Board of Managers. Under the new plan the Board of Managers was replaced by a Staff Advisory Committee of twelve members, two selected by each of the two unions, four selected by the nonunion members of the staff, and four selected by the Librarian. The term is for one year, subject to re-eligibility. The Committee elects its own chairman. The monthly Professional Forum meetings continue, under the general supervision of the Staff Advisory Committee.[6]

In a manner somewhat similar to the management training program of the United States Civil Service Commission, staff discussion groups are organized to include the entire staff of the Library. "A division or other separate unit having not more than twenty-five staff members will meet as a single discussion group, except where the work arrangements prevent this, in which case two groups shall be organized. In larger divisions, the staff shall be organized in groups not exceeding twenty-five members each, preferably along sectional lines. . . . Attendance at meetings of the Staff Discussion Groups, as at meetings of the Staff Advisory Committee and the Professional Forum, is part of the work assignment of the persons concerned, and is on official time." [7]

Department directors are responsible for organizing the groups and designating temporary discussion leaders. When the groups assemble, each is directed to elect a group leader and an alternate group leader to serve for one year. Each meeting is divided into two equal parts, the first devoted to a topic set by the Librarian, "which will be the topic scheduled for the following meeting of the Professional Forum." Back-

---

[5] The development of this program may be traced in a series of General and Special Orders of the Librarian. See G. O. No. 1308, December 12, 1946, and S. O. Nos. 275, May 7, 1946; 306, October 15, 1946; 318, December 11, 1946; and 324, January 1, 1947.
[6] To "some thoughtless people" who had questioned the wisdom of providing as much encouragement and organized opportunity for the discussion of issues by the rank and file as this plan affords, the Librarian replied with a quotation from a speech delivered by Mr. Justice Frankfurter at the Willkie Award dinner in Washington, February 28, 1947 (*Congressional Record*, March 3, 1947, p. A843):

The answer to the defects of our society is not denial of the democratic faith. The answer is more loyal practice of that faith . . . a democratic society presupposes confidence and candor in the relations of men with one another and active collaboration for the common ends of life. For we are enlisted in a common enterprise — the bold experiment of freedom. It involves the most exacting collaborative effort. It demands the exercise of reason on the largest scale and self-discipline of the highest order. . . .
[7] On the use of this type of conference procedure, see Lehman, W. P., "The Management Training Conference Plans," *Public Personnel Review*, May, 1942, pp. 138–144.

ground information is provided for these topics. Each group must prepare a summary report of each part of each group meeting and submit it in duplicate to the department director within three days. One copy is forwarded to the Director of Personnel for study and comment and for submission with comment and recommendations to the Librarian. "The Library administration agrees to notify groups of the disposition of any recommendations they may make." This is extremely important, as will be noted later.

Employee Relations

The term "employee relations," as interpreted during the war period, included the whole field covered by this chapter. Postwar developments indicate a tendency — which has been accepted for the purposes of this discussion — to restrict its application to the relations of management to its employees and especially management-labor relations so far as they relate to employee unions, collective bargaining, and the right to strike. Other aspects of the employee welfare program as formerly conceived are now spoken of as employee services; health and welfare activities are usually dealt with separately. These problems will be discussed in the following section of this chapter. Such items as suggestion systems and procedures for the handling of grievances are undoubtedly aspects of labor relations and are considered here.

Suggestion Systems. A development in the public service, during and since World War II, has been the use of suggestion systems. Such systems, coupled with special monetary compensation, were widely used in wartime, but there is no reason why they cannot be equally useful in peacetime, with or without a monetary reward. They are based upon the valid assumption that intelligent employees, engaged in performing an operation, can often see ways and means of producing more with less expenditure of time, money, or effort. Suggestions of this type mean greater efficiency and lower costs.[8] Former Director of the Budget Webb expressed this idea when he said that such systems "not only provide a fresh flow of ideas but can also increase the sense of participation throughout the organization and thus invigorate morale."

In industry employees were often reluctant to offer suggestions

---

[8] See Donaho, John A., "Employee Suggestion Systems in the Public Service," *Public Personnel Review*, October, 1945, pp. 230–235, and Zausmer, Garson, "The New York State Employee Suggestion Program," *ibid.*, October, 1947, pp. 200–204; Staats, Herbert E., *Recognition of Constructive Suggestions by State Employees* (Minnesota Division of Administrative Management, St. Paul, 1943), and United States Civil Service Commission, *Suggestion Systems: A Selected List of References* (Washington, 1944).

either because they thought it might mean fewer jobs for them or larger profits for the company. The monetary reward was necessary to obtain results. In government agencies reluctance was due to the fact that so often after suggestions were turned in, nothing happened or someone else took credit for the improvement. This defect can be over-come — in fact, it must be if the system is to work. Even here a finan-cial reward helps. In May, 1947, the *Washington Post* reported that twenty-seven employees from the District and thirteen states received a total of $1125 for submitting ideas that led to improvements in op-erations. In New York State in the same year employees were awarded cash prizes ranging as high as $500 for suggesting new ways to increase government efficiency.

One of the best plans that has come to the writer's attention is that developed under the leadership of Dr. Luther H. Evans of the Library of Congress. In the staff discussion meetings previously described, Li-brary employees are given an opportunity to offer suggestions on any subject if they believe the idea would contribute to greater efficiency in operations. Record is made of all suggestions, and they are passed up through the Director of the Division, the Director of Personnel, ulti-mately to the Librarian. In his office they are edited, given case num-bers, and mimeographed for distribution at the next Professional Forum meeting. These pamphlets sometimes run to thirty or forty mimeo-graphed pages. The disposition of *every* recommendation is shown. If the Library administration either deems it undesirable or finds it impos-sible to carry out a given recommendation, the reasons are plainly stated.

Grievance Procedures. Another important element in a well-rounded employee-relations program is a formalized grievance procedure. Here again considerable progress was made during wartime, although the need had long been recognized. The United States Civil Service Com-mission has defined a grievance as "an employee's expressed feeling of dissatisfaction with aspects of his working conditions and relationships which are outside his control." The President's Committee on Admin-istrative Management had recommended in 1937 that improved meth-ods for handling grievances be devised.[9] Carefully formulated proce-dures are now in effect in Federal departments and agencies as well as in the more progressive state and local jurisdictions. These plans in-

---

[9] *Report with Special Studies*, p. 66, cited in Knapp, Daniel C., "Administering Federal Grievance Procedure," *Public Personnel Review*, April, 1947, pp. 96–101, which deals particularly with Federal installations in the Columbus area; see also McClure, Rus-sell E., and Wall, Hugo, "Handling Employee Grievances in Wichita," *ibid.*, July, 1947, pp. 127–131.

clude not only the handling of grievances within the agency but possible appeals to a higher authority. The accompanying table for the State of New York indicates the major causes of employee dissatisfaction, the time limits placed upon appeals, and the agency designated to consider them.

New York State Civil Service System

TIME TABLE FOR APPEALS *

ACTION	TIME	APPEAL TO
Disciplinary Action	20 days or 4 months	Civil Service Commission Courts
Examination Marks	20 days to look over papers PLUS 20 days to file appeal after seeing papers	Civil Service Commission
Service Ratings	5 days On unsatisfactory performance reports, immediate request for "Statement of Facts" PLUS 2 weeks after receipt of "Statement of Facts"	Department Appeal Committee, Civil Service Commission
	2 weeks after receipt of "Statement of Facts"	Civil Service Commission
Classification	60 days after notice of action is received from Classification Board No time limit on appeals	Civil Service Commission Classification Board
Salary	60 days after notice of original allocation	Salary Board
Other Grievances	No time limit	Departmental Personnel Officer, Personnel Council

* *State Personnel News*, July, 1947, p. 3.

Both advantages and disadvantages connected with such a plan are generally recognized. Among the former are the bolstering of employee attitudes and morale; the alleviation of pressures by members of the legislative bodies upon administrators in regard to individual employee complaints; bringing to top management information regarding the effectiveness of its first-line supervisors; and the tendency to reduce turnover rates. The dangers lie in the possible undermining of the supervisor's authority through reversal of his decisions and a possible negative effect on employer-employee cooperation in other matters, occasioned by the desire to "get even."

Formal grievance procedures are designed to make mandatory — automatically or upon the employee's request — the formation of an appeals committee when a grievance reaches a designated level in the organizational hierarchy. In field establishments, for instance, this is likely to be the commanding officer or the chief of the local installation. It has been shown that the mere existence of such procedures gives assurance to employees that they can obtain an impartial hearing and this in turn has a wholesome effect on morale. Actually, in a well administered organization the frequent use of such procedures should not be necessary. When used, however, they serve to give uniformity of interpretation to personnel policies.

Employee Unions. A number of unions of government workers have at times and in particular circumstances made some progress in enrolling members. Such progress has on the whole been rather sporadic and has not in most agencies been supported by a continuing interest. The support given unions tends to fluctuate in direct relation to the quality and efficiency of the management. The propriety of such unions has long been questioned. In Great Britain permanent employees are under restrictions which prevent them from joining a union which includes noncivil servants. This traditional position of the government as employer was well stated by the late President Roosevelt in a letter written to the President of the National Federation of Federal Employees in August, 1937: [10]

The desire of government employees for fair and adequate pay, reasonable hours of work, safe and suitable working conditions, development of opportunities for advancement, facilities for fair and impartial consideration and review of grievance, and other objects of a proper employee-relations policy is basically no different from that of employees in private industry. Organizations on their part to present their views on such matters are both natural and logical,' but meticulous attention should be paid to the special relationships and obligations of public servants to the public itself and to the government. All government employees should realize that the process of collective bargaining, as usually understood, cannot be transplanted into the public service. It has its distinct and insurmountable limitations when applied to public personnel administration. The very nature and purposes of government make it impossible for administrative officials to represent fully or to bind the employer in neutral discussions with government employee organizations. The employer is the whole people, who speak by means of laws enacted by the Representatives in Congress.

Mr. Roosevelt recognized full well that "organizations of government employees have a logical place in government affairs." It remained, however, for the Federal Personnel Council, working over this problem nearly a decade later, to attempt to formulate a statement of policy governing the relations of Federal agencies with organized employees. The statement covered six points:

---

[10] Quoted from Ranen, Ellis, *Labor Relations in the Civil Service,* p. 2 (Conference on Civil Service Legislation, New York, 1941); see also La Due, Wendell R., "Significance of Legislation Forbidding Strikes by Public Employees," *Water and Sewage Works,* October, 1947, pp. 353–358.

1. Recognition of the right to organize; this was followed with the proviso that this should not be construed as recognition of the right of Federal employees to strike.
2. Declaration of open shop principle
3. Recognition of the duty of administrative officials to confer with representatives of employee organizations, and urging them actively to seek the advice and recommendations of such organizations in the formulation of policy on such matters
4. Administrative officials are permitted, within limitations established by law, to accord preferred status to a particular employee organization in representing all employees.
5. Agreements reached through conference and negotiation should be reduced to writing, published, and made accessible to all employees affected.
6. Administrative regulations relating to the conduct of such meetings shall be published and made readily accessible to all employees.

Thus while the current tendency is to accept the right of public employees to organize and to bargain collectively within the limits established by law, there is some reason to question the necessity of their doing so, at least in the Federal service, where legislation affecting employees is generally fair and reasonable. In many respects its provisions are generous as compared with conditions generally prevailing elsewhere. Since the hours, compensation, and conditions of work in the public service are largely controlled by law, there is little that a union can accomplish through collective bargaining. Although conditions in many state and local units are not good, little progress has been made in unionizing their employees. Legal limitations in government service are such that unions are obliged to confine their efforts mainly to the securing of better working conditions.[11]

At this point it is important to observe that poor working conditions and efforts at unionization go hand in hand. Week after week, headlines like these appear in the newspapers:

PUBLIC EMPLOYEES MAY FORM UNION
(83 workers in a small city)

CAPITOL HILL EMPLOYEES MAY ORGANIZE UNION
(Jerry Kluttz' Federal Diary tells of efforts of this group to obtain shorter hours and better pay)

CIVIL SERVICE GROUP EXPANDS – SCHOOL TEACHERS NOW ELIGIBLE TO JOIN EMPLOYEES ASSOCIATION

---

[11] Among the more useful titles are Magnusson, and Feldman, Herman, "Public Employees and Unions," National Municipal Review, April, 1946, pp. 161–165; also a report of a panel discussion on "Labor Unions and Collective Bargaining," Public Administration Review, Autumn, 1945, pp. 373–379.

This last item is interesting because it presents the problem in a new field. In the past, efforts at unionization have made little progress among teachers, outside of a few large cities, mainly because as members of a professional group teachers generally felt that trade union tactics had no place in their scheme of things. But this long-suffering group, with years of college work and professional training, observing janitors, charwomen, street cleaners, and garbage collectors receiving higher pay and better hours, were reluctantly forced to turn to unionization. In December, 1946, it was reported that the New York State Department of Labor had given final approval to the Civil Service Employees' Association, Inc., of New York, to extend its membership to eligible workers in all political subdivisions of the state, including school teachers.

Legal Status of Unions; Right to Strike. The growth of unions among government employees has been a more or less natural result of the expansion of government services, the increasing difficulty — if not the impossibility — of individual dealing, and the spread of unionization among workers in private employment. The last factor has undoubtedly had a considerable influence. The National Civil Service League recognizes, for instance, that "in keeping with the times, an administrator should not interfere with the mere act of association by employees." [12] Since the right of employees to organize may imply the right to use the pressure tactics of organized labor in private industry, a particular responsibility is placed upon government so to conduct its employer-employee relationships that public employees will not have need to use devices which, by reason of their status as civil servants, may be denied them.

The right of public employees to go on strike regardless of the seriousness of their grievances is a matter upon which there is wide disagreement. There are those who take the view given classic expression by Calvin Coolidge in terse phrases at the time of the Boston police strike in 1919, that no group of public employees has a right to strike against the public interest in any place or at any time. During the 1947 legislative sessions, after a wave of such strikes in 1946, a number of states undertook to write this philosophy into law. [13] Taking an oppo-

---

[12] *Employee Organizations in the Public Service,* p. 11 (New York, 1946).

[13] At least ten states in 1947 outlawed strikes by some or all public employees. Heretofore, Virginia was the only state to ban strikes by public servants. Michigan, Missouri, Nebraska, New York, Pennsylvania, and Texas passed laws banning strikes by public employees generally, while Indiana, Minnesota, New Jersey, and Washington outlawed strikes for certain groups of public employees. Indiana and New Jersey banned strikes by public utility employees, while Minnesota outlawed strikes by employees of hospitals. For a discussion of the New York law, see "Anti-strike Law for New York Public

site position are those extreme believers in the trade-union principle who profess to see no difference between the obligations of public and of private employment and who therefore view strikes of public employees with complete equanimity as being necessary to obtain recognition of their rights.

Those who take a middle ground seem to have made some progress in gaining public support. This group recognizes the right of *all* employees to strike, whether publicly or privately employed, *except* those who are engaged in rendering services essential to the health and safety of the community. This exception is extremely important and includes some persons in both employment categories. Among public employees it would obviously include fire and police forces, water works employees, garbage and refuse collectors; among private employees, those of essential public utility services such as gas and electricity, public transportation, and possibly communications — all associated with businesses long recognized by law as affected with a public interest. Any general agreement to accept such a principle imposes upon management in these enterprises an especially grave responsibility for so conducting their relations with employees that there can be no conceivable justification for a strike.[14]

The adoption of such a principle does not in any way settle the problem so far as it relates to teachers. During the first half of the school year 1946–1947 twelve major strikes involving more than 2000 teachers and 50,000 pupils were reported. The largest and most significant occurred in Buffalo, New York; many others were threatened but were not actually called, including one in New York City. Educators themselves divide into opposing groups on this question. Schools are essential in the long run of course, but they are not so immediately essential that their closing for a few days is a vital matter. After all they are not in continuous session, the length of the standard school year being approximately 180 days.

Perhaps an answer to the whole problem is being worked out, not by the passage of harsh legislation which may be unenforceable but in the development of self-restraint and a sense of public responsibility on the part of the unionized employees themselves. In this respect the action of the 1946 convention of the twenty-nine year old National Federation of Federal Employees may be significant. This group refused to

Service," *Good Government*, May–June, 1947, and for the general problem, "Have Public Employees the Right to Strike?" *National Municipal Review*, September, 1941. Roger N. Baldwin answers "yes," pp. 515–517; H. Eliot Kaplan, "no," pp. 518–523; Sterling D. Spero, "maybe," pp. 524–528, 551.
[14] With regard to a familiar "solution" of such problems during wartime, see Vietheer, George C., "The Government Seizure Stratagem in Labor Disputes," *Public Personnel Review*, Spring, 1946, pp. 149–156.

invoke the traditional tools of trade unionism to secure higher wages for Federal workers. While it adopted unanimously a resolution calling upon Congress to raise salaries and give a more liberal retirement system, it rejected pleas for the use of collective bargaining, the strike, and the closed shop.[15]

If such a policy were to be generally adopted by government employee organizations, the task of the unions would become one of presenting, with the force of organized numbers behind them, the point of view of employees regarding matters relating to pay, hours, and working conditions. Such a function has its uses from the point of view of management as well as that of the workers. The union serves as a shock absorber for individual complaints. Its constant watchfulness tends to promote the best interests of a career service, and it serves or may serve as a powerful influence for better public relations. It may provide support for top management in resisting unwarranted reductions in force or cuts in appropriations.

Employee Services

The employee welfare program is many sided, including welfare associations, credit unions, recreation programs and associations, counseling, and other types of activities carried on by and for the benefit of employees. Health and safety programs, sometimes considered a separate function, are included here. Some of the more important items are discussed briefly in the paragraphs which follow.

Credit Unions. The first credit union in this country was established in 1909 under a special act of the New Hampshire legislature. Massachusetts followed in 1910. By 1934 state laws were on the books of all but five states, not to mention the Federal Credit Union Act. Under this authorization the employees of most large governmental organizations now operate such a financial institution, a number of them having substantial resources. In the field, membership may be open to all government employees without regard to agency.

A credit union is a cooperative enterprise, an association of employees in a department, agency, or establishment, without regard to rank, pay, race, color, or creed. The members agree to pool a portion of their savings to form a fund from which loans may be made to one another for any "provident and productive purpose." It is organized like a club: one member, one vote, officers elected from the membership. The officers for the most part serve without pay. A board of directors controls

---

15 See Jerry Kluttz, *Federal Diary*, in the *Washington Post*, September 7, 1946, and at the municipal level, volume by Rhyne.

policy. A treasurer appointed by the directors takes care of business details. A credit committee elected by the members passes on applications for loans. A typical charge is $5.50 for $100, if repaid in ten monthly payments.

The financial soundness of the organization is safeguarded in several ways. It may be incorporated under state or Federal law. Its books may be periodically inspected by a supervisory committee, independently of the treasurer. The books may also be subjected to examination by state or Federal authorities, or again, the treasurer and all officers who handle funds may be under bond. In any case, in most agencies management assumes a definite responsibility both for providing necessary facilities (office space, supplies, etc.) and for general supervision of the conduct of the organization. Such supervision is commonly exercised through the employee-relations section of the personnel office.

Recreation Associations. The importance of recreation was early recognized in the training of men in the armed services. Such programs were developed in war plants, both public and private, but it was not until 1942 that the Federal Recreation Committee was established under the leadership of the Federal Personnel Council, to meet the recreation needs of the 250,000 Federal civilian employees in Washington. Sixty major departments and agencies were represented. The Council was charged with responsibility for developing and extending participation among Federal employees in recreation activities provided within the community.

Experience in this important undertaking made possible the establishment of a series of guiding principles of general application for the development of such a program. These may be summarized as follows: [16] The planning of employee recreation and related employee services should be developed as an integral part of the whole employee-relations program of the personnel office. It should be based on the actual needs of employees as revealed by careful fact-finding surveys. Persons engaged in working with groups of employees in the development of a recreation program should stimulate, not manipulate; develop, not sponsor; initiate, not administer. The participation of employees in planning the program is essential. In the planning, careful consideration should be given to factors of age, sex, race, etc., and a special effort should be made to offer a variety and balance of choices. Practical working relationships should be established with community groups and agencies, both public and private, so that the services and

[16] Based on Stalley, Marshall, "Employee Recreation as a Personnel Function," *Public Personnel Review*, July, 1945, pp. 174–178.

facilities of the community may be made available to employees. Only those services should be provided directly by management which are not already available in the community or cannot be made available through community effort. And finally, such a program may be regarded as completely successful only when its activities are well known to employees.

Employee Publications. Included under the heading of employee publications are handbooks and house organs. Each has its sphere of usefulness. An employee's handbook is a pamphlet, either bound or loose leaf, setting forth essential information regarding the organization of the agency, its program and policies, and the rights and privileges as well as the duties of employees. It is prepared by the agency for the information of all employees but is especially useful in the process of inducting new employees into the organization. A house organ, on the other hand, is a serial publication, issued at frequent intervals and edited by and for the employees under the general supervision of management. It provides a medium for the dissemination of "folksy" news about individual employees and their families and at the same time it may be used within limits for presenting to employees messages from management on any matter of current interest and importance.[17]

Counseling Program. One of the most important elements in an employee-relations program as a whole is counseling. This is, indeed, so important that it is being considered separately in the next section. It is mentioned here in order to emphasize the fact that it is really not separate but an essential element in the agency's program of employee relations.

Employee Counseling

The establishment of a counseling office is naturally the first step in such a program. Announcement must be widely disseminated so that all employees know of the availability of the service; this may be done through circulars or by notices on bulletin boards or over loudspeaker systems. The service will ordinarily be set up as a section in the personnel office. There are two fundamental conditions for success: employ-

---

[17] There are multitudes of both of these types of publications; for present purposes the former are considerably more important. See Bentley, Garth, *How to Edit Employee Publications* (Harpers, New York, 1944); Biklen, Paul F., and Brecht, Robert B., *The Successful Employee Publication* (McGraw-Hill, New York, 1945); and articles by Bentley, Garth, "The Employee Publication as a Morale Builder," *Advanced Management,* July–September, 1943, pp. 79–85, 96; Brecht, Robert D., "Trends in the Employee Publications Field," *Personnel,* May, 1948, pp. 413–416; also United States Bureau of the Budget, *The Preparation and Use of Administrative and Employee Manuals: Selected References* (Washington, 1945).

ees must become convinced not only by being told but by their own experience that the counselors are qualified and trustworthy, and they must be assured that they are free to consult them on working time, without prejudice, so far as their relations with their supervisors are concerned.

Qualifications for Counselors. Counseling is a new profession. It requires personnel with a good educational background and certain definite personality traits. Training must be done very largely in the establishment since there are as yet few academic courses of instruction in this type of work. During the war the Counseling Committee of the Community War Services was set up to analyze the personal traits needed for counseling and to formulate certain requirements for the job. With regard to the former, it was suggested that an applicant should possess: [18]

1. Emotional maturity and stability, which means being socially well adjusted
2. Interest in understanding all types of people, which means having a warmth and friendliness that puts people at ease
3. Respect for the rights and dignity of the individual — using tact, showing consideration for people's feelings, and letting people make their own decisions
4. Objectivity — seeing both sides of a question, being impartial without being cold or unsympathetic
5. Maintaining an impartial attitude, and refraining from preaching or moralizing
6. Trustworthiness — refraining from gossiping about workers' problems
7. Flexibility — that is, being adaptable to many types of people and problems

In addition the counselor should be acceptable both to management and to the employees and should be familiar with the techniques of personnel administration and of counseling. He should, furthermore, be familiar with the organization, purposes, and program of the agency and with union organization.

Types of Problems. Over a period of weeks or months, a counselor will be called upon to deal with almost every conceivable type of problem that may beset ordinary human beings. The relations between the agency and the employee unions require the participation of top management, but even here the role of the employee-relations section may be important. The personal problems of individual employees arise from a multitude of different sources, but the skillful handling of all of them is essential to the maintenance of good morale within the organization. Indeed, it has been urged by one of the foremost authorities in the field that there is need to divide counseling into two distinct jobs,

[18] Counseling Committee of the Community War Services, report cited by Cantor, *Employee Counseling*, pp. 137–138.

one to deal with administrative problems, the other to deal with psychological problems.[19]

Some of the complaints are trivial and grow out of petty personal frictions, personal grudges, and mutual dislikes; such problems may often be solved by transferring one of the persons involved to some other section or unit. Some grow out of rumors, many of which are without foundation. Others involve infractions of the rules on the part of some one or more employees and may call for disciplinary action. Still others involve friction in supervisory relationships; these require unusual tact on the part of the counselor, who must present the worker's point of view to the supervisor and the supervisor's point of view to the worker.

Many of the problems arise out of personal and domestic difficulties entirely outside of the establishment. It is here, perhaps, that the counselor is in a position to render his greatest service both to the employee and to the agency. In those instances which lead to formal charges, dismissals, or other disciplinary action, he must be careful to serve the best interests of management without forfeiting the confidence of employees. If confidence is lost his usefulness as a counselor is terminated; there is little that he or anyone else can do to restore this essential condition of successful counseling work.

The Position of the Counselor. Further consideration should be given to the place of the counselor in the organization. He must be qualified both by formal training and experience and by personal characteristics. He must have the confidence of both management and employees, because he serves very often in the role of conciliator. One able counselor has well stated the matter in these words: [20]

The extent of the responsibility and authority of the counselor is one which could be argued endlessly from different points of view. Naturally, the decision lies in the hands of management in the individual agency. Certainly, the counselor should not have the authority to make decisions as to placement, transfer, promotion, or wage increases; nor should the counselor have authority in disci-

---

[19] See Cantor, Nathaniel, and Banning, John C., "Functions of Personnel Counselors," *Personnel Journal*, September, 1944, pp. 104–110; Civil Service Commission's reference list, and McMurry, Robert N., *Handling Personnel Adjustments in Industry* (Harpers, New York, 1944); Goldman, Rosaline, "The Role of Psychology in a Vocational Counseling Service," *Occupations*, May, 1946, pp. 501–505; Rogers, Carl R., "Development of Insight in a Counseling Relationship," *Journal of Consulting Psychology*, November–December, 1944, pp. 331–341; and Snyder, Louise M., "Counseling – Bridge Between Management and Worker," *Factory Management and Maintenance*, January, 1945, pp. 129–133.

[20] Coit, Edith N., "Counseling Activity as an Integral Part of the Employee Relations Program," an address before the Philadelphia Federal Council of Personnel Administration, May 3, 1944; see also Tead, Ordway, "Employee Counseling: A New Personnel Assignment – Its Status and Its Standards," *Advanced Management*, July–September, 1943, pp. 97–103.

plinary matters or in the handling of employees by their supervisors. The counselor must work more subtly than that. He must have pleasant, informal relationships with line supervisors; he must be able to move freely within the organization and have access to executives. When he has an employee problem to discuss, and recommendations to make, he must be tactful and quiet, rather than didactic and blustery. His self-assurance must take the form of intelligent self-control.

In his contacts with employees, he must be just what his name implies — a counselor, an advisor. He should not promise what he himself does not have the authority to carry out. However, on the other hand, nothing can be gained and much may be lost by limiting the employee's access to the counselor. In making such limitations, an immediate desire is fostered in the employee to get past the supervisor. Like any other forbidden thing, the employee desires it because it is forbidden. If the administration has decided that the counseling activity is valuable and has chosen counselors whose judgment can be trusted, surely no harm can be done by those counselors pursuing their activity to its fullest extent.

The counselor is likely to find that his interviews may be classified roughly into three main types: welfare interviews, those in which the employee is asking for adjustment in his work or claiming unfair treatment, and those in which the office serves as a kind of information center for answering questions. The counselor's reports may be made to the director of personnel, but he should function quite apart from other personnel transactions. His work requires and he must be accorded a high degree of personal freedom. Much of the information that comes to him is personal and confidential, not unlike that involved in the professional relations of a physician or psychiatrist with his patients. The confidence must be respected by management.

Counseling Procedure. The work of a counselor is carried on chiefly in personal conferences. His staff should therefore have individual private offices furnished with a desk and comfortable chairs. Each case should have its own file folder in which each conference is reported briefly and objectively. In this way there is a permanent record showing the chronological development of the case. These records may be referred to while the case is in process of adjustment and may be used for informing management when necessary. The record should be made in each instance *after* the interview, since note-taking in the course of the interview is likely to create a barrier between the counselor and the employee. In the actual conduct of the interview, Professor Cantor suggests that the counselor should: [21]

1. Not argue
2. Not give advice
3. Not try to direct the conversation
4. Not force answers

[21] *Op. cit.*, pp. 97–98.

5. Not take sides
6. Listen rather than talk
7. Try to grasp what the employee does not want to talk about
8. Try to grasp what lies *behind* what the employee is expressing
9. Remain impartial and never make moral judgments
10. Above all, communicate to the speaker that he appreciates how he feels

Benefits of Counseling Service

The counselor, if properly qualified and equipped, can render very great service to individual employees in the solution of their personal problems both inside and outside the agency, to management, and to the organization as a whole.

Benefits to Employees. The counselor's work in behalf of employees is undertaken not merely from humanitarian considerations but because a discontented and worried employee is likely to be an indifferent and inefficient workman. If his personal problems can be satisfactorily solved, he will again be able to devote his full mind and energy to the discharge of his responsibilities on the job. There is infinite variety to the number of problems and the number of types of problems that employees — both men and women — will bring to the members of the counseling staff. Mention has already been made of those arising within the agency itself.

Problems arising outside the agency provide tremendous opportunities for personal service; these may involve domestic difficulties, care of minor children left without supervision while both parents are away at work, illness of some member of the family, a wayward son or daughter, or any one of a thousand other problems which at one time or another may confront any individual. Oftentimes the employee does not know what to do or where to turn for help. He broods over his troubles and feels personally embarrassed if not actually disgraced. He worries to such an extent that he is unable to eat, sleep, or concentrate his attention on his work.

It is the duty of the counselor not only to listen to the employee's story in a sympathetic manner but to have a sufficient knowledge of and contact with the social welfare resources of the community to give him assistance and advice. The service rendered in such cases is a real service not only to the employee and to society but to the employer, who will henceforth have the respect and confidence of the employee and the benefit of his full productive effort on the job. The solution of such problems may involve reference of the employee to a physician in his neighborhood or to a family society or other welfare agency; or perhaps it may mean help in securing part-time assistance at home for housekeeping or the care of minor children.

Service to Management. One of the most important services a counselor renders is his service to management as a trouble-shooter. The employee who has a grievance should first discuss it and try to settle it with his supervisor. In some cases this is impossible either because of personality difficulties or because the employee feels embarrassed in discussing the subject with his supervisor. In such instances — if the employee has a legitimate problem — the counselor as an impartial third party may be able to exercise his good offices in working out a solution. At any rate the employee should be perfectly free to utilize the services of any member of the employee-relations staff at any time for advice.

The counselor must proceed with discretion and with due regard to the confidence which the employee has reposed in him. If he violates this, the counseling service will not long survive. A single complaint from a single employee may not be significant, although the attempt must be made to work out a solution. When, however, a number of employees come in with grievances about the same condition or about the same supervisor, it is probable that something is wrong and that some corrective measures are needed. In such cases the counseling staff should have easy access to management — to as high a level of management as is necessary to deal effectively with the problem at hand. The counselor knows the cause of the dissatisfaction, and it is probable that in conference with management a suitable solution can be worked out. At any rate the effort to do so should be made. Success in such negotiations a fair percentage of the time is vital to the continued confidence of employees in the counseling staff and to good morale in the organization.

SELECTED REFERENCES

There are several useful bibliographies in this field: Burnham, Paul S., *Counseling in Personnel Work, 1940–1944, A Bibliography* (Public Administration Service, Chicago, 1944); Davis, Keith, *A Selected and Annotated Bibliography of Recent Literature on Personnel Administration and Industrial Relations* (Bureau of Business Research, University of Texas, 1948); Home Owners Loan Corporation, *A Bibliography on Employee Relations* (Washington, 1939); United States Civil Service Commission, *Employee Counseling: A Selected List of References,* and *Suggestion Systems: A Selected List of References* (both, Washington, 1944)

Cantor, Nathaniel, *Employee Counseling* (McGraw-Hill, New York, 1945). Best general discussion of the subject.

Clapp, Gordon R., and others, *Employee Relations in the Public Service* (Civil Service Assembly of the United States and Canada, Chicago, 1942). Best title dealing with the subject from the point of view of the public service.

Federal Security Agency, *A Guide for Establishment and Operation of In-Plant and Community Information and Counseling Services for Workers* (Washington, 1944). Wartime manual, much of which is applicable to peacetime operations.

Ghiselli, Edwin E., and Brown, Clarence W., *Personnel and Industrial Psychology* (McGraw-Hill, New York, 1948). A current discussion geared to the problems of private industry.

Magnusson, Leifur, *Government and Union-Employee Relations* (Public Administration Service, Chicago, 1945). A labor relations specialist discusses the problem of unionism among government employees.

Metz, Harold W., *Labor Policy of the Federal Government* (Brookings Institution, Washington, 1945). A review, as of the end of World War II.

Meyer, Harold D., and Brightbill, Charles K., *Community Recreation* (D. C. Heath and Co., Boston, 1948). An up-to-date survey of public recreation generally. Ample bibliographies.

National Civil Service League, *Employee Organizations in the Public Service* (New York, 1946). An important citizen group discusses labor organization in the public service.

Pressman, Lee, *Legal Memorandum in Support of the Power of Municipalities to Enter into Collective Agreements* (Congress of Industrial Organizations, New York, 1942). Labor law attorney argues for the affirmative on a much disputed question; for more impartial consideration of the legal aspects of government-union relations at the municipal level, see Rhyne, Charles S., *Labor Unions and Municipal Employee Law* (National Institute of Municipal Law Officers, Washington, 1946).

Staats, Herbert E., *Recognition of Constructive Suggestions by State Employees* (Minnesota Division of Administrative Management, St. Paul, 1943). Describes a specific state program in a long neglected aspect of government personnel management.

Tennessee Valley Authority, *Collective Bargaining in a Federal Regional Agency* (Knoxville, 1941). Describes the TVA experience with collective bargaining.

War Department, Civilian Personnel Pamphlet series:
Effective Employee Relations (No. 2, Washington, 1943).
Exit Interviews (No. 9, Washington, 1943).
Personnel Counseling (No. 1, Washington, 1943).
Planning Employee Services (No. 7, Washington, 1943).
Civilian Personnel Officers' Employee Relations (Army Service Forces Manual M216, Washington, 1945).

11

CONDITIONS OF EMPLOYMENT

In the discussion of employee relations and employee services, certain aspects of the problem of morale have been considered. The services to employees are, for the most part, the extra things that a department or agency does in the effort to keep its employees contented and happy. The conditions of employment now to be considered have likewise much to do with morale, but they represent what may be regarded as the minimum responsibilities of the employer toward his employees. Most of them are now generally accepted as essential to a sound personnel program.

Hours, Leaves, and Attendance

Every large organization has to have rules governing such matters as hours, leave, and attendance. If operations are complicated, these rules are certain to be complicated also, in order to account for overtime, night work, work on Sundays and holidays, coming to work late or leaving early, vacations, and sick leave, to mention only a few of the problems.

Hours of Work. In public agencies the hours of work are established by statute or, in the case of municipalities, by ordinance. These regulations, which apply to all full-time employees, set forth the exact length of the workday and the work week, although administrative officers may be authorized to make such special arrangements as the needs of the service may require. In the Postal Service, for instance, some employees must be on duty at all times if the mails are to be kept moving; and in the custodial and guard services men are needed on duty at hours when the buildings are not open for the transaction of business.

In the Federal service the law now provides for a work week of forty hours, which on the basis of fifty-two weeks amounts to 2080 hours per year. Most agencies specify a schedule of five eight-hour days, although a five and one half day week (such as existed prior to World War II) is still a possibility. During the war the schedule called for a forty-eight hour week or more — six eight-hour days, and no holidays except Christmas. In most agencies, with the best of planning, work does not flow evenly throughout the year. This means that when there are peak loads, some temporary employees must be hired, or regular employees must work overtime.

Overtime may be paid only when authorized by a supervisor who has been given authority to do so. The law specifies time and a half for authorized overtime, but very often agencies with heavy peak loads and limited funds give compensatory time. This solution, of course, allows straight time for overtime, which an employee is not required to accept if he does not wish to do so. At the same time this arrangement has the advantage of increasing the opportunity for vacation leave during dull periods. Compensatory leave must be used up within a reasonably short time after it is earned and not later than the end of the year in which it is earned; it cannot be carried over.

Other phases of the problem of hours include lunch periods, rest periods, and holidays. The lunch period varies from half an hour to an hour, depending upon the nearness and the adequacy of cafeteria or lunchroom accommodations. Ten-minute rest periods in midmorning and midafternoon are commonly authorized. Employees are not required to take them, but those who are engaged in clerical or repetitive jobs usually do so. It has been demonstrated that efficiency in such types of work is improved when rest periods are observed.

The holiday program in most public agencies corresponds rather closely to that normally observed in private industry. At present there are seven paid holidays authorized in the Federal service: New Year's, Washington's Birthday, Memorial Day, July Fourth, Labor Day, Thanksgiving, and Christmas. In addition, time off may be allowed occasionally by Executive Order for excessive heat, severe storms, transit strikes, or similar causes.

In 1947 the Bureau of Labor Statistics completed a survey of the effects of hours of work on efficiency, absenteeism, and work injuries. The results are summarized as follows: [1]

The five-day week and eight-hour day tend to yield better results in terms of efficiency, absenteeism, and work injuries than did longer daily and weekly hours. In most instances, and up to a certain point, longer hours yielded higher levels of total weekly output. But the increase in output did not measure up to the increase in hours. As a rule, workers under wage incentives and at routine and repetitive jobs in which the workers were in complete control over the speed of operations were able to obtain only two hours of output for every three hours of work when hours exceeded forty-eight per week. Up to the forty-eight hour level, efficiencies were fairly well maintained, although the total weekly output level suffered from greater absenteeism and a higher incidence of work injuries. In terms of labor costs, hours in excess of forty-eight per week meant four and one-half hours' pay for two hours of output.

---

[1] Clague, Ewan, Commissioner, Press Release, July 27, 1947.

Types of Leave. Leave policy in the public service has been rather more liberal than in most private establishments. In the Federal service, regulations now provide for accumulation of annual leave at the rate of one day per biweekly pay period, or twenty-six days per year, up to a maximum not to exceed sixty days,[2] and for sick leave at the rate of one and one-fourth days per month, or fifteen days per year,[3] up to a maximum not to exceed ninety days. These two accounts are kept separately for each employee, although the tendency in recent years has been greatly to simplify the system. Formerly Federal leave regulations made special provision for marriage leave, maternity leave, vacation leave, and emergency leave for attendance upon personal business. These have all been eliminated, so that (with exceptions to be noted) all leave requested by an employee for whatever purpose is charged to annual leave.[4]

Sick leave may be taken an hour, a day, a week, or more, as required. It is usually cumulative so that an employee who becomes subject to a serious illness or operation may find that he has leave to cover his absence. In such cases employees are often provided with work they can do at home, thereby reducing somewhat the amount of leave required. Visits to doctor or dentist, for eye examinations or treatment or other necessary purposes related to health, may be charged to sick leave. In normal times in established agencies abuses of sick leave privileges are neither frequent nor numerous. During the war years abuses were quite common, largely because existing policies enforced long hours and an absolute minimum of leave. Cases of abuse can easily be detected by examination of leave records, and disciplinary action in one case is likely to prevent further violations.

Mention has already been made of compensatory leave, which was suspended in the Federal service during World War II. Other special types of leave are military and official. Persons in public employ who are called for a tour of duty in the armed forces need not resign but

---

[2] Wartime conditions caused many regular employees to accumulate huge amounts of annual leave. The Comptroller General ruled that such leave might be carried over, so that no employee would be penalized. In mid-1947 it was provided that no employee who had less than sixty days on July 25th of that year, could carry over more than that amount at the end of the year. This regulation was designed to protect the agencies in the future from the heavy costs involved in terminal pay for such employees when transferred to another agency or separated from the service.

[3] The Civil Service Assembly recommends one and one-half days per month. A spot check shows one day a month in New Jersey and New York, Niagara Falls, Seattle, San Mateo. Wichita has a sliding scale arrangement, depending on length of service. Tacoma and Aberdeen, in Washington, allow five days and six days respectively. See New Jersey Chamber of Commerce, *An Analysis of Sick Leave Programs for Government Employees* (Newark, 1944).

[4] It is usually the policy, for instance, to excuse employees on election day, for not more than two hours, for purposes of voting, without charge of leave.

may make request for military leave, which will automatically be granted. Official leave is granted for jury duty, for appearing as a witness in court, and for attendance at meetings of the Federal Business Association, personnel or finance councils, or professional meetings relating directly to the work of the employee. Leave without pay may be granted to regular employees who for health or other reasons find it necessary to be absent from their jobs for a prolonged period of time.

Attendance. The administration of the leave system requires at best an elaborate system of accounting and record keeping. Requests for annual leave for any lengthy period must normally be filed in advance and, for obvious reasons, approved by the supervisor. Suspension of leave privileges or loss of leave may be resorted to in disciplinary cases.

Leave records are necessary in connection with payroll work, but analysis of them may be extremely useful to the agency in other ways. For instance, they may indicate either good working conditions and good morale or bad working conditions and poor morale. It is part of the responsibility of management to check these records at frequent intervals, to keep itself informed, and to take corrective measures if necessary.

There is no uniformity of practice in different jurisdictions with regard to the keeping of leave, attendance, and payroll records. It is now generally accepted that this is not properly a function of the personnel office but rather an accounting and fiscal function. In the Federal government this position was taken officially in 1946 by the House Appropriations Committee and in a decision of the Comptroller General. Most of the records may now be kept by accounting and bookkeeping machines.[5]

In this procedure the basic data for each pay period must be furnished by the personnel clerks in the operating units. Employees are usually required to sign in each day on "sign-in sheets," which are made up from the preceding payroll list. The personnel clerk forwards these to the payroll or disbursing office, together with whatever other forms may be required. For such purposes it is essential that standard forms and terminology be used.[6]

See Hawthorne, Joseph W., and Morse, Muriel, *Business Machines in Public Personnel Administration* (Los Angeles City Civil Service Commission, 1940), and Horchow, Reuben, *Machines in Civil Service Recruitment* (Civil Service Assembly of the United States and Canada, Chicago, 1939); Kidneigh, John G., "Record Keeping in the Merit System Office," *Public Personnel Review*, October, 1944, pp. 221–226; Stockard, James ?., "The Punch Card in Personal Administration," *Personnel Administration*, November, 1946, pp. 29–33; and Wilgus, George, "Mechanizing Routine Personnel Operations," *Public Personnel Review*, January, 1947, pp. 23–29.

For discussion of standard terminology, see "Records and Reports" in the *Federal Personnel Manual*.

The task of the payroll office is now greatly complicated by a considerable number of deductions, some of which apply to all employees and all of which may apply to a few. The income tax deduction is made for all employees on the basis of their signed statement regarding number of dependents. But there may also be deductions for bond purchases, hospitalization, community chest, or other purposes for which employees have signed authorization. In a large organization the volume of work involved in making these deductions is so great that it is customary to stagger them as much as possible. This is a benefit to the employee also, inasmuch as it distributes the deductions over two or more pay periods.[7]

Absenteeism and Turnover. In well-established organizations absenteeism and turnover do not constitute much of a problem. They may, however, grow to serious proportions in rapidly expanding units, as many agencies discovered to their dismay during the war period. They may be due to salary and wage differentials in a tight labor market, to the character of the work, or to some other external factor, but on the other hand they may be due to poor supervision and incompetent administration within the agency.[8]

Whatever the causes of absenteeism and excessive turnover, the fact remains that both are a serious obstacle to the efficient operation of any enterprise. Employees who are on hand have to be temporarily assigned to the work of the absentees, often to the neglect of their own duties. Not only that, but turnover is expensive. A new employee is in most jobs of little use. Much time must be spent in giving him necessary instructions, and whatever work he does must be checked for accuracy. The more complicated the work, the longer it takes before he is in a position to produce. Some jobs require an initiation period of a year or more.

The Rights and Duties of Employees

Public employees have all civil rights of citizens with the exception of such political rights as will be discussed later in this section. Their corresponding duties, stated in general terms, include the following: to discharge faithfully and to the best of their ability the responsibilities of their respective positions; to support loyally the existing form of

---

[7] See *Pay-Roll Deduction Methods*, a management practices pamphlet issued by the Policyholders Service Bureau, Metropolitan Life Insurance Company.

[8] Numerous studies of this problem were made during the war, as for instance: *Controlling Absenteeism*, and *The ABC of Absenteeism and Labor Turnover* (Division of Labor Standards, Washington, 1943 and 1944); *Control of Absence* (Policyholders Service Bureau, Metropolitan Life Insurance Company); and Palmer, Dwight L., and others, "Why Workers Quit," *Personnel Journal*, September, 1944, pp. 111–119.

government; and to abstain from all conduct or activities incompatible with their position as a civil servant. This position, it may be said, imposes the duty not only of abstaining from improper activities but of abstaining from conduct that might have the appearance of being improper. Specific restrictions governing the conduct of officers and employees of the Federal government are set forth in the *Civil Service Act and Rules;* they include the following items: removal or destruction of records or documents, private use of government vehicles, use of appropriated funds to influence Congress, purchase and sale of office, making gifts to superior officials, engaging actively in partisan politics.

Loyalty Investigations. Periods of war and the unsettled international conditions which follow war seem to precipitate political and/or popular hysteria about the loyalty of public employees. During and after World War I even duly elected representatives were excluded from their seats in legislative halls — Victor Berger of Wisconsin from the national House of Representatives, five Socialist members from the New York State Assembly. Conditions generally seemed pretty bad to some who believe in freedom of thought and expression.

In World War II the record was considerably better. With a President and an Attorney General who refused to countenance political persecution, the war period passed with relatively few significant abuses of the civil rights of citizens. When peace came, the so-called radicalism of the administration became the theme of various Congressional inquiries.[9] The administration, presumably as a measure of political defense, requested legislative authority and an appropriation of $25,000,000 for a large-scale investigation of the loyalty of all Federal employees. On March 25, 1947, the President issued Executive Order No. 9835, which prescribed "procedures for the administration of an employees' loyalty program in the Executive Branch of the Government." Shortly before adjournment the First Session of the 80th Congress enacted the Federal Employees Loyalty Act of 1947 and appropriated $11,000,000 for its administration. It created a Loyalty Review Board, assigning responsibility for the administration of the program to the United States Civil Service Commission and the Federal Bureau of Investigation, the former to make record checks and inquiries with regard to new employees, the latter to make loyalty investigations chiefly with regard to incumbent employees.

On this general question, see Cushman, Robert E., "The Purge of Federal Employees Accused of Disloyalty," *Public Administration Review,* Autumn, 1943, pp. 297-316; Mitchell, Harry B., "The Employee Loyalty Order," *Personnel Administration,* July, 1947, pp. 1-3; Schlesinger, Arthur M., Jr., "What Is Loyalty? A Difficult Question," *New York Times Magazine,* November 2, 1947, pp. 7, 48-50; and issue of *Editorial Research Reports,* September 11, 1946.

The Hatch Acts: Restrictions on Political Activity. Employees in the classified civil service are regularly prohibited from engaging in certain political activities. In the Federal government, where such restrictions had been in effect for many years, substantially all employees in the executive branch were brought within their purview by the Hatch Act of 1939. State employees whose principal employment is in an activity financed in whole or in part from Federal funds, were made subject to these prohibitions in an amendment adopted the following year. All such employees are now prohibited from active participation in partisan politics.

The Commission has listed and explained some of the more important types of political activity in which government employees may not engage.[10] For instance, political activity by indirection is prohibited; that is to say, any activity which is prohibited in the case of an employee acting independently is also prohibited in the case of an employee acting in open or secret cooperation with others. Candidacy for or service as delegate, alternate, or proxy in any political convention or service as an officer or employee thereof is prohibited, but attendance as a spectator is permissible. Likewise an employee may attend primary meetings, conventions, caucuses, and the like as an observer but not as an active participant. Service on or for any political committee or similar organization is prohibited. Employees may be members of political clubs but it is improper for them to be active in their organization or to serve as officers in such clubs. They may make but not solicit, collect, or receive political contributions.

Service in preparing for, organizing, or conducting a political meeting or rally, addressing such a meeting, or taking any part except as a spectator is prohibited. Employees may not march in a political parade nor organize or be an officer of or leader of such a parade. They may

---

10 *Political Activity and Political Assessment of Federal Officeholders and Employees.* Overacker, Louise, *Presidential Campaign Funds* (Boston University Press, 1946) contains an excellent discussion of the effectiveness of the Hatch Act, on the interpretation and application of which see: Friedman, Joseph M., and Klinger, Tobias G., "The Hatch Act: Regulation by Administrative Action of Political Activities of Governmental Employees," *Federal Bar Journal*, I, October, 1945, pp. 5-22; II, January, 1946, pp 138-167; Heady, Ferrel, Jr., "The Hatch Act Decisions," *American Political Science Review*, August, 1947, pp. 687-699; Howard, L. Vaughn, "Federal Restrictions Upon the Political Activity of Government Employees," *ibid.*, June, 1941, pp. 470-474; Levitan, David M., "The Neutrality of the Public Service," *Public Administration Review*, Autumn, 1942, pp. 317-323; Marx, Fritz M., "Comparative Administrative Law: Political Activity of Civil Servants," *Virginia Law Review*, August, 1942, pp. 52-91; Merriam, Charles E., "Some Aspects of Loyalty," *Public Administration Review*, Spring, 1948, pp. 81-84; Mosher, Lester E., "Government Employees Under the Hatch Act," *New York University Law Quarterly Review*, April, 1947, pp. 233-264; Unsigned, "Civil Servants and the Right to Engage in Political Activity," *Indiana Law Journal*, April 1947, pp. 246-252. The 80th Congress in 1948 did away with the Hatch Acts, as such, incorporating their provisions in the Criminal Code.

sign petitions but must not initiate, circulate, or canvass for signatures on them. They may not publish a newspaper nor write nor comment in the columns of a newspaper on political matters, whether the articles are signed or unsigned. On the other hand there are two or three important things which employees may do. Activity in organizations having for their primary object the promotion of good government or the local civil welfare is not prohibited, provided such activities have no connection with the campaigns of particular candidates or parties. They may express opinions on political matters, privately but not publicly. They have the right to cast their votes but not otherwise to participate in the conduct of elections, that is, to serve as judge of elections, inspector, checker, teller, watcher, or as an election officer of any kind.[11]

In general, state or local officeholding by Federal employees has been prohibited since 1873. While this has been interpreted as applicable to candidacy or the preliminary steps in lining up support which precede formal announcement of candidacy, numerous exceptions have been made in the case of certain offices of a minor character and in certain municipalities adjacent to the District of Columbia. Added to all these restrictions are, of course, those relating to political assessments, political coercion, and the purchase or sale of public office, all of which are included in the United States Criminal Code. The constitutionality of the Hatch Act has been affirmed by the United States Supreme Court [12] although the decision was by no means clear cut.

The purpose of all this legislation has been "to prevent pernicious political activities." This is, to be sure, a very commendable purpose, but the method of accomplishing it does raise some difficulties. The meaning of some of the provisions of the law is so vague that most employees hesitate to avail themselves of even those political privileges (except actual voting) which seem to be open to them, lest they be judged to have overstepped the mark. Since the type of person who is interested in the public service is likely also to be interested in politics, he finds it doubly difficult — at least upon entering the service — to adjust himself to these restrictions upon his accustomed freedom of action and expression.

Dual Officeholding. An important condition of employment is found in the well-nigh universal restriction upon dual officeholding. This restriction applies to officers and employees in all three branches of the government — legislative, executive, and judicial — and to all positions

---

[11] No less than twenty-six states had, by mid-1946, adopted legislation embodying one or more of the provisions of the Hatch Act. See report prepared by Norman J. Small, State Law Section, Legislative Reference Service, May 1, 1946.
[12] United Federal Workers of America v. Mitchell, 91 L.Ed. 509, 1947.

of profit or public trust within the jurisdiction as well as to positions in other levels of government. In the Federal service, employees have been prohibited from holding any other Federal, state, or local position since 1873, when an Executive Order to this effect was issued by the President. Such a provision is now incorporated in the *Civil Service Act and Rules.*

State employees are often expressly prohibited from holding either Federal or local office or employment in addition to their state positions. The following provision from the Constitution of Illinois will serve to illustrate: [13]

> Nor shall any person holding any office of honor or profit under any foreign government, or under the government of the United States (except postmasters whose annual compensation does not exceed the sum of $300) hold any office of honor or profit under the authority of this State.

Since the Federal regulation applies throughout the service and in all states, no state employee in any state may simultaneously hold Federal employment except in those areas specifically authorized by law, in which joint Federal-state programs are authorized. Prohibitions similar to that in Illinois are found in approximately half the states. Thus, in these jurisdictions, citizens interested in public employment are subject to dual restrictions with regard to this important point.

Forms and Methods of Discipline

In all jurisdictions there are laws, ordinances, rules, and regulations governing the conduct of employees on the job. Some of these, of the types just discussed, apply to all employees in a particular jurisdiction; others relate to matters of internal policy within the department or agency. The management of an agency is concerned with infractions of rules of either type. Its responsibility with regard to the former is normally shared with the central personnel agency, while it has sole responsibility for the enforcement of the latter. The necessity for the use of disciplinary measures — for trying to make certain that the punishment fits the crime — probably constitutes the most unpleasant aspect of the whole problem of personnel management.

Causes and Types of Disciplinary Actions. Infractions of the rules are not uncommon, but the number of serious violations is relatively small. The need for disciplinary action arises under a great variety of circumstances, most frequently where temptation is greatest and pressure most severe, as in police departments. The ordinary causes which put in mo-

---

[13] Art. IV, Sec. 3; see also Providence Governmental Research Bureau, "State Constitutional Provisions Against Dual Office Holding," Supplement to bulletin, April, 1936.

ion some form of discipline include, according to Professor White, the following: [14] (1) inattention to duty — tardiness, laziness, carelessness, breakage or loss of property, etc.; (2) inefficiency; (3) insubordination, violation of law or regulation, disloyalty; (4) intoxication; (5) immorality; (6) lack of integrity, including violation of a recognized code of ethics, failure to pay debts, soliciting or accepting a bribe, or deliberately neglecting to enforce the law.

In order to cope with this variety of methods of wrongdoing, an impressive list of disciplinary actions has been evolved. Of these, some are formal; others are quite informal, involving nothing more than "a chill in the atmosphere" or a reprimand. Formal types of discipline vary from a timely notice to judicial prosecution. Some of the well established types of penalty include, to quote again from Professor White, "informal notice and warning; reprimand, with or without entry on the record; requirement of overtime; loss of seniority rights or delay in salary increment; suspension; demotion; removal for cause; judicial prosecution."

Discipline for Minor Offenses. Employees guilty of relatively minor offenses may be reprimanded and given a warning against repetition of the offense, with or without entry on the record. This may be done by the immediate supervisor, but it is likely to make more impression if done by a higher officer. In other instances, especially in police departments, discipline may consist of overtime for such offenses as taking a nap on the steps of a church, neglecting to call the station house, or leaving an intersection without relief. Other ways of handling such cases include demotion, withholding an expected promotion or salary increment, suspension of leave privileges, or loss of leave.

Discipline for Serious Offenses. Suspension, a form of discipline which may be used in serious situations that do not warrant separation, has been defined as the enforced relinquishing of duties for a specified period without pay. The *Federal Personnel Manual* lists the following as among the grounds for which suspension is frequently imposed: failure to follow an agency's requirements regarding attendance or reporting for work; violation of safety and security regulations; and personal misconduct on the job. Suspension may also be imposed pending regular action to separate an employee for disability or to transfer him, or pending investigation of evidence with regard to questions affecting his suitability for public employment.

---

[14] *Introduction to the Study of Public Administration,* Third Edition, p. 423 (Macmillan, New York, 1948), and Magoun, F. Alexander, "Principles of Disciplining," *Personnel,* November, 1945, pp. 161–170.

The most serious penalty, applicable only to major offenses, is separation, removal, or dismissal, with or without prejudice. While the general subject of separations is reserved for later consideration, it may be noted that they may be effected for disciplinary reasons for such offenses as the following, listed in the *Federal Personnel Manual:* criminal, infamous, dishonest, immoral, or notoriously disgraceful conduct intentional false statements as to any material fact, or deception or fraud in securing examination or appointment; habitual use of intoxicating beverages to excess; or a reasonable doubt as to the employee's loyalty to the government of the United States.

In all cases involving disciplinary actions the employee has the right of appeal within the agency itself, and if this does not obtain for him a modification of the original decision, he may resort to appeal procedures provided by the central personnel agency or to the courts. Procedures in this matter show the widest diversity. The best interests of the service require that the aggrieved employee have some opportunity for securing the correction of error or injustice, involving appeal to higher authority or to an appeal board; they are not generally served, however, by setting up a procedure which makes dismissals next to impossible and which have the effect of putting on trial, not the offending employee but management.

Health and Safety

Health and safety were formerly regarded as part of the employee relations or welfare program, but the present tendency is to consider them separate functions which may or may not be carried on under the general supervision of the personnel office. Actually, of course, the physical conditions of work have an important bearing on the health, safety, and well-being of employees. They cannot be expected to maintain a high degree of efficiency if they are compelled to work in poor light, in cramped quarters, in unnecessary noise, or in a poorly ventilated room. Providing suitable working conditions in clean and pleasant surroundings is indeed a first responsibility of management not only in connection with the health and safety of employees but in its own interest as an important means of achieving maximum efficiency in operations.

There are, in fact, many health and welfare influences for which management can and should be responsible. In addition to the maintenance of proper working conditions, it is responsible for the safety education of its personnel and, when accidents do happen, for proper care of the injured. Causes of accidents and sick leave also should be an lyzed with a view to correcting unsatisfactory conditions. Management should provide adequate facilities for lunches, recreation, and rest rooms and carry on a broad program designed to meet the particular needs of its employees.

Even in the absence of an adequate health program there are many things that can be done — and that were done during the war — to safeguard health and prevent loss of valuable working time. One is the chest X-ray program. The Philadelphia Federal Council of Personnel Administration put on an intensive drive in two successive years to induce all agencies and all employees in the metropolitan area to avail themselves of the opportunity to obtain chest X-rays. While they did not get 100 per cent compliance, they did achieve a substantial measure of success. Follow-up was made by the agency medical officer if there was one or by the Council Committee on Health and Safety and the local tuberculosis association. A later campaign sought to achieve as nearly complete coverage as possible in the use of the Wassermann test. When a smallpox scare developed, employees were vaccinated on a wholesale basis. These programs were possible through cooperation between the Council and local health agencies.[15]

The New Federal Health Program. Any organization with a thousand employees or more can and should provide health services for them. Small organizations can provide an emergency room with a full-time nurse in attendance, while large ones can provide a full-time health unit with physicians and nurses. Such services have been practically nonexistent in state and local units and until lately, because of lack of specific authorization, they have been rare in the Federal service also. In the early forties, Representative Jennings Randolph introduced a bill to provide a health program for Federal employees. For a time there were high hopes of its passage, but it fell by the wayside until in the 79th Congress it was enacted as Public Law 658.

This law made it possible to establish a preventive medical program for Federal employees. Heads of departments and agencies, including government owned and controlled corporations, after consulting with the United States Public Health Service and after consideration of its recommendations, may establish programs to promote and maintain the physical and mental health of their employees. Such programs have been urged for years; many industrial organizations and commercial

---

[15] It is not meant to imply that this was a unique program. State workers in Connecticut have been X-rayed and have been immunized against influenza in 1946 and 1947. A District of Columbia chest X-ray drive began in the fall of 1947 and continued through the winter of 1948; it included all Federal workers.

establishments have demonstrated that they pay dividends in increase efficiency and in decreased loss of time due to illness.[16] There is ever reason to believe that the same will be true in government service Prompt treatment of minor injuries and ailments may ward off seriou consequences, causing loss of time or impaired efficiency on the job.[17]

The terms of the act apply to both physical and mental health. De partments and agencies may within the limits of their appropriation "establish by contract or otherwise health services for employees unde their supervision." They may in fact establish and operate their ow health service program, contract for it, or combine the two systems The program includes treatment of on-the-job illness and dental con ditions requiring emergency attention, pre-employment and other ex aminations, referral of employees to private physicians and dentists and preventive programs relating to health. The United States Publi Health Service has worked out in detail the proposed standards to gov ern the operation of such a program, specifying that it shall be pre ventive, under competent professional supervision, and adequately pro vided for in terms of space, facilities, and supplies.

Mental Health. Mention has already been made of the mental-healt aspects of this program. Of course only large organizations can main tain an adequately staffed mental hygiene unit, but smaller ones car pool their resources and maintain such a service on a cooperative basis During the war the Mental Hygiene Unit of the United States Publi Health Service in Washington was instrumental in solving many per sonnel problems and was able to recommend adjustments that held in the government service many individuals who might otherwise have left. It is sound logic to assume that if such a service can be of signifi cant assistance in an emergency period, it can be equally valuable in so-called normal times.[18]

The Safety Program. Another phase of the health program includes ac cident prevention and the care and compensation of accident victim where preventive methods fail. During the war, accident preventio was emphasized in all industrial agencies — shipyards, arsenals, aircraf

[16] In the course of the debate, Representative Randolph pointed out that, while pri vate organizations with 1000 employees commonly have a medical officer, many gov ernment agencies with employees ranging in number from 10,000 to 50,000 had none For his discussion of the government's sick leave experience, and of the comparison o the cost of proper medical care with that of excessive sick leave, see his remarks in the *Congressional Record*, August 1, 1946.

[17] See Harvey, Verne K., "An Industrial Health Program for Federal Employees," *American Journal of Public Health*, March, 1945, pp. 239-242; Wittmer, J. J., "A Co operative Health Program," *Executives*, February, 1944, pp. 1-2, 6.

[18] See Cronin, John W., and others, "An Industrial Hygiene Mental Program for Fed eral Employees," *Public Health Reports*, November 9, 1945, pp. 1323-1336.

ictories, warehouses, and the like. Each agency had a safety commit-
ie which made periodic inspections to determine the presence of acci-
ent hazards and to remove them.[19] In any large organization the regu-
r employment of a safety engineer is highly desirable. In clerical and
ffice work, however, there has always been a tendency to minimize
ie possibility of accidents; but accidents caused by tripping over open
le-drawers or over telephone wires stretched across aisles, the falling
f piles of material insecurely stacked, and so on, are actually quite nu-
ierous. Accidents which could have been prevented cost the Federal
overnment approximately 17,600 man-years in 1943.[20]

When accidents do happen, the injured party must immediately file
report with his agency and with the United States Employees Com-
ensation Commission, which was established under an act of Congress
. 1916. This act provides compensation benefits, including medical
ire, for those who suffer personal injuries in the performance of offi-
al duty. The Civil Service Commission has no responsibility and issues
o instructions with respect to this act. The employee must take up
atters arising under it with his own department or agency or with the
imployees Compensation Commission. Notices of injury and claims
ir compensation must be filed within the period prescribed by law.[21]

he Prestige Value of Public Employment

i an earlier chapter some consideration was given to the problem of
iorale or what one might call the psychological climate within the
ency. Closely related to morale within the agency is the prestige of
ie agency outside, the esteem in which it is held by potential appli-
nts and by citizens generally. It is unfortunate that in this country
ie public service has not been held in very high regard in spite of a
gh level of efficiency in many quarters. The degree of prestige grad-
illy increases with the size of the unit, it being nil in many cities and
iunties, not too good in the states, and only fair in the Federal gov-
nment.

There have been few studies of this problem, perhaps because it is

---

See Herrick, Carl E., "The USDA Safety Council," *Personnel Administration*, No-
mber, 1947, pp. 24–25, 38.
For an excellent discussion of this problem, see Zimmerman, R. R., "Are Federal
mployees Expendable Too?" *Personnel Administration*, April, 1944, pp. 1–5. Also
dress by Brayer, Edward F., on the Federal accident prevention program of the
ited States Employee's Compensation Commission, in minutes of the New York
deral Council of Personnel Administration, August 20, 1945.
See *Safety Through Management Leadership* (Division of Labor Standards, Special
lletin No. 15, Washington, 1944); *Safety and Health Handbook* (Soil Conservation
rvice, Washington, 1944); *Health and Safety for TVA Employees* (TVA, Chatta-
oga, 1944); *Safety Code for Employees* (Bureau of Maintenance, Ohio Department
Highways, Columbus, 1944).

difficult to evaluate so intangible an element on a scientific basis. Professor White did attempt such a study in Chicago some twenty years ago, in which more than 5000 persons of all classes were interviewed and their answers carefully tabulated and analyzed. The returns indicated that in Chicago municipal employees enjoyed an unsavory reputation. Majority opinion rated them below corresponding employees in private business. Professor White properly assumes that the "morale (and hence in part the efficiency) of any group is affected by the group's conception of its social evaluation." This relationship between prestige and efficiency served as the justification for his study.[22]

The public service at all levels suffers from (1) the firmly established habit of Americans to regard it as a fundamental right to denounce the government and those who work for it; (2) vicious statements, which are given wide publicity, issued by people in responsible positions who ought to know better, to the effect that no sensible person wants to work for the government and take the abuse which is heaped upon government officials and employees. In December, 1947, for instance, the president of a great midwestern university announced that he could no longer in good conscience advise faculty members and graduates to go into government service. Such statements are absolutely inexcusable when the need for trained men in government service is so great and when so much effort is being expended in the effort to obtain them.

No one need expect that the public service will be free from abuse. The nation's greatest political leaders — Washington, Jefferson, Lincoln, Cleveland, Wilson, and the two Roosevelts — have all been subjected to outrageous personal vilification and abuse.[23] Lesser figures cannot escape and need not expect to do so. The ability to take criticism and abuse is apparently part of the job. Every occupation has its drawbacks, and this is one which prospective applicants should consider and recognize. This does not mean that there is not much that can and should be done to create public understanding that will in the end reduce the amount of unjustifiable and malicious criticism.

That the picture is not wholly black, not nearly so black as one might suppose from the stories of unfortunate cases which receive wide publicity, is shown by numerous recent and current developments. The universities have made real progress in training and placing young people in government service at all levels. The Federal government itself is now developing, through an interagency committee, a plan to sen

22 See *The Prestige Value of Public Employment,* Revised Edition (University of Chicago Press, 1932).
23 For a full account, see Pollard, James E., *The Presidents and the Press* (Macmillan, New York, 1947).

hundreds of government workers to college, with salaries and expenses paid, on the theory that a few thousand dollars invested to train a good man for an important job may well save many times that amount.

Still another encouraging sign is to be noted in the results of a Gallup poll, published August 30, 1947, which indicates that 41 per cent, or two in every five Americans, say they would rather work for the government than for a private firm. Two others would rather work in private employment, and the fifth one is impartial. Thus those who have a definite preference are about evenly divided — a result which compares very favorably with the findings of a similar poll conducted in England where the tradition of the public service is much more firmly established than it is in the United States.

SELECTED REFERENCES

Attorney General's Committee on Administrative Procedure, *United States Employees Compensation Commission* (Washington, 1941). Survey of administrative practices in the agency administering the employees compensation program for Federal workers.

Department of Agriculture, *Safety and Health Handbook* (Soil Conservation Service, Washington, 1944). Manual of instructions on health and safety matters for employees.

Department of Labor, *Safety Through Management Leadership* (Washington, 1944). On the organization and management of a safety program. *Hours of Work and Output* (Bureau of Labor Statistics, 1947) analyses relation between these two important factors in industry.

Magnusson, Leifur, *Workmen's Compensation for Public Employees* (Public Administration Service, Chicago, 1944). Subtitle: An analysis of state and Federal legislation.

Meriam, Lewis, *Public Personnel Problems from the Standpoint of the Operating Officer* (Brookings Institution, Washington, 1938) and Mosher, William E., and Kingsley, J. Donald, *Public Personnel Administration,* Revised Edition (Harpers, New York, 1941) both include some consideration of problems discussed in this chapter.

New Jersey State Chamber of Commerce, *An Analysis of Sick Leave Programs for Government Employees* (Newark, 1944). Survey of practices in other jurisdictions undertaken because of allegedly unsatisfactory conditions existing in the New Jersey state government.

Tennessee Valley Authority, *Health and Safety for TVA Employees* (Chattanooga, 1944). Employee manual on health and safety.

From the United States Civil Service Commission:

Health and Medical Services for Public Employees: A Selected Bibliography (Washington, 1944).

Political Activity and Political Assessments of Federal Officeholders and Employees (Washington 1939).

12

CHANGES OF STATUS

MANY difficult placement problems arise within the organization during the individual's period of service, such problems as promotions, demotions, transfers, and salary increases. These result in "personnel actions," each of which involves some change in the status of the employee. It now becomes necessary to consider the meaning of "status" and "changes of status" and to examine the basis upon which all such changes should be made — the service record of the individual employee.

The Concept of Status. The word "status" has come to be part of the jargon used in connection with merit-system administration. The concept is vitally important to the individual employee, for it affects his rights in the service and indeed the very security of his job. It relates to his position under the Civil Service Act and under the rules and regulations that have been promulgated under its terms, whether he is a permanent or a temporary employee, his seniority rights, re-employment rights, rights to within-grade increases, and the like.[1] As of any given time he enjoys "status" in a particular position, in a given service, at a specified salary and grade. If for any reason any of these aspects of his employment are changed, he is said to have had "a change of status." Every employee watches carefully to see that he is given the benefit of every advantage to which he is entitled under the act and rules. Although these rules are often exceedingly complicated, seasoned employees acquire complete familiarity with them and exceptional skill, after the manner of a constitutional lawyer, in developing plausible interpretations which will react to their own advantage.

The concept of status has been worked out to give a fair degree of security to the career employee. While generally speaking this is desirable, it has often been stretched to imply a degree of security impossible to achieve in government service or anywhere else. Permanent tenure under the law is of little value if one's job is abolished, if the function as a whole is discontinued, or if the legislature fails to appro-

---

[1] See Barnett, Robert M., and Harrington, Helen F., "Problems of Personnel Status in the U.S.E.S.," *Public Personnel Review*, October, 1945, pp. 219–229.

priate funds from which one's salary can be paid. To be sure, the possession of tenure may give one rights to prior consideration for some other position in the service or may even make it possible to "bump" some other employee with lesser status out of his job, as happened so often during the Federal reduction-in-force program following World War II.

The Service Record. When a new employee enters on duty, a personal record card and a personnel folder are set up for him. On the card will be entered from time to time all personnel actions affecting him as he goes on from year to year: when he entered on duty, where he was assigned and in what position, and what promotions, transfers, salary increases, service ratings, and disciplinary actions (if any) have affected him in the course of his employment. If he resigns or is dismissed and is later reinstated, full information about each period of service should be indicated. The record should include the estimates of his superior officers regarding such personal qualities as are essential to his work, and all correspondence, commendatory or otherwise, relating to his employment.

The service record becomes the basis for determining practically all personnel actions. Without such records it is impossible to have any fair and defensible system of promotion and to avoid personal and political influence and favoritism. This is often true merely because men's memories are so short. Examination of the record enables management to determine at a glance the seniority rights of one employee or a group of employees and to see what progress they have made in the organization during the period of their employment. In disciplinary cases the record shows whether the current charges represent a first offense or whether the employee is an habitual offender.

Service Ratings [2]

Service ratings have already been mentioned as an essential part of the employee's personnel record. While they constitute a part of the record as a whole, they should always be given special consideration when personnel changes are contemplated. Existing rating systems are far from perfect, but when conscientiously used, they are infinitely preferable to no formal ratings at all. The present systems are the result of many years of effort and experimentation, in both public and private

---

[2] The most comprehensive discussion of this subject now available will be found in the author's *Efficiency Rating Systems*, which contains an extensive bibliography of recently published materials. For other bibliographies, see Aronson, Mahler, and United States Civil Service Commission. Aronson, in twenty-six pages, lists essentially all available materials, as of date of publication.

employment, to evolve some scientific means of evaluating the contributions made by individual workers. Such systems have been variously designated: "efficiency rating," "merit rating," "service rating," and "performance rating."

Fundamentally the purpose of such a system, whatever it may be called, is to eliminate so far as possible the variable human factors in judging an employee. It seeks to substitute the impartial use of established forms and procedures for personal favoritism, whim, caprice, and the like. It attempts to introduce an element of precision into the measurement of intangible personal qualities and characteristics which seem so difficult to evaluate fairly and objectively. One Federal agency evolved the following statement of purposes and objectives: [3]

A service rating plan is a systematic method by which supervisory judgments of employee performance may be recorded regularly through a process of analysis and synthesis. The recorded rating of an employee in accordance with a systematic plan is a consciously directed formalization of the continuing process of evaluation involved in supervision.

The basic purposes in establishing a formal evaluation plan are to have recorded judgments which will serve in connection with other legitimate and more objective evidence as a means of improving supervision, as a means of improving performance, and as a basis of personnel actions. In the operation of a rating plan, it is highly important that no one of these purposes should be emphasized at the expense of another.

The ultimate objective of a service rating plan in a public agency coincides exactly with the ultimate objective of every public agency: namely, the provision of fully adequate service in accordance with the purpose and functions of the agency.

Efficiency Ratings in the Federal Service. Efficiency ratings in some form have been used in the Federal service since 1887, although the period of their most significant development and use dates from the first World War. The Bureau of Efficiency, established in 1916, served as adviser and consultant to departments and bureaus in the establishment of rating systems. Under the terms of an Executive Order of the President, issued October 24, 1921, the head of each executive department and independent establishment was required to set up "a system of rating of employees of the classified service of the Federal Government in the District of Columbia." Within the framework of this statute and Executive Order, the Bureau of Efficiency formulated the first uniform rating system in the Federal government.

The Classification Act of 1923 contained provisions for the establishment of the Personnel Classification Board, whose duty it should be to "review and revise uniform systems of efficiency ratings established

---

[3] Beers, Fred S., "Draft Definition, Purpose, and Objectives of a Service Rating Plan" (Mimeographed, Social Security Board, Washington, November, 1942).

under the terms of the Act." These provisions made necessary certain changes in the system previously established. Other changes have occurred since. The uniform system promulgated in 1922 was superseded in 1924 by a graphic rating system which was approved by the Personnel Classification Board and retained until 1935.

Since the passage of the Classification Act the United States Civil Service Commission has been responsible for the administration of some system which should be uniform throughout the several departments and agencies of the Federal government for all employees in the classified service. The Commission revised the graphic rating system in 1935 and substituted the plan which is in substance still in effect. Changes have, to be sure, been made in it from time to time as necessary, as when positions under the salary schedules in Executive Order No. 6746 were changed in 1941 to conform with the requirements of the Mead-Ramspeck Act of August 1 of that year.

For many years the uniform system of the Federal government called for regular ratings for the period ending March 31st of each year. Beginning in 1947, an option was offered to agencies between this plan and ratings given one year after entry on duty, and annually thereafter, thus spreading the work throughout the year. Every employee who has been on the job for six months or more must be given a probational or trial period rating. With the elimination of special ratings, all new employees are given an entrance rating, which is their last official rating if they enter by transfer; a rating of Good if they are entering the service. A rating chart has thirty-one elements (the last eleven of which apply to supervisory positions only); a limited number of these are selected in each case as being applicable to the duties of the position filled by the employee being rated. Those elements that are most important in relation to the position are given special emphasis by underscoring. Each element is marked plus, minus, or check, indicating respectively superior performance, weak or unsatisfactory performance, or performance which meets adequately the requirements of the position. The following rules are set forth on Form 51 for determining the final adjective rating (the long established practice of translating adjective ratings into numerical ratings was discontinued in 1949):

Rating Standards

Deviations must be explained on reverse side of this form

All underlined elements marked plus, but no element marked minus	Excellent
A majority of underlined elements marked plus, and no element marked minus	Very good
All underlined elements marked at least with a check, and minus marks fully compensated by plus marks, or	Good
A majority of underlined elements marked at least with a check and minus marks not fully compensated by plus marks	Fair
A majority of underlined elements marked minus	Unsatisfactory

The immediate supervisor normally serves as rating official, the supervisor next removed as reviewing official. All ratings are tentative until they have been discussed with the individual employee and reviewed by management. The employee who believes that he has been dealt with unfairly has the right of appeal to the efficiency rating committee within his agency, or if he prefers, he may file his appeal with the Efficiency Rating Board of Review.

In spite of the so-called "uniform" system, which the Hoover Commission would scrap in favor of another, no better if as good, there are half a dozen others in operation in the Federal government. Among them are the systems used by the Departments of the Army and of the Navy for rating ungraded employees, the postal service system, and the system used by the TVA. The latter is an interesting example of the facts-of-performance type which represents an attempt to escape from making judgments regarding the personal qualifications and characteristics of employees and to report upon easily ascertainable and observable facts regarding what the employee actually does on the job.

Merit Rating in State and Local Units. The number of state and local merit rating systems is legion, for the idea has spread rapidly during the last quarter of a century. Their development has more or less coincided with that in the Federal government. In New York State, for instance, the first steps were taken in 1917 and 1918. The city of Cincinnati has had merit rating almost from the beginning of its civil service, several different types having been tried since 1915. The development in New York City dates back to 1883, the year in which the Pendleton Act was passed. Thus it is that in all types of governmental units — states, cities, counties, school systems, park systems, and so on — merit rating systems are now in common use.

Most states that have a merit system applicable to all or most of the employees in the executive branch of government, make provision for rating, whether the basis be constitutional (as it is in eight states), or statutory, or a combination of the two. The systems, however, in their diversity reflect the lack of agreement among students regarding the major characteristics of an ideal system. Although the desire to keep uniformity within a given jurisdiction is everywhere apparent, it has usually been found necessary to make modifications based upon fundamental differences in types of jobs — labor, clerical, or professional.[4]

Types of Rating Systems. The first type of rating system is the rating scale or schedule, of which there is also a bewildering variety — de-

---

[4] For a description of these systems in about one third of the states, see the author's *Efficiency Rating Systems*, Part III and Appendix A.

scriptive scales, man-to-man scales, numerical, alphabetical, graphic, and lineal scales. Of these, the graphic is perhaps most widely known. It consists essentially of two elements: (1) a list of traits or activities arrived at by an analysis of factors leading to success or making for failure on the job and (2) various descriptive phrases or adjectives denoting the several degrees of a particular activity or trait which may be shown by an employee. The form of the device is as follows:

KNOWLEDGE OF WORK	Thoroughly familiar with all phases of work	Well informed, has mastered most details	Adequate knowledge, knows job fairly well	Limited knowledge of job	Inadequate comprehension of work

The Probst system is another which is well known and has been widely publicized. It undertook to provide:

1. That the performance of an employee be reported in statements of fact or specific and verifiable judgments, rather than in general and highly subjective conclusions, such as had characterized most previous rating systems
2. That these be stated graphically in terms of the everyday thinking of the supervisors
3. That a sufficient number of behavior qualities or specific judgments be included to permit the supervisor to report only those which he had personally observed
4. That the scoring system be such as to make subsequent "adjustments" of ratings unnecesary

The facts-of-performance plan is relatively recent and particularly promising. It is now in use in the TVA, in California, and in New York City. Recent developments in the uniform Federal system indicate a strong tendency in this direction. In this and other systems similarly designed, effort is directed toward giving an accurate report of the employee's on-the-job performance rather than describing his character, attitudes, and other personal qualities. In this respect the report of performance represents a fundamentally different approach to the whole problem. Indeed, great emphasis is laid upon the fact that the supervisor is not grading or rating his employee but rather that he is giving what purports to be a factual and unbiased account of work done. This whole procedure is based upon the fundamental assumption that the personal characteristics, peculiarities, and idiosyncrasies of the individual are more or less irrelevant and that both management and the employee want to know the answer to such questions as: How well or how badly is the job being done? If it is not being done well, why isn't it?

Administering the Rating Program. Much might be written about the problems involved in administering the rating system. Most important, perhaps, is that of obtaining full cooperation on the part of both supervisors (rating officials) and employees. This can be done only by a carefully planned educational campaign designed not only to develop understanding of the nature and purpose of the system but to overcome two common weaknesses in its administration: (1) hasty and ill-considered ratings; (2) predetermined ratings, in which the elements are marked, high or low as the case may be, in order to justify a rating that had been decided upon before the process was actually begun. Again, because men's memories are short and because there are constant changes in the personnel of any large organization, this educational work must be done over and over again, prior to each succeeding rating period. There are a score of special problems which arise or may arise.[5]

A program for the training of rating and reviewing officials must be so planned and carried out that each such officer will be thoroughly familiar with the nature and purposes of the system. As part of the program the personnel office should prepare an element chart, indicating those elements on the efficiency rating form that are applicable to each position or type of position in the agency. Not all the elements on most forms are applicable to all types of positions. The more intelligently the elements are selected in relation to the requirements of each position, the more accurate the ratings will be. One Federal agency has adopted a system by which the supervisor and the employee or employees discuss and come to a written agreement on the elements to be used for a particular position.

Once the committees have been appointed, the training of officers carried on, and the elements relating to each position selected, it is possible to proceed with the rating. In the uniform Federal system the elements from which selections are to be made in connection with any given position are classified in two groups, as shown in the table on page 217. The elements of general application appear in column 1; those applicable to supervisory positions only are listed in column 2. Those that are regarded as fundamental in connection with that particular job are weighted or underscored; others, important but not fundamental, are circled. In connection with each element, the rating officer (i.e., the immediate supervisor) assigns a plus, a check, or a minus mark. A plus mark means outstanding performance; a check means adequate; a minus means weak. If the system provides for the use of sepa-

---

[5] For consideration of these, see *Efficiency Rating Systems,* Part IV. The Federal Personnel Council's report on problems relating to efficiency rating administration mentions no less than twenty specific problems (80th Cong., 2nd Sess., House Report No. 1428).

rate rating charts for each job group, as do the state systems in California and Wisconsin, the individual work assignments must be examined and classified in order that the proper rating form may be supplied for each employee.

Report of Efficiency Rating
U.S.C.S.C. Standard Form No. 51

RATING ELEMENTS

1. Maintenance of equipment, tools, instruments
2. Mechanical skill
3. Skill in the application of techniques and procedures
4. Presentability of work (appropriateness of arrangement of work)
5. Attention to broad phases of assignments
6. Attention to pertinent detail
7. Accuracy of operations
8. Accuracy of final results
9. Accuracy of judgments or decisions
10. Effectiveness in presenting ideas or facts
11. Industry
12. Rate of progress on or completion of assignments
13. Amount of acceptable work produced (Is mark based on production records?)
14. Ability to organize his work
15. Effectiveness in meeting and dealing with others
16. Cooperativeness
17. Initiative
18. Resourcefulness
19. Dependability
20. Physical fitness for the work

21. Effectiveness in planning broad programs
22. Effectiveness in adapting the work program to broader or related programs
23. Effectiveness in devising procedures
24. Effectiveness in laying out work and establishing standards of performance for subordinates
25. Effectiveness in directing, reviewing, and checking the work of subordinates
26. Effectiveness in instructing, training, and developing subordinates in the work
27. Effectiveness in promoting high working morale
28. Effectiveness in determining space, personnel, and equipment needs
29. Effectiveness in setting and obtaining adherence to time limits and deadlines
30. Ability to make decisions
31. Effectiveness in delegating clearly defined authority to act

Uses of Efficiency Ratings. The usefulness of efficiency ratings is threefold; they produce information that can and should be used by the operating agency, by the supervisor, and by the employee. From another angle one may cite the list of uses of such ratings suggested by the Civil Service Assembly of the United States and Canada:

1. For use in promotion tests
2. To provide one basis for making salary increases or decreases within the scale of pay for a given class
3. For use in the evaluation of test results
4. To determine the order of layoff and re-employment
5. To ascertain if a worker's value is increasing or decreasing
6. To use in discovering employees who are to be transferred or demoted
7. For use in cases of removal:
   a. By the personnel agency on account of low ratings
   b. By the department head when preferring charges
   c. By the employee in case of appeal

Promotions

Planning and executing a sound promotion policy is one of the most difficult problems facing an agency. It must be solved, however, for there is no more certain method of killing the interest and initiative of employees than to have them become convinced that the organization offers no opportunity for advancement. The establishment of a policy does not, of course, guarantee that all who deserve promotions will secure them, because budgetary limitations or legislative interference may prevent; but it does give employees some assurance that the unworthy will not be advanced in preference to the deserving.

Promotion has been defined as a change from one position to another of higher grade or higher minimum salary within the same agency and without a break in service. This means change to a position involving more difficult and important duties, greater responsibilities, and usually a higher salary.[6]

Methods of Promotion. Such changes may be brought about in a number of ways. A vacancy may occur in a position for which an employee already in the organization is qualified by training and experience. In such a case a subordinate replaces a superior or is given a position at the same level as that of his former superior. In an expanding organization a new position may be created which may be filled by promotion. Or it may happen, as it often does, that the individual will remain in the same position, which by reason of a greater volume of work and increased responsibilities may be reclassified to a higher grade at a higher salary.

The technique by which promotions are made depends to a large extent upon the personnel system in effect in the jurisdiction or agency and upon the type of work. In administrative and supervisory positions at the higher levels, decisions with regard to promotions are made by management after careful consideration of the qualifications of available personnel, usually without formal examination. In lower-grade positions where there is a large number of potentially eligible candidates, promotion examinations may be given and promotion registers established, from which vacancies in a higher grade are filled in a manner parallel to that in which the original appointments were made. Thus a promotion register of CAF–2 eligibles may be set up for the filling of CAF–3 vacancies.

Progressive organizations now frequently attempt to secure employee participation in carrying out a promotion program. This demo-

---

[6] *Federal Personnel Manual,* P3–4; see also Civil Service Assembly of the United States and Canada, *Placement and Probation in the Public Service,* Chapter 4.

cratic procedure can be made effective through the establishment of a promotion board for the agency, the members of which are chosen by the employees. The board, sitting with representatives of management, may help to decide promotion standards and qualifications and may assist in establishing promotion registers for some positions and in applying standards to applicants in other cases. Such a procedure is valuable in a number of ways. It gives at least a few employees some insight into the difficulties involved in making the decisions that have to be made, and it gives to employees generally the assurance that all promotion applications have fair and impartial consideration.[7]

Major Problems in Promotion Policy. A number of underlying conflicts confront management in the execution of a promotion policy. The first is the necessity of striking a balance between the desire on the one hand to recruit new people from outside, thus "bringing new blood into the organization," and the necessity on the other of giving recognition to those employees who by reason of the quality of their work and the length of their service have a right to expect that they will be considered in connection with filling vacancies in grades higher than their own. Such situations sometimes resolve themselves into a choice between a promotion which will benefit the morale of the employees and the appointment of a new person who will add strength to the staff.

In the solution of this dilemma, management is often confronted by a scarcity of good material for promotion, due very often to the failure of preceding administrations to recruit and hire the right type of employee. One is thus brought face to face with the fact that a sound promotion policy is possible only where special attention has been given to the selection of a high type of individual who is capable of growth and development in the service. Unless this is done first, promotion is impossible; no conscientious administrator can promote when he has no one qualified for promotion. Such a situation, when it exists, is a reflection on management itself, past or present; hence care must be taken to make certain that it actually does exist. A further obstacle arises from the fact that management too often comes to think of its employees in terms of the positions they have and fails to realize that they have the capacity for handling greater responsibilities.

Another serious problem arises out of the generally prevailing attitude toward seniority. There are too many individuals, both in and out of government, who appear to believe that by merely remaining physi-

---

[7] See Johnson, W. C., "Employee Participation in the Promotion Program," *Personnel*, May, 1947, pp. 429–439.

cally alive and reporting for work regularly, they will one day arrive in some important post. To be sure, many have done exactly that. Seniority is important and should be considered, but it should not be the deciding factor *unless* two candidates, one with and one without seniority rights, appear to be equally qualified in other respects.

The proper weight of efficiency ratings in determining eligibility for promotion is another thorny problem. Those who have seniority regularly protest against what they regard as undue emphasis upon efficiency ratings, while those who lack seniority and have high efficiency ratings claim that efficiency should count most. It probably should, but in practice it rarely does, for the old-line employees are usually able to carry their point with regard to seniority. This was illustrated by the changes made in the transition from the reduction-in-force regulations to the retention-preference system at the close of World War II.

The basis for a sound promotion policy consists in recruiting and appointing competent persons, training them and encouraging them by increases in both grade and pay as fast as the opportunity presents itself and as fast as they demonstrate their capacity to assume greater responsibilities. It is a fine thing for the messenger boy to become chief chemist, but in such an instance the messenger boy must become qualified as a chemist. Only on this basis can promotions be made consistent with the best interests of the agency or of the service as a whole.

Other Types of Personnel Actions

In addition to promotions there are no less than half a dozen types of personnel actions in the placement field — transfer, demotion, reassignment, re-employment, reinstatement, and nonduty status including both furlough and extended leave. With regard to all these types the service record, the last efficiency rating, the length of service, and veterans' preference are important.

Transfers. Transfers may be either interagency or intra-agency. The latter involves change of position within the same agency from one official headquarters to another or from one organizational unit to another, without break in service. The interagency transfer involves a similar shift across departmental or agency lines, also without break in service. The shift may or may not be accompanied by a change of salary and grade. The occasion for the change may be readjustments within the agency, the desire of another unit for the services of the employee in question, or the employee's personal dissatisfaction and desire for a change. When transfers are made, employees are normally extremely careful to protect as fully as possible their rights under the law.

The Civil Service Assembly's Committee on Placement in the Public Service discusses a number of the more common reasons for which transfers are made or requested. Among the reasons that obviously motivate the employee are the desire to avoid "blind alley" jobs, to facilitate school attendance, to avoid an unmerited demotion, or to escape friction with the supervisor. Among the reasons motivating the agency may be mentioned the leveling off of "peaks" and "valleys" in employment, technological changes, considerations of training, and readjustments within the agency. The Hoover Commission recommended that departments and agencies be required to work out promotion programs and that the Civil Service Commission facilitate transfers of competent personnel across agency lines, as a means both of developing and of strengthening the career service. The number and variety of these reasons illustrate a point thoroughly familiar to every administrator, namely, that changes in personnel and in the assignment of personnel are the ever-present characteristics of any working force.

Special mention should be made of the fact that transfer may be extensively and effectively used in periods of retrenchment and reduction-in-force in a particular agency — unless, of course, most other agencies are at the time facing the same problem. In the period of readjustment following World War II, for instance, the disbanding war agencies set up special out-placement officers to render every possible aid to employees whose separation notices had been issued. Where opportunities for placement were found in other government agencies, they were normally effected by transfer.[8]

Demotions. Demotions are personnel actions in which an employee is retained in the service at a lower grade and reduced salary. Sometimes they result from decisions in disciplinary cases where the offense is serious and the investigation establishes beyond reasonable doubt the guilt of the accused. In other instances they may be the result of the "down-grading" that may occur after the agency has suffered a serious cut in appropriations. Or after a period of inflation and scarcity of personnel, during which jobs have been "blown up," it may be resorted to as a necessary means of getting things back to normal. Management is naturally anxious to spread its limited resources as far as possible, and this means may appear justified in order to prevent a virtual collapse of the agency's program.

---

[8] See Brody, William, "Personnel Administration in a Liquidating Agency (NWLB)," *Public Personnel Review,* January, 1946, pp. 25–30; Kealy, Walter G., "Out-Placement Programs of the Federal Government," *Personnel Administration,* September, 1947, pp. 30–32; and Kronemeyer, Robert E., "Manpower Problems in Demobilizing the Navy," *Personnel Administration,* May, 1947, pp. 32–40.

While down-grading and demotions do not seem fair to employees, they are often accepted, at least when jobs are scarce, on the theory that some job is better than no job, which is usually the only alternative. In another sense the practice may be defended on the ground that it is preferable to impose some injury on many employees than to inflict severe hardship on a few. The demoted employees are apt to complain to their representatives, who then criticize management for pursuing policies necessitated by their own failure to provide necessary operating funds.

Reassignments. A reassignment involves a change without promotion or demotion under any one of the following circumstances: (1) from one position to another in a different line of work, such as clerk to stenographer, or chauffeur to guard; (2) in the same line of work within the same department or agency; or (3) from one service to another, as from subprofessional to clerical, administrative to fiscal (CAF). Changes of this character are more common in the early stages of an employee's connection with an agency than in the later. If the new employee does not do well on his first or second assignment, he may be tried on a third or a fourth. It is regarded as good personnel practice to make a serious effort to find some work that every employee can do well; it is cheaper to teach an employee a new job than to orient another new employee and teach him the work besides. Reassignment is the technique by which this is done. Reassignment may also become necessary when an office or agency is subject to reorganization.

Re-employment. An employee who resigns from the service or who is separated through no fault of his own, retains — at least for a limited period — a right to re-employment if there occurs a vacancy for which he is qualified and in which he is interested. The veterans are the most numerous group claiming re-employment rights.[9] The theory is here, also, that an experienced employee familiar with the nature and purposes of the organization is preferable to a new one. When numerous employees are separated in a reduction-in-force program, it is customary to give all who are interested in a possible return to government service an opportunity to have their names placed on the re-employ-

---

[9] *Federal Personnel Manual* (P3–8) has this to say on re-employment: "Whenever an agency is considering filling any position by promotion from within the agency, it may give the same consideration to a former employee who has been transferred from that agency under the war service regulations, with reemployment rights in the agency, as he would have received if he still occupied the position he left. Such a former employee may be selected for the promotion, and if he is not authorized to return at that time to the position to which promotion is made, his reemployment rights at the time application is made for reemployment in the agency will be applicable to the position to which promotion was made during his absence."

ment list in order that they may be called back when and if a suitable opportunity occurs.

Reinstatement. Re-employment and reinstatement are usually considered together. The individual who is re-employed may or may not be brought back in his old job. In a reinstatement he is restored to the same position or a position similar to that which he formerly held. An examination of the Federal rules and regulations governing reinstatement suggests that careful attention must be given to the circumstances under which the employee left the service. Very often an employee separated for cause (for political activity, for disability, or for disciplinary reasons), having spent many years in the service, desires to be reinstated in order to complete the minimum number of years necessary for retirement. All such cases, unlike those of employees who voluntarily resign to accept other employment, require careful investigation.

Nonduty Status. Employees may be in nonduty status either through their own initiative or that of the agency. In the former case, when leave has been requested exceeding the amount of annual leave accumulated to their credit, they may be put on leave without pay (LWOP), while in the latter the agency may put them on administrative furlough. This also is a nonduty, nonpay status. In either case they are entitled to return to their positions and to be placed on the active rolls at the expiration of the specified period of leave or furlough.

SELECTED REFERENCES

Most of the literature, aside from articles in periodicals and professional journals, deals with the practices in private industry. Bibliographical lists on efficiency or merit rating will be found in Aronson, Albert H., and others, *A Bibliography of Service Ratings* (Social Security Board, Washington, 1939), Mahler, Walter B., *Twenty Years of Merit Rating, 1926–1946* (Psychological Corporation, New York, 1947), and in Graves, cited below; on seniority, in Thompson, Laura A., *Seniority in Industrial Relations: A Selected List of References* (Department of Labor, Washington, 1944).

Dartnell Corporation, *Employee Rating Programs,* 2 vols. (Chicago, 1944). Extensive discussion of plans used in large industrial establishments; for another excellent study of practices in selected private firms, see National Industrial Conference Board, *Efficiency Ratings: Methods of Appraising Ability, Efficiency, and Potentialities* (New York, 1942).

Graves, W. Brooke, *Efficiency Rating Systems* (Legislative Reference Service, Library of Congress, 1947) and in Senate Committee on Post Office and Civil Service, *Hearings* on Efficiency Rating System for Federal Employees, Appendix, pp. 185–251 (80th Cong., 2nd Sess., 1948). Discusses the history, development, and administration of such systems in government, both Federal and state.

Marble, Samuel D., *The Application of Psychological Techniques to Employee Service Rating* (Maxwell Graduate School, Syracuse University, 1941).

Probst, John B., *Service Ratings* (The Author, Minneapolis, 1931), and *Measuring and Rating Employee Value* (Ronald Press, New York, 1947). The originator of a system of rating widely used in both industry and government presents his views.

Smyth, Richard C., and Murphy, Matthew J., *Job Evaluation and Employee Rating* (McGraw-Hill, New York, 1946). One of the latest and one of the best general discussions, geared, however, to private employment.

Wortham, Mary E., *Rating of Supervisors* (California Institute of Technology, Industrial Relations Section, Pasadena, 1943). Analysis of a much discussed aspect of the merit rating program.

From the United States Civil Service Commission:

Efficiency Rating Manual (Washington, 1942).

Efficiency Ratings, 1940–1945: A Selected List of References (Washington, 1946).

Rating Official's Guide (Washington, 1946).

13

SEPARATIONS AND RETIREMENT

THE final event in a career in the public service — be it long or short — is separation, which may be brought about by death; by resignation, either voluntary or involuntary; by dismissal, by reason of reduction in force; by removal for the good of the service, either for inefficiency or for cause (disciplinary); or by retirement, which may take place on age, length of service, or disability. There is some tendency among personnel people at present to minimize the importance of these problems and to regard separation as a more or less incidental aspect of the placement function (it creates a vacancy and requires a new placement) and retirement as a record-keeping activity which really does not belong in the personnel office anyway. The fact remains that these activities are important, tremendously so to the employee, regardless of where they are performed or by whom.

Separations by Death or Resignation

It is true of most vacancies caused by the death of an employee that the agency has no responsibility. In some cases, however, where death is caused by an accident that might have been prevented or by illness brought on by unfavorable working conditions, the agency has a very real responsibility. Such cases cause suffering to the employee and to his family and unnecessary expense to the government. The sooner the conditions are corrected, the better for all concerned.

Resignations. Resignations may be either voluntary or involuntary. Little time need be spent on the latter, for the employee would probably be removed anyway and is given the special consideration of an opportunity to resign in order to keep his record clear and not impair his chances of obtaining other employment. The number of voluntary resignations is likely to be a fairly good barometer of general business conditions. When they are good and jobs are reasonably plentiful, the rate is apt to be rather high; but under contrary circumstances few employees will resign except perhaps for reasons of health. A high percentage of resignations means of course a high rate of turnover, which is an indication to management that something is wrong.

While the cause may or may not be under their control, there are measures that management may take to combat high turnover. A good employee-services program will help develop a favorable opinion of the agency as a place to work. Attention to improving methods of supervision and supervisory relationships will help greatly. The regular use of exit interviews will aid in determining the specific causes of dissatisfaction. Reclassification of individual positions or groups of positions may help improve the situation in a highly competitive labor market. In an organization expanding under the pressure of war or other emergency, rapid promotions also help an agency to retain its employees and thus reduce waste. The agency may not save any money by this means, but it will have a much more competent working force.

Removals

There is a widespread but erroneous belief that it is well-nigh impossible to fire a public employee or, to put it another way, that it is next to impossible for a public employee to do anything that will actually bring about his dismissal.[1] The task of making a removal is of course likely to come under the heading of unpleasant business, and this may explain why administrative officers have often shown a deplorable reluctance to perform their duty in cases where the facts indicated only too clearly that use of the removal power was in order. Any management which performs its duty not only can but will dismiss an employee for either of two major reasons: (1) for incompetence and inefficiency; (2) for cause, which of course indicates dismissal for disciplinary reasons. The present discussion is not concerned with the problem of removals except in the classified service; officers selected under political appointment hold only for stated terms or at the pleasure of the appointing authority. Those that are elected may normally be removed only by impeachment or recall.

Removals for Incompetence or Inefficiency. Employees may be dismissed for incompetence or inefficiency at any time. In the case of those who are still serving in their probationary period, making a dismissal

[1] On this point, see Kaplan, H. Eliot, "Removals in the Civil Service," *Public Personnel Review*, January, 1946, pp. 31–32. In January, 1948, the Civil Service Assembly of the United States and Canada reported the results of a detailed analysis of the dismissal practices of 111 civil service agencies in state and local government; in these jurisdictions, 5018 civil service employees were dismissed during 1946. Although 2568 of these could have taken their cases to civil service appeal boards, only 330 did so. Appeal boards backed up the original decisions to dismiss employees in two thirds of the contested cases. In short, the dismissing authorities' action "stuck" in over 95 per cent of the cases open to appeal. The study also focused on civil service dismissal cases referred to the courts. During 1946, only thirteen of the 5018 dismissals studied were appealed for judicial review. Of the thirteen, nine were settled during the year. Seven decisions previously made by appeal boards were upheld, while two were reversed.

should create no serious problem.[2] It is, in fact, the purpose of the probationary appointment to give management an opportunity to determine whether or not the employee can perform satisfactorily the duties of the position and also to give the employee an opportunity to judge whether or not he can do the work and is interested in the position.

Failure on the part of management to exercise its judgment as to the fitness of the probationer before the expiration of this working test often has extremely unfortunate consequences. The service may be saddled with an unsatisfactory employee for the remainder of his natural life. Sometimes the failure to terminate the appointment is due to carelessness, poor judgment, or unwillingness to go through with an unpleasant task. Whatever the reason, the unfit probationer who is permitted to slide through into the status of a permanent employee becomes a problem in the service for years to come. As he stays on, the seniority he acquires creates a serious problem which in fact reflects upon management. It should not take two years or five years or ten years to discover that an unfit employee is unfit and if it does, there is something radically wrong with management.

Removals for Cause. Removals for cause are made for violations of the act and rules governing the conduct of employees and are discussed in an earlier chapter on the conditions of employment. It is one thing to read the legal prohibitions and another to visualize the cases that actually arise. Several store clerks under the Liquor Control Board in one state were dismissed on charges of bribery and favoritism — accepting gifts of money from licensees, withholding well-known brands from sale and saving them for tavern proprietors, and the like. A cook in a state hospital in another state was fired for "misconduct toward female patients," though he claimed, as is usually the case, that he was dismissed for "political, religious, or racial reasons." Twelve employees in another state hospital in the same state were found to have been running a small-loan business among patients; others were taking patients out of the institution on parties and using the patients' money to pay the bills. Still others had borrowed money from patients. The records of any central personnel agency will provide abundant illustration of the various infractions of the regulations which employees may be guilty of.

Removal Procedure. While the procedure in removing permanent employees is less simple than that in the case of probationers, a simple statement of the reasons, signed by the administrator, is regarded in some

[2] See Civil Service Assembly's *Placement and Probation in the Public Service;* Short, Oliver C., and Dow, Edward F., "Drop Duds During Probation," *Personnel Journal,* November, 1938, pp. 168–174.

jurisdictions as adequate and final. A common provision specifies that no employee in the classified service shall be removed, discharged, or reduced in pay or position — except for just cause, which shall not be religious or political, and except during the probationary period — until he has been furnished with a written statement of the reasons for such action and has been allowed to give the removing officer a written answer. Usually also a copy of the statement of reasons and a copy of the written answer must be furnished to the central personnel agency, whether or not provision is made for appeal.[3]

While the rules vary greatly from one jurisdiction to another, the dismissed employee may usually file an appeal and request a hearing before the civil service commission or some other agency specified by law. A recent New Hampshire statute, for instance, constitutes the governor and council as a state employees' appeal commission.[4] Except for those subject to the merit system, any regular classified state employee who is discharged may appeal to this commission for a review of his case and for reinstatement. The commission is required to hold a public hearing and may summon witnesses. If after such hearing the commission shall be of opinion that the employee was discharged without just cause, it may order his reinstatement to the same position and at the same salary. There are two obvious objections to this arrangement: the governor of the state should not be burdened with routine problems of this character, and the state should not be operating without merit system legislation in which the central personnel agency would be responsible for the performance of such duties.

In other jurisdictions the recommendation of the administrative officer goes directly to the commission, which schedules a hearing. If the employee does not contest the dismissal, the case can be quickly disposed of; if he does contest it, the hearing assumes many of the characteristics of a trial in which the administrative officer appears as the plaintiff, and the dismissed employee as the defendant. Some indication of the size of the task is indicated by an announcement from the Illinois Civil Service Commission in 1941. Whereas previously the Commission itself had conducted hearings on all charges filed against civil service employees, the president of the Commission then appointed two investigating boards to conduct hearings, one in Chicago, the other

---

3 An Executive Order of President Truman, effective May 1, 1947, made it plain that agencies are responsible for the demotion or firing of inefficient employees and that the only procedure necessary to fire a permanent employee is to give him a copy of the charges against him and to allow him a reasonable time to answer them. The general rule is that no formal hearing is required except where the statute specifically so provides. See Short and Dow, op. cit.
4 Laws, 1947, Chapter 89; on this whole problem, see Illinois Legislative Council, Right of Appeal From Removals Under the Merit System.

ownstate, and to report their findings to the Commission for final action. In making the announcement, the president stated that this arrangement would greatly expedite the work of the Commission and would give him "time to direct activities in the offices of the Commission and to oversee the work generally."

It is desirable for the central personnel agency to exercise some supervision over dismissals in order to avoid abuses,[5] but the procedure ought not to be so difficult and complicated that the administrative officer would be disposed to endure almost anything rather than the ordeal of presenting a case for action. Nor should the system be one which in operation has the effect of putting management rather than the deficient or delinquent employee on trial. Nor should one assume that reinstatement as a result of such hearing is an unmitigated blessing, even when there might be reasonable doubt of the adequacy of the reasons upon which the dismissal was based. The employee may return with an objectionable attitude and openly gloat over the fact that he has proved himself stronger than the management of the agency. This certainly is not a "healthy" situation.[6]

Reduction-in-Force

The number of persons employed in public service at all levels has risen enormously since 1933, primarily because of economic depression and war, and also because of the fact that citizens demand more and better service in many different fields. Taking the Federal government as an illustration, the Byrd Committee reported the following figures: [7]

In December, 1932, there were 563,805 civilian employees in the executive branch of the government. The payroll amounted to $1,016,150,000.

In December, 1939, there were 928,936 civilian employees (excluding 57,918 emergency relief employees), with a payroll amounting to $1,692,811,000.

By December, 1941, the war activities had so increased the number of civilian employees that the number stood at 1,647,308, with a total payroll of $2,628,-71,000.

Then came Pearl Harbor. By June, 1943, there were 3,095,463 civilian employees.

By V–J Day, August, 1945, the executive branch had a total of 3,649,769 civilian employees and a payroll of $8,014,096,000 — about eight times what it had been in 1932.

By June 30, 1947, the payroll had been reduced, after stupendous efforts, to a estimated 1,850,000 civilian employees.

See McCloskey, Robert G., "The Case for 'Foot-in-the-Door,'" *National Municipal Review*, March, 1945, pp. 122–124, 128.
The strongest opposition to civil service review of dismissals came some years ago from the city manager group. For an excellent discussion of the issues involved, see letter from Messick, Charles P., in *National Municipal Review*, June, 1927, pp. 419–420.
Joint Committee on Reduction of Nonessential Federal Expenditures, *Federal Postwar Personnel* (April, 1946).

At this point consideration of our present problem, reduction-in-force really begins.

Efforts at Reduction in 1947. In his annual message to the Congress in January, 1947, President Truman recommended severe cuts in the personnel of the executive branch — cuts as drastic and as deep as the administration felt it was safe to go without serious injury to the service. With the advent of the 80th Congress, the executive departments and agencies put in seven hectic months, for reasons which are clearly indicated by the newspaper headlines quoted below, chiefly from the *Washington Post:*

MARCH 22, 1947:
    Labor Dept., NORB, FSA Funds Pared
    Appropriations Unit Recommends Cuts; 100 Denied Salary in Conciliation Service

APRIL 22, 1947:
    GAO Will Cut Staff by 2000 in 2 Years, Warren Asserts

MAY 26, 1947:
    8000 More U. S. Employees to Get Notices by Thursday
    Most of Those Affected Were Warned; 100,000 Will Be Cut From Field Rolls

JUNE 11, 1947:
    VA Orders Job Cut of 400 Here
    Agriculture Dept. Cuts Started in Virginia

JUNE 25, 1947:
    Maritime Lays Off 2800 Until July 1

JULY 26, 1947:
    Conferees Eliminate 18,000 War Dept. Jobs

Reduction-in-force may occur in any government unit at any time. It is usually necessary after any large emergency situation has passed. It is bound to be a difficult and trying experience, in which some employees lose their jobs. But there are right ways and wrong ways of going about it. The methods pursued by the 80th Congress, for instance, completely demoralized the personnel in the Federal service. Long-time observers of the Washington scene testified that the morale of Federal workers had never before within their memory been so low as it was in 1947. Headlines like those above and constant reiteration of the claim that the cuts would be wide and deep, that more were still to come, that the economy drive might cost the jobs of a million workers, kept thousands in such a state of apprehension that normally efficient operations were impossible. Other factors contributed to the general demoralization; the loyalty investigations, for instance, aroused fear, not because of what an employee had done but because of what he might be accused of having done. And after all the hullabaloo, the actual cuts — serious though they were in some instances —

amounted to less than 200,000 out of the total of 500,000 or 1,000,000 that had been promised.

The reductions actually made emphasize another important point. One would naturally assume that an effort would have been made to keep the best qualified and most competent employees, as the Hoover Commission has recommended should be done. In practice it was very largely "rights," not qualifications and competence, that finally determined what ones were to be retained and what ones were to go. War-service employees, many of whom were far better qualified than the individuals who replaced them, were eventually out, almost automatically. Permanent employees were supposed to be restored, but they were often passed over in favor of a veteran. This is the kind of situation that may greatly undermine the strength of the civil service.

The whole truth of the matter is that little progress in actual reduction *can* be made. Someone is interested in every activity that government carries on; otherwise it would not have been initiated. It is easy enough to talk of unnecessary expenditures and unneeded personnel, but it is usually quite another thing to find them.[8]

Reduction-in-Force Procedure. Where a small cut in personnel is contemplated, it can usually be accomplished within a short time by permitting vacancies caused by transfers, resignations, and normal turnover to go unfilled and by making internal adjustments (transfers and reassignments) within the agency. In the case of a severe reduction, certain definite procedural steps have now been pretty well established. These are:

1. Determination of the personnel ceiling
2. Establishing the register
3. Locating the "retention point"
4. Internal adjustments
5. Notice to employees to be separated
6. "Placement in reverse"
7. Report to the central personnel agency

The Federal procedure with regard to these steps is exceedingly complicated. The requirements are established under the applicable statutes by the head of the government and by the central personnel agency; the actual application of them rests with the departments and agencies under the general supervision of the central personnel agency.

For discussion of these matters, see Brody, William, "Personnel Administration in a liquidating Agency (NWLB)," *Public Personnel Review*, January, 1946, pp. 25–30; Kealy, Walter G., "Out-Placement Programs of the Federal Government," *Public Administration*, September, 1947, pp. 30–32; and Kronemeyer, Robert E., "Manpower Problems in Demobilizing the Navy," *Personnel Administration*, May, 1947, pp. 32–40.

The idea of a personnel ceiling is relatively new. Budgetary procedures have long been used for controlling the amount of money to be spent by a given agency for personal services; now, in addition, they exercise a further control by determining also the number of persons — regardless of salary and grade — who may be employed by the agency. This "personnel ceiling" is subject to periodic revision, in connection with which management must present specific information regarding the workload for the ensuing period. The idea seems to have originated with the Byrd Committee and to have been officially adopted as an amendment to the Federal Employees Pay Act of 1946.

The second step is the establishment of the retention register. For this purpose full and up-to-date information with regard to the service and status of each employee is essential. The Department of the Army solves the problem by having each employee fill out a personal information sheet. In order to select employees for separation the personnel officer has to put the employees in the levels affected in a retention order. This order is shown for a particular level on a retention register, which serves to indicate how many employees there are in the competitive level, what kind of employees they are, and where they are in the organization, so that the personnel officer can plan how many to separate. The register also indicates the basis for separation when the personnel officer explains the action to the employees or to the commission.

The third step involves the location of the retention point. If transfers and turnover will take care of the excess personnel within the time limit assigned, no actual separations may be necessary. The retention point is, in the language of the *Federal Personnel Manual*, the credit point on a retention register (identified by the number of retention credits) above which employees are retained and below which employees are separated unless retained by specific exception. Along with the effort to locate the retention point, attention must be given to the possibility of readjustments within the agency itself which will either reduce the number of separations that would otherwise be necessary or obviate the need for making any. Reassignments may be made to positions which have been left unfilled. Requests for extended leave may be granted or administrative furloughs used. Some employees may be loaned or transferred to other agencies not at the time in the throes of reduction-in-force. In many ways by careful planning and by skillful management an agency can soften the impact of the blow both upon itself and upon its employees.

When all possible adjustments have been made and the retention point determined accordingly, the next step is to serve notice upon

ose employees who are to be separated. In this connection, absent
nployees with re-employment rights must be taken into consideration,
r a place must be made available to them when and if they return.
he notice must be an individual one and served in writing not less
an thirty days prior to the date upon which the separation is to be-
me effective.

The final step in the procedure is the report to the central personnel
ency. Under the Federal plan, the Civil Service Commission is sup-
sed to be notified of a reduction as soon as the employees are notified.
a series of reductions in the same area are to be made within a ninety-
y period, the report should be sent as early as the first notice to an
nployee, for the simple reason that in the past the Commission has re-
ived reduction-in-force appeals from employees before any official
port of a reduction was received from the agency.

tirement

lthough the history of public-employee retirement systems extends
ck over a century, most of the significant advances have taken place
nce World War I. In this development private employers have been
r in advance of government,[9] where aged and infirm employees were
pt on the rolls as messengers or clerks long after they had earned the
ace and quiet of their own firesides. This was done because at the
ne there was nothing else to do. The salaries were not adequate to
able employees to acquire a competence for their old age, and there
as no provision for retirement.

There are various ways in which the needs of such employees can
met. One obviously is a retirement system.[10] Another, which might
pplement rather than supplant a retirement system, is a group insur-
ce program such as was recommended in Massachusetts in 1942 by a
cial legislative commission.[11] Still another would be to bring public
nployees under the coverage of the social security plan. In testifying
fore the Ways and Means Committee of the House of Representa-
es on this subject in April, 1946, Earl D. Mallory, Director of the
nerican Municipal Association, stressed the fact that his organization
d repeatedly urged the adoption of such a policy. It may be noted,
cidentally, that the only reason this was not done in the original act
as the existence of legal questions regarding the means of imposing

---

he Bell System, for instance, boasts that it was a pioneer in pensions, "long before
re was any thought of Social Security or of pensions by most companies. The Bell
tem instituted a pension plan for its employees which went into effect in 1913."
See Weinberg, A. A., "Retirement Plans in Relation to Public Personnel Administra-
n," *Public Personnel Review*, July, 1943, pp. 153-164.
House Committee Report No. 147, December 1, 1942.

upon the states and municipalities the taxes necessary to support the system.[12]

Purposes of Retirement Plans. The purposes of retirement plans may be variously classified. One writer says they are humane and administrative. Another groups them under three headings: (1) to provide means of support for those superannuated employees who can no longer work with reasonable efficiency;[13] (2) to care for disabled employees, whether the disability is due to occupational or nonoccupational causes; (3) to provide some financial assistance for the dependents of employees whose death results from occupational hazards or otherwise. The desirability of meeting these needs is now generally recognized in government at all levels. As the author has observed elsewhere, the establishment of a retirement system based upon sound actuarial standards and competently administered is a great benefit not only to the employees but to the government as well through the improved efficiency and morale in the public service as a whole.

Different Types of Retirement Systems. Retirement systems, regardless of the size of the governmental unit within which they operate, may be classified according to the source of funds and according to the method by which provision is made for meeting liabilities, that is, for the payment of pensions. Funds for the payment of claims may be provided by the government alone, by the employees alone, or by contributions from both. On this basis, retirement systems are usually classified as contributory and noncontributory. It is now generally believed that the contributory plan is preferable; if the security which the system provides is worth having, then the employee ought to be willing to make some contribution toward achieving it.

Pension payments may be made on either a cash-disbursement basis or on a strictly actuarial basis. Under the first plan, no particular reserve is built up and the payment may not correspond to the actuarial value of the contributions. Under the second the pension is paid from an accumulated reserve and based on the actuarial equivalent of the contributions which have been made by the employee and/or the government in his behalf. The actuarial plan is regarded as highly preferable; it is of little value to have a pension plan on the statute books if funds are not available to meet claims when they come due.

In general, in the operation of pension plans the cash-disbursement

---

[12] Mr. Mallory's testimony appears in the published hearings, and was reprinted in a number of the journals of the state leagues of municipalities. See also Corson, John "Can Municipal Employees Get Federal Insurance?" *New Jersey Municipalities,* March 1941, pp. 4–6.

[13] White, L. D., *Introduction to the Study of Public Administration,* p. 404.

nd noncontributory features are usually associated, while the actuarial nd contributory systems likewise go together. The former combina- ion is the simpler. Since no provision is made for the accumulation of eserves, funds must be appropriated as required to meet whatever bur- len is placed upon the system. Only two states, Connecticut and Maine, mploy this system; it has, however, been used extensively by local nits, especially for such groups as firemen and policemen. The princi- al weakness of this type arises from the fact that the retired or disabled mployee has no guarantee that the funds for the payment of his allow- nce, particularly those to be provided by the government, will be orthcoming. This rather tragic situation has developed time and again n local systems, in which diversion of funds and poor management ave caused many a scandal.

The actuarial plan is scientifically much more sound than the cash- lisbursement plan, and at the same time it is much more difficult to in- titute and operate. In most cases, contributions planned on an actuarial asis are provided for on an equal basis by both the government and he employee; the employee builds up an annuity which becomes effec- ive at the time of his retirement. In some jurisdictions the contributions re on a sliding scale, the rates depending upon the life expectancy of he employee according to age and sex. Three states — Colorado, Min- esota, and Ohio — do not contribute to their retirement funds and con- equently act merely as trustee of the annuity funds which are built up y regular deductions from the salaries of employees.

Retirement in the Federal Government. The first law creating a retire- ent system of general application for Federal employees was approved n 1920, amended four times two years later, and re-enacted with nu- erous changes in 1926. These changes provided for more liberal cov- rage; for an increase in the percentage contributed by employees from ½ to 3½ to 5 (it is now 6) per cent of the basic annual salary; for full redit for every year and every month of service up to thirty years; for n increase in the maximum annuity from $720 to $1000; and for com- ilation of more complete and more valuable records.

In the last twenty years numerous further amendments and im- rovements have been made, the most recent in 1948, when Congress assed the Langer-Chavez-Stevenson Retirement Act. It is a compul- ory contributory system in which the government matches the contri- utions made by the employee. It applies to all civil service employees nd to certain other specified classes of employees of the Federal gov- rnment, as well as to the regular annual employees of the District of Columbia. The administration of the system, formerly under the Com-

missioner of Pensions in the Department of the Interior, is now a re
sponsibility of the Civil Service Commission.

The principal provisions of the new Civil Service Retirement Act o
1948 may be summarized as follows: [14]

1. After April 1, 1948, an employee must have at least five years of *civilian* serv
   ice to qualify for *any* annuity benefits.
2. The age requirements (70 years mandatory, 62 optional with fifteen years c
   service or 60 with thirty years) remain the same except that you may now re
   tire at 55 with thirty years' service with 3 per cent deducted from your annu
   ity for each year you are under 60.
3. The retirement deduction will be increased from 5 to 6 per cent in July, 194?
   and interest on the money in the retirement fund is reduced from 4. to 3 pe
   cent, effective January 1, 1948.
4. An immediate annuity is available, under certain conditions, to employee
   who leave the government after twenty-five years of service. This applies to
   person who is separated through no fault of his own (in a reduction-in-force
   for example). This portion of the new law was made retroactive to July 1
   1947. The amount such a person receives will not be a full annuity if he is les
   than 60 years old. It will be scaled down at the rate of ¼ of 1 per cent pe
   month (3 per cent per year) for each full month under 60 at the date o
   separation.
5. After April 1, 1948, there is but one age at which annuity starts for those pe:
   sons who work for the Government for at least five civilian years and the
   leave before reaching retirement age. That age is 62. In connection with thi
   if a person serves at least five civilian years, but hasn't reached the twenty
   year mark, he has the choice of taking a refund of all the money to his credi
   in the Fund (including interest) or leaving it in the Fund for annuity pu
   poses when he reaches age 62. If he takes the refund, no annuity is possible
   (This was amended in 1949 to permit withdrawal of funds up to twent
   years.)
6. The method of computing annuities is now a simple basic formula. This is it
   when the person's average salary for his highest five consecutive years of Fe
   eral service is $5000 or more, we merely take 1½ per cent of that average an
   multiply by the total number of years of service. If the person's five-year ave
   age salary is less than $5000, we take 1 per cent of it, add $25 to that, an
   then multiply by the total years of service. The result is the annuity which
   payable.

[14] From *Information Bulletin*, Library of Congress, March 23–29, 1949; other sum
maries by Edward H. Rees, Chairman of the House Committee, in *Congressional Rec
ord*, March 5, 1948, and Office of the Quartermaster General, OQMG Bulletin No. 3
March 8, 1948; Myers, Robert J., "Recent Amendments to the Civil Service Retiremen
Act," *Social Security Bulletin*, April, 1948, pp. 9–17, 44. For summaries of the prov
sions of the old law, see the following publications of the United States Civil Servic
Commission: *The Civil Service Retirement Act, with Annotations and Regulation*
(1942); *Annual Report* of the Retirement Division; *Retirement in Brief* (1944); *You
Retirement System: Questions and Answers Concerning the Federal Civil Service Re
tirement Law* (1944).

The Federal retirement provisions discussed up to this point relate to classified employees under the civil service (mainly executive), approximately 97 per cent of the total number. The remainder are covered by the provisions of no less than nine different laws, a situation that results in what one writer has referred to as the jumble of public retirement systems. The list follows:

Alaska Railroad Retirement Act
Panama Canal Zone Retirement Act
Foreign Service Retirement and Disability Act
Federal Reserve Act of 1913 and Banking Act of 1933
United States Naval Academy (civilian employees)
Comptroller of the Currency (Examining Division)
Tennessee Valley Authority System, established 1939
District of Columbia Policemen's and Firemen's Relief Act
District of Columbia Teachers' Retirement Act

The first two of these systems are administered by the United States Civil Service Commission, while the last two correspond to municipal systems. The others are administered by the departments or agencies to whose employees the laws apply. All are contributory systems.[15] In addition, within a period of twenty years Congress has enacted a retirement plan for railroad employees and an old-age and survivors insurance plan for the majority of workers gainfully employed and for their dependents.

Legislation is also in effect applicable to officers and employees of other branches of the government service. Members of the judiciary may retire on full pay at age seventy. The Legislative Reorganization Act of 1946 provides for retirement of members of the Congress. Other legislation strengthens the retirement and disability provisions relating to members of the Foreign Service of the United States. Legislative employees have been under the provisions of the Civil Service Retirement Act for many years. The provisions relating to members of Congress may be summarized as follows: [16]

Coverage is optional and may be elected within six months of either the date the legislation was enacted or the date on which the Member of Congress takes his oath of office. There is no compulsory retirement age. Monthly benefits are payable for disability after five years' service, or for age-and-service retirement at age sixty-two, after six years' service. If a member with six years' service or more

See Brannon, Thurza J., *Outline of Federal Retirement Systems* (Federal Security Agency, Washington, 1948), and Pizer, Marguerite L., "The Jumble of Public Retirement Systems," *George Washington Law Review*, December, 1943, pp. 57–71. Ruth Sticker had useful discussions of these problems in the *Social Security Bulletin*, April, 1941, and January, 1942.
Social Security Bulletin, November, 1946, pp. 44–45.

is not re-elected before age sixty-two, the first payment is deferred to that age. If an annuitant returns to Congress, benefit payments are suspended, and he may increase his subsequent benefit amount by resuming contributions. If a disability annuitant recovers before retirement age but is not re-elected within the year following recovery, monthly payments are suspended until he attains age sixty-two.

A Member of Congress, like a civil service employee, may arrange for a survivor annuity by electing a reduced employee annuity at the time of retirement; a lump sum consisting of the unexpended balance of his contributions (with interest) is payable when death occurs before retirement or on the death of an annuitant who has not elected a survivor annuity. Refunds of contributions on separation from service, however, are made only if the Member served less than six years (instead of five as for civil service employees) and was not retired for disability. If he is later re-elected, the Member must redeposit the amount refunded, with interest, before he may become eligible for an annuity.

State Retirement Systems. Sporadic attempts to provide pensions for certain groups of public employees in specific areas began in some jurisdictions as much as a century ago. An historical survey of pension fund legislation in Illinois, for instance, shows that such legislation was first enacted in that state in the year 1849 and that by 1939 there existed the same kind of jumble of legislation which characterizes the pension situation in many other jurisdictions: [17]

Illinois appears to have been one of the first states to provide a retirement plan for any class of public or quasi-public employees. As early as 1849 there was established a benevolent association to give relief to volunteer firemen of the City of Chicago who became disabled as a result of their duties. While this act was private legislation — not public — it was the first of nearly 200 original and amendatory statutes relating to the pensioning of public employees in Illinois.

The twenty-seven public pension systems in Illinois affect about 110,000 public employees, of which about 17,000 were being paid pension benefits in 1939 while the balance were still in active service.

Of the twenty-seven pension systems, the application of seventeen is confined to employees of Cook County, the City of Chicago, or of special districts whose boundaries approximate those of the county or city names. One plan applies only to Peoria policemen, while five relate to particular groups in the state outside Chicago; and four are of general application for particular groups of employees state or local as the case may be, without any limitation to particular governmental units. While there are only twenty-seven pension systems in Illinois, the number of separate public pension funds is 127, since many municipalities may maintain pension funds under a single statute. Thus, the statute relative to pensions for policemen outside Chicago governs the operation of funds maintained by fifty-three different municipalities, while forty-nine are maintained under the corresponding statute relative to firemen.

---

[17] Illinois Legislative Council, *Factors Involved in Pension Legislation for Governmental Employees in Illinois*, pp. 3–4; see also Illinois Department of Insurance, *Report of Examination of Public Pension Funds, 1939* (Springfield, 1939).

The first state-wide retirement system for teachers was set up in Rhode Island in 1907. Others followed from time to time, until thirty years later there were fifteen such systems. In 1937 six new laws were adopted, and in the decade from 1937 to 1947 the number increased to such an extent that teachers in all states except Idaho were covered. The movement for the coverage of public employees generally began a little later and progressed more slowly. Massachusetts adopted the first law in 1911, Connecticut and Maine following in 1919. By the end of 1940 there were only thirteen laws, but by the end of the 1947 sessions there were thirty-two. All of this means that more systems were set up in the last seven years than in the preceding thirty.[18]

State employee retirement systems are of several types. In one type all employees except perhaps a few elected or appointed officials are covered. In another, teachers, who have a separate system of their own, are excluded. In still other types coverage of employees of local units is compulsory, or optional, or authorized but not utilized by the local units, or not even authorized. The prevalence of these various types is shown in the 1948–1949 edition of the *Book of the States*. Considering the tremendous number (approximately 1800) of retirement systems in existence for state and/or local employees, the coverage is poor. Forty-eight systems protect over 76 per cent of California state and local employees; 196 systems protect 65 per cent of Massachusetts employees. The national average ratio of covered to total employment, which is 46 per cent, is exceeded by only fifteen states. In contrast, less than 10 per cent of the state and local employees were protected by retirement plans in twelve states, aside from Idaho which has no system. Perhaps a more illuminating index is that of state, city, and other local personnel, exclusive of school employees. In only ten states was the ratio of covered to total nonschool employment more than 46 per cent; while in half the states over 90 per cent of nonschool employees lacked pension protection.[19]

Study of an analytical table of state retirement laws compiled by A. A. Weinberg, actuary, shows that in most states sixty years is the minimum age for retirement. The number of years of service required varies from two and a half in Iowa to thirty in Indiana. Retirement is usually compulsory at seventy. In most states no limitation is specified on the maximum earnings covered. The percentage of employee con-

---

[18] The best of the older works covering retirement systems is Conyngton. The best current discussion of the teacher systems is in the NEA research bulletin, *Statutory Provisions for Statewide Retirement Systems;* and for the systems applicable to public employees generally, Weinberg's "Retirement Planning for Public Employees," which has an excellent table setting forth the essential features of all the state systems.
[19] These figures are from *Retirement Systems for State and Local Government Employees: 1941*, p. 6 (Governments Division, Bureau of the Census, Washington, 1943).

tributions is normally set at 4 or 5, the state contribution ranging from 2 to 3½. The employee's contribution is deducted from his salary; that of the state is commonly provided by legislative appropriation. California has sought contributions large enough to provide a more adequate pension; rates range from 4.82 to 11.61 per cent for employees and 7.2 per cent for the state. The average monthly payment per beneficiary, for all systems in 1941 was $72.00. State systems for state and local employees were the lowest at $59.00, while city and district systems were the highest at $78.00.[20]

Allowances for disability constitute an important consideration in a retirement plan for public employees, and most plans make some provision for such allowances. One authority on the subject defines disability as (1) the impairment or loss of physical fitness or (2) mental incapacity resulting from illness or injury. Under many of the retirement plans now in force which embody a disability provision, a benefit is granted when the employee cannot properly perform the duties of the position occupied at the time of disability.[21]

In most states refunds are permitted, normally with interest varying from 2 to 4 per cent, when employees leave the service. The formulae for determining benefits to annuitants and to dependents vary greatly from state to state, the most common for annuitants being one sixtieth or one seventieth of the average final salary per years of service. Not more than half of the systems provide occupational death benefits, although most of them do provide both occupational and nonoccupational disability benefits; naturally, they provide for the former at a higher rate than for the latter. The administration of the system is usually under a retirement board; the secretary of the board serves as administrative officer.

Retirement Systems in Local Units. Provision for retirement of employees of municipalities and other local units has gone through an interesting series of changes. As has been indicated by reference to the Illinois experience, the early acts were not only local in application but each was restricted to a particular type of employee in a designated governmental unit. Most common were pension funds for firemen, policemen, and teachers; many of these systems continue to this day. The next step provided for city-wide or county-wide systems, embracing all employees of the unit in question or all not already covered by special systems of their own. Finally came the modern period of general state legislation covering all local units, either authorizing coverage in

[20] *Ibid.*, p. 31.
[21] See Hoge, Wilson E., "Disability Provisions," a mimeographed report prepared for the Committee on Public Employee Retirement Administration of the Municipal Finance Officers Association (Chicago, 1942).

the system established for state employees or setting up a separate system for all local employees. The latter arrangement, of course, resulted in the operation of two separate and independent pension plans.

The basis for the initiation of the first type is well illustrated by the findings of a recent survey of fire-fighting activities in Pennsylvania, findings which are typical of other jurisdictions: [22]

> Originally, all firemen in Pennsylvania were volunteers and, although they risked injury or death in service to the community, they were not considered municipal employees. It became necessary to organize private associations to give financial aid to disabled firemen and to widows and orphans of firemen. The first of these organizations was the Philadelphia Association for the Relief of Disabled Firemen, chartered in 1833.

A few years later, in 1857, a 2 per cent tax was levied on the premiums collected by foreign fire-insurance companies; after this was declared unconstitutional by the courts in 1879, a state tax of eight mills on the dollar was substituted, on the gross amount of premiums collected by insurance companies incorporated for profit in the state. Ten years later a tax of 2 per cent was imposed on premiums of insurance companies of other states and foreign countries doing business in the Commonwealth. In 1895 the 2 per cent tax was limited to fire-insurance companies, one-half of the net amount received from the foreign fire-insurance tax being paid to city and borough treasurers on the basis of the returns of this tax from such units. Although many additional changes have since been made in the law, close to $2,500,000 was paid by the state to the local units in a recent year for firemen's pensions. In 1946 the state Police Pension Fund granted to 171 municipalities a much smaller allocation of funds for police pensions.

The second type of pension plan mentioned above is that of city-wide application, with the possible exception of existing special systems such as those for police and firemen. Such systems exist in many cities, large and small, throughout the country. The major difficulty with both of these types — the specialized group plan and the local unit system — arises from the fact that they are often incompetently managed and consequently have serious financial difficulties. This is, in fact, a major reason for the trend toward the third type, the state-wide system for local government employees. The management of any such enterprise is a highly technical job requiring observance of established actuarial standards; it is one which small cities as a rule are not equipped properly to discharge and which numerous large ones have failed to discharge for other reasons.

When planning a retirement system for the officers and employees

---

[22] Smedley, Elizabeth, "Early Efforts Toward Firemen's Relief," *Bulletin* of the Department of Internal Affairs, April, 1947, pp. 9–13.

of a local unit, several major problems arise: Who shall be included in the membership? What kind of system shall be established? When shall retirement become effective? With regard to coverage it may be said that inclusion of all permanent full-time officers and employees should be compulsory and that firemen and policemen should be included by consolidation of existing systems if such exist. Part-time, seasonal, and casual employees should not be included. The answer to the second question has already been indicated. The third question itself presents a number of subsidiary questions, such as age for voluntary retirement, age for normal retirement upon the initiative of the city, and age for compulsory retirement. The answers to these questions depend in part upon the individual employee and the nature of his work and in part upon actuarial experience which applies to any retirement system regardless of the size of the unit in which it operates.[23]

As of 1947 there were twenty-four states with laws providing for state-wide retirement funds to cover local government employees. The great majority had been established since 1938; ten of them were created or extended to cities by legislation passed in 1945. Fourteen of the twenty-four have a single public employees' retirement fund for state and local governments; [24] the remaining ten established separate municipal retirement funds administered on a state-wide basis.[25] With two exceptions, states in this latter group maintain independent state employees' retirement plans.

In the operation of these systems the term "municipality" is very broadly construed to include (as in Michigan) "any county, city, village, or township," or corporation established by, supported by, or engaged in the performance of any governmental function.[26] Entry into the system may be voted either by the governing body of the local unit or by a majority of the electorate in that unit. It is often provided that entry becomes effective at the beginning of the next calendar year.

---

[23] See Gabriel, A. G., "The Who and When of a Municipal Retirement System," *The American City*, April, 1947, pp. 111–112.

[24] See Kansas Legislative Council, *Retirement of Municipal Employees*, p. 1. These states are: Alabama, California, Colorado, Indiana, Iowa, Maine, Maryland, Montana, New Hampshire, New Jersey, New York, Oregon, South Carolina, and Virginia.

[25] *Ibid.;* these states are: Connecticut, Illinois, Michigan, Minnesota, Nebraska, North Carolina, Ohio, Pennsylvania, Texas, and Wisconsin.

[26] Good descriptive material is available on some of these systems: Michigan Municipal League, *Explanation of the Michigan Municipal Employees' Retirement Act*, and *Some Questions and Answers about the Michigan Municipal Employees' Retirement System* (Ann Arbor, both 1946); Lee, Earl J., "The Nebraska Municipal Retirement Law," *Nebraska Municipal Review*, December, 1946, pp. 2–17; North Carolina League of Municipalities, *The North Carolina Local Governmental Employees Retirement System* (Raleigh, 1941); "Texas Municipal Retirement System," *Texas Municipalities*, August, 1947, pp. 166–183; Wisconsin Municipal Retirement Fund, *Handbook of Information* (Madison, 1944).

While the establishment of a single state system for all employees, state and local, is preferable, the local units usually urge a separate system on the theory that their problems are "different." [27] Whatever the solution, the administration of retirement systems necessitates a high degree of interlevel and interjurisdictional cooperation.

SELECTED REFERENCES

Bankers Trust Company, *106 Retirement Plans, 1944–1945* (New York, 1945). Analysis of retirement plans in private firms.

Brannon, Thurza J., *Outline of Federal Retirement Systems* (Federal Security Agency, Washington, 1948). Best survey of existing Federal systems.

Illinois Legislative Council, *Factors Involved in Pension Legislation for Governmental Employees in Illinois* (Springfield, 1940). Other studies dealing with pension and removal problems include: *Right of Appeal from Removals under the Merit System* (Springfield, 1937), and *Pensions for Firemen and Policemen* (Springfield, 1945).

Kansas Legislative Council, *Retirement Systems for State Employees in Kansas* (Topeka, 1937); see also *Retirement of Municipal Employees* (Topeka, 1946).

Larsen, Christian L., and Cowan, Conrad, *South Carolina Public Employee Retirement Systems* (Bureau of Public Administration, University of South Carolina, 1947).

McCamman, Dorothy F., *The Scope of Protection Under State and Local Government Retirement Systems* (Bureau of Statistics and Research, Social Security Board, 1944). The most recent and the best general survey available.

Meriam, Lewis, *The Principles Governing the Retirement of Public Employees* (Appleton, New York, 1918). This is the original work on the subject; for another survey, made ten years later, see Conyngton, Mary A., *Public Service Retirement Systems: United States, Canada, and Europe* (Bureau of Labor Statistics, Bulletin No. 477, Washington, 1929).

Municipal Finance Officers Association, *Retirement Plans for Public Employees* (Chicago, 1946); for other studies at the municipal level, see Association of Washington Cities, *Analysis of Selected State-wide Retirement Systems for Municipal Employees* (Olympia, 1945); Kansas, *supra;* North Carolina League of Municipalities, *The North Carolina Local Government Employees Retirement System* (Raleigh, 1941).

National Education Association, *Statutory Provisions for State-wide Retirement Systems* (Washington, 1946). This survey is limited to teachers; for an earlier one in the same field, see Studenski, Paul, *Teacher Pension Systems in the United States* (Institute for Government Research, Washington, 1930).

Pouder, Margaret K., *State Retirement Systems for Public Employees* (Tennessee State Planning Board, Nashville, 1947).

United States Bureau of the Census, *Retirement Systems for State and Local Government Employees, 1941* (Washington, 1943).

United States Civil Service Commission, *Civil Service Retirement Act, with Annotations and Regulations* (Washington, 1943), and *Retirement Systems for Federal Employees: A Selected List of References* (Washington, 1946).

Weinberg, A. A., "Retirement Planning for Public Employees," in *Book of the States, 1948–1949*, pp. 204–221 (Council of State Government, Chicago, 1948). Includes an extremely valuable comparative table on coverage, qualifications, and contributions.

---

[27] For a good presentation of the problem of local participation, see *County Participation in the State Employees' Retirement System* (California Department of Justice, Sacramento, 1944).

14

MODERN PERSONNEL
MANAGEMENT

In the preceding chapters of Part II the operating problems of personnel administration have been discussed. The major concern has been with what happens in a department or agency when employees are hired, placed, disciplined, fired, promoted, or confronted with problems regarding which they may seek the aid of the employee counselor. It now seems appropriate to look at the whole personnel-management program of the government as it appears from the vantage point of the central personnel agency. In this connection attention will be given to the central agency, its organization, duties, and responsibilities, and to some of the modern mechanisms in the form of councils and committees which are used to make the program effective. Finally some consideration will be given to personnel utilization.

The Central Personnel Agency

The prevailing form of organization for the central personnel agency is a board or commission of three members. This pattern was established by the provisions of the original Pendleton Act of 1883, at a time when the Hydra-headed body was widely in vogue for all sorts of administrative purposes — health, police, water, parks, and public works. Unfortunately, many jurisdictions continue to follow this pattern, although the trend is now definitely in the direction of the single administrator. Where the board is still retained, as it usually is in health administration, it is an advisory and rule-making body rather than an administrative body.

United States Civil Service Commission. The Civil Service Act specifies that "the President is authorized to appoint, by and with the advice and consent of the Senate, three persons, not more than two of whom shall be adherents of the same party, as Civil Service Commissioners," the said Commissioners to hold no other official place under the United States. The President, the act continues, "may remove any Commissioner" and may fill any vacancy so as to conform to the conditions governing the original selections. The original salary was $3500; it is now $10,000.

The act charges the Commission with certain specific duties, the first of which is to formulate and adopt suitable rules and regulations for carrying the act into effect. It is further specified that these rules shall provide:

1. That open competitive examinations shall be held for testing the fitness of applicants
2. That all positions shall be arranged in classes and grades
3. That appointments in the departmental service shall be apportioned among the several states according to population
4. That a period of probation shall precede any absolute appointment
5. That no civil service employee shall be required to contribute to any political fund or to render any political service
6. That no civil service employee has any right to use his official authority or influence to coerce the political action of any person or body
7. That noncompetitive or qualifying examinations may be given in proper cases
8. That the appointing power shall notify the Commission of selections made from certificates issued to it, and of other personnel actions

The Commission is further authorized and directed to enforce its regulations, to make investigations pertinent to the discharge of its responsibilities, to keep records, and to make an annual report to the President. As a standard-setting agency it has a particular responsibility to formulate and carry out a sound personnel program within its own organization.

The Central Agency in the States. The type of organization used for the state personnel agency will depend in the first place upon whether or not the state has a civil service law. It is possible, of course, to have a classification of positions and uniform salary schedules within these classifications without having civil service. It is also possible to keep reasonably adequate service records without civil service, although the rate of turnover is naturally higher in jurisdictions where political acceptability takes precedence over merit. In fact the major difference between the application blank which the applicant fills out in a state with civil service and the blank he fills out in a state without civil service, may consist in the presence or absence of a form requiring the signature of a political sponsor. This may be the most important part of the application in states without civil service, but even at that the importance of the form depends upon the character of the administration and the pressure upon its members to provide jobs for the faithful. Even in such a system, there is usually a central personnel office where records are kept and through which all questions relating to personnel are cleared.[1]

Civil service laws now exist in more than half of the states.[2] In such jurisdictions it is customary to have a commission of three, not more than two of whom shall be members of the same political party, to administer the law. The commissioners are appointed by the governor for terms of from three to six years, and are usually confirmed by the senate.[3] Overlapping terms are frequently prescribed. The compensation of commissioners is inadequate in all states except Maryland, New York, and North Carolina; in many states expenses incurred in attendance at meetings are allowed. The commission is usually authorized to employ an executive officer who is responsible for the actual administration of the system.[4]

Municipal Organization. The same problems of organization arise in the cities as well, though the operations are with a few exceptions on a smaller scale. The lines of development have been the same. Starting with the independent commission, which is still retained in some jurisdictions, the trend has been toward integration of the personnel setup with the administration either by employing an executive director for the commission or by creating a director of personnel, with or without an advisory committee of citizens. Pfiffner identifies these types as the independent, the completely integrated, and the partially integrated forms of organization. The new type of personnel department is gradually replacing the old type of civil service commission especially in the constantly increasing number of city-manager cities, in which the manager is made legally responsible for the administration of the personnel system.[5]

The Single Commissioner. The preference of students of personnel administration has been shifting from the commission form toward a single commissioner. The Maryland Civil Service Law (1920), which has been reasonably successful in operation, provided from the beginning

---

[1] For a description of such a system, see Joint Legislative Committee on Finances, *A Survey of the Government of Pennsylvania,* pp. 47, 611–617 (Harrisburg, 1934), and Michigan Civil Service Study Commission, *Report,* pp. 20–21 (Lansing, 1936).

[2] See the author's *American State Government,* Third Edition, pp. 491–497 (Heath, Boston, 1946), and *The Book of the States, 1948–1949,* pp. 195–201.

[3] The Louisiana law provides a unique system of selection. The presidents of five leading educational institutions in the state (state university, leading non-sectarian university, and three sectarian institutions) each nominate three candidates, from which list the governor appoints a commission of five members.

[4] For descriptions of the organization in specific states, see titles in Selected References; also Olson, Emery E., "A Personnel Board in Action" (California State Personnel Board), *Public Personnel Review,* October, 1946, pp. 200–208.

[5] These questions are discussed in the standard texts on municipal administration by Hodges, MacCorkle, Munro, Pfiffner, and Reed.

for a single commissioner.[6] All the state-wide civil service laws enacted since 1936 place the administrative functions not in a board or commission but in the hands of one official, known usually as the personnel director. Moreover, three states which started with board administration have since amended their laws to provide for a single administrator. Only five of the twenty-five state-wide merit systems existing in 1945 still retained board administration. Serious consideration was given in 1947 in both New York and Ohio to a change from board administration to a single commissioner type.[7]

Under existing arrangements in the Civil Service Commission there is no head. There are conflict and division of authority within the Commission itself, and a serious absence of that close relationship with the head of the executive branch which should exist with the over-all personnel agency of the Federal government. It is significant that both the President's Committee on Administrative Management and the Hoover Commission recommended drastic changes in this setup for the administration of the Federal civil service. The former proposed a single executive officer to be known as the Civil Service Administrator, and a nonsalaried civil service board of seven members to serve primarily in an advisory capacity. The basic structure recommended by the Hoover Commission calls for a Director of the Office of Personnel in the President's Office, who would serve as Chairman and Administrator of the Civil Service Commission. Under this plan the Commission's work in standard-setting and top policy determination would be emphasized, while responsibility for the multitude of personnel transactions would be shifted to the operating agencies.

The Personnel Program

Defining the Personnel Function. There has in the past been wide variation in practice, if not actual disagreement in principle, as to what the personnel job really is. Personnel officers like other "bureaucrats" have tended to stretch their operations into more and more different fields of

---

[6] See Short, Oliver C., "The Maryland One-Man Civil Service Commission," *National Municipal Review*, March, 1926, pp. 153-157; Howard, L. Vaughn, "Maryland's Single-Commissioner Civil Service System," *Public Personnel Review*, April, 1946, pp. 73-80.

[7] The following are the states which entrust the administration of their state-wide merit systems to a single administrator, either with or without a board for rule-making, the hearing of appeals, and the determination of policies. The year of the adoption of the present merit system is shown in each case. A board for nonadministrative functions exists in all but Maryland and Virginia; in Connecticut, its powers are only advisory.

Alabama — 1939	Louisiana — 1940	Minnesota — 1939
California — 1913	Maine — 1937	Rhode Island — 1939
Connecticut — 1937	Maryland — 1920	Tennessee — 1937
Indiana — 1941	Massachusetts — 1884	Virginia — 1942
Kansas — 1941	Michigan — 1937	Wisconsin — 1905

activity. The situation became so confused that in the summer of 1947 the Bureau of the Budget called upon the Federal Personnel Council for help. There were up to that time no staffing standards for personnel offices, no established bases upon which reliable budget estimates could be made for carrying on the personnel function in a given agency. And obviously, no such standards could be established until the proper boundaries of the personnel function were marked out and agreed upon.

The task was indeed difficult; perhaps that was the reason why so little work had been done upon it. Many people were involved in an extensive effort during a period of three weeks — the Council's Committee on Personnel Management, a subcommittee, a work group,[8] and a considerable number of personnel technicians.

Activities of Personnel Administration

The Work Group

1. Direction and Administration of the Personnel Program
2. Position Classification and Compensation
3. Employment, Placement, and Separations
4. Training
5. Employee Relations and Services
6. Health and Safety
7. Personnel Actions, Records, and Reports
8. Services Performed as Agents for and under the Direct Supervision of the Civil Service Commission

Federal Personnel Council

1. Position Classification
2. Salary Administration
3. Employment
4. Placement
5. Efficiency Rating
6. Training
7. Health
8. Safety
9. Employee Relations
10. Employee Counseling
11. Employee Services
12. Separations
13. Leave
14. Advice and Consultation to Management
15. Personnel Research
16. Procedures and Records

---

[8] Ralph M. Hogan, Navy Department, Chairman; Kenneth B. Atkinson, then Assistant Director of Personnel, Department of Commerce; Harrison E. Meyers, Director of Personnel, Federal Works Agency; E. J. Sheppard, Jr., Bureau of the Budget; Ward Stewart, Director of Personnel, Atomic Energy Commission; and the author. The War Department, in Civilian Personnel Circular No. 38, June, 1947, had undertaken to state, for its own uses, some "Tentative Staffing Standards for Civilian Personnel Offices." The following are the best of the printed statements: Couch, Virgil L., "The Scope of Personnel Activities in the Federal Service," *Personnel Administration*, January, 1948, pp. 1–14, 18; Donovan, Jeremiah J., "The Classification of Subject Matter Dealing with Public Personnel Administration," *Public Personnel Review*, January, 1941, pp. 36–39; Hubbard, Henry F., "The Elements of a Comprehensive Personnel Program," *ibid.*, July, 1940, pp. 1–17; National Roster of Scientific and Specialized Personnel, "Description of the Profession of Personnel Administration" (leaflet); Unsigned, "The Field of Personnel Administration," *Personnel Administration*, April, 1945, pp. 16–18; and "The Profession of Personnel Administration," *Personnel Journal*, January, 1946, pp. 265–269.

The first item in the Work Group classification is concerned with the personnel function at the top management level — policy determination, planning, and developing and supervising the execution of the policies decided upon. Items 2–6, inclusive, should at this stage of the discussion be more or less self-explanatory. There were questions on some items, such as the propriety of including separations with employment and placement and the desirability of separating employee services from employee relations, and safety from health. Major questions of policy developed regarding both of the last two items. As for item 7, every major phase of personnel work involves "records and reports." The question was whether this activity should be broken up so that the records and reports relating to each element in the program would be maintained by those responsible for its administration or whether the whole record-keeping operation should be centralized. The latter alternative was agreed upon because the committee was at the time concerned with functions and not with organizational structure. It was not meant to imply that this would serve as an organizational pattern.

The final item raises the question of the labor boards which perform services as the agents of and under the direct supervision of the United States Civil Service Commission. The present system is manifestly bad. The legislatures — Federal and state alike — have never been willing to give the central personnel agency sufficient funds to enable it properly to perform its job; on the Federal level, therefore, the Commission has been obliged to borrow personnel (and indirectly, funds) by shoving off on the departments and agencies functions that it should itself perform. The departments are really doing the Commission's work and paying the bill besides. The members of the Committee felt that this undesirable practice should be brought out into the open.

One other matter deserves mention. The Committee took the position that certain activities that relate to personnel are not a proper part of the personnel program. In excluding from this classification the items of leave accounting, pay-roll accounting, and retirement accounting, the Committee was merely confirming earlier decisions to the same effect by the Office of the Comptroller General and by the Chairman of the House Committee on Appropriations. While these items relate to personnel or may even be considered borderline cases, their fiscal and accounting aspects take precedence over any relationship they may have to the personnel function.

Responsibility of the Commission. The Commission, as the central personnel agency of the government, is responsible for the personnel program in all departments and agencies. Our consideration will have to be centered not so much on the program itself as on the nature and extent of the responsibility of the central personnel agency for it and the means by which it is to be carried out.[9]

If this responsibility is to be adequately discharged, there must be "some changes made" both in the general attitude toward personnel administration and in the attitude of the personnel agencies themselves. The public as represented in the legislature must get over the idea that personnel administration is a luxury, a nice thing to have if there is plenty of money. A sound personnel program is no luxury; it is a necessity in any well-administered organization, either public or private. It will pay dividends in the long run in many ways. But it will not run itself. It requires intelligent leadership and time and money and effort.

The general attitude is illustrated by what happened in the Federal government at the end of World War II. During the war the Commission had been able to obtain more adequate financing than ever before; but as soon as the last shot was fired, the situation changed. For the first time in its history the Commission had a trained staff and resources, in the central office and in the field, with which to do a well-rounded job. Before long, the staff was scattered, although reduction-in-force, administration of veterans' preference, and the loyalty program meant more work rather than less. The Commission, left without necessary funds, inaugurated its big "decentralization program," farming out its work on the departments and agencies, not because anyone seriously believed that this was the thing to do but because there was no alternative.

On the other hand some personnel people and even some personnel agencies have the wrong attitude toward their job. In the old days the chief function of the Commission was that of a policeman. The purpose was to "keep the rascals out" and to do what could be done to prevent the occurrence of the more glaring abuses. Under such circumstances the personnel agency was bound to be more or less unpopular. But times have changed, and the duties have changed or should have changed with them. The major purpose is no longer to exclude the incompetent but rather to recruit the competent, hold them in the service, and develop and improve the service.

Assistance to Operating Agencies. The major function of the agency involves over-all planning of the program in each of the areas discussed

[9] See Bureau of the Budget, "Organization and Responsibility for Personnel Administration," *Personnel Administration*, May, 1943, pp. 3–5; Short, Oliver C., "Internal Management of a Central Personnel Agency," *Public Personnel Review*, January, 1942, pp. 7–10; and Wright, James F., "Making the Most of Personnel Staffs," *Personnel Administration*, November, 1947, pp. 39–42.

in the preceding chapters — recruitment, placement, training, employee relations, public relations for the service as a whole, and so on. This can best be accomplished by developing a pattern for personnel office operation and by giving assistance and full cooperation to the operating agencies. Assistance can be rendered through representatives assigned to each of the agencies to confer with them in working out solutions of their personnel problems. The representatives serve in a liaison capacity between the agency and the various sections of the central office. They have at their disposal the facilities of the office as well as the advice of experts in various phases of personnel work. The representatives are — or should be — able and mature persons, with a well-rounded knowledge of the whole personnel setup.[10]

The government's personnel program is in a very real sense a program affected with a public interest. The establishment of good relations between the personnel agency and the operating agencies — important as that is — is not enough. The program itself has to be formulated, and it should be formulated by democratic processes. The central agency should not be in the position of telling operating agencies what they must do, or else; the two together should work out a program acceptable to both.[11] The best means yet discovered for doing this is the Council of Personnel Administration. When so formulated, the operating agencies are willing to cooperate in carrying out a program which they have helped to develop, which they understand, and which in most cases is in general harmony with the conditions confronting them, as they say, "in their own shops."

Equally important is the developing of decent public relations. In this area personnel agencies have been negligent. The public will support a public service and a personnel program that it knows and understands. The central personnel agency is primarily responsible for this understanding. Press and radio releases for the general information of the public are useful, but a successful public relations program requires

---

[10] For comment on this general problem, see Cushman, Charles H., "Relations Between the Commission and the Executive Officer," *Public Personnel Review*, April, 1947, pp. 67–72; Jouno, Randolph J., "Establishment Boards in the Federal Civil Service," *American Political Science Review*, October, 1947, pp. 955–962; Luikart, Fordyce W., "The Civil Service Commission's Inspection Program," *Personnel Administration*, May, 1947, pp. 16–18, 54; McDiarmid, John, "Attack Personnel Problems Cooperatively," *Public Personnel Review*, April, 1946, pp. 57–65 and "The Changing Role of the United States Civil Service Commission," *American Political Science Review*, December, 1946, pp. 1067–1096; Moyer, Lawson A., "The Work of Boards of United States Civil Service Examiners," *Public Personnel Review*, July, 1941, pp. 192–198; Warner, Kenneth O., and Zook, Donovan F., "Improving Relationships Between the Personnel Office and the Operating Offices," *Personnel Administration*, September, 1946, pp. 2–9; and Webb, James E., "Relations Between the Budget and Personnel Agencies," *Public Personnel Review*, January, 1947, pp. 14–16.
[11] See Bratton, Barbara L., "Putting Personnel Policies in Writing," *Public Management*, February, 1946, pp. 42–45.

much more than this. If it is to succeed in attracting and holding capable people in a career service, the full cooperation of educational institutions and professional organizations is highly essential. This also can be accomplished through proper organization — in this case, committees working in close cooperation with all the available sources of supply of personnel possessing the requisite educational and professional qualifications.[12]

Councils of Personnel Administration

The first Council of Personnel Administration (now known as the Federal Personnel Council) was established in 1931. It was reconstituted in 1939 under the terms of the same Executive Order of the President which directed departments and agencies to establish personnel divisions under qualified directors. In 1947 the system was further modified. The Council is an interdepartmental committee on Federal personnel matters, composed of the directors of personnel of the various departments and agencies in the departmental service in Washington, together with representatives of the Civil Service Commission and the Bureau of the Budget. Under the guidance of Dr. Frederick M. Davenport and a staff which has purposely been kept small, it demonstrated its usefulness to such an extent that steps were taken by the Civil Service Commission early in 1943 to create similar field councils in the larger cities where there were considerable concentrations of Federal employment.

In fact, an experimental field council had been set up in Cleveland in October, 1942, and another for the New York metropolitan area in December of that year. The Philadelphia Council, largest and most active of the group, was organized in August, 1943. A couple of years later there were approximately thirty field councils functioning in continental United States.[13] In the meantime the idea has spread to the states and cities. A personnel council as a division of the Department of Civil Service was established by Governor Dewey in an Executive Order issued in June, 1945. In Los Angeles a personnel coordinating council was established in May, 1948, under the sponsorship of the city Civil Service Commission and the Bureau of Budget and Efficiency.

---

[12] On these questions, see the Civil Service Assembly's *Public Relations in Public Personnel Agencies* (Chicago, 1941).

[13] On the central council, see Executive Order No. 9830 of February 24, 1947, and "The Personnel Council System," a leaflet issued by the Federal Personnel Council, March, 1947. Information on the field councils is based largely on the *Statement of Purposes, Scope and Methods of Personnel Councils in the Field* (Federal Personnel Council, Washington, 1947), and an article by the author, growing out of his own experience with that organization: "The Philadelphia Federal Council of Personnel Administration," *Public Personnel Review*, October, 1945, pp. 240–247.

The New York Council is composed of a chairman appointed by the governor, a member suggested by the Department of Civil Service, one suggested by the Division of the Budget, and an official representative designated by each department. Weekly meetings are held by the three members, and monthly meetings by the full Council. In addition the Council has a small technical and clerical staff. Uniform rules have been established for all departments. The Council functions through committees established to recommend to the Civil Service Commission uniform practices which are acceptable both to the administration and to employees.[14] No field councils are at present contemplated in New York. The states of Maine and Maryland and the city of Detroit are also experimenting with the council idea.

Purposes of the Council Movement. The purpose of the Council, "functioning as an advisory body, is to promote through study and discussion the application, interpretation, and development of personnel policies and practices. Through common understanding and effort it seeks to improve personnel administration throughout the Federal service." The statement of purposes adopted by the Washington Council has been generally followed in the field. These purposes may be summarized as follows: (1) to serve through its committee organization as a fact-finding and coordinating body; (2) to serve as a central forum for the exchange of views and the formulation of common policies and procedures; (3) to serve as a clearinghouse for the dissemination and exchange of information on new policies, emergency situations, and so on; (4) to serve as another means of contact between Washington and the field, making available a two-way line of communication with regard to personnel policies and problems. The central council gives guidance to field councils but does not direct them; it furnishes them with its own minutes and digests of field council minutes, with a checklist of personnel legislation before Congress, and with other information services.

Membership. The problem of membership is always a difficult one. The central council, in spite of rigid limitations admitting only directors of personnel, has grown to twice its original size and is now so large that it crowds the supposedly ample quarters provided for it. In the field each council decides the size and inclusiveness of its own membership. Designations are made either through the appropriate field officials or the director of personnel of the department or agency. The membership problem is even more difficult here, for each of the larger departments has a number of installations, establishments, and offices

---

[14] Letter to the author from the Chairman of the Council, October 27, 1947.

in each large city, operating quite independently of one another and often located miles apart. To admit to membership only one representative of a department would clearly defeat the purposes of the movement. Virtually every department and agency in the government is represented in field councils throughout the nation.

The membership problem arises in another form, so far as subordinate officials in the personnel offices are concerned. The council can perform a tremendously useful training job — if the section heads are present at meetings. They will not come unless they have some status and are made to believe that their presence is desired. The Philadelphia Council solved this problem by establishing an associate membership to which were attached nearly all the privileges of regular membership, with a series of training groups in specialized areas for staff members. With the cooperation of top management in the various agencies and of most regular members, these arrangements proved highly satisfactory.

Committee Organization and Activities. Much of the work must be done through committees, which are regarded as the backbone of the council program. The table on page 255 shows the list of eleven committees of the central council as of 1947, the list of nine committees in the Philadelphia Council as of 1945, and the committee setup in the state council in Albany. The committees of the central council were set up in accordance with the sixteen elements of personnel administration developed by the Council.[15] In the Philadelphia list these elements have been combined even further, but the effort is still made to cover the whole field on a logical basis. This Council has, in addition, a small executive committee for the purpose of saving time in council meetings and relieving the membership from consideration of many problems involved in council management.

The Philadelphia Committee on Personnel Management was composed of the chairmen of all other committees. It had as its province important questions not covered by other committees and, in general, questions of sufficient scope to impinge upon the special fields of study assigned to two or more other committees.

The activities of the committees vary greatly from one council to another. They must, of course, study and report upon any question referred to them by the council, but they should in addition function as small councils in their respective subject-matter fields and exercise their own judgment and initiative in undertaking and carrying through

---

[15] See page 248, and Federal Personnel Council, *Committee Work in the Personnel Council System*, Revision 1 (Washington, May, 1946).

Council Committee Organization

FEDERAL DEPARTMENTAL SERVICE (WASHINGTON)	FEDERAL FIELD SERVICE (PHILADELPHIA)	NEW YORK STATE (ALBANY)
Personnel Management	Personnel Management	Agenda*
Classification and Salary Administration	Classification and Salary Administration	Examinations
Employment	Employment and Placement	Publications
Placement	Efficiency Ratings	
Efficiency Ratings	Training	
Training	Health and Safety	
Health and Safety	Employee Relations	
Employee Relations	Veterans' Affairs	
Separations	Executive	
Leave		
Records and Procedures		

* As of February, 1949, a permanent committee structure had yet to be determined; special committees were functioning on recruitment and supervisory training. Special committees on service ratings and tardiness had reported and had been dismissed.

worth-while projects. The extent to which they do this will depend largely upon the qualifications and the leadership of the committee chairmen, for here as elsewhere a good chairman can make a committee, while a poor one can ruin one. They may present findings and recommendations for council action and may inform the council of current developments in their particular subject-matter fields.

It is impossible to lay out a pattern for council-committee activities, for the nature of these will vary with time and circumstance. They represent, as does the council itself, an effort to develop decisions and administer policies through the cooperative effort of many units and many individuals. The following projects which were carried on by committees of the Philadelphia Council illustrate the types of work which such committees may properly undertake. Since a large number of agencies were conducting training programs of various sorts, the training committee undertook to establish some standards for the evaluation of these programs. Other committees prepared and circulated lists of materials, summaries, and outlines in their respective subject-matter fields or arranged for special courses to be given in local educational institutions. They developed and carried out plans for assisting agencies in handling specific problems, such as the annual efficiency rating program. They organized institutes or short courses, under the auspices of the Council, for the improvement of supervision or the utilization of community resources in counseling work.

Council Meetings and Activities. In the central council most of the weekly meetings are devoted to consideration of committee reports and discussion of current problems presented by members. In the field, where meetings are less frequent and where conditions are different, it is not possible, even by putting a good deal of pressure on committees, to obtain a sufficient number of discussible reports to occupy the attention of the council for any considerable portion of its meeting time. Consequently most sessions have to be planned to include talks, followed by discussion, and panel discussions, on timely topics in the personnel field.

Among the numerous activities of the councils mention has already been made of the training program conducted for personnel-office staff members and for the training of counselors on community services. Furthermore, the councils organized personnel management conferences; the one in Philadelphia provided a three-day program that would have reflected credit on a national association in the personnel field. Additional conferences were planned, but the exigencies of wartime transportation intervened. The Council was also active in the field of health and safety, carrying on a number of different programs under the leadership of its committee in that area. It sponsored chest X-ray campaigns, immunization programs, and Wassermann tests for as many Federal agencies and employees in the metropolitan area as were willing to cooperate.

One of the most important projects undertaken by the New York and Philadelphia councils was their scholarship program, which was worked out in cooperation with major educational institutions in each city. For a number of years two universities in Philadelphia have each offered one new scholarship a year for a three-year term to a Federal employee selected by the Council's scholarship committee. The selections have been made very carefully from among numerous applicants, after examination of each one's record and a personal interview. Only those who meet the full requirements of the universities are considered. No "strings" are attached to the scholarships, but the effort is made to select candidates who seem to have sufficient interest in the public service to warrant the expectation that they will continue in it.

Present Status and Future Prospects. The central council in Washington continues to function effectively, but the present status of the field councils is not too good because of the reduction-in-force program in the Federal service. Some areas no longer have enough personnel people to keep a council in active operation, and even in those areas where they still function, their effectiveness is impaired by lack of competent leadership. The drastic cuts in the Commission's budget and staff have resulted, in other words, in de-emphasizing council work.

This curtailment has been a serious mistake legislatively and administratively. The future prospects of the movement are good, provided at least one full-time professional person with necessary secretarial assistance is made available for each field council. This is not too much to ask because the guidance of a council program requires an enormous amount of work in planning and administration, in correspondence, and in individual contacts both in person and by telephone. The council movement should be regarded not as a fad of wartime but as an important aid in the development and execution of a sound personnel program at any time.

Committee on Administrative Personnel

In December, 1941, the Civil Service Commission established a national Committee on Administrative Personnel, composed of outstanding individuals in the field of management both public and private. Its objective was set forth in the following language:

To aid in the discovery and identification, in and out of the Federal service, of persons performing, or competent to perform, the functions of management, direction, and supervision; and to aid in their evaluation and placement in the Federal service at the point where they may be most useful to the nation; and to stimulate the development of administrative competence.

Thus the purpose was to aid the Commission in developing plans and programs for recruiting qualified people for higher-grade positions in the Federal service. As was noted earlier, this kind of recruiting requires special techniques if it is to be successful in bringing into the government service the highest type of individual. Like the personnel-council movement which preceded it, it proved so successful that it was believed that similar advantages might be realized from the establishment of similar committees in the field.

In 1944 the Commission accordingly directed its regional directors to organize regional committees on administrative personnel. The directors were given a good deal of freedom in determining the size of the committee and the character of the membership. Some regions set up a large committee composed of "big name" individuals in key positions — presidents of universities, business corporations, and the like. The Third Region proceeded on an entirely different principle. It made an effort to balance the committee with representatives of three groups: personnel officers in government, representatives of universities and governmental research organizations, and personnel officers in private business. "Big names" were sought not as such but as men who had some knowledge of and some interest in personnel problems; the theory was that they would be better able to attend committee meetings and in a far better position to contribute to the committee's deliberations. The result was a fine working group of very high caliber. The organization of such a committee is simple. It has a chairman and a secretary. Regular meetings of the full committee are held quarterly, but short monthly meetings are held for members residing in the metropolitan area. All members are kept constantly informed by mail and at the committee meetings regarding the government's needs for high-grade personnel. Blanks are furnished to members, who are urged to use them in referring individuals or in suggesting the names of persons who should be contacted by recruiting representatives or who might be sources of the type of personnel desired. Since committee members are purposely selected from various parts of the region, it sometimes happens that they are able to supply valuable local information regarding sources of supply of specialized personnel.

Since the end of the war the committees have been continued, but the emphasis has changed somewhat. Attention is no longer focused entirely on top-level personnel but is directed rather to the problem of drawing able persons into a career service. This naturally emphasizes contacts with the universities and colleges. Thus the Third Region sponsored early in 1947 a Federal Agency–College Conference which was attended by eighty representatives of educational institutions and Federal agencies. This conference established three working committees in the general fields of physical, political, and social science. Later in the year all three committees were asked to help publicize the Junior Professional Assistant Examination among the seniors of all universities and colleges in the region.[16]

Personnel Utilization

The movement for better personnel utilization has passed through two phases and is now in a third. The first, which lasted about fifty years, was dominated by the reform element, whose chief concern was to curb the evils of patronage. The second phase began at the end of World War I with the passage of the Classification Act of 1923. The standard pay scale was developed and great progress made in applying scientific methods to various aspects of the personnel management job. The third phase began with the initiation of the plan for departmental and agency personnel offices and for the personnel-council movement just described.

As the war progressed, the man power situation became everywher

---

[16] See Olson, Emery E., and Pollock, Ross, "Staffing and Training for Administrativ Competence in the Federal Service," *Personnel Administration*, September, 1945, pp 8–14.

more and more acute. Tremendous efforts were made to stretch existing resources to the utmost by: (1) recruiting and training women for as many jobs as possible; (2) calling back into active service many persons who had retired but were still able to work; (3) lowering age requirements and easing restrictions so that younger workers might be employed; (4) studying the physical requirements of all types of jobs in order that the physically handicapped might be fully utilized; and finally, (5) studying jobs and people in the effort to bring about the best possible placement and to utilize fully the highest skills of each worker.

Personnel utilization is simply another name for good personnel management. Although emphasis on the idea grew out of the man power shortages of the war years, the principal features of the program are equally applicable to peacetime. With the nation committed to the idea of full employment for all persons able and willing to work, it is important that the services of each be utilized as far as possible on a full-time basis at highest skill. It is thus important, economically as well as administratively, that management be conducted with a maximum degree of efficiency.[17]

In any program for the better utilization of personnel, the central personnel agency has a major responsibility in planning and training. The program will have to be carried out in the individual operating agencies under their directors of personnel, but the central personnel agency cannot escape responsibility for the planning and coordination of the program as a whole. Such a program involves, in the first place, a careful survey of the situation in each department or agency. Upon the basis of the information so obtained, a utilization program can be planned around the following major considerations: [18]

1. Obtaining the support of top management for the program
2. Improvement of supervision
3. Using position classification as a tool of supervision and management
4. Internal placement for maximum utilization
5. Training for maximum utilization
6. A program for economizing in personnel
7. A progressive employee-relations program
8. Improved working conditions; health and safety program

It will be observed that these items include practically all aspects of the personnel program heretofore discussed. The Commission went on

---

[7] See Emmerich, Herbert, "Good Personnel Administration Is Good Administration," *Public Personnel Review,* January, 1945, pp. 1–5.

[8] See United States Civil Service Commission, *Better Use of Personnel;* also Department of Agriculture, *A Guide to Better Management* (Washington, 1944) and Navy Department, *Navy Management Program* (Washington, 1943).

to emphasize the responsibility of the director of personnel in the operating agency for the following aspects of the program:

Efficiency ratings	Employee grievances
Health and safety programs	Exit interview program
Help-sharing plans	Maximum use of available man power
Induction and orientation of new employees	days
	Promotion from within
Skill training	Supervisory training
Utilization of handicapped employees	Work simplification
Employee counseling	Utilization surveys

The Navy Department, in describing its program, declared that it was "sparked by a principle and a conviction. The principle is: management is not the direction of things but the development of people for better performance. The conviction is: the men and women in any unit possess the intelligence to determine how they can improve the operation of themselves as individuals and their group as a whole." That is better personnel utilization and that is better management. The Navy Department proceeded to outline six steps toward achieving this goal:

1. Job Clarification
   What is the job, what are the steps in performing it, where does it fit into the organization?
2. Standards of Performance
   List of desirable work and conduct conditions that will result from satisfactory performance; a basis for evaluating efforts of the individual
3. Performance Review
   Periodic comparison of the employee's performance with the above standards
4. Help and Information
   Aid that appears needed from the performance review
5. Source of Information
   Determination by the supervisor of the best place to find the help or information needed
6. Time Schedule
   Planning the work of the unit so that the employee who needs the training can be spared from his work long enough to acquire it

In the face of widespread criticism of the growing power of the executive branch and increasing concern about the Federal bureaucracy, it becomes urgently necessary to select the right employees, assign them to the right positions, develop them into satisfactory producers, and see that they receive fair treatment. In the long run the quality of government that will be experienced by some 146,000,000 American citizens will depend to a large extent on the functioning of approximately four or five million employees of the Federal, state, and local governments

How is the central personnel agency to assist the officials in operating agencies to accomplish these objectives? Assuming that the planning has been done, how shall the central agency carry out the training function? Many devices are available for this purpose, as those who had any active part in management during the war period well know. The central personnel agency can furnish information on the basic principles of organization and management, in condensed and usable form. It can organize and direct conferences with operating officials, explain the program, foster discussion of it, and answer questions. It can work with operating officials in planning personnel surveys and interpreting the results, and in developing training programs and institutes as indicated by the results.[19]

SELECTED REFERENCES

Bibliographical aids in this field are quite numerous; the following are both recent and good: Tennessee Valley Authority, *Personnel Administration in the TVA: A Selected List of References* (Knoxville, 1948), and United States Civil Service Commission, *Personnel Administration and Civil Service: A Selected List of References* (Washington, 1946).

From the Civil Service Assembly of the United States and Canada:
Digest of State Civil Service Laws (Chicago, 1940).
Policies and Practices in Public Personnel Administration (Chicago, 1943).
Public Relations in Public Personnel Agencies (Chicago, 1941).
Readings in Public Personnel Administration (Chicago, 1942). Selected articles from various issues of the *Public Personnel Review*.

The Commission of Inquiry on Public Service Personnel, through its report (*Better Government Personnel* – McGraw-Hill, New York, 1935) and a series of supporting monographs, gave real impetus to the then lagging movement for better personnel administration. *Problems of the American Public Service* (McGraw-Hill, New York, 1935) was a cooperative product, while Julius Wilmerding, Jr., wrote: *Government by Merit* (McGraw-Hill, New York, 1935).

The Commission on Organization of the Executive Branch of the Government, *Personnel Management*, and *Task Force Report on Federal Personnel* (Appendix A) (Washington, 1948). Contain significant recommendations for the improvement of the federal personnel system.

Hendrickson, Roy F., *The Personnel Program of the United States Department of Agriculture* (Civil Service Assembly of the United States and Canada, Chicago, 1939). This study, by the then Director of Personnel, describes the main features of the Department's program, the historical development of the first fifty years of which is described in Stockberger, Warner W., and Smith, Virginia B., *Personnel Administration Development in the United States Department of Agriculture* (United States Department of Agriculture, Office of Personnel, 1947).

Among the better recent articles, see Appleby, Paul H., "Reorganization for Personnel Administration," *Public Personnel Review*, April, 1942, pp. 100–106; Belsley, Lyle, "Personnel Administration in the Modern State," *Social Education*, December, 1939, pp. 623–627; Devoe, Maxwell A., "Administrative Relationships of Public Personnel Agencies," *Public Personnel Review*, January, 1941, pp. 18–27; Emmerich, Herbert, "Good Personnel Administration Is Good Administration," *ibid.*, January, 1945, pp. 5; Hubbard, Henry F., "The Elements of a Comprehensive Personnel Program," *ibid.*, pp. 1–17; Kaplan, H. Eliot, "Standards of Public Personnel Administration," *Good Government*, April–June, 1934, pp. 9–15; and Lilienthal, David E., "Modern Tools for a Modern Job," *Personnel Administration*, April, 1945, pp. 1–5.

Several interesting surveys have been prepared of personnel practices in individual states:

Holloway, W. V., *Personnel Administration in the States* (Oklahoma Legislative Council, 1948). Prepared for the information of the Constitutional Survey Committee.

Illinois Legislative Council, *State Personnel Administration in Illinois* (Springfield 1946).

Shumate, Roger V., *State Civil Service in Nebraska* (Nebraska Legislative Council Lincoln, 1938).

University of Denver, *Civil Service in Colorado* (Bureau of Business and Social Research, Denver, 1945).

Jamison, Judith N., *Intergovernmental Cooperation in Public Personnel Administration in the Los Angeles Area* (Bureau of Governmental Research, University California at Los Angeles, 1944); for further and more recent information relating to the same area, see Los Angeles Bureau of Budget and Efficiency, *Report of Administrative Survey of the Civil Service Department: Administration, Organization, Management* (Los Angeles, 1948).

President's Committee on Civil Service Improvement, *Report* (77th Cong., 1st Session House Document No. 118).

From the Public Administration Service:

Merit System Installation (Chicago, 1941).
Personnel Programs for Smaller Cities (Chicago, 1940).
Personnel Administration and Procedure (Chicago, 1938).

From the United States Civil Service Commission:

Annual Report (Washington, annually).
Evaluating Personnel Management (Washington, 1945).
Federal Employment Under the Merit System (Washington, 1940).
History of the Federal Civil Service, 1789 to the Present (Washington, 1941).
Wartime Policies of the United States Civil Service Commission (Washington, 1942

War Department, Committee on Classification of Personnel, *The Personnel System the United States Army*, Vol. I, History of the Personnel System; Vol. II, The Personnel Manual (Washington, 1919).

White, Leonard D., *Research in Public Personnel Administration: An Outline of Suggested Research Topics* (Social Science Research Council, Committee on Public Administration, Washington, 1942). See also the excellent volume which he edited on *Civil Service in Wartime* (University of Chicago Press, 1945).

PART III

FISCAL MANAGEMENT

15

FISCAL PROCESSES
AND ORGANIZATION

BEFORE undertaking an extensive analysis of the various elements in the fiscal process, it seems advisable to attempt an over-all view of what that process is and of the conditions under which it operates. First the legal concept of the fiscal year will be considered. Then follows a definition and brief explanation of the basic elements of the fiscal process and some of the essential facts regarding the historical background of its various problems. Finally the problems of coordination as between departments and agencies of the same governmental unit are considered in the concluding section of this chapter as they appear at the Federal level.

The Fiscal Year

The term "fiscal year" is used to mean the twelve-months period for which a unit of government ordinarily reports on its financial operations. A study made by the Bureau of the Census in 1945 disclosed that of the 155,115 governmental units then existing, 104,000 or 67 per cent ended their fiscal year in June, while 25,000 or 16 per cent ended theirs in December. While this heavy concentration of fiscal years ending in June is due largely to the inclusion of 99,000 school districts whose fiscal years naturally end in that month, there has of late been a definite tendency away from the former practice of having the fiscal year of governmental units correspond with the calendar year. The end of a fiscal year brings heavy responsibilities to officials and, if it comes at holiday time, may cause great inconvenience to citizens.

The fiscal year of the Federal government runs from July 1 of one year to June 30 of the next. Thus fiscal '48 began on July 1, 1947, and fiscal '49 began on July 1, 1948. All but seven of the states begin their fiscal years on July 1. The exceptions are: Ohio, January 1; New York and Washington, April 1; Pennsylvania, June 1; Texas, September 1; Alabama and Wyoming, October 1. Many of the states operate on a biennial budget, and where this is the case, the biennia (with the exceptions noted) begin on July 1.[1]

Book of the States, 1948–1949, pp. 184–189.

So far as the practice of cities and other local units is concerned there is wide diversity. This is the more remarkable in view of the number of local governments which operate on the basis of laws providing for state-wide uniform fiscal years. In eight states (Massachusetts, Montana, Nevada, New Mexico, North Carolina, Oklahoma, Oregon, and West Virginia) all local governments end their fiscal years on a common date, ordinarily coinciding with that prescribed for the state itself. In six additional states (Indiana, Mississippi, New Jersey, Ohio, Utah, and Washington) a uniform fiscal year is prescribed for all local units except school districts. In the other thirty-four states no uniformity exists.[2]

These extreme variations tend not only to complicate the collation and analysis of statistical information but also to make it unusable for purposes of comparison between governmental units. In order to obtain comparable data much time must be spent in checking data and, in the case of the Bureau of the Census, in planning the routing of field agents and the timing of canvasses. The fact that the census report gives five tables of fiscal years for states, cities, counties, and townships, demonstrates the almost insuperable difficulties in issuing statistical data for governmental units.[3]

Basic Elements in the Fiscal Process

It is the purpose of this section to show, as clearly as one can, what might be called the natural history of a tax dollar. First, the dollar has to be obtained; that involves the assessment and collection of taxes. Then it has to be held for safekeeping until its expenditure is authorized; that involves the custody of funds and possibly their investment. If there are not dollars enough on hand to meet known or expected obligations, borrowing may be necessary; that raises the problems of incurring, managing, and ultimately retiring debt. The next step is financial planning or budgeting, which is the name applied to the planning of the spending program. When such a program is formulated and approved, it must be enforced; that raises the problem of fiscal supervision. Procurement involves the acquisition of necessary property and supplies. When the goods have been received and found acceptable or

---

[2] For specific illustrations in representative units, see: ILLINOIS: Illinois Legislative Council, *Property Tax Dates* (Springfield, 1939); Mathews, Thomas A., "1944–1945 Municipal Calendar of Statutory Duties for Illinois Municipal Officials," *Illinois Municipal Review*, January, 1945, pp. 13–16. PENNSYLVANIA: "Tax Collection and Assessment Calendar," *County Commissioner*, March, 1946, pp. 9–11. ST. LOUIS: "Time to Change the City's Fiscal Year," *Dollars and Sense in Government*, May 15, 1945. In this city the fiscal year begins on the second Tuesday in April, resulting in years of irregular length.

[3] See Hemenway, H. Harrison, "Fiscal Years of State and Local Governments," *State and Local Government Special Study No. 29* (June, 1945).

National History of the Tax Dollar

FINANCIAL ACTIVITY	FEDERAL	STATE	MUNICIPAL
Assessment and Collection of Taxes	Bureau of Internal Revenue Bureau of Customs	Department of Revenue Department of Taxation and Finance State Tax Commission	Department of Finance Board of Assessment and Revision of Taxes
Custody of Funds	Treasurer of the United States	State Treasurer	City Treasurer
Borrowing and Debt Administration	Treasury Department	State Treasurer	City Treasurer
Financial Planning	Bureau of the Budget, Executive Office of the President	Budget Office Finance offices of the departments	Budget Office Finance offices of the departments
Financial Supervision	Bureau of the Budget General Accounting Office	Budget Office Board of Administration and Finance Department of Taxation and Finance	City Comptroller
Procurement	Division of Procurement Treasury Department	Department of Property and Supplies State Printing Board Department of Public Works	Department of Purchases Department of City Property
Disbursement	Treasurer of the United States	State Treasurer	City Treasurer
Financial Reporting	Treasurer of the United States	State Treasurer Auditor General	City Treasurer
Audit and Control	General Accounting Office	State Comptroller State Auditor Auditor General	City Auditor City Comptroller

When personal services have been rendered, they must be paid for; this involves disbursements, and financial reporting so that the public may know what is being done with its money. Finally, the whole record must be checked for accuracy and to make certain that the transactions reported are in accordance with the provisions of law. This concluding task is the responsibility of the auditor. These steps, together with the names of the fiscal officers ordinarily responsible for their administration at the various levels of government, are shown in the table which appears above on this page.

Assessment and Collection of Taxes. The history of tax collection is as old as government itself. For generations it has been said that two things are certain: death and taxes. In olden times the king's ministers deter-

mined how much tribute could be collected from a given area and sol
the privilege of collection to an individual who turned over to the gov
ernment the amount specified and kept whatever he was able to collec
in excess of that amount. In modern times the methods have not been so crude, but they di
not greatly improve in efficiency from the public's point of view unt
comparatively recently. Originally the states relied upon the genera
property tax as a chief source of revenue. The administration of th
tax, however, was a function of the local governments rather than c
the state. Local officials assessed the property and collected the tota
tax, from which a prescribed proportion was remitted to the state fc
its support. As other forms of tax were imposed, provision was made b
law for collection in each jurisdiction by a different tax collector, an
each collector was paid on a fee basis. Thus there were limits — thec
retically, at least — to what the collector could obtain for himself, bu
the rules regarding fees were such that the annual return was in man
cases vastly in excess of a reasonable compensation for the service rer
dered. In addition the taxpayer was subjected to the inconvenience c
having to conduct as a separate transaction the payment of each ta
provided for by law.

All regular Federal taxes are now collected by two agencies: the Ir
ternal Revenue Service and the Customs Service. In many states withi
the last few years collection of taxes has been centralized under a sing]
department or agency, and a system of centralized collection of loca
taxes on a county-unit basis has become the accepted procedure. Th
multiplicity of agencies engaged in the collection of revenues in son
states is so great as to stagger the imagination — ten, twelve, or eve
more.

Custody of Funds. "If all the public revenues could be so timed as t
arrive in the government's hands exactly at the moment they wei
needed," wrote Harold M. Groves, "the custody of public funds woul
be a negligible problem." Because this is not done or perhaps because
cannot be done, there arises a considerable problem of the custody an
investment of funds. When in ancient civilizations taxes were paid i
kind, the public treasury consisted of warehouses; later, when pay
ments were made in cash, the treasury had to provide facilities for tl
storage of coin and bullion. In modern times, when taxes are "paid pre
dominantly in credit, the storehouse idea gave way and governmen
chose to carry their excesses in the form of bank balances with a go\
ernment bank or one or more selected private banks." [4]

[4] Groves, Harold M., *Financing Government*, Revised Edition, p. 595 (Holt, Ne
York, 1945).

Before the development of this credit economy and the facilities of ommercial banking, the treasurer was responsible for holding in cus-)dy and for safely transporting the actual gold. Before the centralized easury system went into effect, any department, board, or commis-on collecting money for the government had authority to deposit it ι any of the designated depositories. This practice caused much criti-ism and complaint. Under the centralized treasury system the treasurer the custodian of all funds. Willoughby wrote many years ago that the duties of the treasurer may be briefly defined as those of receiving, olding in safe custody, and disbursing upon proper order all public ınds, and of safekeeping all financial securities and papers of like char-:ter. From the accountability standpoint, the responsibility of this of-ce may be reduced to the single obligation of being able at all times to :count for all moneys and securities coming into its possession. His ac-)untability is, thus, not unlike that of the ordinary banking institu-on." [5]

orrowing and Debt Administration. When the recommended or ap-roved expenditures exceed the anticipated revenues, the difference ιay have to be made up by borrowing, if the budget is to be balanced. ι such cases the treasury becomes responsible for preparing the speci-cations for the bond issue, for advertising for bids, and for selling of ιe bonds. After the bonds have been sold, the treasury is again respon-ble for the administration of the debt, a procedure which involves the ιpervision and maintenance of the sinking fund (if there is one) or ∶eping the necessary records for serial bonds — maintenance of rec-:ds with regard to ownership, accumulation of the funds, and paying ᵮ the bonds according to schedule.

It often happens that the treasury has on hand funds which cannot ∶ expended for ordinary governmental purposes — trust funds and the come from public lands and from trust funds. These cannot be per-itted merely to lie in the vaults for safekeeping; they must be in-∶sted. Making these investments in accordance with the provisions of w and the decisions of the investment board, and the general vigilance ver their safety becomes the responsibility of the treasury. When the :oblem becomes as vast as it is in the larger units of government today, ιis is no mean responsibility.

inancial Planning. Budgetary procedures developed in the govern-ents of foreign states and in American business long before they ap-∶ared, early in the present century, in American government. To be ιre, an attempt to establish such procedures had been made when the

Willoughby, William F., *Principles of Public Administration,* p. 508 (Johns Hopkins ess, 1927).

government of the Confederate States of America was set up, but th
effort was short lived.[6] Budgeting procedures were well established i
most of the states and in many cities before the Federal Budget and Ac
counting Act of 1921 was adopted. The first state legislation wa
adopted in 1911 in California and Wisconsin; by 1926, when the Rhod
Island budget law was passed, some kind of budget law existed in a
the states. This was an amazing record of speed in the legislative ado
tion of a new idea. Some of the early laws were inadequate and no
very satisfactory when judged by modern standards, but they pro
vided the beginnings out of which present-day executive budget sy:
tems have developed. The following list shows the years in which th
first budget legislation was enacted in various states: [7]

Dates of Initial Adoption of State Budget Laws

1911   California and Wisconsin
1913   Arkansas, Ohio, and Oregon
1914   Louisiana
1915   Connecticut, Iowa, Minnesota, Nebraska, North Dakota, and Vermont
1916   Maryland, New Jersey, and Washington
1917   Delaware, Illinois, Kansas, Missouri, New Mexico, South Dakota, Te:
       nessee, and Utah
1918   Georgia, Kentucky, Massachusetts, Mississippi, Virginia, and West Vi
       ginia
1919   Alabama, Arizona, Colorado, Idaho, Maine, Michigan, Montana, N
       vada, New Hampshire, North Carolina, Oklahoma, South Carolin
       Texas, and Wyoming
1921   Florida, Indiana, and New York
1923   Pennsylvania
1926   Rhode Island

The early laws provided a wide variety of budget organizatio
Some types were executive, some legislative, and some a combinatic
of the two. Indeed, for many years a spirited controversy was carrie
on regarding their relative merits. On the basis of experience opinion
now united in favor of the executive budget. This does not imply th
there may not be a place for the legislative budget also, although th
purposes of the two are somewhat different. The Legislative Reorgan
ization Act of 1946, indeed, makes specific provision for a legislativ

[6] Perkins, John A., *The Role of the Governor of Michigan in the Enactment of A
propriations*, p. 181 (Bureau of Government, University of Michigan, 1943).
[7] White, Leonard D., *Trends in Public Administration*, p. 189 (McGraw-Hill, Ne
York, 1933); Cleveland, Frederick A., "Evolution of the Budget Idea in the Unit
States," *Annals*, November, 1915, and Buck, Arthur E., "The Development of t
Budget Idea in the United States," *ibid.*, May, 1924. For a classification of types
budget systems, see White, p. 191, and Carleton, Robert L., *The Reorganization an
Consolidation of State Administration in Louisiana*, pp. 33-36 (Louisiana State Unive
sity Press, 1937). For a table on current state budgetary procedure, see page 310.

udget in the Federal government in addition to the executive budget
stem, which remains as before. The various elements involved in the
roblem of expenditure control — of which budget formulation is but
ne — are indicated in the table below.

ements of Expenditure Control

UDGET FUNCTION	METHOD OF EXECUTION	CONTROL EXERCISED INTERNALLY	EXTERNALLY
dget Formulation	Preparation, consolidation, and justification of estimates	Top management and fiscal officers	Budget office
dget Authorization	Legislative action	Appropriation committees; hearings	Investigators
dget Execution	Control of amounts and purposes of expenditure	Top management and fiscal officers	Budget office
dget Accountability	Scrutiny of individual expenditures by auditing and accounting procedures	Fiscal officers	Independent auditor general or comptroller

As this table clearly shows, the budget must go through several
ocesses if it is to serve as an effective tool. Generally these processes
gin with the submission of requests by the various departments and
encies. These requests are analyzed and correlated by the financial
ficer or budget director. Then they are submitted to and studied
the responsible central executive officer — the President, governor,
ayor, city manager, superintendent, or what not. The discretion of
e planners is limited to the extent that important expenditures have
en made mandatory by law. The chief executive usually confers with
e heads of the submitting departments and holds conferences or pos-
ly hearings on the requests. He then makes such changes as he deems
cessary in the best interests of the government and the taxpayers in
ew of the general policies of the administration and the financial
tus of the unit at the time.

nancial Supervision. A financial plan, i.e., a budget, however good is
little use unless some adequate provision is made for carrying it out.
wer and responsibility should be centered in the chief executive. His
dget report embodies a plan of action for the future; after enactment
to law, it becomes a guide for the present. The process is continuous:
e budget is being executed while the next one is being prepared. The
dget must be comprehensive, taking cognizance of all income and all
penditures and of all financial requirements. Its advantages redound
the benefit of the executive, the legislature, and the public. The first

is obliged to plan ahead; the legislature has a basis for intelligent action
the public is provided with essential information on government oper
ations and proposals.

Other essentials of such a system are a uniform plan for the classifi
cation of the items of expenditure, a uniform accounting system, an
means for preventing overspending or spending so much in the earl
part of the year that there is not enough left to maintain operations dur
ing the latter part. The normal procedures for realizing this purpos
involve (1) the allocation of specific sums for specific purposes for
specified period of time and (2) in connection with the accounting sys
tem, the establishment of encumbrances by which funds are set aside t
make payment for goods or services when the commitment is made, no
when the goods have been received and the bill becomes due. Obvi
ously, no further commitments can be authorized when the total actu
ally spent plus the total encumbered equals the amount of the alloca
tion.

Procurement. Every department or agency of government, whethe
line or staff, has procurement problems of two types — personnel, an
property and supplies. Since recruiting and placement were considere
at length in Chapter 7, the present discussion may be limited to the ac
quisition and custody of property and supplies. Among the major prob
lems to be considered here are the establishment and enforcement o
standards and specifications in the purchase of commodities; centra
purchasing vs. central contracting; questions which arise in connectio
with the acquisition and custody of property — options, contract
searching of title, and so on. The purchase, maintenance, and contro
of the use of government-owned automobiles, and the enforcement o
regulations affecting travel, communications, and postage are often dif
ficult problems to solve. The construction and maintenance of publi
buildings, and printing, both present specialized problems of procure
ment which, because of their importance, will be given special con
sideration.

Disbursement. Disbursement involves the actual payment of money b
the treasurer or his representative for goods received or services ren
dered. After the revenues have been collected, they are held in the cus
tody of the treasurer, who should be — but rarely is — the disbursin
officer of the government. He is, in fact, the least important of the fisca
officers, his duties being largely ministerial in nature. "He is controlle
in all his actions by the auditor. The treasurer can no more refuse t
cash a properly drawn warrant of the auditor than a bank can refuse t

cash a properly drawn check of a depositor." [8] The treasurer in the states really enjoys a higher constitutional status than his duties warrant. In no state does he have a part in the formation of policy. Like the treasurer of a commercial company, he is under bond, a fact which undermines the theory upon which the office has been made elective in all states and cities. His related functions include the disposition of unusable and unwanted property, the handling of claims against the government, the bonding of public officers and employees, the insurance of public risks, and oversight of the grant-in-aid system.

Financial Reporting. Financial reporting is of relatively recent origin. In years past, financial reports were published — but what reports! They were large and cumbersome. The printing was poor, the binding was terrible, the usual black cloth covers gave a funereal appearance. No more attention was paid to the contents than to the outward appearance. Great masses of detailed and undigested statistics and financial data and records of countless individual transactions were included indiscriminately. The contents were the raw material out of which a good report might possibly have been made. Badly edited and poorly organized as they were, the hardy soul who ventured to examine them received little reward for his effort. They provided no means by which he could get a clear picture of what his government was doing.

Good financial reporting is designed to be illuminating. The report does not have to be large; preferably, it should be rather small. It should contain selections of material and summaries of operations presented in such form that an intelligent citizen can obtain a clear understanding of major programs and policies and how they are working out in practice. The text should be readable and supplemented by charts, graphs, tables, and pictures wherever these devices can be used to advantage. The format should be sufficiently attractive to challenge the prospective reader's attention, and the contents good enough to sustain his interest. In all fairness it should be said that the modern type of financial report is rapidly replacing the old.

Audit and Control. The organization for fiscal control varies greatly from one jurisdiction to another. The Federal government organization, which is far from satisfactory, was established under the provisions of the Budget and Accounting Act of 1921. The General Accounting Office is in charge of both accounting and auditing. The head of this Office, the Comptroller General of the United States, is ap-

---

[8] Sappenfield, Max M., *Financial Administration in the States of Illinois, Ohio, and Indiana*, p. 7 (Thesis abstract, University of Illinois, 1934).

pointed by the President, by and with the advice and consent of the Senate, for a term of fifteen years. This unusual length of term was decided upon in order to insure his independence of the executive.

In the states there are several different possible solutions of the problem of the location of the accounting functions in the governmental structure. The budget bureau does the work in some jurisdictions. There may be a department of finance, of taxation and finance, or of finance, budget, and business, as in Illinois, New York, Ohio, and Washington. There may be a board of administration, a board of control, or a commission on administration and finance, as in Alabama, Oregon, and Massachusetts, and formerly in Minnesota. Finally the work may be done by the comptroller or comptroller general, as it is in the Federal government and in the states of California, Georgia, Maryland, South Carolina, and Texas.

The accounting function usually is and should be in the hands of one officer; auditing, in the hands of another. Although the office of auditor exists by constitutional requirement in practically all the states, comptrollers are provided for in less than half of them. The majority of states and cities choose their accounting and auditing officers by popular election. According to a study made by the Association of State Auditors, Comptrollers, and Treasurers, nine state auditors are selected by methods other than popular election, three being appointed by the governor, two appointed by the governor with the consent of the legislature, and four elected by the legislature.

Fiscal Coordination

The over-all problem of fiscal management and control is not solved either by central planning and supervision or by good accounting procedures and practices within the individual departments and agencies, vital though both of them are. Even where both exist, there is always the danger that diverse interpretations may be given to the same rules and regulations with the result that contrary and sometimes contradictory policies are followed by different agencies within the same governmental unit. This type of thing leads to confusion and frustration. The public does not understand it, and the morale of some employees is undermined.

The remedy lies in some form of coordination. The word "coordination," although a perfectly good one, has been much abused. It suggests practices and procedures designed to secure uniformity. The need for it arises from inherent difficulties in the use of words to convey ideas. No matter how clearly and precisely one aims to express himself, he is almost certain to discover later that different individuals have in all sincerity given varying interpretations to what he has written. Thus there is need not only for clearly written instructions but for assistance in interpreting and applying these instructions in such a manner as to produce decisions and actions by numerous officials and agencies consistent with some uniform policy.

This principle, like many others, is relatively easy to state but difficult to put in practice. How does a top administrator go about the task of preventing different parts of his organization from proceeding in all directions simultaneously? How, in other words, does he coordinate their activities in a given area? In the field of fiscal administration two important developments have taken place in recent years at the Federal level, and these may exert a strong influence in the coordination of policies. Although the same need exists at the state and local levels, no comparable developments in either are known to the author.

Bureau of the Budget Field Offices. As a beginning toward the coordination of policy among Federal agencies in the field, particularly on fiscal matters, the United States Bureau of the Budget has established offices in Chicago, Dallas, Denver, and San Francisco. The plans have been developed cautiously and experimentally; if they succeed reasonably well in accomplishing their purpose, more may be established later. Four methods of coordination are being used by these offices: conciliation, calling groups together, providing continuing unofficial consulting services, and creating committees.

It is well known that jealousy and friction sometimes develop between agencies whose programs are closely related if not overlapping. When such cases occur in the field, the representatives of the Bureau of the Budget, acting as management consultants rather than as fiscal officers, are sometimes able to bring the contending parties together to mediate or conciliate their differences. Where more than two agencies are concerned with a problem, a conference may be arranged between representatives of the agencies and of the public. Field representatives who possess the know-how of getting things done within the limitations of government procedure and who have the willingness to do so, can often exercise a good deal of discretion without violating either the law or their instructions.

Field representatives often need assistance on purely administrative problems. In most cases they could obtain it from their own departmental offices but for the barrier created by distance. Since the Bureau of the Budget has assumed responsibility for management consultant work within the Federal government, its field representatives are frequently able to render assistance to field officers of other agencies. Again, where the interests of several agencies or groups are involved, the Bureau representative may use his good offices in establishing a committee to stay with the problem until a solution is found. Some of these are *ad hoc* committees, while others deal with continuing problems and may function on a more or less permanent basis. In such situations the Pacific Coast Board of Intergovernmental Relations described in Chapter 5 has proved itself useful.

Field Councils. In Chapter 14 the development of field councils of personnel administration has been described. The author, because of his close connection with one of these councils during the war period and his knowledge of its usefulness, suggested to the Director of the Budget that the same type of organization of fiscal officers in some of the larger metropolitan areas might be equally useful. Although no attention was paid to this suggestion, the fiscal officers of Federal agencies in the Chicago area got together informally — wholly on their own — and in mid-1945 were organized as the Federal Finance Conference.

Since that time the Bureau of the Budget has discovered that the idea does have possibilities. It has not only given the Chicago Conference its approval but has incorporated the council idea into its field program wherever its field offices are located. At a meeting of the American Society for Public Administration held in Washington in March, 1947, a representative of the Bureau listed four specific services that field councils can render:

1. Exchange information at monthly meetings
2. Discuss problems of overlapping and duplication and of Federal-state relations
3. Discuss over-all problems of management, such as recruitment, wages, etc.
4. Secure top-management sponsorship of specialized programs

The Chicago Conference, formally organized in 1946, performs all these functions for the larger agencies in that area represented in its membership. Its constitution states as its purpose fostering "the exchange of information and views on major problems concerning fiscal and related over-all management functions common to the Federal agencies represented, with the further object of improving existing practices and studying and developing new procedures that may be proposed for the benefit of such agencies in Chicago." Membership is restricted to one per agency, not more than thirty in all. Each member must occupy a position of authority and responsibility in his agency for "fiscal, budget, or related management functions." Each may designate an alternate with similar qualifications, and each may bring one or more officers from his agency when some subject of special interest to them is to be discussed. The organization is simple and relatively informal: monthly luncheon meetings are held throughout the year to discuss problems of common interest. The early history of the Conference was well summarized by its secretary-treasurer: [9]

Early in 1945, the administrative officers of the various war agencies in Chicago organized an informal luncheon group at which our common problems were discussed and persons invited to present various administrative problems. We used this technique as a supplement to the official channels of communication and found it to be extremely effective. This was particularly true at the time the Division of Central Administrative Services of the Office for Emergency Management was liquidated in November, 1944. CAS had acted to some extent as a unifying, coordinating tool and a center of communications for those of us responsible for the administrative functions of the war agencies.

The organization, however, remained very informal and, in the press of other business, eventually discontinued meeting. The friendships and acquaintances which had been developed, however, remained in effect until the summer of 1945 when the Chief of the Chicago Field Office of the Bureau of the Budget proposed the establishment of a formal organization which would perform for the larger Federal agencies in Chicago some of the functions which it had been previously hoped would have been exercised by the Federal Business Association. A small organizing committee met and proposed the formal organization which in June, 1945, was named the Federal Finance Conference. The name stemmed from the primary interests of a large portion of the members who were responsible for the budget and fiscal activities of the decentralized departmental agencies located in Chicago, and the larger Federal field establishments located here also.

SELECTED REFERENCES

Since most of the problems discussed in this chapter are considered at length in the chapters which follow, the references regarding these topics are presented in connection with the appropriate chapters.

[9] Letter from Marvin B. Osterman to the author, March 8, 1946.

16

ASSESSMENT AND

COLLECTION OF TAXES

Organization for Tax Collection

Federal Organization. In the early years the Federal government depended very largely on customs receipts as a source of revenue. It is not surprising therefore that the Customs Service is the oldest administrative agency of the United States, its history extending back to 1789.[1] Reorganized from time to time, it derives its present powers from the Customs Reorganization Act of 1927, by which the Secretary of the Treasury is authorized to confer upon the Commissioner of Customs or other officer in the Bureau "any of the rights, privileges, powers, or duties, in respect to the importation or entry of merchandise into, or exportation of merchandise from, the United States, vested in or imposed upon the Secretary. . . ."[2]

While the Bureau is charged with numerous duties, its oldest and most important function is that of collecting duties on imports. Under the Tariff Act of 1930, merchandise intended for import must first pass the scrutiny of customs officials, and any duties due thereon must be paid. While the responsibility for collecting these duties is assigned to the Secretary of the Treasury, this official has by a series of directives delegated all his authority under the act to the Bureau, with the exception of certain matters which the Attorney General has ruled must be subject to his personal action.

Domestic taxes are collected by the Internal Revenue Service, an agency dating from 1792, when provision was first made by act of Congress for a "Commissioner of the Revenue" as an officer of the Treasury Department. It was not until 1862, however, that the Bureau was established on a permanent basis. It is now, as formerly, a branch of the Treasury Department. Although the Commissioner is appointed by the President, by and with the advice and consent of the Senate, he acts

---

[1] Act of July 1, 1789, 1 Stat. 29. The history of the Service is described in Bureau of Customs, School of Instruction, Lesson Paper No. 03 (1939).
[2] See Attorney General's Committee on Administrative Procedure, Monograph No. 27, and Act of March 3, 1927, 44 Stat. 1382, 5 U.S.C. § 281 b. For exceptions later referred to, see 35 Op. A. G. 15 (1925).

under the direction and supervision of the Secretary of the Treasury. The Commissioner is charged with "general superintendence of the assessment and collection of all taxes imposed by any law providing internal revenue," the task being accomplished through the Internal Revenue Service.[3]

Original Decentralized State Organization. The type of organization previously existing in all the states and still existing in a majority of them permits many different agencies to collect taxes. It is reported that in California revenue administration in its entirety involves almost every department and agency of the state. "There is scarcely a division of government which is not responsible for the collection of funds in some form."

The same condition existed prior to 1938 in Kansas, which had six agencies and now has two administering state taxes. Out of well over a dozen tax forms adopted between 1861 and 1937, the State Tax Commission administered nine. The Department of Registration and Inspection, the Insurance Commissioner, the Secretary of State, the Motor Vehicle Commissioner, and the State Corporation Commission each administered one or two. In addition the Treasurer, the Auditor General, and the county treasurers were all charged with some tax collecting functions. Furthermore, since taxes are not always paid voluntarily, the office of the Attorney General was actually the final collecting agency in many cases.[4]

In Pennsylvania prior to the adoption of the Fiscal Code of 1929 a similar situation prevailed. Since the general property tax was not used for state purposes, it was not affected by the reorganization of state fiscal agencies. The capital stock tax on corporations, the tax on corporation loans, the utility gross receipts tax, and numerous others were collected by the Auditor General. Insurance taxes were collected by the Insurance Commissioner; incorporation fees by the Secretary of State; and the liquid fuels and the motor registration fees by the Department of Highways. As in Kansas, the county treasurers collected many taxes. The Budget Office had existed only since 1923; the Auditor General, acting as tax collector, did no auditing but hired commercial auditors to go over the books of the various departments, agencies, and institutions. Before bills could be paid and warrants drawn, they had to be approved both by the State Treasurer and by the Auditor General. Not only did

---

[3] I. R. C., § 3901 (a) (1).
[4] Kansas Legislative Council, *Concentration of State Tax Administration*, p. 2. ILLINOIS: Illinois Tax Commission, *Fifteenth Annual Report*, 1933, pp. 255–261, including organization chart (Springfield, 1934). OREGON: Oregon Tax Study Commission, *State and Local Tax Administration*, p. 2 (Salem, 1946).

the state lack an organized plan for the collection of taxes but the entire machinery for fiscal administration was highly disorganized.

The same situation still exists in Michigan, which established a Department of Revenue in 1942 but without any serious attempt at unification of the tax collecting function. As late as 1944 it was possible for an investigating agency to report that "over half a hundred state departments, boards, and commissions now act as cashiers for the state, accepting money for taxes, licenses, fees, rentals, and other miscellaneous purposes. Collection of the more important revenues is divided among eleven of these agencies. Miscellaneous licenses and fees are collected by forty-five others."[5]

The most common form of organization has been the state tax commission. The movement for the establishment of tax commissions extended over many years — from 1865 to 1929. Those in Massachusetts (1865), California (1879), and Vermont (1886) were established prior to 1890; in the succeeding ten-year period, eight more were set up, including Michigan, New York, and Wisconsin, making a total of eleven at the beginning of the twentieth century. Eight more were established between 1900 and 1909, ten between 1909 and 1914, nine between 1915 and 1919, and seven between 1920 and 1924. Since that time the only new commissions have been in Washington (1925), Iowa (1929), and Pennsylvania (1947).

The powers that a state tax commission should exercise were summarized some years ago in the Model Tax Plan issued by the National Tax Association: [6]

1. Original assessment of all property or business that has a state-wide rather than a local character, all financial institutions, and public utility companies of every description

2. The assessment of the personal property tax and the tax on business incomes . . . , also the administration of inheritance taxes and any other state transfer taxes

3. The equalization of property assessments for the purpose of state taxation and the equalization of county taxes whenever there are different assessment districts within a county

4. Directive and supervisory powers over the assessment of property, including the power to order reassessments and, if necessary, to appoint appraisers to reassess any property that local officers have not assessed in accordance with law

[5] Michigan Public Expenditure Survey, *Save in the State to Save the Nation*, pp. 3-4 (Lansing, 1944), and Ford, Robert S., and Landers, Frank M., *Property Tax Administration*, p. 4 (Bureau of Government, University of Michigan, 1939).

[6] Appears in *Proceedings*, 1933, p. 408; see also Lutz, Harley L., *State Tax Commission* (Harvard University Press, 1918), and the following articles: Cooper, Lewis B., and Holland, N. S., "An Adequate State Tax Commission," *Tax Magazine*, September, 1936; Hogan, Willard N., "Growth of the Kentucky State Tax Commission," *ibid.*, January, 1936, pp. 1-12.

5. Power of removal, after a hearing, of local assessors for inefficiency and misconduct

6. Authority to act as a board of appeal in such cases as may be necessary

7. Authority to investigate the entire subject of taxation, and to gather and publish comprehensive statistics concerning all matters of taxation and public finance

When the states were almost wholly dependent on the general property tax for their revenue, there was no need for a Department of Revenue. As this situation changed by degrees to the complicated tax structure of today, the legislature was obliged, every time a new tax was added, to assign its collection to some existing agency or to establish a new agency. The result was extreme confusion. Secretaries of state, state treasurers, state auditors, state insurance commissioners, state highway departments, state public utility commissions, and a host of other agencies in addition to the state tax commissions were performing tax collection functions which were wholly unrelated to their major duties and which they were ill prepared to perform efficiently and economically.

The Integrated State Agency. A careful check of the agencies responsible for the administration of the major types of state taxes, made by the Federation of Tax Administrators in 1940, showed that there were only eight states in which a substantially complete integration of the tax collecting function had been achieved.[7] In 1947 only nine states might be regarded as integrated, sixteen as partially so. Some progress toward integration has been achieved in many states in the past few years, and plans for it are under consideration in many more. The integrated, single-headed form of organization is, of course, highly preferable for the regular work of administration. Its advantages include a substantial reduction in collection costs, economy in the use of specialized personnel, the possibility of using assembly-line techniques in handling routine tasks, unification of tax policy so that the application of tax laws will cause a minimum of discrimination, obtaining better compliance and more effective collection, and making auditing more effective and economical.[8]

---

[7] There seems to be little agreement as to what constitutes integration. One writer put the number at fifteen in 1938, another at ten. Two surveys, however, come out with approximately the same results. Barthell and Campbell reported in 1947 on 1945 data; Charles F. Conlon of the Federation of Tax Administrators reported in 1948 on 1947 data (*Book of the States, 1948-1949*, pp. 227-235) as follows: one agency in nine states; two agencies in sixteen states; three agencies in thirteen states; four agencies in eight states; five agencies in two states.

[8] James W. Martin has written extensively on tax administration: "Comparative Efficiency of Tax Administration – Records, Audits," *Taxes*, April, 1944, pp. 164-169, 185; "Cost and Efficiency of Tax Administration: Policies," *ibid.*, June, 1944, pp. 263-271;

COMMONWEALTH OF KENTUCKY: DEPARTMENT OF REVENUE*

ORGANIZATION

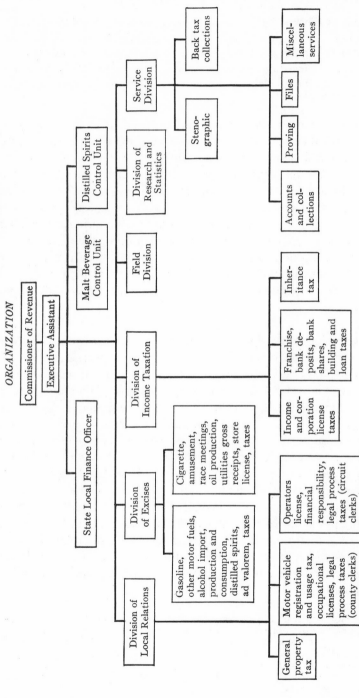

* From Kentucky Department of Revenue, *Twenty-fifth Annual Report*, 1943, p. 6.

There are, in fact, three types of organization used in integrated departments: the commission, the single-headed department, and the combination of the two. Approximately half the states have a department of revenue, department of taxation, department of finance, or department of taxation and finance. Approximately one fourth have a tax commission alone; under this form all duties and powers of tax administration and review are exercised by the commission. The commission is usually composed of three appointed or elected members with staggered six-year terms. Taxes are collected in three of the remaining states by the state board of equalization, in three by the comptroller, and in the others by officers functioning under a bewildering variety of names. In a good many states in which there is some form of combination of single administrator and commission the administrative duties may or may not be divided but the review functions will normally be exercised by the commission.

The internal structure of the department of revenue varies greatly from state to state according to the tax pattern. The organization of the Department of Revenue in Kentucky, in the planning of which James W. Martin was highly influential, is shown in the chart on page 282. Under the head of the department are his immediate assistants and the chiefs of the various divisions and bureaus. There should be a bureau of research and statistics, and there must be a field service. The breakdown of the remainder of the department into divisions, bureaus, and units depends obviously upon the nature of the taxes to be collected. Since no two states have the same pattern, it is practically impossible to classify state tax-collecting agencies according to organizational type. Whether taxes are collected by a commission or a department, the bureau structure will be essentially the same. Where a commission exists in addition to a department, its duties may well be confined to the settlement of appeals and to research. In this case the commission becomes a quasi-judicial rather than an administrative body.

Field Organization. Revenue collection is obviously a function that must in the larger units be largely decentralized not only in the interests of economy and efficiency but as a matter of accessibility and convenience to the taxpayer. This point is well illustrated by the fact that in 1939 the personnel of the Customs Service numbered approximately 8252, all but 189 of whom were employed in the field. In the Internal

---

"Costs of Tax Administration," a series of four articles in *Bulletin* of the American Tax Association, January, February, March, and April, 1944; "Tax Administration Structures," *Taxes*, May, 1944, pp. 220-227; and "Tax Administration," a series of three articles in *State Government*, March, April, and May, 1944.

Revenue Service there were 22,600 employees, all but 4200 of whom were in the field. While the number of these employees greatly increased during the war years, when millions of new income-tax payers were brought under the requirements of the law, the ratio of employees in the departmental and field services did not materially change.

Because of the nature of the service the number of field offices is larger in Internal Revenue than in most other Federal departments and agencies. In addition to three field services supervised from Washington there are five major divisions — the Collection Service, the Field Audit Service, the Supervisory Field Service of the Alcohol Tax Unit, the Field Divisions of the Technical Staff, and the Field Divisions of the Salary Stabilization Unit. The first of these, the Collection Service, may be taken as illustrative.

The President is authorized by the Internal Revenue Code to establish not to exceed sixty-five "convenient collection districts" and may from time to time alter them. The sixty-four existing districts have been established by a series of Executive Orders issued over a period of time, the last on February 1, 1927. In all such orders involving the creation, alteration, or consolidation of districts the territory in each is designated by state and county. In addition to these sixty-four main offices there are twenty branch or division offices, eighty-one branches of main offices which sell revenue stamps, and numerous zone offices consisting usually of desk space in a post office or Federal building, assigned to a deputy zone collector working out of a collector's office in a near-by city.

Each district has a Collector of Internal Revenue, appointed by the President by and with the advice and consent of the Senate. Since this is one of the far corners of the Federal government which the civil service system has never penetrated, the Collector in each district nominates his own staff, subject to the approval of the Commissioner and of the Secretary of the Treasury. While Collectors have been given instructions as to the qualifications for the various types of positions to be filled by them, less attention is paid to qualifications and more to political considerations than in most other branches of the Federal service.

In the states a similarly extensive field organization is required. In Pennsylvania, for instance, where a well-organized Department of Revenue exists, the central office at the Capitol exercises supervision and control over institutional collections by establishing procedures and practices for revenue accounting and collection work. One revenue agent of the Department is placed in each state-owned institution, and examiners are assigned to county and state-aided institutions, one examiner being responsible in some instances for the examining of records and investigation work in several institutions. In order to avoid excessive travel, the sixty-seven counties of the state have been divided into eight field districts, each of which has a central office and staff sufficient to handle field work required by the various bureaus of the Department. This arrangement has proved very satisfactory.[9]

Assessment of Taxes

After a tax bill has been passed and has been signed by the executive, it becomes necessary for the department or agency responsible for tax administration to organize itself and proceed with the assessment of the tax. Assessment involves the determination of the taxable object and the calculation of the amount of tax due, or as another writer has said, "the locating, listing, and valuing of property for taxation." The first step is taken care of largely by the provisions of the law itself as interpreted by the department and as supplemented by rules and regulations issued by it. In some cases the actual process of assessment is simple; in others, quite difficult. Where the taxable object is known, as in the case of a motor vehicle, and the necessary information regarding it is available, the determination of the amount of tax due becomes a mechanical process of applying the rules. The owner of a car which has once been registered in the state may then be billed. In the case of the Federal automobile stamp tax which was levied during World War II, merely purchasing the stamp at any post office and affixing it on the windshield of the vehicle was all that was required.

In other cases it is necessary for the property owner and taxpayer to file a report showing the nature and extent of his holdings, his income, or the volume of his business, before the tax can be computed. Even in such a case the responsibility for the original computation of the tax may be placed upon the taxpayer or upon his employer,[10] the collecting agency merely reviewing the return for the purpose of ascertaining that the payment submitted is not either larger or smaller than it should be. The Federal tax system and the systems in many states are basically self-assessments either by the taxpayer himself or by his employer, as in the case of income and social security taxes. Examiners are usually stationed at convenient places in all centers of population to assist taxpayers in making out their returns.

---

[9] For map, see Joint Legislative Committee on Finances, *Survey of the Government of Pennsylvania*, p. 375 (Harrisburg, 1934).

[10] For a rather spectacular exception to this point of view, see the case of Vivien Kellems, Westport, Connecticut, manufacturer who in 1948 discontinued withholding Federal income taxes from employees; she contended that she must be appointed an Internal Revenue agent, be paid for her services, and be reimbursed for collection expenses incurred. She offered to fight the issue out in the courts, but later retracted.

The growing complexity of modern life has enormously complicated the task of the assessor. Where the work originally involved simple enumeration and computation, the evaluation of the reports of modern business and the properties utilized by them requires the services of experts. The situation is still further complicated by the urgent need for revenue: "governmental operations were meager and required little in the way of financial support. Public functions were direct and apparent. The taxpayer could easily see the purpose for and application of his contribution. The ratio of his tax to his income was small, and he was comparatively unconcerned about the tax question." [11] He might have served at some time as a tax official himself, and moreover the assessment rolls were readily available for inspection. The two factors which contributed to the disruption of this satisfactory situation have been stated by the same writer as follows:

With the increase in public expenditures and the consequent growth in the significance of tax contributions, underassessment became a politically tempting practice. In this way the assessor, who more and more assumed the character of a permanent, professionally political official, appealed for electoral support by the only device his duties provided — discrimination and underassessment. Since state taxes were apportioned for local collection, and since the township or county having the lowest ratio of assessed to true value escaped its proper contribution to the central government at the expense of its neighbors, a policy of general and repetitious underassessment was particularly popular. This practice actually became a contest between assessors of different jurisdictions, while within a specific jurisdiction discrimination became the device for currying the support of influential individuals.

The second factor was the development of vast diversification in the property which the assessor was called upon to evaluate. Public utility properties, industrial plants, and residences of the wealthy with their rich furnishings and art objects were impossible of accurate appraisal by the untrained, elected official. In some localities the assessor attempted to load local government costs on corporative property; in others these and certain other valuable classes of property almost escaped taxation entirely. Neither practice was conducive to confidence in the tax system or its administration.

The establishment of state boards of equalization, later to be considered, and the allocation of tax sources between the state and the local governments, provided some solution for these difficulties. Allocation, often informal rather than legal, reserved certain tax sources to the Federal government and certain others to the states and left to the local units those types of property to which the general property tax might apply. This arrangement was satisfactory until all units of government, pressed for funds, began to grab at everything in sight and until complaints arose regarding the burden of taxation and the gross inequali-

---

[11] Campbell, *State Fiscal Organization*, p. 5.

ties resulting from a lack of coordination in tax policy between the different levels of government.

Determination of Tax Liability. Although, as has been said, the Federal tax system is basically one of self-assessment in which it is the taxpayer's duty to determine correctly and to pay promptly taxes imposed by Federal statute, the Internal Revenue Service is constantly checking on taxpayers. Its powers in this respect are very broad, including not only the right to examine the return to determine its accuracy but the right to require access to books, records, and premises of taxpayers and to compel the testimony of taxpayers and others. The taxpayer must pay the amount assessed whether or not he believes an error has been made, at the same time filing claim for refund or abatement with the Service. This may be either allowed or denied; if denied, the taxpayer still has access to appeal procedures, later to be discussed.

As in the case of the Federal government, every state revenue department or commission has a schedule of the dates upon which taxpayers must file returns under the various tax laws in force. An effort is made to stagger these due dates, partly for the convenience of taxpayers and partly to distribute more evenly throughout the year the workload of the department. Payment may be made all at one time, or partial payment may be made under an installment plan. The department checks each return and takes up with the taxpayer any questions that may arise regarding it. The department has power to settle the amount of tax due, subject to such provisions regarding appeal as may have been established either by law or by departmental regulation.

The department or commission may have, as in New York, the task of assessing special franchises. If the Commission had, in the days when the general property tax was being used for state purposes, assessed all such franchises, wherever located, at 100 per cent of their full value, those located in Sullivan County would have been grossly overtaxed by the local governments in comparison with other property upon which the assessment rate averaged 33 per cent of full value. The property tax rates imposed by the local units in this county upon franchises were based upon their value as determined by the Commission. Again, the New York State income-tax collections are distributed among the local units on the basis of property valuations. If this money were distributed on the basis of the original valuations without equalization, Tioga County would, because of its practice of assessment at 95 per cent of full value, receive more than its fair share, while Sullivan County with its low rate would receive much less than its fair share. For these reasons equalization is necessary whether state funds are distributed to the local units or collected from them. In most states the central boards do not readjust the valuations of individual parcels of property; they merely revise the average or aggregate valuations of the various taxing districts.[12]

The research and investigating function of the state tax commissions has two important phases: the collection of data on tax matters for the state and all its political subdivisions, and the carrying on of independent research. The work of the Wisconsin Commission has been outstanding in the collection of statistical data, while that of the New York Commission has been noteworthy in connection with research. Wisconsin publishes an annual series of bulletins giving detailed information on assessments and collections of taxes for every unit of local government within the state; the same type of data, along with much other information, is contained in the reports of the Comptroller of the State of New York, issued under his authority as supervisor of the accounting of local units. On the research side, the New York State Tax Commission, working in cooperation with various universities in the state, turned out in the decade of the thirties a notable series of studies of tax problems.[13] This type of work is exceedingly important and will continue to be so if the states are to develop a more rational system of taxation and solve some of the perplexing problems of overlapping and multiple taxation.

Assessment of Local Taxes. Local taxes for the support of counties, cities and boroughs, towns and townships, villages and school districts have been chiefly property taxes and, within this category, largely taxes on real estate. For years the prevailing assessment procedure was for the elected assessors or viewers to go around "viewing" or gaping at the properties to be assessed and by a curious mixture of guesswork and political favoritism determining the amount at which each property within their jurisdiction would be assessed. This procedure has gradually given way in progressive communities to the use of scientific methods of tax assessment. The constitutions of all but three states require full-value assessment, but this requirement is honored more in the breech than in the observance.

The first step in the actual process of assessment is to discover the

---

[12] National Industrial Conference Board, *State and Local Taxation of Property*, pp. 65–66 (New York, 1930); also Connecticut Development Commission, *Basis of Property Evaluation for Tax Purposes* (Hartford, annually).

[13] The following titles are illustrative: Ford, Robert S., *The Allocation of Corporate Income for the Purpose of State Taxation;* Girard, Richard A., *The Scope of Uniformity in State Tax Systems;* Hinckley, Russell J., *State Grants-in-Aid;* Pond, Chester B., *Full Value Real Estate Assessment as a Prerequisite to State Aid in New York;* Silverherz, Joseph D., *The Assessment of Real Property in the United States;* Spangler, Frank LeRoy, *Operation of Debt and Tax Rate Limits in the State of New York;* and Tower, Ralph B., *Luxury Taxation and Its Place in a System of Public Revenues.*

properties to be taxed. For this purpose tax maps of numerous varieties are necessary — land value maps, tax district maps, public utility maps, soil maps, land use maps, contour maps, and zoning maps.[14] Outside of the large, well-equipped city tax offices it is necessary for the state to aid if this map work is to be adequately done. In Illinois a project whereby every tax district in the state was mapped, was begun in 1934 and completed in 1938. It was found, incidentally, that there were no less than 15,079 units in which it was possible for a person to be a resident of twelve different taxing districts.[15]

Once the properties are located, it is necessary to apply the rules for determining the valuation. For the guidance of assessors about half the states have prepared handbooks or manuals.[16] It is now the aim to secure competent personnel by examination and to apply principles in such a manner that two people working independently can arrive at the same result. This means that the land and the improvements on the land will have to be considered separately, the value of the property being determined by adding these items together. There are some kinds of assessment work that local authorities are not fitted to perform even with assistance, such as that involving railroads and other public utilities. As an illustration, the valuation per mile of main-line track and right of way of the New York Central Railroad varies from about $2000 per mile in Rome to about $46,000 per mile in Yonkers.[17]

It is impossible to consider the many problems connected with assessments and assessment procedure. The historical background is interesting, as are many of the current problems.[18] Many of the latter are peculiar to rural areas,[19] and many proposals for reform have been suggested, such as equalization, the inducement of full value assessment, and so on.[20] Although state use of the real estate tax is steadily declining, the states are more and more recognizing their responsibility for assessment supervision and state-wide reassessment programs. In 1948 at least four states were engaged in such programs at an average cost of $100,000 per state.

Question may be raised as to whether the fundamental basis of our

---

[4] National Association of Assessing Officers, *Construction and Use of Tax Maps;* California State Association of County Assessors, *Assessors Maps* (State Board of Equalization, Sacramento, 1943).

[5] Illinois Tax Commission, press release, March 13, 1938.

[6] For a list of these, see National Association of Assessing Officers, *Study Guide for Assessing Officers,* pp. 14–15. Many new ones have been published since, and a good many of the older ones are revised from time to time.

[7] New York State Constitutional Convention Committee, *Report,* Vol. 10, p. 165 (Albany, 1938). Many similar illustrations might be presented from other states.

[8] See Silverherz, *op. cit.,* Part I, historical background; Part II, present organization in each of the forty-eight states.

[9] For lists of these studies in the various states, see the successive editions of the author's *American State Government* (Heath, Boston, 1936, 1941, 1946).

[10] Silverherz, *op. cit.,* Part III.

assessment procedure is correct. Assessment here is based upon the theory that property as such has value; the English proceed upon the theory that the value lies in the income-producing power of the property. This seems not only to be more rational but to provide partial solution of the difficulties that arise in times of depression, when the value of real estate declines and the rentals derived from it diminish.[21]

In the late thirties much attention was given to problems of assessment throughout the country, and a large part of the literature dates from that period. The National Association of Assessing Officers has outlined briefly and clearly — although in some eighty items — the principles that ought to govern assessment organization and procedure. Because of the excessive length of this list it cannot be quoted here; but another, showing common defects in assessment procedure together with proved remedies, will indicate the nature and range of the problems in this field.[22]

The Review of Assessments

There are a number of different devices for the review of assessments and the elimination of inequalities: an intradepartmental board, an interdepartmental board, an independent agency such as a state tax commission or a state board of equalization, and a local board of review. Each of these will be briefly considered.

Intradepartmental Boards of Review. Passing upon the complaints raised by taxpayers is always difficult. Because of the quasi-judicial nature of the work, the department may find itself serving as both prosecutor and judge unless it sets up a system of intradepartmental boards of review. Such boards serve a threefold purpose: (1) giving the department an opportunity to obtain a review of the findings of its own officers and employees; (2) assuring the complaining taxpayer that he will have a hearing before an unprejudiced and relatively disinterested board; and (3) protecting the government itself against any possibility of any bureau chief's favoring or discriminating against any taxpayer for whose account he is responsible. The boards tend to absolve the department from the charge that as judge it finds correct a decision it has previously determined administratively.

21 See Reed, Thomas H., and Chubb, L. R., "Rental Value as a Measure of Ability to Pay," *National Municipal Review*, July, 1936; Zangerle, John A., "Assessing Real Estate on Its Income — Is the English System Preferable?" — an address before the National Association of Assessing Officers, Knoxville, 1935.
22 See *Assessment Principles and Terminology*, Chapter 2, and Welch, Roland B., "Improving Assessments in the Small City and Town: a Survey of Maine Assessment Statutes and Procedures," *New England Townsman*, August, 1942, pp. 3-4, 14-15, on which the table here is largely based.

he Assessment of Taxes on Real Property

COMMON DEFECTS	PROVED REMEDIES
ssessment districts too small	Create larger districts
se of boards of assessors	Unanimous opinion of authorities in public administration that assessment function is better performed by a single assessor
ssessors elected to office	More fearless and equitable assessments secured by appointment of assessors
o tests of fitness are applied in selection	Make selections on basis of technical qualifications for the work
erm of office often only a year	Make appointments for indefinite tenure, as a means of developing a career service
here is practically no method of removal before expiration of term	Method of removal, for cause only, should be available
aid on a per diem basis, for part-time work	Put on an annual salary, for full-time work
adequate funds provided for the work	Appropriate adequate funds
ssessors required to make piecemeal assessments of such properties as public utilities	State agency should assess public utilities and other properties located in part in numerous districts
nnual assessment is often required by law	Frequent revaluation is necessary; it should be a continuous process
uch property is escaping taxation	Inaccuracies can be prevented by adequate tax maps and other tools of the trade
uch property improperly described in assessment records	Here also good tax maps will help to correct the situation
phabetical listing of properties on the rolls often used	Real estate should be listed on the rolls in geographical order; this is facilitated by good tax maps
any districts have inadequate inventories of buildings and other improvements	Inspect all improvements and make records in permanent form, to be used from year to year, as long as the building is in service
o serious effort is made to separate valuations for land and improvements	Separation of the value of an improved parcel provides better basis for comparisons among parcels
ttle or inadequate use made of sales data	Sales data should be systematically collected, verified, and studied, for each transfer
ttle or inadequate use made of land classification maps	Land classification maps an important aid in computing value of rural land

The Processing-Tax Board of Review in the Treasury Department, omposed of eight members, was established to adjudicate claims for efund of processing taxes collected under the Agricultural Adjustment ct. All the members, as provided in the Revenue Act of 1936, were fficers or employees of the Treasury Department, designated by the ecretary of the Treasury. The Board was given exclusive jurisdiction ver processing-tax refund claims, the District Courts and the Court of laims being wholly deprived of such jurisdiction.[23]

The same type of board has been developed at the state level. The ennsylvania Department of Revenue devised some years ago a group f six nonstatutory boards of review to assist in the final settlement of any of the more perplexing problems encountered by individual buaus of the Department. The personnel was selected in some cases

Attorney General's Committee on Administrative Procedure, *op. cit.*, p. 15.

from among the officials and employees of the bureau with whose prol
lems the board was to be chiefly concerned, and in others from ind
viduals selected across bureau lines. The list of these boards follow
with brief comments about the nature of each. In no case do membe
receive additional compensation for this work. Proceedings before th
boards are conducted in accordance with rules of practice and pr
cedure formulated by the Department.[24]

Board of Corporation Tax Resettlements. This Board, created purely for a
ministrative purposes, is composed entirely of employees of the Department
Revenue who are appointed by the Secretary of Revenue, and of the Audit
General's Department who are appointed by the Auditor General. The perso
nel usually consists of a Deputy in charge of the settlement of taxes and at lea
two taxing officers from each department.

Board of Enrollment and Disbarment. This Board is constituted for the pu
pose of determining the eligibility of lawyers and others to practice in the D
partment of Revenue. The personnel is composed entirely of employees of th
Department who are appointed by the Secretary.

Board of Institutional Management. This Board consists of one Deputy fro
the Department of Revenue, one from the Department of Justice, and one fro
the Department of Welfare. It passes upon institutional policies that affect re
enue and that affect functionally the work of the Department of Welfare. F
instance, should the Department of Revenue try to collect for maintenance in
state hospital from a poor board which has sent one of its inmates from the poo
house to that hospital for treatment? Large numbers of such questions arise.

Board of Liquid Fuels Tax Redetermination. This Board is composed of en
ployees from the Department of Revenue, who serve with a Deputy from th
Department of Justice appointed by the Attorney General and a Deputy fro
the Department of the Auditor General appointed by the Auditor General. The
duty is to function in relation to the liquid fuels tax, in a manner similar to th
in which the other boards function.

Board of Official Inspection Stations. This Board, composed entirely of mer
bers of the Department of Revenue, hears complaints where official inspectic
stations have had their appointment canceled.

Board of Suspension of Licenses. This board is likewise composed entirely
members of the Department of Revenue, serving at no additional compensatio
It sits to hear appeals from persons whose licenses have been suspended for i
fraction of the Motor Vehicle Code.

Interdepartmental Boards of Review. If an aggrieved taxpayer is unab
to obtain satisfaction by means of a review of his case within the d
partment — either by the bureau chief concerned or by means of a
intradepartmental board — he may in some jurisdictions appeal his ca
to an interdepartmental board for a final administrative hearing befo

---

[24] Joint Legislative Committee on Finances, *op. cit.,* pp. 297–298. On the question
rules of practice, see Martin, "Practice Before the Kentucky Department of Revenue
Kentucky Law Journal, November, 1939, pp. 3–17.

aking court action. The Board of Finance and Revenue in Pennsylvaia is such an agency; a somewhat similar ex officio agency exists in ?eorgia. While the Pennsylvania Board has certain duties of its own to erform under the provisions of the Fiscal Code of 1929 as amended, ` may receive appeals from any of the six intradepartmental boards aleady mentioned. Its membership includes the State Treasurer, who is hairman, the Attorney General, the Auditor General, and the Secreiry of Revenue. Decisions must be by a majority of the members.

The duties of the Board are to revise any settlement made by the)epartment of Revenue, by the Department of the Auditor General, r by the Treasury Department; to grant permission to the taxing deartments to make resettlements under certain conditions; to decide isputes between the taxing departments when they are unable to agree;) hear and determine petitions for the refund of taxes and, upon the lowance of any such petition, to refund such taxes or to credit the ac-)unt entitled to such refund; to authorize the refund of moneys sub-:ct to escheat which have been paid into the state treasury; to select id designate state depositories. When exercising the latter function, ie Board is authorized to invite the Secretary of Banking to sit with id advise it; to fix the rate of interest collected from active and inac-ve state depositories; to approve surety bonds or collateral given to rotect state deposits; and to administer various sinking funds and spe-al funds.

If a taxpayer is aggrieved by action of the Department of Revenue,)proved by the Auditor General, on his petition for settlement which : files within the ninety-day period, then he may within a thirty-day :riod petition the Board of Finance and Revenue for review. In order) prevent the filing of petitions merely for the purpose of delaying iyment of the tax, the petitioner is required to file an affidavit. The ise thing for the taxpayer to do is to pay as much of the tax as he ad-its to be due, so that interest does not accumulate against taxes that he iows he must pay. The Board must act upon petitions for review ithin ninety days after they are filed; nonaction is equivalent to re-sal. If the petitioner still feels aggrieved after the decision of the)ard, he may then proceed to the Dauphin County courts, at any time ithin sixty days after the decision of the Board. The Board has, how-`er, never failed to act upon a petition. It has done its work thor-ighly and carefully and has been generally satisfactory in operation.[25]

dependent Commissions and Boards of Appeal. Perhaps the best illus-ation of the independent appeal board or commission is the Federal

Board of Tax Appeals, which is composed of sixteen members ap
pointed by the President by and with the advice and consent of the Sen
ate for overlapping terms of twelve years. The power of remova
which may be exercised only for cause, has never been used. Each mem
ber has been designated as a division, and each is authorized to hear an
decide cases. The chairman is directed by law to fix the times an
places of the meetings of the divisions with a view to making it possib
for taxpayers to appear with a minimum of inconvenience. Forty-eigl
cities have been designated for the docketing of cases, and hearings ar
usually scheduled in a given city as soon as a sufficient calendar hε
accumulated.

The Attorney General's Committee on Administrative Procedur
thus summarizes the provisions of the Internal Revenue Code goverr
ing the organization and functioning of the Board: [26]

Under the present law, a case may be docketed with the Board by filing pe
tion for review within ninety days after the mailing by the Commissioner of tl
statutory notice of deficiency in income, estate, or gift taxes. The Board's dec
sion becomes final three months after rendition unless petition for review by a
appropriate appellate court is filed within that period. Upon such review the Ci
cuit Court of Appeals or the Court of Appeals for the District of Columbia mε
"affirm or, if the decision of the Board is not in accordance with the law, . .
modify or . . . reverse the decision of the Board, with or without remanding tl
case for a rehearing, as justice may require." The judgment of the appellate cou
is final, except that it is subject to review upon certiorari by the Supreme Cou

Most of the states have tax commissions of the type previously d
scribed, usually charged with responsibility for equalization. In fac
the members of this commission constitute the board of equalizatio
or act in this capacity in about one fourth of the states, while i
others the two functions are performed by separate bodies. Most of tl
early boards were ex officio bodies and accomplished little. By creatir
separate boards or assigning this function to the tax commission the r
sults have been more satisfactory.

The Federation of Tax Administrators made a survey of state boar
of tax appeals a few years ago.[27] Nine states and the District of Colun
bia had then established such boards; at least one other has been estal
lished since. The states are Delaware, Louisiana, Massachusetts, Micl
gan, Minnesota, New Jersey, Ohio, Pennsylvania, South Carolina, ar
Wisconsin. Georgia has an ex officio board, and several other states pr
vide for administrative review of the determinations of the reven
commissioner. Most of the boards have three members, although son
have more; all are appointed by the governor with the advice and co

---

26 Joint Legislative Committee on Finances, *op. cit.*, pp. 12–13.
27 Research Report No. 13 (Chicago, 1942).

sent of the senate, subject in some instances to requirements relating to professional or political qualifications. The salary arrangements are fairly good. Generally speaking, the boards have rather broad jurisdiction; the New Jersey board, for instance, reviews all appeals concerning the assessment, collection, apportionment, or equalization of taxes.

Appeals are taken to the boards by petition, notice of appeal, or sworn statement. Each has established and published rules of practice and procedure to which all appellants must conform.[28] In some jurisdictions a stenographic reporting of all hearings is mandatory. In general, requirements as to who may practice before the boards are similar, appearances being authorized for attorneys, certified public accountants, and the appellant or his representatives. Special reference is made in most cases to the question of refunds, and it is often required that funds be set aside to take care of them. The net cost to the states is small, most of it being offset by additional receipts. Where questions of law are involved, appeal may be taken to the courts.

Boards of Equalization. The term "equalization" means the adjustment by a central board of the aggregate assessed valuations of several subdivisions of government in such a way as to allocate equitably to the various taxing jurisdictions the property of organizations that are centrally assessed. In some states county boards equalize the assessments made by smaller units, but the term usually implies the adjustment of relative aggregate valuations between counties and cities by a state equalization board or tax commission. The purpose of this procedure may be clearly shown by specific reference to the Sullivan County-Tioga County situation in New York in 1928, to which reference has previously been made (see page 287). New York State now publishes equalization tables for each county, showing rate of assessment, assessed value, 100 per cent value, equalized value, percentage added or deducted, and amount added or deducted. These become official figures for the year to which they apply.

The distinction between tax commissions and boards of equalization should be emphasized. Either may exist in a given state without the other, or both may exist together. The former is conceived in broader terms; it is a general state agency concerned with all phases of the state tax program. The latter is, as the name suggests, concerned chiefly with

---

The fourteen rules of practice and procedure of the Wisconsin Board cover the following topics: business hours, appearance and practice, petitions for review, form and style of papers, docket, amendments, motions, extensions of time, hearings, briefs, evidence, proposed findings of fact, practice and procedure, and amendment of rules. The rules of practice and procedure "shall substantially follow that before the Circuit Courts of this State." On this Board, see Slater, Harry, "Functions and Procedures of the Wisconsin Board of Tax Appeals," *Taxes*, December, 1940, pp. 749-754, 770.

the elimination of inequalities in the administration of the general property tax. Since the real estate tax is now used largely as a source for local revenues, the board of equalization does not collect the money, as the tax commissions formerly did. Where a tax commission exists alone, it performs both functions. The equalization function carries with it responsibility for the collection and for the analysis and publication of information on assessments and collections in each of the counties of the state.[29]

Local Boards of Review. The need for a review of local assessments is indicated in the table below, which compares the assessments of certain residential properties in a California city.[30] The inadequate character of

Comparison of County Assessed Value to City Assessed Value
of Sixteen Homes in Piedmont, California

	COUNTY ASSESSED VALUE — 1929	CITY ASSESSED VALUE — 1929	RELATIONSHIP IN PER CENT *
1.	$3600	$3830	93.99
2.	2150	3030	70.96
3.	5050	6260	80.67
4.	2200	3100	70.97
5.	2450	2280	−6.94
6.	2400	2320	−3.33
7.	5250	4900	−6.67
8.	3750	3950	94.94
9.	5550	7840	70.79
10.	2950	3600	81.94
11.	3650	5000	73.00
12.	1650	2550	64.71
13.	4050	3720	−8.15
14.	2200	3300	66.67
15.	3250	3280	99.09
16.	2200	2180	− .91

* City assessment equals 100 per cent.

the work of local boards of review in the correction of such condition has been pointed out many times and is all too often obvious to anyon who takes the trouble to investigate conditions in his home com munity.[31]

One method of improving this situation is to educate the member of these local boards. Such a move was inaugurated in Illinois in 193-

[29] The California State Board of Equalization is an excellent example of this type (board; see its biennial reports, and such supplementary publications as *Assessed Va ues for 194–*.

[30] California Assembly Interim Committee on Assessments and Appraisals of Re Property, *Report*, p. 23 (Sacramento, 1937).

[31] See, for instance, Simpson, Herbert D., *Tax Racket and Tax Reform in Chicag* pp. 376–377 (University of Chicago Press, 1930).

hen review-board officials from the 102 counties of the state were in-
ted to a conference organized and planned by the state tax commis-
on. It was reported that the local assessors, review-board members,
d county treasurers regarded these sessions with approval because
ey found in them a clearinghouse for information and experiences
lculated to help them solve their individual problems of assessment
d review.

Pointing out that the completion of the assessment roll by the town,
llage, or city assessor is not always the final proceeding in the deter-
ination of the assessments of individual parcels of real or personal
operty, Professor Goodman of the University of Wisconsin outlines
me of the essentials of the procedure that should be observed by
ards of review: [32]

A board of review is not an assessing body.

A board of review can make changes in individual assessments only upon oral,
sworn testimony, committed to writing by the clerk of the board.

Assessments of particular taxpayers cannot be increased by the board without
giving notice to the affected taxpayer in time to appear before them.

A board has no power to reduce the valuation of the property in question if
no evidence under oath has been given before it.

A board cannot disregard unimpeached evidence showing that the assessor's
testimony is incorrect.

Within these limitations, Wisconsin courts have taken a very reasonable attitude toward allowing boards to exercise their judgment on contested property values.

e Collection of Taxes

he collections have risen enormously since 1941. Tax revenues for
47 in thirty-five states were 51 to 148 per cent greater than in 1941,
average for the six-year period being 58 per cent.[33] Similar increases
ere reported in the cities. The first question regarding the collection
taxes involves the distinction between the determination of the tax
d the actual process of collecting the money. Here are two distinct
erations; should the same agency be required to perform both of
em? As Willoughby pointed out long ago, although opinion and
actice differ widely, most states and cities distinguish clearly be-
een the two, vesting their performance in separate agencies.[34]

The collection of the money by the same agency that determines
e assessment makes it somewhat easier to achieve a high degree of ef-

---

See Goodman, A. B., "Essentials of State Assessment Supervision," *Taxes*, Novem-
, 1946, pp. 1049–1053.
See releases by Tax Foundation, Inc., New York City, in 1948.
Principles of Public Administration, pp. 505–506 (Johns Hopkins Press, 1927).

ficiency in collection and more difficult to check one of these operatio
against the other. Independent assessment and collection services ma
be more expensive because of the necessity for maintaining separate o
ganizations. "The best method would seem to be that of concentratir
in a single service the duty both of assessing the sums due and of the
collection, and of organizing the service in such a way that the two o
erations are entrusted to distinct subdivisions of the service."

A separate account of individual ledger sheets must be maintaine
for each taxpayer for each type of tax administered. This necessitates
modern, mechanical system of accounting, in the operation of whi
the record is kept constantly up to date. These ledger sheets shou
show instantly each remittance received and credited to the taxpaye
each assessment made, as determined by an audit of the taxpayer's r
turn; each supplemental charge, if any, found necessary to be made
the taxpayer's account; any delinquent assessment or unpaid porti
thereof; and any refund found to be in order, the reason for approvi
it, and upon whose authority it was made. In addition, revenue contr
accounts make immediately available the total of all assessments, c
lections, refunds, delinquencies, etc., to date, classified as follows: [35]

a. For each source of revenue
b. For each of the counties of the state
c. And, in the case of certain taxes, the amounts contributed by each of the f
   lowing groups: domestic and foreign taxpayers, common carriers, insuran
   companies, banks, public utilities, building and loan associations, trusts

The actual processes of collection are fairly simple in most cases.
may be advisable, as Willoughby points out, for the collecting agen
to separate its receipts into three classes: taxes, revenue producing e
terprise receipts, and miscellaneous. When the receipts come in, us
ally in the form of checks, they are credited to the proper account
indicated above, and the funds are transmitted at regular and freque
intervals to the treasurer, who gives the collecting agency a receipt a
holds the funds themselves in custody.

There are numerous ways in which the government can give co
sideration to the taxpayer without serious disadvantage to itself. Acc
mulation of tax burdens at some specific time, as January 1, can
avoided by staggering due dates on the various tax forms. Since a ve
large number of people live on salaries, installment payments may
authorized. Both of these devices, in fact, benefit the government l
maintaining a steady flow of revenue into the treasury. Staggered d

[35] Tennessee Taxpayers Association, *Analysis of Semi-Annual Yields of Reven*
. . . , p. 2 (Nashville, 1937). Similar compilations and analyses are frequently p
lished by official bodies.

ates aid in achieving a more even workload in the revenue depart-
nent. For the convenience of local taxpayers arrangements may be
aade with banks to act as receiving stations, the banks turning over
eir collections at regular intervals to the appropriate official.

ollection Problems. A collecting agency is responsible for finding or
ying to find the most economical and efficient method of collection.
)ften it has a wide latitude under the law, and if not, the law can be
mended. It is important to keep costs at a minimum consistent with
fficient collection; no tax is a good one that eats itself up in costs of
ollection. In the case of the gasoline tax, for instance, it is possible to
ollect from each retailer over the state who sells gasoline from a pump,
ut it is far cheaper to collect from the big oil companies and whole-
ulers. In the one case, the collecting agency has many thousands of
pen accounts; in the other, there are only a few hundred, so that op-
ortunities for evasion are greatly restricted. Similarly, some taxes like
ie unemployment compensation tax or the sales tax are of such a na-
ire that businessmen and firms can be pressed into service as collectors.

Considerable diligence must be exercised to prevent tax dodging
ad evasion. Some taxes, of course, lend themselves more readily to
iese practices than do others. Tax evasion is not illegal; like "honest
raft" it involves violation of the ethical rather than of the legal code.
'ax dodging, on the other hand, is a deliberate attempt to escape a
nown and recognized obligation under the law. The collecting
gency, of course, is interested in stopping these loopholes. Money
)ent in developing an adequate, trained staff to handle these cases pays
ig dividends in increased revenues. When the Tax Division of the De-
artment of Justice put on a drive in 1946, the "snoopers" probed the
nancial records of large spenders at exclusive resorts and brought mil-
ons of dollars into the Treasury. More than a hundred thousand "chis-
ers" paid up — one of them to the tune of $2,000,000 — to avoid
narges and penalties. The Attorney General reported that for every
ollar spent for personnel in this Division over a period of five years,
ie return had been $320. The record in states and cities is not always
) dramatic, but it nets substantial returns for the public treasury.

The problem of delinquency is quite different in character if not in
fect. Here the difficulty usually arises not from unwillingness to pay
ut from inability. If the central office fails to make a collection, the
ise is assigned to the appropriate field agent; if he fails, then it may be
ecessary to secure the assistance of the attorney general, who may in-
itute proceedings or take such other steps as may seem to him advis-
)le in order to protect the interests of the government. In the local

units, where property taxes are chiefly involved, the normal procedui is a tax sale, although distress sales, receiverships, scavenger acts, ta reversion laws, attachments, and personal judgments may be resorte to. When tax delinquent properties are offered for sale and there are r buyers, the government may find itself holding the properties in que tion and faced with the problem of managing and disposing of them.

Centralization of Tax Collection. Centralized tax collection has alread been mentioned as a phase of the organization of the collection fun tion. Not only should it be entrusted to a single department which h no other duty to perform, but many of the taxes now collected l cally should be collected by this department. The situation in Pennsy vania — which is not at all peculiar to that state — provides a strikir example of what a state tax collection system ought not to be. As fa back as the legislative session of 1933, Governor Gifford Pinchot pr posed the adoption of measures that, it was estimated, would brir $17,000,000 of additional revenue into the state treasury each ye without imposing a single new tax or raising the rate on any existir tax. These proposals were:

1. Transfer the collection of the four mill personal property tax from the counties to the Department of Revenue, guaranteeing to the counties as much as they had been collecting them-selves, and dividing the rest between the counties and the state $13,000,0(

2. Transfer the collection of the mercantile license tax from the counties to the Department of Revenue; additional revenue to be derived thereby   1,700,0(

3. Authorize the Department of Revenue to collect all inheritance taxes directly, instead of indirectly through the counties; addi-tional revenue   2,300,0(

      Total additional revenue $17,000,0(

This illustration shows what is possible in a single state if a centralize system is substituted for the old-fashioned, relatively inefficient syste of county collection.

Centralization goes farther, however, if the most efficient plan is 1 be employed. In the past, it was customary to have a separate collecto

---

[36] See Illinois Legislative Council, *Collecting Delinquent Property Taxes.* On tax sale Ford, Robert S., and Wood, William B., *Tax and Salvage Sales* (Bureau of Gover ment, University of Michigan, 1939), and Abbott, Peyton B., "What's Wrong wi Tax Titles?" *Popular Government,* May, 1944, pp. 3–11, in which it is contended th the summary foreclosure procedure in North Carolina may produce titles more marke able than those under court action. On tax-reverted properties: Arkansas State Pla ning Board, *Arkansas Tax-Forfeited Land: Manual of Policies and Procedures* (Litt Rock, 1941); Hillhouse, A. M., and Chatters, Carl H., *Tax-Reverted Properties Urban Areas* (Public Administration Clearing House, Chicago, 1942).

r each type of local tax, in each political subdivision. A citizen might ve to pay his real estate taxes to a county collector, to a township llector, and to a collector for the school district. If there was a separate poll tax, road tax, or other special levy, there would probably be her collectors for each. Until recently this condition generally prevailed; now more than three fourths of the states have a centralized tax llection system on a county unit basis, and other states are moving in is direction. The county collector is authorized to establish branch ffices as required for the proper performance of his duties, but in many stances he utilizes the banks and branch banks within the county. The nk receives the payment and gives a temporary receipt; once a month turns over to the county collector any amounts it has received. hen the collector's office is able to issue an official and permanent ceipt.[37]

LECTED REFERENCES

rthell, Russell, and Campbell, Helen, *State Organization for Tax and Revenue Administration* (Bureau of Public Administration, University of California, 1947). Earlier studies by the same organization include: Campbell, O. W., *State Fiscal Organization* (1937) and Culver, Margaret S., *State Tax Administration* (1939).

deration of Tax Administrators, *State Boards of Tax Appeals* (Chicago, 1942). A survey of appeals agencies and procedures.

rd, Robert S., *State Tax Administration* (Bureau of Government, University of Michigan, 1940), and with Landers, Frank M., *Property Tax Administration* (1939).

nsas Legislative Council, *Concentration of State Tax Administration* (Topeka, 1938) and *Reorganization of Kansas State Financial Administration* (1940). Deals with the application of the principles of centralized tax administration in a particular state.

patrick, Wylie, *State Supervision of Local Finance* (Public Administration Service, Chicago, 1941). Ways and means of state control essential to good local financial administration.

tz, Harley L., *The State Tax Commission* (Harvard University Press, 1918). A pioneer work, still very useful.

rtin, James W., and Morrow, Glenn D., *Organization for Kentucky Local Tax Assessment* (Bureau of Business Research, University of Kentucky, 1941). On state supervision of assessment procedures in a particular state.

om the National Association of Assessing Officers:
  essment Principles and Terminology (Chicago, 1937)
  nstruction and Use of Tax Maps (Chicago, 1937).
  oceedings of the National Conference (Chicago, annually).
  udy Guide for Assessing Officers (Chicago, 1937). Contains extensive bibliography and list of state manuals for assessors, available now in most states, and frequently revised.

tional Association of State Auditors, Comptrollers and Treasurers, *Tabular Analysis of State Fiscal Offices* (Chicago, 1938). A valuable compilation of information.

For what the late Clyde L. King called "the most thoroughgoing study of the costs d procedure of collecting local taxes in this country," see Nicholson, Blake E., *Col-tion of Local Taxes in Pennsylvania* (State Department of Revenue, Harrisburg, ;2).

Analysis of the financial procedures of particular states, prepared by the Public Adm istration Service:

Handbook of Financial Administration, Commonwealth of Kentucky (Chicago, 193 *Manual of Financial Administration for the State of Rhode Island* (Chicago, 1939) *Report on Financial Administration in the Michigan State Government* (Chicago, 193

Sappenfield, Max M., *Financial Administration in the States of Illinois, Ohio, and In ana* (University of Illinois, 1934). Thesis abstract.

Shumate, Roger V., *Assessment and Collection of Property Taxes in Nebraska* (N braska Legislative Council, Lincoln, 1941). Survey of procedures and methods.

Silverherz, Joseph D., *The Assessment of Real Property in the United States* (N York State Tax Commission, Albany, 1936). Standard title, up to date of pub cation.

17

PUBLIC BUDGETING:
FORMULATION AND ADOPTION

The Rise of Budget Systems

Federal Budget System. The real drive for the adoption of Federal budgeting procedures began with the report of President Taft's Commission on Economy and Efficiency, which strongly recommended the establishment of a Federal budget and went so far as to publish in 1913 a model budget for the year 1914. Congress stubbornly resisted the idea, even going so far as to forbid the President to submit the estimates in any other than the customary fashion. This action, which the President regarded as a legislative intrusion upon the executive prerogative, aroused his ire, and he submitted the budget in a new form anyway.

In 1917 Congress did pass a budget act, but this was vetoed by President Wilson on the basis of his objections to certain of its provisions. This action was the more remarkable when one realizes that the fundamental point was the establishment of the principle and that later amendment of any such law might always be regarded as a possibility. At any rate, the question was made an issue in the Presidential campaign of 1920, the Republican candidate promising that if elected, one of his first acts would be to press for the enactment of a Federal budget law.

In 1921 the Congress passed and President Harding signed the present Federal Budget and Accounting Act.[1] This was a double-barreled act, Title I of which created the Bureau of the Budget under a Director and an Assistant Director appointed by the President and serving during his pleasure. Senate confirmation was not required. Title II of the act created the General Accounting Office under a Comptroller General, also appointed by the President but, in order to achieve his complete independence from the administration and from the party in power, for a term of fifteen years without eligibility for reappointment. Under the leadership of General Charles G. Dawes, who was appointed by President Harding as the first Director of the Budget, the new office got off to a good start.[2]

---

42 Stat. 20; 31 U.S.C. 11-16.
For an account of the establishment, see Mr. Dawes' book.

The Budget Office was originally located in the Treasury Depar
ment where, beginning in 1933, the Director — a permanent employ
of the Treasury — worked in close cooperation with the President an
the Secretary of the Treasury. Mr. Buck, analyzing this situation
1937 for the President's Committee on Administrative Manageme
and apparently viewing it with approval, foresaw the possibility th
the Secretary of the Treasury might eventually function in the capa
ity of an American Chancellor of the Exchequer. Not long after,
1939, President Roosevelt transferred the Bureau of the Budget fro
Treasury to the Executive Office of the President, where it has sin
become the major staff agency of the chief executive.[3]

The functions and duties of the Bureau of the Budget were s
forth specifically in the following terms in Executive Order No. 824

1. To assist the President in the preparation of the budget and the formulati
   of the fiscal program of the government

2. To supervise and control the administration of the budget

3. To conduct research in the development of improved plans of administrati
   management, and to advise the executive departments and agencies of t
   government with respect to improved administrative organization and practi

4. To aid the President to bring about more efficient and economical conduct
   government service

5. To assist the President by clearing and coordinating departmental advice
   proposed legislation and by making recommendations as to Presidential acti
   on legislative enactments, in accordance with past practice

6. To assist in the consideration and clearance and, where necessary, in the pre
   aration of proposed Executive Orders and Proclamations, in accordance wi
   the provisions of Executive Order No. 7298 of February 18, 1936

7. To plan and promote the improvement, development, and coordination
   Federal and other statistical services

8. To keep the President informed on the progress of activities by agencies
   the government with respect to work proposed, work actually initiated, a
   work completed, together with the relative timing of work between the se
   eral agencies of the government; all to the end that the work programs of t
   several agencies of the Executive Branch of the government may be coor
   nated and that monies appropriated by the Congress may be expended in t
   most economical manner possible with the least possible overlapping and d
   plication of effort

[3] See Reorganization Plan No. 1, July 1, 1939 (76th Cong., 1 Sess., House Docume
No. 262), and Executive Order No. 8248 (*Federal Register*, September 12, 1939, p. 386
For discussion of this transition, see Smith, Harold D., *The Management of Your Go
ernment*, Chapter 5 (McGraw-Hill, New York, 1945), and the following articles: Ma
Fritz M., "The Bureau of the Budget: Its Evolution and Present Role," *American P
litical Science Review*, I, August, 1945, pp. 653–684; II, October, 1945, pp. 869–8
Pearson, Norman M., "The Budget Bureau: From Routine Business to General Staf
Public Administration Review, Spring, 1943, pp. 126–149; and Wilkie, Horace V
"Legal Basis for Increased Activities of the Federal Budget Bureau," *George Washin
ton Law Review*, April, 1943, pp. 265–301.

The primary duty of the Bureau under this statute is to assist the President in the preparation of the annual budget, which he is required by law to transmit to the Congress. It is revealed, as a matter of fact, by the committee hearings and reports and by the debates, that'the purpose was to fasten responsibility upon the President for the estimates submitted to Congress. To this end the act authorized the Bureau "to assemble, correlate, revise, reduce, or increase the estimates of the several departments and establishments." The act also provided that, at the direction of the President, the Bureau should make detailed studies of the departments and establishments with a view to "securing greater economy and efficiency in the conduct of the public service," taking into consideration changes in methods, activities, organization, or appropriations. In view of the provision for a legislative budget in the Legislative Reorganization Act of 1946, it is interesting to note that in one respect the Bureau was also to serve the Congress, in that the act required it to render to any revenue or appropriations committee of either House such aid and information as might be requested.

In its early years the Bureau functioned with inadequate financial support considering the magnitude of the tasks assigned to it. It had a small staff, partly because it lacked funds and partly because it had a narrow conception of its duties and responsibilities. Harold D. Smith, a career man in the public service who had previously served with distinction as Budget Secretary for the state of Michigan, brought with him a broader concept of the office. He believed that spending more money to staff the Budget Office adequately would in the end save many times the cost. And so it has. For the first time the office began to function not only in planning the over-all spending program of the Federal government but as an active instrument for the control of Federal expenditures. In addition to the formulation of the budget report this growth involved, as the list from the Executive Order of the President has shown, advisory functions to the President, to the departments, and to Congress; general staff services; and functions in connection with administrative management, executive reorganization, and legislative reference. The extent of the Bureau's growth is illustrated by the fact that as late as 1937 it had only forty-one employees, whereas in February, 1947, it had 582.

The Bureau's activities are at present conducted by five major divisions and a field service in addition to a Federal Board of Hospitalization which serves as an advisory agency. The activities of these divisions are outlined in the *United States Government Manual* as follows:[4]

---

[4] 1948 Edition, pp. 58–59; these were discussed by Harold D. Smith in his address before the American Political Science Association, Washington, December 28, 1939, on

Division of Estimates. Through the budget officers of departments and agen cies this Division collects, reviews, and holds hearings on annual budget esti mates, revising and preparing them for the President's consideration and his pres entation to Congress in the Annual Budget; reviews supplementary and deficiency estimates; continuously studies and analyzes the operations and financial require ments of all agencies of the Federal government; and reviews at quarterly inter vals the apportionments of appropriations and allocations and the estimated civil ian personnel requirements of all agencies.

Division of Legislative Reference. This Division reconciles, and clears, for conformity with the established policies of the President, recommendations of the various departments and establishments with respect to proposed legislation, enrolled bills, Executive Orders, and other executive documents.

Division of Administrative Management. This Division advises and assists de partments and agencies of the Federal government on problems of organization, administrative procedure, and management.

Fiscal Division. This Division examines and reviews for improvement the op eration of government systems of financial reporting; studies governmental fiscal programs in relation to economic and fiscal trends; and supervises the prepara tion of the Annual Budget document.

Division of Statistical Standards. Under the Federal Reports Act of 1942, this Division provides coordination and promotes improvements in the statistical serv ices of the Federal government by analyzing and clearing plans and report forms used by Federal agencies in obtaining information from the public and other agencies and by other means described in the act.

Field Service. The Field Service aids the Bureau in investigating Federal field operations, counsels with Federal agencies in order to improve coordination of field activities, consults with state and local officials with respect to Federal pro grams, examines and recommends improvements in the utilization of supplies and equipment in the field, and promotes economical, effective, and efficient ad ministration in the field establishments of Federal agencies.

Budget Systems in the States. In 1926, as has been noted, every state had some kind of budget law. The various types of such legislation in the various states at the close of the decade of the twenties were thus classified by A. E. Buck, eminent authority on budgetary problems:[5]

1. *Executive Type.* This type, under which the governor is responsible for preparing the budget to lay before the legislature, was used by 1945 in all but nine states.[6]

"The Role of the Bureau of the Budget in Federal Administration." In actual practice there is a large amount of interdivisional cooperation in carrying out Bureau functions.
[5] *Public Budgeting,* pp. 28–29 (Macmillan, New York, 1929); see also Sundelson, J. Wilner, *Budgetary Methods in National and State Governments* (New York State Tax Commission, Albany, 1938). For studies of budget systems in individual states, see: Alyea, Paul E., *Alabama's Balancing Budget* (Bureau of Public Administration, Uni versity of Alabama, 1942); Martin and Briscoe; Gulick, Luther, *Evolution of the Budget in Massachusetts* (Harpers, New York, 1920); Miles; Parish; Perkins; and Tenner.
[6] The test case in New York was significant and widely discussed; see Crawford, Finla G., "The Executive Budget Decision in New York," *American Political Science Review,* May, 1930, pp. 403–408; Guthrie, William D., "The New York Executive Budget," American Bar Association *Journal,* February, 1930, pp. 83–98; and Swenson, Rinehart J., "The New York State Budget Controversy," *New York University Law*

2. *Administrative Board Type.* A group of administrative officers, usually including the governor or some of his appointees, is made responsible for preparing the budget. The purpose of this arrangement may be either to associate the more important of the independent administrative officers with the governor in the formulation of the budget or to surround the governor with a board so constituted as to restrict his influence on financial planning. This type is used in five states — Delaware, Florida, Montana, Texas, and West Virginia.

3. *Administrative-Legislative Board Type.* In this type the board is composed of administrative officers, including the governor and members of the legislature. The chief design of this agency is to bring the legislature into the initiating stages of the budgetary procedure; it is used in three states — Indiana, North Dakota, and South Carolina.

4. *Legislative Type.* This leaves the preparation of the budget to a committee of the legislature. This practice, once quite common, was last used in Arkansas, which changed to an executive type of budget in 1937 and reverted again to the legislative type in 1943.[7]

Thus there was a rather surprising uniformity among the states regarding the organization and functioning of the budget agency. With the exception of those still using the administrative-legislative board type, the preparation of the state budget was exclusively an executive function assigned, if not to a budget officer, to some other department or agency in the executive branch. A study of the state fiscal offices made a decade later by the National Association of State Auditors, Comptrollers, and Treasurers showed that more than half the states had created an office of budget director or had established a budget division. Other states had simply added budgetary duties to those of an already existing executive or administrative officer.[8]

By the late forties and at the close of still another decade in the development of state budgeting, it was found that substantial progress had been made in improving procedures. The governor is now the budget-making authority in all but nine states. As noted, Arkansas re-established its legislative budget in 1943 under a Legislative Budget Commission composed of nine members of the House and seven of the Senate. In Delaware, Florida, Illinois, Montana, North Dakota, South Carolina, Texas, and West Virginia there is an administrative board or a legislative-administrative board of which the governor is chairman. Although there are numerous exceptions, staff work is normally done in a budget office immediately under the governor or functioning as a bureau in the department of finance.

Quarterly Review, September, 1929, pp. 174–181, and "New York Court Sustains the Executive Budget," *National Municipal Review,* February, 1930, pp. 81–88.

[7] For a summary of the debate on the relative merits of this and the executive budget, see Gruenberg, Frederick P., "The Executive vs. the Legislative Budget," *National Municipal Review,* March, 1918, pp. 167–173.

[8] *Tabular Analysis of State Fiscal Offices,* pp. 44–49 (Chicago, 1938).

The Budget as an Instrument of Fiscal Policy. A budget system ha
been defined by Buck as "the process by which the financial policy o:
the government, including its monetary requirements, is formulated
adopted, and carried into effect." President Roosevelt in his budge
message of 1941 said that "it reflects in money terms what the govern
ment does for the people and what the people contribute to the government." Another writer emphasizes the three essentials of formulation
submission, and approval: "The budget is a plan for financing an enterprise or government during a definite period of time, prepared by a
responsible executive, and submitted to a representative body for thei
approval or authorization." Harold D. Smith in an address at Alleghany
College in 1940 used these words:

> The budget is now regarded as a useful tool for the efficient execution of the
> functions and services of government; as a body of policies having tremendou
> economic and social implications for every citizen; and as a potent stabilizing
> force in a fluctuating national economy. It is a device for consolidating the vari
> ous interests, objectives, desires, and needs of all our citizens into a program
> whereby they may jointly provide for their safety, convenience, and welfare.

The purposes of a budget system have been variously classified and
described. By providing a plan for spending, a plan for coordinating
expenditures with revenues, and a plan for controlling spending wher
authorized, the system seeks to accomplish its major purpose of promoting the well-being of the public it serves. Those who are responsible
for the formulation and execution of the budget must take into account
the probable total economic and social effect upon the life of the nation of the tax collecting, borrowing, and spending program recommended. The process by which this end is accomplished has been described by Allen D. Manvel, formerly of the Bureau of the Budget, as
encompassing no less than five different aspects of policy determination
as follows: [9]

> 1. *Economic Policy* — involving the relationship between government expend
> iture and all income or expenditure. Economic policy involves the question
> "How much of the economy should government comprise?"
> 2. *Debt Policy* — involving the relationship between total government ex
> penditure and current government revenues. Debt policy deals with the prob
> lem, "When, how, and to what extent should government incur and retire debt?"

[9] "The Philosophy and Essentials of Budgeting," in Seckler-Hudson, Catheryn, *Budget
ing: an Instrument of Planning and Management,* Unit I, pp. 58–66. This volume, a
well as Unit IV, contains many excellent articles and papers; there is an extensive
bibliography in Unit I. See also Holcombe, Arthur N., "Over-all Financial Planning
Through the Bureau of the Budget," *Public Administration Review,* Spring, 1941, pp
225–230; Perloff, Harvey S., "Budgetary Symbolism and Fiscal Planning," in Friedrich
Carl J., and Mason, Edward S., Eds., *Public Policy,* II, pp. 36–62 (Harvard University
Press, 1941); Smith, Harold D., *The Management of Your Government* (McGraw
Hill, New York, 1945); Walker, Robert A., "The Relation of Budgeting to Program
Planning," *Public Administration Review,* Spring, 1944, pp. 97–107.

3. *Revenue Policy* — involving the relative magnitude of various sources of revenue. Revenue policy is mainly concerned with the question, "What taxes should be imposed?"

4. *Expenditure Policy* — involving the relative magnitude of governmental expenditures for various purposes. Expenditure policy considers the question, "What is the comparative value or importance of different government activities?"

5. *Operating Policy* — involving the relationship between the cost and the results of particular government activities. Operating policy is concerned with the question, "How effectively is government organized and operated to achieve its purposes?"

The same writer has stated in convenient form a series of criteria by which one may decide whether a given budget is good or bad. These criteria are, in other words, basic essentials of budgeting, a process which involves the intelligent cooperation of top management and all levels of supervision. The budget program must take account of the fiscal effects of the policies recommended and must make provision for effectuating these policies. The five major qualities essential to effective budgeting are: [10]

1. *Responsibility:* clear and authoritative responsibility for the various aspects of the budgeting function, that is, a single point of final executive decision and responsibility

2. *Comprehensiveness:* the entire fiscal program should be assembled and summarized for evaluation

3. *Flexibility:* the presence of a reasonable degree of policy choice in budget formulation and of administrative discretion in budget execution

4. *Reliability:* involving not merely the accuracy of the information used in the formulation and enactment of a fiscal program but also the availability of such information in sufficient detail and meaningful form to permit its intelligent evaluation

5. *Integrity:* that the fiscal program as enacted will be carried out substantially as intended

Preparation of the Budget Report

Budget formulation has been defined as "the preparation and adoption of a plan for activities in a time period, relating the activities to cost and resources." The budget report, which is the result of this process, is the document submitted by the executive to the legislature and it contains his recommendations for the ensuing fiscal period. After the legislature has approved the plan and made the necessary appropriations, the budget report as modified by the legislature becomes the

---

[10] Another list which appears to be of ancient origin, includes eight items: publicity, clarity, comprehensiveness, budget unity, detailed specification, prior authorization, periodicity, and accuracy. See Smith, Harold D., "The Budget as an Instrument of Legislative Control and Executive Management," *Public Administration Review*, Summer, 1944, pp. 181–188.

budget enforceable by the proper authorities. Before the report can be compiled, an important preliminary step must be taken: the estimates of the revenues that may be expected during the ensuing fiscal period, from the existing tax laws, must be prepared.

Budgeting Time Tables. A definite schedule must be set up for the handling of budgetary matters; this should be done on an annual basis, although most of the states are still functioning on the antiquated biennial system. Under such circumstances certain steps must be taken in the even-numbered years in preparation for the legislative session in the odd-numbered years. In the odd-numbered years other steps are taken, all but the first of which relate to the enforcement of the budget after it has been approved and adopted by the legislature. This topic will be considered later.

Budget Time Table in a Biennial System
Commonwealth of Kentucky [11]

In the even-numbered years:

SEPTEMBER 1. Budget estimate-forms are distributed to all departments and other agencies with detailed instructions for the preparation and submission of the estimates to the Division of the Budget.

OCTOBER 1. Final date for the return of estimates to the Division of the Budget.

OCTOBER 1 to 31. Review, analysis, and preliminary revision of estimates.

NOVEMBER 1 to 30. Conferences with department heads, discussion of estimates with the governor, and final revision of the estimates.

DECEMBER 1 to 31. Consolidation of estimates and preparation of proposed budget document.

In the odd-numbered years:

Not later than the third Monday after convening of the General Assembly in regular session, the printed budget document is submitted to the House of Representatives for its consideration.

MAY 1. Request for allotment form distributed to department heads.

MAY 31. Final date for submission of requests for allotments to the Division of the Budget.

JUNE 1 to 20. Study and revision of requested allotments.

JUNE 20. Advices of allotment for first quarter sent out by Division of the Budget.

SEPTEMBER 20. Advices of allotment for second quarter sent out by Division of the Budget.

DECEMBER 20. Advices of allotment for third quarter sent out by Division of the Budget.

MARCH 20. Advices of allotment for fourth quarter sent out by Division of the Budget.

Sequence of Steps in Budget Formulation. Budgeting is or should be a continuous process. The preparation of the budget report, which is only one aspect of that process, requires a period of several months and includes the steps listed in the timetable on this page. In an annual system, of course, the tempo is accelerated so that the whole process can be completed in a single year. The process requires the participa-

---

[11] Kentucky study, *op. cit.*, p. 23; Alyea covers Alabama, while Sundelson comments on budget schedules in each state.

tion of a very large number of officials. The request forms are distributed by the budget office to the heads of all spending agencies some time prior to the date at which they must be returned. Each department head is responsible for the estimates for his agency. He is expected to know the need for each item and its relative importance as part of the whole. The budget officer must coordinate these requests with each other and with the prospective income for the next fiscal period, the estimates for which are usually made by the comptroller or treasurer.

The original requests — no matter what instructions are issued to the contrary [12] — are almost invariably padded, on the theory that by asking for more than is needed or more than is expected it may be possible to bargain for an amount adequate for the needs of the department. The total of all the requests always vastly exceeds the most optimistic estimates of probable receipts. The amount of such excess having been determined, the spending agencies are asked to reduce their estimates accordingly. Some reductions may be brought about by this process, but they are usually not significant. Next come the conferences of the representatives of the spending agencies with the budget officer for the purpose of justifying the requests;[13] at these conferences each item is discussed and the arguments in favor of all except the most routine and obviously necessary items are presented. Overlapping and duplicating requests, as between departments, must be eliminated. The final decision rests theoretically with the chief executive, actually in most cases with the budget officer.

A research report on budgetary procedure and control in Detroit in 1946 indicates a number of ways in which the budgetary practices of that city might be improved. Since these suggestions apply with equal force in many other jurisdictions, they are listed below:[14]

1. The compilation and use of general background information, such as forecasts of revenues, price changes, etc. in preparing the budget
2. Outlining by the mayor of the significant policy matters to be kept in mind by departments in preparing budgetary requests
3. The justification by departments of their requests in writing, such justifications to be based so far as possible on estimated work and cost units
4. Development of cost and work units
5. Establishment of cost and work unit standards

---

[12] The Federal government, as well as most states and cities, publishes handbooks of instructions for use in preparing and submitting estimates; some of these include the classification used for items of expenditure, under the uniform accounting system.
[13] Budgets should be based on estimated work and cost units and on comparisons with standards of performance and appraisal of results; see Tenner, Irving, "Justifying Budgetary Requests," *Public Management*, October, 1946, pp. 297–299.
[14] Bureau of Governmental Research, *Budgetary Procedure and Control*.

6. Use of cost and work unit standards to determine whether the budgetary requests are proper

7. Reorganization of the Budget Bureau to carry out the foregoing suggestions most effectively

The budget officer is in a strategic and powerful position; it is of the utmost importance, therefore, that he have proper qualifications and training. From the vantage point of his office one may obtain a more comprehensive view of the government as a whole than from any other position except that of the chief executive himself. In connection with the preparation of the budget report it is necessary for him to weigh the value of each activity in each department to determine, in accordance with his best judgment and the fullest information obtainable, which activities are absolutely essential and which can be reduced or eliminated. He must take into account the number of persons benefited by the service, the effectiveness of the departmental organization, and many other factors. He must ferret out inefficiency as well as overlapping and duplication of services. He must carefully scrutinize the requests for salaries and for materials and operating expenses. He should, where possible, suggest savings through consolidations, the standardization of procedure, or such changes in administrative procedure as will result in a more satisfactory distribution of the workload throughout the year. At the same time it should be remembered that he does not make policy; that is done by the legislature and the chief executive. What he does is to try to translate these over-all policy decisions into terms of a fiscal program for the operating agencies of government.

Professor Key pointed out some years ago a basic defect in budgetary theory which is as true now as it was when he wrote in 1940: so far there are no recognized principles or standards to guide a budget officer in deciding to allocate x dollars to activity A instead of to activity B. The decisions are largely a matter of personal judgment; some may even be arbitrary. That the judgment is that of a trained and informed person is good but not enough. The budget officer in the center of the conflict between representatives of interest groups competing for financial support for their particular programs should have some sounder basis for his decisions than now exists; "the most advantageous utilization of public funds" should not resolve itself, as it now does, "into a matter of value preferences between ends lacking a common denominator."[15]

Actually, the area within which any official may exercise discretion in the allocation of funds is often severely limited. At the Federal

---

[15] Key, V. O., Jr., "The Lack of a Budgetary Theory," *American Political Science Review*, December, 1940, pp. 1137–1140.

level the cost of past wars (including interest on the public debt), national defense requirements, and a new foreign policy add enormous expenditures which cannot be cut to any appreciable degree. In the state and local units there are comparable charges for retirement of the public debt. The state budget planners are bedeviled by earmarked funds — often under constitutional mandate and sometimes absorbing as much as 75 or 80 per cent of the revenues — as well as by continuing appropriations. In the local areas, there are mandatory expenditures, i.e., items which must be included in local budgets under requirements of state law.[16]

Nor do reductions in other items come easy, and the cuts that are made are likely to be insufficient to offset the harm they may cause. Nearly everyone thinks the total of public expenditures is too high, but when pinned down on the question as to where savings may be made, he either comes out with some vague generalization about reducing waste and inefficiency or about eliminating some service which does not, so far as he knows, benefit him personally and about which he knows nothing. The trouble is that someone else feels this service is highly essential but views as unnecessary some other activity in which the first critic is interested. Serious efforts already made have largely eliminated actual waste; cuts in other areas are likely, in the long run, to cause injury to essential services.

The method of applying the basic principles of budgeting is well illustrated by the transformation of the Federal Bureau of the Budget, reference to which has already been made. Under such a plan the budget becomes a real tool for financial management. In developing its new control machinery, the Budget Office has employed a considerable number of high-grade employees in the capacity of budget analysts, each one of whom is assigned to work on a particular department or agency. They study its financial records, program, organization, and needs, frequently visiting both its departmental and its field offices. On the basis of the information thus acquired, they may recommend changes in organization or procedure which might result in greater economy of operation or in greater efficiency. While the agency is not bound by law to heed such advice, it may well do so, for future requests for funds are apt to be decided on the assumption that these recommendations have been carried out.

Here arises the situation of a staff agency telling an operating agency how to run its business. Sometimes, of course, it needs to be

---

[16] See "$37,527,917,167," *Fortune*, March, 1947, pp. 110–115, 215–218, and "$39,668,-993,983," *ibid.*, March, 1948, pp. 102–107, 188, 191–192; references on earmarked funds in the states in Chapter 21; and Carter, Edward W., *Mandatory Expenditures of Local Governments in Pennsylvania* (University of Pennsylvania, 1934).

told, and sometimes the judgment of the budget analyst is quite as competent as that of the operating official. There are, however, other cases in which the operating agency must depend upon the judgment of highly specialized technical people on its own staff. In such instances the budget analyst should be aware of his own limitations, recognizing that in many fields he is himself a layman. If he fails to use caution in trying to impose his views regarding technical or professional problems upon an operating agency, the control system may harm rather than aid the cause of good administration.

Content of the Budget Report. The budget report is a kind of financial road map that shows three things: (1) the financial condition at the close of the last fiscal period; (2) for the current period both the present situation and the expected condition at the close if existing policies and commitments are faithfully carried out; (3) expected results in the ensuing fiscal period if the anticipated revenues are received and if the recommended expenditures are made. This is not a simple matter, for it involves consideration of many factors such as estimates of tax yields, expenditure needs, and forecast of economic conditions, all of which are surrounded by uncertainty. All told, the document must give a complete and accurate picture of the financial condition of the governmental unit.

If the budget report is to be the most effective instrument for the information of the legislature and the public, it should present an understandable and workable financial plan for the management of the government. As a matter of fact, few such budget reports have done this. The Hoover Commission severely criticized Federal budget practices on this score, noting that in spite of its colossal size the Federal budget fails to give a complete picture of the cost of specific services or functions. Items relating to a specific function are so scattered (and sometimes hidden) that even after careful search the full cost of the performance of the function is not apparent. This situation is aggravated by putting emphasis on "objects of expenditure" such as personal services, supplies, and equipment, rather than on the work or service to be performed.

In order to correct this situation, the Commission recommended the adoption of a "performance budget" to be achieved by the refashioning of the whole Federal budgetary concept, showing the cost of functions, activities, and projects instead of individual items for personnel, supplies, and equipment. It was further recommended that the budget estimates of all operating departments and agencies should be divided into two primary categories — current operating expenditures and capital outlays. These proposals, it may be noted, are in general accord with the requirements of the Government Corporation Control Act of 1945. At the state level the content of the budget is likely to be influenced by various factors within and without the control of the administration. There may be constitutional or statutory limitations, or both, applying to types and rates of taxes. Economic conditions will affect both tax yields and expenditure requirements. Within this framework the administration may exercise discretion in developing its own policies and financial program. The contents of the document which it formulates are in more than half the states prescribed by law, while in most of the remainder the laws not only prescribe certain contents but stipulate in what form they shall be presented. Such items as the following may be included either in response to such legal requirements or because the budget officer believes them essential to the realization of his purpose: [17]

A consolidated fund balance sheet
Balance sheets by funds
Summary statement of general fund operations and of all special fund operations
Analysis of changes in deficit and surplus for the general fund and for each special fund
A statement of debt
A summary of all estimated tax receipts by source
A summary of all estimated nontax receipts by source
A summary of estimated expenses, in some such form as is indicated below
A summary of expenditures made

In some cases this information should be given, for comparison, for two or more fiscal periods. The summary of estimated expenditures may be broken down by character and object classification and by fiscal periods. The breakdown by character would show estimates for current operating expenses (personal services, materials and supplies, etc.) and for capital outlay (land, buildings, machinery, and equipment). The object classification would indicate proposed expenditures for these items by funds (general, road, etc.) and for two or more fiscal periods.

Presentation of the Budget Report. When the preparation has been completed and the document approved by the chief executive, it must be sent to the printer. Seeing the report through the press is a difficult assignment and requires constant watchfulness and vigilance. The Federal Budget in 1947 weighed seven and one half pounds; that for 1948,

---

[17] Martin, *op. cit.*, pp. 72–73.

six and three fourths pounds. There is, as Professor Martin points out, nothing approaching uniformity in the format of the state reports: [18]

In physical appearance budget documents exemplify all sizes from regular octavo to large atlas and vary in length from eighteen pages, as in the Nebraska report for the 1941–1943 biennium, to over 700 pages, as in the current New Mexico and California documents. New York's executive budget is printed in two volumes, each of which contains over 500 pages. Sometimes the budget documents contain only expenditure data without even a brief statement of governmental income. Some states do not publish their budgetary plan for general circulation in any form; no effort is made to issue the estimates for public information.

Some give a summary of the budget recommendations in one volume, and supporting statistical data in another. Others include both in the same volume. A few are even mimeographed. Nearly all are put out on pages of large and unusual size, which makes for difficulty in handling.

In most jurisdictions the printing must be completed early in January so that the report may be submitted to the legislature when the chief executive presents his budget message. This message calls attention to the general features of the report, but it is expected to discuss unusual features such as new items, significant increases or decreases, or recommendations which will require the levying of new taxes or the exercise of the borrowing power. In such cases he must clearly indicate his proposed policy.

Consideration of the Budget by the Legislature

Under the Anglo-Saxon tradition, the elected representatives of the people have control of the purse. The problems involved in the discharge of this responsibility may be grouped under four headings: (1) the difficulties the legislature faces in securing sufficient information for making intelligent decisions; (2) procedure both in committee and in consideration on the floor; (3) the extent to which the legislature should change or modify executive budget recommendations, and the circumstances of such changes; and (4) the type or form of the legislation when final action is taken.

The Legislative Budget. The Legislative Reorganization Act of 1946 contains in Section 138 specific provision for a legislative budget. The two committees — one from each House — concerned with finances

are authorized and directed to meet jointly at the beginning of each regular session of Congress and after study and consultation, giving due consideration to the budget recommendations of the President, report to their respective Houses

---

[18] *Op. cit.,* pp. 67–68.

a legislative budget for the ensuing fiscal year, including the estimated over-all Federal receipts and expenditures for such year. Such report shall contain a recommendation for the maximum amount to be appropriated for expenditure in such year, which shall include such an amount to be reserved for deficiencies as may be deemed necessary by such committees.

If the estimated receipts exceed the estimated expenditures, the report shall contain a recommendation for a reduction of the public debt; if the estimated expenditures exceed the estimated receipts, a concurrent resolution shall be submitted providing for an increase in the public debt.

The first two years of experience under the law do not indicate that any great progress has been made. The joint committees with their 102 members are more like a town meeting than a committee. This unwieldy group established a working subcommittee of twenty members to go over the whole budget by February 15 to present to Congress its recommendations as to the maximum amounts to be appropriated for the coming fiscal year. The report was to be accompanied by a concurrent resolution and to come before the two Houses for debate. Three weeks is not much time to accomplish such a task. The subcommittee is confronted, furthermore, with a high percentage of "fixed" items which cannot be reduced.

The future of the legislative budget remains a question of great uncertainty. In 1947 the two Houses failed to come to an agreement, and the legislative budget died in conference. In 1948 agreement was reached. In 1949 some members favored abandoning what they regarded as a futile effort; others proposed that the effort be continued but that the date for the report be set later in the session, thereby allowing the committee more time and giving members a better opportunity to size up the general situation.

Difficulties in Consideration. While it is essential to the preservation of democratic procedures that the legislature approve the spending program, current conditions make increasingly difficult the legislature's proper discharge of this responsibility. Under the American system of the separation of powers, there is a certain amount of jealousy between the executive and the legislative branches — a desire on the part of each to preserve its established prerogatives. This usually prevents full cooperation between the two branches and very often leads to open conflict. This situation may exist even when both are under the control of the same political party, but the rivalry is likely to be more acute where the legislative majority and the executive are of opposite parties or opposite factions of the same party.

The legislature's jealousy of its prerogative is nourished by its almost inevitable and almost complete dependence upon the executive for information essential to the consideration of the budget, and members are extremely resentful of what they regard as lobbying and pressure-group tactics by executive departments in behalf of their appropriations.[19] The budget office is under the President, the governor, or the mayor. The departments responsible for the administration of the various programs have the financial data and statistics on workload that the legislature needs. The legislature might develop means of securing adequate information by duplicating records and facilities, but only at excessive cost. So it goes on; reliance largely upon data received from the executive, and loud complaints about executive usurpation.

Legislative Procedure on the Budget. It is customary for the budget report and supporting bills to be referred to the appropriation committees of the two Houses. (The executive's budget message and the budget report are usually accompanied by draft bills which would, if enacted, carry out the recommendations contained in the report.) The members of these committees, which are regarded as among the most important committee assignments, have through years of service become somewhat familiar with the program and the functions for which the governmental units spend their money. In the absence of adequate information, the members of the legislature are in turn largely dependent on the recommendations of the members of these committees.

In most jurisdictions hearings on important items are scheduled. In Washington, representatives of each spending agency have an opportunity to appear before the appropriate subcommittee and present arguments and factual data in support of the official budget recommendations relating to their own agency and its program. A similar procedure is followed in many states and cities. If some members of the committee are hostile to the agency or to some portion of its program, the representatives of the agency are likely to be subjected to intensive grilling.

In some jurisdictions legislative trips for on-the-ground inspection of institutions are made during the session. In Michigan, where such inspection trips have been a traditional feature of legislative procedure, this practice is justified by the claim that the legislature cannot rely on the judgment of the budget director alone as to the needs of institutions. In addition to the fact that one member of the legislature doubted

---

[19] For a classic statement, see Committee on Appropriations, Digest of Statement of Hon. Styles Bridges, Chairman, "Savings Resulting from the Economy Program of the 80th Congress," December 17, 1947.

whether the visitors would "know any more when they got back than before they left," their absence on one occasion so reduced attendance in the Senate as to make it impossible for that body to proceed with the consideration of bills of a controversial character.[20]

All these procedures consume much time. Data on California, for instance, show that in this state consideration has usually extended over a period of 110 days on the average.[21] Over the period from 1929 to 1943 the budget was received from the executive later and later in January. The constantly growing size and complexity of the state program explained this fact and also the steady increase in the length of time consumed in consideration. The legislature tackled this problem, with the result that in 1945 substantial progress was made in shortening the time. The extent of this progress is indicated in the report of the Joint Budget Committee: the 1943 Budget Bill was signed on April 2, whereas the one for 1941 was not approved until June 5, more than two months later.

The use of joint legislative committees for consideration of the budget would be most helpful. This device, long common in New England, is now used rather extensively and is preferable to the separate committees which were once the rule. It saves the time of members both in the study of items and in the conduct of hearings. It insures that the representatives of both Houses will have before them the same information, in the same form, and at the same time. It also saves the time of department and agency representatives who may tell their story once instead of being obliged to repeat it. And by eliminating duplication and making greater efficiency possible, it is obviously less expensive.

The Committee on State Government of the National Municipal League gave careful consideration to the question of the most desirable procedure in legislative consideration of the budget. The results of its deliberations are set forth in the following language in the *Model State Constitution:*

Section 704. *Legislative Budget Procedure.* No special appropriation bill shall be passed until the general appropriation bill, as introduced by the governor and amended by the legislature, shall have been enacted, unless the governor shall

---

[20] Perkins, *op. cit.,* pp. 167–168; these trips were evaluated as far back as 1918 by the Budget Commission of Inquiry: "As a usual thing, the time spent by the committee at the institution is wholly inadequate for getting anything but meager information, and most of that is furnished by the executive officers of the institution. Furthermore, the members of the committee are not usually men who have made a study of state governmental business and financial affairs. It should not be expected, therefore, that they gain very much knowledge as to actual conditions, other than what they are told, by a few hours' visitation."

[21] California Legislature, *Report of Joint Legislative Budget Committee,* p. 34 (Sacramento, 1945).

recommend the passage of an emergency appropriation or appropriations, which shall continue in force only until the general appropriation bill shall become effective. The legislature shall provide for one or more public hearings on the budget, either before a committee or before the entire legislature in committee of the whole. When requested by not less than one-fifth of the members of the legislature, it shall be the duty of the governor to appear in person or by a designated representative before the legislature, or before a committee thereof, to answer any inquiries with respect to the budget.

The legislature shall make no appropriation for any fiscal period in excess of the income provided for that period. The governor may strike out or reduce items in appropriation bills passed by the legislature, and the procedure in such cases shall be the same as in case of the disapproval of an entire bill by the governor.

Modification of Budget Recommendations. The second paragraph of this section raises the question of the extent to which the legislature should modify the recommendations in the budget report. Whatever its action in this regard, the legislature has an obligation to act promptly and complete the consideration of the appropriations well in advance of the date on which they become effective. Failure to do so may cause great hardship in the executive agencies, as was the case in 1947 and 1949 when the Congress did not act upon the appropriations until midsummer.[22] Many agencies faced the new fiscal year without funds; the situation was so serious that there was even talk of providing interim funds. Agencies which maintained their existing staffs were faced with the problem of absorbing later the amount of overexpenditure made during this waiting period.

In general it may be said that if the budget has been carefully prepared, it should be approved by the legislature in substantially the form in which it was submitted. There are at least three important reasons for supporting this view. The first is the fact that the legislature often lacks important information — in spite of the hearings which are regularly scheduled — which presumably was taken into account in the budget office. In the second place, the recommendations of the report may be assumed to accord with the major policies of the administration. In recommending specific amounts for various purposes, the relative value of increasing or decreasing expenditures for these purposes will presumably have been carefully weighed. If this is true, it is not necessary to make many changes — a slight increase here, a small decrease there — to throw the whole plan out of gear. One may well contend that any reasonably careful plan is preferable to the hit-or-miss allocation of funds that is likely to result from too much legislative tinkering. Finally, observation serves to show that legislative changes

---

[22] Due partly to the shift in party control and partly to the new procedures necessitated by the passage of the Reorganization Act of 1946.

n the spending plan are, more often than not, based on political considerations and the personal likes and dislikes of the members who propose them. Many of the proposals are vicious and definitely contrary to the public interest — attempts to freeze out agencies by withholding unds; [23] attempts to get rid of administrative officers by reducing or withholding their salaries; attempts to advance the interests of some pressure group at the expense of the public interest.

Sometimes the legislature attempts to exercise its control by the insertion of positive or negative requirements. For instance, it may be provided that "no portion of this appropriation may be used for payment of the salary of . . . [some individual administrator whom the legislators do not like]." This represents a type of petty but annoying interference with the exercise of normal administrative discretion in the selection of personnel. In other instances, where no specific directive is included, legislative understandings or gentlemen's agreements may exist between the legislative leaders and the executive officers to whose departments appropriations are made.

All these considerations relate to the wisdom of legislative tinkering with budget recommendations. There is the further consideration of the power of the legislature to increase or decrease the amounts recommended in the budget. In the Federal government and in all but four states as well as in most cities this power is unlimited. In Maryland, Nevada, New York, and West Virginia the legislature may strike out or reduce but not raise items in the budget. Since the executive departments are rarely hesitant about asking for funds, it is a little ridiculous for the legislature to insist that they need more money than has been asked for by the governor. If the three branches of the government are to be retained independently, the legislature cannot be denied the right to increase or decrease the amount of its own appropriation, but in those states where the governor has power to reduce items, an increase may later be negatived.[24] The same right on the part of the legislature would probably exist with regard to appropriations for the judiciary.[25]

The Director of the Division of Labor Standards was obliged, on March 24, 1947, send out the following notice: "I regret to inform you that we will be unable to continue our bi-monthly Legislative Report for the present sessions of the state legislatures. The House Appropriations Committee has made no provision for the continuance of the Division of Labor Standards for the next fiscal year. We have been advised to separate personnel immediately so that terminal leave may be paid out of current appropriations."

See Wells, Roger H., "The Item Veto and State Budget Reform," *American Political Science Review*, November, 1924, pp. 782–791, and Smith, Dick, "New Financial Procedures in Texas," *State Government*, May, 1947, pp. 144–145, 154.

White, *Introduction to the Study of Public Administration*, p. 268, reports a provision in the Maryland Constitution (Article III, Section 52) as follows: "The governor's estimates for the executive branch cannot be increased, but may be reduced . . .

If the system of control is well administered, measures providing fo either supplementary or deficiency appropriations should be rare in deed and occur only in real emergencies. A word may well be added regarding the general effect of legisla tive consideration of the budget report. The original departmental re quests are always high and are cut down by the budget officer. Exam ination of the record justifies the generalization that part of the cu will be restored in the legislature. These restorations do not occu straight across the board; some items will probably be increased, othe reduced, but total increases will exceed total reductions. In Minnesot in 1937 the legislature exceeded the recommendations on a large num ber of specific appropriations but cut below on university, educationa and building appropriations, with the result that the total was less tha the recommendations.[26] Normally, however, the actual amounts ap propriated will fall at some point between the budget recommendatior and what the operating agencies originally requested.

Types of Appropriation Legislation. A good many questions arise re garding the manner in which appropriations should be authorizee Should they be made directly to operating units or to the chief execu tive or department head? What are the relative merits of lump su and of specific allotment or detailed appropriations? What is mean by continuing appropriations, revolving appropriations, conditional c variable appropriations, permanent or "no-year" appropriations, an when is their use justifiable? When may the use of "sum-sufficient" ap propriations be justified in preference to appropriation of defini amounts? Should appropriations lapse at the end of the fiscal perio or hold over until some later date? And what of legislative directio contained in appropriation measures and of legislative understanding never formally recorded?

Prior to the development of budget systems there were likely to l as many appropriation acts as operating agencies, a practice which "f cilitated the pleasant practice of voting for all appropriations an shrugging off responsibility for the grand total at the end of th session." Conflict and confusion were widespread as departments we independently to committees with proposed legislation and appropri tion requests. The tendency in the budget era has been drastically

the estimates for the courts (prepared by the judges) cannot be reduced, but may I increased; and estimates for the legislative branch may be either increased or reduced
[26] For excellent illustrative material, extending over a twelve-year period, see Sho. Lloyd M., and Tiller, Carl W., *The Minnesota Commission of Administration ai Finance, 1925–1939*, p. 74 (University of Minnesota Press, 1942), and Illinois Legislati Council, *Appropriation Requests and Enactments, Illinois 1947 General Assembly*, p. (Springfield, 1947).

:duce the number of acts, so that in some jurisdictions appropriation f all funds necessary for the regular operation of the government is overed in one bill. The form may vary, funds being allocated to invividual establishments or to such specific purposes of expenditure as ersonal services, supplies and equipment, etc., with a breakdown nder each showing allocations for the purpose to individual departents and agencies.

The question has recently arisen as to whether the Congress should uss a number of separate appropriation bills, as it has been doing, or hether all of them should be consolidated into a single bill.[27] As things ow stand, money is appropriated on a piecemeal basis and no one can sualize how much "the whole works" is going to cost. The confusion made worse by continuing appropriations and by the failure to disnguish between appropriations and contract authorizations, so that in y given year there may be no visible relationship between total appriations and total expenditures. Another suggestion of a somewhat pposite nature calls for the establishment of a "double budget," i.e., a an under which operating expenditures would be listed in one budget, vestment or nonrecurring items in another. When receipts were suffient to cover the former (including service charges on government vestments), the budget would be said to be in balance.

A lump sum appropriation provides a specified amount for the partment or agency indicated. Under a specific allotment approprian, the legislature places a clear limitation on each item of expenditre and upon the amount that is authorized. The more minutely it earrks the purposes for which funds are to be expended, the greater e degree of control it exercises. By the same token, the more specific e legislative control over spending, the more difficult becomes the ecutive's task of efficient management. This brings one face to face th the question of lump sum versus specific allotment appropriations. ne specific allotment system was necessary before the installation of oper control procedures;[28] under present conditions they are not ly unnecessary but they constitute, by reason of their inelasticity, an stacle to effective administration. Since such appropriations tie the nds of the administrator, they make it impossible for him to accom-

---

See Senate Committee on Rules and Administration, *Hearings* on S. Con. Res. 6 to lude all general appropriation bills in one consolidated appropriation bill, March 24, y 1, and June 24, 1947. The Hoover Commission called attention to the confusion sing from the use of several different types of appropriation acts — annual, no-year, manent, reappropriations, contract authorizations, etc. — and recommended that the ngress make a complete survey of the appropriation structure without delay.
In Texas, where this system is used, specific allotment is carried to such lengths as include appropriations not only for individual schools and colleges within the state versity but for each faculty rank or grade in each department of the university.

plish adjustments made desirable by changed conditions or the needs of emergency situations.

On the other hand lump sum appropriations are sometimes abused by departments. A small agency, for instance, may request a total appropriation of $30,000, of which two thirds is asked for personal service. A lump sum of $30,000 is appropriated, but the department subsequently increases its payroll by adding one or two new employees and skimping on other items of expense. In this way the purpose of the budget is defeated. Or a highway department may request funds for general highway purposes, specifying amounts to be spent for street cleaning, sidewalk construction, street repairs, lighting, and other activities. Subsequently the department may spend its lump sum appropriation in wholly different proportions from those specified in the estimates, again defeating the purpose of the budget. Such defects in legislation can of course be minimized by the California practice of specifying the amount available for each of three objects of expenditure — personal services, operating expenses, and equipment, or they can be prevented by proper administrative controls.[29]

The use of continuing appropriations is often a temptation to the legislature, but when they are made, they are likely to constitute a serious problem for the budget office.[30] This type of appropriation may be used to insure the continuance of a new program over a specified period of time, for which a grant-in-aid may be provided on a diminishing basis. There is, however, a well-established principle of law that one legislature cannot bind a succeeding legislature. Thus any succeeding legislature — legally, if not morally — has the right to revoke or modify such an appropriation. This device was used in Alabama for years when the legislature met in quadrennial session. When the grant of funds is permitted to stand without modification, it assumes the nature of a mandatory expenditure, provision for which must be made in all succeeding budgets during the life of the grant.

Conditional or variable appropriations may also be used under variety of circumstances. The legislature may be without adequate information regarding some matter for which financial provision must be made, or it may desire to give the governor greater freedom in the

---

29 For Governor Lehman's views on a legislative proposal to substitute a lump sum budget for the line item Executive budget system in effect for more than a decade see Legislative Document (1939), Nos. 87, 88, and 89.

30 In California, approximately 60 per cent of the budget falls into the category of fixed charges, i.e., appropriations which have been written into the state's constitution by the people or continuing appropriations enacted into law by the legislature. There remains only approximately $25,000,000 out of the $640,000,000 budget for 1947-19 over which the budget director may exercise some degree of control. See Links, Fred W., "Budgetary Control Over State Expenditures," on California, State Government, May, 1947, pp. 136-137. The situation in Michigan and some other states is as bad worse.

exercise of administrative discretion by making an appropriation conditional upon his approval. When there is uncertainty as to the probable amount of future revenues, appropriations may be made in whole or in part conditional upon a surplus in the general fund. There are a number of ways in which the device of the conditional appropriation would seem to promise interesting possibilities if properly employed.[31]

Clarification of Terminology. At this point, when it may be assumed that the budget report has been enacted into law through the passage of the appropriation act or acts, it is important to differentiate between the budget and the appropriation. The difference is very significant. The annual (or biennial) appropriation act (or ordinance) passed by the legislative body determines the maximum amount of money that may be expended during the fiscal period for the specific purposes for which the appropriation is made. The appropriation limits only the total expenditure during the fiscal period for each of the designated purposes of expenditure, with respect to the department or agency for which the appropriation is made. It may not be modified or amended except by formal legislative action. It does not fix the rate or time schedule of expenditures. The principal disbursing officer cannot approve a claim that would exceed the total appropriation against which it is to be charged. The control of expenditures, which is the subject of the following chapter, rests with the chief executive — president, governor, mayor, or city manager.

The budget, on the other hand, is a detailed estimate of the several kinds of work or activities proposed to be performed and of the persons and things proposed to be used, in accomplishing the objectives contemplated by the appropriation. For convenience of accounting and for control the estimate is built up by items according to the account classification, and each one of such classified items constitutes a definite requirement of the plan of work estimated and proposed at the time of making the budget. The budget, therefore, becomes a picture in words and figures of what the appropriation contemplates, the total amount of each being the same. The budget of itself does not authorize expenditures; no expenditure contemplated by the budget can be made or obligated until it shall have been authorized by law, and then only in conformity with prescribed procedure.

A word of caution should also be added regarding the difference between an appropriation and an authorization. The appropriation makes funds available for a specified purpose while an authorization makes legal the accomplishment of a given purpose or program, when and if the funds are provided for it. Legislatures have given their bless-

Alyea, *op. cit.*, pp. 105–107.

ing to countless things for which they have later failed to provide funds. Appropriation of funds for a given purpose may, however, be assumed to carry with it authorization to do that for which funds were granted, even though there is no specific legislative authorization. An authorization, on the other hand, may be carried out only when funds are appropriated for that purpose or when the responsible agency has on hand to its credit unexpended and unattached funds in the treasury.

SELECTED REFERENCES

Buck, Arthur E., *The Budget in Governments of Today* (Macmillan, New York, 1933). Latest of several volumes on public budgeting by an outstanding authority.

California Legislative Auditor, *Analysis of the Budget Bill* (Sacramento, annually). Extremely interesting annual analysis of budget recommendations.

Commission on Organization of the Executive Branch of the Government, *Budgeting and Accounting*, and Task Force Report on *Fiscal, Budgeting, and Accounting Activities* [Appendix F] (Washington, 1949).

Dawes, Charles G., *The First Year of the Budget of the United States* (Harpers, New York, 1923). History of the establishment of the Federal budget, by its first Director.

Ensley, Grover W., *The Role of Budgeting in Government* (Tax Foundation, New York, 1941). A good brief exposition by a competent student.

Kilpatrick, Wylie, *State Supervision of Local Budgeting* (National Municipal League, New York, 1939). Well known student of local finance analyzes methods of state control over local budget making.

There are a number of good studies of budgetary procedures in particular states among them:

Martin, James W., and Briscoe, Vera, *The Kentucky State Budget System* (Bureau of Business Research, University of Kentucky, 1945).

Parish, William J., *The New Mexico State Budget System* (Division of Government Research, University of New Mexico, 1946).

Miles, Hooper S., *The Maryland Executive Budget System, 1916–1941* (Annapolis, 1942).

Perkins, John A., *The Role of the Governor of Michigan in the Enactment of Appropriations* (Bureau of Government, University of Michigan, 1943).

Tenner, Irving, *Michigan's Budget System* (Bureau of Governmental Research, Detroit, 1946).

Municipal Finance Officers Association, *Municipal Budget Procedure and Budgetary Control* (Chicago, 1942). Procedural manual for use of municipal finance officers.

Naylor, Estill E., *The Federal Budget System in Operation* (The Author, Washington, 1941). A very good exposition of Federal budgetary procedures.

Princeton Local Government Survey of New Jersey, *The Budget Process in Local Government* (Princeton, 1936). Analysis of local budgetary process in a state which pioneered in the supervision of local units.

Seckler-Hudson, Catheryn, Ed., *Budgeting: An Instrument of Planning and Management*, 4 vols. mimeographed (American University, Washington, 1944). An extensive compilation of the best published articles on Federal budgeting.

United States Department of Agriculture, *Guide to Working Materials on Federal Budgetary and Financial Administration* (Washington, 1944). Manual for use of departmental fiscal officers in the central office and in the field.

Willoughby, William F., *Principles of Public Administration* (Johns Hopkins Press, 1927). Excellent chapters on budgeting by one of the framers of the Federal Budget and Accounting Act.

18

PUBLIC BUDGETING: EXECUTION

HIS chapter is concerned primarily with the enforcement of the
budget. Budget administration may be defined as "the management of
plan of activities, previously approved in the form of a budget, ac-
ording to a schedule, and at a cost within the resources available." It
important, however, to keep in mind that in the vast field of financial
dministration with its many ramifications it is essential that there be
ne person in whom is centered responsibility for financial operations.
his point was admirably stated by Henry Morgenthau, Jr., at the
onclusion of his long tenure as Secretary of the Treasury in 1945. In
s Summary Report for the year, which was really a summary report
r the years 1934–1945, he said:[1]

To me, the outstanding weakness in the management of Federal fiscal busi-
ss is the absence of a single, responsible officer to whom the President may
ok for complete and comprehensive policy direction over the entire field of bor-
wing, lending, spending, and insuring. During the period of my Secretaryship,
has become increasingly apparent that the many segments of important finan-
l activity that are managed administratively by agencies other than Treasury
ould be drawn together for purposes of policy coordination. Since the Treasury
cretary is charged with the responsibility for raising the funds, managing the
blic debt, collecting the taxes, maintaining the accounts, and reporting to
ngress on the financial condition of the nation, he is identified as the Chief
cal Officer. Yet, in actual practice, the area of control and influence exercised
the Secretary of the Treasury is largely limited to one side of the ledger. He
not in a position to exert proper influence over the use and disposition of the
ds he must raise and account for to the nation. This weakness is a material
ndicap to the functioning of the Treasury Department and, moreover, to the
lerly and unified conduct of this government's financial affairs. . . .
Generally, I proposed that Treasury's influence be extended to embrace these
as:
A. Policy control and correlation of programs relating to banking, insurance,
ding, and borrowing, now spread principally in the Departments of Agricul-
e, Interior, and Post Office (Postal Savings), the Federal Loan Agency, the
tional Housing Agency, and the Federal Deposit Insurance Corporation.
B. Policy influence with respect to the money and credit markets of the coun-
, typified by activities of the Board of Governors of the Federal Reserve Sys-

---

ummary Report of the Secretary of the Treasury, 1945, pp. 103–106 (Washington,
y 15, 1945).

tem, the Federal Open Market Committee, and the Securities and Exchang
Commission.

C. Policy direction over Federal revenue and expenditures typified by tł
President's budget and proposed legislation submitted to the Congress from tł
standpoint of a unified fiscal program.

The plan for accomplishing the necessary degree of integration in this ar
of fiscal management contemplated first the establishment of a National Cor
mittee for Fiscal Affairs chairmaned by the Secretary of the Treasury and cor
posed of representatives from each of eight subcommittees covered these fields:

1. Industrial Finance	5. Money and Credit
2. Agricultural Finance	6. Housing Finance
3. Foreign Finance	7. Public Works Finance
4. Maritime Finance	8. Federal Budget

Thus the Secretary of the Treasury would be in a position to oversee the fisc
programming of all constituent organizations without disturbing the basic corp
rate patterns, regulatory and insuring controls, or operational practices of su
agencies. . . .

Elements of Expenditure Control

If the task of executive budgeting is to be adequately performe
there must be a uniform accounting system and a uniform system f
the classification of items of expenditure. It is essential that each spen
ing agency be required to live within its income; appropriate devic
for attaining this requirement are a system of allotments or allocatio
and the encumbrance of funds for each purpose of expenditure and f
each quarterly period. Unless some such devices are used, agenci
will be found at the end of the fiscal period to have exceeded the a
propriations made to them as they did in the prebudget era; and th
either a supplemental or a deficiency appropriation will be necessar
The Federal government has its so-called Anti-Deficiency Act, ar
some states and cities now have strict legislation prohibiting spendi
or commitment of funds in excess of appropriations. In California, f
instance, "to assure that the provisions of the fiscal year budget as a
proved by the Department of Finance are followed, any person w
incurs any expenditure in excess of the allotments or other provisio
of the fiscal year budget is liable both personally and on his offic
bond for the amount of the excess expenditures." [2] The same authori
continues:

---

[2] Links, Fred W., "Budgetary Control Over State Expenditures," *State Governme*
May, 1947, pp. 136–137, and California Government Code, Sec. 133370. The origi
Federal Anti-Deficiency Act (31 U.S.C. 665) was enacted in 1870 and was amended
1905 and 1906 to require that expenditures from most appropriations be made at suc
rate as to insure availability of funds during the entire year, and to impose penalties
violation. Executive Order No. 8512 of August 13, 1940 broadened the coverage to
appropriations.

In addition to this control, no department may create any new position without specific approval of the Department of Finance. Documents which are submitted to the state's civil service agency to establish a new position must first have the approval of the Department of Finance before that agency may authorize a position to be filled. All contracts entered into by any state agency for rent of space or services of any kind must be approved by the Department of Finance before such contracts have legal effect.

All purchase orders for materials, supplies, and equipment must be submitted to the Department of Finance for procuring of bids and issuing of purchase orders for such items. All printing requisitions, likewise, must be submitted to the Department of Finance for approval. The Purchasing Division and the State Printing Plant both are in the Department of Finance.

Expenditure control involves two separate and yet closely related functions. One is the immediate problem of enforcement and execution, the other the longer-range problem of supervision and control of expenditures. In the handling of these problems there are responsibilities, some internal, some external, as judged by their relation to the operating agencies to which funds are appropriated. The budget is a plan for spending. In the execution of such a plan, the agency itself through its own personnel and fiscal officers is responsible for staying within the limits of its appropriations. This is a task for internal management and control. Externally, from the point of view of the operating agency, it is the responsibility of top management to see that this is done. This is normally accomplished through the budget office.

The supervision and control of expenditures involve much more than a mere enforcement of the budget plan as established by law in the appropriation act or acts. It means, in addition to checking the availability of funds and ascertaining that their expenditure is authorized for the purposes indicated, the broader considerations of control of policy; scrutiny to prevent misappropriation of funds, by means of administrative audits, approval of contracts, supervision of procurement, personnel control, and supervision of transfers and emergency funds; control to prevent deficits; and control to insure the wisdom and reasonableness of expenditures.[3] These processes must be initiated early if they are really to be effective.

These objectives are achieved mainly through accounting, auditing, and reporting procedures which are supervised by management and used for this purpose. Since these procedures will be considered in later chapters, no comment is necessary at this point beyond emphasizing their importance as instruments for effective control. Such control is usually a function of the central financial agency, very often

---

For a discussion of these points, see White, *Introduction to the Study of Public Administration*, Third Edition, pp. 281–288 (Macmillan, New York, 1948).

the budget office. Management relies upon the internal or pre-audit within the agency; and externally it relies upon the independent or post-audit. The former protects the administration while the latter assures the public and the legislature, after the transactions are completed, that the records are correct and that the expenditures have been made in accordance with law.

Perhaps there is no better way of emphasizing the benefits of good financial management than by showing the consequences of bad. Many years ago, when the struggle for public budgeting had still to be won, an advocate of budgeting chanced to discover the following item in *Collier's Weekly:* [4] "It was on the 31st of October that the charwomen and the rest of the mechanical force which manage the Capitol building in Washington were given their pay for the month of June." One is impressed not only with the picture of poor men and women waiting four months for their pay but with the insight which this incident gives into the running of national affairs. Only where there is no budgeting and no proper method of fiscal control, can such situations arise.

The late Harold D. Smith, on the basis of years of experience in the Federal, state, and municipal service, undertook to set forth, tentatively to be sure, a series of principles governing good budget procedure in a democratic society. These principles, he hastened to add, are designed from the point of view of executive management, "and in this respect are as one-sided as those designed for legislative control. Democratic budgeting requires the reconciliation of these two distinct approaches." [5]

Principles of Executive Budgeting

1. *Executive Budget Programming.* Budgeting and programming are the two sides of the same coin; both must be under the direct supervision of the chief executive.
2. *Executive Budget Responsibility.* The responsibility of seeing that agency programs are brought into accord with legislative intent and are executed with the greatest possible economy.
3. *Budget Reporting.* Budgeting must be based on full financial and operating reports flowing up from the administrative units.
4. *Adequate Budget Tools* such as proper staff, and authority to institute and enforce proper control procedures.
5. *Multiple Procedures in Budgeting.* Varying procedures to fit the needs of different types of operations, such as everyday administration, long term projects, quasi-commercial transactions, etc.

---

[4] Fitzpatrick, Edward A., *Budget Making in a Democracy*, p. 85 (Macmillan, New York, 1918).
[5] *The Management of Your Government*, pp. 90–93.

Executive Budget Discretion. To the executive branch should be left the determination of the precise means of operation to achieve the purposes set forth by the law.

Flexibility in Timing. The budget should contain provisions that permit immediate adjustment to changing economic conditions with which fiscal policy must cope.

Two-way Budget Organization. Efficient budgeting requires the active cooperation of each agency and its major units; there must be in each a budget office for that agency with functions similar to those of the government-wide budget office.

lotments and Encumbrances

n appropriation is not an order to spend; it is, rather, an authorization spend up to the amount appropriated, when and if these funds are quired for the proper operation of the agency and for the accomishment of the authorized purpose. The fact that the legislature has proved a given amount does not mean that it has to be spent willy-lly. While department and agency heads probably know this, they ten fear that if they turn back anything into the treasury, the legisure will conclude that in the next budget the agency can get along less — an assumption that may or may not be justified. As one rmer Member of Congress expressed it, the only arithmetical process ith which the average Member is familiar is subtraction.

he System of Allotments. Of the numerous devices for enforcing the dget and controlling expenditures, none is quite so useful or important as the system of allocations or apportionment of funds. This s been defined as the determination by the budget officer of the ount of obligations which may be incurred under an appropriation contract authorization during a specified period. It is an administrae device used not only in government but in business and other types organizations for delegating financial authority and for controlling availability of funds for specific purposes within a monetary limitan. Further distributions of an allotment to lower levels of management by the recipient, i.e., the head of a department or agency, are quently called "suballotments."

The use of allotments is a relatively recent development. The dee seems to have originated in Illinois in 1917 as a part of the reornization movement of that year. In 1930 ten states had a general otment law. In 1933 Professor White reported a couple more. The stem is now used not only in the Federal government but in two rds of the states and in cities throughout the country. The allotnt states have enacted legislation applying to all appropriations; in ne others the system has been put in operation on the basis of the authority of the executive to supervise and control expenditures.[6] In the administration of an allotment system the first step follows immediately the approval of the budget by the legislature. The enforcing agency, normally the budget office or the comptroller, lifts the totals from the appropriation act or acts and divides them up into quarterly allotments — equal for agencies with an even flow of work, unequal for others, for the various purposes and objects of expenditure.

If the unit operates on an annual budget, as do the Federal government, some states, and all cities, appropriations will be broken down into fourths for each department or spending agency. If the unit is a state operating on a biennial budget, one half of the appropriation for each spending agency must be reserved for the second year and the yearly allotment broken down into quarters. Allotment accounts differ from expenditure distribution accounts in that an allotment sets a definite limit on the amount chargeable to the account, while an expenditure distribution account is merely one class in a classification series for the collection of financial data without regard to limits. While a separate account is necessary for each allotment, expenditure distribution accounts may be established to yield information on a much more detailed basis than that upon which allotments are made. The original lump sum allocations are made for the agency by the budget office; the more detailed allocations, according to object of expenditure, are normally made by the agency itself.

Allocations cannot be made on a purely automatic and arithmetical basis either in the budget office or in the operating agencies. Some of the agencies do not spend their money at the same rate throughout the year. While the quarterly allotment is the normal procedure, allotments may be made for greater or lesser periods where the quarterly period is impractical.[8] Forest fires are most likely to occur in late summer or fall; snow removal from highways is necessary only in the winter months; and so on. In spite of all efforts it is impossible in some agencies to develop an even workload throughout the year. In making allotments, this must be taken into account. Agency officials must be free to develop allotment classifications suited to their needs, provided

---

[6] Kansas Legislative Council, *Reorganization of Kansas State Financial Administration,* pp. 41–54 (Topeka, 1940), and White, *op. cit.,* pp. 288–292.

[7] See United States Bureau of the Budget, *Budget Administration Conference Material,* Section 5, on "Allotment Structure and Methods" (Washington, 1947). This compilation contains a great deal of valuable up-to-date material.

[8] In such instances the budget officer may be authorized by law to prescribe a different period, suitable to the circumstances, this period not to exceed six months nor extend beyond the end of the fiscal year. In other instances where special conditions exist, monthly allocations may be specified. The State of New York is experimenting with a system, to be described later, in which monthly and quarterly reports indicate the trend of expenditures are substituted for the more rigid system of allotments.

assification of the Objects of Expenditure

UNITED STATES	COMMONWEALTH OF VIRGINIA	CITY OF DETROIT *
Personal Services	11 Personal Service	100 Salaries and Wages
Travel	12 Contractual Service	200 Contractual Personnel
Transportation of Things	13 Supplies	Services, Fees, Commissions
Communication Services	14 Materials	300 Supplies, Materials and
Rents and Utility Services	15 Equipment	Expense (Deptl. Classific.)
Printing and Binding	16 Land and Structures	400 Supplies, Materials and
Other Contractual Services	17 Current Charges and	Expense (Uniform City
Supplies and Materials	Obligations	Classific.)
Equipment	18 Pensions and Retirement	500 Equipment
Lands and Structures	Salaries	(Replacements)
Grants, Subsidies and	19 Rotary Fund	600 Unclassified Appropriations
Contributions		700 Fixed Charges
Pensions, Annuities and	CAPITAL OUTLAYS	800 Equipment
Insurance Losses	25 Equipment	(Nonreplaceable)
Refunds, Awards and	26 Land and Structures	900 Capital Improvements
Indemnities		
Interest		* Supplementary classifications
Public Debt Retirement		by function and of funds are
Investments and Loans		used in the Detroit system.

tailed Breakdown in Classification
the Objects of Expenditure

PENNSYLVANIA	VIRGINIA
3. Transportation, Communication, and Information	12. Contractual Service
	121 General Repairs
a. Traveling Expenses	122 Motor Vehicle Repairs
b. Motor Vehicle Supplies and Re-pairs	123 Light, Heat, Power, and Water
	124 Traveling
c. Freight, Express, and Cartage	125 Transportation
d. Postage	126 Communication
e. Telephone and Telegraph	127 Printing, other than Office
f. Newspaper Advertising and Notices	Supplies
	128 Other Expenses

ey observe the requirements of the uniform accounting system, use
ndard symbols, etc. Deviations are ordinarily discussed in personal
nferences between the budget officer and the heads of the operating
ncies. When more money is to be expended in one quarter than in
other, the allocations for other quarters must be so reduced that the
al for the year will not exceed the appropriation.

The second step is the breakdown of these quarterly allotments
cording to the major objects of expenditure, illustrations of which
given in the table on this page. While these classifications all have
same essential purposes and bear some obvious elements of similar-
, there is no uniformity among them, even as between different

units at the same level of government. Only the skeleton outline of tl classification used in the three jurisdictions is shown. In practice ea major item is broken down into its component parts. The breakdow in the table on page 333 illustrate this point. They also illustrate tl variations which creep into the handling of the same problem in diffe ent jurisdictions.

Control over an object class or certain types of transactions with an object class may be necessary in order (1) to comply with legal 1 quirements as to amount of money to be spent, number of artic which may be purchased, or unit prices; (2) to avoid abuses, as in u of communications facilities; (3) when individual transactions a large in amount, as in purchases of land or equipment; (4) when ce tral procurement or storage is economical; (5) to provide for a techr cal or policy review at a high level, in order to insure compliance wi technical or policy requirements. Establishment of controls over ar object class opens up the possibility that the use of alternative metho or objects may prove as costly as or more costly than the ones orig nally chosen.

The extension of the allotment system always meets with resistan and sometimes with temporary abandonment. Every agency head w agree that controls are necessary and ought to be established, but n one of them wants his own operations or those of his department su jected to control. Professor Pray presented in 1947 a full report (the struggle to establish postappropriation controls in the Oklahor state government. In this instance there were constitutional and leg barriers to overcome as well as the normal and expected resistance department and agency heads.[9] In many states there is hostility of t courts to any effective executive control.

Establishing Encumbrances. Setting up an allotment system is n enough. It will not enforce itself; it will not be observed at all unl definite steps are taken to carry it out. The allotments indicate mere the maximum limits of expenditure for the fiscal period for whi they are made. Good financial management must do more; it must pr vent unwise or unnecessary expenditures even though funds may ha been authorized and are available to pay for them. As a means of esta lishing such controls, the budget office must examine each requisiti to determine that the proposed expenditure is a proper one and th funds are available to meet it. This is especially important as the er of the fiscal period approaches, when agencies often attempt to spe

[9] Pray, monograph, and "Post-Appropriation Financial Control in the Oklahoma St: Government," *State Government*, June, 1947, pp. 168–171, 179.

r encumber) any remaining balances before the fiscal period ex-
res.

In order to make sure that funds are available, two sets of records
1st be kept. One shows the cash on hand for the agency and for the
rpose. Entries are made in this account when goods or services have
en received and payment for them is being made. But when requisi-
ns are received, the funds that will be needed to meet the charge
1st be set aside so that they will be available when needed and so
1t the agency will not be able to exceed its allotment. This is called
encumbrance, i.e., reservation of a portion of an allotment at the
1e a commitment is made in order to assure that this amount will be
1ilable to provide payment when the goods are delivered or the serv-
s rendered. When an agency has encumbered all its funds for a given
rpose, it must stop making new commitments, even though it may
1l have cash on hand.

Experience with control methods has occasionally made possible
: development of new techniques. One of these appeared in the
deral government during World War II — the practice of putting
:eiling on the number of employees in a department or agency in
dition to the limitation on the amount that could be expended for
rsonal services as determined by the allotment for that item. This
1 a tendency to induce agencies to examine closely their supervisory
ffs, whose salaries were obviously higher. Yet at the same time the
:ncy had to maintain some proper balance between supervisory
ff and operating personnel, since full production cannot be ex-
:ted when supervision is either inadequate or nonexistent. It did,
wever, tend to prevent "chiseling" on salaries through reclassifica-
1 and/or downgrading, since under the personnel ceiling the agency
1ld employ only the specified number of employees anyway.

tablishing Reserves. Another device that has been found useful in
:ping within appropriation limits and in preventing the need for de-
iency appropriations, is the establishment of reserves. Reserves may
established legislatively but are commonly of administrative origin.
1ly three weeks after the Budget and Accounting Act was passed,
:neral Dawes, the first Director of the Budget, issued a Budget Cir-
lar providing for the establishment of reserves. This early circular
he basis for the General Reserve System in operation in the Federal
vernment today. Under it each department or agency is required to
aside as a budget reserve at the beginning of each fiscal year a cer-
1 percentage of the funds appropriated to it for that fiscal year.
he department or establishment must operate without this reserve

fund except that, in case of absolute necessity, such funds may
obligated by an order of the head of the department or establishme
after its release by the Bureau of the Budget. The purpose of such
system is to require a department or establishment to be conservative
the expenditure of appropriated funds and to do away with the nece
sity for deficiency appropriations." [10]

A reserve of this character is to be distinguished from an admin
trative reserve which may be established by a department or agen
and is subject to its own discretionary disposition or use. This practi
is now found in a number of jurisdictions as a means of making certa
that funds are available to cover promotions and within-grade increas
to which employees may become entitled during the budgetary peric
How often has one heard the lament that no funds were available
meet an increased expense for personnel? Such situations, damagi
as they are to employee morale, need not occur if this simple conti
device is employed: at the beginning of the fiscal period determine a
set aside the amount required to cover any increase or promotion
which any employee in the department or agency may become e
titled during the year. Not all of this sum will be required, but wi
such a plan in operation no employee will be denied a deserved i
crease in compensation because of lack of available funds. In Ca
fornia it is reported: [11]

> The budget act provides that each fiscal-year budget shall make provision
> a salary savings reserve to which shall be transferred at the close of each quan
> the unencumbered balance remaining in each allotment for salaries and wag
> This reserve is not available for expenditure thereafter, unless the Department
> Finance authorizes transfers therefrom to meet necessary expenditures for sa
> ries and wages.

While the application of an allotment system must be comprehe
sive if it is to be effective, exemptions to it are frequently authoriz
In the case of continuing appropriations, which are ordinarily sin
purpose items specifically provided for by act of the legislature, t
use of allocations is obviously less necessary. Other funds provided
the legislature for specific purposes are or may be exempted — the
called special fund and designated or earmarked appropriations. Tr
funds are exempted of necessity. This whole matter may be stated
another way: the allotment system is used chiefly, if not exclusive
for the control of general fund expenditures. Coverage of operati
funds in Minnesota is so complete that regardless of source the or

---

[10] Naylor, Estill E., *The Federal Budget System in Operation*, pp. 129–130 (
Author, Washington, 1941).
[11] Links, *op. cit.*, p. 137.

exemptions are appropriations made to the legislature, the courts, and the state university.[12]

Modification of the Budget. In the process of financial control the budget office is frequently called upon to make changes and adjustments in the budget as originally set up. A budget is made to be followed, and under normal conditions it is followed; but conditions do not always prove to be "normal." In an uncertain world, revenues may be more or less than anticipated, needs for expenditures greater or less. And in such instances it is not intended that a budget shall be a financial strait jacket. There must be flexibility as well as control. The budget office has the authority (or ought to have it) to make necessary modifications to meet emergencies, and it should not hesitate to use this power. In some jurisdictions the budget officer is required by law to make such adjustments:[13]

The provision of the Minnesota law, which creates the necessary safety devices, and makes the flexibility mandatory, is that in case the budget commissioner shall discover at any time that the probable receipts from taxes or other sources for any appropriation, fund, or item, will be less than was anticipated, and that consequently the amount available for the remainder of the term of the appropriation or for any allotment period will be less than the amount estimated or allotted therefor, *he shall* with the approval of the governor, and after notice to the agency concerned, reduce the amount allotted or to be allotted so as to prevent a deficit. From this, it is readily seen that appropriations made by the Minnesota legislature are not full authority for the departments to spend. . . .

This goal of flexibility may be achieved in part by action of the legislature itself. The United States Department of Agriculture is authorized by law to make shifts in the purposes for which funds are spent, up to 20 per cent of the amount appropriated. Several different types of budget modification may be used as conditions indicate.

The exercise of this power may sometimes require transfer of funds. The budget office does not have the power to take funds from one agency and give them to another, once the legislature has approved the budget report and passed the appropriation acts; but it can modify the original allocations set up for a particular operating unit, transferring funds from one division or one category to another within the agency when deemed to be in the best interests of the government. Such transfers may relate to either purpose or time. Perhaps a change in the work program of the agency makes desirable a different use of funds than seemed necessary when the budget plan was formulated.

Driscoll, Theodore G., "Budgetary Control Over State Expenditures," (in Minnesota) *State Government*, May, 1947, pp. 137–138.
Driscoll, *op. cit.*

This involves budget office approval of a change from one purpose to another. Or perhaps the time schedules of work in the agency have been changed because of bad weather, a heavy burden of other types of work, or other causes. In such a case the agency may wish to shift certain funds from one quarter to another or, under a biennial budget scheme, from one year to another. The approval of such changes is entirely within the province of the budget office.

Emergency needs may also arise to create the necessity for fund transfers. In some instances departmental appropriations carry a small emergency item, but it is rarely large enough to take care of an emergency of considerable proportions. Floods, droughts, or other natural catastrophes are cases in point, as might be an outbreak of domestic violence. The department or agency concerned would be under obligation to take prompt and appropriate action, but it could scarcely be expected to bear the cost out of regular operating funds. In such cases the chief executive and the budget officer must work out the financial arrangements, unless or until the legislature is in session to provide the necessary funds. If the legislature is not in session, transfers may be resorted to where possible under the law. While the authority in the case of transfers rests with the chief executive, the budget officer ordinarily acts in his behalf except in the most important cases, where the matter will be brought to his personal attention.

In a governmental unit whose fiscal program is well administered strong controls will have to be established over spending. Controls imposed to bring about economy and prevent deficit financing must not, however, be permitted to become so rigid and bureaucratic that they obstruct the operation of government departments and agencies. It is not the proper function of the budget officer arbitrarily to substitute his opinion for that of the departments and agencies in the determination of departmental policies. Policies are established by law and by the administration in power, usually after consultation with department heads. Rather should the budget officer recognize his position as that of a service agency in a governmental organization whose accomplishments will be measured by the quantity and the quality of the performance of its operating departments.

Other Methods of Budget Enforcement

There are, in addition to the allotment and encumbrance system, numerous other methods which can be used to enforce the budget and control expenditures. The use of the allotment system does not exclude the use of these devices, many of which, in fact, supplement and strengthen the controls built up under it. While the major respon

sibility rests upon the budget office, enforcement demands cooperation from departments and agencies and all fiscal officers of the government, be it national, state, or local. This point is well illustrated by
a report on expenditure control in local government in the state of
Rhode Island. This survey, made by the Institute of Public Administration, recommended a five-point program of fiscal reconstruction: [14]

1. Reorganization and integration of the fiscal offices and agencies in each of the
   city and town governments
2. Establishment of a central agency in the state to formulate, promulgate, and
   administer a general fiscal policy for all local governments
3. Systematic budgeting and debt supervision, all local governments to follow a
   uniform practice in budgeting, and bond issues to be approved by the central
   agency before application made to the legislature
4. Uniform accounting, comprehensive reporting, and competent annual post-
   auditing to be emphasized
5. Establishment of a uniform fiscal year for all local units, with which the appropriation year should be made to coincide

Requiring Regular Reports. The budget office may require, on forms
prescribed by it, regular monthly and/or quarterly reports of expenditures from each department or agency under the administrative control of the chief executive. While the budget office should already
have, from the requisitions which flow through its office, most of the
information which the reports contain, they provide an opportunity
for checking and comparing records and ascertaining that both the
budget office and the operating agency have the same understanding
of the facts of the current situation. The Budget Director of New
York State thus describes the comparative statement of three-year
monthly trends of expenditures required of departments in that state: [15]

This serves as a rough indicator because only general categories of expenditures are used and only cash items are covered. It affords the Budget Division a
criterion for judging whether or not departmental operations are following their
anticipated pattern, and it calls attention to conditions which may be causing deviations from the pattern.

A second device used in the same state consists of a monthly statement of cash expenditures, unpaid obligations, and unencumbered
balances on a monthly and cumulated basis:

This more detailed analysis of expenditures is compared each month against
the expenditure pattern projected for the fiscal year, by each department. These
projections are set up at the beginning of the year and reflect the anticipated ex-

[14] Buck, Arthur E., *Local Finances in Rhode Island* (Rhode Island Public Expenditure
Council, Providence, 1945). For a general statement on methods of control, see White,
op. cit., pp. 267–278.
[15] Burton, John E., on New York, *State Government*, pp. 138–140, 153.

penditures for each month of the year. The cumulated expenditure projection is transferred to the monthly report, and the expenditure position relative to this pattern is established.

These devices, concludes Budget Director Burton, "provide a current expenditure control over spending agencies without forcing them to comply with a rigid system of monthly or quarterly allotments. They also aid the budget director in appraising departmental policies and provide him with a current over-all pattern of state expenditures which is studied in relation to the current revenue outlook."

These reporting procedures may be supplemented by budget office examinations of the records of the departments and agencies. Such reports and examinations are a regular part of Federal procedure, as they have been of the procedure in most states for many years. Indiana put such a system in operation in 1909, Louisiana in 1910, California in 1911. By 1933 such practices had been introduced in about half the states, and they have since become standard practice among them as among all well-administered municipalities.

Determining the Propriety of Expenditures. As previously indicated, it is not sufficient that a proposed expenditure be legal or that the agency have a large enough unencumbered balance to cover it. The budget office, which is responsible for over-all control of the spending program, must have authority to reduce expenditures under appropriations, if the legislative intent may still be accomplished and at least in unusual cases also pass upon the wisdom, expediency, and necessity of proposed expenditures. In some cases this means setting up the judgment of the budget office against that of the operating agency. The position of the latter may be right from its point of view; but from the point of view of the jurisdiction as a whole and the fiscal situation at the time, the budget office may be right. At any rate the budget office has, and it must have, the final word. Otherwise no effective financial control is possible.

In another respect also the budget office review becomes a matter of vital importance. That office must watch not only the rate of expenditure but the rate of income. If it becomes apparent that for any reason receipts are falling below estimates, the budget office has the power and the duty to see that current operating expenses are reduced enough, if at all possible, to offset the decline in revenues. Here again one must remember that an appropriation is not an order to spend; it is an authorization to spend, if necessary and if there are funds. The budget office will not cut so severely as to impair essential services, but there are always with governmental agencies as with individuals some expenditures that can be postponed until a later time. By eliminating such items the budget office can at least shorten the gap between expenditures actually authorized and the funds available to meet them. This type of control is common practice at all three levels of government.

Examination and Approval of Vouchers. Effective financial control requires not only supervision of financial commitments but a careful scrutiny of actual expenditures. There is no uniformity in practice as to the location of the agency responsible for this operation. Sometimes it is in the budget office, sometimes in the comptroller's office, or it may be under the auditor general. Before vouchers, bills, and claims are approved for payment, however, they must be examined to make certain that the expenditures were originally authorized, that the prices charged are reasonable for the goods or services provided, and that there is no misappropriation of funds. In all jurisdictions this type of control is now a matter of regular procedure.

Study of Administrative Organization and Procedure. If the public is to receive 100 cents' worth of goods or services for each tax dollar it contributes, there is urgent need for the continuous study of organization and procedure in the operating agencies. Only recently has the importance of this function come to be realized. No such effort was made in the Federal government prior to the Smith era in the Bureau of the Budget, and few indeed are the states that have seriously undertaken the performance of this function.

In an earlier chapter mention was made of the manner in which the Federal Bureau of the Budget, through its budget analysts, studies the organization and operations of the various departments and agencies. In the states it has been proposed that as the governor has a budget officer and a personnel officer on his staff, he should have also an administrative officer who would study problems of administrative organization and procedure in a manner similar to that in which the other two study the problems of their respective fields. In Massachusetts, where the Board of Administration and Finance has been in operation since 1921, some attention has been given to these problems. Also in Minnesota, where the idea of an administrative manager has been put in actual operation, progress has been made in solving the day-to-day problems arising in the administrative field.[16] Later, Michi-

16 See King, Stafford, "Financial Reorganization in Minnesota," in a bulletin of the National Association of State Auditors, Comptrollers and Treasurers (Chicago, 1940); Short, Lloyd M., "Minnesota Brings Her Government Up-to-date," *State Government*, August, 1939, pp. 137–138, 148–149; Stassen, Harold E., "Managing Minnesota," *National Municipal Review*, July, 1939, pp. 495–498, 508, and "Minnesota Points the Way,"

gan set up its Department of Business Administration, while New York City has for years had its Department of Investigation.

The question may well be raised as to where the responsibility for the discharge of this function should be located. In the Federal government it is in the Bureau of the Budget. In the two states mentioned, it is independent of both the budget and the personnel agencies. Some, incidentally, have argued that the central personnel agency should assume this function; and to a limited extent during World War II the United States Civil Service Commission with its personnel utilization program did assume it. Actually the function belongs to neither one. The budget office is likely to view its responsibility chiefly as an opportunity to practice economy, while the central personnel agency would view the problem largely in terms of personnel.

The function should be performed by an independent officer or agency, under the chief executive and of equal standing with the other two. Management is a science in and of itself. It is more than financial control, although that is an important element in it. It is more than good personnel management, although that too is vitally important. Management involves the coordination of three things — finance; personnel; organization and planning. Each one is so dependent upon the other two that no one of the three can function independently in interpreting agency program and policy. The task of the management specialist is one of coordination and adaptation. He must adjust both fiscal policy and personnel policy to the over-all policy and program of the agency. His function cannot be performed to the best advantage by either of the other major parties at interest — the finance officer or the personnel officer.

SELECTED REFERENCES

For bibliography on the Federal budget, see Fuller, Grace H., *Federal Budget: A Selected List of References* (Division of Bibliography, Library of Congress, 1940). Some of the titles cited in the preceding chapter are also useful here; for methods of control in additional states, see:

Alyea, Paul E., *Alabama's Balancing Budget* (Bureau of Public Administration, University of Alabama, 1942).

Barth, Harry A., *Financial Control in the States with Emphasis on Control by the Governor* (University of Pennsylvania, 1923).

Cline, Denzel C., *Executive Control over State Expenditures in New Jersey* (Princeton University Press, 1934).

Pennsylvania Budget Office, *The State Governmental Budget and Its Place in the Present Fiscal Structure* (Harrisburg, 1930).

Wisconsin Citizens Public Expenditure Survey, *A Brief Survey of Financial Administration and Organization in Wisconsin* (Madison, 1945).

ibid., January, 1941, pp. 4–7, 21; "Michigan's Department of Business Administration," *ibid.*, September, 1943, pp. 448–449. The New York City Department of Investigation has made numerous studies of administrative organization and procedure in that city.

Benson, George C. S., and Litchfield, Edward H., *The State Administrative Board in Michigan* (Bureau of Government, University of Michigan, 1938). For another historical survey of this once popular method of commission control of fiscal matters, see Short, Lloyd M., and Tiller, Carl W., *The Minnesota Commission of Administration and Finance, 1925–1939* (University of Minnesota Press, 1942).

Buck, Arthur E., "Financial Control and Accountability," in President's Committee on Administrative Management, *Report with Special Studies*, pp. 135–138 (Washington, 1937). Recommendations for improvement in Federal procedures.

Commission on Organization of the Executive Branch of the Government, *Budgeting and Accounting*, and Task Force Report on *Fiscal, Budgeting, and Accounting Activities* [Appendix F] (Washington, 1949).

Kull, Donald C., *Budget Administration in the Tennessee Valley Authority* (Bureau of Public Administration, University of Tennessee, 1948). Useful and up-to-date.

Lewis, Verne B., *Budgetary Administration in the Department of Agriculture* (Public Administration Service, Chicago, 1940). Practices of an important Federal department. (Appears also as Appendix A in Gaus, John M., and Wolcott, Leon O., *Public Administration and the United States Department of Agriculture* (Public Administration Service, Chicago, 1940).

Mansfield, Harvey C., "The General Accounting Office," in President's Committee on Administrative Management, *Report with Special Studies*, pp. 169–202 (Washington, 1937), and his *The Comptroller General* (Yale University Press, 1939). For earlier discussions, see Willoughby, W. F., *The Legal Status and Functions of the General Accounting Office of the National Government* (Brookings Institution, Washington, 1927) and Benson, George C. S., *Financial Control and Integration* (Harpers, New York, 1934).

Millett, John D., *Research in Public Budget Administration* (Committee on Public Administration, Social Science Research Council, New York, 1941).

Pray, Joseph C., *Post-Appropriation Budgetary Control in Oklahoma* (The Author, Norman, 1946).

Smith, Harold D., *The Management of Your Government* (McGraw-Hill, New York, 1945). Late Budget Director discusses Federal control procedures.

Sundelson, J. Wilner, *Budgetary Methods in National and State Governments* (New York State Tax Commission, Albany, 1938). Standard title on the subject.

United States Bureau of the Budget, *Budget Administration Conference Materials* (Washington, 1947). Excellent training materials; see also Department of Agriculture, *Guide to Working Materials on Federal Budgetary and Financial Administration* (Washington, 1944).

19

PROCUREMENT

THE supply activities of government can best be carried on through a central agency of supply designed to insure the establishment and enforcement of systematic procedures and basic standards, while the operating aspects of the work are so far as possible decentralized among the departments and agencies. The Hoover Commission, in its report on the Office of General Services, lists seven primary phases of the supply operation; namely, specification, purchasing, traffic management, inspection, property identification, storage and issue, and property utilization.

Standards and Specifications

The first step in purchasing should be the establishment of standards and specifications for all articles (excepting fuel and perishable foodstuffs for institutions) which the government is obliged to buy in quantity and with any degree of frequency. A specification is a word picture of the subject of a contract; it may be one sentence long or it may consist of a complete book accompanied by drawings. Federal specifications are "standards prepared by the United States government to aid Federal purchasing agents in procuring most advantageously materials, equipment, and supplies required by the Federal government." They are intended primarily for the benefit of government buyers but anyone may use them. The bureau or division of standards in the purchasing department furnishes standard specifications for all items commonly in use by all departments, agencies, and institutions in the government.

Establishment of Standards and Specifications. In the performance of its functions the division of standards must compile information from all operating agencies regarding the products required by them. As the work progresses, a catalogue to be used by officials in requisitioning materials may be prepared. The General Schedule of Supplies for the Federal government in 1938 listed 56,000 items; its successor, the Index of Federal Specifications, starts with acetone, a solvent, and ends with zinc-yellow, a paint pigment. In between lies a vast field of commodities, some commonplace, some unusual.[1]

Such a service, properly administered, can materially improve the quality of the goods procured and can accomplish substantial savings for the governmental unit. The Federal Director of Procurement states:[2]

The primary objective of a purchase specification is, simply stated, to inform the vendor what the purchaser wants. In that connection, a "standard" has been defined as a "criterion, measure, or example of procedure, process, dimension, design, extent, quantity, quality, or time, which is established by authority, custom, or general consent, as a definite basis of reference or comparison." Similarly, a "standard of quality" is a carefully drawn description covering the characteristics of a material, some supply article, or a piece of equipment, and should cover all of the variations which it is desirable to consider at the time the standard is adopted. Tolerances allowable, desired quality in this sense is that characteristic or combination of characteristics which renders a product suitable for a given use. "A product is not simply good, it is good for a certain purpose." In considering the quality of an article, the intended use should be kept uppermost in mind. Economic utility of a commodity is likewise related to intended use. Thus the real cost of an article is the price of that article divided by the service it will render.

In drawing up specifications, the agency may obtain aid from a number of different sources. The United States Bureau of Standards issued its *National Directory of Commodity Specifications* in 1925 and has revised it from time to time since. Other directories in more limited fields are also available. To facilitate the use of specifications, the Bureau of Standards inaugurated a certification plan and has compiled lists of manufacturers who have indicated their willingness to comply with selected Federal specifications and commercial standards. They agree to certify to purchasers, upon request, that the materials supplied by them are guaranteed to comply with the requirements and tests of the specifications and standards.[3]

Manufacturers often give valuable assistance; they may be called in with representatives of departments or institutions for an exchange of ideas. The specifications finally determined are an attempt to reconcile the ideas of these two groups by adjusting government requirements to the practical problems of manufacturing.

Federal specifications are developed under the supervision of the

---

[1] Bureau of Federal Supply, Standards Branch, *Why Federal Specifications?* p. 2 (Washington, 1946).

[2] Mack, p. 124; within quote from Harriman, N. F., *Standards and Standardization*, pp. 24 and 131 (McGraw-Hill, New York, 1928).

[3] See Bureau of Standards, *Services of the National Bureau of Standards to Governmental Purchasing Agencies*, and references contained therein (Circular Letter LC-497, Washington, 1937).

Federal Specifications Board, composed of representatives of ten Federal departments and establishments. An Industry Advisory Council has been set up in order that the specifications adopted may conform to industrial practices as well as to government requirements. A standard Outline of Form has been established:

> A — Information regarding other Federal specifications to which references are made
> B — Types, classes, grades, sizes, and colors of commodity covered (limited to types suitable for government requirements)
> C–D–E — Outline of the requirements for the commodity
> F — Methods of sampling, inspecting, and testing
> G — Packaging, packing, and marking for shipment
> H — Requirements applicable to individual government departments
> I — Special notes

Changes in specifications may be made from time to time as required, by application of the same procedures.

Uniform specifications protect both the government and the producer by clarifying requirements and making them definite. By uniformity, attained through the elimination of unnecessary varieties and grades, they make possible volume purchases at reduced cost. The benefits to government and industry may be summarized as follows: [4]

Benefits of Purchasing Specifications

TO GOVERNMENT	TO INDUSTRY
Reduced cost through more competition	Reduced cost of production
Better deliveries	Reduction of types produced
No sales pressure on buyer	Elimination of nonstandard items
Minimum confusion over interpretation of requirements	Establishment of well-defined purchase standards
	Simplification of supply

For purposes of cooperation with the budgeting and accounting offices, it is customary to classify the commodities purchased according to type and to assign a symbol to each type. Classifications of procurement specifications resemble rather closely the classification of objects of expenditure, illustrated in the preceding chapter.

Inspection and Testing. Without enforcement, standards and specifications are worthless. The most convenient means of enforcement are inspection and testing. "Inspection," writes Mr. Mack,[5] "is the natural

---

[4] For extensive discussion of this point, see Forbes, Russell, *Centralized Purchasing: A Sentry at the Tax Exit,* Revised Edition (National Association of Purchasing Agents, New York, 1941).
[5] *Op. cit.,* p. 94.

complement of procurement's component processes. Without systematic, searching inspection, other functions, however efficiently discharged, must suffer in consequence. Inspection is the counterbalance for the exact, written specification and for the scrupulously executed contract." Inspection and testing require careful planning. Each test or series of tests should cover a definite portion of product in order that there be no loopholes for evasion or for the substitution of inferior goods.

The states and cities as well as the Federal government are doing extensive work in this field, both for the establishing of standards and for inspection, especially of materials used in the construction of highways and public works. They have been notoriously lax with regard to purchases of other types; state after state has no central laboratory or inspection facilities but relies upon operating departments to report shortages or deviations from such specifications as exist.[6]

Acquisition and Custody of Property and Supplies

Prior to the development of centralized purchasing, goods were bought in the open market at prevailing prices (or higher) not only by individual departments and agencies but by each separate bureau, division, or section. Favoritism, price juggling, and rake-offs were the rule rather than the exception. Every officer and employee bought what he wanted, when he wanted it, from whomever he chose.

One service might buy a typewriter for $98, another a machine of the same make and model for $128. An official with $500 for furniture might spend it all for a rosewood desk and ask more money the next year to equip his office. In New Jersey, as late as the days of the depression, when prices were low and while the Governor was urging economy, departments were buying such items as:[7]

One Guernsey cow	$950.00	One bookcase	$124.00
One fountain pen	20.00	One picture frame	125.00
Three desk lamps, each	20.00	One swivel chair	51.00
One desk	157.00	One upholstered chair	79.50
One desk pad	9.00	Two radiator covers	99.55
One box of cigars	7.00	One electric clock	8.50

The wastes of old-fashioned, decentralized purchasing methods are well illustrated by examples of purchasing in Chicago as disclosed by a survey made at approximately the same time.[8] The city then paid

[6] Council of State Governments, *Purchasing in the States,* and supplements on inspection and analysis of goods by state purchasing departments, March and May, 1947.
[7] *New York Herald-Tribune,* August 27, 1932.
[8] Chute, Charlton F., *The Public Material Problem in the Chicago Metropolitan Region* (Distributed by the University of Chicago Library, 1937).

average annual prices of 11.7, 14.33, and 16.33 cents a gallon for gasoline, depending upon whether that commodity was bought by one
department or another. Similarly the city paid average yearly prices
ranging from $1.98 to $2.51 a barrel for cement. Lake sand cost $1.53
to $2.11 a cubic yard.

In the paragraphs which follow on the acquisition and custody
of property and supplies, attention will be given first to the stores
cycle, then to the individual steps in that cycle — purchase organization, purchase procedure, central storeroom, cooperative purchasing,
land purchasing, and an evaluation of the centralized purchasing plan.
The problem of the disposition of surplus or unusable property will be
considered in Chapter 21.

The Stores Cycle. The procurement function involves a number of
related activities, which have been variously classified. The flow-chart
on page 349, prepared in 1944 by the Navy Department, which was
responsible for many shore establishments, shows three major functions: purchasing; storage and warehousing; issue. The chart also
indicates quite clearly the interrelationships between these three
functions.

Purchase Organization. The Federal government, nearly all the states,
and a great many cities have a central purchasing office or agent.[9] The
movement began late in the last century when Iowa in 1897 established a board of control with power to supervise all purchases for
state penal and charitable institutions. After 1910 progress was more
rapid. A report put out a decade ago by the National Association of
State Auditors, Comptrollers, and Treasurers showed that "in thirty-
eight states purchasing agencies are truly centralized offices and are
empowered to buy supplies for all state departments and agencies with
but a few minor exceptions. Some fifteen of these states, however, provide for one or more such exceptions," most of them relating to institutions.[10] In only five states was this agency so limited in authority
that it could buy only for certain institutions such as hospitals and
prisons. These systems are based on statutory law; some of them prescribe the purchasing procedure in minute detail, "leaving very little
latitude for adaptation of the administrative methods to changing needs

---

[9] For a history of Federal procurement from the earliest times to the present, see
Mack, *op. cit.,* Part I; for recommendations of the Hoover Commission, see *Office of
General Services: Supply Activities,* and *Task Force Report on the Federal Supply
System* [Appendix B] (Washington, January, 1949). In 1949, Congress enacted the Federal Property and Administrative Services Act, thereby taking a long step toward the
strengthening and improvement of this phase of Federal administration.
[10] *Tabular Analysis of State Fiscal Offices,* pp. 61–63; for the early history, see Buck,
op. cit.

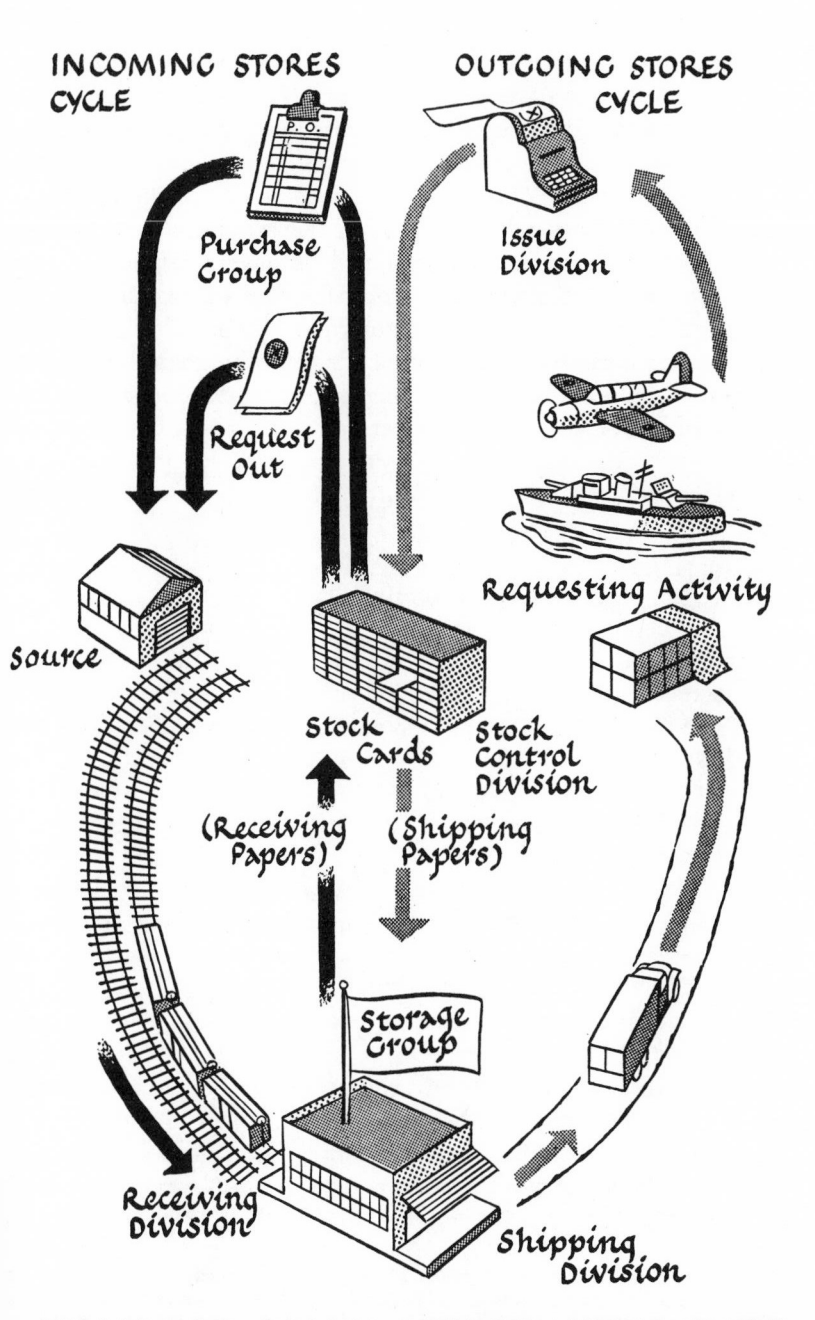

INCOMING STORES CYCLE

OUTGOING STORES CYCLE

Purchase Group

Request Out

Issue Division

Source

Requesting Activity

Stock Cards

Stock Control Division

(Receiving Papers)

(Shipping Papers)

Storage Group

Receiving Division

Shipping Division

STANDARD SUPPLY DEPARTMENT ASHORE
UNITED STATES NAVY DEPARTMENT

and conditions, while other laws merely skeletonize the purchasing organization, leaving the details to administrative rules and regulations to be adopted and changed at will by the official or body in charge of the office." [11]

In 1947 the Council of State Governments reported that centralized purchasing systems were in effect in all but six states, while the remainder were giving serious consideration to the establishment of such an agency. Indicative of the trend toward integrated financial control, purchasing agencies in eighteen states were located within a unified finance department which had accounting and budgeting as well as purchasing functions. Purchasing agencies in nine states operated under and reported to an administrative board or commission. The remaining fifteen either give the purchasing agency separate departmental status or place it within the executive department or make it an independent office reporting to the governor.[12]

Only a few counties have adopted centralized purchasing, but where it has been established, the purchasing agent is appointed by the elected county board and operates under its supervision.[13] Central purchasing procedures are used in most large cities and in some small ones. In these units the purchasing office is usually a separate department. The duties performed in the smaller units duplicate on a smaller scale those performed in the larger ones already described.[14]

Purchase Procedures. Purchasing is an essential function of government. Centralized purchasing, like finance and personnel, is a staff function which came into existence because purchasing for operating departments can be done more efficiently and economically by an

---

[11] Forbes, Russell, *The Organization and Administration of a Governmental Purchasing Office*, Revised Edition, p. 8 (National Association of Purchasing Agents, New York, 1941).

[12] *Purchasing in the States* (Chicago, 1947).

[13] See Bradshaw, H. C., and Hervey, E. J., *Purchasing in Texas Counties* (Texas Agricultural Experiment Station, College Station, 1944), and Miller, Loren B., *Purchasing in Newark* (Bureau of Municipal Research, Newark, 1940); and the following articles: Gehringer, Verne O., "Buying for a Big County's Needs" (San Diego County, California), *Better Roads*, August, 1943, pp. 21–23; Martino, Robert A., "County Purchasing Methods Reviewed," *National Municipal Review*, June, 1940, pp. 388–395; Mispley, J. F., "Centralized Highway Buying," *Better Roads*, January, 1942, pp. 19–21; also Municipal League of Seattle, *How Good Is King County Centralized Purchasing?*. (Seattle, 1947).

[14] On municipal purchasing, see Abbott, Lyndon E., *A Purchasing Manual for Texas Cities* (University of Texas Bulletin, 1935); Forbes, Russell, *Purchasing for Small Cities* (Public Administration Service, Chicago, 1932); Herlands, William B., *Purchasing of School Supplies in New York City* (New York, 1942); New York City Department of Purchases, *A Decade of Centralized Municipal Purchasing* (New York, 1944) and *The War Years, Report on Wartime Activities, 1942–1945* (New York, 1945); Miller, *op. cit.*, and Webb, Malcolm L., *Centralized Purchasing Administration in Philadelphia* (unpublished thesis, Philadelphia, 1940).

agency whose personnel is specialized in purchasing procedures and who give their full time to this work.

The purchasing agency should be so organized that it can study requisitions presented to it by operating departments for the purchase of all classes of materials and can, by use of specifications, standardize and purchase uniformly many of the items used. Where, for instance, sixteen different kinds of pencils were once used, five may be adequate.

Contrary to popular notion a purchase involves a series of steps and procedures rather than a single operation. So far as the Federal government is concerned [15]

Normal purchase derives from the preparation of specifications adequately defining the items required, a determination of sources of supply, and the preparation of bid invitations — in that order. Bids in turn are received, opened, tabulated, and evaluated, after which contracts are prepared and mailed to the contractor (successful bidder) directing delivery of the goods. Upon receipt of evidence of satisfactory delivery, vouchers are prepared authorizing payment to the contractor. Aside from the technical aspects of specifications, sources of supply, transportation, and price, each step advancing a purchase must be in strict accordance with all applicable provisions of law.

The procedure in New Jersey may be taken as illustrative of that followed in the states: [16]

1. *Detailed Applications* — prepared by operating agencies, showing anticipated needs for the next three or six months

2. *Bids* — from vendors, solicited by the departmental buyers on a proposal form asking lowest prices and cash discount for the items listed. Specifications are furnished to prospective bidders

3. *Bids Requiring Contracts* — purchase proposal in an amount of $1000 or over requires advertising in the newspapers and a contract with the vendor

4. *Price Agreement* — used with larger purchases for the purpose of maintaining the price at a certain level, where additional purchases of the same item are contemplated

5. *Purchase Orders* — successful bidder receives an order form from the Purchasing Department stating the quantity desired and the place and date of delivery. This amounts to an "award of contract."

6. *Payment of Vendors* — original and duplicate invoice form must be used by vendors who have sold goods to the state

---

[15] Mack, *op. cit.*, p. 48; for fuller discussion, see pp. 48–62.
[16] Burger and Graves, pp. 19–33. For a survey covering all states, and including in appendix a sample law, organization chart of a typical agency, and flow chart of requisition procedure, see Council of State Governments study; for data on Maryland, Massachusetts, Missouri, New York, and Virginia, see Naylor, E. E., *Purchasing by State Governments* (National Association of State Auditors, Comptrollers and Treasurers, Chicago, 1940); for Alabama, see Alabama Legislative Reference Service, *Alabama State Purchasing* (Montgomery, 1946); for North Carolina, Larsen, Christian L., *Centralized Purchasing for States* (Bureau of Public Administration, University of South Carolina, 1947).

7. *Receipt of Goods* – operating department is responsible for receiving and inspecting goods, since Purchasing Department has no inspection division

8. *Laboratory and Testing Facilities* – Purchasing Department uses Highway Department Laboratory, United States Bureau of Mines Laboratory, and private laboratories when necessary

9. *Payment of Invoices* – operating departments send invoices to Comptroller's Department, with proper forms, for audit and payment

In this state, as in most others, direct purchase orders for perishable foodstuffs may be placed by institutions when granted permission by the Purchasing Department. Emergency orders, when they are legitimate and when the operating agency does not abuse the privilege, are handled expeditiously. A gradual decrease in the number of such orders may be taken as an index of the efficiency of the central purchasing agency.

The law governing contracts invariably specifies that the award must be made to the lowest responsible bidder. While this requirement seems definite and clear, the phrase has led to much controversy. Nelson Rosenbaum has defined the lowest responsible bidder as the one who submits the lowest bid and at the same time has business experience and common sense and can produce. He must have: [17] adequate financial resources; honesty; experience in the type of contract to be let; promptness in performance and deliveries; satisfactory previous work; facilities and equipment to do the work; facilities for continuing public service, such as ability to supply parts.

A serious problem arises when identical bids are entered for a given contract. This, in fact, very often happens. The late Herman Oliphant, legal expert in trade practices, stated that he had repeatedly observed that when the government entered the market, it was unable to obtain competitive bids but encountered monopoly practices and monopoly prices. Also, in periods of scant supply private purchasers are frequently given preference over government in the matter of deliveries.

Some items, not used frequently or in large quantities, may be bought by specification on order for immediate delivery either to the warehouse or to an operating agency or institution. In the case of such items as office supplies, it is advantageous to contract for a year's supply, deliveries to be made at intervals throughout the year. Thus the advantages of both central purchasing and standardization of commodities are preserved. The government is able to purchase in quantity at lower prices and is freed from the necessity of handling and storing huge quantities of material; the manufacturer is able to maintain an even working force and an even level of production.

---

[17] See Rosenbaum, Nelson, "Criteria for Awarding Public Contracts to the Lowest Responsible Bidder," *Cornell Law Quarterly*, November, 1942, pp. 37–53.

Centralized contracting often eliminates some of the practical objections to centralized purchasing that arise from operating departments and institutions. Such complaints are more likely to be the fault of the persons entering them than of the system, but they are still a source of dissatisfaction. For instance, a storekeeper at an institution may not report the fact that the supply of flour is low; later, when the supply is exhausted, management is surprised and annoyed to discover that it takes time to order and obtain delivery. The emergency order system may be used in such instances, but it is by no means a desirable solution of the problem. Another complaint arises from the tendency of some centralized purchasing offices to dictate to the operating agencies, to assume that they know better what the agency needs than the officials of the agency themselves.

Storage and Issue. The central purchasing agency is responsible for traffic management, i.e., the transporting of property from the point of purchase or storage to the point of need, and for the stewardship of materials during the period of storage. No item for which the turnover rate is less than four times a year should be stored. Articles of great bulk should not ordinarily be stored. Total stock investment and overhead costs should both be kept as low as possible, compatible with efficient operation of the service. Absolute control by the purchasing department should be maintained over the stock, and a running inventory should be kept. Such rules should in general guide the purchasing agency in the administration of the storeroom, the main purpose of which is to insure prompt service to departments in obtaining goods constantly in demand.[18]

Exceptions may be made in the application of the central purchasing plan, as when departments are authorized to make direct emergency purchases not in excess of $50 or, in the case of institutions, not in excess of $100. Such exceptions are reasonable and justifiable; failure to recognize this fact may be the cause of much dissatisfaction among the departments and agencies served. As an administrative device designed to expedite the procurement process, a revolving fund may be established. This fund may be reimbursed from the allocations to departments and agencies for particular types of supplies, upon bills rendered by the purchasing agency. In some jurisdictions, the general fund has been charged for heat, light, power, rent, and telephone service fur-

---

[3] Indianapolis Chamber of Commerce, *Shall the City of Indianapolis Establish a Central Storeroom?* and *Problems to Be Considered in the Establishment of the Indianapolis Central Storeroom* (Indianapolis, 1935). For discussion of the problem at the Federal level, see Mack, *op. cit.*, p. 82 ff. and in the states of Connecticut, Minnesota, and Washington, "Inventory Control Plans in the States," *State Government,* August, 1946, pp. 201–205.

nished to special fund agencies. If such funds are to be maintained, they should bear their share of the cost of these necessary services, lest they become an unnecessary and unjustifiable drain upon the general fund. Organized lobbies are often powerful enough to prevent the passage of legislation making the principle of self-support universally applicable to special fund agencies.[19]

The central procurement agency is responsible for property identification, that is, the cataloging of property under some standard system to facilitate identification, and for property utilization, that is, the task of seeing that property is efficiently used and is suitably disposed of when no longer needed. It is also regarded as good management to invest this agency with responsibility for the disposition of unused or unneeded personal property.

Evaluation of Centralized Purchasing. An observer who attempts to evaluate the work of a centralized purchasing agency must admit that the plan presents some difficulties as well as many notable advantages. The former can be largely eliminated by making necessary exceptions and by using centralized contracting for certain types of purchases. The advantages can be obtained in no other way: lower prices and higher quality result in substantial savings. This is due not merely to the advantages of large quantity purchasing but to such other factors as the exercise of greater intelligence and efficiency in purchasing, and the elimination of favoritism. That the actual savings are significant is shown by the fact that Vermont was able to make substantial savings in the purchase of paper stock. Before the new methods were adopted, job lots and seconds were frequently bought.[20] Purchases were made on a hand-to-mouth basis in small lots as needed. Through centralization, paper stock was bought in quantities, usually in ton lots. Bond paper was contracted for in the four grades most commonly used, in 5000 pound lots, thereby saving approximately one third of the former price. This situation is quite in accord with that in three midwestern states covered by a survey of financial administration more than a decade ago. "The experience of each of these states shows that centralized purchasing is a source of much economy and is worthy of the title conferred upon it by Russell Forbes when he called it 'a sentry at the tax exit gate.'"[21]

At the local level, Pittsburgh saved money on 160 out of 187 item

[19] Joint Legislative Committee on Finances, *Survey of the Government of Pennsylvania,* Chapter 26, on the Game and Fish Fund (Harrisburg, 1934).
[20] *Biennial Report* for the two years ending June 30, 1936, p. 6 (Montpelier, 1936).
[21] Sappenfield, Max M., *Financial Administration in the States of Illinois, Ohio, and Indiana,* p. 17 (Thesis Abstract, University of Illinois, 1934).

during the first year of centralized purchasing — on some of them comparatively little but on others as much as 50 per cent or more.[22] Dayton, which began centralized buying in 1914 when the city adopted the council-manager plan, saved $83,000 during the first year, including savings of 50 per cent and 40 per cent, respectively, on such important items as fire hose and coal. Winnetka, Illinois, a town of only 12,000, saved considerably more than $1000 a year by consolidating all departmental requirements for gasoline and oil and placing contracts for the total year's supply in advance. Fayette County, Pennsylvania, saved nearly 50 per cent in its first year of centralized purchasing.

Centralized purchasing not only saves money but it makes possible a central audit of all purchases, better supervision of purchases, and elimination of questionable methods. A central agency is less susceptible to the influence of personal favoritism and to high pressure salesmanship, both of which curtail if they do not eliminate free competition among manufacturers. When officials specify a particular brand of merchandise, higher prices for that commodity are almost certain to follow. By minimizing such factors the central purchasing organization is able, to a large extent, to compel competition; the government benefits not only in price but often in quality.

Cooperative Purchasing. Just as centralized purchasing makes possible substantial economies within a given governmental unit, so joint or cooperative purchasing makes similar savings possible as between a number of political subdivisions situated geographically proximate to one another. In the last decade considerable progress has been made in developing these procedures in a number of areas. A survey made in 1941 showed such plans in operation in Cincinnati and Hamilton County, among various governmental entities in the Milwaukee area, in the Los Angeles and San Diego metropolitan areas,[23] in Chicago's North Shore, and in Pennsylvania. In many areas cooperative school purchasing is being made through a revolving fund, and excellent work is being done by state leagues of municipalities in Michigan, North Carolina, and Oregon.

In Pennsylvania, for instance, legislative authorization for joint pur-

---

[2] *Joint Purchasing and Its Possibilities for Certain Local Governments in Pennsylvania, op. cit.,* pp. 7–8. Chicago set up a central purchasing bureau in 1947, expected to result in thousands of dollars of savings. For other late developments at the municipal level, see Public Administration Clearing House release, December 10, 1947.
[3] As far back as June, 1914, the Tax Association of Alameda County was asking: Why not ONE central purchasing agency for Alameda County and its cities, instead of SIXTY-FOUR? Is $250,000 worth saving? If you were spending $1,000,000 a year and someone showed how to save 25 per cent of it, wouldn't you sit up and take notice?

chasing by local units was given in 1937. Such units may enter into agreements with each other to establish buying pools, the form of the agreements being left to the discretion of the participants. Joint purchases involving expenditures of more than $500 must be in writing and must be advertised, and the contract must be awarded to the lowest responsible bidder. At least one representative from each of the political subdivisions joining in the purchase shall be present at the meeting in which the bids are opened.[24]

In a study of the operation of this act, covering three townships and three boroughs in a county in the Philadelphia metropolitan area, and including eight selected and widely used commodities — gasoline, motor oil, fuel oil, asphalt, sand, cement, crushed stone, and police cars — it was found that each of the six communities would save on at least five of the eight and that two of them would save on seven out of the eight. In a situation in which, under previous purchasing practices, prices varied from 7.5 to 384 per cent, it was conservatively estimated that none of the six communities would save less than 5 per cent and all six together would save 7.9 per cent on the amount spent at the time of the survey on these eight commodities alone. In terms of dollars it was shown that $4625 could be saved out of a total expenditure of $58,470.

Another influence toward cooperation is the National Institute of Governmental Purchasing, which seeks to improve the organization and administration of governmental buying through:

1. A regular and systematic interchange of information and experience among governmental buying agencies
2. Consultation with legislative bodies, departments of government, and others on legislation and problems affecting governmental purchasing
3. Cooperation and assistance in the development and promotion of simplified standards and specifications for governmental buying
4. Developing and furnishing information regarding uniform laws and procedures for governmental buying and for the disposition of surplus or obsolete supplies, materials, and equipment
5. Promotion of public understanding and support of professional government buying
6. Continuous research in the organization and administration of centralized governmental buying agencies
7. Stimulation of and advisory assistance in the preparation of in-service training materials and programs for governmental buying agencies

---

[24] Act of April 29, 1937, P. L. 526, discussed in *Joint Purchasing*. See also Becket Paul, and Plotkin, Morris, *Governmental Purchasing in the Los Angeles Metropolitan Area* (Bureau of Governmental Research, University of California at Los Angeles 1941), which contains an extensive bibliography, and Forbes, *op. cit.*

8. Issuance of certificates and awards for merit and proficiency in governmental buying
9. Other activities having a bearing on the professionalization of governmental buying

Public Printing and Duplication

The history of public printing in America is a sordid story of personal favoritism and political manipulation. In state after state and city after city private printers who have monopolized the public printing have grown immensely wealthy at the public's expense. A survey of the administration of municipal printing in New York City, made by the Commissioner of Investigation in 1940, describes what has been unfortunately a typical situation: [25]

Frequent investigations have demonstrated that for almost a century, city printing has been characterized by collusion among printers, political brokerage, extravagance, gross inefficiency, and willful waste of public funds. Each investigation has revealed that the same pattern for plunder was followed by each successive dictator of city printing.

City printing procurement has followed the same pattern in good administrations and bad. . . . Frequent exposures have had no therapeutic effect. Without variation the monopoly has continued from before the days of Tweed until recently. During the last two years, the latest monopolistic ring of city printers has been broken; but this result, the study indicates, will be little more than temporary unless the basic method of procuring city printing is changed.

Types of Control. The control over public printing is handled in various ways. In the Federal government and in the states of California, Kansas, Nevada, Oregon, and Washington the government does its own printing in its own plant. In all other states and in the cities the work is done on a contract basis, with monopoly contracts, class printing contracts, or individual contracts, and more or less frequent use of open market orders. The supervising agency may be in charge of purchases, functioning in a separate bureau or not, or it may be under a board of control. Iowa has such a separate board. In Pennsylvania there is a Bureau of Publications in the Department of Property and Supplies. Reference has already been made to the Commission on Administration and Finance in Massachusetts, where an elaborate and effective system for the supervision and control of printing has been developed.

Under the Massachusetts plan no document may be published without the sanction and approval of the Commission; in fact, this is always noted in two lines which appear at the bottom of the title page of each document: *Publication of this document approved by the Com-*

Herlands, pp. 1, 23.

mission on Administration and Finance. Each document has a P.D. (Public Document) number, as well as an account number for office records and symbols indicating the number of copies ordered and the date of the order. Regular reports keep the same P.D. number from year to year, as is the case in a number of other states.[26] A similar system of numbering serial publications is used in New York State.

In a centralized agency the duties include editing of all reports, bulletins, and other publications of departments and agencies, legislative and judicial as well as executive. A large government agency requires a vast assortment of printed materials, including steel-engraved liquor stamps, illustrated annual reports, special licenses, general acts of the legislature, state codes, maps, traffic violation tickets, inspection stamps and tags, accounting forms, fingerprint record cards, letterheads, and printed labels.[27] Procurement involves classification of printing and binding; obtaining the printing from a government plant or through advertising and awarding of contracts; copyright of some publications; accumulation and sale of waste paper, documents, and other materials no longer required; processing of requisitions received from operating agencies; packing, mailing, shipping, and distribution of publications.

Some documents may be sold, albeit at a nominal price. In California, for instance, the office functions in a manner comparable to that of the Superintendent of Documents in Washington. In Pennsylvania the law requires that all departmental publications costing more than five cents must be sold at cost of publication. Such a procedure, however, produces little revenue — scarcely enough to offset the inconvenience and annoyance to the citizen. Oftentimes the agency refuses to accept stamps for the small amounts involved. Printing may be a large item, running into many hundreds of thousands of dollars each year, but it is surely not the way to effect economy by making it as difficult as possible for the citizen to obtain information about his government and its operations.

Different Contract Systems. A comprehensive survey of state printing practices, made a number of years ago, showed that the contract system was the prevailing one. Contracts may be made with a number of different printers or with one; in the latter case a monopoly situation develops. In eighteen states a class system of letting printing contracts prevails, under which "bids are taken on large amounts of

---

[26] For a further description of this system, see the author's "Public Reporting in the American States," *Public Opinion Quarterly,* April, 1938, pp. 211–228.

[27] Alabama Legislative Council, *Alabama State Printing,* Introduction (Montgomery 1946).

printing, and contracts awarded for a period of time; specific publications are not mentioned in the contract." The various types of contracting systems in use are shown in the table below.[28]

State Printing: Contracting Systems in Use

I. CLASS SYSTEM	II. INDIVIDUAL JOB SYSTEM	III. MIXED SYSTEM
A. *Statutory*	Georgia	Arkansas
Alabama	Maryland	Connecticut
Colorado	Massachusetts	Florida
Illinois	Nebraska	Iowa
Kentucky	New Hampshire	New York
Louisiana	New Jersey	Wisconsin
Maine	Oklahoma	
Minnesota	Rhode Island	
Missouri	South Dakota	
North Dakota	Utah	
Ohio	Vermont	
Tennessee	Virginia	
West Virginia		
B. *Administrative*		
Indiana		
Mississippi		
Montana		
North Carolina		
Pennsylvania		
Texas		

Typical classifications of printing, as used in the operation of the class systems in Alabama and Kentucky, are shown in the table below.

Classification of Printing in Selected States

CLASS	ALABAMA	KENTUCKY
I	Reports of decisions of Supreme Court and Court of Appeals	Legislative printing; printing and binding of all reports and miscellaneous printing for executive departments
II	Legislative printing—general, local, revenue, and pamphlet acts; Senate and House journals	All blank books used by the counties
III	Annual and biennial reports; handbooks, pamphlets, and reports	Lithographic printing
IV	Bills, forms, calendars, and reports for legislature and for executive departments; binding for the courts	Paper for state printing

Sparlin, *Administration of Public Printing in the States*, pp. 10–11, and several articles by the same author. Of the states not included in this list, three (Arizona, Delaware, and New Mexico) have no centralization of printing procurement and thus no contracting systems. Five states, noted earlier, have state printing plants, while no information was available regarding the practices of four states: Idaho, Michigan, North Dakota, and Wyoming.

It can be readily seen that there is no logic behind either of these classifications; in Kentucky practically all the state printing is included in Class I. Statutes require the contract to be let for four years in Kentucky, while in Alabama the period is five years for Class I and two years for other classes. The usual bidding processes are followed, the contract being awarded to the lowest responsible bidder; but as Dr. Sparlin notes, printers in the state — except the one who held the previous contract — are about as competent to furnish such a bid as the ordinary layman. The printer who held the contract has the plant and equipment, or should have it; he feels that he has acquired a vested right to continue. Other printers probably do not have the necessary equipment and do not want to invest in it without some assurance that they will be permitted to continue the work. This fact in itself tends to give a competitive advantage to the holder of the contract.

Thus it is that the monopoly system of printing develops. In Kentucky and in such other states as Missouri, New York, and Pennsylvania, one firm does all the work, operating on a long-term contract, during one contract period after another. At the same time it is contended that the individual job system used in twelve states overcomes most of the defects of the class system and that its use makes possible great financial savings. Under this system "specifications are written on each printing job so there can be no doubt by either the state or the printers as to what is desired by the former and what the latter expects to deliver." The Massachusetts Commission has developed this system to a high state of efficiency. In the same year that Missouri received only a single bid on half a million dollars' worth of printing, Massachusetts utilized the services of 151 different plants. "It was nothing unusual for the Bay State to have fifteen or twenty firms bidding on individual items of printing advertised by the Commission." [29]

Problems in the Control of Printing. The agency may prepare and execute contracts, after such advertising as is required by law, not only for the printing but for the purchase of paper stock. In order to have the contracts properly drawn, the specifications should be prepared in accordance with accepted standards, thus making possible substantial savings below the regular commercial rate charged for individual small printing jobs. Against these contracts orders may be placed on receipt of requisitions from the various departments and institutions — perhaps as many as 10,000 a year; these require careful analysis and editing to make sure that the departments receive the proper type of work. Close supervision should be given to the work as it comes through the press

[29] Sparlin, *op. cit.*

The adjustment of the workload is a very difficult thing. When the islature is in session, the resources of the agency are severely taxed the volume of legislative printing. Departmental reports — annual or nnial — of the various departments, boards and commissions, and in- utions, are likely to be received about the same time and should be ued as promptly as possible. The writing and editing of the state nual entails a large volume of work in the collection and compila- n of statistics and other information. In addition to these regular as- nments, there is a steady flow of departmental bulletins, regular and cial, reports, circulars, and forms that must be provided for depart- nts, often on short notice.

vernment-Owned Printing Plants. There has been much discus- n of the relative merits of public printing under contract versus vernment-owned and operated printing plants. On the one side it is imed that the work will not be done as cheaply, as efficiently, or as ll in a government-owned plant and that the government has no ht to invade a legitimate field of private endeavor, thereby removing m private business a large volume of work.

On the other hand it is argued that substantial savings are possible ough a government-owned plant and that there is no need for gov- ment to pay, in addition to the actual costs of materials and labor, element of profit which enters into all contracts made with private cerns. In support of the latter position one can point to the Govern- nt Printing Office in Washington and to the successful operation of h plants in five states, as well as to the widespread abuses in those isdictions which operate under a contract system. Government op- tes business enterprises efficiently in other fields — state liquor stores, nicipal utilities, and the like. Furthermore, the excessive costs under itract arrangements will inevitably cut down the amount of print- the departments and agencies should get for their money and may n interfere with the efforts of departments to secure necessary or irable printed materials.[30]

It is not without significance that after a careful study of experience government-owned plants in other jurisdictions the two most recent estigations have either definitely sponsored a government-owned nt (New York City) or recommended it after certain alternative thods of correcting abuses had been tried without success (New rk State). Some comparative plant production figures for govern- nt-owned plants are shown in the table on page 362.

---

ee Sparlin, *op. cit.*, Chapter 9, and Nystrom.

State Printing Plants: Plant Production Figures

	CALIFORNIA (1939)	OREGON (1940)	WASHINGTON (1(
Total mechanical employees	220	34	60
Total mechanical production	$735,211.17	$106,617.00	$139,987.65
Total annual output	$1,229,110.94	$250,915.47	$274,031.60
Average annual production per mechanical employee	$3324.00	$3136.00	$2333.00

Similar figures were not available for the other two states, Kan and Nevada. The report called attention to the fact that the avera annual production figure for employees in the industry, as reported the Department of Commerce Census of Manufactures for 1933, 19 and 1937, was $3566, a figure which presumably includes a profit. special report on state printing costs in Kansas, prepared by the Kan Legislative Council in 1941, indicated, however, that the plant in t state operated to meet the printing needs of the departments and ag cies more economically than they could be met by other means. I were true that, on the average, government-owned plants are no m economical than private printing would be, they have other advanta such as the elimination of abuses. In other words the financial cons eration alone should not determine governmental policy in this matt

Duplication. Every agency has frequent need for duplication se ice — the reproduction of forms, instructions, and intra-office men randa through the use of some quick and relatively inexpensive fo of reproduction. Many such methods are now available: mimeogra hectograph, multilith, multigraph, photostating and photocopyi blueprinting, and microfilming.[31] Economy and efficiency may be tained by careful analysis of the nature of the work, its purpose, nu ber of copies needed, and frequency of issue.

While most agencies are quite liberal in meeting requests of s members for duplicating service, questions do arise in its administrat and control. The natural preference of every operating agency — sm as well as large — is to have duplicating facilities immediately at ha They assume that in this way they can establish their own priori and be more certain of securing prompt handling of rush ord These benefits are by no means certain to follow. A small duplicat office, with inadequate staff and equipment, may be bogged down always behind schedule.

---

[31] For a description of each of these, see Bureau of Budget and Efficiency, *Prin and Duplicating Service* (Los Angeles, June, 1947).

A centralized duplicating service, on the other hand, for all the of-
es or divisions of an agency or for a number of agencies need not of
cessity be remote in distance from those it serves, or lacking in re-
onsiveness and willingness to meet their needs.

ansportation and Communication

overnment transportation is a major item of expense and creates an
portant problem in administration and supervision. Not only do gov-
nments operate a very large number of cars and trucks but they now
vn airplanes,[32] and some own patrol boats and other vessels. Prior to
'orld War II there were approximately 30,000,000 registered motor
hicles in the United States. Although registration methods in many
ites make segregation difficult, it was estimated that there were a few
s than 400,000 owned and operated by government agencies. Of this
imber the Federal government had something less than one third.[33]

overnment-Owned Motor Vehicles. The Automobile Division of
e Pennsylvania Department of Property and Supplies, which may
taken as illustrative, controlled in 1945 the operation of 1836 cars
d 664 trucks, not including the equipment used by the Department
Highways. That there has been a steady increase in the use of such
uipment as the number and scope of government activities have in-
eased, is clearly shown in the table below.

mmonwealth of Pennsylvania — Registered Motor Vehicle Equipment

DATE	NUMBER OF PASSENGER CARS	NUMBER OF TRUCKS	TOTAL
June 1, 1929	681	284	965
January 24, 1931	890	285	1175
December 1, 1932	839	290	1129
January 1, 1939	1808	624	2432
January 1, 1941	1787	633	2420
January 1, 1943	1856	588	2444
January 1, 1945	1836	664	2500

nserviceable vehicles are, of course, sold. In the performance of its
ties the Division maintains approximately twenty-five employees,
cluding a mechanical inspection unit whose work results in a con-
lerable saving in operating costs.

More than one third of them; see Barthell, Roger V., "Airplanes for State Gov-
iments," *State Government*, June, 1941, pp. 136–139, with tables.
"Publicly Owned Motor Vehicles in the United States," *American City*, December,
9, pp. 64–65.

This raises the question of organization. The central agency shou be authorized to make or to contract for the making of all repairs government-owned vehicles; for gasoline, oil, and tires used in the operation; and for the necessary repair parts. Some units have had e perience with both of these methods. At one time the Pennsylvar Department of Highways operated a central garage to which all mot equipment owned by the Department was brought for maintenan and repairs. This was found to be an extremely costly method, a losses in driving time and in wear and tear on equipment made it u desirable. The central shop also proved to be too large for efficie management, and it was subsequently abandoned in favor of garag in each of the highway districts into which the state is divided.

In contrast to the regional garages of the Highway Departmer the Automobile Division of the Department of Property and Suppl has entered into some 1400 contracts with service stations througho the Commonwealth, providing for the repair of state-owned equi ment as required from time to time. These contracts cover minor r pairs with reliable repair shops, all of which are classified and careful checked. Members of the inspection unit go over all vehicles perio cally, to check brakes and equipment and to insure safety and oper ing efficiency. Under the jurisdiction of the division a central gara is operated at the capital for storing and repairing all equipment l cated in the capital city and within a radius of ten miles. By requiri departments to keep accurate records of operations and to subr monthly reports on the operation of equipment assigned to them f daily use, it was possible — prior to World War II — to reduce t operating costs of all motor equipment to an average of approximate two cents a mile.

The central agency should assign all automobiles to the various c partments, agencies, and institutions, and it may furnish cars with without chauffeurs for the temporary use of other departments up request. This necessitates the maintenance of a fleet of cars for t use of departments which do not have constant need for equipmel Such a fleet makes for better utilization of equipment and keeps do expenditures for new cars, which are purchased on a competiti basis.[34]

There are in all jurisdictions some officers and employees w

[34] For rules and regulations regarding the use of city-owned passenger cars in sev large cities, see New York State Bureau of Municipal Information, Report No. 2 (Albany, February 14, 1946). For a table showing private car mileage rates in forty-eight states, prewar, see Kansas Legislative Council, *Regulation of State Tra Expenses*, p. 23. See also United States Bureau of the Budget, Circular No. A-30, standard cost and reporting system for government-owned motor vehicles (Revis May, 1948).

ive their own automobiles on official business and receive reimburse-
ent or "mileage." Such travel may be undertaken only when prop-
y authorized, only on official business, and only within the ter-
orial limits of the jurisdiction when this mode of travel is cheaper
an rail transportation would be. In the Federal government this
mmonly means within the borders of the district, zone, or region
ved by the office to which the employee is attached. Approximately
lf of the states place special restrictions on out-of-state travel in
ivately owned automobiles. Mileage rates vary from four to seven
d a half cents a mile, with widely divergent regulations regarding
sts of lodging, meals, and incidental expenses.[35]

During the war all governmental units effected substantial savings
critical materials and of expense by a strictly controlled use of gov-
nment-owned motor equipment. In 1943 OPA asked such units to
duce their mileage to 40 per cent of their 1941 levels. This was
ne not only by severely restricting the use of cars but by reducing
ed limits, organizing car pools, and so on. At least one third of the
tes established car pools based upon the New Hampshire plan.[36]

forcement of Travel Regulations. As the activities of government
ve grown more diversified and as the trend toward decentralization
s carried more and more work into the field, expenditures for travel
ve steadily increased in both national and state jurisdictions. The
gulation and control of these expenses is a problem common to both
vate and public employers but it is probably a more difficult one
 the latter. Public agencies, in an effort to eliminate the evils at-
dant upon the familiar "swindle sheets" reporting travel expenses
 individuals privately employed, have often made necessary travel
 public employees extremely difficult and sometimes a financial
rden on the employee.

The legislative branch of government can enact legislation to
vern such expenditures, but it must of necessity be broad in its pro-
ions. Specific rules applicable to one department or activity may not
 especially suitable for another. To a certain extent the legislature
1 limit travel expenditures by its appropriations, but in the final
alysis the control rests with the executives who are empowered to
thorize travel. The fact that the travel expenses sustained by a rela-

---

Shumate, pp. 22–25. In Pennsylvania for years, the maximum allowances for meals
re: breakfast, $.65; lunch, $.85; dinner, $1.25.
See Brewster, R. Wallace, and others, "The States and Mileage Conservation,"
te Government, October, 1943, pp. 211–213; "State Car Pools Cut Mileage," *Better
ads,* March, 1943, pp. 17–18; "Governor Olson Issues Executive Order Ratifying
gulations for Pooling All State-Owned Automobiles," *California Highways and
blic Works,* October, 1942, pp. 1–2.

tively small state like Nebraska for the fiscal year ending June 1939, amounted to well over $600,000 seems to indicate the seric nature of the problem.[37]

All things considered, the allowance of a reasonable per diem pro ably represents the most satisfactory solution of the problem. T Federal government has followed this policy for some time. Fede employees are furnished with travel requisitions for all official trav since these are universally accepted by public transportation co panies, employees do not have to advance money. The per diem de ing and following World War II was $6, an inadequate amount view of room rates and the prices of meals in city hotels and resta rants. After years of effort to increase the per diem to $8 or $10, leg lation passed in 1949 permitted a maximum of $9, leaving to t agencies some discretion as to the amount authorized under various c cumstances. A rate which may be sufficient in rural areas (which e ployees of many governmental agencies rarely have occasion to visit official business) is apt to be quite insufficient in the larger towns a cities. Under rather severe restrictions, claims for taxi fare, streetcar bus fare, and checking of baggage are allowed.[38]

Advances for travel expenses are regularly made to employees private industry; their use in government is possible but not ordinar encouraged.[39] If advances are not to be used extensively, certainly go ernment employees have a right to expect prompt processing and pa ment of their travel vouchers. During World War II there were ma Federal employees whose duties required them to travel extensive who had several hundred dollars tied up in travel accounts. With t establishment of field offices by Treasury Disbursement, the spe with which these accounts were handled was materially increased.

Communications Control. All government agencies of necessity ma extensive use of the mails. In the Federal government, penalty e

---

[37] Shumate, *op. cit.*

[38] Juran, J. M., *Bureaucracy: A Challenge to Better Management*, pp. 43–46 (Harpe New York, 1944) discusses these problems at some length under the heading: " Errors at All Costs." While railroad rates and per diem are both standardized, cessive time and effort is expended in analyzing these minor items, many of wh are "disallowed." "There are," he says, "hundreds and hundreds of auditors going o thousands and thousands of vouchers in which the total money disallowed is m less than the salaries of the auditors. Not only that, the amount of money disallow is for the most part less than the cost of keeping it."

[39] See *Statutes, Rules, and Regulations Relating to Transportation and Subsistence Civilian Officers and Employees of the Federal Government Traveling on Offi Business* (Government Printing Office, Washington, October, 1942). Employ whose work requires them to travel extensively may, by obtaining a bond for not than $1000, secure advances in moderate amounts, but in no case in excess of estimated needs for a given period, for the travel directed.

:lopes are provided under Congressional authorization for all official
isiness. In the past little effort was made to control the volume.
nder regulations put in effect in 1945 the outgoing mail of all agen-
es must be weighed and the agency charged accordingly. Special
inpenalty envelopes are provided for interoffice communication,
ereby accomplishing a saving. Careful inventories are kept of pen-
ty envelopes in each agency.

The operations of modern government frequently require speed,
hich in turn justifies the use of the telephone [40] and telegraph. Regu-
tions regarding the use of these methods of communication vary
idely. In the Federal government during World War II many un-
:cessary long-distance calls were made. Control is difficult. If too
any persons are authorized to approve such calls, laxity often re-
ilts; if controls are too rigid, there may be obstacles to the efficient
induct of the work of the agency. A little advance planning will
ten prevent the development of "emergencies."

A survey which included analysis of data from exactly half of the
ates in 1940 showed the following variations in control practices at
iat level: "One state permits such expense (apparently without re-
riction), one does not permit it at all, three states allow it 'in case of
nergency,' six leave this to the discretion of the several spending
gencies, and thirteen permit such expense 'for official business only'
id allow claims 'when properly itemized.' " [41]

onstruction and Maintenance of Public Buildings

or many years the construction and maintenance of public buildings
·as, like purchasing, scattered among various departments and agen-
es. Gradually the idea took hold that this work represented a gov-
·nmental function in and of itself, and centralized departments were
tablished for its performance. This development took place in some
ates in connection with the reorganization movement, before it ap-
eared in the Federal government in 1939 [42] with the establishment
f the Public Buildings Administration. In 1949 the Hoover Commis-
on recommended that this service, along with other central services
f supply, be placed in a new Office of General Services, under a

---

Telephone Service: Basic Elements of Necessity and Use (Bureau of the Budget,
pril, 1947) deals with the problem of telephone installation and control from the
andpoint of management.
Shumate, *op. cit.*, p. 24.
The Public Buildings Administration was established as part of the Federal Works
gency under the provisions of Reorganization Plan No. 1, pursuant to provisions
f the Reorganization Act of 1939. Prior to July 1 of that year, the component parts
: the PBA operated as units of the Procurement Division in the Treasury Depart-
.ent and of the National Park Service in the Department of the Interior.

Director appointed by and responsible to the President. This propos
was effected by the passage of the Federal Property and Administr
tive Services Act of 1949, under the terms of which the Federal Wor
Agency and all of its component parts, including the Public Buildin
Administration, were absorbed in the General Services Administratio
The old PBA became the Bureau of Public Buildings in the new A
ministration.

The Bureau is responsible for the administrative, technical, ar
clerical functions incident to the design, construction, maintenanc
and repair of Federal buildings, performing the following functions:

Operates, maintains, and protects all buildings under the jurisdiction of tl
Administration

Determines the need of and arranges for the repair and preservation of buil
ings, including leased properties, operated by the Administration

Performs all moving operations of government agencies into, out of, or with
buildings operated, maintained, and protected by the Administration

Collects and prepares for submission to the Bureau of the Budget and tl
Congress data and estimates for the construction and repair of Federal buildin
and for the general administrative expenses of the Administration

Acts on a joint committee with representatives of the Post Office Depa
ment in the selection of sites for public buildings outside the District of C
lumbia

Determines the sufficiency and applicability of appropriated funds in conne
tion with contracts and changes thereof and for other purposes

Effects final settlement of contracts

Collects preplanning data for use in the determination of building projec
within and outside the District of Columbia

Makes recommendations on the assignment of space in new and existi
buildings throughout the country

Administers rental and lease contracts

Prepares preliminary sketches and estimates leading to the establishment
a program of Federal building construction

Is responsible for the architectural and engineering design

Conducts activities required for the development of tentative drawings, cab
net sketches, working drawings, and specifications for all projects authorized u
der the various Federal building programs

Land Acquisition. Land acquisition is an important first step in an
public works project. Although it is a purchasing operation, it diffe
in important respects from purchases of commodities and equipmen
There are, in fact, many governmental activities in connection wit
which land has to be acquired — agriculture, airports, forestry, fis
and game, highways,[43] and institutions. Where parcels of land ar
needed for a specific purpose, they may be acquired through the ex

[43] Public Roads Administration, *Bibliography on Land Acquisition for Public Roa*
(Washington, March, 1947).

ercise of the power of eminent domain. In this connection, incidentally, individuals often value their property highly although at assessment time they contend that it is not worth much.

All basic laws, constitutions, and charters contain provisions designed to protect citizens from a taking of their property for public
use (it may never be taken for private use) without just compensation. The process involves proposal and counterproposal, with final
resort to the courts if agreement cannot be reached otherwise. The
property must be surveyed and the title abstracted. These operations
can best be performed by a central agency responsible for all acquisitions for all departments and agencies. Both services require the use
of a field force. The surveying must be done by employees working
out of field offices near where the properties are located, while the
title abstracting must be done by members of the legal staff similarly
situated.

For such purposes as the development of forests or of fish and
game preserves, government can often afford to wait to secure land
rather than pay the high prices that might otherwise be asked. It is
customary, therefore, to wait to secure suitable properties at tax sales.
In other types of undertakings such as the construction of highways or
other public works government often cannot wait. It is torn between
the desire to proceed with dispatch in a new undertaking and the
necessity of protecting the public treasury from collusion to raise the
price of the land required and from other forms of extortion.[44]

Construction. The construction aspect of the public buildings function involves the construction or contracting for the construction of
all new buildings and the alteration or repair of existing structures
costing more than some specified sum — often $10,000. The agency
may be authorized to rebuild, restore, or replace property damaged
or destroyed; prepare or cause to have prepared plans and specifications; have contracts executed; and supervise the erection, construction, or replacement of property damaged by fire or other casualty.
The staff consists of experts in general and mechanical construction
of buildings, essential for the supervision of a vast program. Competent architects [45] and engineers are employed to prepare plans and

---

[44] This was the type of thing which George Washington Plunkett called "honest
graft" — a situation in which a public official, on the basis of inside information, went
in with his relatives and friends to buy or take option to buy land required for some
prospective public improvement.
[45] The selection of suitable professional personnel is no easy task; see Council of State
Governments, *Architects for Public Projects: Selection and Compensation* (Chicago,
1949). For a description of the methods used by the Oklahoma City Board of Education in selecting an architect, see *School Board Journal*, May, 1946.

specifications. Work is advertised and contracts awarded to meet specific building needs of departments, agencies, and institutions. The latter are responsible for organizing their needs in the form of projects which must be approved by the budget officer and may be executed only in accordance with appropriations made by the legislature for the construction work involved.

The construction agency must give proper supervision and inspection to both work and materials as the projects progress; it may in some instances purchase the materials itself.[46] It arranges for prompt payments to contractors, enforces the bonds relating to performance of labor and delivery of materials, compels maintenance of fair and equitable wages in contracts for public works,[47] and enforces the state requirements for the use of materials manufactured within the state if such exist. Among the benefits resulting from the work of this agency are the reduction of costs, closer inspection to see that the government actually receives what it pays for, raising standards in public building work, savings in advertising for bids, and taking the responsibility for supervising construction work away from operating departments not equipped to handle it properly.

The Authority. The Authority as a type of administrative organization was mentioned briefly in Chapter 1. The Authority is a corporation created by the state or municipality under state authorization with power to borrow independently of the debt limits imposed by law, for the purpose of carrying on one or more important public construction projects. Examples are found in the numerous public housing authorities and in the Pennsylvania Turnpike Commission. While there are obvious immediate advantages to this device, there are also serious objections. The Authority is not legally a part of and cannot be effectively controlled by the governmental unit creating it; the debt which it creates is practically but not legally a part of the public debt and is not subject to the same protections and guarantees that govern the public debt. It represents, furthermore, an unwise scattering of administrative authority.

Space Procurement. The steady expansion in the number and scope of governmental services and the growth in the number of public

---

[46] In a year and a half, beginning January, 1946, the California Department of Public Works reported savings of more than $1,000,000 on purchases of war surplus. See Fulton, Rex, "Public Works Department Saves More than Million Dollars on Purchase of War Surplus," *California Highways and Public Works*, May–June, 1947, pp. 1–3, 8
[47] The Federal Walsh-Healy Act of 1936 requires that all those who contract with agencies of the government for materials the value of which exceeds $10,000 shall not work employees more than eight hours a day or forty hours a week; that they will pay the prevailing wage rates in the industry; and that they will not employ child labor on government work.

employees has created serious housing problems for public agencies — national, state, and local. Older types of public building construction were supposedly ornamental but contained so much waste space that they were ill adapted to present-day needs. For fear of public criticism and because of lack of funds, legislative bodies have been reluctant to authorize new construction even when the need for it is clearly indicated. The result has frequently been serious overcrowding and the renting of space in commercial office buildings, often at excessive cost.

This result has been especially apparent during emergency periods (depression, defense, and war) and in the expansion of field services — both Federal and state — into many new communities. During World War II the Federal government took over under lease in many cities so much office and warehouse space that private firms and individuals were unable to find desirable space. Poor planning of even recent structures had in many cases provided little or no room for expansion. In Washington the situation was even worse. A building program extending over many years, moving some whole agencies out of the city, the construction of the Pentagon, vast as it is — all these failed to solve the problem. "Temporary buildings" put up during World War I are still in daily use. In state after state, authorities struggled with the problem of office space for necessary state employees.

In 1942 the Virginia Advisory Legislative Council made an analysis of office space occupied by state agencies located in Richmond. Of 506,127 square feet occupied, 168,143 square feet was rented at an annual rental of $120,746. The space occupied was at the time inadequate to the extent of 48,431 square feet. The amount of rented space plus the deficiency gave a total deficiency in state-owned space amounting to 216,574 square feet, an amount approximating two fifths of the total amount of state-owned accommodations then in existence. In Indiana in 1944 the Indiana Economic Council found state agencies faced with a shortage of one third of the space required. The data shown in the table on page 372 are the more significant because of the usual reluctance of taxpayers' organizations to make recommendations involving increased expenditures or capital outlay.[48] New Jersey, faced with a similar situation, undertook in spite of postwar construction difficulties the construction of a new state office building in 1946.

Maintenance. The duties performed in connection with the maintenance of public buildings include the supervision, control, and protec-

---

[48] See Virginia Advisory Legislative Council, *Office Space Requirements* (Senate Document No. 3, Richmond, 1942), and Indiana Economic Council report.

tion of three major types of buildings: (1) the central group in the capital city, housing the legislative, executive, and judicial branches of the government; (2) major penal, correctional, and welfare institutions scattered over the nation or the state; (3) education buildings, including institutions of higher learning. In spite of some increase in the number and types of public buildings in recent years, no dominant pattern for their administration has as yet emerged.[49]

The central agency must make all repairs, alterations, and improvements in and about the buildings and grounds, as well as cleaning, caring for, and policing them. A distinction may be made between the

Indiana State Office Space Requirements — 1944

	AREA NOW OCCUPIED (IN SQUARE FEET)	AREA REQUIRED (IN SQUARE FEET)
Offices in State-owned Space	405,203	665,355
Offices in Rented Space	9,389	11,153
Total	414,592	676,508

mechanical and electrical work on the one hand, and maintenance work of a nontechnical nature on the other — work such as that of the janitorial force. Many different types of craftsmen are employed — painters, carpenters, electricians, plumbers, steam fitters, marble mechanics, locksmiths, hardwood-floor finishers, upholsterers, charmen, charwomen, clock repairmen, typewriter repairmen, and many others. In Pennsylvania, which has an exceptionally fine set of state buildings, the total amount of floor space in the capitol group approximates 1,000,000 square feet, for the maintenance of which about four hundred persons are required, half skilled workers and half janitors.

In addition to actual maintenance work, the buildings must be operated for the accommodation of the public, thus requiring elevator operators, guides, police, and others. Care of the grounds is entrusted to an experienced landscape gardener whose duty is to maintain and beautify the land surrounding the buildings. In one sense, this work may not seem particularly important, but the efficiency with which it is done has much to do with the first impressions which many citizens gain when they visit the seat of government. The roads and approaches must also be kept in repair.

[49] Very little study has been given to this problem, but see Council of State Governments survey, state by state, which includes an excellent summary chart, pp. 20–24.

SELECTED REFERENCES

Purchasing. There is much literature on purchasing; an annotated bibliography, at the Federal level, will be found in: *Procurement and Disposition of Federal Property* (Bureau of the Budget, Washington, 1948). There is also a manual for the information of Federal purchasing officers: Mack, Clifton E., *Federal Procurement* (Washington, 1943). Naylor, E. E., in *Federal Contracts and Procurement Procedures* (The Author, Washington, 1943) describes these procedures. For experience at other levels, see:

Beckett, Paul, and Plotkin, Morris, *Governmental Purchasing in the Los Angeles Metropolitan Area* (Bureau of Governmental Research, University of California at Los Angeles, 1941).

Burger, Alvin A., and Graves, Thomas J., *The State Purchasing Department: An Administrative Survey* (New Jersey State Chamber of Commerce, Newark, 1941).

City of New York, Department of Purchases, *A Decade of Centralized Municipal Purchasing* (New York, 1944). See also: Herlands, William B., *Purchase of School Supplies in New York City* (New York, 1942).

Council of State Governments, *Purchasing by the States* (Chicago, 1947). The most recent and the best of several studies at this level.

Forbes, Russell, *Governmental Purchasing* (Harpers, New York, 1939). The foremost authority on public purchasing sets forth the principles involved, and the more desirable practices. See also his numerous pamphlets dealing with specific aspects of the subjects, put out by the National Association of Purchasing Agents.

James, Herman G., *The Protection of the Public Interest in Public Contracts* (Public Administration Service, Chicago, 1946).

Larsen, Christian L., *Centralized Purchasing for States* (Bureau of Public Administration, University of South Carolina, 1947).

Oklahoma Legislative Council, memorandum on *Centralized State Purchasing* (Oklahoma City, 1948).

United States Bureau of Standards, *Services of the National Bureau of Standards to Governmental Purchasing Agencies* (Washington, 1937).

Printing. The literature on public printing is much less voluminous, but there are several good titles: For the war program, see *Public Printing in Peace and War: Development and Administration of the War Program by the Government Printing Office* (Washington, 1947).

Herlands, William B., *Administration of Municipal Printing in New York City* (New York, 1940).

Kansas Legislative Council, *Analysis of State Printing Costs* (Topeka, 1941); also *Appropriation and Control of Funds for State Printing* (Topeka, 1938).

Los Angeles Bureau of Budget and Efficiency, *Printing and Duplicating Service* (Los Angeles, 1947).

Nystrom, Wendell C., *Development of State Publication of Textbooks in Kansas* (University of Kansas, 1937).

Sparlin, Estal E., *The Administration of Public Printing in the States* (University of Missouri Studies, Columbia, 1937). Much the most important work on the subject.

Transportation and Communication. The literature in this area is very scant. The following may be useful:

Bureau of the Budget, *Telephone Service, Basic Elements of Necessity and Use* (Washington, 1947). A brief manual for the use of Federal people.

Kansas Legislative Council, *Regulation of State Travel Expenses* (Topeka, 1940).

New York State Bureau of Municipal Information, *Rules and Regulations Regarding the Use of City-Owned Passenger Cars* (Albany, 1946).

Shumate, Roger V., *Expense Accounts of State Officers and Employees in Nebraska* (Nebraska Legislative Council, Lincoln, 1940).

Construction and Maintenance. Here again the literature is very lean:

Colorado State Planning Commission, *The Building Program of the State Institutions of Colorado* (Denver, 1947).

Council of State Governments, *The Administration of State-Owned Buildings* (Chicago, 1944).

Indiana Economic Council, *State Office Space Requirements* (Indianapolis, 1944).

Santa Clara Council on Intergovernmental Relations, *A Survey of Government Buildings in San Jose* (San Jose, 1947).

20

CUSTODY OF FUNDS

The Treasury

Historical Background. The history of the custody of Federal funds is characterized by repeated change and much controversy. Prior to 1791 the funds were deposited in such state banks as were then in existence. From 1791 to 1811 they were deposited in the first Bank of the United States; from 1811 to 1816 again in various state banks. In the interval from 1816 to 1833, they were gradually withdrawn from state banks and deposited in the second Bank of the United States. From 1833 to 1840 this practice was reversed. In 1836 occurred the distribution of the surplus. The Independent Treasury Act of 1840, under which vaults and safes were provided in the Treasury in Washington and subtreasuries were established in New York, Boston, St. Louis, and Charleston, remained in effect until 1863, when the National Banking Act was passed. National banks established under this act were eligible for the deposit of Federal funds. Then in 1913 came the Federal Reserve Act, basis of the present system, under which the Federal Reserve Banks act as the government's special instrumentality for assistance in its financial operations.

In the state and local governments chief reliance has been upon banks as depositories. A few states have experimented with an independent treasury, a solution of the problem too expensive for intermediate or local governmental units. In the administration of a bank depository system such questions as the selection of depositories, the determination of the rate of interest to be paid by them, the distribution of funds among them, and the security to be furnished by them must be dealt with. The standards of conduct governing state and local treasurers in the performance of these duties have improved greatly in recent years.

Treasurer of the United States. The Treasurer of the United States is charged with the receipt and disbursement of public moneys that may be deposited in the Treasury in Washington and in the other depositories authorized by the Secretary of the Treasury to receive deposits of government funds for credit in the account of the Treasurer of the United States. The summary of the duties of this officer continues:[1]

Funds advanced to disbursing officers for the use of Government departments and establishments under the appropriation of Congress are credited in the accounts of such disbursing officers on the books of the Treasurer, and the disbursements therefrom are made by checks drawn by the Treasurer. In his Office are prepared and issued, for the Secretary of the Treasury, the daily Treasury statement of the United States, the monthly preliminary statement of the public debt, and the monthly preliminary statement of classified expenditures of the Government; the monthly statement of the outstanding paper currency of the Government is also published. The Treasury general ledger accounts of the trust fund, the reserve fund, the gold certificate fund, and the general fund, and other important accounts are maintained in his Office.

He prepares the annual report of the Secretary of the Treasury. The Treasurer is fiscal agent for the issue and redemption of United States currency, for payment of principal and interest of the public debt on obligations the principal and interest of which are fully guaranteed by the United States, for payment of principal and interest on bonds of the Puerto Rican government (of which the Secretary of the Treasury is the transfer agent), and for the redemption of national bank notes, Federal Reserve notes, and Federal Reserve bank notes. He is the treasurer of the board of trustees of the Postal Savings System, trustee for bonds held to secure public deposits in national banks and bonds held to secure postal savings in banks, and custodian of miscellaneous securities and trust funds.

There are in the Office of the Treasurer six divisions: Administrative Division, Accounting Division, Cash Division, Currency Redemption Division, Division of General Accounts, and Division of Securities.

The State Treasurer. The office of state treasurer is provided for in every constitution except that of New York. In all but five states the choice is by popular election. The legislature selects the treasurer in Maine, Maryland, and Tennessee; in Virginia he is appointed by the governor with the approval of the legislature; New York, as noted, has no officer with this title. The title is either State Treasurer or Treasurer of State in all but two states; in Rhode Island, he is officially designated the General Treasurer, and in Massachusetts, Treasurer and Receiver General. In over half the states the term is two years; in twenty states, four years. "Only seven state treasurers have a staff of more than fifty, whereas eighteen have a staff of ten or less. Nevada has but four on the treasurer's staff. This should be contrasted with Pennsylvania, which is one of the few states having over fifty employees. The State Treasurer in Pennsylvania has a staff of 375, and the combined office forces of the treasurer and auditor total 1023 employees, enough to form a fair-sized community of themselves."[2]

---

[1] For latest information on duties of all Federal officers and agencies, see current issues of the *Congressional Directory* and the *United States Government Manual*.

[2] National Association of State Auditors, Comptrollers and Treasurers, *Tabular Analysis of State Fiscal Offices*, Part I. In Pennsylvania both of these offices have for

Over half of the states charge the treasurer, either by constitutional provision or by statute, with "(a) receiving all or most of the state moneys; (b) holding custody of special or general funds; (c) disbursing moneys, usually on warrant of the auditor or other fiscal officer; and (d) keeping a record of state receipts and disbursements. In some jurisdictions, the treasurer may have power to issue and register bonds, sell bonds, sign bonds, and pay interest on bonds. Some miscellaneous duties include the sale of tax stamps and the payment of bonuses."

Selection of Depositories. When the treasurer (or other responsible officer) is in receipt of funds from taxes, licenses and fees, fines, gifts, "conscience money," escheats, etc., it is necessary to take care of them promptly. A simple deposit is all that is required for receipts to be credited to operating funds (unless there is a surplus), but in other cases the problem of more or less permanent investment arises. In such instances the first major step is the selection of a depository or some form of investment. Depositories were formerly chosen on the basis of personal and political favoritism with little regard for the safety of the funds and none for the return to the state in the form of interest. The custodial officer, long permitted to profit personally from the interest paid on funds belonging to the government, is no longer permitted to do so. Professor Faust, who has made the most extensive studies of the custody of public funds, has enumerated the factors which now control the distribution of such funds:[3]

1. Amount of funds available
2. Capital stock and surplus of the depositories
3. Amount and kind of security they furnish
4. Amount of state funds derived from taxation in the localities wherein the banks are situated
5. Seasonal demands of different communities for funds
6. Amounts requested by the banks
7. Maximum sums set by statute for deposit in any one bank
8. Interest rate the banks will agree to pay

As a result of the application of such guiding principles, the selections are made. The number of depositories in a given state will vary according to the size of the state, the density of population, and the

---

years been considerably overstaffed in comparison with the work which they actually perform; see Joint Legislative Committee on Finances, *Survey of the Government of Pennsylvania*, Chapters 4 and 6 (Harrisburg, 1934). Analysis of the powers of the office will be found in numerous state surveys.

[3] *The Custody of State Funds*, pp. 9–10.

number, size, and location of banks. Not all the depositories carry active accounts; as a matter of fact, only a very small number will be used for checking purposes. At a fairly recent date Pennsylvania deposited money in twenty-eight different funds in 773 separate accounts in 516 bank depositories, but only seven of these were active checking accounts. Wisconsin had 655 accounts. An example of what happens in practice may be seen in the following excerpt from a typical newspaper account of state deposits:

New York State has $491,000 of its funds on deposit in three Watertown banks, according to the official report of the Department of State issued late Wednesday. Of the three, the Northern New York Trust Company has the largest deposit, $300,000. The Watertown National Bank has $100,000, and the Jefferson County National Bank, $91,000. Institutions sharing in the distribution of the state deposits and funds reposing with the various banks and trust companies follows:

    Amsterdam — City National Bank, $25,000; First National Bank, $175,000; Montgomery County Trust Company, $175,000

    Barneveld — First National Bank, $5000

    Boonville — National Exchange Bank, $17,000

    Camden — First National Bank and Trust Company, $20,000

    Canastota — First National Bank, $10,000; Canastota State Bank, $16,000

    Carthage — Carthage National Bank, $45,000; National Exchange Bank and Trust Company, $85,000

    Cazenovia — Cazenovia National Bank, $10,000

The operation of the system in three midwestern states is thus described by Sappenfield:[4]

The legal provisions governing the deposit of public funds in Illinois and Ohio are very similar. Each provides for awarding portions of the state's funds to those banks which, after proving their soundness and the deposit of reliable securities as a guarantee of state funds deposited with them, offer to pay the highest rates of interest for the use of a portion of the state's funds. The actual placing of the state funds on deposit is done by the treasurer of the state under the direction of a board of officials of which he is also a member. The depository law of Indiana does not follow the plan of that in Illinois and Ohio in every particular. The granting of deposits is done by a board, but the banks do not have to deposit collateral securities and the rates of interest are set by law rather than being set by competitive bidding among the banks. Instead of requiring the deposit of collateral securities as a guarantee of the deposited state funds, Indiana has created a "sinking fund" for this purpose. This fund is built up and maintained by diverting the interest earned on public deposits to this fund. The fund's maximum amount is set by law at $3,000,000 and the minimum to which it may fall without calling for further diversion of earned interest to it is at $2,000,000.

4 *Financial Administration in the States of Illinois, Ohio, and Indiana*, p. 8 (Thesis abstract, University of Illinois, 1934).

Protection of Deposits. Many different devices have been used for the protection of public deposits. The total amount of such deposits, as Professor Faust has shown, is large enough to be a significant factor in the banking life of the community. For generations they have been accorded preferential treatment. They had priority under the common law, and statutory provisions have continued to provide such treatment. Classified on the basis of the essential protective features involved, the various methods used can be summarized as follows:[5]

1. Granting governmental units the status of preferred creditors upon the closing of a bank and the liquidation of its assets, either by statute or by judicial construction

2. Relying largely upon national and state banking supervision to afford adequate protection for the public deposits

3. Holding the official custodian and his surety liable for the safety of the public funds in bank depositories

4. Requiring banks in order to qualify as public depositories to file either personal or corporate surety bonds and holding the sureties liable for the safety of the public funds while in depositories

5. Requiring banks in order to qualify as public depositories to pledge assets in the form of specified collateral security in an amount equal to or slightly in excess of their public deposits, and in the event a bank becomes unable to repay its public deposits, acknowledging the right of depositing units to liquidate the pledged collateral

6. Depositing public funds in a banking institution wholly owned and operated by the state or in a bank in which the state owns a controlling interest

7. Establishing a state insurance or guarantee system with a fund built up and maintained from interest paid or premiums levied upon the interest of all public deposits, such fund to be used to reimburse depositing units to the extent that their funds at any time become tied up in closed banks

8. Permitting only such banks to qualify as public depositories as can comply with and maintain a standard of strength and measure of liquidity prescribed within limits by law and specified in detail and enforced by an administrative board

The same author has discussed elsewhere the more important types of irregularity in the custody of funds.[6] While this article deals with the situation in the state of Missouri, the abuses described are not peculiar to any one state. The salary of the treasurer is inadequate, and the office is tied up with many official duties entirely foreign to its

---

[5] Faust, *The Security of Public Deposits,* p. 6; this study analyzes each of these methods. See also Chatters, Carl H., and Draper, Ben, "Legal Provisions for the Protection of State and Local Deposits of Public Funds, as of July 1, 1937," in *Tax Systems of the World,* Seventh Edition, pp. 234–237 (Tax Research Foundation, New York, 1938).

[6] Faust, Martin L., "Irregularities in the Custody of State Funds in Missouri," *National Municipal Review,* February, 1931, pp. 74–77.

main function. The constitutional, elective basis upon which it is established is basically unsound. In Missouri the amount of state funds placed in any one bank does not necessarily bear any relation to the capital and surplus of the institution; hence one finds hundreds of thousands of dollars poured into obscure banks which can pledge collateral which satisfies the legal requirements but is inadequate for the protection of the state.

As a means of eliminating these irregularities and promoting greater safety, Professor Faust suggests the adoption of improved fiscal practices.[7] Governmental units might reduce bank balances; one officer went so far as to say, partly in jest, that it would be best not to have any public deposits. It is a sound principle of business management to maintain a sufficient cash balance in the bank to meet the obligations of the government as they arise but not, as has so often been the case, to maintain a balance greatly in excess of immediate needs. Other recommendations involve a reduction in the number of special accounts, the investment of surpluses, limiting deposits to the stronger banks, and refraining from using as depositories too many small banks. In this connection national banks were safer prior to the establishment of the Federal Deposit Insurance Corporation; deposits might well be limited to banks that are insured by that Corporation. A strengthening of the present inadequate limits on the amount of deposits permitted in any one bank would also be helpful.

Requiring bank depositories to pay interest on state deposits has become standard practice. In 1936 Alabama was the only state which was not receiving interest on its bank balances. Interest rates may be regulated in any one of four ways: (1) a specific rate may be established by law; (2) the treasurer or the depository board may fix the rate at an amount not less than is specified by law; (3) these authorities may fix the rate without statutory restrictions; or (4) the law may require the fixing of rates on the basis of competitive bidding. The latter is the most modern method, but it is still used in only a few states. Theoretically such a system represents an attempt to apply the principle that a state should receive the highest rate consistent with safety that the depositories are willing to pay. In practice, however, such a system presents difficulties, especially in preventing collusion and in actually maintaining the competitive principle. The availability of funds and their security are important factors that may be dangerously compromised in such a system. An examination of interest rates received on state deposits shows that banks pay the highest rates in those states where the deposits are distributed on this basis.

---

[7] *The Security of Public Deposits*, Chapter 9.

A study of state fiscal organization made a few years ago evaluated the manner in which this work was commonly done, in the following words: [8]

The main source of current criticism of the treasury function arises from the choice that may be exercised as to the deposit of surplus public funds. Since the use of these funds offers opportunity for profit, the official responsible for selecting depositories may be subjected to considerable pressure, criticism, or temptation by those who are willing to pay for the temporary loan of idle government money. Although most states have passed laws preventing an official from appropriating the interest from public sums to his private use, there is still opportunity for informal agreements and collusion.

These forms of malfeasance are difficult of detection and are not entirely susceptible to correction by a readjustment of organization. However, the assignment of this relatively minor and routine duty to an officer specifically created for the purpose does overemphasize the importance of the function and weakens responsibility. The independent treasurer has little incentive for effective or efficient performance, and the officials deeply concerned with this objective have no influence upon him. The combination of custodial care with those accounting and budgeting functions assigned directly to a responsible executive branch of the institution is now the customary practice in both public and private affairs. By this allotment, accountability is made more direct, and economy and efficiency are promoted.

Purchase and Custody of Securities. In nearly all jurisdictions the treasurer plays an important part in the investment of funds. The report of the National Association of State Auditors, Comptrollers, and Treasurers showed that he is the sole officer charged with such investments in eight states; that he with another official or agency performs the function in ten states; and that in fourteen he serves as a member of an investment board. Some other official or agency performs the function in ten states. "Some of the states have loan boards, sinking fund commissions, or some special body established for this purpose. New York stands alone in conferring power to invest state funds upon the Comptroller. Kentucky delegates this authority to the Commissioner of Revenue, Pennsylvania to the Board of Finance and Revenue. Frequently special bodies, set up to perform a particular function, will also handle the investment of any funds which pertain to the administration of that function. For example, the board of education in Iowa and the school fund commission in Kansas are authorized to invest school funds, and the industrial commissioner of Colorado may invest the state compensation fund."

The custody of bonds representing the investment of state funds, and of collateral deposited by banks to secure or indemnify the deposit

---

[8] Campbell, O. W., *State Fiscal Organization*, p. 12 (Bureau of Public Administration, University of California, 1937).

of state funds, is an important function of the treasury in many states. Securities may have been bought out of moneys belonging to sinking funds, to retirement funds, or to the state workmen's insurance fund as well as from surpluses developing in the general fund. In Pennsylvania the Bond and Surety Bureau has custody of about $155,000,000 worth of securities. The Bureau clips coupons on the securities and credits them to the proper funds. As indicated in the preceding chapter, accurate and up-to-date records must be kept of securities held and of changes that may occur in the holdings of the state. This is important in order to secure the prompt collection of interest and to enable the state to dispose of holdings whose further retention cannot be justified on principles governing sound investment.

Fund Maintenance

The problems of fund maintenance are legion. In addition to the general fund, one finds in most jurisdictions a sizable number of special, segregated, or designated funds, earmarked for the purposes of some particular group, the members of which have paid the license, fee, or tax by which the fund was created. Next there are a good many public land or trust funds maintained on a custodial basis, not to mention such miscellaneous funds as the conscience fund and funds derived from escheats. Since administratively the problems of the special funds are most difficult, special emphasis will be given them in this discussion.

General Funds. In many jurisdictions there is no definition of the general fund in either the constitution or the statutes. Recognizing this fact, the legislature of Kansas in 1937 defined the general revenue fund as "the fund into which shall be placed all public money and revenue coming into the state treasury not specifically authorized by the constitution or by statute to be placed in a separate fund, and not given or paid over to the state treasurer in trust for a particular purpose." In the Federal government general funds comprise money available for general government purposes.[9]

The reports show that in the states the general fund was originally the chief if not the only basis of support for most agencies prior to 1900. During the present century, parallel with the rise of pressure groups in American politics and due very often to the influence of these groups, a multiplication of special funds has been permitted to cut deeply into the revenues of the general fund, until that fund is

[9] *General Statutes,* 1937 Supp. 75-3036, cited in Kansas Legislative Council, *The Problem of Special (Fee) Funds in Kansas,* p. 8, and Naylor, Estill E., *The Federal Budget System in Operation,* p. 146 (The Author, Washington, 1941).

often actually smaller and less important in the financial picture in the state than are a number of the special operating funds. Under such circumstances it becomes impossible to consider state finances without extended reference to them. In a comparative study made at the University of Alabama in 1943, it was reported that [10]

> In comparison with other states, Alabama has more special funds and her general fund is of much less consequence as regards both receipts and disbursements. All of the thirty-one states for which data are available handle a greater percentage of their total net receipts through their general funds, while thirty of the thirty-one employ their general funds to greater extent as disbursing agents. Of twenty-four states for which this information could be secured, seventeen use fewer funds.

Surplus Funds. During World War II, while the Federal government was accumulating a larger and larger debt, the states and cities were able very greatly to improve their financial condition. Without imposing any new taxes or raising the rates on existing taxes, they were able simultaneously: (1) to balance their budgets; (2) to accelerate the reduction of their outstanding debt; (3) to accumulate considerable surpluses. No unusual skill was required to accomplish these results in spite of the claims made by some candidates for office.[11] Swollen tax receipts from the boom of war industry made such a result well nigh inevitable. Although commonly spoken of as surplus funds, these funds were not actually surplus in any real sense. The money was "saved" because at the time the states and cities could not spend it.

These funds were needed for normal governmental purposes which because of scarcity of man power and materials could not be met in wartime. In many jurisdictions some portion of them was earmarked for public works, for expenditure at such time as labor and materials might become available. The remaining "surpluses" were quickly exhausted as one pressure group after another — often for the best of purposes — made a raid upon them, particularly for increased state aid for schools, highways, and other purposes. The long-range consequences of this series of events are not yet fully revealed; it appears, however, that spending patterns have been established which it will be exceedingly difficult to maintain from regular tax receipts under the more normal conditions of peacetime.[12]

---

[10] *Alabama State Funds* p. 1.

[11] Governor Walter S. Goodland of Wisconsin gave an excellent statement on this situation; see his *Executive Report on State Finances and Messages*, pp. 9–10 (Madison, 1943).

[12] See Tompkins, on California, and Rightor, Chester E., and Ingersoll, Hugh D., "How to Use State Surpluses," *State Government*, March, 1942, pp. 57–58, 71–72; Unsigned, "Disposition of State Surpluses Analyzed," *ibid.*, September, 1943, pp. 463–464; Wychoff, Vertrees J., "The Surplus Concept in State Finance," *ibid.*, December, 1943, pp. 238–240, 251.

Special Funds. Special funds are variously referred to as segregated, designated, or earmarked funds; they contain money pledged by law to specific purposes. Their history in the states during the past half century has been an interesting one. The philosophy of the special fund is easy to understand. A particular group of taxpayers, being required to pay licenses or fees, feels that the revenues derived therefrom belong to them as a group. If they are motorists paying gasoline taxes, motor license fees, and operators' license fees, they feel that this money should go into the highway fund and be used for road construction and maintenance, and they resist *en masse* any attempt at diversion, regardless of the worthiness of the purpose. If they are hunters or fishermen, they feel that the funds derived from their license fees should be used for the acquisition and stocking of additional game preserves and streams and not for the regular operating expenses of government.

Most of these groups are strongly organized and are able to bring pressure to bear upon the members of the legislature at times when they think their interests are at stake. So effective were the lobbies for special groups in state after state, that the number of special funds grew to unreasonable proportions. It was only when the administrative absurdity of the situation thus created became apparent that it was possible to do anything toward decreasing the number. A state might find that its balance in the general fund was low and so might be obliged to borrow money from commercial banks to meet current obligations, or issue tax anticipation warrants, while at the same time there were significant balances, perhaps much larger than the sums borrowed, lying idle in some of the special funds. All receipts belong to the state, but those in special funds cannot be used; instead, the state pays out considerable sums in interest on short-term loans. This situation, occurring repeatedly, brought about a gradual decrease in the number of special funds in some states. Sometimes the principal was preserved by a guarantee to the special groups affected that they should be entitled to an appropriation from the general fund approximately equal to the amount which they paid in the form of licenses and fees.[13]

The process of establishment is simplicity itself. Take Colorado, as an illustration: [14]

Having been admitted to the Union in 1876, the First Assembly lost little time in passing a general appropriation act. That meant that everybody in the

---

[13] For a general comment on special funds, see Willoughby, William F., *Principles of Public Administration*, pp. 495–497 and Chapter 27 (Johns Hopkins Press, 1927).
[14] Department of Government Management, *Earmarking of Public Revenues*, p. 5 (University of Denver, 1940).

state government was assured of a pay check. Taxes were antied into one pot (the General Fund) and debts were dealt with as they became due and payable. Such an arrangement kept the state's finances directly under the fingers of the Legislature. These first legislators were well aware that the power to pay was the power to control, and were not passing out any cash without administrative strings tied to it.

Such uncomplicated management of finance did not last. An up-and-coming state like Colorado must have institutions of higher learning. Constitutionally provided state revenues were insufficient, so the Legislature declared a special mill levy, and allocated the proceeds to certain school funds . . . the Colorado College of Agriculture, School of Mines, et cetera. And so the first legislatively "earmarked" revenue was shunted into special funds.

This was in accord with the traditional American policy of trying to keep the schools "free from political entanglement." Then came the stockmen and in succession a host of others.

These groups do not confine their efforts to a single state or to any single campaign. They are well financed, well organized, and persistent. They work both in Washington and in the state capitals. The highway organizations secured an antidiversion clause in the Hayden-Cartwright Act of 1934 and promptly set to work to obtain antidiversion amendments to the constitutions of the several states. And they have made progress — if such it may be called. In the 1945 sessions the subject was considered in eighteen states and, in five, amendments received legislative approval. By 1948 twenty states had adopted such amendments. Similarly, tax funds are earmarked for educational or welfare purposes in a growing number of states.[15]

The situation in a particular state may be shown by reference to Pennsylvania, in which the number of operating funds (including the general fund but not the so-called custodial special funds) reached a maximum from 1923 to 1927, there being a total of twenty-seven during that four-year period. In the biennium of 1913–1915 the Commonwealth had only two funds, the general fund and the sinking fund. In the following biennium there were five. Another peak was reached in the period referred to above, but by 1931–1933 the number had been reduced to seven. Then it began to grow again. In 1933–1935 it went up to seventeen, and by 1941–1943 it had risen to twenty-one, the total amount involved being about three times as much as it had been twenty years earlier.

Bad as is the situation in this state, that in other states is not only

---

[15] National Highway Users Conference issues at intervals a pamphlet, setting forth "progress" in protecting highway funds and giving an "honor roll" of the states having antidiversion constitutional amendments, and the text of the amendments; see also Clague, Ewan, and Gordon, Joel, "Earmarking Tax Funds for Welfare Purposes," *Social Security Bulletin*, January, 1940, pp. 10–20.

as bad but often many times worse. According to official reports, Alabama had seven funds in 1900; fifty-four in 1936; and one hundred in 1942, which expended 91 per cent of the total net disbursements made by the state.[16] In Kansas it is reported that "by a curious patch-work process extending over a period of more than sixty years, Kansas has built up a large number of these funds, in which at the present time more than four fifths of all state receipts are set aside for specific pur-poses. Such funds are more than bookkeeping accounts; they represent actual physical segregation of cash resources."[17] A few years ago there were thirty-two such funds in California and sixty-five in Louisiana. In Illinois there were four general revenue reserve funds, forty-two special funds, and sixteen separate funds which may be regarded as trust funds, for various types of Federal grants. Large numbers exist also in Missouri, New York, and Ohio. A few years ago New Jersey had more than forty, controlling approximately three fourths of the state's revenues.[18]

But it would be difficult indeed to surpass the record of Colorado, in which it is reported that there are 231 special funds;[19] of South Da-kota, where the number has varied between 454 and 530 since 1930; or of Oklahoma, where the mere line-by-line listing of funds and ac-counts required six mimeographed pages. The general fund revenues in this last state have been declining progressively for a number of years, the figures for 1937, 1938, and 1939 being, respectively, 40.5, 32.7, and 29.8 per cent.[20]

Examination of selected municipal reports shows that the cities are about as badly off as the states and for substantially the same reasons. Philadelphia had about twenty-five funds in 1944. Years ago, however, the National Committee on Municipal Accounting recommended that the resources, obligations, and financial transactions of the cities should be classified under the funds to which they relate and that the number of funds should be small. The following, the Committee believed would ordinarily be sufficient: General, Special Revenue, Working Capital, Special Assessment, Bond, Sinking, Trust and Agency, and Utility. Only those additional funds required by law should be estab-lished.[21]

---

[16] *Alabama State Funds*, p. 1.

[17] *The Problem of Special (Fee) Funds in Kansas*, p. 10.

[18] For an excellent description of this situation, see Cline, Denzel C., *Executive Con-trol over State Expenditures in New Jersey*, pp. 12, 29-30 (Princeton Universit Press, 1934).

[19] *Earmarking of Public Revenues*, pp. 11-16.

[20] Oklahoma Tax Commission, Know Your Government Series, Bulletin No. 1 Table 4 (Oklahoma City, 1946), and Weaver, *Oklahoma's Deficit: A Study in F nancial Administration*, Chapter 3.

[21] *Municipal Funds and Their Balance Sheets*, p. 1 (Chicago, 1935).

This vicious system reacts to the serious detriment of governments and people in a number of different ways. It prevents any over-all planning of the fiscal program of the governmental unit as a whole. The money is there but the hands of management are tied. In the second place the legislature, whose responsibility it is not only to lay and collect taxes but to spend the receipts in the best interests of all the people, abdicates its responsibility every time it submits to the demands of a persistent pressure group representing some part of the public. And again, the operation of the system makes needlessly difficult the payment of the state's bill when due; often there is money in the treasury, but if it is earmarked for some other purpose, it cannot be used. Finally, the system may lead to still another unfortunate condition — the expenditure of a major portion of the government's total receipts by an agency supported by earmarked revenues, without appropriation. In Oklahoma, for instance, more than half of the money of the state is spent without appropriation and therefore without normal and necessary controls either by the executive or by the legislature. The effects of the system are so bad that Professor Weaver lists it as one of the three major causes of Oklahoma's deficit and financial difficulties.

Trust Funds and Other Types. In addition to the separate operating funds in states and cities, there is a considerable number of custodial and trust funds which contain money in the custody of the government as trustee, for expenditure in accordance with the terms of the trust. Examples include a manufacturing fund for prison industries, state employees' and school employees' retirement funds, state workmen's insurance funds, public lands and trust funds, funds from Federal grants, and sinking funds for the retirement of outstanding debt. In 1938 Kansas had twenty-three different trust funds, seven special funds for grants received from the Federal government, and four custodial funds. In Kentucky the Public Administration Service found it necessary to deal in its survey not only with different funds but with different types of funds, including in addition to the general fund the following: [22]

1. Revolving, Trust, and Agency — a group of related funds
2. State Road
3. Highway Bridge Bond
4. Highway Bridge Bond Sinking
5. National Industrial Recovery Act Highway

Handbook of Financial Administration, Commonwealth of Kentucky, Chapter 4 (Chicago, 1937).

6. County Road Trust
7. Special Deposit Trust
8. State Fire and Tornado Insurance
9. Unemployment Compensation

No uniformity whatever exists among the states with regard to the special funds established; aside from the general fund, which exists in all states, no two of the lists bear any resemblance to each other.

Sometimes individual funds in particular states represent something quite different from what one might expect. In Kentucky, for instance, a revolving fund means a state treasury account accruing to the credit of a budget unit from operating receipts, fees, gifts, or appropriations which may be used in defraying maintenance and operating expenses of activities and agencies which are in whole or in part self-supporting. Under the law such accounts may be established by appropriation for financing the operations of industries, farms, hospitals, dormitories, dining halls, etc. and/or by depositing the operating receipts of such activities and agencies in the state treasury to the credit of the respective revolving account. On such a basis the possibilities of establishing special operating accounts are almost unlimited.

In Nebraska the lands and funds held in trust have been classified as follows: [23]

Classification of Lands and Trust Funds in Nebraska

PERMANENT LAND ENDOWMENT	PERMANENT TRUST FUNDS	CURRENT OR TEMPORARY TRUST FUNDS
Common School Lands	Permanent School Fund	Temporary School Fund
University Land	Permanent University Fund	Agricultural College
Normal School Lands	Normal School Endowment	Income Fund
Agricultural College	Fund	University Income Fund
Lands	Agricultural College	Normal School Income
Saline Lands	Endowment	Fund
	Bessey Memorial Fund	Bessey Memorial Income

Conclusions. The excessive number of special funds creates an il logical and difficult situation. They undermine legislative control ove finances; activities operating on appropriations must secure annual o biennial legislative approval while functions operating from earmarke funds may continue their existing program if the legislature does nc direct otherwise. Likewise, administratively there is little or no justi cation for them. All of the money in all of the funds belongs to th people and their government, but as long as it is divided into a larg

[23] Shumate, *op. cit.*, Chapter 4.

number of special funds, these funds are not available for use when and where needed.

Some would go so far as to eliminate all of them — except those of a custodial or trust nature — crediting all receipts from whatever source to the general fund. It will be a long time before such a step can be taken, desirable though it might be. In Pennsylvania in the session of 1933 it proved impossible even to make all of the special funds self-supporting to the extent of requiring them to reimburse the general fund for their operating costs. The pressures that were strong enough to get these funds established were still strong enough to protect them even from the pressure for good financial management.

Debt Administration

People have always worried about the public debt. As one looks back from the vantage point of 1949, it would seem that they had little to worry about. A new philosophy regarding the public debt has in late years been advanced — a reassuring philosophy which, if valid, gives little cause for concern even now as one faces the very sizable debts accumulated during two world wars, a major depression, and the demands of a new foreign policy. It may nevertheless be worth while to take inventory of what has happened.

The Federal Debt. The Federal government commenced operations in 1790 with a gross national debt of $75.8 million or $19.2 per capita. The debt rose to a peak of $127.3 million in 1816, following the War of 1812, but by 1836 was entirely liquidated. Receipts were chiefly from customs duties. In 1860 the debt was only $64.8 million, or $2.06 per capita. In 1866, following the Civil War, the debt was $2.8 billion or $77.69 per capita. Thereafter the debt was gradually reduced until in 1893 it amounted to $961.4 million or $14.49 per capita. Various internal taxes began to supplement customs duties as sources of revenue. The Spanish War and a falling off of customs revenues caused an increase in the debt in 1899 to $1.4 billion or $19.33 per capita. Except for a demand for government bonds as security for national bank notes, the debt might have been paid off in the early years of the present century. The debt of March 31, 1917, just prior to our entry into World War I, was $1.3 billion or $12.36 per capita. The developments through the next three important epochs may be summarized as follows: [24]

World War I. The peak of the World War I debt was reached on August 31, 1919, with a total of $26.6 billion or $250.18 per capita. The debt on June 30, 1920, stood at $24.3 billion, a reduction of $1.1 billion having been made during

---

These figures are summarized from *Tax Digest*, November, 1945.

the preceding fiscal year. The lowest postwar debt was $16 billion or $129.66 per capita, on December 31, 1930.

The Depression. The fiscal year 1930 was the last in which the budget was balanced. The debt commenced its upward climb, reaching $42.9 billion or $325.63 per capita on June 30, 1940, at which time expenditures in the defense program were commencing to be made. The total on November 30, 1941, just before our entrance into World War II, was $55 billion or $412.32 per capita.

World War II. The debt rose rapidly during World War II. The total gross debt on June 30, 1942, was $72.4 billion or $537.35 per capita; on June 30, 1943, $136.7 billion or $1001.55 per capita; on June 30, 1944, $201 billion or $1456.54 per capita; on December 31, 1944, $230.6 billion or $1662 per capita; and on June 30, 1945, $258.7 billion or $1855.58 per capita. The gross public debt on August 14, 1945, when the Japanese accepted surrender terms, stood at $262.6 billion, in addition to which there was $505 million in guaranteed obligations.

State and Local Debt. Comparable increases, for somewhat different reasons, have taken place at both the state and local levels. The trend in state debts during the last two or three generations is indicated in the table below; that on city and county debts, in the table on page 391.[25]

Trend in State Debt, 1870–1946

YEAR	TOTAL FUNDED DEBT	PERCENT INCREASE OR DECREASE
1870	$ 341,245,198	. . . . .
1880	286,818,453	−15.94
1891	238,283,071	−16.92
1900	253,331,203	6.31
1910	311,093,349	22.80
1912	362,159,272	16.41
1922	1,106,078,000	205.41
1932	2,593,666,000	134.49
1937	3,186,043,409	81.40
1942	3,104,000,000	−10.30
1946	2,344,000,000	−35.10

Miss Trull found that for 1937 there was "a total of nineteen states with per capita net debts below $10; seven with debts between $10 and $20; nine between $20 and $30; five between $30 and $40; five between $40 and $50; and three over $50, two of these falling between $50 and $60 and one close to $80 per capita." When the states were grouped by per capita net supported debt, state and local, there were two with debts between $20 and $39; ten between $40 and $59; nine between $60 and $79; eight between $80 and $99; eight between $100 and $119; six between $120 and $139; two between $140 and $159 and three with debts of $200 and over.

[25] Trull, Edna, *Resources and Debts of the Forty-eight States*, 1937, p. 2 (Dun Bradstreet, New York, 1937), supplemented by United States Bureau of the Census figures.

During the war period both the total amount of state debt and the
r capita averages steadily declined. Net long-term debt amounted to
750 million at the end of the fiscal year 1946, indicating a decrease
7.4 per cent during the year, and of 33.4 per cent since the end
1940. Nevada continued to be debt free. All but seven of the reining forty-seven states reduced their gross debt in 1946; new bor-
wings were made in these seven states. Per capita gross debt at the
d of 1946 was largest in Arkansas and Louisiana, $75.64 and $64.38
pectively. Per capita debt of three states was between $40 and $59,
d of five between $30 and $40. At the other extreme, four states —
orida, Idaho, Iowa, and Nebraska — had gross debt outstanding of
s than $1 per person. Ten states had over $30; fourteen had more
in $15 but less than $30; twelve had between $5 and $15; while
·ven had less than $5.[26]

In 1947, Dun & Bradstreet made an analysis of the per capita net
bt on an over-all basis for the two hundred largest cities in the
ited States, and seventy-five metropolitan counties. The results
: shown in the table which appears on this page. The figures used
the compilations are as of various dates in 1946; while they are
ghtly higher than the low reached in 1945, they reflect only the be-
nings of postwar borrowing.

ge in Per Capita Debt
Jnited States Cities and Counties

TY SIZE GROUP	HIGH IN GROUP	MEDIAN IN GROUP	LOW IN GROUP
r 500,000	$241.82	$111.02	$26.82
000 to 500,000	155.20	100.34	38.40
000 to 250,000	237.72	66.80	13.58
•0 to 100,000	471.79	62.08	0.00
largest cities	471.79	69.20	0.00
aajor metropolitan unties	275.72	81.69	10.78

nstitutional Limitations. There are no debt limitations in the Federal
·nstitution, the maximum limitation being fixed by statute from time
time as required. Practically all the state constitutions and city
arters, however, impose some limitations upon the power to incur
bt and indicate more or less specifically the purposes for which debt
y be incurred. Although numerous purposes are mentioned, they
y be grouped — so far as the states are concerned — under four
·dings, as indicated in the table on page 392.[27]

Bureau of the Census reports, and *Book of the States, 1948-1949*, pp. 248-249.
Manning, John W., "Constitutional Limitations on State and Local Indebtedness as

Constitutional Limitations on State Debt

1. For general or public purposes — twenty-five states
   California, Colorado, Idaho, Illinois, Kansas, Louisiana, Maine, Maryland, Massachusetts, M
   tana, Nebraska, Nevada, New Jersey, New Mexico, New York, North Carolina, North Dak
   Ohio, Oklahoma, Oregon, Pennsylvania, Rhode Island, South Carolina, Virginia, and Washing

2. For casual deficits, deficiencies in revenue, and existing emergencies — twenty states
   Arizona, Delaware, Florida, Georgia, Idaho, Illinois, Indiana, Iowa, Kentucky, Massachuse
   Michigan, Missouri, Nebraska, Ohio, Oklahoma, South Dakota, Utah, Virginia, Washingt
   and West Virginia

3. For improvements and public works — nine states, or eleven if California and New York are inclu
   whose constitutions specifically mention highways
   Alabama, Colorado, Idaho, Kansas, Maryland, New York, Oregon, South Dakota, and Utah

4. Miscellaneous — various such purposes are mentioned:
   Soldiers' bonus, war, or to repel invasion — four states
     New York, Ohio, Pennsylvania, and Texas
   Bonds to pay existing debt, or for funding — three states
     Arkansas, Colorado, and Texas
   Extraordinary expenditures — two states
     Minnesota and Wisconsin
   Determined by the legislature — two states
     New Hampshire and Tennessee
   For utilities — one state
     Alabama

In some states a definite limitation upon the amount is impose either on a percentage basis or in the form of a maximum amou Nevada, Virginia, and Wyoming limit the amount of debt to 1 cent of the total property valuation; Utah to 1½ per cent; No Carolina, to 7½ per cent; and South Carolina, to 8 per cent. T amount may be fixed by the legislature in Delaware and New Han shire. Maximum amounts are indicated for twenty-five states in t table below.

Constitutional Limitations on Amount of State Debt

$2,000,000 — Idaho	300,000 — California
1,000,000 — Kansas and Pennsylvania	250,000 — Illinois, Iowa, Minnesota, and Miss
750,000 — Ohio	200,000 — New Mexico, North Dakota, and T
500,000 — Georgia and Kentucky	100,000 — Montana, Nebraska, New Jersey,
400,000 — Oklahoma and Washington	South Dakota, and Wisconsin
350,000 — Arizona	50,000 — Michigan, Oregon, and Rhode Islan

Complicated schedules of limitations for specific purposes are p vided in the constitutions of three states. Maine limits general debt $300,000 and highway debt to $2,000,000, but New York has no li on either. Maine's limit for wharves and ports is $1,150,000; for s diers' bonus, $3,000,000, as against $45,000,000 in New York. T latter has a limit of $300,000,000 for grade crossing elimination, h

of July 1, 1937," *Tax Systems of the World,* Eighth Edition, pp. 236–237; and Rat ford, B. U., "Constitutional Provisions Governing State Borrowing," *American . litical Science Review,* August, 1939, pp. 694–707.

of which is borne by the state, and $10,000,000 annually for public works. Colorado and Maryland have very complicated limitation provisions.

Slightly more than half of the states make some provision for exceeding the debt limits, in case of emergency (Idaho, Kentucky, Maine, Minnesota, Nevada, Oregon, and Wisconsin); to repel invasion (Michigan); in case of invasion and insurrection (Nebraska and North Dakota); or in case of war (Oregon); for losses in school funds (Iowa); for public buildings and for agricultural credit (Minnesota). Two different processes are prescribed, one legislative, the other popular. Of the legislative type, one state provides for action by the assembly (Delaware); two for determination by the legislature (New Hampshire and Pennsylvania); and one for a two-thirds vote of the state legislature (South Dakota). Of the popular type, four states provide merely for a popular vote (Rhode Island, Virginia, Washington, and Wyoming); five for a majority vote (Illinois, Montana, New Jersey, New Mexico, and Oklahoma); and two for action by two thirds of the electors (Missouri and South Carolina). In some cases, as in Pennsylvania, the procedure amounts to an amendment of the state constitution.[28]

Some states impose specific limitations upon the term of debts, ranging from five to seventy-five years, as indicated in the table on this page.

Constitutional Limitations on the Life of State Debts

years — Wisconsin	30 years — Kentucky and North Dakota
years — Missouri (soldiers' bonus)	35 years — Missouri (highways), and New Jersey
years — Idaho, Iowa, Nevada, Washington, and West Virginia	40 years — South Carolina
	50 years — New Mexico and New York
years — Arizona	75 years — California

ess than half of the constitutions mention this particular phase of the subject. Minnesota specifies that the life of its debts shall be for not less than ten nor more than thirty years; Montana and New Hampshire state that the matter may be determined by the legislature; and Kansas leaves the matter indefinite. There has been considerable discussion of the wisdom of imposing specific limitations in amount and

Ratchford, op. cit., in a slightly different classification, groups the states as follows:
In the Electorate —
    By constitutional amendment — seventeen states
    By referendum — seventeen states
In the Legislature — fourteen states
r discussion of the history of limitations on temporary debt in New York, see New rk State Constitutional Convention Committee, Report, Vol. 10, Chapter 3 (Albany, 1938).

in time upon emergency debts. During the depression there was much dissatisfaction in Pennsylvania with the $1,000,000 limitation, which was regarded as a limitation upon emergency debt, but all efforts to change it either by general revision or by specific amendment failed. In New York a limitation of one year upon the life of emergency debts was one of the problems analyzed by the Constitutional Convention Committee, which developed at some length the arguments for and against the broadening of the powers to contract deficit loans.[29]

A few constitutions provide extraordinary debt limits, and some prohibit debts of particular types. Loans for the benefit of corporations, companies, or railroad corporations are prohibited in thirty-five states; for the benefit of individuals or persons, in twenty-two states; of associations, in twelve states; and for local government units of various types, in three states. In South Dakota the matter is left to the determination of the legislature. In most constitutions the type of bonds to be issued is not specified; the following are the types specified where the subject is mentioned at all:

Funding or refunding — Delaware and North Carolina
Registered — Minnesota and South Carolina
Serial — Arkansas, California (highways), New York, and West Virginia
Sinking fund — Michigan, Ohio, and Pennsylvania
Term — California (general); Idaho, Kentucky, Maryland, Missouri (soldiers benefit); and New York

In all the states where the subject is mentioned, warrants may be issued; similarly, it is provided in most cases that the debt is to be amortized by an annual tax. The maximum interest rate is specified in a few states at 4 or 6 per cent, or at such other rate as may be specified by law.

Limitations on municipal debt may be found in the state constitutions, in state laws requiring submission and approval of bond issues by a state agency, or in their own charters. The latter usually relate to the total amount of debt that may be incurred, measured in terms of a percentage of the total assessed valuation for one or more years and exempting self-supporting debt, i.e., debts producing revenue sufficient to meet carrying charges, such as transit facilities or water works. The limitations applying to the city of Philadelphia may be taken as illustrative.[30]

---

[29] *Ibid.*, pp. 72–73; the chapters which follow deal with other important aspects of the problem of borrowing in New York: Chapter 4, Requirements for State Bond Referenda; Chapter 5, Prohibition against the Lending of State Credit; Chapter 6, Incurrence of Debt to Repel Invasion; Chapter 7, Provisions for the Repayment of State Debts.

[30] Bureau of Municipal Research, *Philadelphia's Debt Limit* (Philadelphia, 1945).

Under the Philadelphia charter the city may incur debt up to 10 per cent of the last assessed valuation of taxable property. Since this arrangement permits the debt limit to rise in prosperous times when borrowing should be at a minimum and tends to restrict it in periods of depression when heavy borrowing may be necessary, Professor Karl Scholz has since 1935 advocated the adoption of a borrowing base computed on a ten-year average of total assessed valuations. This would tend not only to stabilize the base but to raise it when economic conditions were bad and reduce it in periods of prosperity.[31]

Instrumentalities of Public Borrowing. When the issuance of bonds has been authorized, in accordance with the prescribed rules and regulations and subject to such limitations as may be provided by law, the issue must first be advertised — normally by the Treasury.[32] Very often the sale is on the basis of competitive bidding, in which case the rate will be determined largely by the judgment of Wall Street as to the soundness of the credit of the governmental unit, the extent to which it has already exhausted its borrowing power, the purpose for which the money is to be expended, and many other factors. Numerous types of obligations are issued by governments. National governments may issue non-interest-bearing notes in the form of legal tender or "greenbacks." In times past, citizens might be forced to make loans to the government, but modern governments arrange loans on a contractual basis. Obligations may differ also in their time of maturity. To quote Professor Groves: "Governments may borrow for a few days or for many years. Many European bonds have been issued with no definite maturity at all. They are a perpetual obligation of the government so far as interest is concerned. In general, borrowing is usually classified as short term, intermediate, and long term." [38]

Short-term borrowing in the form of bank loans or tax anticipation warrants may be used to tide over emergencies, but even these forms require the cooperation of the banks and financial interests. Callable bonds may be used for short but indefinite periods. Short-

"Municipal Borrowing and Legal Debt Limits," *National Municipal Review*, June, 35, pp. 323–327, and *Municipal Borrowing Power, Debts, and Unemployment* (Pennvania State Planning Board, Harrisburg, 1937). The New York State Constitutional Convention Committee proposed a five-year moving average (*Report*, Vol. 10, pp. 7–311). Approval of both of these proposals is given by Hansen, Alvin H., and Perloff, Harvey S., *State and Local Finance in the National Economy*, p. 207 (Norton, New York, 1944).

Louisiana has used a Board of Liquidation for the administration of its state debt three quarters of a century; see Moak, Lennox L., *Louisiana's Little Legislature: A Study of the Board of Liquidation of the State Debt, 1870–1945* (Bureau of Governmental Research, New Orleans, 1945).

Groves, Harold M., *Financing Government*, Revised Edition, p. 546 (Holt, New York, 1945).

term loans are commonly used to meet payrolls or for other urgent expenditures, during a lean period that may develop prior to the receipt of new tax revenues. With good management such emergencies should not arise often, but if the credit of the government is good, there should be no difficulty in disposing of such offerings on favorable terms when necessary.

The duration of loans made for longer periods will be determined partly by the financial condition and prospects of the governmental unit, partly by the purpose. Intermediate loans may be made for public improvements, especially those that will have a limited period of usefulness or that can be expected to pay off out of earnings. For the latter, revenue bonds are often used.[34] In no case should loans be contracted for longer periods than the probable life of the improvements; otherwise the public will find itself paying for a replacement before the original loan has expired. Long-term bonds may be issued where the cost is great, as for such items as a soldier bonus or some improvement of exceptionally long life, like a permanent housing development.

Repayment of loans was formerly handled by the establishment of a sinking fund; modern practice favors the use of serial bonds which are cheaper, since the periodic retirement of a portion of the debt reduces the interest charges. Furthermore the very presence of a sinking fund provides a constant temptation, especially in times of economic stringency. The money lies there, and officials are tempted to borrow it to tide over the emergency or to finance the beginning of some new project. The situation resembles that of the bank teller who "borrows" a few dollars to help him over a critical situation; he thoroughly intends to return the money, but ill luck follows bad and he keeps taking more rather than returning what he originally borrowed, until finally his peculations are discovered. Furthermore, when funds are short, there is always the temptation to postpone payment to the sinking fund until better conditions prevail. Thus the obligation which should come first from the point of view of the maintenance of sound credit comes last or perhaps not at all.

Management of the Public Debt. With the growth of the public debt to the unprecedented proportions previously indicated, the question of its management becomes of vital importance. As the total kept mount-

---

[34] For ordinary bonds the full faith and credit of the government is pledged, supported by the taxing power; revenue bonds are payable solely from the revenues of the enterprise they have financed and carry no obligation whatever for support from taxes or general fund appropriations: see Bird, Frederick L., *Revenue Bonds* (Haynes Foundation, Los Angeles, 1941).

ing, there was much speculation as to how large a debt the nation's economic structure could support. Although the record of the post-war years demonstrates that these particular worries were not justified, there are other questions still to be answered.

Should these debts be retired and if so, how fast? Most Americans were brought up to believe that any debt was bad; now there are those who maintain that public debts are not bad and that there is no particular urgency about paying them off or reducing them.[35] The majority opinion among both scholars and informed citizens is probably to the effect that the debt should be reduced as rapidly as circumstances will permit, both to reduce the carrying charges and to increase the capacity for future borrowing should another emergency arise. If such a policy is to be followed, taxes should be left substantially as they are in order that the maximum reductions in the debt might be made in a period of full employment, high wages and high prices, and huge corporate profits. To reduce the taxes under such circumstances would serve only further to increase prices and profits and the inflationary trend, while at the same time it retarded debt retirement.

In this connection still another problem arises — the age-old controversy between pay-as-you-go and borrowing or deferred payment for public works. There is no dogmatic answer for this question; borrowing may sometimes be justifiable or even necessary. Generally speaking, pay-as-you-go is cheaper, and the public receives more for its money. A sizable portion of the expenditure is not eaten up in carrying charges. But it takes longer to accomplish objectives, and it requires both a continuity of policy and a persistent and determined effort that are difficult to achieve under our political system. As Alfred E. Smith said years ago while Governor of New York, "The trouble that under this policy we do not pay and we do not go." Milwaukee citizens recently voted, after many years of pay-as-you-go, to incur debt to obtain necessary improvements.

There are other means than debt retirement of reducing the debt and the burden it entails. One of these is refinancing. In a period of falling interest rates a government may sometimes call in existing loans, pay off part, consolidate the remainder, and float a new loan at lower rates. Monetary devaluation helps government borrowers, as it does private ones. And, of course, there is always the possibility of repudiation or partial repudiation, or scaling down of public debts — a pro-

See writings of John Maynard Keynes, Alvin H. Hansen, and others, and for the contrary view, Abbott, Charles C., *Management of the Federal Debt* (McGraw-Hill, 1946) and Moulton, Harold G., *The New Philosophy of Public Debt* (Brookings Institution, Washington, 1945).

cedure not unlike that resorted to when an individual or a corporation goes into bankruptcy.

The problem of tax exemption raises another important policy question, especially in a Federal system such as ours. Under the doctrine of McCulloch v. Maryland [36] it was long accepted as public policy that the officers, agencies, and instrumentalities of one unit of government (Federal, state, local) should not tax the officers, agencies, and instrumentalities of the others. Government securities were included in this arrangement until in recent years the Supreme Court has in a reversal of policy gradually whittled away these intergovernmental tax immunities. The result is that any tax exemption provided in connection with any given issue applies only to taxes levied by the issuing jurisdiction.[37]

SELECTED REFERENCES

Abbott, Charles C., *Management of the Federal Debt* (McGraw-Hill, New York 1946). Discussion of debt policy at the Federal level.

Blair & Company, *A Record of Debt Change in the Ninety-one Largest Cities of th United States, 1935-1944* (New York, 1944). Historical and statistical record o prewar and wartime municipal developments.

Bureau of Municipal Research, *Philadelphia's Debt Limit* (Philadelphia, 1945). Di cussion of debt limit problems in the nation's third largest city.

Bureau of Public Administration, *State Funds in Alabama* (University of Alabam 1943). For discussion of the problem of special funds in another state, see Kans Legislative Council, *The Problem of Special (Fee) Funds in Kansas* (Topek 1940).

Committee on Public Debt Policy, series of six reports on the National debt (Ne York, 1948). Deal with administration, effect on the national economy, etc.

Faust, Martin L., *The Custody of State Funds* (National Institute of Public Admini tration, New York, 1925) and *The Security of Public Deposits* (Public Admini tration Service, Chicago, 1936). These are the only available studies of this in portant question.

Joint State Government Commission, *Fiscal Analysis of the Operating Funds of t Commonwealth of Pennsylvania, 1923-1943* (Harrisburg, 1944) and *The Debt the Commonwealth of Pennsylvania and Its Local Subdivisions* (Harrisburg, 194: Two excellent case studies.

Ratchford, B. U., *American State Debts* (Duke University Press, 1941). Standard tit

Shumate, Roger V., *The Administration of State School Lands and Public Trust Fur in Nebraska* (Nebraska Legislative Council, Lincoln, 1940).

Studensky, Paul, *Public Borrowing* (National Municipal League, New York, 194 Excellent analysis of existing procedures with recommendations for improveme

Tompkins, Dorothy C., *The General Fund Surplus Problem in California* (Bureau Public Administration, University of California, 1943). Excellent discussion o pressing wartime problem in states and cities.

Weaver, Findley, *Oklahoma's Deficit: A Study in Financial Administration* (Univ sity of Oklahoma Press, 1940). A good case study.

---

[36] 4 Wheaton 316 (1819).
[37] See Powell, Thomas R., "Intergovernmental Tax Immunities," *George Washing Law Review*, June, 1940, pp. 1213-1220, and other articles by the same author.

21

DISBURSEMENT OF FUNDS

Disbursements

THE procedure involved in making disbursements is fairly simple, although numerous agencies may be involved. In the Federal government, with a few specific exceptions, the function is exercised by the Chief Disbursing Officer in the Treasury Department. The Comptroller General may provide for the payment of accounts or claims adjusted and settled in the General Accounting Office, through disbursing officers of the several departments and establishments, instead of by warrant — which has long been regarded as the normal method of operation. The Federal procedure in making funds available for disbursement and in the actual payment of obligations is set forth in the two charts appearing on pages 400 and 402–403.[1]

In the centralized treasury systems of the states and cities accounts presented for payment are audited by the auditor or comptroller and, if found valid, are then sent to the disbursing officer for payment, accompanied by the proper warrant. A study of fiscal officers made by the National Association of State Auditors, Comptrollers and Treasurers showed that the auditor and comptroller are the disbursing officers in the states, over three fourths of which have empowered the same official to draw and sign the warrants. The auditor performs both duties in half the states, the comptroller in twelve. The remaining states have different officials to draw and to sign warrants. The governor has relatively little responsibility in the actual disbursement of funds.

"In no state is money paid out until a warrant therefor has been duly drawn and signed. In the majority of states, warrants are used as authorizations to draw checks. In four states, however, warrants when signed by the proper official may circulate as bank checks, and it is therefore not necessary to issue checks. In thirty-seven states, the treasurer signs the checks, but in four of these, he does so jointly with the auditor, jointly with the comptroller in three, and jointly with the director of accounts in one. The auditor signs them in five states, the

See United States Bureau of the Budget, *Budget Administration*, Training Conference Manual, Section 3 (Washington, 1947).

PRINCIPAL STEPS CUSTOMARILY TAKEN IN MAKING FEDERAL EXPENDITURES

MAKING FUNDS AVAILABLE FOR DISBURSEMENT

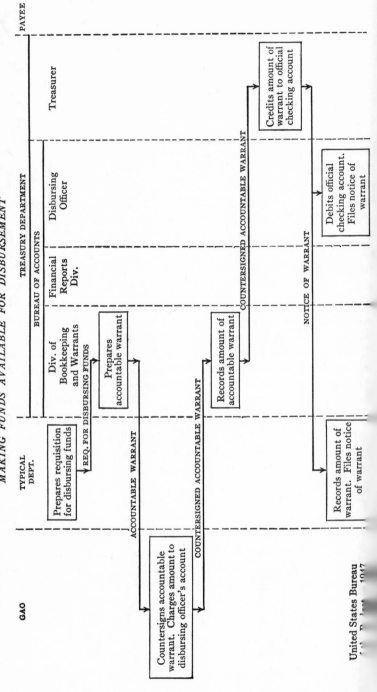

commissioner of taxation and finance with the comptroller in one, and the trustee of the particular fund involved in one."

Check Writing. During World War II the War Department's Office of Dependency Benefits wrote checks by the million. Benefits went to one tenth of the American people, by one of the greatest accounting-machine operations in business history. Housed, in Newark in a twenty-story office building that looked like a big factory, some 8500 civilian employees and about 175 army officers turned out 7,500,000 family-allowance and allotment-of-pay checks every month. The checks went to soldiers' dependents in the forty-eight states and in one hundred foreign localities from Tanganyika to unoccupied China. A survey of this tremendous operation, made by *Fortune*, reported that [2]

> The ODB check-writing factory is the world's largest disbursing agency under one roof. It distributes more checks every month than any government agency or private business ever did before, by means of the most elaborate clerical production-line system and the newest business machinery to be found anywhere. Over 60,000 incoming communications a day are acted upon and answered within forty-eight hours, and checks are mailed within five hours of the date when due. It is not surprising, therefore, that insurance-company executives, bankers, and other businessmen have journeyed to Newark to see what the ODB's techniques could offer in the way of clues to their own clerical and accounting problems.

For the Federal government as a whole during the last fiscal year in the long regime of Henry Morgenthau as Secretary of the Treasury, it was reported that the Division of Disbursement issued nearly 82 million checks, amounting to over $10 billion. All told, the Treasurer of the United States paid over 332 million checks involving $189 billion. In the states as well as in the Federal government there has been an enormous increase in the number of checks written. This may be accounted for by the great increase in the number and scope of state activities, resulting in a much larger number of state employees. Expenditures made in connection with unemployment relief and work relief programs during the depression period, with and without Federal aid, account for many more.

In Pennsylvania, which may be taken as a representative state, some twenty-five or thirty check writers were employed a number of years ago. The checks, in sheets of four, were typed in triplicate for record keeping. The use of a mechanical device made it possible to sign all four simultaneously; in fact, the process as a whole has long been

---

"Checks by the Million," *Fortune*, December, 1944, pp. 151-154, 194-196.

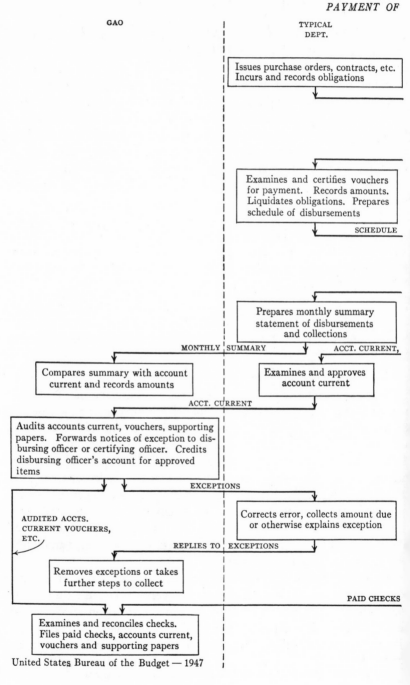

GAO

TYPICAL
DEPT.

Issues purchase orders, contracts, etc.
Incurs and records obligations

Examines and certifies vouchers
for payment.   Records amounts.
Liquidates obligations. Prepares
schedule of disbursements

SCHEDULE

Prepares monthly summary
statement of disbursements
and collections

MONTHLY SUMMARY   ACCT. CURRENT,

Compares summary with account
current and records amounts

Examines and approves
account current

ACCT. CURRENT

Audits accounts current, vouchers, supporting
papers.   Forwards notices of exception to disbursing officer or certifying officer. Credits
disbursing officer's account for approved
items

EXCEPTIONS

AUDITED ACCTS.
CURRENT VOUCHERS,
ETC.

Corrects error, collects amount due
or otherwise explains exception

REPLIES TO EXCEPTIONS

Removes exceptions or takes
further steps to collect

PAID CHECKS

Examines and reconciles checks.
Files paid checks, accounts current,
vouchers and supporting papers

United States Bureau of the Budget — 1947

IN MAKING FEDERAL EXPENDITURES

OBLIGATIONS

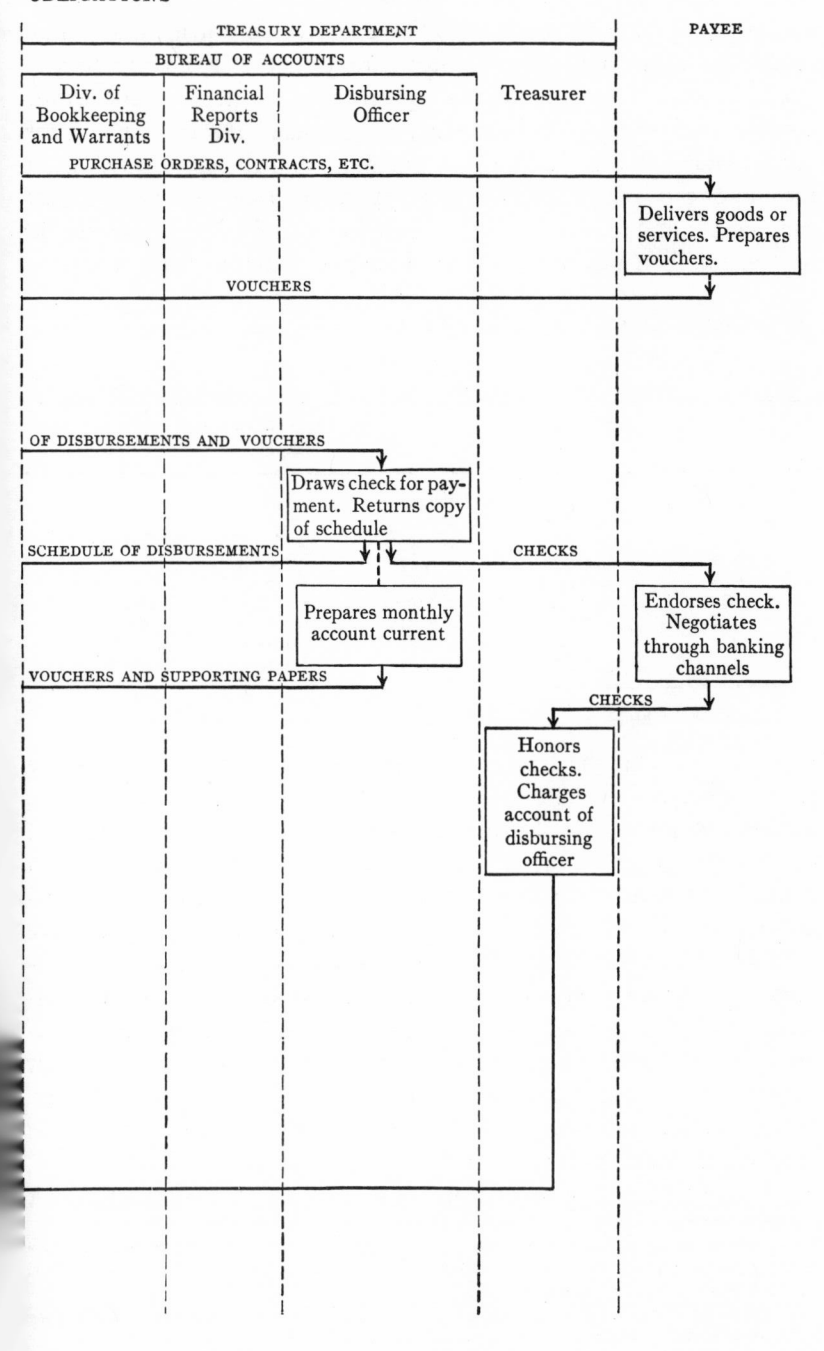

as completely mechanized as possible. The number of checks issued in this state increased tremendously in the last quarter of a century, as is shown in the table on this page.[3] These figures do not include public assistance or unemployment compensation checks. Even in the war years, when there was a minimum of unemployment, relief checks for a single week in the month of June, 1943, totaled 28,522, while in the corresponding week in 1944, the number was still high – 21,914. At the end of the war, in the spring of 1946 public assistance checks were running about 250,000 a month, unemployment compensation checks over one million a month – a total of about 15 million checks a year.

Commonwealth of Pennsylvania: Checks Written
by the State Treasurer – Selected Years, 1923–1945

YEAR	GENERAL FUND	MOTOR FUND	MISCELLANE- OUS FUNDS	TOTAL
1923	174,373	176,602	34,283	385,238
1928	272,805	386,637	216,257	875,699
1933	834,693	787,360	1,169,183	2,791,236
1937*	2,121,760	1,248,757	548,647	3,919,164
1938	1,596,274	547,163	512,942	2,656,379
1942	1,027,148	564,191	582,493	2,173,832
1943	967,138	456,367	502,305	1,925,810
1944	896,468	421,813	478,966	1,796,247
1945	922,586	477,932	511,291	1,911,809

* Highest year.

It is plain that the treasury's business is one of the largest in any given jurisdiction. It has, in fact, become so great that decentralization has become imperative if the work is to be performed efficiently. In the Federal government, Treasury Disbursement has not only been obliged to establish field offices but, as has been shown, to handle disbursements for some important functions separately.[4] The states have been faced with similar problems on a smaller scale. With the exception of public assistance, however, all state disbursements in Pennsylvania are handled at the capital, even those for unemployment compensation. Public assistance checks are written in four offices so that they may be rushed to the needy with all haste. One is located in Pittsburgh, servicing western counties, one in Philadelphia for eastern counties, the other two in Harrisburg and in Scranton.

A public disbursing officer, like an individual, must constantly look

[3] Joint Legislative Committee on Finances, *Survey of the Government of Pennsylvania*, p. 115 (Harrisburg, 1934), and letters to the author from the State Treasurer, September 28, 1939, and April 18, 1946.
[4] As the War Department; see Technical Manual TM14–500, *Organization and Functions of Disbursing Offices* (Washington, May, 1945).

ahead, planning his work so that funds will be on hand to meet urgent needs as they arise. In this establishment of priorities he may have legal assistance. To refer again to Pennsylvania, the State Constitution provides that "the moneys held as necessary reserve shall be limited by law to the amount required for current expenses." [5] Working under this mandate, appropriations have as a precautionary measure been classified as preferred and nonpreferred, and the duty is placed upon fiscal officers to first protect preferred appropriations if at any time sufficient cash is not available in the Treasury to meet all classes of appropriations.

Disposal of Property. Governments frequently find it necessary to dispose of surplus or unserviceable property — land, buildings, supplies, equipment, and the like. The Federal Constitution provides that "the Congress shall have power to dispose of and make all needful rules and regulations respecting the territory and other property belonging to the United States," and similar authorization is to be found in the basic law of many states and cities. Prior to World War I the sale of land was the major disposal problem of the Federal government; following two world wars, the chief concern has been to dispose of surplus war materials and supplies. In the states the governor controls all or substantially all state property; in Alabama, for instance, the governor's department of finance has the duty "to sell, exchange or otherwise dispose of any personal property of the state determined by the Director of Finance not to be needed for public use or to have become unsuited to such use." [6]

This is not the place to review the history of the public land policy of the United States; the present discussion will, therefore, be limited to the disposition of relatively small and more or less isolated parcels of land formerly used for public purposes and no longer required. There are three ways in which the Federal government may dispose of land: (1) sale or lease; (2) use in conjunction with different governmental functions or even to produce other property which in turn is subject to disposition, as in the TVA; (3) conveyance of the land on condition that the grantee use it in a specified manner and with a grant-in-aid.[7] The magnitude of the problem after World War II was staggering, as one surveyed the number of war plants and air fields,

Article IX, Section 13; for interpretation, see Commonwealth *ex rel.* Schnader v. Liveright, Secretary of Welfare, *et al.*, 308 Pa. 55, 1932.
[6] *Code of Alabama*, 1940, Title 5, Sec. 145 and 181; Title 45, Sec. 3.
[7] See note in *Michigan Law Review*, April, 1941, pp. 1020–1023, which deals primarily with the third method as discussed in United States v. City and County of San Francisco, 310 U.S. 16, 1940.

the Federal Public Housing Authority (which grew out of war demands), and many other remainders from the war. Since 1944, when the Surplus Property Act was passed, there has been under consideration the need for permanent legislation covering the procurement, utilization, and disposition of Federal property. This was done in the Federal Property and Administrative Services Act passed in 1949 by the 81st Congress.

In the field of personal property the problem is likewise of tremendous proportions. Before the operations of government became so complex, most obsolete or surplus property was sent to the dump, was stowed in a remote storeroom, or was the object of petty graft. In 1946 it was reported that, in Alabama, state agencies conducted sales to the public of personal property, exclusive of alcoholic beverages, amounting to at least $2.1 million. Items included cotton cloth, agricultural produce, used automotive equipment, official publications, scrap, seedling trees, hides, baby chicks, and all types of obsolete equipment.[8] This figure may not seem large when compared with the war surplus of the Federal government, but it is still a fair amount for a moderate sized governmental unit.

Salvage of surplus and scrap offers significant possibilities in the larger units of government. This may, in fact, be made an important part of the supply program. Surplus paper forms, for instance, may be converted into scratch pads, and crankcase drainings may be used as road oil or for lubricating crude machinery. But when it is found that there is no means of using the surplus or of converting waste material for use, it is necessary to dispose of it by sale.[9] Common deficiencies in the disposition of unneeded or unserviceable property at the state and local levels are failure to centralize responsibility for the disposal function; lack of procedural requirements prescribing the manner of making a public sale; failure to coordinate the needs of the whole governmental unit with the disposal process; and absence of a vigorous check over the custody or disposition of such property.

When the amount is large, as in the case of war surpluses, the task becomes exceedingly difficult. The determination of a suitable organization to perform the work is in itself a problem, as witness the series of attempts to arrive at a satisfactory organization following World War II — the Surplus Property Board, the War Assets Administration, and finally the use of the Reconstruction Finance Corporation. The intricacy of the problems almost defies solution and

---

[8] Alabama Legislative Reference Service, *The Disposal of State Personal Property.*
[9] On the salvage program in New York City, see address by Flood, Leo P., "Salvage Surplus and Scrap," before National Institute of Governmental Purchasing, Chicago, August 21, 1946.

there is, furthermore, the virtual certainty that, no matter how well the job is done, few will be satisfied.[10]

There is need for all reasonable speed lest the material spoil or deteriorate in value before it is offered for sale; yet at the same time proper procedures must be established to prevent favoritism, collusion in bidding, or disappearance of the property to be sold — all of which require time. These problems were further complicated after World War II by an intricate system of priorities established to permit Federal agencies, state and local government agencies, and veterans to have an opportunity to purchase before the sale was opened to the general public; this took still more time. Adequate solution of these questions was vital because of the effect of disposal upon the economic life of the nation.

The supply department should see that agencies requiring goods be informed when disposal items are available. Reference has already been made to the substantial savings realized by the California Department of Public Works through the purchase of surplus goods. The state and local units generally showed real interest in the opportunity for such savings. The National Institute of Governmental Purchasing developed an elaborate twenty-point plan for the disposal of surplus property to the local governments and nonprofit institutions under the Surplus Property Act of 1944 — a weak and inadequate piece of legislation which was shortly afterward replaced.

Claims Against the Government

One of the essential elements in the theory of the state and of sovereignty has long been the idea that, as a supreme authority, the state could not be subjected to the indignity of being sued in a court of law. Yet it has also been recognized that individuals do on occasion suffer loss as a result of governmental action or of negligence on the part of the state or its officers. The problem has been — and still is — to provide means by which persons subjected to *bona fide* injury may recover (for the state does not desire to evade its just obligations) without (1) impairing the dignity of the state or (2) opening up the possibility of recovery on bogus or unjustified claims.

The doctrine of immunity from suit finds expression in various ways in the state constitutions. Many of the states by specific provision recognize their responsibility before their courts, but the pro-

---

10 For a discussion of the legal problems involved, see Olverson, John B., "Legal Aspects of Surplus War Property Disposal," *Virginia Law Review*, June, 1945, pp. 550–612; and for a study of the disposition of a major project, Howard, Dorothy B., *History and Disposition of a Powder Plant Project, Nitro, West Virginia, 1917–1942* (Bureau of Labor Statistics, Washington, 1945).

visions regarding suit are much more lenient in some jurisdictions than in others. The data in the table below are based on a report which was compiled in 1944.[11]

State Constitutional Provisions
Regarding Recovery in Claims Against the State

1. Permit suit to be brought in such manner and in such courts as the legislature may provide — 19 states
   Arizona, California, Delaware, Florida, Indiana, Kentucky, Louisiana, Nebraska, Nevada, North Dakota, Ohio, Oregon, Pennsylvania, South Carolina, South Dakota, Tennessee, Washington, Wisconsin, Wyoming

2. Supreme Court shall hear all claims against the state, but its decision is recommendatory only and shall be reported to the next session of the legislature — 2 states
   Idaho and North Carolina

3. State shall never be a defendant in any court of law or equity — 4 states
   Alabama, Arkansas, Illinois, West Virginia

4. Miscellaneous provisions — 4 states
   Michigan, Montana, New York, Utah

5. Constitution silent on liability or suability in the courts — 19 states
   Colorado, Connecticut, Georgia, Iowa, Kansas, Maine, Maryland, Massachusetts, Minnesota, Mississippi, Missouri, New Hampshire, New Jersey, New Mexico, Oklahoma, Rhode Island, Texas, Vermont, Virginia

From the variety of these provisions it appears that there must inevitably be wide diversity in the practice in the several states not only with regard to the actual procedure governing the institution and conduct of proceedings but in the willingness of the states to entertain consideration of certain types of claims at all. The determination of this procedure is a legislative matter in nineteen states by constitutional mandate; in nineteen others, where the constitution is silent on the subject, it may reasonably be presumed that the legislature has power to act, although as one writer has observed, "the courts have always looked upon legislation that is in derogation of sovereignty or state power with a cold eye, and have tended to restrict it to narrow limits," often putting a narrower construction upon it than was intended by the legislature.

The virtual immunity of the state from suits in tort suggests that the citizen is, practically speaking, at the mercy of the state and its agents. This, however, is wholly contrary to the basic assumptions of our legal philosophy. Under the common law doctrine that there is no wrong without a remedy, the citizen has legal means of maintaining his rights even against the sovereign. Actually, one of the oldest efforts to give the citizen redress for wrongs inflicted by agents of government is found in the application of "the rule of law" which makes public

---

[11] Illinois Legislative Council, *The Suability of the State*, pp. 1-2.

officials personally liable to suit for unauthorized property damage, false arrest, abuse of power, and other wrongful acts. The only valid defense which the official may offer is that he acted within the scope of the authority conferred upon him by law, and even then he may be held liable if perchance the act itself is invalid. The obligation may be moral as well as legal.[12]

Types of Claims. If it may now be assumed that provision has been made, either by constitutional or statutory authorization, for the settlement of valid claims against the government, it becomes pertinent to inquire what these types of claims are. Under what circumstances, in other words, are citizens justified in making claim against the state for financial reimbursement? So far as the states are concerned, no better answer to this question can be found than by referring to the actual experience of one state during a typical year for which figures are available.

The Kansas experience in 1939 is revealed in a study made by the Kansas Legislative Council in 1940.[13] In this instance 123 claims were considered by the legislature's Joint Committee on Claims and Accounts, of which exactly two thirds (82) were allowed, one third (41) were denied. Financially, the claimants did not fare so well. The eighty-two claims totalled $172,857, of which only $66,953 was allowed — a figure which represented approximately one sixth of $235,-614, the total amount claimed by the 123 claimants. The basis of these claims was varied. There were twenty involving torts of state agents, resulting mainly in injuries to persons, a few to property. Seventeen arose under the workmen's compensation law. Forty-six desired refunds either for tax overpayments or of unused deposits. Twenty-one made claim for goods or services rendered to state agencies, six for reimbursement of payments made in behalf of the state. There were five military claims, three of them growing out of the Civil War. A small number of others grew out of obligations owed local governments, outlawed warrants, and other miscellaneous causes.

The settlement of these many types of claims by procedures fair both to the government and to the injured citizen presents a difficult problem. Analysis of the methods in common use in the various juris-

---

[12] For discussion of these questions, see Shumate on tort claims against state governments, and Dworkin, Harry J., "The Immorality of Moral Claims," *State Government,* December, 1941, pp. 291-292, 298 (on irregularities in Maine).

[13] *Claims Against the State,* pp. 4-9. For a similar analysis for Nebraska for 1939 and 1941, see Shumate, and for a number of cities, Gravlin, Leslie M., *A Brief Report on Hartford Claim Costs* (Governmental Research Institute, Hartford, 1944).

dictions suggests three main categories — legislative, executive, and judicial.

Judicial Settlement. There are two main types of arrangements for the judicial settlement of claims against the state. The first involves the adjudication of claims of authorized types, in such regular courts in law or equity as may have been specified by law. The Tucker Act of 1887 gave the Federal district courts the same jurisdiction over claims against the United States as that given to the Court of Claims, and the Federal Tort Claims Act of 1946 authorized suit against the government irrespective of the amount of the claim. Because of the immunity-from-suit doctrine, suit in claims cases may be brought only with the consent of the government.[14] Since it would be difficult to give consent in each case individually as it arose, blanket authorization may be given in advance in certain specific types of legitimate cases which arise more or less frequently. While every reasonable effort may be made to protect the government from the successful prosecution of bogus or unwarranted claims, due regard must be given to the basic legal requirements of due process and equal protection.[15] In most jurisdictions the judgment of the court is final, although in some it is regarded simply as a recommendation to be referred to the legislature for its consideration.

The second type of judicial settlement involves the use of specialized courts, which are in turn of two types. Some of them, like the United States Court of Claims and those found in the four states noted below, have a general claims jurisdiction, being authorized by law to hear and decide any claim case which may lawfully be considered. The Federal court consists of five members, appointed by the President by and with the advice and consent of the Senate. This court was established by Congress in 1855 under its power to appropriate money to pay the debts of the United States, primarily for the purpose of investigating contractual claims against the government.[16] The states

---

[14] This rule is strictly construed in the Federal courts; see United States v. Sherwood (312 U.S. 584, 1941) in which it was held that a district court had no jurisdiction in a suit against the government in which the plaintiff was joined by a private party, since Congress had never consented to suits of this nature.

[15] In Jacob v. City of New York (315 U.S. 752, 1942), plaintiff had been injured while using a defective wrench. The trial judge had refused to let the case go to the jury on the basis of the "simple tool doctrine," i.e., that the master is not negligent in the case of defective simple tools because the possibility of injury from such tools is so slight as to impose no duty on him to see that they are free from defects. The Supreme Court held that "a due respect for the statutory guaranty of the right of jury trial, with its resulting benefits, requires the submission of this case to the jury."

[16] See *Code of the Laws of the United States* (1934), 1260–1266; also Naylor, Estill E., "The United States Court of Claims," *Georgetown Law Journal*, March, 1941, pp. 719–738.

which follow the Federal plan are among the most heavily populated. The New York court, which has existed for three quarters of a century, disposes of claims against the state amounting to several million dollars a year. The Illinois court was established in 1903 and reconstituted in 1917. West Virginia came along in 1941. The Michigan statute of 1939 does not represent a particularly desirable type, since instead of providing for regular full-time judges, use is made of existing circuit court judges on a part-time basis.

In other states these courts are specialized not only in the sense that their jurisdiction is limited to claims cases but also that it is limited to particular kinds of claims cases. Thus in Nebraska in 1935 a Workmen's Compensation Court was established, with authority to administer and enforce the workmen's compensation law. This is a three-man court, the members of which are appointed by the governor, under certain restrictions regarding previous experience and political affiliation, for a term of six years. These specialized courts — if such they may be called — are not too clearly distinguishable from administrative boards created in other states for the performance of precisely the same functions.

The Joint Committee on the Organization of Congress, which submitted its report in 1946, took a strong position in favor of the delegation by Congress to the courts of the power to settle private claims — a duty which had up to that time consumed session and committee time out of all proportion to the importance of the subject matter. After commenting on the lack of fitness of the Congress to handle individual claims, the Committee continued, in support of its recommendation: [17]

> The United States courts are well able and equipped to hear these claims and to decide them with justice and equity both to the government and to the claimants. We, therefore, recommend that all claims for damages against the government be transferred by law to the United States Court of Claims and to the United States district courts for proper adjudication.

This recommendation was enacted as Title IV of the Legislative Reorganization Act of 1946 and is known as the Federal Tort Claims Act. Provision is made for the administrative adjustment of claims of $1000 or less by the various departments and agencies of the executive branch and for suits in Federal district courts which are authorized "to render judgment on any claim against the United States, for money only, on account of damage to or loss of property or on account of personal injury or death caused by the negligent or wrongful act of any employee of the government" while on official duty, if a private

---

[17] *Organization of the Congress*, p. 25 (79th Cong., 2nd Sess., Senate Report No. 1011).

individual would be liable to such claim under the laws of the jurisdiction in which the loss or injury was sustained. Provision is made for the establishment of rules of procedure and for appeal. A one-year statute of limitations applies. Although the enactment of this legislation has removed from the Congress an enormous burden of unnecessary work, examination of the pages of the *Congressional Record* during the 80th Congress indicates only too clearly that the twelve exceptions provided in the act are much too numerous and too extensive. The problem has not been solved, but a beginning has been made.[18]

Administrative Determination. Prior to the Federal Tort Claims Act, the Federal government made practically no provision for the administrative determination of private claims. This act authorized such settlement on claims of $1000 or less, specifying that all such determinations should be final and conclusive — in the absence of fraud — upon both the claimant and the agency. The head of the agency shall make payment of the award out of appropriations that may be made therefor, and he shall annually make a report to the Congress of all claims so paid.

Although some states rely upon this method of settlement, there is little uniformity among them with regard to organization or procedure. Some provide for the reference of claims to administrative boards or commissions, usually ex officio bodies composed of state executive officers. Michigan did this prior to the establishment of its Court of Claims, using a state administrative board composed of seven principal executive officers in the state. Pennsylvania uses a Board of Arbitration consisting of three members appointed by the governor. There is a filing fee of $50. The Board must file a written opinion, and its decision is final. The award, if any, is paid by the department involved out of funds appropriated for the original contract or pur-

---

[18] For comments on the first year of operation, see Baer, Herbert R., "Suing Uncle Sam in Tort," *University of North Carolina Law Review*, February, 1948, pp. 119–138; Foley, George F., and Heuser, M. M., "The First Year Under the Federal Tort Claims Act," *Federal Bar Journal*, October, 1947, pp. 23–32; and Jackson, E. J., "The Tort Claims Act — the Federal Government Assumes Liability in Tort," *Nebraska Law Review*, November, 1947, pp. 30–42. During the second year of the operation of the law, the Senate Committee on Expenditures in the Executive Departments held extensive hearings; in its report, *Evaluation of Effect of Legislative Reorganization Act of 1946* (80th Cong., 2nd Sess., Senate Report No. 1175), the Committee recommended bans on the following types of bills: private bills which could have been instituted under the Federal Tort Claims Act; private bills of all kinds which are more than ten years old; private bills which the President has vetoed, unless substantial new evidence is introduced; private bills previously rejected by committee, unless substantial new evidence is introduced; bills based on tort claims accruing prior to January 1, 1945, and extending to such claims the jurisdiction heretofore granted to administrative agencies and district courts over claims accruing thereafter.

pose. A number of states have provided for investigation of claims prior to legislative action, by a state board of examiners or state claims commission. In any case where both administrative and judicial procedures are available for the proof of claims, the claimant must exhaust all administrative remedies before resorting to court action.[19]

The lack of uniformity in policy governing recovery is quite as pronounced in the cities as in the states, by whose laws the cities are bound. A study of practice on "snow and ice" cases in cities in the northeastern states in 1944 showed not only a wide variation in fundamental policy but a resultant variation in per capita cost of damages allowed in such claims, as between cities in different states. Since these claims may develop into considerable expense to a city, many of them have gone to great lengths to oppose tort claims against them. Boston, for instance, employs skilled investigators in its law department. "These men collect evidence, photographic and otherwise, question witnesses, doctors, and claimants, and present a complete picture of the case to the city attorney. 'Nuisance value' of claims is not recognized and the practice is to force the claimant into court unless the city is quite clearly liable. In Chicago, no suit is settled without proof of a *prima facie* case, and claims paid by the City Council are limited to actual expenses proved to have been paid as a result of the tort. . . ." [20]

Legislative Adjudication. Legislative adjudication is the only method of claims settlement in some jurisdictions and may in any one be regarded as a final resort. In democratic countries the legislature has always been regarded, in a special sense, as the guardian of the people's rights. In all such countries the right of petition for the redress of grievances is recognized as a vital element in the democratic process, and the petition is usually addressed to the legislature. On this point Professor Shumate observes: [21]

The legislature thus became the first agency for adjudicating claims against the state, and even today it remains the most important one. In states which do not permit suit, and which have not set up special claims commissions, the legislature is the only body through which redress can be secured. Furthermore, where permission to sue is given, it usually does not cover all cases, and cases arising outside the jurisdiction of the courts will normally be presented to the legislature. Finally, even where suit is brought against the state, the litigant may, in some instances, still take his claim to the legislature if he fails to secure satisfaction in the courts.

Most state legislatures receive scores, if not hundreds, of claims at each ses-

---

[19] Dworkin contends that in the handling of "moral claims" against the state responsibility should be vested in an independent agency operating under definite rules.
[20] Gravlin, *op. cit.*, pp. 3–4.
[21] Shumate, *op. cit.*, p. 11.

sion. As a result, they have adopted a regular procedure for dealing with these claims. Normally, there is a committee on claims, or one with some similar title, charged with hearing claims. The committee reports its findings to the legislature in the form of a bill listing each claim which has been approved, together with the amount allowed. This bill, if approved by the legislature and signed by the governor, becomes an appropriation authorizing the payment of the amount specified to each claimant.

The *control* over this matter is clearly a legislative responsibility, but serious question may be raised as to whether the handling of individual claims is a proper legislative function. Short legislative sessions at two-year intervals may amount to a substantial denial of justice, regardless of the final disposition of the case by the legislature. Incidentally, the courts also might be quite as slow. Other critics have pointed to the ever-present possibility that personal and political considerations may be given undue weight. Most significant, however, is the question as to whether the handling of such claims is a proper legislative activity. It requires fact-finding, which is primarily an administrative activity, and adjudication, which is principally a judicial function. Under such circumstances it would appear that the legislature might well confine itself to making available to citizens suitable and adequate administrative and judicial procedures by means of which any legitimate claims against the government could be promptly processed.

This point of view is forcefully stated in the excellent report of the Joint Committee on the Organization of Congress, whose recommendation on this matter has already been cited. The Committee says:

Congress is poorly equipped to serve as a judicial tribunal for the settlement of private claims against the government of the United States. This method of handling individual claims does not work well either for the government or for the individual claimant, while the cost of legislating the settlement in many cases far exceeds the total amounts involved. Long delays in consideration of claims against the government, time consumed by the Claims Committees of the House and Senate, and crowded private calendars combine to make this an inefficient method of procedure.

These observations are quite as applicable to the state legislatures as they are to the Congress.

Insurance of Public Risks

Government faces many of the same risks as do corporations and individuals. There is the danger in both cases that employees who handle large sums of money or securities may misappropriate some portion of them. Government property is likewise subject to such casualty risks as fire, theft, and tornado. The law usually requires that certain officers and employees whose duties are of such a nature as to provide unusual temptations for the individual and danger of loss to the government, be bonded. Losses may occur as a result of embezzlement, theft, or malfeasance on the part of such individuals. The problem arises in part from the frailties of human nature and in part from the fact that there is in this country so little by way of a corps of trained, professional public servants. One commentator lays great stress on this point: [22]

Unfortunately we have in this country little in the way of tradition of public service. Vast sums of public money are not administered and heavy responsibilities of public affairs are not borne as a rule by men trained for a lifelong, whole-time career of civil service. Our public business is managed and our public purse is controlled in the main by the butcher, the baker, and the candlestick-maker, equipped for the task by the training provided by their trades, and performing the task all too often while they are still chiefly concerned with butchering, baking, and candlestick making. We even find at times these large sums and heavy responsibilities controlled by third assistant apprentices of such worthy tradesmen.

In the early days public risks were left without protection or else public employees obtained personal surety through the signature of some friend or a director of a bank in which funds were deposited. The courts were so lenient in their estimate of the liability of such sureties that little protection to the public was afforded. At present there are two methods by which the problem may be handled. Surety bonds and casualty insurance may be taken out with commercial companies at the usual commercial rates, or the government may become self-insurer by setting aside in separate accounts sums sufficient to cover any ordinary losses. Where government property is widely distributed, it is regarded as cheaper to assume the risk than to carry insurance.

Extent of the Bonding Problem. Some idea of the extent of the bonding problem may be obtained from a study of the practices in a relatively small state, for which, however, complete data are available. The Nebraska state Constitution requires the bonding of all major officers for a sum in no case less than $50,000, while scores of other officers and employees are required to furnish bond in varying amounts. All but eight of fifty-seven departments, boards, commissions, and agencies of the state government reported in 1943 that one or more of their officers and/or employees were under bond. The summary table showed a total of 528 bonded employees with a total coverage of $3,476,680. Out of a total premium of nearly $12,000 an-

[22] Anderson, Hale, *The Public Official Problem*, p. 3 (Association of Casualty and Surety Executives, New York, 1935).

nually, a little more than one third was paid by employees, a little less than two thirds by the state. (In all jurisdictions except Iowa and Nebraska the state pays all bond premiums.) The mere listing of the bonded positions under the state government required sixteen pages, running from twenty-five to thirty entries to the page.[23]

In the constitutional and statutory provisions governing bonding requirements there is little uniformity or consistency. In one agency the three commissioners and the secretary had no bond, while eight subordinate employees did. A current survey of tax collectors' bonds in third-class cities in Pennsylvania showed little relationship between the premium rate and the risk involved. This report continues: [24]

The study of the cost of treasurers' bonds in the forty-six third-class cities, made in 1943, disclosed that the amount of coverage varied from less than 10 per cent to more than 50 per cent of the tax duplicate. There was no connection between the size of the bond taken and the amount of the tax duplicate. The surety companies make it almost impossible to secure a small bond, and if one is obtained, the premium is just as high. Also losses were so few as to have no fixed relationship to the size of the bond. For example, the greatest loss in any city in the ten-year period covered by the survey was $21,612.54 paid to a city which purchased a $250,000 bond to cover duplicates of $3,227,712.79.

Commercial Bonding. There are various classes of surety bonds commonly used; government is or may be interested, in one way or another, in most of them. Contract bonds are important in connection with contracts for public work, although a bond guaranteeing faithful performance on the part of the employee bonded, comes under this grouping and may be required of fiscal officers. A fidelity bond makes the surety liable for losses resulting from embezzlement or other acts of dishonesty on the part of the officer or employee. Depository bonds are used in connection with deposits of public funds etc.

In all bonding arrangements there are three parties at interest: the one in whose favor the bond is written — the government; the party in whose behalf the bond is written — the officer or employee; and the party who acts as guarantor, known as the surety.[25]

When any individuals or corporations enter into an agreement, that is, a contract, they are bound only to each other, and to no others, for faithful compliance with such agreement; but the moment that a bond or instrument of indemnity is executed for the purpose of protecting one of the parties to such an agreement, the contract ceases to be a two-party agreement, and becomes instead

---

[23] See Shumate, *Bonding of State Officers and Employees.*
[24] Smedley, Elizabeth, "Cost of Tax Collectors' Bonds Surveyed," *Bulletin* of the Department of Internal Affairs, March, 1946, pp. 13–18.
[25] Knight, Herbert M., "Surety Bonds and How to Negotiate Them," *Civil Engineering,* November, 1935.

a three-party obligation. The party protected by such indemnity is then bound to the surety to perform his obligations under the contract as implicitly and as completely as is the principal, the party in whose behalf the bond is written.

Of the five most common forms used in the bonding of public employees the great majority of jurisdictions use the individual form, which covers the individual but not the position. The position form covers the position but not the person who holds it. The blanket form covers all positions regardless of the person or persons holding them; the University of Nebraska, for instance, has more than 800 employees covered by a blanket bond. Finally, the name schedule form covers a specific group of individually named employees, while the blanket personal form covers a specific group of employees.

State Bonding. The premiums paid to commercial bonding companies in many jurisdictions amount to thousands of dollars a year; if lesser amounts were put aside annually in a fund established for the purpose, and the fund were permitted to grow to adequate size, the government could obtain the same protection at far less cost. Once the fund was properly built up, further contributions could be omitted during following years in which there were no losses or only minor ones. Such a proposal has been recommended from time to time — by the Hoover Commission in 1949, and in the states by the Joint Legislative Committee on Finances in Pennsylvania in 1933. Alabama enacted a modified form of state suretyship in 1935. North Dakota has for years operated a state bonding department, the history of which was described in an annual report many years ago: [26]

The State Bonding Department . . . did not come into being as a spontaneous outburst of some legislative assembly, but instead came about as a consequence of a long demand from the various political subdivisions. Charges were made by individuals holding official positions that discrimination and unjust rates were being charged by private companies. It was brought to the attention of the 1915 legislative session and a law was passed establishing a department for the purpose of bonding public officials.

Private companies attacked the law declaring it was unconstitutional and their contention was sustained by the court. Complaints continued to be heard, the legislature of the year 1917 enacted another law eliminating the unconstitutional features of the previous law. The new law was likewise attacked but this one was declared constitutional by the United States Supreme Court. As a result of the court procedure the department was not permitted to function until the last part of the year 1918. The 1917 law was amended during the session of 19. Since that time there has been no practical opposition to the department. . . .

Alabama *Laws*, 1935, p. 365; Hopton, Harold, "History," in North Dakota State Bonding Fund, *Complete Report, 1929*, pp. 5-8 (Bismarck, 1930).

The State Bonding Department has served the state well in two ways: first, by being a financial success thereby saving the taxpayer; second, by making uniform and stabilizing the rates on bonds of public officials. Had not the department been in existence during the past few years of financial distress it is reasonable to assume that the rates on public officials' bonds would be so high as to make such bonds almost prohibitive.

Not all the experiments in state bonding have been as fortunate in their results as the one in North Dakota. The neighboring state of South Dakota established a State Bonding Company in 1919, in the office of the Commissioner of Insurance, with an appropriation of $25,000. The premiums were set at the rate of twenty-five cents per $100, with a minimum premium of $2.50. This rate was to be effective until the fund reached $100,000, after which rates were supposedly so regulated as to keep the fund at that figure.[27] Largely because the fund was poorly managed, the state returned to the practice of using corporate surety companies in 1933. In spite of the apparent failure of this experiment, it is still possible that with good management and proper safeguards the practice might effect substantial savings.

Insurance of Government-Owned Physical Property. The problems presented in the insurance of government-owned physical property are in some respects parallel to those relating to suretyship. The purpose here, as elsewhere, is to spread the risk. The relatively few who suffer loss are reimbursed from the premiums paid by the many. Every policyholder contributes a little each year, that no one may suffer a major loss. In 1942 two surveys of prevailing practice in the insurance of public-owned physical property were published.[28]

Fifteen of the thirty-six states which replied to the Council of State Governments inquiry rely on private insurance companies for the protection of the major amount of their physical property. These are Arkansas, Connecticut, Delaware, Idaho, Indiana, Louisiana, Maine, Montana, Nevada, New Mexico, North Carolina, Utah, Vermont, Virginia, and Wyoming. Nine states reported carrying individual insurance on individual buildings. Seven had blanket coverage of all buildings. Two states — Delaware and Idaho — carried blanket insurance for each group of buildings; for example, all university buildings might be covered under one policy, all state office buildings under another. Four states had made recent changes in the administrative arrangements for the handling of this problem:

---

[27] League of South Dakota Municipalities, *Insurance Costs and Practices in Governmental Subdivisions in South Dakota*, p. 25 (Vermillion, 1946).

[28] Most useful is Everstine, *Self-Insurance of State Property*, and Council of State Governments study. Since neither agency was able to secure replies from all states, the data are not complete.

Self-Insurance of Physical Property
in American States and Cities

	STATES		CITIES
With No Fund	California	New Hampshire	Boston
	Kansas	New York	Buffalo
	Massachusetts	Ohio	Chicago
	Minnesota	Oklahoma	Cincinnati
	Mississippi	Texas	Columbus, Ohio
	Missouri	Washington	New York City
	Nebraska		(except schools)
			Seattle
			Washington, D.C.
With Special or Limited Fund	Illinois	Maine	
	Iowa	South Dakota	
With an Insurance Fund	Alabama	Oregon	Ann Arbor
	Colorado	Pennsylvania	Baltimore
	Florida	Rhode Island	Detroit
	Kentucky	South Carolina	Philadelphia
	Michigan	Tennessee	Providence
	North Dakota	Wisconsin	

The most recent was in Louisiana where the new Fiscal Code, which became law in 1940, centralized all purchasing operations for all State departments under the Department of Finance. Prior to this time, all of the bureaus, commissions and departments of the state were making their own individual purchases for their insurance requirements. From the information given, Kentucky (apparently) switched over in 1936 from private insurance companies to its own state fund; Minnesota changed from individual insurance companies to a form of self-insurance in 1923; South Carolina's own Sinking Fund Commission was established in 1900, but no information was received on the situation prior to that date.

Self-Insurance. As is shown in the table on this page, a very substantial number of states and cities carry some form of self-insurance, covering all or — in the cases of Florida and Maine — part of their insurance needs. No sensible individual who owns property would think of going without fire insurance and, depending on where the property is situated, tornado or other forms of casualty insurance. Yet more than a dozen states and a very sizable number of large cities carry no insurance and likewise have no insurance fund, relying on current appropriations to care for such losses as may occur. Many of these jurisdictions report that since they have rarely if ever suffered substantial loss from fire, such insurance is unnecessary — a claim which could be made by many individuals who still believe it wise to carry insurance.

The members of a second small group of self-insurers are difficult to classify. These states "can be classed neither with those having no fund nor with those having an orthodox fund. In each state, the legis-

lature makes regular appropriations to care for losses from fire. T
appropriations are made before fires occur, but unused portions
them are not allowed to accumulate into a regular fund." [29]

Twelve states and five large cities operate regular insurance fund
following in most respects the basic principles of commercial fire i
surance companies. While most of the states include only state pro
erty in their funds, Alabama, South Carolina, and Wisconsin have e
tended coverage to county property to such a degree that sometim
well over half of all the property insured belongs to counties and loc
school districts. In most jurisdictions it has been the practice to requi
the fund to accumulate its own reserve, with no moneys except the
coming in from the premiums paid by the various departments ar
agencies whose properties are insured. After a careful study of t
experience of the various jurisdictions operating these funds, Carl I
Everstine concludes: [30]

> The general experience with state and municipal insurance funds has be
> satisfactory. Occasionally there are reports that a large loss could not be n
> from the fund, but for the most part the funds operate at a substantial profit.
> public fund may save money because of the low loss ratio on public prope
> (which in some cases has enabled governments to secure reduced rates from co
> mercial companies), and at the very least can save the money going to pay t
> administrative expenses of the private underwriters. Against these factors it is
> gued that a large loss may bankrupt the fund, that the presence of the fund
> vites diversion, and that state insurance is an invasion of private business.

These arguments have not deterred the states from entering oth
phases of the insurance business, for self-insurance obviously ne
not be confined to the insurance of physical property. For many yea
a large number of states have operated their own funds for the i
surance of workmen's compensation risks. While these facilities a
available to private employers desiring to benefit by the lower ra
these funds can offer, the facilities may also be employed for the i
surance of those state employees whose duties require the state,
employer, to carry workmen's compensation insurance upon the
The Virginia State Highway Department has been self-insured sin
1919. Its experience has been that the costs are lower, that rehabili
tion of the injured is more likely, and that employees favor the plan

Similarly North Dakota, which has since World War I carried
the most extensive state insurance program, operates a bonding fu

[29] Everstine, *op. cit.*, p. 11.
[30] *Op. cit.*, p. 16.
[31] See Robertson, Giles M., "We Save by Carrying Our Own Workmen's Insuranc
Better Roads, December, 1942, pp. 19, 28. See also McCahan, David, *State Insurance
the United States* (University of Pennsylvania Press, 1929).

for state and local officers, a fire and tornado fund under which it carries fire and windstorm insurance on the greater portion of its own property, and a hail insurance program at rates in 1946 ranging from 17 to 45 cents per acre for $5.00 insurance and from 27 to 72 cents per acre for $8.00 insurance. In 1946 nearly 16,000 farmers took out policies on more than 1,800,000 acres (an average of 118 acres per farmer), at a total premium cost of approximately $1,000,000, part of which was produced by tax levy, part by cash premiums on special policies. The risk covered was over $14,287,363; the surplus fund at the close of the business year was over $3,500,000. The loss ratio was 5.48 per cent. Policies may be placed through the local assessor or the county auditor.[32]

The Grant-in-Aid System

Origin and Development. A discussion of problems relating to public spending would not be complete without some mention of the grant-in-aid system now used so extensively for a variety of purposes at both the Federal and state levels. The pattern for Federal aid was established as early as 1787 by the provisions of the Northwest Ordinance; it was further developed in the provisions adopted in 1803 admitting Ohio to the Union and reserving one section, later two sections, of land in each township for school purposes. The surplus in the Treasury in 1837 was distributed among the states in "proportion to their respective representation in the Senate and House of Representatives of the United States."

Under the terms of the Morrill Land-Grant Act of 1862 the states were given Federal lands, on the same basis of apportionment, for colleges of agriculture and mechanic arts. Each state was granted 30,000 acres of land or its equivalent in land scrip for each member in Congress apportioned to it under the census of 1860. This was the last of the general land-grant acts, the first to aid a state function for which the Federal government later assumed a continuing responsibility. The lands allotted to the older states along the Atlantic coast were located in the West; in these cases the lands were sold or leased or the natural resources were exploited, the income being used for the support of higher education. These laws provided the patterns around which the present system of Federal grants-in-aid has been built.[33]

In the twentieth century, when the system of monetary grants came into general use, the passing years witnessed not only a steady increase in the number of purposes for which grants were made and

See Annual reports of the North Dakota Insurance Department; also of the State Bonding Fund, and the Fire and Tornado Fund.
See Council of State Governments, *Federal Aid to the States* (Chicago, 1949).

in the amount of the grants but, for a time at least, a standardizati
of the procedure which one might summarize as follows: [34]

The term "Federal aid" referred to annual, recurrent lump grants made
the Federal government to participating state governments. Each state legislat
wishing to take advantage of Federal aid for a particular function would first
up or designate a state agency with power to perform the work involved. T
state agency, in turn, would periodically draft a program to be submitted to
Federal government for its approval. Upon such approval being given, Fede
funds would be turned over to the state. The state agency would then be
pected to carry out the program, meeting at least the minimum standards p
scribed by the Federal grant unit. Finally, the usual grant-in-aid statute c
tained a provision for "matching" funds; that is, to be eligible for its "quota"
Federal funds, each participating state was obliged to supply at least one dolla
state or local moneys for every Federal dollar received.

In the decade of the thirties the established pattern was modif
as the necessity for more liberal terms encouraged making outrig
grants to both states and cities for some purpose such as relief, a
the making of what have been called "quasi grants" in connection w
the work programs of WPA, CWA, and PWA. The latter agenc
differed from each other in important respects but were "alike in th
common emphasis upon the giving of employment" and in their te
ency "to veer away from traditional Federal aid procedures in or
to find the most appropriate means of carrying out their purposes."
At the turn of the century the amount of the grants was not gr
they did not then nor do they even now constitute a large percent
of the $35 to $40 billion Federal budget or of the total receipts of
state governments. In 1930 three-fourths of the Federal grants went
highways, the remaining fourth for emergency relief, public wo
and education. In 1940, out of a total nearly six times as great, m
more than half went into social security and related programs, alm
one-third for highways, the balance for miscellaneous programs. In
table on page 423 figures are presented at significant intervals fr
1900 to 1946 inclusive.[35]
The pattern for state aid was established in the early years of
century when financial assistance was given in New Jersey and ot
states to local communities for highway purposes. The growth of
system in the states has been parallel with its growth in the Federal g
ernment and for much the same reasons. It has been used extensiv
and in increasing amounts to aid health and welfare services, educat

---

[34] Williams, Bitterman, also: Johnson, Byron L., *The Principle of Equalization*
plied to the Allocation of Grants-in-Aid (Federal Security Agency, Washing
1947), and Macdonald, Austin F., *Federal Aid* (Crowell, New York, 1928).
[35] For a comparable analysis, see Johnson, *op. cit.*, p. 8, compiled from the annua
ports of the Secretary of the Treasury.

Federal Grants-in-Aid to States (in millions)

FUNCTION	FISCAL YEAR ENDING JUNE 30					
	1900	1920	1930	1935	1940	1946
TOTAL	$2.9	$34.0	$100.5	$2,196.6*	$567.5	$757.8
Social security and related programs	.9	2.9	1.3	2.8	359.2	611.5
Public assistance	...	...	...	...	271.1	421.2
Employment security	...	...	...	1.3	51.7	55.7
Health and welfare	.9	2.9	1.3	1.5	26.4	134.6
Education	1.2	4.8	10.1	12.7	24.7	34.3
Public Roads	...	20.3	75.9	274.7	164.5	74.5
Natural Resources	.8	6.0	13.2	14.5	29.1	37.5
Emergency Relief and public works	...	...	...	1891.9	...	...

Regular grants, excluding $304.7 for emergency relief and public works.

nd highways, until the payments to the local communities now con-
ume anywhere from one fourth to one half of the total expenditures
f the state governments. The aid comes in the form of grants or shared
axes and from statutory provisions for refunding some specified por-
on of collections. As the difficulty of raising additional revenues for
xpanded service requirements in cities and counties increases, the pres-
ure for more and more state aid becomes intense. In the postwar years
ontinuing statutory commitments have raised serious financial prob-
ms for a number of states.

uestions of Policy. The growth of the grant-in-aid system has been
phazard, the decisions in individual cases being commonly made on
e basis of political considerations and pressure group influences. New
ants such as those for hospital surveys and construction and for air-
rt construction have been added from time to time, but few of the
lier purposes have been abandoned. Numerous questions of policy
ve arisen with regard to the operation of the system. One of these is
 allocation formula, which varies somewhat according to the purpose
 the grant; in some instances, as in highways, a number of different
ments are combined in the same formula. In the vocational education
gram the basis of apportionment may be urban population, rural
ulation, farm or nonfarm population. In agricultural extension work
mp sum of $50,000 is allotted to each state, while three additional
s are apportioned on the basis of rural population, farm population,
 special needs.

In all the early grants matching provisions were included, the recipient units being required to supply for the specified purpose an amount equal to the grant. This practice was modified in the states as well as in the Federal government during the depression era. Outright grants and more liberal matching provisions replaced the old 50-50 formula, but the requirement that the funds should all be used in accordance with the conditions of the grant continued to be employed.[36] Similarly, in the states, previously accepted methods of allocation were modified as efforts were made to expand the highway program to provide work for persons who would otherwise have been on relief, or as direct grants were made to "financially distressed" local units.

The states and the local units alike resented the "interference" which resulted from the acceptance of the grants. The states protested loudly about Federal invasion of "State rights," while representatives of the local units gave expression to similar concern about "home rule." The states as recipients of Federal aid resented the same types of control which they themselves imposed upon their local units. No unit of government, Federal or state, can afford to give outright grants without any attempt to ascertain that the funds are used properly and for the purpose intended. If the recipient unit does not like the conditions of the grant, it has a simple and obvious solution: it can refuse to accept the money. But they rarely do; they feel that the money belongs to them by virtue of the taxes their citizens have paid and that if they do not use it, some other state will get it. They want it, and they want the services which the additional money will provide; but they resent the controls. When the question of the constitutionality of the Sheppard-Towner Infant and Maternity Hygiene Act was brought before the Supreme Court by Massachusetts in 192 the Court in upholding the validity of the act very clearly stated the position.[37]

One of the most perplexing problems in recent years has had to do with the budgeting of aid funds by the receiving unit, state or local. While it is obviously desirable to include such funds in the budget as practically all other types of receipts are included, practice with regard to this matter differs widely. A survey made by the Council of State Governments in 1947 showed that about one half of the states

---

[36] The enforceability of such provisions was sustained by the Supreme Court in Ervein v. United States (251 U.S. 41, 1919), in which New Mexico had attempted to divert a small portion of a grant for educational purposes to publicizing the advantages of the state.

[37] Massachusetts v. Mellon, 262 U.S. 447, 1923, and Frothingham v. Mellon, 262 U.S. 447, 1923.

budgeted Federal grants-in-aid more or less in the same manner as they budget state money, but three fourths of the state budget officers felt that such controls were not satisfactory. In very few states were requests for grants channeled through the state budget office either on the way to a Federal agency or on the way back to the state department. Very few state budget offices were participating in the advance planning of Federal aid programs. For this there are a number of reasons. Normal controls have been difficult as long as heads of state agencies could go directly to the Federal government and ask for funds. Another difficulty has been based upon a misconception of the funds, a tendency to regard them as a gift for which it was unnecessary to account in the usual manner.[38]

Advantages and Disadvantages of the System. The real questions concerning the merits of the system relate not to supposed "interference" with State rights and home rule but to the political difficulties which hamper (if, indeed, they do not prevent) the use of the system for the accomplishment of its intended purposes. The grant-in-aid system (formerly called the subsidy system) rests upon the basic New Testament philosophy that man is his brother's keeper. Applied in this area, it imposes upon the wealthy and populous states a responsibility for the maintenance of minimum standards of government service in states that are smaller and lacking in wealth and resources. It assumes that the United States is "one country," in which accepted minimum standards of education and of health and welfare services should not be denied to any citizen because by accident he happens to have been born or to reside in one of the less favored sections.

If this doctrine were applied in practice as it is accepted in theory, grant-in-aid funds would be allocated on the basis of need. This is rarely done; representatives of the large states in Congress and of large cities in the legislatures rise to insist that they get their share. The result is that every allocation formula represents a compromise between need for financial assistance on the one hand and the voting strength of wealth and population on the other. The supporters of any given measure barter away as much of their original demands as they are obliged to do in order to get the bill through the legislature. Thus funds are given to those who have and are withheld from those who are not — given to Illinois and New York and withheld from Arkansas and Nevada; given to Philadelphia and Pittsburgh and withheld from upstate rural counties. More money is spent for the purposes of the

---

ee "Coordination of Grants-in-Aid at the Receiving End," summary of a panel discussion in *Public Administration Review*, Spring, 1948, pp. 152–153; this question dealt with in the report issued by the Council of State Governments.

grant, to be sure, but the bulk of it is not spent where it is needed most.

Some consideration must be given to the principles upon which allocation formulas are constructed. Generally speaking, the character of the formula is determined by the purpose of the grant and bears some direct relation to it. In education it may be population and average daily attendance or total assessed valuation; in highways, population, area, and mileage. Or allocation may be on some arbitrary basis such as a percentage of collections of a certain tax (liquor taxes in the states and liquid fuels taxes are sometimes so distributed),[39] or the administrative costs incurred in connection with a certain program (social security). Some of these factors emphasize need while others reflect the influence of power and wealth.

Improving the Grant-in-Aid System. From the discussion so far several possible methods of improving the operation of the grant-in-aid system are obvious. The program could be planned and the money distributed where the need was greatest. In many cases the smaller unit could perform the function unaided, if the larger unit would permit it access to adequate sources of revenue. These changes are easy enough to state, but their accomplishment is essential if the American federal system is to be preserved. Preliminary work must, in the mean time, be done along two different lines.

It is urgently necessary to find out as nearly as possible what functions of government are to be performed and at what levels or combination of levels. The existing arrangements are the result of inheritance from the past plus miscellaneous casual additions. There is need for specific information as to exactly what is being done, by what units, and at what levels. It would then be possible to determine which units were best equipped to perform the various functions required and to provide the most efficient service at the least cost. It has been proposed that a temporary National Commission on Intergovernmental Relations be created to conduct such a survey and make recommendations, that the commission be allotted sufficient time and financial support adequate to permit it to do a thorough job, and that a staff officer to carry out such a program be provided for in the Executive Office of the President.[40]

---

[39] See Pennsylvania Economy League, *Liquid Fuels Tax and Grants to Local Governments* as provided in Acts Nos. 320 and 400 of 1945 (Pittsburgh, 1946).
[40] The author developed such a plan at some length in "Readjusting Government Areas and Functions," *Annals*, January, 1940, pp. 203–209, and in "Federal Administrative Areas; An Historical Record of Confusion in Wartime and a Suggested Program of Action," *Western Political Quarterly*, March, 1948, pp. 54–70. Several such measures, the best by Representative Caleb Boggs and Senator Robert C. Hendrickson

Such a survey would certainly include the problem of financial support. It is necessary to determine what portion of the national income is to be spent for public service and what portion of the latter amount should be covered by grants-in-aid. This amount could then be budgeted so that each proper function for which aid is required would receive its fair share of the total funds available. Such an arrangement would tend to bring order out of chaos and to substitute careful planning for haphazard arrangements.[41]

Administrative Controls. The final consideration relates to the methods used by the Federal government in the states and by the states in the local units to enforce the conditions of the grants made by them. Among the more important of these methods are: [42]

1. Inspection and field service
2. Audit
3. Records and reports
4. Role of associations and conferences
5. Control over personnel
6. Antidiversion provisions
7. Threat of withdrawal of funds

No service can rise appreciably higher than the caliber of its field personnel, and no field service, however able its members, can be turned loose to function without some supervision from its central office. Among the various methods by which supervision may be exercised are regular or periodic inspections, or compliance surveys, to ascertain deviations from approved plans and regulations. Another important control device is the requirement of uniform specifications for accounts and the regular submission of designated records and reports. These provide the granting agency a basis for comparing the efficiency and cost of operations in different jurisdictions as well as for observing the degree of compliance with conditions governing the grant. The post-audit of accounts provides opportunity for determining whether compliance with regulations has been observed.

Understanding and support of a program not only on the part of

(H.R. 2389 and S. 810), were introduced in 81st Cong., 1st Sess. Extensive joint hearings were held (and published) by the subcommittees on Intergovernmental Relations of the Expenditures Committees, in May, 1949. This proposal was endorsed by the Hoover Commission and has the support of state and municipal organizations. See the Council of State Governments' Task Force Report for the Hoover Commission, *Federal-State Relations* (Senate Document No. 81, 81st Cong., 1st Sess., 1949).

On these problems, see especially Harris, Joseph P., "The Future of Federal Grants-in-Aid," *Annals*, January, 1940, pp. 14–26.

These are discussed in Key and in Williams.

the public but of the staff that is responsible for administration are one of the most effective means of securing compliance. If the program is to be effective, the field offices must have considerable latitude — within the framework of prescribed policies and procedures — to adapt their methods to local conditions in carrying it out. Under such circumstances control over personnel becomes a very important instrument for securing compliance.

Fiscal controls are, perhaps, most important of all. Most drastic method of control, commonly used only after prolonged disregard of the authority of the supervising agency, is the withdrawal of or threat to withdraw funds. Antidiversion programs have been instituted to prevent the siphoning off of local funds which might be used for the benefit of the aided activity, as for example, in the Hayden-Cartwright Act of 1934. In the states the same device has often been used to compel local units to provide adequate support for school facilities, to correct unsanitary conditions, etc.

SELECTED REFERENCES

The Bureau of the Budget prepared an annotated bibliography, *The Procurement and Disposition of Federal Property* (Washington, 1948); the materials listed below relat chiefly to the state and local levels:

Alabama Legislative Reference Service, *The Disposal of State Personal Propert* (Montgomery, 1946). A brief but excellent discussion of the problem in a partic ular state.

Bitterman, Henry J., *State and Federal Grants-in-Aid* (Mentzer, Bush, Chicago, 1938) A good general treatise on the subject.

Council of State Governments, *Insurance of State-Owned Physical Property in Thirt) six States* (Chicago, 1942), and on the same subject, Everstine, Carl N., *Sel Insurance of State Property* (Maryland Legislative Council, Baltimore, 1942).

House Committee of Expenditures in the Executive Departments, Hearings on the *Fe eral Property Act* (81st Cong., 1st Sess., 1949). The corresponding Senate Com mittee also held hearings on this act.

Illinois Legislative Council, *The Suability of the State* (Springfield, 1944), and on t) same general subject, Kansas Legislative Council, *Claims Against the State* (T peka, 1940), and Shumate, Roger V., *Settlement of Claims Against the Sta* (Nebraska Legislative Council, Lincoln, 1941).

Key, V. O., Jr., *The Administration of Federal Grants-in-Aid* (Public Administr tion Service, Chicago, 1937). Best treatment of administrative aspects of t subject.

League of South Dakota Municipalities, *Insurance Costs and Practices in Gover mental Subdivisions of South Dakota* (Vermillion, 1946), and Wilson, Hilliard] *Municipal Insurance Costs and Practices* (American Municipal Association, C cago, 1939).

McCahan, David, *State Insurance in the United States* (University of Pennsylva Press, 1929). Though old, it is still the only thorough treatment of the subject.

Shumate, Roger V., *Bonding of State Officers and Employees* (Nebraska Legislat Council, Lincoln, 1944).

Williams, J. Kerwin, and Edward A., *Grants-in-Aid Under the Public Works ministration* (Columbia University Press, 1939). Administration of a grant-in program in a depression agency.

On the financial aspects of the grant-in-aid program, see Maxwell, James A., *The Fiscal Impact of Federalism in the United States* (Harvard University Press, 1946), and as related to a particular governmental function, Quattlebaum, Charles A., *Federal Aid to Elementary and Secondary Education* (Legislative Reference Service, Library of Congress, 1948).

On the administration of grant-in-aid programs at the state level, see:

Carr, Robert K., *State Control of Local Finance in Oklahoma* (University of Oklahoma Press, 1937).

Crouch, Winston W., *State Aid to Local Governments in California* (University of California Press, 1939).

Malone, Paul E., *Fiscal Aspects of State-Local Relationships in New York* (New York State Tax Commission, Albany, 1937).

Snavely, Tipton R., and others, *State Grants-in-Aid in Virginia* (Century, New York, 1933).

Stout, Randall S., *State Grants-in-Aid in Pennsylvania* and *Recent Trends in State Grants-in-Aid and Shared-Taxes* (Both, Pennsylvania State College, 1945 and 1948, respectively).

22

ACCOUNTING, AUDITING,
AND FINANCIAL REPORTING

The Accounting System

THERE are several possible solutions of the problem of the location of the accounting function in the governmental structure. A survey by the National Association of State Auditors, Comptrollers and Treasurers disclosed that forty-three states have a centralized accounting office, thus making it possible to secure practically any financial information about the government from a single source. There are a few exceptions, where not all the records are subject to the authority of the central office:

> In seventeen states, accounting is centralized in the office of the comptroller. Seventeen other states have placed this responsibility upon the auditor. . . . In only one state, Vermont, is the treasurer alone vested with this accounting responsibility, while in another, North Dakota, the treasurer and auditor share the responsibility.

The offices of auditor and treasurer exist in practically all states, but the office of the comptroller had been created in less than half of them – twenty-two. The survey concludes with regard to the powers and duties of this officer that

> In more than 50 per cent of the states having a comptroller, he has power to pre-audit claims, post-audit receipts of accounts of state agencies, draw treasury warrants, keep state accounts, and prescribe accounting forms – all functions of the state auditor in other states. In only a few states is there some overlapping of the auditor's and comptroller's duties. . . . A few of the more scattered duties sometimes imposed on the state comptroller are to assist in the preparation of the state budget, to supervise state banks, to apportion interest on school funds, to sell state bonds, to approve pension applications, and to direct the prosecution of officials for financial delinquencies.

Quite in contrast to the nondescript character of this office in the states is the extent to which the General Accounting Office in addition to its auditing functions has succeeded in establishing control of administrative accounting methods in the Federal government. To be sure, this control has been subjected to criticism on the ground that the function properly belongs to the executive. Harvey C. Mansfield, writing in the Report of the President's Committee on Administrative Management, emphasized the fact that "the methods and results of financial management alike should receive the criticism of an external, independent auditor. Yet how can the Comptroller General criticize what he has himself prescribed? And who is to do it for him, since he is responsible to no one?" President Hoover in 1932, several years before the President's Committee was created, recognized the strength of these arguments and recommended the transfer of the Comptroller General's power over administrative accounting to the Bureau of the Budget. The Hoover Commission, although without unanimous agreement, recommended in 1949 drastic changes, including the establishment of an Accountant General in the Treasury "to prescribe general accounting methods and enforce accounting procedures."

Of the board type of organization, the Commission on Administration and Finance established in Massachusetts in 1922 is an excellent example. The Commission consists of a chairman, the comptroller, the budget commissioner, and the purchasing agent. Certain duties are assigned to these men acting together as a commission, and certain others are assigned to them individually. Collectively they exercise complete supervision over all expenditures and over the entire system of accounting, record keeping, etc. This function, of course, is the particular responsibility of the comptroller. The Alabama board which was created the following year is divided into five departments: executive, purchasing, accounting, prison affairs, and state insurance. The Oregon board is ex officio, consisting of the governor, the secretary of state, and the state treasurer — obviously a much less desirable arrangement than that in Massachusetts.[1]

The accounting system may be considered from two angles, that of control of expenditures and that of general record keeping. The function of the budget office is to pass upon the propriety of expenditures and their conformity to administration policies; the function of the central accounting office (which may be a part of the budget office) is to pass upon the classification of expenditures and the availability of funds. This purpose can best be accomplished by accounts kept on an accrual basis.[2] On the record keeping side the function should be cen-

For studies of such boards in other states, see Benson, George C. S., and Litchfield, Edward H., *The State Administrative Board in Michigan* (University of Michigan Press, 1938); Short, Lloyd M., and Tiller, Carl W., *The Minnesota Commission of Administration and Finance, 1925–1939: An Administrative History* (University of Minnesota Press, 1942).

As in Illinois and Ohio; see Sappenfield, Max M., *Financial Administration in the States of Illinois, Ohio, and Indiana*, p. 15 (Abstract of thesis, University of Illinois, 1934).

tralized, and the nature of the records to be maintained should be prescribed by this central accounting office. Preferably this agency should prescribe the accounting forms to be used.

Principles of Government Accounting.[3] While it is true that the general principles of accounting apply uniformly to all kinds of accounts, it is equally true that many of the rules followed in private affairs are definitely out of place when dealing with the public business; at the same time the latter makes some demands upon its accounting system which are not made by privately operated enterprises. The essential differences between public and private accounting rest upon three considerations: in the public business the efficiency of the operation is measured in terms of service to the public, while in private business it is measured in terms of profit; the assets of a public corporation are not in any sense a basis for determining the financial strength of the enterprise, while in private business they are; again, "the necessity for strict limitation of the activities of officers, boards, and appropriating bodies as to the amount and purpose of expenditures puts a require ment on the accounting system not essential to that of a private concern."

With these differences in mind it may be appropriate to recorc some principles tentatively agreed on by a national committee of out standing authorities in the field of municipal accounting. With sligh modification they may be accepted as a set of basic standards for publi accounting at any level.

1. *Centralization of Accounts.* The accounts should be centralized under th direction of one officer, who should be made responsible for keeping or supervi ing the keeping of all financial records and preparing all financial reports.

This does not necessarily mean that all accounts must be kept i one office or at one place. It does mean that all accounts necessary fc the governmental unit concerned should be coordinated and unifie an end which can be attained only when the entire accounting syste: is under the supervision of one responsible officer. What it means n to have a centralized accounting system is vividly told in a report r lating to the city of Pittsburgh.

As late as 1942 Pittsburgh had no department of finance. Becau there was no central administrative accounting system and becau reports were not furnished to the supervisory employees, every c

---

[3] Condensed from an outline of principles of municipal accounting, recommended the National Committee on Municipal Accounting, January 6, 1934, and Morey, Llo "Fundamentals of Municipal Accounting," an address before the Municipal Finar Officers Association.

partment independently maintained and often duplicated its own financial records for limited distribution. The records kept by the city comptroller were primarily a legislative bookkeeping system which failed to provide information for quarterly allotment budget control; on the cost of services, activities, and projects; on the control and distribution of commodities purchased; on what assets the city owned in the way of facilities, equipment, or commodities. "The city, in other words, has no fixed capital accounting." A report prepared by the Western Pennsylvania Division of the Pennsylvania Economy League continues: [4]

These are facts an administrator simply must have if he is to have tools to evaluate the effectiveness with which services are performed. They are facts he must have if he is to assay the assets acquired by the city's money. The absence of a system by which such facts are produced almost automatically brings a train of inefficiency and waste.

2. *Character of the Accounting System.* The general accounting system should be on a double entry basis with a general ledger maintained in accordance with the following principles:

(a) The accounts should be classified in balanced fund groups.

(b) Asset accounts for permanent property not available to meet expenditures or obligations should be segregated from other fund assets and the equity represented by them not included in the current surplus of any fund.

The requirement of the centralization of accounts can be made effective only if the general system be of a double entry character with a general ledger in which all accounts are contained or controlled. "Only through the operation of a general ledger in which all assets, liabilities, and equities appear and in which all transactions finally rest, either individually or in total, can there be assurance that the accounting system is comprehensive and complete and represents a full control over all financial transactions."

3. *Classification of Funds.* A classification of funds, such as is suggested in the accompanying table, is essential in order that the assets, liabilities, and proprietorship of every fund or group of funds may stand out as a separately balanced group of accounts.[5] In meeting this requirement, the accounts of the general

---

[4] *P. E. L. Newsletter*, "A Central Administrative Accounting System for the City of Pittsburgh," June, 1942, p. 3; see also Mayor's Committee on Central Administrative Accounting, *Report*, April 10, 1942.

[5] In this connection Mr. Morey explains that it is essential to understand the meaning of the term "fund." In its narrow sense, a fund is a sum of money or other resources designated to defray expenditures for a certain purpose. In governmental accounting, the term embraces all accounts necessary to set forth the resources, obligations, and net worth or surplus resulting from such a designation. Each fund is a separate financial entity. The use of funds is necessary in government accounting to guarantee the autonomy and integrity of money which is restricted as to purposes for which it may be used.

ledger must be subdivided in such a manner as to set out separately all accounts relating to any fund or group of similar funds. As a result a complete balance sheet may be compiled for every fund, and such an arrangement is essential to a properly prepared financial report.

4. *Budgetary Control Accounts.* The general accounting system should include budgetary control accounts of revenues, expenditures, appropriations, and encumbrances.

The budget is the heart of the financial system of the governmental unit to which it relates. If it is to operate effectively, it must be re-

Classification of Funds for Governmental Accounting Purposes [6]

STATE	MUNICIPAL
Maintenance and operation of state departments and institutions	General fund
Personal service	Special revenue fund
State aid to localities and other statutory payments	Utility funds
	Bond funds
Highway construction and maintenance	Special assessment funds
Social welfare	Trust and pension funds
Unemployment insurance	Agency funds
Receipts by the state and refunds paid by it of taxes, escheated funds, and miscellaneous revenues	Sinking funds
Expenditures of special funds	

flected in and controlled by the accounting system. A budget that is operated independently or in loose relation thereto, cannot be carried out with a full degree of security. The presence of budgetary accounts in the general accounting system is a positive necessity for showing the current fiscal condition of the funds and of the unit. The separation of budgetary accounts from other accounts is not only unnecessary but is a means of encouraging needless duplication of records in some cases and of incomplete records in others. The accounts necessary for budget control include those dealing with estimated revenue, with appropriations, with encumbrances, and with unappropriated surplus. The exact titles may vary but their substance is essential for every governmental accounting system.

5. *Revenue Accounting.*[7] Revenue should be accounted for through the budgetary control accounts. Whether revenue is accounted for on the accrual basis or the cash basis, all items of a nonrevenue character should be excluded from reports of revenue. Revenues should be classified by fund and by source, in accordance with standard classifications.

---

[6] Todd Company, *Positive Disbursement Control Applied to Public Funds*, p. 1 (Rochester, 1940). This is a description of the procedure employed by the New York State Department of Audit and Control.

[7] See Office of the Comptroller, *Manual of Revenue Accounts* (New York, 1942).

If revenue is accounted for on a cash basis, meaning that an item is considered revenue only when it is collected in cash, the reports should be prepared on that basis. If revenue is accounted for on an accrual basis by taking into the accounts each item when it becomes due or a bill is issued for it, the reports should be prepared on that basis. The latter is not only preferable but is regarded by authorities as essential to good accounting.

6. *Expenditure Accounting.* Expenditures should be accounted for through budgetary control accounts and on such a basis as will take into the accounts all material used and services rendered during a given period.

The same considerations which make accrual accounting so desirable in dealing with receipts apply with equal force in expenditure accounting. Of course, the same type of system must necessarily be used for both types of accounts. Suitable provision should be made out of the appropriations of the current period for encumbrances for which material has not yet been received or services have not yet been rendered. Expenditures, like revenues, should be classified by fund, by department, and by activities (and by object, if desired), in accordance with standard classifications.

7. *Cost Accounting.* There should be a system of cost accounting in which costs are allocated to the various activities in the respective departments. This system should be coordinated with the general accounting system.

A system of unit cost accounting whereby the cost of various items of operation in various departments can be accurately determined is highly essential to a good accounting system. Cost accounting is possible only if there is effective control over labor and materials. It provides for adequate time records [8] and for a check on the service of every employee. It provides for handling materials through a central storeroom and for recording them in perpetual inventory records. "The system for unit cost accounting," says Mr. Morey, "should be subsidiary to the general accounting system and should be properly linked to that system. It should not be operated independently from the general ledger but should be constantly balanced to control accounts maintained in that ledger. Only in this way can accuracy and completeness be assured. Only in this way can a budgetary control over work projects be maintained." [9]

There is a widespre: i impression to the effect that such records are prohibited in he Federal service; for discussion of such basis as there is for this belief, see the uthor's *Efficiency Rating Systems* (Legislative Reference Service, Library of Congress, Washington, 1947) and Senate Committee on Post Office and Civil Service, Subcommittee Hearings on *Efficiency Rating System for Federal Employees*, Appendix, p. 185–251 (80th Cong., 2nd Sess., 1948).

Such a system may provide an effective yardstick for management. Uniform county highway cost accounting systems in Minnesota and Wisconsin make possible valuable comparisons between the work of all the county departments in the state, and of the

8. *Property Inventory Records.* There should be inventory records of both consumable and permanent property, and the records of property should be subsidiary to and controlled by accounts in the general accounting system.

The asset accounts of property should be maintained on the basis of original cost, estimated cost if the original cost is not available, or, in case of gifts, the appraised value at the time received. If current valuations are desired for insurance or for statistical purposes, they should be computed independently from the books and not carried into the accounts. It is not necessary to account for depreciation on general government property except for unit cost purposes, unless cash can legally be set aside for replacements.

9. *Accounting for Business Enterprises.* The accounting for utilities operated by a city or for other business enterprises operated by the government should follow the standard procedure employed by similar enterprises under private ownership. The accounting for public institutions such as colleges, hospitals, and libraries, should follow the standard procedure employed by each class of institution.

Accounting Records. In a general survey of the principles of administrative organization and procedure it would be inappropriate to attempt to describe in detail the accounting system in use in any single jurisdiction or to state in detail and in precise terms just what such a system should be. Because of individual differences, such systems vary widely even on essential matters. Many of them are not very satisfactory.

A number of years ago the Public Administration Service made an intensive analysis of the administrative procedures in the fiscal area employed in the states of Kentucky, Michigan, and Rhode Island, together with recommendations for their improvement.[10] This organization took the position that the following records must be maintained: general ledger, journal voucher, daily summaries of financial transactions, encumbrance and expenditure ledger, detailed expenditure analysis ledger, institution ledger, receipts ledger, record of depository balances, and the investment record. It will be observed that in general

---

costs of maintenance for different types of construction. It is claimed that it fosters a spirit of competition between administrators, thereby promoting greater efficiency in all county highway operations. See United States Bureau of the Budget, *Budget Administration,* Training Conference Manual, Section 9 (Washington, 1947), and Olson, Carl A., "Does Your Accounting System Really Work for You?" *Better Roads,* August, 1946, pp. 27–30 and September, 1946, pp. 31–34; Stebbing, R. F., "Uniform Cost Accounting for Minnesota Counties," *ibid.,* March, 1946, pp. 19–22; Thelen, A. J., "Wisconsin Counties Install Uniform Cost Accounting," *ibid.,* March, 1948, pp. 29–30, 42–50.

[10] *Handbook of Financial Administration, Commonwealth of Kentucky,* Chapter 7; *Report of Financial Administration — State of Rhode Island,* Chapter 12.

these requirements are in accord with the principles of accounting and the requirements of fund classification previously set forth.[11]

The practical value of such records may be shown by further reference to the Pittsburgh situation. Where adequate records are not maintained, not only are officials themselves operating in the dark but citizens are unable to exercise their right to analyze and criticize the management of the public business. Such records, in other words, in addition to serving as tools of management serve also as instrumentalities for the popular control of administration. In the Pittsburgh report it was urged that the adoption of proper methods for the administrative control of accounting procedures would have a number of specific benefits that were absent under the system then existing. These objectives, which are listed below, are likewise completely in harmony with the accounting principles previously outlined.

1. *Budget Allotment and Encumbrance Control.* The reports prepared on encumbrances and on quarterly allotments will form a basis for proper current budgetary control and for good budgeting in the future. They will furnish to each department, to the Mayor, and to the City Council, accurate information that will make possible intelligent consideration of all appropriation items.

2. *Commodity Control.* The control outlined will prevent the breakdown of operations due to the fact that required materials are not in stock. It will prevent loss from accumulation of obsolete stock. It will provide a means of using up unusable stocks of one department which can be used by other departments. It will save money by making it possible to reduce inventory to a minimum with safety. It will conserve floor space. It will disclose materials and supplies which are unaccounted for and which the management will therefore have to keep close watch on to see whether discrepancies are due to wastage or to theft.

3. *Purchase Analysis.* Under the proposed plan it will be possible to prepare data which can be used for the reducing of the frequency of ordering, the combining of purchase requirements, the reducing of quantities purchased to a minimum, and the reduction of orders under $25.00 to absolute necessities. It will be possible to tell how much to buy, what to buy, when to buy. This information will make it possible to determine what items should be stored and the storeroom to which such items should be assigned.

4. *Cost Accounting.* The advantages of cost accounting are self-evident. Almost everyone who has any connection with administration knows that operations cannot be carried on effectively without current reports of the costs involved. Operating without cost reports is operating blindly.

5. *Property Records.* There are now no city-wide records kept of the machinery, equipment, or other property owned by the city. Under the present system, equipment can be either lost or stolen with the possibility that such loss may never be known. Under this proposed system, an inventory will be taken of all personal property except commodities included in the commodity control in-

---

[11] For definition of these and other terms commonly employed in the field, see National Committee on Municipal Accounting, *Municipal Accounting Terminology for State, Municipal and Other Local Governments.*

ventory. An identification number will be set up for each item of personal property and recorded in the most practical manner on the item, either by stencil, tag, or other means. It will then be possible to account for all such items and disclose discrepancies due to either waste or theft.

Payroll Accounting. So large a portion of the expenditures of most government agencies is for personal service as to justify some mention of the peculiar problems of payroll accounting. The procedure differs somewhat from that used for other purposes and is often handled outside of the general accounting office. In the Federal service it is definitely regarded as a fiscal rather than a personnel function.

Federal employees are paid every two weeks throughout the year (twenty-six times), with the agency schedules so staggered as to even out the work in Treasury Disbursement. State officers and employees are paid in some states monthly, in others semimonthly. The first step is getting the names officially on the payroll. The signing of the oath of office and the personal affidavit constitute the basis for this action. When it is completed, the personal fanfold can be set up for the new employee in the personnel office.

The evidence required on payrolls includes the separate listing of new positions, additional identical positions, vacant positions, changes of name, and leaves of absence. In each instance the date of appointment must be shown, date of entry on duty, and date of signing the oath of office and personal affidavit. Shortly before the checks are to be issued, personnel change sheets must be filed with the disbursing officer by each department or other employing agency. With this information at hand, payroll vouchers may be prepared. A separate voucher is made up for each department or agency.

The procedure should be uniform for all departments, and it should be centralized, a standard voucher being used for all. The following information is included in the sheet heading of the voucher: the name of department or agency, the name of the division or institution, the number of the allotment or account to which the payroll is chargeable, the name of such account, and the period covered by the payroll. The items entered in the sheet columns should show the name of each employee, the title of his position, the rate of compensation; insurance retirement, and other deductions; and, for salaried employees, the amount payable after deductions have been made. In the case of employees compensated on a daily or hourly basis, the gross amount payable is left blank, for subsequent insertion by the department before the voucher is certified for payment.[12]

[12] Public Administration Service, Kentucky study, Chapter 10, and Burger an Tegnell.

Further steps in payroll accounting include verification (i.e., certification, signature of persons certifying, checking for accuracy, etc.), routing to and from the disbursing office and within the agency, and the use of payroll data as a source for records and reports. The preparation of payrolls is very largely a repetitive process. While it is essential that employees be paid on time, all reasonable precautions must be taken to prevent "check raising" or other forms of defalcation. It does not follow that the work is difficult merely because the need for care, accuracy, and speed is great. A New Jersey survey showed that with the exception of highway department laborers and institutional attendants state employees' pay checks remain constant 95 per cent of the time. Under these circumstances it is evident that the preparation of payrolls lends itself to the extensive use of mechanical equipment.

Mechanical Equipment and Modern Methods. In former times the keeping of public financial records consisted largely of "bookkeeping." But the spectacle of a thin, pale, anemic-looking man, sitting on a high stool with a visor over his eyes, is as out-of-date as are other characteristics of the horse and buggy era. Modern management has found that with a greatly increased volume of work and higher standards of completeness and accuracy antiquated methods made it impossible or excessively costly to get the work done. The survey of payroll accounting methods in New Jersey during World War II pointed out that "the glaring weakness in the present state payroll system is its antiquated, inefficient, and costly preparation procedure," involving reliance on manual repetitive work and other types of inefficient, wasteful, and duplicating effort. The report continued: [13]

Although the state government personnel has increased over fivefold in the past twenty-five years, the payroll preparation system has remained relatively unchanged. During this time, efficient cost-saving devices have been developed and are in wide use, but it would appear that the New Jersey state government administrators and legislatures have been reluctant to adopt these new methods.

The same kind of situation is found in many county offices, where clerks sit day after day laboriously copying by hand documents which could be photostated in a few minutes and at a tremendous saving of time, energy, and money. For these reasons many public agencies at all levels have resorted to the use of mechanical and electrical equipment for their financial and record-keeping operations. Manufacturers of such equipment have developed accounting and bookkeeping machines that can with slight modifications be adapted to the

---

[13] Burger and Tegnell, *op. cit.*, p. 4.

requirements of any record-keeping operation. Company experts in forms and procedures are available for consultation. With their help the management of any department or agency can evolve methods and procedures that will accomplish their particular job at a substantial saving of time and personnel costs and at great improvement in the efficiency of operations.[14]

Auditing

In the Federal government the auditing function is performed by the Comptroller General of the United States; indeed, an analysis of the terms of the Budget and Accounting Act of 1921 would seem to indicate that this was his original and primary purpose. In the states the office of the auditor — variously designated as the auditor, auditor of state, or auditor general — exists in all but five jurisdictions, usually by constitutional requirement. The exceptions are: California,[15] New Hampshire, New York, Rhode Island, and Tennessee. The survey made by the National Association of State Auditors, Comptrollers and Treasurers found that

> Twenty-three auditors are elected or appointed for a term of four years, and seventeen auditors for a term of two years. Thus a total of forty auditors are in office for a four-year or a two-year term. Of the three remaining states having auditors, five years is the term in New Jersey, and no definite term is specified in Nevada and South Carolina.

This same survey disclosed that the number of employees ranged from two in Nevada to 648 in Pennsylvania; it continues:

> Over one-half of the states having auditors employ between ten and fifty persons; four states employ between fifty and 100; and five states employ between 100 and 500. The economic character of the state as reflected in the amount of revenue collected does not seem to explain entirely the number of fiscal employees. The states having less than ten employees in the auditor's office include Delaware, Maine, Montana, Nevada, New Mexico, and Wyoming; the states having more than 100 employees are Illinois, Iowa, Michigan, Missouri, Ohio, and Pennsylvania. On the other hand, New Jersey, Massachusetts, and Wisconsin each have only a staff of fifty employees or less. A more influential factor is whether the auditor's office includes field examiners for the enforcement of some fiscal law or laws.

---

[14] The International Business Machines Corporation has published an elaborate series of manuals, sample copies of which are available on request, setting forth the methods and procedures used in different types of accounting operations as well as in other phases of taxation and finance, personnel administration, and general law enforcement activities.

[15] A special Assembly committee on auditing in California recommended in 1937 a permanent joint standing committee on state audits and accounts, after finding that the state had "no thorough or complete system of auditing and accounting in its administrative departments."

Under the provisions of the New York Constitution the state comptroller is required to audit all vouchers before payment, and all official accounts; to audit the accrual and collection of all revenues and receipts; and to prescribe such methods of accounting as are necessary for the performance of the foregoing duties. The payment of any money of the state or of any money under its control or the refund of any money paid to the state, except upon audit by the comptroller, shall be void. The legislature may define his powers and duties and may also assign to his supervision the accounts of any political subdivision, but it shall assign to him no administrative duties except such as may be incidental to the performance of these functions.

Types of Auditing Work. Accounting has been defined as "the art of recording, classifying, and summarizing in a significant manner and in terms of money, transactions and events which are, in part at least, of a financial character, and interpreting the results thereof." Auditing is defined as "a systematic examination of the books and records of a business or other organization, in order to ascertain or verify, and to report upon, the facts regarding its financial position and its financial operations." [16] These definitions serve to differentiate accounting and auditing and to indicate their respective places in the general accounting field. As Professor Tannery has observed, accounting is constructive and auditing analytical. [17]

There are two types of auditing work — the internal or pre-audit, and the external or post-audit. The first is concerned with the examination of the elements of a transaction before it is completed and recorded in the final accounting records; it is a tool of management, an administrative check upon the accuracy and legality of transactions still in process within the department or agency. Post-auditing, on the other hand, is concerned with the examination of the records after the transactions have been completed and recorded. The Federal government, all but three states (Michigan, New York, and Rhode Island), and most cities provide for such an independent post-audit.

Pre-Auditing. In the Federal government the responsibility for both types of auditing rests in the hands of the Comptroller General. As has already been suggested, it is unfair to management to place the control over spending elsewhere than in the hands of those who are responsible for administration, and it is not logical to have the same officer checking upon expenditures both before and after the transac-

---

[3] Montgomery, Robert, *Auditing Theory and Practice*, Fifth Edition, p. 3 (Ronald Press, New York, 1935).
[7] Tannery, *State Accounting Procedures*. Chapter 14 deals with the post-audit.

tions are completed. When an effort was made to limit the powers of the Comptroller General, tremendous objection was raised, mainly for political reasons. His office had not existed prior to 1921; yet it was now alleged that the pillars of the Constitution would crumble if his sacred powers were changed by one iota!

At the state level the report published by the National Association of State Auditors, Comptrollers and Treasurers indicates clearly the significance of the pre-auditing of expenditures as an aid to budgetary control:

> Three main steps are usually involved in a pre-audit. First, claims are examined to determine if they fall into the proper budgetary or appropriation classification. Then the appropriation account is investigated to determine whether it is sufficient to meet the obligation and whether cash is on hand to pay the claim. Then, the final step is to determine whether the claim presented is a legal obligation of the state or any of its agencies. . . .
>
> Greater emphasis is placed upon pre-auditing for availability of funds and legality of the expenditure, however, than upon proper classification. . . . The comptroller or auditor is usually charged with the pre-auditing duties. In thirteen states, all three pre-audit steps are performed by the comptroller, and in seventeen states by the auditor, either singly or with another fiscal agency. . . . Most of the states having a central accounting office provide that the same agency shall also pre-audit state expenditures. In twenty-nine states, the central accounting office is the main pre-audit agency for all three steps, and in eleven other states the central office is responsible for one or two of the steps. In only three states, Indiana, Montana, and Vermont, is the pre-audit for all three steps performed by an office different from the central accounting office.

Post-Auditing. While the post-audit is primarily an external responsibility, work of this character may be done by either government auditors or private auditors employed by the government, or both. As Professor Tannery explains, an internal post-audit is performed by employees of the organization being audited, who are therefore directly responsible to the administration; [18] an independent post-audit may be made either by the state post-auditing agency, independent of the administration, or by private accountants employed on a per diem contract basis. This, incidentally, is an unnecessarily expensive method. At any rate the independent post-audit must be performed by a person who is not an employee of the administrative organization being audited and who is free of administrative responsibility and influence.

In the Federal government the General Accounting Office, as has been noted, performs both types of auditing work, responsibility for

---

[18] *Op. cit.*, p. 400. A large highway department, for instance, may assign certain employees (field auditors) free of operating responsibilities to the task of determining whether operating policies and procedures are being carried out by subordinates to whom authority and work have been delegated.

which is assigned to the auditor in half the states, to the comptroller in six others, and in the remainder to officials variously designated. The objectives of such an audit, as enumerated by Professor Tannery, are: (1) to provide the general policy making and appropriating authority with a control over administration that does not interfere with its day-to-day functions and operations; (2) to furnish the legislature and the public with an independent appraisal and report of the activities performed by the operating officials; (3) to give the executive a significant check on the work of his departmental staff and advice on current problems of management in which accounting is an important factor, thus increasing the efficiency of the department and the use and accuracy of the state's accounts; (4) to serve as a means of preventing and detecting fraud and dishonesty. While this last item may occasionally be important, it is much less so than the improvements in administration that may result from thorough auditing.

Independence of the Auditor. Sound policy indicates independence for the auditor. He should be relieved of all functions that do not relate to auditing, and he should be completely independent of the executive but not, as in the case of the Comptroller General, of all external authority. It is commonly believed that in order to achieve independence this officer should be popularly elected; but this is by no means essential. Legislative selection is a possible substitute. It has also been assumed that the auditor ought not to be appointed by the executive, although he is so appointed in the Federal government and in some states. Sound policy likewise dictates that the legislature, having made appropriations for specified purposes, should carefully and zealously seek to ascertain that its mandates have been observed. It should also decide whether administration has been economical and efficient. Members of the legislature, who are responsible to the people, should be aware of the burden of taxation.

The report of the President's Committee made no specific recommendation of change regarding the method of selection, but it did propose changes of title in accordance with recommended changes of function. "Since the functions of this officer would be restricted to auditing in the proper sense of the word, 'Auditor General' would be an appropriate title. For the agency that he would head, 'General Auditing Office' or 'Office of the Auditor General' is suggested. This would emphasize the basic theory upon which the substantive changes are made." The report continues:

The powers of the Auditor General should be defined to include audit and investigation, and they should extend to all governmental agencies whatever, unless specifically exempted by Congress. His organization should provide for regional auditing offices paralleling the disbursing system, but they should be under his full administrative control. . . .

Frequency of Audits and Promptness of Reports. The law commonly requires that state books shall be audited annually; this requirement is as often honored in the breach as in the observance. Reference has already been made to California and Pennsylvania; note now the following comment on the practice in Illinois, Indiana, and Ohio: [19]

Investigation has shown that an audit of all state agencies in Ohio is not made annually. The auditing work is done in Ohio and Indiana by staff auditors; in Illinois part of the work is done by staff auditors and part of it by outside auditing firms. Since there are only two staff auditors in the employ of the auditor of public accounts in Illinois, the auditing of the larger and more important state agencies is done by outside firms. The office of the auditor of public accounts is audited annually along with the rest and by an outside auditing firm. The auditor's office in Ohio is not audited annually; it is audited only when one man retires from office and is succeeded by another. Since the auditing agency in Indiana keeps none of the state's accounts and is not an operating agency, it has no important accounts to be audited. However, the department calls in an outside auditing firm annually to make an audit of the receipts and expenditures of the department.

Prior to 1929, when the Fiscal Code was enacted, the situation in Pennsylvania was equally unsatisfactory. Outside auditors were employed to examine the records of the various departments of the state government; the auditor general's department did practically no auditing work. As late as 1934, when the department was doing some of the work it was supposed to perform, it was from one to four years behind in the audit of the various departments, and this in spite of the fact that it was heavily overstaffed.[20]

In the typical auditing procedure the auditor is charged with final responsibility for all disbursements except those from rotating or other funds exempted by law from his control. The value of the work depends largely upon the promptness with which the report is rendered — as any businessman well knows. It is only by a prompt report that those in charge are informed of conditions which need correction and are able to apply corrective measures before substantial losses have been sustained as a result of long-continued use of improper methods. This is particularly true in a governmental organization subject to periodic changes of administrative control. One administration will often have passed into history before any effort is made to audit the

[19] Sappenfield, *op. cit.*, p. 21.
[20] Joint Legislative Committee on Finances, *Survey of the Government of Pennsylvania*, Chapter 3 (Harrisburg, 1934).

accounts of some of its departments. A new administration will likely show little interest in a detailed analysis of the financial transactions of departments prior to the beginning of its term of office, for whose conduct, in a period covered by the audit, they could have had no possible responsibility.

Probably the best solution of this problem is to be found in the continuous audit. With proper organization this is easily possible. Under a centralized purchasing agency all the vouchers come from one source rather than from the several departments. Payroll requisitions follow a generally similar procedure. But the auditor who contents himself merely with verifying the mathematical accuracy of the records is of little use to management. Management needs warning of unusual trends, analysis of factors causing them, and forecasts of their probable effect. One writer has summarized these duties of the auditor and comptroller in five words: Record, Compare, Analyze, Question, Forecast.[21]

Financial Statements and Reports

Only recently has much attention been given to governmental reporting, of which financial reporting is a very important aspect — especially so if citizens are to understand the public business. Alfred E. Smith claimed that he had acquired most of his tremendous knowledge of state government through careful study of the way the state obtained and spent its money. Good financial reporting serves the budgetary process, informing both the executive and the legislative branch and the public about the nature and scope of governmental activity. Since official records are available to government people, informing the public is the most important purpose. The table on page 446 shows two different ways in which public financial reports may be classified.[22]

Professor Lepawsky found that the reports for all the states were varied and numerous; in the biennium 1936–1938 at least 317 separate series came to the attention of the Library of Congress. This is an average of about six and one-half different reports per state. There is some correlation, although not an exact one, between the number of report series in a given state and the number of reporting agencies. Of the latter 304 were discovered, including the names of all the types of fiscal officers found in any of the states and distributed as shown in the table on page 446. A complete list of agencies, by states, is given in

[21] Goldie, R. J., "A Managing Executive's Concept of Controllership," *The Controller*, October, 1945, p. 513.
[22] Lepawsky, Albert, "Financial Reporting by States," in Wilcox, Jerome K., Ed., *Manual on the Use of State Documents*, pp. 47–54 (American Library Association, Chicago, 1940), and City of Wichita, *Accounting Procedure Manual*, pp. 52–56.

Classification of Public Financial Reports

ACCORDING TO CHARACTER OF FINANCIAL TRANSACTION (LEPAWSKY)	ACCORDING TO TYPE OF REPORT (WICHITA)
Revenue — taxes and nontax revenues Expenditures — total for the fiscal period, and by functions, objects, or departments Budgets — estimates and appropriations, and specific itemizations for activities, salaries, and purchases Debts — total debt, funded and short-term debt, interest and debt retirement data	Budget report Annual financial report — presenting a financial picture for and at the close of the fiscal year Quarterly reports — showing expenditures by activity within each fund, and revenues by source within each fund Monthly reports — showing a considerable number of items for each activity appropriation, classified by operating departments Treasurer's financial statement — quarterly, listing for each fund the cash balance at the beginning of the quarter, receipts and disbursements, and cash balance

the Lepawsky article. An exactly parallel situation prevails in the cities. A study made in 1945 in the United States Bureau of the Census, Division of Governments, reported on data received from 364 cities; there were no less than 992 reports put out by 779 issuing departments. Of these, 890 were annual; five were semiannual; twenty-one, quarterly; and seventy-eight, monthly.

Financial Reporting in the States, 1936–1938

NUMBER OF STATES	NUMBER OF REPORTING AGENCIES	NUMBER OF REPORTS ISSUED
1	3	3
2	4	8
11	5	55
14	6	84
10	7	70
6	8	48
4	9	36
48	42	304

From this information it is clear that among fiscal officers there is no clear understanding of what financial reporting is or why it is necessary to make such reports at all. Actually the preparation of financial statements and reports is one of the most important functions of accounting officers. The reports should be designed to furnish information to the general public and to groups especially interested in the financial condition and operation of the government. It is not enough that reports be issued; their form and content is of vital importance. In the past, many of them have been excessively long, frequently containing large quantities of unimportant and nonessential material and usually presenting dreary, repetitious reading.[23]

A great many of the published reports show what has happened, but without supplemental information they do not give a clear picture of what is happening. To do this, it is necessary to know not only what revenues have already been collected and what expenditures have already been made, but approximately how much will be collected and how much may be spent. Then the reader can tell whether his government is tending toward insolvency or whether it is in sound financial condition. Of course, annual reports can be supplemented by monthly or quarterly statements presenting such information as the following, in accordance with the practice of the Federal government and of many state and local units:

1. Balance in each fund at the beginning of the fiscal year
2. Receipts to date by each fund
3. Anticipated payments into each fund during the remainder of the fiscal year
4. Payments from each fund to date
5. Anticipated payments from each fund to the end of the fiscal year
6. Anticipated surplus or deficit of each fund at the end of the fiscal year

Essential Qualities of Financial Reports. The way to improve public reports is to make them attractive, readable, and informative. The first step after convincing public officials of the desirability of a new form of report is to centralize responsibility for its production in one person who should, if necessary, call in professional assistance from a printing house and/or an advertising agency to deal with format, illustration, color, design, etc.

Irrespective of the specific purpose of any one report, high standards of accuracy, clarity, completeness and continuity, and timeliness are obviously essential.[24] Unfortunate and disastrous consequences may result from policies and actions predicated upon inadequate or inaccurate financial data. The analysis of financial transactions must be correct and the component parts of each transaction correctly classified; the use of accounts and account titles must be correct, and uniform

---

[23] Massachusetts Federation of Taxpayers Associations, *Pruning the Municipal Budget,* Part II, Analysis of Staff Functions (Boston, 1942), presents the following list of unnecessary information frequently found in reports of cities and towns in that state: by-laws; departmental reports of receipts and payments; lists of dog licenses, taxpayers in arrears, library acquisitions, voters (poll lists), jury lists, school graduates, births, marriages, and deaths, street lists, hydrant locations — not to mention technical detail n departmental reports and unimportant school programs.
[24] These qualities are discussed in Tannery, *op. cit.,* pp. 290–291; see also Branscomb, nd United States Bureau of the Budget, *Budget Administration,* Training Conference Manual, Section 10 (Washington, 1947).

terminology must be employed to describe the elements of transactions and accounts; and the preparation and processing of supporting papers and documents must be uniformly handled, as well as the asbstracting of facts from the accounts for presentation. Clear presentation involves care and accuracy in the wording of titles so that the headings do not lead one to expect either more or less than the figures justify; and the exact period of time covered by the data should be clearly indicated. To be of most use, statements should be complete in the sense of including data on all aspects of the financial operations without giving such great detail that the reader becomes lost in a mass of minutiae; completeness, in other words, does not demand the printing of every item in every expense account or even the printing of individual expense accounts at all, but rather the totals for various types of expenditures such as those contained in all travel vouchers for the period covered by the report. The usefulness of reports is impaired if there are gaps in time or if the data are lacking in continuity. Furthermore, they must be as nearly up-to-date as possible; the sooner the reports can be completed and distributed after the close of the fiscal period covered, the more likely they are to be of value. Nothing is duller or ordinarily more useless than financial records of transactions long since concluded.

Conditions for Effective Reporting. The requisites for a timely and effective system of fiscal reporting, in addition to a set of financial records maintained in accordance with established principles of governmental accounting, are as follows: [25]

1. A properly organized and integrated fiscal administrative structure for the governmental unit as a whole. It is especially important that the relationship of the central accounting office with other agencies be carefully defined and clearly understood and that the operations of the central accounting office be coordinated with those of the offices of the treasury, budget, purchases, revenues, and personnel.
2. A sound and logical organization within the central accounting office with the duties and responsibilities of the staff definitely fixed and clearly defined
3. A statements and statistical unit within the central accounting office, headed by a person thoroughly trained and experienced in governmental accounting and reporting directly responsible to the chief accounting officer
4. Procedures in the operating agencies and in the central accounting office that facilitate the efficient and speedy processing of documents that relate to financial transactions
5. A trained office staff and modern office equipment for handling a large volume of work with dispatch and efficiency

---

[25] Tannery, *op. cit.*, pp. 291–292.

The United States Bureau of the Budget in 1945 formulated a check list for the evaluation and improvement of fiscal records and controls. It indicated some of the major steps in the administration of fiscal activities which should be examined periodically in each fiscal unit of the departmental and field offices to insure that backlogs of work are eliminated, records are posted to date, payroll deductions are recorded accurately, and all subsidiary records have been properly reconciled. The check list contained a total of thirty-eight questions, all designed to show the extent to which agency records were up to date. This is a prime prerequisite of good financial reporting.

Illinois and Michigan have done noteworthy work in financial reporting. The Illinois Department of Finance has put out several editions of a small volume entitled *The A–B–C of Illinois State Finance*. The annual reports of the Michigan Auditor General are put out in two large volumes attractively designed and executed, the first containing explanatory comments and related financial data in condensed form; the second, underlying financial statements, both in summary and in detailed form. Part II is broken down into three sections, dealing respectively with revenues, expenditures, and appropriations. Monthly financial statements pertaining to the major operating funds are issued in addition, as well as a summary statement in leaflet form for wider distribution.

As for local units, the Director of Finance in Saginaw, Michigan, did an excellent job with his annual report for the fiscal year ending June 30, 1947. Vermont towns, under the stimulus of a state-wide campaign, have responded well. A number of local units in Alabama, Pennsylvania, and other states have obtained assistance in report preparation from their local university bureaus of public administration. There are thus many examples which could be cited of new and improved financial reporting.

SELECTED REFERENCES

Accounting. Perhaps the best authority on governmental accounting is Lloyd Morey who, following several earlier works on the subject, collaborated with Robert P. Hackett on *Fundamentals of Governmental Accounting* (Wiley, New York, 1942). Significant works dealing with accounting problems at the three levels of government are listed below:

Federal: Bartlett, E. F., *Accounting Procedures of the United States Government* (Public Administration Service, Chicago, 1940); Naylor, Estill E., *Federal Government Accounting* (Daniel Press, Washington, 1944); and Commission on Organization of the Executive Branch of the Government, *Budgeting and Accounting*, and Task Force Report on *Fiscal, Budgeting, and Accounting Activities* [Appendix F] (Washington, 1949).

State: Tannery, Fladger E., *State Accounting Procedures* (Public Administration Service, Chicago, 1943).

Municipal: Chatters, Carl H., and Tenner, Irving, *Municipal and Governmental Accounting* (Prentice-Hall, New York, 1940). Important are the numerous publications of the National Committee on Municipal Accounting in Chicago, covering terminology, standard classification of revenues and expenditures, bibliography, etc. Numerous states have issued manuals for their municipalities, among them the League of Minnesota Municipalities, Association of Washington Cities, Nebraska Auditor of Public Accounts; see also the Kalamazoo Bureau of Municipal Research, and the City of Wichita.

Special problems in governmental accounting are dealt with by Fishack, Howard G., and Miller, Loren B., *Mechanical Aids in Tax Accounting* (Newark, 1939); Burger, Alvin A., and Tegnell, G. G., *A Centralized Payroll System for Our State Government* (New Jersey State Chamber of Commerce, Newark, 1941).

Auditing. For references on the work of the Comptroller General, see those listed at the end of Chapter 18. Much less has been written on auditing than on accounting, but the following are of interest:

Bureau of Municipal Research and Service, *Auditing Policies and Practices of Oregon Cities* (University of Oregon, 1942).

Martin, James W., and others, *The State Auditor* (Bureau of Business Research, University of Kentucky, 1942).

Shumate, Roger V., *Proposed Audits for the Departments of Roads and Irrigation and Board of Control* (Nebraska Legislative Council, Lincoln, 1944).

Sikes, Pressley S., *A Manual for County Auditors in Indiana* (Bureau of Government Research, Indiana University, 1946).

On financial reporting

Branscomb, Marjorie S., *A Decade of Improvement in Public Finance Reporting: Guides and Techniques for Improving Reporting* (Municipal Finance Officers Association, Chicago, 1947).

Clickner, Louise H., *City Periodic Financial Reports* (United States Bureau of the Census, Division of Governments, 1946). Shows prevalence of regular financial reporting in the cities of the country.

23

PUBLIC WORKS
AND FINANCIAL PLANNING

THERE are two major aspects of the planning of public works: the planning of the physical structures themselves, and the financial planning to provide the funds required. The second is necessary in order to synchronize public investment with economic conditions, to take up the slack as soon as opportunities for private employment diminish, on the theory that, to use the words of the International Labor Organization's Philadelphia Charter of 1944, "poverty anywhere constitutes a danger to prosperity everywhere." The emphasis in the present chapter will be on financial planning, the budgeting of capital outlays, and the relations of the works program to the general economic situation. Certain questions with regard to building needs which apply to both aspects of planning will be considered first.

Historical Development and Postwar Needs

After long years of neglect many jurisdictions in the era following World War I found it necessary to enlarge greatly their building programs. In the decade of the twenties funds were easy to raise either by taxation or by borrowing. Many states and cities relied upon borrowing, often to the point of exhausting their borrowing capacity. After interruption in the early part of the depression, spending for public works continued on a still larger scale during the late thirties — then, however, largely with Federal funds, for the states and cities with shrunken revenues and little or no free borrowing capacity were in no position to finance the extensive construction program which their own needs or the seriousness of the depression required.

Thus it was that in the interval between the two World Wars considerable progress was made in the more adequate housing of public offices, institutions, and agencies. Whereas the Department of Public Works in New York spent on an average $3 million a year before the consolidation act, it afterward spent on an enlarged program approximately $65 million annually. Enlarged building programs were going forward in many states; the list which follows is more illustrative than comprehensive. All of this construction — and more — took place within the capital cities; in addition there were office buildings to house activities in the field, and improved facilities at institutions.[1]

Louisiana, Nebraska, North Dakota, Oklahoma, Oregon, and West Virginia each erected new main capitol buildings.

Massachusetts erected a new office building across the street behind the capitol, and connected it with the main building by means of a viaduct over the street.

New York erected a thirty-two story office building at the rear of the capitol.

Ohio erected a new office building and a building for the Supreme Court.

Pennsylvania began the construction of a group of four office buildings, the last of which was completed in 1938.

Tennessee put up a new state office building and a new Supreme Court building.

West Virginia completed two office buildings.

Construction Program After World War II. The needs for public building and construction after World War II surpassed anything known in the history of the country. In the field of highway construction, the current needs were tremendous. The motoring public, in which most of the general public is included, wants more and better roads. The highways built during the twenties and thirties are now kept in service only with increasing maintenance costs, and many of them are in serious need of reconstruction. Repair and maintenance are consuming so large a portion of motor fund receipts that there is little left for new construction, and new construction of the types now desired is far more expensive than ever before not only because of increased costs of labor and materials but because of more elaborate design. The public wants wide, limited-access superhighways or "free ways" with cross traffic eliminated for through travel, and expressways which avoid local traffic through congested areas.

The needs of public institutions are likewise tremendous. Many factors have contributed to the growth of populations in medical and surgical hospitals, mental hospitals, and welfare and correctional institutions. The population of the country has increased. Minimum standards of care are much higher than formerly. Many types of cases, once neglected, are now subjected to treatment. Provisions for the housing

---

[1] The following are representative reports during this period: Maryland State Planning Commission, *Ten Year's Expenditures for Public Works, 1924–1933* (Annapolis, 1936); Minnesota State Planning Commission, *Report, 1931* (St. Paul, 1931); Missouri State Building Commission, *Report No. 1* (Jefferson City, 1934); Smith, Alfred *Progress in Public Improvements* (Albany, 1928); Oregon State Planning Board, *First Report on the State Capitol Building Program* (Salem, 1935); and *A Report on State Building Needs in Salem and Capitol Group Planning* (Salem, 1936).

and care of the "wards of the state" have rarely if ever been adequate, and in many jurisdictions, both state and local, the overcrowding and neglect have been a disgrace to a supposedly civilized society. Not only do existing structures provide a totally inadequate amount of space and number of beds, but the buildings themselves are so unsafe as to constitute a safety hazard to patients or inmates and staff alike. In many cases repairs and remodeling are no longer possible; new construction and expansion are the only answer.

In education, also, building needs are great. Space needs, of course, are constantly changing because of shifts in population and increase or decrease in the school population in particular age groups or communities. After a period of declining figures, it now appears that as a result of many wartime marriages most communities must look forward to meeting the need for increased school facilities during the coming years. The load will soon reach the elementary schools, and in a few years more it will be felt in the secondary schools. Particularly in suburban communities the need at the secondary school level is already acute, buildings now housing twice as many students (or more) than they were originally planned to accommodate.[2]

Other urgent needs include office space for governmental agencies at all levels; the development of air transport facilities, including airports, terminals, and landing strips; water systems, sewers, and sanitation facilities; parks and recreational projects — to mention only a few. One may readily envision the magnitude of the task if he recalls the size of the program of the Public Works Administration in the depression era or if he examines any of the current state reports on approved projects.[3] In all these fields new construction was practically suspended

See "Report of the Executive Director to the Board of Managers," of the Council of State Governments, *State Government*, January, 1945, pp. 4–5. At the same time, the largest first-class township in Pennsylvania was warned by the Middle States Association of Colleges and Secondary Schools that its senior high school might lose its standing as an accredited secondary school the next year, on account of inadequate facilities. The building, put up to accommodate 700 pupils, now houses a registration of 1,900. Other nearby townships face conditions that differ only in degree.

See, for instance, Colorado State Planning Commission, *The Ten-Year Building Program, 1937–1947, of the State Institutions of Colorado* (Denver, 1945), and *The Building Program of the State Institutions of Colorado* (Denver, 1947); Maryland Commission on Post-War Reconstruction and Development, *Maryland Post-War Public Works Program* (Baltimore, 1945) and *Six-Year Capital Improvement Program for Maryland* State Planning Commission, Baltimore, 1947); New York State Postwar Public Works Planning Commission, *Approved State and Municipal Projects* (Albany, 1945); the latter requires seventy pages for the mere listing of the projects throughout the state. Council of State Governments, *Public Works in the States* (Chicago, 1945) and Applebee, Inez A., and Rothenberg, Leon. "City Capital Outlay from 1937 through 1943," Bureau of the Census, *City Finance, 1943*, April, 1946, entire issue, contain much valuable information.

during World War II, and even necessary and urgent repairs which would in normal times have been made without question, were held at an absolute minimum.

Some Aspects of Physical Planning

Two major aspects of physical planning will be considered here: the function of over-all planning, carried on by city and state commissions, so far as it relates to planning the building construction program; and the more detailed planning of the structures themselves by the art commission, state architect, or department of public works.

Over-all Planning. Unlike many developments in American government which have begun at the top and filtered down, over-all planning began in the cities, appeared next in the Federal government, and spread from there to the states under the impetus of Federal aid. City planning commissions have functioned in many communities throughout the country during the present century, but the idea failed to gain acceptance at the upper levels of government prior to the early thirties. In 1932 President Hoover's Committee on Social Trends recommended the establishment of a National Resources Planning Board, which was created by President Roosevelt by Executive Order in 1934. This Board, functioning under various names, made a significant contribution to American civilization by its studies of the human and natural resources of the nation, until by a shortsighted action of the Congress in 1943 funds for its continued existence were withheld. The Board concerned itself with over-all trends and planning, not with the details of individual construction projects.

The spread of planning among the states was rapid during the middle thirties, largely because of Federal encouragement and aid in the form of financial grants and loan of personnel. Planning commissions, both state and local, are commonly composed of five, seven, or nine members appointed by the chief executive for a term of three years. Often the law provides for a number of ex officio members from such departments as finance, public works, or natural resources, the remainder consisting of lay members. Provision is also made for a director and staff to perform the technical work.

In the states the planning and development agencies in nearly all jurisdictions have tackled not only the over-all problems of their respective areas but the building and construction needs of the various departments, agencies, and institutions. As World War II wore on toward a conclusion, many states — some of which had abandoned their planning commissions when Federal aid for the purpose was disconti ued — established new commissions for postwar planning. In some cases, as in Pennsylvania, this move resulted in the duplication of facilities which could have handled the new problems of reconstruction quite adequately. In California in 1943 the legislature went so far as to abolish the State Planning Board, creating instead a State Reconstruction and Re-employment Commission to which were assigned all powers, duties, and jurisdiction of the State Planning Board as well as duties relating to reconstruction and the aiding of returned veterans. In 1947 the legislature abolished this agency and established in its place the Office of the Director of Planning and Research.[4]

Again, in this connection, Federal aid provided an important stimulus. During the war the President established the Public Works Reserve to assist the state and local units in the development of their capital investment plans and to develop a unified fiscal policy for all levels of government. Its function was to secure and prepare information and estimates to be used in the establishment of a reservoir of useful public projects to absorb the expected postwar unemployment — which was long delayed. Although the funds allotted to it were small indeed, the agency became the victim of hostility on the part of many members of Congress, which refused to appropriate for it only one and a half years after its establishment. The abolition of this agency, along with the National Resources Planning Board, left the United States without any Federal agency "with authority and funds for the planning of public investment on a national scale."[5]

Regardless of the level of government involved, the primary and fundamental purpose of a master plan is to guide the unit in its future growth and development. Such a plan must be carefully prepared. It should be easily comprehended and draw the outlines of the state or city of the future. Its intent is to coordinate all future improvements so that the utmost efficiency and economy can be realized. The plan, once adopted, should be amended and revised as often as changing conditions may require if its value as a guide is to remain unimpaired. In this way all improvements will become an integral part of the over-all master plan.

The Virginia State Planning Commission thus describes the various

For up-to-date information on the financial support of all these agencies, see *Expenditures and Budgets of State Planning and Development Agencies, 1946–1949* (Association State Planning and Development Agencies, Chicago, 1948).

For an excellent account of PWR, see article by Higgins, Benjamin, "The United States Public Works Reserve," *International Labor Review*, November, 1944, pp. 581–2. The Bureau of Community Facilities of the Federal Works Agency (now General Services Administration), however, took over some of the duties of PWR: see its *Report on Plan Preparation of State and Local Public Works* (Washington, 1946), and Advance Planning Regulations.

steps in developing a building construction program for the city of
Richmond: [6]

The work done by the City Planning Commission in the past four years has
been of immense value to the city. It has gathered and made available in convenient form pertinent data which is constantly being used by both the administrative and legislative branches of the city government in reaching a decision on the merits of many proposed projects involving the expenditure of public
funds. The Planning Commission, in the preparation of a comprehensive plan,
has taken a long range view of the future city and has endeavored to lay out and
chart all improvements in advance of their needs so that these may be executed
in an orderly and economical manner, consistent with the city's ability to finance.

Simultaneously with the studies now being made by the Planning Commission,
the Department of Public Works was recently called upon to submit a program
of capital improvements covering the entire needs of the city for the first four
postwar years. After canvassing all departments of the city government, and receiving from them a list of recommended projects, tabulation and summary of
cost was made wherein it was found that practically every type of improvement
common to urban development was listed, totaling in estimated cost a little
more than $21,000,000.

A breakdown by departments, showing general type of improvements and estimated cost for each department for a four year period is as follows:

Public Works: Opening and widening streets, general street improvements, paving, bridges, sewers, airports, parks, swimming pools, incinerators, flood control, etc.	$ 9,855,000
Public Utilities: Gas and water production and distribution, electric power and street lighting	4,765,000
Public Safety: Three new fire engine houses, fire fighting equipment and underground signal system	444,000
Public Health: Health Center, six clinic buildings, and improvements to Pine Camp Hospital	1,360,000
Public Welfare: New City Home, and replacement of city market	1,000,000
Public Library: Seven new branch libraries	360,000
Public Schools: Construction of new Technical Institute, four new school buildings, and additions to two existing schools	3,650,000
GRAND TOTAL, all departments	$21,434,000

Planning of Individual Projects. In former times little attention was
paid either to planning or to the appearance of public buildings; it was
customary to determine how much floor space would be required and
to put a wall around a sufficient number of square feet to provide it
with suitable openings for doors and windows. This may have been

---

[6] *Municipal Planning Institutes,* Section 3, *Planning for Public Works,* pp. 3-4 .(Richmond, September, 1945).

sufficient in a day when the energy of the people was devoted to the settlement and development of a new continent, but it is by no means satisfactory in a country with an advanced civilization. Many capitol buildings were expensive and ornate but were so poorly planned as to provide wholly inadequate office facilities for expanding governmental services. Most jurisdictions have since provided some agency — a state or city architect and/or art commission — to pass upon appearance and aesthetic qualities before construction is begun.

In the Federal government this work is part of the responsibility of the Bureau of Public Buildings. The State Art Commission in Pennsylvania, created in 1919, may be taken as a representative state organization. It is composed of five members, appointed by the governor, with power to examine and approve or disapprove the exterior design and proposed location of all public monuments, buildings, and other structures as well as private structures proposed to be erected on state or municipally owned land anywhere in the Commonwealth other than in first and second class cities. It supervises the erection and construction of certain memorials that involve the services of a sculptor. This Commission has reviewed and approved, over the years, hundreds of plans submitted by architects, as required by law, to a total value of many millions of dollars. It collaborates with the engineers of the Department of Highways in the designing of bridges, and with the Department of Public Instruction in the development of "standard" designs for various types and sizes of public school buildings.

The Commission, instead of merely approving or disapproving the designs submitted to it, has acted as a consulting body, offering constructive criticism in the form of pencil studies and the like whenever it seemed advisable to do so. The suggestions have been offered with the idea of reducing costs and in most instances improving appearance as well; and they have effected savings to the county, borough, municipality, or the Commonwealth itself. In the prewar years the quality of architectural designs improved greatly, due in some measure, no doubt, to the influence and efforts of the Commission. In general, architects have come to recognize the value of this service to the public bodies of the state as well as the benefit to the profession resulting from unbiased criticism of the designs. The Commission is entirely separate from the Department of Property and Supplies, which has charge of actual construction.[7]

In New York the Department of Architecture became a division of the Department of Public Works after reorganization in 1927. This

---

[7] See Joint Legislative Committee on Finances, *Survey of the Government of Pennsylvania*, pp. 313-314 (Harrisburg, 1934).

agency has important responsibilities in connection with the planning of construction. In some jurisdictions, however, planning has been done by special legislative committees, by commissions authorized by legislative act, or by other departments. The Division of Architecture in the California Department of Public Works has been functioning since 1907 and is the agency through which all the obligations of the Department in connection with some fifty or more state departments and institutions are discharged. Its duties include preparing all plans and specifications, superintending construction of new buildings, and remodeling or repairing old ones. It designs and installs all heating, lighting, ventilating, refrigerating, water supply, mechanical and electrical plants, landscaping, and water engineering of various types.

Financial Planning

Former Absence of Capital Outlay Planning. In the past the methods for allocating funds for new construction as well as for the rehabilitation of existing structures were largely haphazard. Each project was built as a complete entity with little or no relation to any other public work. No one knew what the real needs were, for there were no plans.[8] Department heads competed with each other for available funds, and they as well as pressure groups lobbied among the members of the legislature for their favorite projects. Local newspapers and organizations took sides in public debate in which the project either became an issue in an electoral campaign or culminated in a popular referendum. In either case all too often the result was that, instead of placing funds where they were most needed and where they would do most good, they were placed where the pressure and influence were strongest. It was a case of the wheel that squeaked the loudest getting the grease.

This system — or lack of system — was widespread. Its results were obviously unsatisfactory. There was no assurance that needs would be met in the order of or in proportion to their urgency or even that urgent needs would be met at all. Some businesslike plan under which funds were allocated in accordance with need and in which the government received a full dollar's worth of value for every dollar spent, was

---

[8] For a contrary view, see Goodrich, Carter, "National Planning of Internal Improvements," *Political Science Quarterly*, March, 1948, pp. 16–44. Goodrich contends that while the term "economic planning" came into general currency recently, economic planning itself is no new thing in American history, citing especially the movement for internal improvements in the first half of the nineteenth century. On the history of planning in the United States, see Gaus, John M., "The Planning Process in Government," in McCormick, Thomas C., Ed., *Problems of the Postwar World* (McGraw-Hill, New York, 1945), and Linford, Alton A., "Public Work and Fiscal Policy in the United States," *Social Service Review*, September, 1944, pp. 295–317.

imperative. It has been suggested that the requirements of such a plan were fourfold: [9]

1. That care be exercised to determine that every building project undertaken actually is needed
2. That provisions be made for over-all long-range plans to meet the state's building needs from the standpoint of the state as a whole
3. That a system of priorities be set up to determine which building projects come first
4. That sound provisions be set up for maintenance

There was not only gross carelessness in the selection of projects but even greater laxity in the determination of fiscal arrangements. In the absence of a capital budget making annual provision for some portion of the construction needs of the government, reliance has been placed upon bond issues, and a substantial portion of the burden has thus been shifted upon the taxpayers of future years. This has been justified by a number of arguments: (1) that the cost was too great to be borne in a single year but could be more easily disposed of if spread over a number of years; (2) that capital improvements are services which will be utilized over a period of years, as a result of which payments for them should be made as the benefits from them are derived; (3) that benefits from construction made by one generation of taxpayers may extend into the life of another. Therefore, they say, it is proper for those who benefit to share in the cost.

These arguments in themselves admit the lack of a planned program of expenditures. Dr. David H. Kurtzman has given a clear statement of the disadvantages of the older established procedure: [10]

With a proper master plan and the automatic inclusion of a capital outlay program in the annual budget, what is there to gain by prolonging the liquidation of the liabilities? What is the difference between raising revenue for a current improvement or paying for an improvement made sometime in the past? Certainly, so far as the taxpayer is concerned, he gains nothing from such an arrangement. On the other hand, he stands to lose by long-term financing. Every municipality must pay for the convenience seemingly gained from bond issues. Even in the days of low interest rates, a serial bond of $1,000,000 bearing an annual interest rate of 2½ per cent will cost $387,000 in interest before final maturity. If term or sinking fund bonds are sold, the interest cost would amount $750,000 less the earnings of the sinking fund investments. Bond issuance involves, in addition to interest charges, an annual state tax of four mills, the cost of advertising, cost of printing, and cost of legal opinions. In addition, there is the cost of bookkeeping necessary to keep track of all the bond funds and sinking funds.

Edward Staples, executive director of the Missouri Public Expenditure Survey, quoted in *National Municipal Review*, November, 1945, p. 515.
"Financial Planning," *Progress* (published to promote the Pittsburgh Plan), October, 1948, p. 3.

Elements of Financial Planning. The preparation of plans and specifications for public works projects well in advance of actual construction is a new approach to the problem of economic stabilization, the
object, of course, being to obtain a shelf of useful projects that can be
put under way the moment privately financed construction lags. No
plan for such construction can be made for any community unless certain elementary facts are available: where the government obtains its
money, what it is used for, how much debt there is, and how much
debt may be legally incurred. One must know also what economic
resources the community has; this factor, along with the community
income, will largely determine the kind of program that can be carried
out. Finally, one ought to know whether the community has any financial plan or objectives already established or whether it has been merely
drifting along toward whatever chance happens to bring.[11]

The next requirement is that there should be a comprehensive survey of existing facilities and of present and future needs. This determination may be made by the departments and agencies concerned or
as a result of legislative investigation. When the information is available
for all agencies, a program of capital budgeting can be worked out by
the planning commission. The size of the program, when finally completed, will depend upon many things: the size, wealth, and population
of the governmental unit; the extent of the building needs; the extent
to which the cost is to be borne out of current revenues or is to be met
through exercise of the borrowing power. At any rate such a plan will
show what the needs are, how they can be met, how long it will take
to meet them, and what the cost will be.

It is important to emphasize the fact that such a plan rests not on
guesswork and favoritism but on careful analysis of the best data available in the light of the best interests of all citizens and all parts of
sections of the state or city. Since it is impossible to accomplish so
vast a program all at one time, a priority system based upon degrees of
urgency must be established. Such a system will probably be to some
extent a compromise between the desire to meet first needs first, regardless of the department or agency concerned, and a desire to give
recognition at an early date to the most urgent needs of all departments.

The plan must also provide for maintenance. In the past, many public buildings, and buildings for private institutions as well, became virtual white elephants in the hands of their owners because no provision
had been made for maintenance and repair. In some types of building

---

[11] Chatters, Carl H., *Financing Local Improvements*, p. 1 (Bulletin No. 22, American
Public Works Association, Chicago, 1944).

this is an extremely important item, and failure to provide for it may impose an almost impossible burden on current revenues. In late years some private institutions have even gone so far as to refuse gifts of buildings unless an endowment fund of suitable size is provided for maintenance.

The actual operation of this procedure may be illustrated by further reference to the experience of the city of Richmond, as recounted by the Virginia State Planning Commission: [12]

Our next step (after completing the tabulation of projects and summary of cost) was to call upon the City Comptroller for an analysis and forecast of the city's income and expenses over a like period of time in order that a program of construction may be adjusted to the city's ability to pay. With this information at hand, and having in addition thereto the benefit of the over-all long range views of the Planning Commission setting forth an orderly and coordinated scheme of proposed improvements, the city authorities are peculiarly well equipped to formulate and adopt, at this time, a program of postwar construction for execution immediately following the cessation of hostilities.

It is generally conceded that the city is in no position, financially, to carry out at the end of the war, a program of public works construction costing in excess of $5,000,000 annually. Curtailments of projects recommended by various departments will, therefore, be necessary in the belief that a minimum program of approximately $3,000,000 per year for the first four years is possible of accomplishment, since the latter sum is more in keeping with that which has been expended by the city within the past two decades prior to the beginning of World War II, and that a program of public works improvements in Richmond adjusted to its ability to finance and in harmony with its future plans, should be adopted now for the immediate postwar period.

Summarizing, we in Richmond, through studies and preliminary plans made, are in position and prepared as never before to formulate and adopt in advance an intelligent postwar construction program. We have carefully inventoried our needs in the order of preference. We are in position to adjust urgently needed capital improvements to the city's ability to pay for such improvements. The work done by the City Planning Commission in analyzing and recommending the future needs of the city serves as an invaluable guide in the integration and coordination of a public works program which would be in harmony with the orderly development of the proposed master plan of the city, even though such plan has not yet been officially adopted by Council.

The Timing of the Public Works Program

The physical and financial planning of the public works program, indispensable though that is, solves only half the problem. As a result of experience between two World Wars, our people have learned that there is a right way and a wrong way to execute the programs. In the boom period of the twenties both states and cities engaged in extensive building operations. It is true that the need was great, for World War I

Op. cit., p. 5.

had interrupted construction for public purposes, as war always does, and there had been a long period of neglect before that.

Lessons From Experience Between 1920 and 1940. While most of the construction may have been desirable, it had not been properly planned, and it was not all necessary — at least under the circumstances. Some of it could have been deferred. There were three major defects in the procedures followed at that time: the now familiar lack of over-all planning, the method of financing, and the timing in relation to the general economic conditions then prevailing. These last two items require additional comment and explanation.

There is always a disposition to believe that borrowing is the best and easiest way to obtain public improvements. Sometimes it is necessary when the total cost of the improvement is greater than can be met from current tax receipts, but it is seldom the best and never the cheapest. When it is used, great care should be taken that the life of the bonds does not exceed the probable life of the improvement. The tendency to resort to borrowing is further encouraged by the unwillingness of legislators to impose new taxes or to raise the rates on existing taxes. The idea generally prevails that by borrowing, the other fellow will have to pay the bill. Current taxpayers get the benefits of the improvement and escape much of the burden of paying for it. In the twenties both states and cities acted upon these erroneous conceptions. Although economic conditions were good and taxes could have been increased, both states and cities borrowed, often to the full extent of their borrowing capacity and to the verge of impairing their credit standing. When they could have raised taxes, they did not. When they should have conserved their borrowing power, they exhausted it.

The public improvements of the twenties were unduly expensive another way. In a boom period, construction costs are high because there is competition for the available supplies of labor and material. Employment opportunities are good. Labor is scarce and wages are high. The cost of materials is high and profits are high. Beyond the minimum of absolutely necessary construction and repair, why should government in such a period enter into a highly competitive market, making it still more competitive by bidding for labor and materials already scarce and thereby contributing to inflationary tendencies already well under way? The simple fact is that it should not, but that is exactly what it did.

Then came the great depression of 1929 and the years following. The states and cities desperately needed their borrowing power to meet the ever-growing demands for relief. While these demands increased, tax receipts declined. The fixed charges on a heavy debt thoughtlessly incurred in a period of prosperity consumed a steadily increasing percentage of the meager tax revenues they were able to collect. These units had, by their own action, brought themselves into a situation in which many defaulted on their obligations and many more escaped defalcation by the narrowest possible margin. Had it not been for the timely assistance of the Federal government, the state and local financial situation would of itself have become a major national catastrophe. The Federal government made huge expenditures for public works whose contribution to recovery was, as Harold D. Smith reports, large, but not decisive." The 1933–1938 average of $1.6 billion a year was nine times the yearly average of 1925–1929, "yet the increase in Federal expenditure was almost entirely offset by a sharp contraction of state and local expenditures for construction, a contraction necessitated by severe declines in revenue, unfavorable bond-market conditions, and lack of reserves." [13]

Program for the Future. This analysis of developments in the interwar period has been thus extended because it provides a basis for the establishment of certain principles which, it is now believed, should guide policy in the years ahead. These are:

Development of a long-range plan for capital improvements
A year-by-year program covering work to be done and the method of financing it
When economic conditions are good, hold public construction to a minimum and pay the cost of such improvements as nearly as possible out of current tax receipts plus any grant-in-aid that may be available for the purpose.
When economic conditions are poor, speed up the public construction program, lowering taxes if necessary and making use of the borrowing power to carry forward large projects that will help take up the slack in private employment and increase the demand for construction materials, heavy machinery, etc.

In other words, in good times prepare for bad. Long-range programming and the establishment of protected reserves will help governments through depressions without "cramping their style" in boom periods.[14] By the exercise of such foresight they can so protect their financial standing that they will not, when and if the next depression

The Management of Your Government, p. 130 (McGraw-Hill, New York, 1945).
See Nourse, Edwin G., "Public Administration and Economic Stabilization," *Public Administration Review,* Spring, 1947, pp. 85–92; and Parker, William S., "In Good Times Plan for Bad," *National Municipal Review,* January, 1948, pp. 13–15, 68, and "Programming Municipal Expenditures," *Journal* of the American Institute of Architects, August, 1946, pp. 59–63.

comes, have to travel to Washington, hat in hand, in search of financial assistance.

In 1945 Major General Philip B. Fleming, formerly Administrator of the Federal Works Agency, appointed a Public Works Construction Advisory Committee to study the problem of timing public works construction as a measure for stabilizing the construction industry. The conclusions of this Committee were summarized in their report as follows: [15]

1. Substantial good can result from a well-organized program for increasing th volume of construction during a period of depression by advancing the timin of sound public works projects that have been fully planned for ultimate cor struction although the immediate need for them may not be imperative.

2. Relatively little reduction in the total volume of construction is to be ol tained at the crest of an upswing in the economic cycle by deferring cor struction of public works.

3. Completion of plans and preliminary arrangements for an adequate volun of local public works in advance of the need for them depends upon ava ability of funds for the purpose. We believe that the current policy of advan ing Federal funds, to be repaid when the work is undertaken, to local gover ment agencies for the purpose of planning is helpful and that this progra should be continued with adequate appropriations.

This Committee, noting that the construction industry has expei enced extreme fluctuations far more pronounced than the upward ar downward variations in the over-all economy, emphasizes the fact th by "stabilization" it does not intend to imply stagnation or freezing the total construction volume at any given level, either high or lo "The contemplated objective is the adoption of measures, under o competitive economy, which may lessen the extremes of fluctuati that have characterized this great industry in the past. If the heights uncontrolled peaks, such as have occurred in the cycle, can be reduc and if the valleys can be partially filled, the result will be a health tendency toward stabilization."

It is also worth noting that the construction industry is one of t largest segments of the country's economy, comprising approximat one eighth of the national income in periods of prosperity. Public c struction comprises about 33 per cent of the total construction. If could be "stabilized" to some degree, it would contribute greatly the stabilization of the country as a whole. During the large road-bu ing program in Pennsylvania during the thirties, it was estimated t for every man employed in actual construction work there was a ch

15 "Timing of Public Works Construction as a Measure for Stabilizing the Cons tion Industry," American Highways, January, 1946, pp. 7–8, 18–19, 22, and Ge Fleming's address on the subject in Better Roads a few months later.

of five men given employment in industry to supply equipment and materials. If this estimate was even approximately accurate, it is obviously important to the well-being of the national economy that governments should do all they can by correlating their construction plans with the indexes and analyses of general business conditions.

The achievement of such an objective is no simple matter, as the Committee clearly points out:

Experience has shown that there is an unavoidable lag between the conception of any construction project and the time when construction can be started. Plans must be prepared, legal difficulties overcome, sites acquired, contracts let, and all of these steps are time consuming. Frequently, preparations for construction take longer than actual construction. This has an important bearing on the long-term problem of using public works to sustain construction activity. In order for public works construction to be effective as a means of stimulating the industry at a time when the trend of activity is downward, it is vital that projects be ready for prompt starting of construction. Hence, it is highly important that an adequate volume of projects be fully planned and ready for prompt initiation in time of emergency. Such projects should be useful in character, and ultimately necessary, although the immediate need may not be imperative. With a continuing volume of such projects, normally scheduled for building from year to year over a period of three years, it would be feasible to advance the timing of some to swell the volume of construction.

By way of general conclusions the Committee says:

Evidence favors adoption of a policy of stabilization through effective timing of public works. This does not mean that public works should be subjected continuously to deliberate manipulation as a means of attempting to control business activity or labor conditions. It is anticipated that private and public construction will continue unhampered and in favorable relation to each other during long periods. Only at times when the approach of critical conditions can be recognized should regulation be introduced. In the past, public works have been undertaken on much the same basis as private construction work, namely, on the basis of apparent need, ability to finance, and willingness to undertake the work at a given time. Experience has been that when times are prosperous both private and public works have gone forward in increasing volume and that when times are dull they had dwindled together. The objective should be a modification of these historic tendencies.

Private enterprise should take the lead in construction, being supplemented by necessary public work. Through intelligent timing of public works, there would be brought about a regulated supplementation of private endeavor with the result of a more uniform flow of construction and substantial stabilization of the construction industry. That would be a constructive accomplishment.

Many difficulties beset the administration of such a program. One is the peril imposed by periodic threats of change — if not actual changes — in administration. Such programs, carefully worked out, are business plans which ought to be largely exempt from partisan manipulation, but this is not always the case. When so-called surpluses have been accumulated and earmarked for public works construction, further questions are bound to arise. When is the proper time to spend? Are prices right? Is the necessary man power available? Will materials be diverted from more important needs? Clearly, some flexibility must be provided in the administration of such a program. Effective controls such as have been employed in New York since 1945 are necessary. The Budget Director in that state reports: [16]

For two years prior to 1947, all appropriations for capital outlays except for highways, grade-crossing elimination and housing were subject to release or certification of availability by the budget director so that a program-wide, uniform policy could be maintained in weighing the urgency of projects against all the questions of prices and shortages. In 1947–1948, all capital outlay programs are restricted by the requirement of a budget certificate of availability before construction can proceed so that proper timing of all capital programs can be maintained. Ordinarily these questions would be settled before the appropriations were made, but now it is necessary for a sound financial program that appropriations exceed the amount of construction that should take place in one year

SELECTED REFERENCES

American Public Works Association, *Financing Local Improvements* (Chicago, 1944). *The Status of Public Works Planning and Its Relation to Full Employment* (Chicago, 1945) — and other publications.
Bemis, George W., *Coordinated Public Works for Metropolitan Los Angeles* (Haynes Foundation, Los Angeles, 1945). Public works planning in one of our largest cities
California Reconstruction and Reemployment Commission, *Study of Timing of Public Works in California* (Sacramento, 1946) — and other publications.
Chamber of Commerce of the United States, *The Use of Public Works to Sustain Construction Activity* (Washington, 1945). Gives somewhat grudging assent to the idea.
Clark, John M., *Economics of Public Works Planning* (Brookings Institution, Washington, 1945). Competent analysis by a leading economist.
Council of State Governments, *Public Works and the States* (Chicago, 1945). A study made for the guidance of the states at the close of the war.
Federal Works Agency, *Report on Plan Preparation of State and Local Public Works* (Washington, 1946). Report on a small postwar planning program, carried on for a time during the war.
Gayer, Arthur D., *Public Works in Prosperity and Depression* (National Bureau of Economic Research, New York, 1935). One of the earliest studies of this important problem.
Lorwin, Lewis L., *Time for Planning* (Harpers, New York, 1945). A strong and effective plea for intelligent planning; see also Villard, Henry H., *Deficit Spending and the National Income* (Rinehart, New York, 1947).
Waterman, Patricia L., *The Role of the States in Postwar Aviation* (Bureau of Public Administration, University of California, 1945). Includes consideration of place of this important function in the planning program.
Wootton, Barbara, *Freedom Under Planning* (University of North Carolina Press, 1945). Provides an answer to the much publicized *The Road to Serfdom*, F. A. Hayek (University of Chicago Press, 1944).

[16] Burton, John E., in a symposium on "Budgetary Control Over State Expenditures" *State Government*, May, 1947, pp. 138–140, 153.

PART IV

INTERNAL MANAGEMENT
AND CONTROL

24

PLANNING: POLICY FORMULATION

In the analysis of administration so far, the problems of over-all organization, including staffing and financial organization and control, have been considered. Part IV is concerned with getting the job done, that is, with the problems of internal management and control. These involve the use of the combined personnel and financial resources of the agency, within the established organizational framework, for the accomplishment of whatever functions have been assigned to the agency by law. This is production, whether it be letters typed, hearings conducted and concluded, or objects manufactured. It involves both administration and management, which are the core of the whole administrative process.[1] All that has preceded has been designed to make possible the accomplishment of this basic objective.

The task of management in carrying out an agency program involves five principal aspects, which constitute the subject matter of the several chapters of Part IV. A failure of management in any one of these areas will seriously hamper if it does not defeat the success of the undertaking. These areas are:

1. Planning: determining what is to be done and how it is to be done
2. Organization: the adaptation of structure to function
3. Production: turning out the finished product
4. Supervision: establishment of the necessary controls
5. Leadership: the responsibility of management for giving direction to the undertaking, and guidance and encouragement to the staff

Administrative Planning

'If we could first know where we are and whither we are tending," Abraham Lincoln is reported to have said, "we could better judge what to do and how to do it." Since modern concepts of management had yet to be developed, probably Lincoln did not visualize this as planning, yet that is clearly what he had in mind. Planning, in its simplest terms, is orderly preparation for administrative action. It is necessary if

---

On the basis of Glaser's theory that administration is concerned with "what," management with "how." See his book, p. 70, and later in this discussion, pp. 477-478.

decisions are to bear any relation to reality, for decisions must be based upon some forecast of the future. "If action in accordance with the forecast is to be methodical and orderly, purposeful, and not at the mercy of each new circumstance," says Urwick, "there must be a plan." [2]

Planning as a basis for agency management involves no less than five different phases: the determination of purpose, policy, procedure, progress, and program. Planning as to purpose involves attention to aims and objectives. Planning of policy has to do with establishing guides to action. Procedures planning is concerned with determination of the methods by which the desired results are to be attained. Progress planning involves the development of yardsticks for the measurement of achievement. Program planning is the consolidation of all these into a master plan for the operation of a program or an agency as a whole. It is important, however, that planning should not attempt to go too far into the technical details of operation.

Purpose: Aims and Objectives. Let it be assumed that a law has been passed establishing an important new function, which may be assigned either to a new agency or to one already in existence. The first step now is to determine in broad terms what the aims and objectives of the organization ought to be, and then to divide the function or project into major tasks and to assign priorities. The nature and complexity of this procedure depends largely upon the character of the act. Long ago Freund pointed out the possibility of distinguishing roughly three grades of certainty in the language of statutes of general operation: "precisely measured terms, abstractions of common certainty, and terms involving an appeal to judgment or a question of degree. The great majority of statutes operate with the middle grade of certainty." [3] Approaching the problem from another angle, Hart distinguishes four

---

[2] *Elements of Administration,* p. 34. Planning means different things to different people — a fact which causes confusion in any discussion of planning. There are city planning, economic planning, natural resource planning, and various other types. Management planning is to be clearly distinguished from each of these. As regards natural resource planning, formerly carried on by the National Resources Planning Board and still carried on by various state planning boards, see Millett volume, and Durr, John F., "State Planning and Development Agencies," Part 3, Multi-Purpose Planning and Development Agencies, *State Government,* June, 1947, pp. 172–178; Merriam, Charles E., "The National Resources Planning Board: A Chapter in American Planning Experience," *American Political Science Review,* December, 1944, pp. 1075–1088; and Rockwell, Landon G., "The Planning Function of the National Resources Planning Board," *Journal of Politics,* May, 1945, pp. 169–178.

[3] "The Use of Indefinite Terms in Statutes," *Yale Law Review,* March, 1921, pp. 437–455, and his *Administrative Powers over Persons and Property* (University of Chicago Press, 1928), both cited in Wayne, A. R., "Ethics and Administrative Discretion," *Public Administration Review,* Winter, 1943, pp. 10–23.

grades of administrative discretion, as follows: discretionary, judgment passing, fact finding, and ministerial. The point is that agency planning must be carried on strictly within the limits provided by the statute. Whatever those limits are, they must be flexible and capable of adjustment to changing conditions.

Policies: Guides to Action. When it is determined what is to be done, it becomes necessary to decide how it shall be done; that is, to distribute and assign personnel and to schedule operations within the limits of the man power, facilities, and time available. Decisions — important policy decisions — must be made in rather general terms regarding the methods to be employed in realizing the objectives; for example, whether enforcement is to be sought mainly through education rather than through prosecution. Work plans must be developed and approved, work units set up, and time schedules and deadlines established. When this task has been done, the available personnel must be distributed according to manning tables, and equipment must be assigned. As much as possible of this work must be done in advance, although modifications based upon actual work experience will almost certainly be necessary. In other words, management must translate the activities into specific programs by forecasting the volume of work, its location, and the clientele to be served, in the light of (1) the aims and objectives that have been determined and (2) the resources of money, man power, and skill available to get the job done.

In order to do any type of planning successfully, the planning staff must be provided with all essential information. Henry Fite has well illustrated the need for basic data in dealing with the goals of "how much," "how soon," and "how well." [4] Assume, for instance, that a city-wide chest X-ray program is to be conducted to try to identify the tuberculars before they have gone too far for successful treatment.

If we were to tell an analyst to design a procedure to carry out this mission, and tell him nothing more, I do not think he could do it. There would be some questions he would have to ask. He would have to ask: "How complete a job do you want done?" "Do you want every single man, woman, and child in the city of Albany examined?" "How much money do I have to spend on it?" and "How soon must it be done?" "Do you want it done this year, or can this carry over until fiscal '52?" All of these things are things that he has to know. That is what I have in mind in saying that procedures must be designed both in the light of program goals and administrative goals.

Scheduling, as has been indicated, is controlled largely by legislation. Dates are prescribed by law for filing income tax returns and for

---

[4] Address in *The Role of the Planning Staff in State Agencies*, p. 6.

the renewal of licenses for notaries, real estate brokers, barbers, and cosmetologists and for motor vehicle and operators' licenses. Within the statutory framework, however, scheduling is a means of spreading peak loads, determining time cycles or limits within which operations should be performed. It is a standard device for preventing workloads from piling up on one another, a device which may also provide the basis for making shifts of personnel from one unit to another as the workload shifts. For other than volume operations, it means primarily the setting of completion dates based upon workload, performance, and personnel data, or sometimes merely determining priorities in long-range programs.

Procedures Planning. The planning of the practices and methods by which the desired results are to be attained — the designing of operating procedures — may be achieved through the use of surveys, job analyses, work-flow charts, and questionnaires. The broad objective of the procedural planning unit is to promote efficient production and build up morale through (1) the clarification of duties and responsibilities; (2) securing agreement as to acceptable standards and methods of performance; (3) giving employees at all levels an understanding of operating objectives and their relations to policy decisions. The activities of such a unit may include any or all of a wide variety of procedures, such as spot investigations; over-all surveys of a whole section or of the activity of several sections; studies of structure; occasional reviews of administrative orders, instructions, or other documents of administrative application; consultation with regard to new forms, and a systematic review and improvement of existing forms; and miscellaneous studies.

Most of these activities, it will be observed, call for surveys of one type or another. Surveys, which may be made by function, by units of organization, or by flow of work, according to the requirements of the moment, are necessary in order to obtain basic information. The methods used in survey planning likewise are many and varied. Job analyses by function, by units of organization, by project, or by administrative sequence, may all be useful; such analyses, including review of work, make possible the outlining of new operations and procedures or the improvement of existing ones. Sample organization, process, or work-flow charts may be constructed on the basis of physical layout, of the processes involved, of the forms and equipment required, or of the time involved. Questionnaires, conferences and interviews, and hourly records of work performed may all be used. Other methods include extended observation of all operations and activities, usually in small units and for a limited period of time; investigation of forms, papers, and reports required; or the study of files and case histories of operations similar to the one under observation. Many of these devices are time consuming, but the careful analysis of operations involved in working them out often reveals weak spots which can be discovered in no other way.

Over-all surveys of operating procedures in several sections or divisions, carried on simultaneously, may give consideration to such matters as simplicity of procedure, clarity of instructions, methods of avoiding or clearing up arrearages and backlogs, duplication of effort, full utilization of mechanical equipment, cost, and availability of existing or proposed material and of personnel. Where the survey is directed toward a study of organizational structure rather than of procedure, some of the significant questions cover the jurisdiction of the several units, lines of authority, span of control, coordination of related activities, staff facilities and services, lines of (and opportunities for) promotion, and adequacy of personnel for positions presently existing or contemplated. If the service is an expanding one, flexibility is an important factor.

Occasional reviews of administrative orders, instructions, and forms may serve a very useful purpose. Such items have a strong tendency to multiply, often with little or no consideration of what has gone before. They should be examined for internal consistency and for conformity with existing policy and with administrative practice and requirements as well as for consistency in relation to other pronouncements of policy and general timeliness and suitability. Just as the codification of statutes brings to light many inconsistencies and provides opportunity for clarification at many points, the same type of beneficial result may be expected from the careful study of agency rules and regulations. Analysis of forms often reveals an amazing duplication, which can be kept under control only by constant watchfulness and periodic review.

The procedural planning unit may be called upon to make miscellaneous studies. It may be asked, for instance, to standardize the reports of supervisors in order that they may be compared with one another. Office layout and office management, including the use of mechanical equipment, is another type of study it may undertake. But there is little use in making such surveys unless the constructive suggestions emanating from them are put into effect. In such a case two specific steps are necessary: (1) instruction and assistance must be given to line supervisors in the installation of the required changes; (2) there must be follow-up to see that action has been taken by the various supervisors. Where a modification of records and forms is involved, changes should not ordinarily be made without consulting other departments or agencies that may be concerned, such as the budget office, the personnel office, the central statistical office, or the division of administrative management.

Progress: Measurement of Achievement. Progress planning involves the development of yardsticks for the measurement of achievement. This is possible through setting standards for unit production, standards of quantity and quality, of job methods, and of reporting units for control purposes. Such procedures, which will be considered more fully later in this chapter, will enable management to evaluate accurately the existing performance and to forecast personnel needs for the future.

The procedural planning unit may be called upon for assistance in developing standards of quantity, that is, production measurements. In some work this is not difficult because simple counting of completed units is all that is necessary. Where the work is more complicated, as in the handling of legal matters extending over a long period of time, suitable techniques may have to be developed. A different type of measurement problem is presented in the development of standards of quality: How well is the job being done? What are the minimum requirements of satisfactory performance? Such standards may have been developed by the personnel office in administering the efficiency or merit rating system.

Program Planning. Program planning is the consolidation of all other types of planning — determination of aims and objectives, policy, procedures, and measurement of achievement — into a master plan for the operation of the agency program as a whole. With these matters disposed of, management is in a position to settle many of the over-all problems, such as budgeting expenditures and determining space and equipment requirements. It can develop plans for the direction and supervision of personnel and for reporting the accomplishments of its employees on the job. Reports may be in terms of quantity (production reports) or in terms of quality, describing the character, significance, and effect of the work performed. Both types of reports may be of great value later on in the justification of budget requests.

Where a program is already in operation, the indication of need for clarification or change of procedure usually appears in the form of unreasonable delays, accumulation of backlogs, backtracking of papers and other work units, or the development of conflicts between organizational units regarding authority. Once the decision is made to do intensive work in this field, the first step is to gather essential background information through systematic analysis of existing operations, the preparation of process charts, etc.

In making a systematic analysis each operation must be examined to ascertain its purpose. Each must be broken down into its component parts in order to determine its necessity, its relation to the whole, the time consumed in its performance, the supervisory approvals required, and other pertinent factors. Process charts help the investigator to visualize the actual functioning of the operation. They enable him to detect lost motion and the relations between different parts of the procedure and to follow the logical sequence of the procedure.

Areas of Planning

ADMINISTRATION (WHAT)		MANAGEMENT (HOW)
DIRECTIVE (*Top Level*)		
	With	Determine frame of organization
Define major objectives	} respect	Assign major fields of activity
Establish basic scheme of operations	to	Locate and define general channels of responsibility and coordination
Establish general policies and standards of accomplishment	major functions	Establish administrative procedures (in broad terms)
ADMINISTRATIVE (*Middle Level*)		
Break down operations into specific functions and projects		Make specific assignment of duties to subordinate units of organization
Set standards of accomplishment; quantity and quality		Establish specific procedures
		Time and schedule operations
Assign priorities within organization and major divisions		Provide means of observation and direction
OPERATIVE (*Bottom Level*)		
Divide functions and projects into tasks		Assign tasks to individuals
Assign priorities within units		Establish work procedures
Specify individual and group jobs		Establish flow and timing of tasks
Prepare plans of unit production (work budget)		

The procedure in planning a new program depends to a large extent upon the level for which the planning is being done. Actually there are three types — directive planning at the top level, managerial planning at the middle executive level, and operative planning at the bottom level. Each has its distinguishing characteristics; for purposes of comparison these have been indicated in the table which appears above.[5] Urwick enumerates six characteristics of a good plan, namely, that it [6]

1. Is based on a clearly defined objective
2. Is simple
3. Provides for a proper analysis and classification of actions, i.e., that it establishes standards
4. Is flexible
5. Is balanced

---

[5] Based on Glaser, *op. cit.*
[6] Urwick, *op. cit.*, p. 34.

6. Uses available resources to the utmost before creating new authorities and new resources — really a special application of the principle of simplicity

Installation of a Program

New programs come into existence in various ways. They may be the result of the work of the planning staff, they may be proposed by the head of an operating unit, or they may grow out of the employee suggestion system. Unless they do originate with the planning unit, they should be studied by that group to detect possible defects and possible conflicts with the established policy of the agency, to determine exactly what changes will be necessary if the proposal is adopted, and to secure from higher authority whatever authorization may be necessary.

Tentative schedules on personnel, equipment, supplies, and space, as well as tentative procedures, are usually adopted for a trial period. Several different types of organization for the testing of a new plan are possible. The first is to set up an experimental unit — a "pilot unit." Such a unit is nonproductive; its purpose is solely to see how the plan works and to discover the "bugs" in it. The second type is a complete installation on a small scale to take over some separable portion of the regular workload. Another type — a risky one in a large organization — is to make a complete installation, taking over for the entire organization the full load of the work in question.

At the end of the trial period a decision will have to be made regarding the adoption of the new plan. Operating manuals or instructional materials prepared for the trial period will have to be carefully examined and revised in the light of experience. Operating schedules will have to be set up in cooperation with the planning unit, for personnel, including induction and training; for equipment, including purchase and installation; for supplies, including purchase and storage; and for obtaining and preparing necessary space.

Many special problems are likely to arise during the period of installation. For instance, can actual operations be started during this period so that the new program can be started gradually? If the new program requires less personnel — which is a common goal in such changes — what is to be done with the excess? Can they be placed elsewhere in the organization or must they be terminated? How and when does training in operating (not installation) procedures begin? Who will assume responsibility for answering questions and clearing up "bugs"?

It requires leadership and driving power to put a new program in operation, especially when it is a substitute for previous procedures. Without leadership, older employees who resist change are likely to give grudging cooperation, if indeed they do not attempt to sabotage the whole program. In this way many a good plan never has a chance to be put into active operation. Sometimes the failure is due to a lack of understanding which in turn may be ascribed to failure to sell the program to the employees. Whatever the reason, planning data are of little use unless they are put to work.[7]

Production Controls

Success in an administrative enterprise is dependent upon competent leadership at the top level and an informed and cooperative working force. The top executive should be free to deal with policy, to confer with the heads of his operating units, and to promote coordination. For the performance of these duties he should have intelligence, courage, decisiveness, a technical mastery of the field, and the ability to work with people — for that is a major part of any executive's job. There must be delegation of adequate authority and a system for enforcing the accountability of supervisors. It is all very well to define objectives, to lay out a concrete program, and to set up a fine organization for carrying it out, but someone has to make sure that the whole thing is operating according to plan. There must be a mechanism for control.

The purpose of this mechanism is to provide management with the information it must have. It must know that the program being carried out is the program that it planned to have carried out, that it is more or less on time, that it is operating within allowable limits of expense and within allowable limits of quality. Management also needs to provide itself with data from the outside about the impact of the program on the community it is trying to serve, to make sure that the program is relevant and is effective with respect to the need it is supposed to be meeting. There must also be information on internal operations, information which indicates whether the limits on cost and quality are being observed.

Since information is of little use unless it is analyzed, interpreted, and applied, the need of a staff of specialists qualified to do this work is indicated. The head of any large organization will readily agree that all members of his top management group — staff executives, department heads, and operating officials — should have a uniform understanding of the answers to certain basic questions. Carlson lists five such ques-

---

See, for instance, Crawford, J. C., "Putting Planning Data to Work," *Better Roads*, May, 1948, pp. 21-22, 34-35, in which it is argued that local road administrators will make more rapid progress in solving their problems by increasing the use of traffic, financial, road-inventory, and other data collected by the state-wide highway planning surveys, and that joint planning activity will link state and local officials with new bonds of confidence and understanding.

tions and suggests the basic tools through the use of which the answers should be found; the corresponding procedures are suggested, for the most part, by Taylor.[8] The two are combined in the table which appears on this page. A management staff to handle these matters is essential in a large organization because the task becomes too large for the top executive to handle. The authority resides in him, but it is hu-

Basic Procedures and Tools of Sound Management

QUESTIONS	PROCEDURES	MANAGEMENT TOOLS
What are we doing?	Analyze the organization Operating method Structure and staff Procedures	Organization manuals
Where is it done?	Analyze the workload Work reporting Standards Types of work	Functional charts
Who does it?	Set up production planning mechanism Tools Routing Scheduling Dispatching	Organization charts
When is it done right?	Set up control procedure Basic process of control Controls and indexes	Standard practice instructions
How well are we doing it?	Set up standards of performance and yardsticks for the measurement of achievement	Periodic appraisals of performance

manly impossible for him to do all the work. Hence he has a personnel office, a budget office, — and a management staff, the size and type of which will vary according to the size of the organization, the nature of its work, the ability of the chief executive to utilize staff aides, and other factors.

Organization Manuals. The organization manual should clearly indicate to both management and the working force "what we are doing." It should, says Carlson, "outline clearly and definitely the nature and extent of the objectives, the policies, and the activities of the organization as a whole; the various activities and functions of all organizational

---

[8] See Carlson, Dick, "Five Basic Tools of Sound Management," *Personnel Administration*, March, 1947, pp. 16–17; Taylor, Herbert O., Jr., "Production Planning and Personnel Administration," *ibid.*, July, 1947, pp. 49–51, 57; and Werolin, A. E., "Effective Controls for Top Management," *Advanced Management*, September, 1947, pp. 120–12 Hoslett, Schuyler D., uses a similar list in *Aspects of Army Post Administration*, p. (American Historical Company, New York, 1945).

units; the relationships of organizational units to one another and to the organization as a whole, and their crisscrossing channels of communication. It should also explain the scope of authority, the duties and responsibilities of each major position within each organization unit," so that:

1. All channels of communication, up and down, are perfectly clear
2. The relationships and interrelationships of each position and each organizational unit are commonly understood
3. The different ranks of authority and the range of duties and responsibilities carried under each title are defined
4. Gaps in responsibility do not occur in certain areas of activity
5. Overlaps of responsibility are correctly interpreted, justified duplications of effort are understood and are integrated into the whole activity
6. A uniform interpretation of the breakdown of all activities into organizational units is readily available

There are scores of such manuals in existence. In 1946, for instance, a procedures manual was prepared for the State Law Section of the Legislative Reference Service, Library of Congress, covering a detailed description of the functions of the Section, the basic tools required, and the procedures preliminary to indexing and digesting state laws, compiling digests of laws for publication, compiling the biennial *State Law Index*, and answering inquiries involving research. Such a manual is usually issued in preliminary form to facilitate correction and revision. The finally completed manual should be put out in loose-leaf form so that it can be readily kept up-to-date. The work of preparation is valuable — if for no other reasons — because it requires careful analysis of procedures and exact statement of their nature and purpose. Such a manual is extremely valuable in training new employees, but there is always the danger that older employees will look at it and put it away so carefully that they seldom refer to it.[9]

Charts: Functional and Organizational. The value of charts in informing the staff "where it is done" and "who does it" arises largely from the same sources that contribute to the value of all visual aids. People do not always fully comprehend or remember what they read, but they seldom forget pictures or graphic presentations. Probably the first thing that most new supervisors do is to study their organization and the charts that have been made of it. New employees likewise find such charts helpful in gaining an understanding of the place of their unit and their own place as individuals in the organization as a whole.

Manual of Instructional Materials for the Staff, State Law Section, Legislative Reference Service (Washington, 1946); Miller, Ray, "Evolution of a Wartime Procedure Manual," *Public Administration Review*, Summer, 1946, pp. 228–234.

A good functional chart presents "in graphic form for ready reference by operating personnel, a composite picture of the activities and functions of the organization and the relationships of all organization units to each other and to the organization as a whole." Work-flow charts may be made on the basis of physical layout, processes involved, forms and equipment used, and time involved. An organization chart, on the other hand, indicates unit by unit the positions — with the grade, salary, and name of the incumbent in each case — established to carry out the activities described in the functional chart. Thus the two types of chart supplement each other, as both supplement the descriptive material contained in the organization manual.

Standard Practice Instructions. Before specific instructions can be prepared, operating procedures and control procedures must be developed, for obviously no one can describe processes that are as yet unknown. Procedures have been defined as the physiology of organization.[10] Operating procedures will be formulated in line with the objective sought; control procedures will be designed to insure, so far as possible, the accomplishment of these objectives. The standard practice instructions which try to show "when the job is done right" describe the best way of performing each specific part of each job. They are, says Carlson, "simply well organized write-ups of established methods of carrying out the work performed by each organization group and each separate function or operation." These, he continues, serve the threefold purpose of instructing new employees, guiding old ones, and informing other organizational units whose work must be coordinated with that of the program under consideration.

Periodic Appraisals of Performance. The answer to the last question suggested by the chart — "How well are we doing now?" — calls for a periodic appraisal of performance, sometimes called a Performance Appraisal Program. It does for an operating unit substantially what merit rating does or should do for the individual employee. In both cases predetermined standards of performance should have been established. The evaluation then consists in comparing what is actually being done with what the standards indicate should be happening. "Such a systematic performance evaluation program," says Carlson, "is recognized as one of management's most effective means of improving supervision and improving the performance of the organization as a whole in the

---

[10] Waldo, in Marx' *Elements of Public Administration* (Prentice-Hall, New York, 1947), points out that they may also be viewed as laws of activity and as institutional habits.

attainment of the objectives and results established by top management."

The designing of these systems for management should be the task of the planning staff. As one writer has expressed it, they are nothing but procedure, and the organization and methods man is in the procedures business. Some of the more important tools of appraisal include the work measurement system, the system of administrative reports, the quality report system, the cost control system, measures of effectiveness, and in general all those other things that management must have to evaluate the performance of its organization. Each of these items will now be given brief consideration.

Work measurement in government is relatively new. It represents the application in the public service of the time and motion study concepts initiated in industry by Taylor and developed since by the Gilbreths, Mogenson, Carroll, and others. Until the period of World War II, when work measurement programs blossomed out under various guises and in numerous places, the subject was always more or less taboo in the Federal service. The basic question may be stated in very simple terms: How long does it take to do how much? Most of this information is actually available to management in its regular operating reports, but during the war the program was emphasized and promoted under such names as functional budgeting, time distribution study, job methods analysis, and the Army work measurement program.

Administrative or operating reports are a basic tool for the control of operations. They are to be confused neither with statistical reports (how much revenue was collected, how much has been paid out in claims, how many took examinations, how many inmates are there in institutions) nor with annual or biennial reports which usually present statistical material as well as a summary of operations. Operating reports provide management with a day-to-day, week-to-week, or month-to-month report of actual work conditions with regard to each major operation. They show the amount of work on hand at the beginning and at the end of the report period, and the number of employees engaged in it. They enable management to maintain a constant check on volume of work in relation to time schedules, arrearages, and the like; to detect changes in workload or in productivity of the staff; to compare present with prior workload and performance and with that upon which the budget was based.

The appraisal system must show not only how much work is being produced but how well it is being done. For this purpose quality reporting is necessary. It will show materials spoiled, work rejected, cases returned for correction, etc., depending upon the character of the work. Some errors are inevitable and are to be expected, but when the percentage rises above the minimum determined to be reasonable, it is a clear indication that something is wrong. It may be poor supervision. It may indicate that training is needed, that materials are of inferior quality, or that procedures should be modified.

Cost controls are another important means of appraising the effectiveness of an organization; because of their importance, they will be considered at greater length in the section which follows.

There are many other measures of effectiveness — measures which may be applied primarily as gauges of over-all performance, the quality of that performance, and adherence to the scheduling of time or cycles. These measures may take the form of monthly or quarterly reports and are prepared on a cumulative and comparative basis. The reports cover such items as the following: [11]

> Percentage of work processed within the time limits set
> Percentage of forms pre-addressed for public use actually used and percentage which had to be returned for additional information or be processed as an exception
> Percentage of delinquency in payment or reporting
> Percentage of appeals from determinations or decisions
> Percentage of machine spoilage and machine idle time
> Comparison of the cost of an operation with the return from that operation, if it is measurable

Measures of effectiveness should indicate the long-range value of operations in terms of results achieved and policies applied. They can be used for over-all evaluation of effectiveness and the determination of areas where operations should be studied.

Personnel and Fiscal Controls

In the two preceding Parts of this volume, the systems for organizing and administering controls over personnel and fiscal matters have been presented. There is no need for repetition here, but it is urgently necessary that one tie into his thinking about planning, the personnel and fiscal aspects of the subject. If the administration is to function efficiently, all three phases of the management job — administrative planning (which includes organization and procedures), personnel planning, and fiscal planning — must be drawn together into an effective working whole.

The administrative planning function in its government-wide aspects is carried on by the staff of the chief executive. Similarly, the

---

[11] Quoted from *The Role of the Planning Staff in State Agencies*, p. 14.

central personnel agency is responsible for the government-wide planning and administration of the personnel program, and the budget office is responsible for the fiscal program. Since each of these functions is so vital a part of operations, important responsibilities with regard to each of them devolve upon the operating units. Accordingly, in each such department or agency one finds along with a planning staff a personnel office and a budget office. The decentralization of authority in these fields does not stop here. The operating units of these departments or agencies may not have separate offices for the performance of these functions (although the larger ones do), but the managerial and supervisory staff must constantly be concerned with problems in these areas.

Personnel Planning. No organization can function without staff. It has been said, in fact, that matters relating to personnel may consume as much as 90 per cent of a supervisor's time. His is the responsibility for setting in motion the machinery for filling vacancies, making promotions, transferring personnel from one unit to another, and assignments and reassignments within a unit. While these things are done at the operating level, the agency personnel office is responsible for reviewing the actions to make certain that each is in accord with the established policies of the agency and with the over-all policies of the government. In the planning of any new operation or in the expansion of an existing one, there should be the closest cooperation between the personnel office and the operating officials in the development of such personnel aspects of the program as recruiting assignment and training.

Financial Planning. Similarly, in the field of fiscal affairs responsibility for budgetary formulation and execution seeps down from the top through every level of supervision, each supervisor working with his immediate superior in the organization, until the plan finally evolved for the department or agency becomes a part of the over-all financial plan for the government. As Professor Dimock has pointed out,[12] the tendency now is for budget planning to be carried on (1) on a democratic basis within the organization, all levels of management participating, (2) on a continuous basis throughout the year. More than that, such planning should be closely integrated with organizational planning and with personnel planning, for the close interrelationships of these three factors render impossible any satisfactory planning in any one of these areas without regard to the other two.

Planning in any one of these fields has to be evaluated in terms of social purpose and objectives. Sound budgeting must be defensible in terms of administrative organization and management efficiency and

The Executive in Action, Chapter 11.

also in relation to the personnel requirements of the agency. The personnel program must fit into the agency organization and into the financial resources available for carrying on its work. Likewise organizational planning must take account of the money and man power resources available. No one of the three can be considered as something remote and apart from the flow of execution; each is actually a part of management itself. Every plan, be it organizational, procedural, budgetary, or personnel, must pass the test of feasibility within the agency.

Thinking particularly of budgetary planning, Dimock raises a series of related questions which must be satisfactorily answered:

What will be the effect upon the organizational structure and the efficiency of operation if the requested expansion is favorably acted upon?

Is it possible to secure the trained personnel needed for the desired increase?

Will the expansion improve the efficiency of operations or have the opposite effect?

Would it be better to combine two low-paid positions into one paying more?

If this new position is created, will jurisdictional lines be sharpened or dulled?

If the new position is that of a technician, would he be appointed at a different level or position in the hierarchy and thus serve a larger area of the organization with a saving of funds and effort?

Instead of increasing the number of positions and the expenditure, would it be possible to achieve the same results by improving the efficiency of the organization and methods of management?

Because of the close interrelationships among these important phases of the planning process, it will be noted that many of these questions relate as much to one phase as to another.

Decision Making

Decision making is the selection, from two or more reasonable possibilities, of a course that will, at the time and under the circumstances, provide the most suitable solution of the problem at hand. The adoption of one possibility necessarily implies the rejection of alternatives. The choice is rarely between a perfect answer and an answer wholly bad; it is more a matter of choosing among different shades of gray. But decisions there must be. Failure to make them when necessary or inability to make them wisely will produce poor administration.

Decisions are made at all levels of supervision at every stage of the administrative process. Theoretically the importance of the questions decided declines gradually as one moves from the top downward. Questions that are passed up to the top are supposed to involve basic policy. The more competent the supervisors at the various levels, the fewer will be the questions that have to be sent up for decision or review.

It should be remembered that there are two major types of decisions: one is concerned with problems of internal management within an agency, the other with problems arising in the field of external relations, such as questions of policy and interpretation in law enforcement work. The present concern is with the first type; the second will be considered in Part V.

Decision making, like administration itself, is a group activity. Important decisions are announced by "the front office" in the form of instructions or by announcement either to individuals or to the staff. It is often assumed, at least by the uninitiated, that they are made there. That is true but only to a limited degree. The front office cannot act without information and advice. The information it receives in the form of reports and memoranda submitted either in the regular course of business or at the request of the executive; the advice comes through discussion in staff meetings and in personal conferences. The decision, ultimately made official by announcement or publication by the executive, is or should be the result of the combined thinking of all the executive staff of the agency who are concerned with the problem. This essential in democratic administration.

In an effort to lay the groundwork for a science of administration, Professor Simon has made a searching analysis of the process of decision making.[13] The following are among his conclusions: The aim of administration is to develop an intellectual climate in which the non-rational elements are reduced to a minimum; in which, therefore, administrative organization as such becomes less important as a determining factor in decisions; and finally, in which the logic of the situation narrows the possible choices to "one right answer." The realization of such an objective would develop a kind of behaviorism, in which the executive's free choice between alternatives would be severely limited.

Appropriateness within the organization and general acceptability of the prevailing social and political order are two other factors that influence decision making. So far as the first is concerned, the superior's power to make decisions implies the willingness of those below him in the scale of authority to abide by the decisions when made. As Professor Simon expresses it: "The most striking characteristic of the 'subordinate' role is that it establishes an area of acceptance in behavior

Administrative Behavior, and Marx, Fritz M., review of this volume, "A Closer View of Organization," Public Administration Review, Winter, 1948, pp. 60–65; also McCamy, James L., "Analysis of the Process of Decision Making," ibid., Winter, 1947, pp. 41–48.

within which the subordinate is willing to accept the decisions made for him by his superior." [14]

Securing Adequate Information. Sound decisions can be made only on the basis of adequate information. In order to have information available, a technical staff working only on such problems is necessary. Since no organization or its problems remain static, the need is a continuing one. The staff will correct cumbersome procedures, develop standards and methods of measurement, improve methods, and analyze need for equipment. It will, in fact, do all those things discussed earlier in this chapter as the functions of the planning unit. Where a special planning staff is not available, consultants may be called in from outside.[15]

The need for information raises the whole question of research and the place of the "expert" in administration. In the days when government and administration were simple, there was little need for either. The executive could proceed on the basis of "sound common sense." But those days are no more. The complexity of modern life and therefore of government requires in many cases detailed analysis and careful research. The old notion that anyone with good intentions and a reasonable amount of common sense can administer public office has been proved a delusion. The Federal government, a few states, and a few cities are now trying to make proper use of technical services. Bernard L. Gladieux of the Bureau of the Budget referred to this movement as "one of the most significant developments in Federal administration in recent years." [16]

Most of the states and most of the cities, however, are still blundering along without any adequate provision for this type of service great as is the need for it. Their hesitation in adopting it is due to two factors: elected and appointed officials do not always realize how badly they need it, and the executive who does avail himself of it is open to the charge that he is relying on a "brain truster." He is thus in the

---

[14] Simon, *op. cit.*, p. 133.

[15] Some cynic has defined a consultant as a man who knows less about your business than you do and is paid more for telling you how to run it than you could possibly make out of it if you ran it right instead of the way he told you. The reception which an organization and methods man gets when he goes in to make an organization survey is often not very cordial.

[16] For some general comments on this movement, see Hodson, William, Jr., *Administrative Planning Agencies in the Federal Government* (War Department, Civilian Personnel Division, Washington, 1942), who includes also a somewhat detailed description of the setup in some sixteen Federal agencies.

[17] See Ridley, Clarence E., "Advisory Services Help Cities Solve Local Problems," *Public Management,* September, 1947, pp. 254-257. Cities now spend less than one-fourth of 1 per cent of each expenditure dollar for research and advisory services — says Ridley — top officials are recognizing the need for making greater use of management tools in improving the administration of local services.

enviable position of imperiling his chances of success at his job if he does not use the results of scientific research, and of imperiling his chances of re-election if he does. His only solution is to keep his expert staff safely hidden in the background while he presents the results of their efforts as the sound solution of a practical man of affairs.

The situation brings up, furthermore, the very critical problem of the division of labor between the organization man and the line operator. Marshall Dimock has said that "in unskilled hands the indiscriminate application of organization theory may become a managerial calamity." On this question of the overuse or the ill-considered use of the expert, he continues that the organization expert, like most experts, may be and often is of valuable assistance to the executive, [but] the creation for him of an ill-considered role may lead to much harm. One of his chief faults is that because of his inevitably limited outlook, he may become dogmatic about his prescriptions. Often he assumes that, as an expert, he knows the one best way of doing a thing and is likely to regard modifications and adaptations as unscientific. . . . Another pitfall of the expert is his often uncritical assumption that stereotypes constitute a reliable guide to action in new situations. But no two administrative situations are exactly alike. In any program there are an infinite number of variables which must be coalesced and it is sometimes the factors least apparent on the surface that must be given the greatest weight." [18]

In view of these differences, the approach should depend upon the nature of the organization and the nature of its major task, not upon the whim of the organizer. For instance, if a local authority were to decide that in the future it would have its streets cleaned systematically, this would require organization from the bottom. The method to be employed and the equipment and staff required, would first be determined, and supervision and service staff would be added in relation to the basic staff. If, however, the same local authority were to decide to develop for the first time a publicity scheme, organization would be from the top. A suitable person would be selected to take charge of the publicity, and staff would be added to carry out the program as it was formulated and approved. It would be absurd in the first case to select a man to take charge of the street cleaning at a predetermined salary before estimating the size and nature of the job to be supervised; it would be equally absurd in the latter case to employ printers and billposters before determining what publicity they would have to handle.[19]

The Executive in Action, p. 163, quoted by Fite.
Based upon a letter in an English publication, cited by Fite.

The more the responsibility for any function is subdivided into
steps assigned to different units in the organization, the more slowly the
process works. Planning is no exception. In a small organization planning is often informal, but in a large organization top management i
confronted with a choice between concentrating it in a single unit and
assigning segments of it to several units. The first alternative is likely
to diminish the soundness of detail and the acceptability of the plan to
operating officials; in the second, the lack of a centralized review weak
ens coordination and leads to waste and duplication of effort. A
Glaser points out,[20] "the administrator necessarily has to judge th
effect of these tendencies on his organization and to choose betwee
evils in laying out his planning machinery."

The planning staff has responsibility for making special survey
One does not, however, make surveys indiscriminately; the subjects ar
carefully selected on the basis of knowledge of the weak spots in th
organization, or they may be made at the request of operating units o
the basis of their own belief that they need assistance in some specif
area. The result is that the planning staff is called upon to deal with
wide variety of subject matter. It may even be suggested that the
service to management is somewhat analogous to that performed f
members of a legislative body by the legislative reference service.[21]

Group Participation in the Process. "It will be admitted that we ne
a greater degree of democracy both in government and in industry
they are to serve populations desiring to lead democratic lives, as co
trasted with lives some few of them privileged and the remainder u
derprivileged in varying degree," writes Morris L. Cooke.[22] "In t
connection," he continues, "the increasing tendency is toward the ov
estimation of the top man in all organizations, whether it be the Pre
dent of the Republic, the general manager of almost any indust
plant, or the foreman of a road gang. Over-rating our leaders not o
burdens them but, perhaps of even greater importance, detracts fr
the dignity and status of everybody below."

In an earlier chapter methods of informing the staff and obtain
their suggestions and ideas with regard to agency problems were
cussed in connection with the management training conference p
Conferences of this type, especially those at the top level, can ren
important assistance not only to the head of the agency but to the

---

[20] Glaser, *op. cit.,* p. 82.
[21] For a description of special studies programs of a state agency in New York
address by Ficek in *The Role of a Planning Staff in State Agencies,* pp. 10–12.
[22] "On Some Commanding Aspects of the American Man of Business," *Adva
Management,* October–December, 1944.

partment heads who, being fully informed as to the nature and purpose of agency policies, are the better able to interpret them and carry them out.

An interesting illustration of this type of democratic procedure is found in the Library of Congress, where the so-called Librarian's Conference has been developed. It is composed of high-level administrators who meet three forenoons a week (from 10 to 12) to consider major problems. The agenda is often long and is seldom completed. Many items must of necessity be carried over, coming up a number of times as information regarding the subject is developed. Sometimes a whole session or even several sessions are spent on a single problem. The discussions are very frank, sometimes heated, often lengthy, but they do insure that policy decisions are made only after full consideration of their implications in the various parts of the Library."

These conferences are used, incidentally, as a training device for members of the supervisory staff at the second level. Three or four such staff members are designated every two months to attend. This experience gives them at least three things: an opportunity to become acquainted with the heads of the several departments and divisions of the Library; an insight into the variety and complexity of the problems involved in the administration of the agency; and some understanding of the procedures by which solutions are sought and finally determined. These conferences are, in fact, a fine example of the use of democratic procedures in the determination of policy in a large agency.[23]

SELECTED REFERENCES

American Society for Public Administration, *The Role of the Planning Staff in State Agencies* (Capitol District Chapter, Albany, 1947). An exceptionally good series of papers, discussing basic problems as they arise at the state level.

Barnard, Chester I., *Organization and Management* (Harvard University Press, 1948) and *The Functions of the Executive* (Harvard University Press, 1945). Two of the best discussions of organization and management, including consideration of the planning function.

Dimock, Marshall E., *The Executive in Action* (Harpers, New York, 1945). An able and realistic discussion of the problems of executive management.

Glover, Comstock, *Administrative Procedure* (American Council on Public Affairs, Washington, 1941). A handbook of procedures for operating executives – and a good one.

Filer, John C., and Maze, Coleman L., *Managerial Control* (Ronald Press, New York, 1937). For comparative purposes, this consideration of instruments and methods of managerial control in industry is interesting and useful.

The Library occupies all of two large buildings and has (because of the complexity assignment) an abnormally large number of departments and administrative divisions and a personnel of approximately 1800. Because of the complexity of its function, it exemplifies nearly all the problems of administration to be found in other agencies with a much larger working force.

Hempel, Edward H., *Top Management Planning* (Harpers, New York, 1945). Stresses the importance of top management planning in industry.

Millett, John D., *The Process and Organization of Government Planning* (Columbia University Press, 1947). A very good analysis of the methods and procedures of government planning.

Mooney, James D., *Principles of Organization*, Revised Edition (Harpers, New York, 1948). One of the better treatises on these problems as they arise in private industry.

Seckler-Hudson, Catheryn, *Budgeting: An Instrument of Planning and Management* (American University, Washington, 1945). Unit IV deals with the relationship of budgeting to planning and management.

Simon, Herbert A., *Administrative Behavior* (Macmillan, New York, 1947). Subtitle a study of decision-making processes in administrative organization.

Smith, Harold D., *The Management of Your Government* (McGraw-Hill, New York, 1945). The late Director of the Budget deals with various aspects of management including some attention to planning.

Stone, Donald C., *Federal Administrative Management, 1932–1942* (United States Bureau of the Budget, 1943). One of the ablest students and practitioners of the administrative art discusses important aspects of it at the Federal level.

25

ORGANIZATION FOR PRODUCTION

ORGANIZATION in public administration has been defined as developing
the structure for carrying out the tasks entrusted to the chief executive
and his administrative subordinates. The broad outlines of executive
organization at the government-wide level were considered in Part I;
our present concern is with organization at the department or agency
level. Organization becomes necessary because of the size and the complexity of modern government. It provides a means of establishing
working relationships within the agency, an opportunity to break
down the activities of the agency according to major functions and to
relate the specialized knowledges and skills of its employees to these
functions.

Organization for production means much more than the determination of structure. After the work of the agency has been mapped
out (see preceding chapter), existing personnel have to be fitted into
the new plan, and additional personnel procured; but more than that,
the staff organization for control must be developed. Space has to be
procured and planned, equipment obtained and installed, and provision
made for necessary services. Procedures have to be translated from
planning to actual operation. All this is a part of organization broadly
conceived, and all of it must be accomplished before production really
gets under way.

Organizational Structure

Organization is a means of establishing an alignment of functions or
activities within an agency that will clearly define the duties and responsibilities of each executive. It defines the limits of authority of
each executive and each segment of the agency, and the proper relationships between them. In setting up a new agency this is difficult because very often there are few precedents and no experience to serve
as a guide. In remodeling an old agency, difficulties arise from other
sources. The existing structure is usually the result of expansion along
lines originally laid down. Those in charge, long familiar with this
plan and able through long experience to make it work, may not real-

ize that it has grown unsuitable or that it makes the discharge of their own responsibilities more difficult. Even if they are aware of this, the fact that changing the organizational arrangements will disturb relationships of top personnel and cause a certain amount of transitional confusion may deter them.[1]

The Organization Process. The process of organization involves three distinct steps: designing the structure, staffing the positions created, and operating the department or enterprise through the organization that has been created and staffed. While the chief concern here is with the first of these steps, the second raises important problems in staff and line relationships that must be considered. The third, relating primarily to production, will be considered later.

The problems confronting management in determining the structure of a department or agency duplicate on a smaller scale many of the problems arising in determining at the top level the number and nature of operating units to be set up. In this task management has no less than four basic approaches: function or purpose, process or profession, clientele or commodity, and area. The application of these bases in illustrative situations, chiefly at the state level, is shown in the chart on page 493.

The structure must not only bear some logical relation to the assignment of the agency but it must also conform to established principles of organization — although, it is often contended, the exact form is considerably less important than the manner in which it is administered. The principles, however, are important, and a few of them discussed in Chapter 3 — may be briefly stated here:

1. There should be a single responsible executive head. If commissions or boards are used at all, they should be limited to purely advisory functions. This the principle of unity of command.

2. The number of operating units under the executive should not exceed reasonable limits, from the point of view of span of control.

3. The principle of homogeneity requires that in the assignment of duties units and to individual employees, the effort be made to group similar duties together and to avoid the assignment of dissimilar or unrelated duties to the same employee or group of employees.

4. The staff facilities provided for the executive should be adequate to permit proper coordination, integration, supervision, and control.

5. Adequate authority should be delegated from the top to the successive levels of supervision to enable each to perform in a satisfactory manner the task assigned to it.

[1] See Rowland, Floyd H., "The Plan of Organization," *Advanced Management*, cember, 1946, pp. 152–166.

Four Bases of Agency Organization: Their Application
in Illustrative Situations, Chiefly at the State Level

FUNCTION OR PURPOSE	PROCESS OR PROFESSION	CLIENTELE OR COMMODITY	AREA
Department of Conservation	*Department of Insurance*	*Department of Education*	*Office of War Information*
Divisions of:	Divisions of:	Divisions of:	Branches:
Water Policy and Supply	Statements and Audits	Administration Kindergarten	Domestic Operations
Fish and Game	Accounts	Elementary Schools	Overseas Operations
Forestry	Examinations	Secondary Schools	Area 1
Parks and Historic Sites	Actuarial Liquidation	Higher Education Special Education	Area 2 Area 3
Shell Fisheries	Complaints	Vocational and Industrial Education	
Geological Survey		Adult Education	Bureaus in:
		Education for Blind and Deaf	New York San Francisco
		Libraries	Los Angeles
Bureau of Inspection	*Bureau of Professional Licensing*	*Department of Insurance*	*Department of the Interior*
Divisions of:	Divisions of:	Divisions of:	Illustrative Divisions:
Bakery and Restaurant	Mine Inspectors	Life	Grazing Service
Building	Architects	Fire	Division of Territories and Island Possessions
Boiler	Dentists	Marine	The Alaska Railroad
Elevator	Undertakers	Casualty	Alaska Railroad Commission
Bedding and Upholstery	Nurses Physicians		Puerto Rico Reconstruction Administration
Mines and Quarries	Veterinarians		Bonneville Dam Administration

If the undertaking is extensive, there must be not only functional decentralization within the organization (see item 5), but there must be also territorial decentralization, i.e., the establishment of field offices and a field organization.

The organization of any department or agency at any of the three levels of government has to be fitted into its proper place in the organizational structure as a whole. Its head may be a member of the cabinet; from that angle, the agency must be "organized for interdepartmental functioning and for better projection of policy and administration into whole-public-interest terms" — nation-wide, state-wide, city-wide. The head of the agency will be dependent on bureau chiefs and on career aides, but he cannot rely solely on either. He must have in addition a small group of trusted personal aides to "extend his reach" and assist him in the discharge of his responsibility for over-all management.[2] A permanent undersecretary has often been suggested

Appleby, Paul H., "Organizing Around the Head of a Large Federal Department," *Public Administration Review*, Summer, 1946, pp. 205-212; Pritchett, C. Herman,

as a means of strengthening departmental leadership and management; but while it is necessary to strengthen the department head through provision for an adequate staff, it is undesirable to restrict unduly his choice of policy aides. At the top level a delicate balance must be maintained between the policy aides chosen by the incumbent head and the contribution which can be made by the elevation of career staff to active participation in departmental leadership and management.

Determining the Basis of Organization. It is possible to organize almost any major activity in several different ways or in a combination of ways. The choice of the method is not easy, because all the advantages are rarely associated with any one type. Sometimes two or more are used in combination, as in the United States Department of Agriculture. The top staff in this agency is concerned with the entire department. The first breakdown is functional, some of the principal units being the Agricultural Research Administration, the Farm Credit Administration, the Rural Electrification Administration, the Commodity Credit Corporation, the Extension Service, the Farm Security Administration, the Office of Marketing Services, and the Soil Conservation Service. The distinguishing feature of a functional organization is that the performance of certain duties at all organizational levels is subject to a separate or central control, whereas in line and staff organization all the work in each department is handled by the department.

Many of these units in Agriculture are broken down in accordance with some other principle. The Office of Marketing Services, for instance, is broken down into branches according to commodities — Cotton and Fibre Branch, Dairy and Poultry Branch, Fats and Oils Branch, Fruit and Vegetable Branch, etc. Similarly, the Bureau of Entomology and Plant Quarantine has divisions responsible for the combating of each of the major types of insect pest — gypsy moth, Japanese beetle, Mexican fruitfly, and others. The Soil Conservation Service has operating divisions on agronomy, biology, cartography, engineering, forestry, nursery, and land management. The Bureau of Agricultural and Industrial Chemistry, on the other hand, has four great regional laboratories — northern, southern, eastern, and western — each responsible for research on the basis of the agricultural products grown in the region it serves.

In smaller units the conflict in principle may be more clearly visible.

"The Postmaster General and Departmental Management," *ibid.*, Spring, 1946, pp. 130–136; and Waldo, C. Dwight, "Organizational Analysis: Some Notes on Methods and Criteria," *ibid.*, Autumn, 1947, pp. 236–244. The latter poses a series of rather basic questions which may well be taken into consideration in the effort to improve existing organization.

alized, as in a state department of insurance or education. In the former the organization may be by type of company under regulation, in which case each division performs all the activities relating to the regulation and control of that type. Or the organization may be, as is shown in the chart, on the basis of the type of work involved, without regard to the type of insurance business under regulation. Similarly, a department of education may be broken down according to level of instruction — kindergarten, elementary, secondary, higher, and special — or according to problems, as administration, curriculum, teacher training and certification, teacher retirement, school buildings, and school finance.

There are no absolute rules governing such matters. Some jurisdictions are able to do a good job with one type of organization, some with another. The decision seems to rest partly on the background and tradition of the department, partly on the personal preferences and characteristics of the head of the department at the time. Since there is no "right way" and "wrong way," it is of questionable value to undertake complete and drastic overhauling of a departmental structure merely to satisfy the whim of a new appointee. Such a course creates confusion and impairs efficiency. Changes should be made gradually as required, one being fully worked out before others are undertaken. Meanwhile every effort should be made to obtain maximum efficiency of operation under the prevailing organization.

Once established, most organizations inevitably assume certain characteristics designed to preserve their integrity and maintain their continuity. "Maintenance of the system" is the organizational equivalent of the individual's urge to self-preservation. Selznick has suggested that "maintenance of the system" as a generic need may be specified in terms of the following imperatives: [3]

. The security of the organization as a whole in relation to social forces in its environment
. The stability of the lines of authority and communication
. The stability of informal relations within the organization
. The continuity of policy and of the sources of its determination
A homogeneity of outlook with respect to the meaning and role of the organization

The Staffing Problem. In setting up its organization structure of divisions, bureaus, sections, and so on, management should be free within the prescribed limits to establish whatever form seems best suited to

---

See Selznick, Philip, "Foundations of the Theory of Organization," *American Sociological Review*, February, 1948, pp. 25-35.

the requirements of the agency. It should do so, as far as possible, without regard to personalities, for the problem of staffing should properly come after the structure has been decided upon. Then the existing personnel may be fitted into the new organization in appropriate places, depending upon their qualifications and the duties to be performed. If additional personnel are required, then management will be confronted with the problems considered in Part II.

The structure of the organization should be designed with primary emphasis on the work to be done because only in this way can the grouping of jobs into operating units be logical and well balanced. Only in this way can the line positions at all levels be made of such size and shape that their incumbents will have time for the discharge of their responsibilities in the field of personnel management.

The most difficult organizational problem in this area is determining the proper relationship between line and staff. For instance, when a new employee is to be selected or an old one dismissed for cause, who makes the decision — top management, the supervisor concerned, or the personnel office? When a change is to be made in the accounting system, who makes the decision — top management, the general accounting office, or the supervisor who has to keep the accounts in question? To decide whether a particular matter should be referred for decision through a line channel if it cannot be decided by the immediate supervisor, or whether it should be referred through a staff channel involves a clear understanding of the fundamental distinctions between line and staff and the responsibilities of each.

In the cases cited in the personnel field, the initial screening of applicants for employment should be done by the personnel office, and the selection should be made by the department heads and supervisor jointly. But the personnel office cannot escape responsibility for maintaining the minimum standards of the company or agency. The final choice of an employee to be placed in a given job is a line decision; is important that the department head or supervisor make the decision rather than the personnel office, if he is to succeed in supervising the new employee on the job. Similarly with dismissal for cause; disciplinary action is a line or supervisory responsibility. The line executive who pass upon such a case should seek and receive the advice of the director of personnel, but a line executive at some level of authority should do the actual discharging, subject of course to resort to such appeal machinery as may have been created to protect employee against unjust decisions.

All these matters, not to mention such others as the need for training or a change in the accounting procedures, are line matters in which the decision should be made by the line supervisor within the limits of general policy established for the organization as a whole. The line makes and executes decisions; the staff advises, informs, and helps in supervision (for instance, by making inspections for control purposes). It is necessary to maintain proper balance and proportion between the two. The responsibility of the line is direct; of the staff, indirect. In every case, however, decisions should be made cooperatively, on the basis of analysis of the facts and after full and free discussion. The situation is somewhat analogous to that between the executive and the legislative branches of government. Unless there is cooperation and teamwork, no worth-while accomplishment is possible. Each must respect the rights and prerogatives of the other while seeking to discharge its own responsibility.

Staff units of whatever type are primarily service agencies, although all managerial services involve some degree of control. They have a twofold responsibility for understanding operating problems and for constructive advice and counsel on such problems. The ideal relationship between staff and line exists when staff groups train operating personnel so that the need for further staff assistance is minimized and when all actions emanating from managerial officials stem from the authority of the agency's executive head.

Staff Organization for Control

The development of staff organization for the control of production requires the formulation and adoption of ways and means of obtaining accurate production information and of instituting simple yet positive controls. Management has come to realize the necessity for centralizing in one group responsibility for the development of its controls, procedures, and routines. In private establishments this new function is usually called industrial engineering. It includes such functions as the following: [4]

The analysis and development of proper lines of responsibility
The development and maintenance of administrative budgets,
The analysis, establishment, and control of all office routines and procedures
Salary and hourly rate structure and job evaluation
Time and motion study
Plant layout
Wage incentives
Manufacturing budgets
Equipment requirements
Production and inventory control procedures and such allied subjects as tool design, methods and routing, and the like

See Louden, J. K., "Staff Organization for Control," *Advanced Management*, January–March, 1943, pp. 17–22.

Some of these items relate more to industry than to government, but many of them apply to both. Some of them have been discussed elsewhere in this volume; others will be taken up in the chapter which follows. The essential point here is that in any efficient organization for production all these diverse elements must be pulled together, each in its proper place in a working organization.

The head of an operating unit is supposed to know his organization thoroughly and to be able to detect weak spots. But working as he is under the pressure of direct supervisory duties, he is in practice frequently unaware of improvements which might be made. Thus arises the need for staff specialists in organization and procedure who have the time and the special training and the responsibility for making surveys and analyses. The function of this staff is to make possible decreasing costs and greater efficiency in operations, to produce a better product at a lower cost and at the right time. Planning and organizing may be largely the responsibility of a special staff, but the final task of making the plans work rests with the supervisors, who must today be managers themselves, knowing how to use the common tools of management.

In situations which involve cooperative relationships between the different levels of government, the local director is nearest to actual administration. In such a field as public welfare, for instance, it is he who should be able to answer such questions as: How large should a caseload be? How many social workers can be supervised effectively by one person? How much clerical work should a social worker perform? What kind of training and experience are required for the job? What kind of office is needed, and what is a suitable floor plan for such an office?

Space Procurement and Layout

Some reference was made in Part III to the problem of space as an aspect of the fiscal program of government. It may be assumed at this point that the normal procedures for the procurement and allocation of space have functioned properly and that the operating agency is now confronted with the duty of utilizing the space assigned to it. This utilization requires careful and detailed planning. The translation of these plans into actuality is an important phase of the problem of overall organization for production.

The basic considerations in space control are the bringing together of processes, thereby making possible the sharing of equipment, and the bringing together of a complete operation, thereby making possible a straight-line flow of work. The space utilized by a given agency should be in one building or in adjacent or adjoining buildings. Scatte ing an agency all over town is wasteful, time consuming, and inconvenient to all concerned.

The primary purpose of space control is to make certain that every employee has a satisfactory physical environment for his work without wasting valuable space. Other purposes include the desirability of providing such arrangements as will facilitate (1) the flow of work within the several units; (2) the integration of the flow of work between units; (3) maximum economy in the movement of personnel, forms, materials, supplies, and equipment. Unnecessary movement of personnel wastes time; unnecessary movement of material wastes both effort and time.

Space can be allocated intelligently only upon the basis of substantially complete information regarding the operations to be performed. Standards have been worked out governing the number of square feet of floor space desirable for individual employees engaged in specific types of work. Adequate light, air, and ventilation are assumed. Management must know how many square feet of space are available, what portion (if any) is usable only for files and storage, how many workers must be provided for, and how many pieces of equipment — and of what types — are required at each point in the normal work flow. Provision must be made for filing and storage space; it is not fair to the file clerks, at least for those files which are in constant use, to use the less desirable space for this purpose. When all these data have been assembled, detailed floor plans may be drawn to scale, showing exactly the location of all duty stations and equipment.

Even where careful planning has been done, minor changes are often necessary. Partitions may have to be moved, lighting fixtures changed, soundproofing installed to reduce noise, and heating and ventilating arrangements changed. Telephones may have to be connected and interoffice communications systems installed.

Proper space arrangements have a great deal to do with the efficiency of an organization. All who had any part in the war effort and worked under the terribly crowded conditions then generally prevailing, know full well the detrimental effects of inadequate working conditions. Basic requirements of efficient operation include properly trained and competent supervisors, ability and proficiency on the part of employees, properly established procedures and routines, and also suitable working conditions and adequate physical equipment.[5]

The United States Bureau of the Budget, in its *Field Service Training Institute Manual on Management Techniques*, includes a "Premises Guide for Field Office Space" (Washington, 1947).

Office Equipment and Communications

Every agency, even one engaged in industrial pursuits or field operations, has to have offices. Many government agencies function exclusively through office operations. The planning of these offices and the procurement and installation of the necessary equipment and communications facilities constitute an important aspect of organization for production. Before this can be done, however, decision has to be made as to the extent to which individual operating units are going to be responsible for their own services and whether this work is going to be centralized.

Office Equipment. In addition to the usual office furniture, some machines and appliances may be required, the number and variety in any given instance depending upon the size and the functions of the agency. Of the many different types, the following are among the more important: adding and calculating, billing and bookkeeping, card punching, sorting devices for filing, mailing equipment for addressing, collating, folding, stapling, etc., and duplicating equipment.[6] The actual procurement and the disposition of surplus equipment and supplies is one of the responsibilities of the central purchasing and procurement agency considered in Part III.

Communications Facilities. Still another aspect of the organization for production includes provision for communications facilities, of which there are three major types: interoffice systems, telephone and telegraph, and incoming and outgoing correspondence.[7] Some interoffice systems operate independently, while others are attached to the outside telephones. Other possibilities include electric paging, telautograph systems, and regular messenger service. The most satisfactory appear to be a complete internal system added to the outside phones, with messenger service at fairly frequent intervals to transfer papers from one individual or office to another.

Adequate telephone facilities are assumed as a matter of course. A great many matters may be adjusted by telephone both inside and outside the organization, thereby saving much writing of letters and mem-

---

[6] Including typewriters, various types of duplicators, and photostat, blueprint, and microfilm equipment. For the discussion of these matters, see Neuner and Haye *Office Management and Practice* (Southwestern Publishing Company, 1941); Wyl Gamber and Brecht, *Practical Office Management* (Prentice-Hall, New York, 1937 and Huff, Warren, *Machine Procedures* (Michigan State Civil Service Commissio Lansing, 1938).

[7] See Leffingwell, William H., *Office Management*, Fifth Edition (McGraw-Hill, Ne York, 1935); Neuner and Hayes, *op. cit.;* and publications of the National Office Ma agement Association.

oranda and a vast amount of time that might otherwise be consumed in attending personal conferences. The use of the telephone in the regular conduct of business varies greatly from one agency to another, depending upon the nature of its work. An effort is always made to discourage its use for personal calls. Permission of a responsible supervisor, authorized to approve them, is usually required for all long distance calls.

Special problems arising in the official use of the telephone include confirmation of conversations, recording of important calls, and training receptionists and others who handle this type of communication. Confirmation by letter is frequently used so that the substance of the conversation may be made a matter of official record. Important calls may be recorded for future reference, either by special equipment or by a stenographer. Training receptionists in handling telephone calls promptly and courteously is essential; the impression they make, especially in the receipt of incoming calls, has an important public relations aspect for the agency. If it is necessary to transfer a call, this should be done, due care being taken to make sure that the correct transfer is made.

Handling Correspondence. Efficient procedures are necessary for the handling of mail. In a large organization this is a difficult assignment and one regarding which there is usually much criticism and complaint. All incoming mail is received, opened (unless marked "personal" or "confidential"), stamped, and sorted in a central mail room. All public agencies attempt to discourage employees from receiving personal mail at the office. Since many staff members need the mail in connection with their work, incoming mail should be sorted and distributed promptly. The same messenger service that delivers incoming mail and picks up outgoing mail can usually handle interoffice communications at the same time.

Outgoing mail must obviously be prepared, signed, and cleared. Theoretically all official mail comes to the agency head and goes out from him. Since in a large agency it would be physically impossible for him to read and sign all outgoing correspondence, authority to sign mail is delegated to heads of operating divisions, who may either sign for the head of the agency or sign their own names, indicating their official position. Employees of professional status are commonly authorized to sign letters relating to their regular work. Others are required to obtain clearance on outgoing mail in order to insure conformity with agency policy.

Without engaging in extended discussion of office management and supervision of the handling of correspondence, it may be noted that letters are judged by content and appearance. Criteria for evaluating the former include completeness, conciseness, clarity, correctness or accuracy, and appropriateness of tone. Appearance is judged by neatness and suitability of form. Many good manuals on the handling of correspondence in general and in particular agencies are available.[8] If the job is to be done properly, there must be constant and effective supervision, and appropriate training programs for those engaged in the work.

Timing, Scheduling, and Work Distribution

Timing and scheduling involve planning but are also a phase of organization for production. The purposes are to avoid lost motion and to reduce or minimize the delays caused by both the organization distance and the physical distance work units must travel. If these operations are properly worked out, the accumulation of backlogs may be prevented and the backtracking of work units reduced to a minimum. After this task has been completed, work assignments must be made both to organizational units and to individuals.

Timing and Scheduling. Timing and scheduling are dependent upon careful analysis of individual and unit tasks. Obviously the same techniques cannot be used for all types of jobs — manual, clerical, executive, and professional. Allowance must be made in the latter for lack of uniformity in the subject matter and for differences in the importance of the work and in its volume. In some types time analyses may be made on a quantity basis, such as number of interviews or telephone calls, number of letters typed, number of cards punched, or number of cases processed. Such information, when assembled, usually lends itself to graphic presentation.

When the administration of a large-scale operation is involved, it is customary to set up a tentative program. The proposed steps should be carefully studied with a view to eliminating the unessential. The time factor and the labor requirements in each operation should be given special attention. Finally, provision should be made for a production control unit — a matter to be briefly considered in the following chapter. Familiarity with assembly line methods in large operations fre-

[8] See United States Civil Service Commission, *Correspondence Manual;* Grady, James F., and Hall, Milton, *Writing Effective Government Letters* (Employee Training Publications, Washington, 1939): and Niemann, Charles H., *"Warizing" Correspondence and Its Management* (United States Civil Service Commission, Division of Training, 1942). Many of the same principles that apply to good letterwriting apply also to the preparation of reports. On this subject, see Bureau of the Budget, Division of Administrative Management, *Suggestions for Writing Division Reports,* and Knappen, Joseph G., *Preparing an Effective Research Manual* (Farm Credit Administration, Washington, 1938).

quently prompts the assumption that all operations must be performed in sequence. This is not necessarily so, for in some types of work the simultaneous performance of tasks pertaining to different aspects of the work is possible.

The last step involves the construction of a final production schedule. Some time must elapse before this is done in order that the schedule may be based upon actual work experience. In the process of developing it, all previous procedural studies must be used; current workload reports, progress reports, and the like must be taken into account. Thus in a central personnel agency, one form may be provided for a one-day report of work performed, another for a time schedule of examinations, designed to achieve a suitable distribution of the workload.

Work Distribution. Along with timing and scheduling, work distribution must be considered. The distribution of tasks, first to work units and later to individuals, can be properly made only after careful analysis of the functions, the administrative sequences, and the work units themselves. Each of these major factors may be broken down into its component parts. Function may be defined as the major purpose to be accomplished. This, it may be assumed, has already been determined, perhaps in the governing statute, perhaps by a higher level of administrative authority. Functional analysis, for the present purpose, requires consideration of the contribution of each task to the basic purpose, the possible combination of similar tasks, the number and length of the administrative moves, and the elimination of formalities and avoidable causes of friction.

In analysis of the administrative sequence, time factors are especially important. Here consideration must be given to the determination of the proper time for the transfer of work between individuals, a major purpose being so to arrange the sequence as to avoid waste of man-hours due to waiting periods caused by poor sequences or bad timing, time out awaiting decisions by higher authority regarding the next step to be taken, etc.

In the analysis of work units, questions of quantity and quality present themselves. The decisions on these matters are largely dependent upon the character of the work to be performed. Other factors include the pyramiding of work, differences between recurring and nonrecurring types of work, differences between the delegation of authority on the one hand and control on the other. Glaser suggests four simple maxims which administrators or administrative analysts should consider: [9]

Glaser, *op. cit.*, p. 164.

1. The basic division of administrative work should be according to the organization's major purpose
2. Responsibility and authority for performance should not be separated
3. Work assignments should allow as short administrative sequences as possible
4. Qualitative and quantitative capacity should be considered

The actual assignment of tasks must be made first to organizational units, secondly to individual employees. The considerations that govern assignments to the former include centralization and decentralization, supervision and control, direct channels of administration, and the effectiveness of the skill and experience of specialists. In the further breakdown of work assignments to individuals, these are the more important considerations: the skill and experience required for the task; the importance of the task in relation to the grade or status of the employee; the degree of discretion, judgment, and authority required by each assignment; the appropriate degree of specialization; and the size of the workload resulting for each individual employee.

The Record System

Form and Records. In every operation records of some kind are necessary. Daily and weekly or monthly reports showing amount of work performed and types of work performed, serve as an important tool of management. In the discussion of timing and scheduling, the need for suitable forms for this purpose was mentioned, but standard forms are desirable for other reasons as well. There are in every operation after the organization is "shaken down" many instances in which the same type of case or situation comes up repeatedly. Common sense dictates that such cases be handled uniformly. The use of a carefully prepared office form is perhaps the most practical method. Office forms have other advantages both for reporting and for handling repetitive operations: they tend to establish a logical sequence of ideas in the presentation of information or in the processing of work, and they facilitate the furnishing of multiple copies when needed.

It is easy enough to decide to develop a form for some specific purpose, but one should not overlook the fact that this decision in itself creates certain problems. There are dangers in developing a multiplicity of forms where one or two would suffice. This means that careful attention must be given to both the authorization and the design of new forms, and that there must be a constant review of forms to make certain that they continue to be suitable to the needs of the organization. If the number is too great, the proper use of them is discouraged. If no one can remember all of them, and some kind of indexing or cataloging is necessary, the system breaks down under its own weight. Rigorou effort must be made to restrict the number of forms and to make certain that there is real need for those that are approved and that there is not already in existence some other form designed to serve the same purpose. It is important to eliminate those which are no longer needed and to combine where possible. A classification according to standardized, comparable elements may effect many economies in operation. An appropriate system of forms, when developed and kept under control, provides safeguards of time and operating information essential to sound management.[10]

In design there are various factors affecting the size, type, color, and general format. The determining criteria should be chiefly utilitarian: what sort of form will be the quickest and easiest to use, the most efficient in the actual work situation? Important factors to be considered are the flow of work, number of copies required, method of making entries (longhand, typing, machine processing), method of filing, etc. Usefulness will depend largely upon the suitability of the arrangement and wording of items and on the quality of paper used, as well as the reproduction process — both of which affect legibility.[11]

Files and Filing. Filing would appear on the surface to be simple; in practice, it is a difficult problem in most organizations and one for which only a few seem to have developed a satisfactory solution. One frequently observes vast quantities of material retained in working files long after the need for it has passed, simply on the ground that if it is sent to the general files, it will be lost beyond all hope of recovery should the need arise.

The major difficulty in filing grows out of the fact that it has normally been assigned to the lowest-grade employees. The success of any system is dependent upon the consistent use of some classification of materials. The decision regarding the heads for particular items can be made only by an individual possessing some fair amount of intelligence and education and above all some familiarity with the subject matter.

The installation of a filing system calls for the selection of one among a number that are available. In this selection management, assisted by experts in the planning, installation, and operation of filing

[10] United States Bureau of the Budget, *Forms Control and Design: Selected References* (Washington, 1945).

[11] For discussion of these problems, see Public Administration Service, *Case Studies in Public Administration*, No. 15, "Standardization and Centralization of Forms" (Chicago, 1940); Niles, Mary C., *Middle Management* (Harpers, New York, 1941); War Production Board, *Principles of Design and Standardization of Forms* (Washington, 1942); Wylie, Gamber, and Brecht, *Practical Office Management* (Prentice-Hall, New York, 1937).

systems, has an important responsibility. The choice hinges upon the nature of the operation, the chief purposes for which the files are used, and the general nature and the bulk of the material. Filing correspondence is one thing; filing memoranda, reports, and miscellaneous documents, another. Filing cards or forms of uniform size and shape is one thing; filing miscellaneous and heterogeneous items is quite another. Management must itself decide the question whether the needs of the agency will best be served by an alphabetic, a geographic, a numerical, a phonetic, or a subject matter system. It must decide whether the files are to be vertical, horizontal, visible, or microfilm. When these basic decisions are made, the administration of the system becomes the responsibility of the supervisors and staff of the filing section. Then there still remains the problem of adopting such common mechanical aids as will facilitate the use of the files. Colored dividers, sheets or cards, signals such as tabs or other identification markings each have their advantages and proper uses. Cut corners may be used to identify certain types of material such as cases that have been closed out. Labels, guides, and cross references are useful in their proper places. Discussion of these questions will be found in volumes on filing and in general treatises on office management.[12]

The management of an extensive filing operation calls for careful administration and supervision. Procedures manuals and established work routines are effective aids in actual administration, while periodic surveys will help in keeping the program on a sound basis. There is need for constant attention to the problem of eliminating materials no longer useful. These should either be sent to archives if of permanent value, or destroyed in conformity with prescribed procedures for the disposition of useless papers. Space in the working files can be saved by transferring inactive material to storage files, or in either case by microfilming material of permanent value and significance. Forms and procedures should be frequently reviewed for simplification and standardization.

SELECTED REFERENCES

There is an enormous literature in this field relating to business and private industry due to long neglect, there is little indeed relating to public agencies. The following are among the better and more recent titles:

Commission on Organization of the Executive Branch of the Government, *Task Force Report on Records Management* [Appendix C] (Washington, January, 1949). A valuable study of record making and record keeping in the Federal government.

---

[12] See Brecht and Glaser, *The Art and Technique of Administration in German Ministries* (Harvard University Press, 1940); Leffingwell, *op. cit.;* and Neuer and Hayes *op. cit.*

Holden, Paul E., and others, *Top Management Organization and Control* (Stanford University Press, 1941). An important work whose principles are applicable both in industry and in government.

Hoslett, Schuyler D., *Human Factors in Management* (Park College Press, Parkville, Mo., 1946). A writer with administrative experience in the armed forces appropriately emphasizes the human factors in management; see also: Appley, Lawrence A., *The Human Element in Personnel Management* (Society for Personnel Administration, Washington, 1941) and Tead, Ordway, *Human Nature in Management* (McGraw-Hill, New York, 1933).

Marx, Fritz M., Ed., *The Elements of Public Administration* (Prentice-Hall, New York, 1947). Contains considerable discussion of production problems in government agencies, including organization.

Niles, Mary C. H., *Middle Management: The Job of the Junior Executive*, Revised Edition (Harpers, New York, 1948). This standard work gives appropriate attention to the organization and production responsibilities of the group immediately responsible for it.

Society for the Advancement of Management, *The Work Unit in Federal Administration* (Public Administration Service, Chicago, 1937). The proper determination of the work unit is a basic problem of organization, having important effects upon production.

Stone, Donald C., *The Management of Municipal Public Works* (Public Administration Service, Chicago, 1939). A case study of organization and management in an important municipal department.

Urwick, Lyndall, *The Elements of Administration* (Harpers, New York, 1943). A standard title on administration devotes appropriate attention to the problems of organization and production.

26

PRODUCTION

WHEN the advance planning has been done and the organization established, actual production may be considered. Here the major problems are work methods, quantity control, quality control, and "work improvement" or personnel utilization programs.

The functions must be analyzed, in the first place, to determine whether each operation provided for is necessary and, if so, whether this is the proper time and place for its performance. The whole operation should be studied to eliminate unnecessary effort or possible duplication. The job descriptions should be examined to make sure that they are accurate and up to date. Because of their influence on efficiency, attention must be given to conditions of work — such matters as noise, temperature, ventilation, illumination, hours of work, rest periods, and, above all, conditions of health and safety.

It is also important to scrutinize the organization in order to clarify lines of responsibility. This is often called organization clarification.[1] Management should assure itself that the form of the organization is in accord with the needs of the agency, and in each instance, without permitting the span of control to spread beyond practical limits, it must seek to avoid unnecessary echelons. The shorter and more direct the lines of authority can be made, the more efficient the operation is likely to be. Observance of these principles, designed to develop an organizational structure with the maximum degree of simplicity, is fundamental to good administration.

Work Methods

In production the object is to secure maximum output with a minimum expenditure of man-hours and materials and with the most efficient use of machinery and equipment. The function of supervision and personnel, working in close cooperation, is to accomplish this objective. Bas-

---

[1] Other items in Lawrence A. Appley's "management formula" are: standards of performance, performance review, help and information, source of help and information and time schedule for supplying help and information; see his *The Human Element in Personnel Management*, pp. 17-22 (Society for Personnel Administration, Washington 1941).

ically the problem is to combine into an effective working arrangement the fundamental principles of good personnel management (set forth in Part II), of good financial management (set forth in Part III), and of accepted standards of organization and control. No one member of management can do the job alone, yet the synchronization of the efforts of these three is a difficult assignment — one, however, which constitutes the very heart of the problem of administration.

Responsibilities of Management. In administration, personnel problems are always of major importance. Management is responsible for knowing that there is sufficient qualified personnel on hand to do the job and that this personnel is properly instructed, trained, and supervised. This responsibility can be met only when accurate and complete workload data are available — data by means of which it is possible to estimate and substantiate present and future personnel needs. And, as has been suggested, this personnel can function efficiently only when adequate information and instructions have been furnished to all employees and when there is proper supervision to see that these instructions are known, understood, and applied by all.

For present purposes it is important to emphasize the fact that modern personnel management avails itself of ideas obtained through employee suggestion systems and that it finds some means of providing suitable rewards for useful suggestions. If such a system is to be really beneficial in any organization, certain conditions must be observed.[2] Employees must not only believe that suggestions are actually desired by management, but they must believe that each idea submitted is given careful consideration. This means in turn that all suggestions must be acknowledged and that their sponsors must be informed at a proper time of the disposition made of them. If a suggestion is not adopted, the reasons should be clearly explained. When one is approved, there should be some appropriate recognition of the employee who originally made it. If it involves a really important improvement in procedure or the saving of an appreciable amount, the employee should be given some reward, the value of which bears some reasonable relation to the value of his contribution.

Budget-making time is an excellent time, as John F. Willmott points out,[3] for capitalizing on a review and appraisal of work methods, types of equipment, and plans of organization. Such a review is going on constantly in any well-managed governmental unit or establishment. In a municipality, for instance, by asking such questions as those listed

---

These problems are discussed at length in Chapter 10.
"Work Programs and Municipal Budgets." *Public Management*, September, 1945.

below, not only at budget-making time but throughout the year, many an administrator has been able to work out improvements which have resulted in substantial budgetary economies.

Do we need two patrolmen in police cars?

Would a machine installation do our accounting and tax billing more economically?

Could certain inspectional activities be conducted more economically if one inspector were assigned to each district and required to make several different types of inspections?

Would a more adequate staff of case workers effect economies in total relief expenditures and at the same time give more adequate service to relief clients?

Would the installation of an equipment inventory system pay for itself by eliminating loss and theft of items in stock?

Cannot the municipal hospital do its own laundry more economically than commercial laundries?

The attitude of management on the subject of financial support is vitally important in its relation to the efficiency of an organization. There is no excuse for wasting money, and good management will not tolerate it. Nor is there any excuse for a penny-pinching type of economy which discharges workers before a peak season or uses third-class mail for important papers. Such practices result in confusion and waste and in inconvenience to the public out of all proportion to the relatively small amount saved.

It is a vital responsibility of management to see that the essentials of organization for production — space, equipment, scheduling, and recording — are handled properly. Supplies and equipment must be adequate in amount and properly placed in relation to the needs of employees. Seemingly slight delays in the receipt of materials or failure to supply them in adequate quantities may frequently result in serious delays in production, and so too may improper layouts which necessitate cross-handling of work although a direct production line layout is possible.

Accountability of Supervisors. For seeing that all these things are done the immediate supervisor is responsible. While the various aspects of supervision will be considered in the next chapter, it may not be out of place to note here that the supervisor has a threefold responsibility in connection with production — responsibility for work accomplished and for the safety and care of both workers and equipment. Responsibility for work includes the planning of unit operations, the delegation of authority, the integration of operations, cooperation with the supervisors of other units in the organization, analysis of operations as the work proceeds, and finally the estimating and later the reporting

operating costs. Under responsibility for property and equipment,
e supervisor looks after layout. He must report breakage, damage,
theft — for the property is issued to him and is charged to him. Un-
:r certain circumstances he may also be responsible for the supervision
protective or janitorial service or for both. His responsibility for
e workers encompasses all phases of a modern program of personnel
anagement as it relates to the work of an operating or line supervisor.

esponsibilities of the Working Force. Each employee must be brought
realize the importance of a frequent review of his or her job to make
rtain that it is being done most efficiently, to make sure that unneces-
ry steps or motions have not been retained. Such an admonition may
und trite, but experience shows that in many cases, even in progres-
/e and well-run organizations, there is a strong tendency to continue
perform operations in a given manner for no better reason than that
ey have always been done that way. During World War II, when
e War Manpower Commission's Job Instruction Training was intro-
iced into large numbers of plants and offices, it was discovered that
:ry often these older methods would not stand close analysis. Job
struction Training encouraged employees to break their jobs down
to their component parts. When this was properly done, it was often
scovered that newer and simpler means of accomplishing the same
sults might readily be employed.[4]

oduction Control — Quantity

ne of the most important functions of the supervisor is making a con-
int check upon quantity of production. Some of the techniques and
:vices used in the discharge of this responsibility include setting stand-
ds of performance, making time and motion studies, regulating the
)w of work, and preparing and analyzing production costs and re-
)rts. Each of these items will now be discussed and illustrated in rela-
)n to actual production.

andards of Performance. It makes no difference what kind of organi-
tion the supervisor directs, whether it is a shop producing airplane
irts or an office processing cases, applications, or other papers. Over
period of time it is possible to develop standards of performance for
ch of the types of work involved, and in the interests of good super-
sion it is imperative that this be done. The nature of the standards de-
:nds obviously upon the general character and the difficulty of the

---

The fundamentals of Job Instruction Training were discussed in Chapter 9; see also
/gh, Milton, "A Program to Improve Supervision in the Federal Service," *Personnel
iministration*, November, 1943, pp. 7-14.

work and upon the quality, training, and experience of the personnel. These standards are especially essential to the supervisor as an objective basis for judgment in making merit or efficiency ratings.

A number of sources of information may be employed in developing standards. Records may be kept of the daily or hourly output of satisfactory work for a number of employees engaged in a particular operation, and averages determined on this basis. Before standards are actually adopted, the requirements should be thoroughly discussed with employees, and agreement should be reached between the supervisor and the employees. Standards once agreed upon should be reviewed periodically and adjusted as conditions and operations change.

As soon as a standard has been set for a particular task, the supervisor is ready to measure his employees' performance against it. If an employee's performance exceeds the standard, it is outstanding; if it meets the standard, it is adequate; and if it falls below the standard, it is weak.

This statement is taken from the foreword to a series of performance standards for typical tasks performed in mail and file rooms, put out in 1945 by the United States Civil Service Commission as a part of the Federal Work Improvement Program. The tasks covered include handling of incoming and outgoing mail and tasks performed in the file room. The handling of outgoing mail was the simplest of the operations analyzed, with appropriate breakdowns under each of the following headings: collecting mail, sorting and delivering interoffice mail, reviewing mail, sorting and routing material for filing, preparing mail for dispatch, and follow-up on unanswered controlled mail.[5]

Since one of the major purposes of standard setting is to provide a fair basis for evaluating the work performance of employees assigned to specific tasks, it is important that the standards be related to the elements employed in any efficiency rating or service rating system used in the governmental jurisdiction of which the agency is a part. One may deduce from a study of the standard Efficiency Rating Chart (portions of which are reproduced, pages 213 and 217) used in the Federal service the elements which are involved in each of the six operations listed above, relating to the handling of outgoing mail.

An interesting formula for estimating custodial workloads has been used in the Pittsburgh school district since 1926; there it has been

---

[5] Committee on Standards of Performance, *Standards of Performance for Typical Tasks Performed in Mail and File Rooms* (Washington, 1945). See also Department of the Navy, Bureau of Yards and Docks, *Manual of Procedure for Work Measurement in Public Works Offices* (Washington, 1948); Civil Aeronautics Administration, *Establishing Standards of Performance* (Washington, 1948); symposium edited by Sweez Eldon E., "Standards of Performance," in *Personnel Administration*, July, 1948, pp. 2-51 — a series of eight articles — and United States Bureau of the Budget, *Work Measurement and Cost Accounting: Selected References* (Washington, 1945).

found that best results are obtained when the workload per employee is set up on a regular five-day schedule, leaving the half day for duties which may be performed with less frequency. The governing data (area in square feet, tons of coal burned, etc.) are converted into standard room-equivalents, which represent the amount of work one employee can do in one day. The number of room-equivalents for a building is divided by twenty-four, the average number of full working days per month; the answer is the regular daily work necessary for proper maintenance. The advocates of this plan warn that constant vigilance must be exercised to see that the work units are revised to take account of changes in the use of building materials and the introduction of labor-saving tools and equipment for the custodial force. Unless this is done, the plan is obviously of little use as a management tool.[6]

Much more difficult than setting up standards of performance for individual jobs is measuring the efficiency of a whole organization — a department, division, or section, or even the government of a whole city or state. To this problem of job evaluation on a large scale a good deal of attention has been given in recent years, especially at the municipal level. Thus one writer suggests that, in order to appraise properly a municipal government administrative organization, it is necessary to take a series of seven steps, in the order named:[7]

. The entire series of governmental purposes or objectives which the administrative organization is expected to achieve must be searched out and defined in measurable terms.

. The legal framework which controls the administrative structure must be set out in detail, including legislative determinations of the administration of particular functions by particular divisions of the administrative structure, so far as they exist.

The series of governmental objectives should be restated in terms of particular administrative functions to be performed by particular divisions of the administrative structure, within the legal framework of that structure.

The totality of resources which the administrative organization has to draw upon to achieve its government's objectives must be detailed, including governmental income, level of administrative ability and skills within the community it has to draw upon, the physical situation of the community, materials available, the adaptability of its citizens to changes foreseen in the accomplishment of governmental purposes, and the degree of cooperation

ee Steen, M. M., "Formula for Estimating Custodial Work Loads," *School Business airs*, November, 1945, pp. 1–3.

ee Clack, pp. 19–20, which presents a good bibliography; also Peel, Roy V., Ed., tter City Government," *Annals*, September, 1938, entire volume; Ridley, Clarence E., Simon, Herbert A., *Measuring Municipal Activities* (International City Managers ociation, Chicago, 1938); and Simon, "Measurement Techniques in Administrative earch," *Civic Affairs* (University of Southern California) May, 1941, pp. 1–2, 5–8.

operating between groups and individuals within the community. So far as possible, all resources should be stated in terms of how they affect money expenditures. Where the consumption of resources cannot be measured with exactness in money terms, the fact of their existence should be acknowledged to indicate that exact measurement is impossible.

5. There must be set up a series of estimates of the level of services (that is, the degree of adequacy of the accomplishment of governmental objectives) which it is possible for the administration to provide with the resources at its disposal, in terms of performance ratings achievable. These achievable ratings should be determined both for the functions and for the entire departments or agencies that perform those functions.

6. The actual level of achievement of governmental objectives by the administrative organization, in terms of performance ratings, must be determined from available data for each function and for each department or agency that performs one or more of the functions.

7. Finally, in order to measure the degree of efficiency of performance of each function, achievable performance ratings must be expressed as a percentage of actual performance ratings — the efficiency ratings — for each function and for each department or agency that performs one or more of the functions.

"Comparing performance ratings," continues Mr. Clack, "will indicate the degree of adequacy of performance of governmental activities and will compare governments as to differences in resources and administrative efficiency. Comparing efficiency ratings will show the differences in administrative efficiency alone. Whether one or the other is used for comparative purposes depends upon the purposes the appraiser has in mind."

Some years ago, an attempt was made to suggest standards by which the effectiveness of state administration might be evaluated. A series of sixteen possible criteria was presented, along with suggestions as to the best sources of information on these various points. Among the criteria were: [8]

> Provision for essential services
> Adequacy of administrative structure
> Minimum standards for administrative services
> Rank of the state with regard to its activity in particular fields
> Unit costs in particular fields, as compared with other states
> Adequacy of fiscal controls
> Standards of personnel administration

Time and Motion Studies. In government work, time and motion studies — one of the cornerstones of production management in private industry — is relatively little used because organized labor has always been opposed to it. In fact there is in the Federal statutes a provision

---

[8] See the author's "Criteria for Evaluating the Effectiveness of State Administration," *American Political Science Review*, June, 1938, pp. 508–514.

prohibiting time and motion study in any Federal department, establishment, or installation.[9] Opportunity for observation will convince anyone that the statute discourages but does not prevent the procurement of such data. Management is more careful than it is in private establishments about collecting and using the material; but it is obtained in many cases and is used for many purposes, including guidance in the development of plans for future improvement of the organization.[10]

State agencies are often free from such statutory restrictions. The Chief of the Division of Research and Statistics in the Nebraska Department of Assistance and Child Welfare reported a few years ago some of the uses of time study as an administrative tool in his field.[11] The data were obtained on work sheets for individual employees and on work tickets attached to documents and to automobiles and other pieces of mechanical equipment. In the case of equipment, the study revealed the hours of work and the hours of idleness and accordingly the oversupply of some types and the need for more of other types. From the work sheets it was possible to visualize daily and weekly work patterns for individuals and for the various units within the organization. Records of case workers showed time spent in the field, in travel, and at a desk and raised anew the old question as to whether case workers were given too many clerical duties. These findings should be an immensely valuable guide to a public welfare executive able to interpret their significance.

Regulation of the Flow of Work. No organization can operate to best advantage if management does not by some means either provide a reasonably even flow of work or make adequate provisions for carrying peak loads. In many instances this problem can be solved by careful planning and scheduling; in others, the nature of the work makes it difficult if not impossible to guarantee an even flow of work. A certain school of administrators would solve the problem by adopting functionalism, under which groups of employees and their supervisory personnel are set up to perform each specialized type of work required in the agency. The practice has been generally accepted when applied to personnel, finance including purchasing, accounting, auditing), and miscellaneous office services, but when carried too far the result may be to create confusion rather than to bring about a minimum waste of time

his question is reviewed in the author's *Efficiency Rating Systems*, a survey of their ory and development. See United States Senate Committee on Post Office and l Service, 80th Cong., 2nd Sess., *Hearings*, Appendix, 1948.

ee Davis, Louis E., "Motion and Time Study in Production Planning," *Modern agement*, January, 1946, pp. 20–22.

ee Wendstrand, John F., "Some Uses of Time Study as an Administrative Tool," *ic Welfare*, October, 1945, pp. 229–230, 240.

and to stimulate smooth operation. The objections are well stated by Comstock Glaser: [12]

Functionalism is particularly bad in administration because it multiplies the number of moves through which each sequence passes. This does not matter in manufacturing, where the production line assures proper timing, but if the work consists of making decisions and giving technical treatment to a series of variable cases, motion delay cannot be avoided. Because so many administrative acts involve the assertion of the human will, dividing the work among too many offices obscures responsibility and causes intense jurisdictional conflicts. It is impossible to conduct an understanding effectively if those engaged in its direct phases are directed by several different chiefs, each with his own policies and methods, who must be wheedled and cajoled before integrated performance can be had.

Glaser further points out that the good results claimed by the supporters of functionalism might be attained by such an alternative as the establishment of an exchange service through which employees would be loaned from one unit to another for brief periods. The arrangement would not, he says, "sacrifice the integrity of line units, nor cause the additional administrative moves produced by functionalism Properly managed with simple procedures, it might reduce the waste of working time."

Work Measurement. Work measurement is essential to cost accounting financial control, and control of operations. It is a method for establishing an equitable relationship between the volume of work performed and the employee-time expended. This relationship provides a basis for comparing employee utilization in like operations performed at different locations and for comparing employee utilization in the same operation at the same location over a period of time. Such comparison furnish management with factual information needed to improve efficiency and to deploy available man-power resources effectively.

The Bureau of the Budget has very clearly summarized these uses of an effective work-measurement system when it says [13] that such a system is one of several devices available to administrators and supervisory officials to enable them to:

1. Compare equitably employee utilization and performance among different organization units engaged in line operations and activities

---

[12] *Administrative Procedure*, Chapter III.

[13] *Work Measurement: A Case Study in Five Parts*, setting forth a plan for a complete system of records and reports for work measurement in the regional offices of a hypothetical Federal agency. The early history and development of the movement traced in the Society for the Advancement of Management's *The Work Unit in Federal Administration*. For application of these techniques in the personnel field, Rosenberg, Herbert H., "Can Work Measurement Be Applied in the Personnel Office *Public Administration Review*, Winter, 1948, pp. 41-48.

2. Isolate those organization units or operations in need of procedural or other management study
3. Attain maximum utilization of available man power
4. Attain effective control of operations
5. Forecast and justify future personnel requirements in relation to projected volumes of work

When it is not possible to establish basic norms with the aid of time and motion studies, observation and experience records may be substituted. These records now become source material; they show the "how much" and the "by whom." They are utilized for measurement purposes by the methods of sampling and of comparison with standard job and process costs. It is needless to say, of course, that after responsibility has been assigned for summarizing the data from these records and for preparing comparative and analytical charts, management itself must use the results for analysis of past performance, for future planning for the organization as a whole, and for the appraisal of individual performance.[14]

Reporting and Cost Analysis. Production management requires the establishment of accurate systems for reporting "input" in the form of equipment, supplies, and materials, and "output" in the form of finished product. By proper analysis and interpretation of such data, unit cost figures may be obtained. If unlimited funds were available — as they rarely are — almost any kind of management could produce a required volume of work, but to accomplish the undertaking at average cost management must be reasonably efficient. To do the job at less than average cost requires superior management, and superior management is rare indeed. Unit cost figures provide a factual basis for the equitable distribution of funds and workloads and for future projections as well.

An integrated reporting system for cost measurement requires:

1. *Basic Records:* uniform records for accumulating data, and instructions for their maintenance
2. *Report Form:* a standard report form for summarizing basic records, and instructions for its preparation
3. *Summary Tables and Charts:* a method of summarizing, analyzing, and presenting data on several reports
4. *Routing Plan:* procedures for routing reports upward through the organization and routing summaries downward

There must, of course, be a prior determination of the work units for measurement, standards of performance, development of plans for measuring output where special types of work are involved, et cetera. See Bureau of the Budget, *Work Measurement and Cost Accounting: Selected References* (Washington, 1945).

Without such a system there will be little or no assurance that data are valid and comparable, that the computations or the conclusions are equitable, or that the results will become available in readily usable form on a timely basis. The components of the system are applicable in either a centralized or a decentralized organization, but no portion of it can be omitted if the data are to serve the purposes for which they are intended.

Mr. Thomas A. Ryan, in a recent analysis of the input variable, differentiates sharply between muscular work and sedentary work in approaching the problem of cost measurement. He evaluates measures of cost in terms of energy expenditure, reduced capacity, metabolic changes, fatigue tests, long-term production trends, etc., and points out the specific limitations of each. In his summary he groups the various measures into three classes: (1) promising indices still in the developmental stage; (2) a few established measures which have limited application; (3) crude indices of limited validity which provide rough solutions until more refined methods become practically useful.[15]

The output or production records must show from the quantity viewpoint: (1) work received; (2) amount of work accomplished in a process or by a unit in terms of quantity, rate of production, acceleration — either positive or negative; (3) anticipated volume of work. Keeping the necessary records involves in itself a considerable problem. The information must be adequate, but in order to keep the cost of paper work at a minimum the forms should be as simple as is consistent with adequacy.

Production Control — Quality

So far attention has been restricted to consideration of quantity control. Important as this is, it is not an adequate measure of performance without parallel consideration of quality. There is no profit in the employee who turns out an abnormal volume of work if much of it is imperfect (shop work) or filled with errors (office work). There is likewise no profit if the employee wastes large quantities of materials and supplies. In other words, quality is also important, and the most valuable workman is the one who turns out the largest volume of acceptable work in a given time with a minimum of spoilage or error.

It is not sufficient to state quality in general terms; management must provide standards as specific as possible depending on the function of the agency and the character of its product, the difficulty of the work, and other pertinent factors. In a factory operation accuracy may be measured in terms of tolerances from a specified size or weight

---

[15] See Ryan volume.

in paper work in an office the criteria may be accuracy, neatness, and exercise of sound judgment in the disposition of difficult cases. The requirements for a particular situation should be worked out between employees and the supervisor in terms satisfactory to both.

There are various techniques that can be used to insure observance of quality specifications, among them inspection, measurement, testing, and sampling. Most important of all, perhaps, is the development of what might be called "quality-mindedness" on the part of employees. This attitude may easily be related to morale, to the feeling of loyalty, and it may be fostered by the usual methods — by conferences and by the daily relationships between the supervisor and his employees.

One note of caution may well be mentioned that is applicable to all types of controls. Their purpose is to prevent losses, but when the costs of operation run higher than the savings they make possible, their continuance becomes questionable. There is no economy in spending $1000 to save $500. Glaser uses the illustration of "a merchant who is losing $1000 a month through errors in checking the credit of customers. He introduces an extra operation which catches half of these errors and saves $500. If the monthly cost of this operation is $200, the net gain is $300. Since there are still $500 worth of errors, he may introduce another control step of similar cost and effectiveness. It catches half the errors — $250 — and costs $200; so the second net gain is only $50. Other things being equal, the two control operations are justified; but if third one is introduced, it will catch only $125 worth of errors — $75 less than it costs. In the language of economists, the second step is marginal and the third is submarginal." [16]

Inspection and Measurement. Inspection is concerned primarily with the inspector's measurement of the product. The process, as J. M. Juran has pointed out, has certain essential characteristics for each inspection item: [17]

1. Interpretation of the specification
2. Measurement of the product
3. Comparison of (1) with (2)
4. A judgment as to conformance
5. Disposition of the product
6. Recording of the data obtained

The rigidity of the inspection depends partly upon the nature of the specifications but partly also on the nature of the item and the purpose for which it is intended. Some inspections may be done visually, by the experienced and practiced eye of the inspector, while others require precise measurement. The limitations on the power of the in-

Glaser, *op. cit.*, p. 116.
Management of Inspection and Quality Control, p. 23.

spector should be kept clearly in mind. It is not his business to decide whether the specifications are wise, appropriate, or correct but only to determine to the best of his ability whether they have been complied with.

Testing. There are many forms of tests — performance, destructive, minimum life, strength, etc. In a performance test, which is suitable mainly in the case of manufactured products, all the items can be tested; the object is to determine whether the individual item fits and whether it will work. In destructive tests such as fire tests for ammunition, blow tests for fuses, or tensile strength tests, it is obvious that not all the product can be tested; "sampling must be done, and the uninspected residue must be judged on the results of inspection of the pieces in the sample." Tests for minimum life, such as a minimum number of hours of burning for incandescent lamps or a minimum number of deflections for a spring, are in the nature of partially destructive tests and may — unless accelerated tests can be devised and used — be time-consuming and expensive. In certain tests the cost factor may be important.[18]

The question of the sequence of inspection arises where there is division of labor or where a number of inspections are necessary in the process of manufacture. Juran points out that in such cases several common-sense rules apply; where these rules conflict, the facts in the case will furnish the basis for a proper decision.[19]

1. The inspection items with the higher per cent of defects should be checked first. This avoids doing additional inspection work on pieces which will be rejected anyway.
2. Inspection operations which might create defects should be done first, since any defects created can be found in other checks.
3. Inspection operations which test the product in a manner simulating field conditions should be performed last. The reason for this should be obvious.

Sampling. Reference has already been made to the fact that in situations where it is impossible or impractical to handle every unit separately, inspection and in some types of testing, sampling is necessary. Juran, who devotes considerable space to the discussion of sampling and sorting techniques used in inspection and quality control, distinguishes between control sampling and acceptance sampling and between operational sorting and corrective sorting. Control sampling may be defined as an inspection, on a sampling basis, for the purpose of securing data for exercising control; acceptance sampling may have the twofold

[18] Juran, *op. cit.*, pp. 37–38.
[19] *Ibid.*, p. 34.

purpose of distinguishing acceptable from nonacceptable lots and of grading the product in lots.

Homogeneity of product may be derived from a common origin rather than from mixture. Juran observes that when such is the case, "measurement of a sample of the product can still reflect accurately the nature of the creating reservoir." He continues with the statement of a principle which, he believes, is equaled in importance by nothing else in his volume: [20]

The inspected pieces, reflecting the nature of the process which produced them, will also reflect the nature of the uninspected pieces produced by the same process. This principle is the root of acceptance sampling. Furthermore, the inspected pieces will also reflect the nature of the unmanufactured pieces. This principle is the root of control sampling.

Operational sorting, which is a manufacturing operation having the outward appearance of a detail inspection, has as its purpose the separation of the good pieces from the bad. Corrective sorting involves an inspection of each item produced when the product contains defects to an extent too great to permit the use of acceptance sorting — that is, sorting on a sampling basis. This is an expensive process and should be used only in emergencies when other methods fail to provide assurance of a product of standard and uniform quality.

Modern Quality Control Systems. Of the many questions which arise relative to a modern quality control system, brief consideration may be given to two: lines of authority in inspection work, and administrative controls over it. The major question regarding the location of responsibility for supervision is the more difficult. Should the inspectional force report to production supervisors in the regularly established administrative hierarchy of the organization, or should the whole organization for the performance of the inspectional function be independent? There are strong arguments on both sides.

In some respects the inspectional function is similar to the auditing function, and the generally accepted arguments favoring an independent audit may be applied to inspection. On the other hand, such independence may be costly and, from the point of view of administrative organization, cumbersome. The inspectors should have adequate authority to perform their duties, but they should not be too independent. The fundamental question is one of establishing a proper balance between cost of quality and value of quantity. It is doubtful whether the usual line supervisor is of a sufficiently high caliber to make this deci-

---

Ibid., pp. 77–78.

sion. Juran, who considers these problems at some length, comes to the following conclusions: [21]

Maintenance of a high level of quality requires an inspection department which cannot be readily overruled by the shop. However, if inspection department independence goes too far, the cost of attaining quality will become unduly high. To achieve economic balance, the first common supervisor of the inspector and the operator should be at the lowest level of authority staffed with executives who reflect the company's policy on the balance between cost of quality and value of quantity.

The inspection department faces difficult problems in maintaining sound working relations with other factory departments. Like any judicial body, the inspection department must keep its integrity above reproach and its judgments sound if it is to command the respect of the other factory organizations.

The basic organization plan of the operating shops is a major factor in determining what is the most suitable type of organization for the inspection department. The decision of how to group the rank-and-file inspectors (whether by operating function, or by type of product, or by inspection function) is strongly influenced by the manner in which the operating function is organized

Administrative control over the inspection force may be developed in various ways. In addition to the normal controls over personnel and budget, special ones may be developed and applied. A quality audit or survey may be made periodically. A quality rating system applicable to the plant and its product may be installed. Complaints may be investigated, and a check inspection department reporting directly to one of the higher levels of management may exercise a general surveillance over the work of the inspection department.[22]

Record Keeping. Performance of the inspectional function brings one face to face with the problem of record keeping, in this case from the point of view of quality control. The figures cover many of the same elements included in quantity control but are now supplemented by additional information regarding the number of acceptable units produced, the number of rejects and errors, and perhaps the nature and causes of the latter. The quality report to top management should be complete and comprehensive and may draw data from suppliers of materials, from customers and users of the product, and from records the inspection department. From such data it should be possible develop control charts. These charts have been likened to a highway whose control limits are the shoulders on one side and the center line on the other: [23]

[21] Juran, *op. cit.*, Chapter VII, at p. 131.
[22] For a full discussion of all of these, see Juran, *op. cit.*, Chapter XII.
[23] See Divine, William R., and Sherman, Harvey, "A Technique for Controlling Quality," *Public Administration Review*, Spring, 1948, pp. 110–113.

No car driving along the highway can maintain a perfectly straight path. Unevenness in the road, play in the steering wheel, gusts of wind, and a host of other factors cause slight variations in the path of the car. It would hardly be worth while to investigate the causes of these small irregularities. However, the moment the car swerves outside one of the limits, an assignable cause can be assumed to exist and an investigation should be begun. The cause may turn out to be a defect in the steering mechanism, a sleepy driver, a "one-armed" driver, or some similar specific correctable factor.

Such charts enable management to draw accurate conclusions regarding the efficiency of the organization at any given time or over a given period of time in the light of such changes as may have been made in procedure, personnel, incentives, or training. In addition to informing management when assignable causes for variations are at work, they contribute an additional advantage in that they publicize production results. They furnish a convenient means of stimulating competition either among groups doing similar work or within the same group by permitting comparison of present and past records.

Work Improvement Methods

In the interests of economy and efficiency, attention should be given to personnel utilization at all times and to improvements in work programs which make more effective utilization of man power possible. What has been said in earlier chapters on organization and planning had to do with these factors in the initial stages of the development of a new enterprise or program; what is to be said now relates to that constant effort which should be made in every well-run organization to make improvements in organization, methods, and procedures. This — or at least it should be — a continuous process, for as conditions change, the needs of the organization and the things essential to a realization of the goals of good management change with them. These things most vitally affect both the quantity and the quality of production regardless of the nature of the organization or the nature of its product. The effectiveness of such a program is measured in the government service not in terms of profit but in terms of service to the public. The wartime goal of maximum service to the war effort becomes in peacetime "better government at less cost."

Such a program involves both staff and operating responsibilities, the nature of which are shown in the table on page 524. Here as elsewhere staff responsibility is for over-all planning and coordination, while that of the line officer is cooperation in carrying out the program the operating level. Certainly no element in the total is more important than the personnel management function; if this is adequately

performed, many of the others — important as they are — will take c
of themselves.

Organization Improvement. The objectives of a work improvem
program, so far as they relate to organization, include the devel
ment of proper lines of responsibility, checking the span of execut
control within the organization, and preparation of written definiti

Staff and Line Responsibilities in Work Improvement

FUNCTION	CIVIL SERVICE COMMISSION	BUDGET OFFICE	MANAGEMENT STAFF	OPERATING AGE
Manpower	Tapping all available sources of supply			Survey existir procedures
Personnel Utilization	Develop interagency programs			Develop intra agency pro
Personnel Management	Develop and install over-all program			Put utilization gram in c tion
Cost Analysis		Establish unit costs for individual operations		Provide req data on o tions
Standards of Performance		Determine item for personal service (personnel ceiling)		Establish ac able stan for jobs an erations
Financial Support		Determine over-all financial needs of agency		Prepare rec and justific for agency' needs
Work Methods			Advise and assist in study of problems	Survey existi procedures
Review of Assignment of Duties			Review of functions and activities on over-all basis	Review of tions and a ties within agency
Structural Improvement			Improvement of over-all organizational structure	Review of in structure

of duties. The analysis and development of proper organizational l
of responsibility would ordinarily call for a detailed study of e
major division in the organization, its duties and responsibilities,
span of executive control, and the lines of responsibility and coord
tion, to make certain that it is as simple and as positive as it should
In such a survey it is not uncommon to discover a supervisor or s
foreman with far too many people reporting to him, or a situatio
which by combining jobs significant savings in personnel costs m
be achieved.

In connection with such a survey an organization chart shoul
set up, implemented with manualized instructions wherein each l

man's duties are defined and described and the extent of his authority indicated to prevent overlapping and misunderstanding. If these steps have already been taken, as they should have been, only a checking and revision of the chart and manual may be necessary. When written descriptions of duties are to be prepared in connection with positions in an industrial engineering installation, standard practice instructions are formulated. Included in these are definitions and descriptions of duties and details of new procedures which serve as a continual guide to the keymen.

During World War II such a program was publicized in the Federal government as "work simplification." The New Cumberland ASF Depot, located in a critical labor area in Pennsylvania, provides an excellent illustration in the field of materials handling. Teams of four, consisting of two laborers, one operator, and one checker, loaded and unloaded cars and performed warehousing work. The work of each individual was carefully studied, and finally it appeared possible to combine the work of the checker and the operator in a "unit," thereby eliminating one person, the checker, in each group of four persons. Since there were ninety-six checkers regularly employed, this elimination was definitely worth while.

The execution of such a plan requires care. In this instance it was necessary first to find and train personnel for the new position of checker-operator; the records of the former checkers who had not been trained as operators had to be reviewed; and the practical value of the plan had to be sold to the supervisory personnel. Then the plan had to be put to work. This was done gradually, one warehouse at a time, partly to eliminate the "bugs" in the early stages and partly to allow sufficient time to train personnel. As a result, when the entire program was in effect, eighty persons who were badly needed in other Depot operations were salvaged at an annual payroll saving, so far as warehousing operations were concerned, of approximately $140.000.[24]

Methods Improvement. Methods improvement may involve the development of improved fabrication and installation practices, plant layout, the proper tooling and use of new machines, and the simplification of methods. The development of good plant layout very often results in substantial saving of time, increased production at little or no increase in capital investment, and a more effective use of facilities. Similar savings may result from improvements in design; from the development of

Condensed from a routine report prepared by Hilbert V. Lochner, August 11, 1944, *Work Simplification*, as exemplified in the Work Simplification Program of the United States Bureau of the Budget.

work standards for speeds, feeds, and the setup of machines; and in general from the development and adoption of better methods. In all these areas permanent benefits can be assured only through consistent follow-up.[25]

The survey is the usual and perhaps the normal method of discovering opportunities for possible improvements. When in the conduct of such a survey work distribution and process charts are used, each supervisor will be able to ask and answer five key questions relating to his own activities and those of the unit for which he is responsible: [26]

1. What are my major activities?
2. Is there misdirected effort?
3. Are skills used properly?
4. Is there overloading or underemployment?
5. Are there too many unrelated tasks?

As has already been indicated, the Army accomplished a great deal in the development of administrative techniques during World War II. One of these was a simplified process chart suitable for general use in its installations. Such a chart, which is one of the most important tools in work simplification, may be defined as "a detailed chronological record of steps in the work process." The number and the character of the symbols used will obviously depend upon the nature of the work. The Army Service Forces, whose installations were responsible for operations largely of a storage and warehousing nature, used five very simple symbols: a large circle for operations; a small circle for transportation; a small triangle for storage; a square for inspection; and a circle with a square for operation and inspection. The significance of these terms was thus explained by an officer of the Kansas City Quartermaster Depot:

An operation consists of work which changes the property or characteristic of an item involved in the process. A transportation takes place when an item is moved. . . . A storage takes place whenever an item is stationary and operation is being performed on it. . . . The storage may be in files, in a mail box, etc. . . . An inspection is a verification that some previous operation has been properly completed.

---

[25] For illustrative purposes, see Fite, Harry H., "Training Supervisors in Management Analysis," *Public Personnel Review*, April, 1945, pp. 92–98, and Graham, Ben S., "Paper work Simplification," *Modern Management*, February, 1948, pp. 22–25. During World War II, the United States Civil Service Commission put out numerous items, such as those listed in the Selected References. It published also at intervals a leaflet on *Supervision Improvement*, and a series of one-page mimeographed notes on better use of personnel. Cases involving misdirected telegrams, handling more tabulating work with a decreased staff, savings resulting from use of simple mechanical devices such as the hectograph, were presented.

[26] Hoslett, Schuyler D., *Aspects of Army Depot Administration*, pp. 27–30, 33 (American Historical Company, New York, 1945).

When connected by vertical lines these symbols indicate the flow of work.

Procedures Improvement. Improvement in procedure may result from analysis and control of the paper work necessary to operate an activity of formidable size and complexity; it includes the improvement of both planning procedure and production controls. Paper-work procedure involves control of office routine and practice, including preparation of a forms manual in which is entered every form used in the organization. A forms survey provides a basis for analysis of existing procedures and for both the simplification of forms and the elimination of those found to be unnecessary.

Procedures improvement contemplates attention to planning, scheduling, and dispatching in the various phases of the agency's operations. The movement of men and materials must be controlled and coordinated as to quantity, time, and place. A constant comparison may be made between actual progress and the planned schedule by the use of boards, charts, and other tools of control — a procedure which makes possible the immediate detection and correction of bottleneck situations. Furthermore, centralized and organized shop planning permits the shop master or foreman and his production supervisors to devote more time to the assignment of men to jobs, job planning, technical supervision, and follow-up. Such an over-all program makes for better utilization of man power and increased efficiency in operation.

SELECTED REFERENCES

Rowe, James M., *An Adaptation of Statistical Quality Control*, Quality Control Report No. 7 (Carnegie Institute of Technology, Pittsburgh, 1945). Consideration of an important means of quality control, vitally essential to control of production.

Barnes, Ralph M., *Motion and Time Study*, Second Edition (Wiley, New York, 1940) and *Work Methods Manual* (Wiley, New York, 1944). An authority on time and motion study discusses the problems involved and provides a manual.

Benedict, Howard G., *Yardsticks of Management*, Second Edition (Management Book Company, Los Angeles, 1946). Treatment of the methods and standards of appraisal necessary for the control of production; see also: Clack, Douglas, *General Appraisal Standards and Methods for Measuring Public Administration* (Institute of Politics, Indiana University, 1942), and Dimock, Marshall E., "Administrative Efficiency Within a Democratic Polity," in Martin, Roscoe C., Ed., *New Horizons in Public Administration*, pp. 21–43 (University of Alabama Press, 1946).

Juran, J. M., *Management of Inspection and Quality Control* (Harpers, New York, 1945). Best discussion of inspection as a means of control over quality.

Ryan, Thomas A., *Work and Effort* (Ronald Press, New York, 1947). A good analysis of the psychological aspects of production.

Taylor, Frederick W., *Shop Management* (Harpers, New York, 1911) and *The Principles of Scientific Management* (Harpers, New York, 1911 and 1934). Founder of scientific management sets forth his views in two volumes, now old, but still standard.

United States Bureau of the Budget, *Work Management: A Case Study in Five Parts* (Washington, 1947), and *Work Measurement and Cost Accounting: Selected References* (Washington, 1945). The Federal agency responsible for the management program deals with problems of work measurement.

United States Civil Service Commission, *Better Utilization of Stenographers and Typists* (Washington, 1944); *Standards of Performance for Typical Tasks in Mail and File Rooms* (Washington, 1945), and *Your Part in the Utilization Program* (Washington, 1945). Maximum utilization of man power is an important means of achieving maximum production, both quantitatively and qualitatively; duties in mail and file rooms are used as a means of illustrating the importance of standards of performance in measuring work efficiency.

War Department, Army Service Forces, *Simplification and Standardization of Procedures*, Control Manual M 703-7 (Washington, 1944) and *Work Simplification* Control Manual M 703-4 (Washington, 1945); Services of Supply, *Work Simplification*, Manual for Control Officers, Vol. III (Washington, 1942). Work simplification is one means of attaining maximum utilization of man power.

27

SUPERVISION

ANAGEMENT has been defined by Lawrence A. Appley as "getting ings done through the efforts of other people." Henry Taylor ex-essed the concept admirably more than a century ago when he wrote at "the most important qualification of one who is high in the serv-: of the state is his fitness for acting *through others;* since the im-rtance of his operations vicariously effected ought, if he knows how make use of his power, to predominate greatly over the importance lich can attach to any man's direct and individual activity." [1]

This concept is valid at all levels — "top-side," middle management) use the now familiar phrase of Mary C. Niles), and supervisory. lis latter group, with which the present discussion is primarily con-rned, consists of supervisors, as they are called in the government 'vice, or foremen, to use the corresponding term employed in private lustry. Approximately 85 per cent of the employees of the Federal vernment work under the direction of "first-line supervisors." The lividuals who function in this capacity, at the lowest rung in the lder of supervision, are referred to in the literature of the American magement Association as "management's supervisory executives." [2]

The supervisor is responsible to management at his particular level the organization. In the eyes of the rank and file of employees, who 'ely have personal contact with the heads of the organization, the pervisor *is* management. He is responsible for production. His duty :o see that the total work of the unit gets done effectively. The gen-l character of the supervisory organization and the three funda-ntal aspects of his job are indicated in the simple diagram on

---

'he Statesman, p. 11 (W. Heffer & Sons, Ltd., Cambridge, 1927), and quoted in lic Administration Review, Spring, 1945, p. 162. This book was first published in 2.

'he Foreman's Basic Reading Kit, Foreword (New York, 1944); also United States t Office Department, Introduction to Supervisory Development (Washington, 1944). rivate industry, and occasionally in government, another character enters into this ure. The steward is to the union what the foreman is to the company; he is the key 1 in the relationship of the union to management and of the union to its members. his responsibility to protect the rights and interests of the union members just as the responsibility of the foreman to protect management's interests. See Depart-it of Labor, The Foreman's Guide to Labor Relations, p. 12.

page 531. The base of the triangle is "human relations," and rightfully so, since the supervisor acts through others; the structure cannot stand or be balanced except on such a foundation.[3]

In the problem of supervision a number of matters now demand our consideration: the methods of selecting supervisors, the personal qualities that make for a good supervisor, the duties and responsibilities that go with supervisory positions, the methods and techniques by which the supervisor discharges these responsibilities, and the responsibilities of management to its supervisors.

Methods of Selecting Supervisors

Prevailing Methods. There are at least half a dozen methods by which individuals may be selected for supervisory positions. Selection on the basis of seniority, which is one of the less desirable methods, produces very uncertain results. One may obtain a good supervisor, or he may get a poor one. The truth of the matter is that length of service is largely irrelevant to the problem at hand, that it is a wholly unreliable method of ascertaining whether an individual possesses those personal qualities that seem to be essential in a good supervisor. All that seniority proves is that the individual has lived so long and that he has neither resigned nor been dismissed.

Sometimes management selects a very efficient workman and makes him a supervisor. Even theoretically there is little justification for such a procedure, since performance in nonsupervisory positions offers little evidence of supervisory ability. There is, in fact, no significant correlation between success in nonsupervisory and success in supervisory positions. The mere fact that a particular employee happens to be able to turn out more and better work than any other in his group offers no assurance whatever that he (or she) has the personal qualities essential to a good supervisor. The effect of such a selection may be and often is to transform an outstanding producer into either a mediocre or poor supervisor.

Other methods of selection include choice on the basis of political pull or personal favoritism and more or less accidental designation of some workman to take over in an emergency, often without any serious consideration of his qualifications or the realization that the assignment may turn out to be permanent.

All these methods of selecting supervisors reflect a peculiarity of American thinking. It is always assumed that just as every attorney

THE SUPERVISOR and HIS JOB

CHIEF

TECHNICAL SERVICES
Machines~Materials~Methods
From higher officials to workers

ORGANIZATION~MANAGEMENT
Finances~Personnel
From workers to higher officials

I SUPERVISORS II

A B SUPERVISORS A B

WORKERS
Human Relations
Production~Morale~Public Relations

ngs to be a judge, every worker desires eventually to occupy a su-
rvisory position. Society seems willing to pay a premium for super-
sory work, although the duties of many workers require greater ex-
rience and a higher degree of professional skill. Because "promotion"
ems to be the way to progress in both prestige and salary, many
orkers who do not really want to be supervisors and who have no
rsonal fitness for the work, succumb to the temptation to try it when
forded an opportunity.

Among the more desirable of the prevailing methods of selecting
pervisors may be mentioned the designation and training of an un-
rstudy for each supervisory position so that there will be some quali-
d person always on hand to take over when the incumbent is absent.
second method is a promotion examination — either a written test or
competitive evaluation of the educational qualifications and experi-
ce of those employees whose length of service and efficiency ratings

warrant their consideration. A promotion committee in which employees have representation may be used to review recommendations, thereby assuring the staff that decisions have been made on the basis of merit. Still a third possibility is the application of scientific methods to the selection.

Scientific Methods of Selection. A study of management's views on supervision, made at Purdue University in 1945, resulted in the conclusion that most of these views are not based upon sound knowledge arrived at by thorough investigation of the problems involved. The report continues: [4]

Hence management has no proper basis on which to select supervisors, to promote them, to train them, or to determine their worth or uselessness to the organization. So the most important link in the management-worker contact is actually in many cases the weakest link. . . . The study showed that the type of supervisory quality that the experts think a supervisor should possess can be measured, but that the vague and conflicting notions of supervisory quality that managements have are so sketchy that they cannot often even be stated, much less measured.

On this basis a clear conflict exists between two opposing points of view — on the one hand that scientific methods of selection are impossible or at least impractical and on the other that they offer the most promising means of avoiding the obvious mistakes so frequently resulting from hit-or-miss methods. Milton Mandell has developed these points of view in parallel form as follows: [5]

Formal Methods of Selecting Supervisory Personnel

ARE PRACTICAL	ARE IMPRACTICAL
A large number of factors are important for supervisory success.	Personal characteristics are important for supervisory success.
A number of these factors can be measured adequately by systematic selection methods while other factors can be assessed to only a limited extent.	Personal characteristics cannot be measured adequately by present formal selection methods.
Therefore, formal selection methods should be used for supervisory selection, supplemented by informal methods to measure those factors which elude precise measurement.	Therefore, formal selection methods should not be used for supervisory selection.

The "personality boys" tend to overemphasize the significance of personal traits and characteristics. No one will deny that these are im-

---

[4] File, Quentin W., "Are Management's Views of Supervision Faulty?" *Personnel* January, 1946, pp. 242–254.
[5] See Mandell, Milton M., "The Selection of Supervisors," *Personnel Administration* November, 1947, pp. 22–23, and references therein on industry experience.

portant, but as Milton Rygh has clearly stated, they are only a part of the equipment of a successful supervisor: [6]

While there probably are certain intangible qualities of "personality" or "leadership" that tend to help a supervisor succeed, these qualities merely indicate an aptitude for leading, and are no more a substitute for skill in supervision than an "ear for music" is a substitute for skill in playing the piano. It is not a simple matter to direct the work of others, as many competent craftsmen have discovered when they were chosen to be foremen. There are definite, specific skills involved in supervising other people, which can be learned precisely as any other skills, and which can be taught as readily.

The weight of the argument seems to be very much on the side of those supporting formal tests. In addition to numerous studies made in industry, several government agencies tried during World War II to devise methods of selection that would tend to minimize guesswork and favoritism. The Navy Department program, which antedates most of the others, utilizes five types of test:

1. Written tests of various kinds, such as supervisory judgment and reading comprehension
2. Oral interviews
3. Experience evaluations
4. Efficiency ratings
5. Formal reports by the current supervisor of the candidate

These types by no means exhaust the list of possibilities. Mr. Mandell adds numerous others,[7] which may be utilized in varying combinations according to the nature of the position to be filled. Since supervisory positions vary greatly in character and requirements, it seems unlikely that uniform methods of selection are either possible or desirable; this does not, however, preclude the use of such tests as may be suitable in any given instance. The pattern of tests should be determined in each case on the basis of careful job analysis, each test item elected being susceptible of justification in relation thereto.

Qualifications of a Good Supervisor

f scientific methods are to be applied to the choice of supervisors, it s obvious that some acceptable standards must be evolved upon the basis of which appropriate tests can be selected or constructed. There s much literature on the qualities of leadership and on the essential

See Rygh, Milton, "A Program to Improve Supervision in the Federal Service," Personnel Administration, November, 1943, pp. 7–14.
These are: interest inventories; mental ability tests; tests of technical knowledge and dgment; candidate's knowledge of the organization, policies, and personnel of his ency; record in supervisory training courses; oral interviews; performance on the job fficiency rating); and background information.

qualifications for supervisors. Believing that much of this writing was based on introspection rather than upon an effort to analyze the elements of strength and weakness in actual supervisors, the Committee on Training of the Philadelphia Federal Council of Personnel Administration undertook in 1944 an extensive analysis of these qualifications as displayed by approximately 1200 supervisors actually on the job in various Federal agencies in the Philadelphia metropolitan area.

The Committee's program involved three distinct steps: the identification of essential qualities, the rating of these qualities so that they might be arranged in order of importance, and the development of a test program. The members of the Committee with the advice and assistance of a distinguished group of consultants in personnel management constructed a list of qualities suggested by the members of the group as being essential. The members of the Committee and later the members of the Council were asked to weight these qualities in accordance with their importance in supervisory work.

This effort brought out very clearly the fact that qualifications vary according to the character of the supervisory work to be done. That is to say, some qualification regarded as essential for a first-line supervisor may not be particularly important in a coordinating supervisor, and vice versa. The Committee then set up two different schedules of qualities, one for each type of supervisor. These lists appear on page 535. The final step in the program was the development of a battery of tests by means of which the presence (or absence) of these qualities in individual aspirants could be discovered. In some cases it was possible to utilize tests already worked out; in others, new ones had to be constructed.[8]

In as much as it is somewhat difficult to draw out of this table the more important qualities essential to each type of supervisor and to compare these qualities, there are listed below the five leading skills required by each type, in the order of their significance as determined by the survey:

FIRST-LINE SUPERVISOR	COORDINATING SUPERVISOR
Training personnel	Selecting personnel
Planning the daily workload	Exercising authority and meriting respect
Making assignments and delegating duties	Planning future operations
Developing teamwork among subordinates	Making assignments and delegating duties
Exercising authority and meriting respect	Knowledge of organization's rules and regulations

[8] Milon L. Brown was the Chairman of this Committee. The data collected have been analyzed for a doctoral dissertation by William J. Eisenberg, formerly Personnel Officer, Philadelphia Signal Depot. On this general subject, see also File, *op. cit.*

Philadelphia Federal Council of
Personnel Administration Committee on Training

TABULATION OF QUESTIONNAIRE ON SUPERVISORY QUALITIES *

FIRST-LINE SUPERVISOR			COORDINATING SUPERVISOR	
Total Vote	Order Number		Total Vote	Order Number
		Skill in:		
1220	17	1. Selecting personnel	1887	1
2195	1	2. Training subordinates	1612	8
2194	2	3. Planning the daily workload	1570	10
1381	14	4. Planning future operations	1802	3
1856	6	5. Analyzing workers as to their capabilities and weaknesses	1670	7
2007	3	6. Making assignments and delegating duties	1799	4
1892	4	7. Developing teamwork among subordinates	1734	6
1699	9	8. Improving job results	1584	9
1509	12	9. Evaluating results of operations	1557	11
1678	10	10. Maintaining records and making reports to ʹ superiors	1434	13
1489	13	11. Rating employees	1400	15
1272	15	12. Encouraging workers to grow in service	1190	20
1736	8	13. All the operations of the unit	1340	17
1872	5	14. Exercising authority and meriting respect	1880	2
1529	11	15. Recognizing and dealing with emotional disturbances that affect production	1452	12
1069	21	16. Conducting group discussions	1410	14
		A knowledge of:		
1808	7	17. Organization's rules and regulations	1786	5
1005	22	18. Organization's promotional policy	1185	21
476	25	19. Organization's wage administration plan	785	24
637	23	20. Organization's employment procedure	891	23
1086	20	21. Organization's plan for handling grievances	1198	19
1185	19	22. Organization's standards of production (quantitative and qualitative)	1344	16
520	24	23. Organization's special services (health and recreation)	610	25
1251	16	24. Related operations to the unit supervised	1229	18
1160	18	25. Health and safety services	790	22

* Results of a survey conducted by the Committee on Training, Milon L. Brown, Chairman (1945).

This is one of the most significant efforts thus far made to deal constructively with the problem of supervisory qualifications, but various other groups and individuals have also given some attention to it. Thomas H. Nelson, member of a New York firm of management consultants, published in 1945 the results of his study of it. Emphasizing strongly his belief that workers' attitudes should be consulted, he developed the following list of major requirements of the executive: [9]

> Technical knowledges and abilities
> Knowledge of organization and administration
> Application of the scientific method of thinking to current problems
> Techniques and skills of effective human relations
> Effective expression
> Self-management
> A philosophy of life

The Supervisor's Job

If it may now be assumed that the supervisor has been selected, preferably by some scientific method, it may be appropriate to inquire into the nature of the duties and responsibilities he is to discharge [10] and into the methods by which he discharges them. It is important to know not only *what* he does but *how* he is expected to do it. Although there are many different types of supervisors and supervisory positions, there are some techniques [11] and procedures which, it is believed, are more or less applicable to all.

Setting up Positions. In setting up positions, the supervisor must do at a lower level the same kind of thing that management at the higher levels does, namely, analyze the work to be done and break it down into its component parts. Ultimately the breakdown progresses to the point where individual positions can be created, a position being a sufficient amount of work of a given type to require the services of one employee full time. The specific steps involved after determining the work assignment are: writing the position descriptions, allocating the positions, and fixing the compensation.[12] If the positions are to be set up properly, there must be careful planning of the work to be done and as accurate a job analysis as possible in advance of actual operations.

Staff Development and Training. Another essential technique of the successful supervisor is the selection of a good staff and the constant strengthening of his organization by doing those things which will draw out the best efforts of his employees and encourage their devel-

---

[9] See Nelson, Thomas H., "Administrator and Executive – Two Different Entities in Management," *Modern Management,* January, 1946, pp. 23–25.
[10] These duties have been variously classified; for simple lists, see Cooper, p. 21, and the National Association of Manufacturers, *Strengthening Management Teamwork.*
[11] Technique has been defined as "the method or style of performance in any art, especially skill in the execution of the details of any performance."
[12] Civil Service Commission, *Position Classification as to Aid to Supervision.*

opment and growth. This may involve selection and training of under-studies and the use of appropriate types of training for individuals desiring to prepare themselves for greater responsibilities. It means that in his relations with employees the supervisor ought to be as under-standing, as encouraging, and as helpful as possible, leading rather than driving them. He should realize that the stronger and more capable his staff is, the stronger and more effective his organization will be. Aside from the disastrous effect upon the morale of the group when the supervisor claims credit personally for everything that is done right and blames someone else for everything that goes wrong, he ought to remember that whatever the organization does well reflects credit upon his leadership and direction. There is plenty of credit in a job well done for everyone who has had a part in it.[13]

One of the most important responsibilities assigned to supervisors is that of training and developing subordinates; the various types of such training, on the job and off the job, have been discussed in Chapter 9. As Professor Hersey has observed, no field of management has been more neglected than that relating to executive and supervisory person-nel. "Executives and supervisors," he says, "are human and subject to the same human failings as workers. They need cooperative guidance and constructive advice just as the workers do."[14] There is no one simple way of selecting, promoting, and improving executive and su-pervisory personnel; the ideal approach is to stress the development of executives and supervisors by individual analysis and attention, utilizing the various methods and tools of individualized training discussed else-where in this volume. These, of course, should be coordinated into an effective program.

It is the supervisor to whom the new employee reports for duty. His function is to show the new man to his duty station, introduce him to his new associates, and explain his duties and the working rules of the shop or office.[15] This is orientation training, but in large establish-

---

[13] Lent D. Upson, in his delightful series of letters from a dean of public administra-tion to his graduates, has some interesting suggestions on these points; as for instance:

"A good administrator hires people who are smarter than he is. Certainly, there is some danger that one of the smart ones may get your job, but if an administrator is smart enough to hire smart people, he probably will be smart enough to keep his job in spite of them."

"Give your subordinates as much credit as you can and still not build their reputa-tions beyond their capacities. In appraising the capacities of subordinates, it is well to remember that they are usually much larger than you believe. . . . At any rate, give the subordinate a chance to do a bigger job. He may do it differently from your way. It may be a better way."

[14] Hersey, *op. cit.*, p. 3.

[15] These will include both external and internal directives, the former consisting of acts, executive orders, decisions of the attorney general, the comptroller general, etc. Internal directives vary with the agency; in the case of the United States Civil Service

ments it may be supplemented by additional instruction relating to the organization as a whole. Refresher courses, promotion or transfer courses, and management training conferences may be arranged for present employees. When new rules or regulations come through, or modifications of old ones, it is the supervisor who in group or individual conferences must discuss them and explain them to the employees. The exact steps in this process have been summarized as follows by Mr. Appley, each one to be worked out with the person involved: [16]

1. Develop a simple outline of the functions and operations to be performed.
2. Develop a simple statement of results which will be considered satisfactory.
3. At regular intervals check actual performance against the standards that have been set up.
4. Make a list of corrective actions necessary to improve performance where such improvement is needed.
5. Select the best sources from which he can obtain help and information.
6. Set aside in advance a time for supplying the help and information that is needed.

In the frequent daily contacts which arise in the course of work, the supervisor is constantly instructing employees and explaining various matters pertaining to their work and its relation to the agency program as a whole. Here also the training section may be called in to handle larger problems which cannot be adequately taken care of by the supervisor in his day-to-day contacts with employees. It is difficult to overestimate the importance of these contacts as they affect not only the productive efficiency of the organization but the morale of employees. It often happens that an employee performing a seemingly unimportant and monotonous job takes a new interest in his work when the supervisor explains to him, as he is often able to do, that this work constitutes a really vital phase of the work program of the agency.

Delegation of Authority. The establishment of lines of authority and definite responsibility for work performance is another device by which the supervisor accomplishes his function. He does this by delegating segments of the authority that has in turn been delegated to him

---

Commission, they consist of Commission Minutes, Departmental Circulars (from th Commission to operating agencies), Circular Letters (staff policies and instructions) *Manual of Instructions, Policies, and Procedures,* as well as other divisional and staf memoranda. When the new *Federal Personnel Manual* is completed, it will replac many of these types of internal instructions and will serve as a guide to all departmen and agencies in personnel matters.
[16] *Foreman's Basic Reading Kit,* p. 22; see also "Introducing the New Employee to th Job," *ibid.,* pp. 75–82.

The amount delegated to any one employee will obviously depend upon the nature of the work and the amount of authority required. The supervisor will not subdelegate all his authority, and manifestly he cannot delegate authority that he does not possess. The sum total of what he delegates must, therefore, be something less than has been entrusted to him by his immediate supervisor. While this subject of delegation is one of the most vital concerns of a supervisor, the characteristics and necessity of such delegations, the relationships between supervisor and employee established thereby, and the requirement that the terms of a delegation should be definite and specific with regard to all essential points, are discussed elsewhere in this volume.[17]

Responsibility for Production. In furtherance of production the supervisor is responsible for planning, organizing, and directing the work of his unit. This involves the coordination of men, money, materials, and machines in order that each type of resource may be used to the maximum benefit of the program. It involves the budgeting and scheduling of each so that there may be as nearly as possible an even flow of work within the unit. On occasion, when difficulties are encountered, he functions as a trouble shooter. He must, furthermore, cooperate with other supervisors so that there will be an even flow of production within the agency as a whole. This is actually only a part of the responsibility for cooperation, which extends upward to higher levels of management and downward to supervisors of lower rank. The best results can be obtained only when there is a free flow of ideas and an exchange of information between all levels. This has been likened to a two-way track, one carrying communications from the bottom up, the other from the top down.[18]

Morale Building. The personal leadership of the supervisor is extremely important in the development of good morale and of a proper mental attitude toward the organization and its work. In fact this is his primary responsibility. It has been said that it is his task not merely to get things done but to do so *harmoniously.* The supervisor untrained or improperly trained in the psychology of supervision represents one of the most significant causes of dissatisfaction and poor morale among employees today. Only to the extent that he is successful in building morale can he expect to secure a high standard of production and limit

[17] For general discussion, see Cooper, and Dimock; for a war agency, O'Brien, John L., and Fleischmann, Manly, "The War Production Board Administrative Policies and Procedures," *George Washington Law Review,* December, 1944, pp. 1–60; and on subdelegation, Grundstein, Nathan D., "Subdelegation of Administrative Authority," *ibid.,* February, 1945, pp. 144–196.
[18] See *Strengthening Management Teamwork, op. cit.,* pp. 16–18.

labor turnover with all its accompanying headaches of waste, training and retraining, and retarded production schedules.[19]

It is the supervisor who must keep the employees informed of agency policies and changes in rules and regulations and explain the reasons for and the purposes of such changes. His is that daily and intimate contact with the employees which gives him the opportunity to discuss their problems with them and to adjust differences and minor conflicts. In a well-organized agency there will, to be sure, be a personnel office with employee counselors, appeal procedures, and other services available to dissatisfied employees, but these services become operative only after the immediate supervisor has failed. They are not equipped to handle *all* the problems in the field of employee relations, large and small, and administratively it is not desirable that they should be. The supervisors with their employees are, so to speak, the unit cells of the organization, and it is only when these cells break down that it is necessary for the central personnel office services to enter into the picture.[20]

Health and Safety. The supervisor is likewise responsible for the physical well-being of his employees. This involves careful attention to space layout for equipment, materials, and supplies and to the conditions affecting health and safety that were discussed in Chapter 11. Safety needs in industrial establishments are more or less obvious, but the protection of office workers from a variety of hazards such as open file drawers, stacks of material insecurely piled, and telephone wires stretched across aisles is no less necessary. The supervisor must watch such working conditions as heat, light, ventilation, drafts, the elimination of unnecessary noises — for all of these vitally affect the health of employees. The supervisor must report accidents when they occur and the amount of time lost through sick leave.

If the agency is large enough to justify it either in its own budget or on a cooperative basis with other agencies, a full-time nurse with a first-aid room or dispensary is an excellent investment. This service has

---

[19] In *Foreman's Basic Reading Kit*, see "Helping the Worried Worker," pp. 97–103 and "The Foreman's Part in Preventing Absenteeism," pp. 107–108.

[20] As one phase of a state-wide supervision improvement program, the New York Personnel Council in 1948 put out a monthly series of attractively designed "Tips to Supervisors" under such titles as:

> Do You Know Any "Conclusion-Jumpers"?
> How Good Do You Think You Are? (a self-evaluation sheet)
> Let's Look at the Record!
> How Low Is Your "Fighting Point"?
> Do You Keep Your Promises?
> Make Up Your Mind
> What Do You Expect Anyway?

a beneficial effect on morale, for the workers feel that management is interested in their welfare. In addition to this, it is well known that the prompt treatment of minor injuries, infections, and ailments will save the agency in the aggregate many hundreds — perhaps thousands — of man-hours a year. The supervisor's responsibility in this connection may include also participation in hospital and medical care cooperatives, credit unions, and similar organizations.

Record System and Reports. The supervisor is responsible also for the keeping of records and the preparation of such reports as may be required by higher levels of management. Whatever the nature of the work done by the shop or office, it is absolutely essential for management to know accurately and at frequent intervals just what the workload is — how many units have been received, how many are in process, how many completed, how much backlog (if any), during the period covered by the report. Management must know whether over a period of time the workload is increasing or decreasing. The upward channels of communication in the submission of such reports may, as Professor Dimock has observed, take many forms: [21]

> Planning is one of these; statistics is another; progress reports constitute a third; special memoranda still a fourth. But not all communications are written. Some of the most important, especially when the executive is interested in attitudes and nuances, are face-to-face relationships. There is a universal tendency to say more orally than is written in a formal communication, because expression and attitude are sometimes more significant to the executive than a combination of words on paper.

The exact nature and frequency of these reports will be prescribed by management at the higher levels. The data from which the complete report will be compiled must be fed up through channels by supervisors at all levels from the first-line supervisor on up. Each must establish such record keeping and reporting procedures as may be required within his own segment of the organization in order to obtain the necessary information within the deadline specified. In order to avoid waste of time in inventory work, it is desirable that the supervisor establish a system of record keeping that will enable him at all times to obtain accurate information regarding the amount and character of the work on hand.

Improvement of Supervision

Much of the regular work which a supervisor does in selection, training, and morale building is performed with an awareness that he must

---

[a] Dimock, *op. cit.*, p. 153; see also Little, Mark D., "Internal Reports to Management," *The Controller*, March, 1945, pp. 503-508, 514.

strive constantly to do a better job, for better management of human relations leads to greater organizational productivity and to greater job satisfaction for the staff. It is common knowledge that most organizations produce far less than they could, but merely wishing or hoping for improvement will not bring it about. More active steps must be taken.

Industry has for some years carried on extensive investigation and experiments in the field of "human engineering." Management in public agencies should keep abreast of these findings and utilize them so far as they may be applicable. By cooperation with researchers in human relations it can at very slight expense support inquiries and experimentation that may in the end so increase production as to save many times the original outlay. Experimentation and demonstration are necessary; they must take place, not in laboratories but in actual work places, in which the results may be promptly utilized.[22]

In the meantime, while new techniques are being developed, supervisors can make full use of the means already known for the improvement of supervision. These include self-evaluation both of the organization and of each individual's performance, the avoidance of common errors in supervision, and the utilization of generally accepted guiding principles.

Self-Evaluation. If the supervisor fails to do his job well, or if he fails seriously with regard to any aspect of it, he will eventually hear about it from his superiors. The prudent supervisor, however, will not wait to be "called on the carpet." He will seek to develop ways and means of informing himself about the adequacy or inadequacy of his own performance so that he may detect weaknesses before they become sufficiently serious to impair production and attract attention.

The supervisor who knows his job will be able to think of suitable means of evaluating his own work and determining the relative efficiency of his organization. How can a supervisor see himself? For one thing, he may find it useful to ask his employees to rate him when service ratings are made. From the point of view of his organization he may employ some such aid as the thirty-minute check-up on administrative management reproduced on page 543. This form can be used with slight modification at any level of management. By such means the supervisor should be able to identify weak spots. Identification is perhaps the most vital step, for remedial measures can be planned only if he knows not only that something is wrong but what is wrong.

---

[22] See Planty, Earl G., "New Methods for Evaluating Supervisor Training," *Personnel,* January, 1945, pp. 235–242.

A Thirty-Minute Check-up on Administrative Management
for Personnel in Federal Agencies *

1. Are we satisfied with the quantity of work output?
2. Are we satisfied with the quality of work output?
3. At what levels are operating difficulties apparent?
4. Are the difficulties due to factors beyond our control?
5. Are there some difficulties that we could control?
6. Do operating and staff officers use accepted methods to identify unsatisfactory situations?
7. Do all of our employees know what duties they are expected to perform?
8. Do all of our employees know how well they are expected to perform their duties?
9. Do all our employees know the relationship of their work to that of other work areas?
10. Are our employees in general working with management or only for it?
11. Are we using the following tools of management to remedy undesirable situations?

> Competent staff assistance
> Increased delegation of supervisory and production duties
> A sane program to train each employee in the skills and knowledges he needs to do his job
> A plan of cross-unit training where practicable
> Requirement of understudies
> Satisfactory employee relations program
> An adequate placement program

12. Where can this agency get assistance in its personnel utilization program?

* Prepared by Milon L. Brown, in 1945, then Chairman of the Committee on Training, Philadelphia Federal Council of Personnel Administration. Obviously, for most effective use within an agency, these various items would have to be broken down into their component parts, for checking purposes.

It is also important for him to discover the effect of his methods and his own personal characteristics upon members of his staff. Many forms have been worked out for obtaining employee reactions on these matters. The reactions may be significant even where the supervisor is doing all right. A story is told, for instance, of one supervisor who lost all his best people because they mistakenly believed that he was trying to steal all the credit. Even in such a case it is extremely important for him to learn that such an impression exists and why it exists, whether or not it is justified. The situation cannot be cleared up until the facts are known.

Some Common Mistakes in Supervision. It is easy enough to say that a supervisor ought to conform as nearly as possible to the generally recognized principles of supervision and that he should avoid actions which violate these principles; but this is easier said than done. Supervisors, as human beings, possess certain weaknesses and peculiarities, some of which result in mistakes in supervisory practice. Some of these are especially common. New supervisors should guard against them, but experienced supervisors should also take an inventory of their methods and habits from time to time to make sure that they have not unwittingly fallen into these errors.

Perhaps the most common error is the failure promptly to delegate authority or, having delegated it, to keep a constant surveillance upon its use without at the same time making the subordinate feel that he has no freedom of action and no opportunity to exercise his initiative. Another common fault develops in those individuals who seem to be inherently unsuited to supervisory work. They cannot always be identified in advance; everyone can recall instances in which persons who were congenial and well liked before being given supervisory authority became unbearable afterward. They simply did not know, and some of them proved incapable of learning, how to exercise authority over others. Another common defect is found in those individuals who go to the other extreme, refusing or at least refraining from exercising their authority at all, and trusting to luck that the organization will run itself — as, of course, it will not.

Some Guiding Principles. Most of these weaknesses in supervision can be avoided, as Walter Dietz has pointed out, by careful attention to certain principles which are basic to good relations between the supervisor and those whose work he directs: [23]

> Treat all people as individuals
> Let people know how they are getting along
> Give credit when due
> Give people a chance to talk over in advance the things that affect them
> Make the best use of people's ability

In handling a supervisory problem the supervisor may well follow the four basic principles which were emphasized in the War Manpower Commission's Job Relations Training Program during World War II:

> 1. Get the facts — be sure you have the whole story.
> 2. Weigh and decide — don't jump to conclusions.
> 3. Take action — don't "pass the buck."
> 4. Check results — did your action help production?

Very often the supervisor finds it necessary to issue orders or instructions. At such times he should bear in mind the fact that orders can be effective only when certain conditions exist. As Chester I. Barnard has pointed out, "a person can and will accept a communication as authoritative only when four conditions simultaneously obtain": [24]

1. He can and does understand the communication
2. At the time of his decision, he believes that it is not inconsistent with the purpose of the organization

---

[23] *The Foreman's Basic Reading Kit*, p. 35; see also Hall, Milton, "Supervising People — Closing the Gap Between What We Think and What We Do," *Advanced Management*, September, 1947, pp. 129–135.
[24] *The Functions of the Executive*, p. 165 (Harvard University Press, 1940).

3. At the time of his decision, he believes it to be compatible with his personal interest as a whole

4. He is able mentally and physically to comply with it

Management's Responsibility to the Supervisor

The role of the supervisor is tremendously important. It is no exaggeration to say that a reliable index of the effectiveness of an organization can be found in the quality of its supervisory personnel. But the supervisor, important as he is, is not all-powerful. He is dependent for results upon his staff and upon the kind of cooperation and support he receives from higher levels of management. This is perhaps another way of saying that management at any level can make or break an organization.

The literature of the field abounds with discussions of the importance of the supervisor or foreman. While his virtues have been extolled, a series of developments in industry in the last decade or more have tended to minimize his standing until there has in fact been little distinction between him and the workers.[25] The trend of opinion now is that this condition must be corrected. As Ellsworth S. Grant observes, industry, to save its foremen, "must first decide they are 'employers' — in both the functional and legal meaning of that word. Next, it must make them think of themselves as employers, as managers, as company representatives. . . . Every level of supervision needs to be convinced that foremen *are* management and to treat them as management." There is an interesting phrase in the English law regarding guardianship and ward — "in loco parentis." The guardian stands legally in the position of the parent in his relation to the ward. So here, in the field of management, the supervisor stands (or should stand), in the position of management in his relation to the employee.

What has been true in industry has also been true in government service, perhaps to a lesser degree. A policy which lets the supervisor or the foreman manage regardless of the size of the agency or of the company, must include such basic points as sound selection, continuous training, adequate compensation, proper status, two-way communication, and individual treatment and recognition. In the preceding section attention was directed to the responsibility of the supervisor to top management, and to the methods by which that responsibility might be discharged. The considerations mentioned here require attention to

---

See Grant, Ellsworth S., "Let the Foreman Manage," *Personnel Journal*, March, 1945, 331–339, in which it is contended that "there is no greater contradiction than that, while a foreman is colorfully pictured as a versatile and indispensable manager, his authority has been modified and side-stepped, his pay differential narrowed and his viewpoint often blindly disregarded."

the opposite aspect of the same problem — the responsibility of management to the supervisor.

Delegation of Authority. One of the most important responsibilities has to do with the delegation of authority. The supervisor cannot discharge his duties unless he delegates authority to members of his own staff, but by the same token he cannot discharge them unless his own supervisor gives him authority commensurate in scope and quantity with the task he is expected to perform. One executive in the field, for instance, while ill in the hospital, told two of his leading staff members when they came to visit him, "You fellows go ahead and do the best you can, but if you do anything that I don't like, I'll undo it when I get back." One can well imagine, under such circumstances, how much these two men could do or would try to do.

Full Confidence and Support. Management is responsible to its supervisors for giving them full confidence and support. Its responsibility to them is not unlike that which the operating supervisor has to his employees. Management chooses its supervisors and it should back them up as long as it retains them in supervisory capacities. If they are not capable of doing the job, they should be reassigned, dismissed, or otherwise disposed of; but as long as they continue as supervisors, they have a right to expect that they will not be ignored, undercut, short-circuited, or by other means have their prestige and authority undermined.

Providing Full Instructions and Information. Management, too, must provide its supervisors with all instructions and all information essential to the proper discharge of their responsibilities. It seems obvious that a supervisor cannot plan his work effectively or gear his activity into the program of the agency as a whole, unless he knows what the agency program is. The passing on of essential information cannot be left to accident or chance. An employee's handbook may be used for basic information about the organization, but a definite policy must be established for the dissemination of current material — special orders, supervisory conferences, or other means. If a manual of instructions is provided, it should be set up in loose-leaf form so that revisions and additional material may be inserted from time to time as required.[26]

In the past, supervisory training programs either have been non-existent or else have lacked planning, consistency of purpose, and continuity. There has been little effort at follow-up to see that the desired results were being accomplished. Such checking is essential if in

---

[26] See Heron, Alexander, *Sharing Information with Employees* (Stanford University Press, 1942) and Sutermeister, Robert A., "How to Interest the Employee in His Job" in *The Foreman's Basic Reading Kit*, pp. 65–72.

long run the programs are to be justified, but valid judgments are difficult if not impossible to reach by traditional methods. More reliable judgments may be obtained from the use of such new techniques as evaluation of conference material, evaluation of participation, and evaluation of leadership.[27]

Voice in Policy Determination. In a democratic system of administration such as this volume seeks to emphasize, management must give its supervisors a voice in policy determination. The supervisor (or foreman) is the one person close to the rank and file employee; under proper circumstances he can be a far more effective member of the management team than he has normally been in the past. Participation in the making of policy decisions not only flatters the ego of the supervisors and makes them feel important, but it gives them prestige in the eyes of their employees. From the point of view of management such participation is a wise policy. There is more wisdom in many heads than in one if proper methods of group participation are employed to develop and utilize it.

The public administrator in a democracy should be encouraged to exercise his skill, to use his judgment, to employ all his talents in performing the functions of government,[28] but there are many technical tools that can aid him in the discharge of this responsibility. Committees — many kinds of committees — may be set up for the purpose of providing employees with an opportunity to participate in the determination of policy and the settlement of disputes.[29] As Mr. Hall points it, there are a lot of basic principles of effective supervision that all know and preach but often do not practice.

Because the supervisors are familiar with the problems encountered the various levels of operation, a better plan should be developed with their participation than without it. Furthermore, the fact that they were consulted, that they were given an opportunity to participate in development, is likely to elicit a far greater effort on their part in carrying it out — a responsibility which will rest primarily with them.

For an excellent discussion of this problem, see Planty, *op. cit.*

See Smith, Harold D., "Management in a Democracy," *National Municipal Review,* October, 1942, pp. 476–480; Arthur, Guy B., Jr., "The Foreman's Place in Management," *sonnel Journal,* June, 1947, pp. 42–44; Grant, *op. cit.;* and Hall, *op. cit.*

In an address before the Federal Personnel Council of Metropolitan New York, December 12, 1944, Eduard C. Lindeman mentioned several: executive committees, to carry out policies; legislative committees, to discuss new policies; administrative committees, to maintain continuity of policy; adjustment committees, to handle grievances; advisory committees, to provide disinterested opinion; and coordinating committees, to develop means of unification in the organization. Another device, the management training conference, was discussed in an earlier chapter; see also Carey, H. H., "Consultative Supervision and Management," in *The Foreman's Basic Reading Kit,* pp. 41–50.

They are likely to feel a certain amount of pride of authorship and to be motivated by a desire to make the plan work, which in itself is a fine illustration of good management in operation.

Other Responsibilities. These are but a few of management's responsibilities to its supervisors. Management should so far as it is humanly possible provide its supervisors with an even flow of work and with an explanation of the nature and cause of any irregularities which cannot be prevented. Just as a supervisor should encourage and aid his employees in preparing themselves for the assumption of greater responsibilities, so management at the higher levels, through supervisory training conferences and other suitable means, should seek to prepare its supervisors for more responsible positions. And, finally, management should provide for its supervisors such standards and yardsticks as may be available or can be worked out, for measuring production and for use by the supervisors themselves in gauging the effectiveness of their own work.

SELECTED REFERENCES

American Management Association, *The Foreman's Basic Reading Kit* (New York, 1944). A very valuable collection of basic information for the use of supervisors.
——, *The Development of Foremen in Management* (New York, 1947). Training and development of new talent, to have replacements in supervisory positions, is a essential responsibility of management; on this matter, see also, Chappell, Gerald C *Training of Supervisors* (Industrial Relations Section, California Institute of Technology, 1943); United States Department of Agriculture, *The Development Administrators* (Washington, 1941).
Broaded, Charles H., *Essentials of Management for Supervisors* (Harpers, New York 1947) and Chapple, Eliot D., and Wright, Edmund F., *How to Supervise People Industry* (National Foremen's Institute, Deep River, 1948). Two good treatmen of the techniques of supervision.
Cleeton, Glen U., and Mason, Charles W., *Executive Ability*, Revised Edition (Antioch Press, Yellow Springs, 1946). An excellent treatise on the discovery and develop ment of executive ability.
Cooper, Alfred M., *Supervision of Governmental Employees* (McGraw-Hill, New York, 1943). About the only manual on supervision techniques written primar for the benefit of supervisors in government.
Dimock, Marshall E., *The Executive in Action* (Harpers, New York, 1945). Conta many helpful suggestions in the field of supervision.
Dornsife, Harold W., *Selection of Supervisors* (Industrial Relations Section, Califor Institute of Technology, 1943), and Hersey, Rexford B., *Individualized Execu Selection, Training and Follow-up* (American Management Association, New Y 1945). Two brief but excellent discussions of a much neglected aspect of sup vision.
Gilbreth, Lillian M., and Cook, Alice R., *The Foreman in Manpower Managen* (McGraw-Hill, New York, 1947) and Knauth, Oswald, *Managerial Enterprise Growth and Methods of Operation* (Norton, New York, 1948). Recent works phasizing the opportunities and responsibilities of the supervisor in man po management.

Hall, Milton, *Employee Training in the Public Service* (Civil Service Assembly of the United States and Canada, Chicago, 1941), and *Training Your Employees* (Society for Personnel Administration, Washington, 1940). A Federal administrator deals with the role of training, including training of supervisors.

Kimball, Dexter S., and Dexter S., Jr., *Principles of Industrial Organization*, Fifth Edition (McGraw-Hill, New York, 1939). A standard work on industrial organization includes discussion of the role of supervision.

Macmahon, Arthur W., and Millett, John D., *Federal Administrators* (Columbia University Press, 1939). Discussion of supervisors and supervision at the top level in the Federal service.

Roethlisberger, Fritz J., *Management and Morale* (Harvard University Press, 1941) and with Dickson, W. J., *Management and the Worker* (Harvard University Press, 1943). Deal especially with the morale and employee relations aspects of management.

Schell, Erwin H., *The Technique of Executive Control*, Sixth Edition (McGraw-Hill, New York, 1947) and Shuman, Ronald B., *The Management of Men* (University of Oklahoma Press, 1948). Recent works on management techniques.

United States Civil Service Commission, *Supervision, A Selected List of References* (Washington, 1945) and *Supervision Improvement Program* (Washington, 1943). References, and a program for supervisors in the Federal Service.

Veysey, Victor V., *Describing the Supervisor's Job; Selecting, Training and Rating Supervisors*, and *Using Descriptions in Supervisor Jobs* (all, Industrial Relations Section, California Institute of Technology, 1943). Brief discussions of various aspects of the supervisory problem.

Walton, Albert, *New Techniques for Supervisors and Foremen* (McGraw-Hill, New York, 1940). An excellent work.

War Manpower Commission, Training Within Industry Service, *The Training Within Industry Report, 1940–1945* (Washington, 1945). Reports on a very significant training project in wartime.

Wortham, Mary H., *Rating of Supervisors* (Industrial Relations Section, California Institute of Technology, 1943). This, together with the second Veysey title above, gives interesting information on an always difficult and long-neglected problem of evaluating the services of supervisory employees.

28

LEADERSHIP IN ADMINISTRATION

FROM the preceding chapters it is apparent that good management is characterized by clearly defined objectives; lines of authority previously defined and reduced to writing in such a manner as to indicate definite limits of authority and responsibility; authority commensurate with responsibility; delegation of authority and responsibility to the maximum degree; simple but effective controls through budgetary procedures, reports, reviews; proper distribution of the workload; and effective supervision at all levels.

All these things are important to the smooth functioning of an organization. Although delegation of authority must be provided for final responsibility rests with top management, which must of necessity make numerous decisions especially when questions of policy are involved or where differences of opinion have arisen between members of the staff. The vital responsibilities of top management for coordination and leadership have yet to be considered. If management discharges adequately all its other obligations and fails in these, it will soon be apparent that there is something seriously wrong with the organization.

Coordination

Coordination means teamwork. It is a primary function of management, essential at all levels of administration but a peculiar responsibility of top management. Its basic purposes are to enable heads of departments to deal effectively with questions of policy formulation and execution, to resolve conflicts at points of interrelationship between different parts of the organization, and to liberate the energy of operating units, each within its own proper sphere of activity.

There are various methods by which coordination may be made effective; since they are not mutually exclusive, they may be used in varying combinations in accordance with the requirements of a particular situation. One is obviously to establish a sound organization with attention to such factors as proper allocation of authority, functionalized supervision, and over-all planning. Another is the use controls — fiscal, personnel, correspondence, work flow, etc. The communications system is a third; this may be made effective through written instructions (orders, directives, memoranda), the reporting system, staff conferences, committees, and special investigations of problems that seem to be causing difficulty. A fourth may be called the dominance of an idea, an objective which may be realized through the development of an intelligent singleness of purpose in the minds of the members of the staff. The cooperation of a staff whose members are thoroughly imbued with a feeling of the purpose of their effort can be further strengthened by morale-building activities of various kinds.

In one sense coordination may involve a synchronizing of time schedules within the organization in order to achieve maximum production with a minimum of friction, delay, and wasted energy. In a larger and more vital sense it involves a reconciling of divergent interests and points of view. In this connection the executive must be willing and able to make decisions. The ideal executive, as Dimock expresses it, "is neither too domineering nor too vacillating." Either attitude is likely to lead to disaster. Nor can coordination be taken for granted or left to chance; "the executive must constantly work at it he is not to be embarrassed by unforeseen developments."

Ordway Tead, who has devoted many years to the study of the problem of leadership, sets forth two related principles which throw considerable light on the methods that will integrate group and individual aims: [1]

1. *The Principle of the Representation of Interests*, which says that every social group's interest is safeguarded only as there is an explicit voicing of that interest in the councils of the organization by a representative chosen by and from that group, when issues which affect it are under consideration.

2. *The Principle of Coordination*, which changes the emphasis from the social groups to the organization and says that the organization functions smoothly only as there is this conscious, coordinative process of advance agreement throughout the organization upon the general policies and methods which give its aims effect; and says that this process requires explicit organized group or functional representation in deliberations upon policies which determine outcomes affecting that group.

While these principles may obviously be applied to the solution of conflicts arising within an organization or between different organizations, they have a major bearing upon the responsibility of management in determining the policy of the department or agency in those areas where policy is not clearly prescribed by law.

Democratic Administration, pp. 17–18.

As a structural aid in reconciling institutional and individual objectives, Mr. Tead suggests that ultimate authority and responsibility be vested in a board "explicitly composed of representatives of the several major subgroups which are found to have distinctive outlook and desires." If such groups are formally organized, they can select delegates who will effectively represent them on the board, the agenda for the meetings of which should be distributed in advance. An executive secretary of the board might be responsible for the execution of decisions. However: [2]

The number of people reporting directly to this executive should be limited to the number with whom he or she can have continuous effective contacts as an executive supervisor or leader. When this number is more than ten, the danger of inadequate supervision creeps in. The fact that the head executive can and should have useful personal contacts with a far larger number of individuals than this should not be confused with this necessary simplifying of his direct supervisory responsibility.

These propositions, Mr. Tead believes, merit serious consideration with a view to direct, even if gradual, application by organizations and institutions for the following reasons: [3]

1. A board thus constituted is representative and democratic in a vital sense. It brings it about that all the special interests which have to be reckoned with in reconciling the aim of the whole with the aims of its parts are being currently taken account of. Real integration of aim, policy, and method can thus take place — if there is proper leadership.
2. The aim of the organization can be kept constantly and clearly in view when all groups participate in considering what the aim is and how it is to be given effect. The danger of institutionalism, of organization for organization's sake, is thus greatly minimized. And positively the sense of responsibility of each member and group for the forwarding of the aim of the organization *as a whole* is thus assured as in no other possible way.
3. The aim of fellowship, with its implications of equal consideration of members and all related groups, is thus translated into administrative structure and method.
4. The controlling attitudes, policies, and methods of the whole organization thus *at the outset and continuously* considered, adopted, interpreted, and transmitted in a way best calculated to assure the advance agreement and eager cooperation of all concerned.
5. Everyone in the organization is thus brought to feel a positive and creative stake in the success of the organization. This is true because each has a share in the initiation and clarification of aims, in the determination of policy relating to sufficiency, security, and status — in short, in seeing to it that organized ends and individual aspirations become harmonized into a cooperative whole.

[2] Tead, *op. cit.*, p. 19.
[3] *Ibid.*, pp. 19–20.

Mary P. Follett states in another way the reasons why the application of these two basic principles is so beneficial to an organization. She believes that conscious attention to the coordinating process assures the success of an enterprise for four reasons, which she states as follows: [4] "(1) It achieves a reciprocal relating of all the factors in a situation; (2) it achieves direct contact of the responsible people concerned; (3) it achieves all this in the early stages of common deliberation; (4) it becomes thus, as it should be, a continuing process."

Leadership

A great deal has been written on the subject of leadership, including efforts to specify rather exactly the personal qualities essential to it. Few of these efforts have attained any large measure of success, because leadership is not a thing for which a formula can be written as for a chemical compound. It is a variable, the component elements of which vary not only with the personal characteristics of individuals but with the nature and purpose of the leadership required in any given situation. That is to say, no two leaders are alike even in the same field, while the personal qualities and techniques that bring success in one field may almost automatically produce failure in another in a different environment.

Leadership is intangible. It is difficult to define, like liberty or justice. While it is, in fact, often easier to tell what it is not than what it is, it is still recognizable even by those who have had no special training. The man in the street, although he may not be able to give any satisfactory explanation of it, almost instinctively recognizes it. He observes the differences in public men — presidents, governors, and mayors; and he observes them also in the management of the organizations and agencies in which he works or with which he deals — departments, bureaus, divisions, and sections. He recognizes the difference between those who possess these special qualities and those who do not.

This brings one face to face with the greatest single need in administration — the need to discover, encourage, develop, and promote the individuals who possess this almost priceless gift of being able to inspire and lead others, those who know how to induce others to work with them, to cooperate for the attainment of the objectives and purposes of the organization. Our present inability to solve this problem with more than accidental chances of success represents the

---

calf, Henry C., and Urwick, Lyndall, Eds., *Dynamic Administration — The Collected Papers of Mary Parker Follett*, p. 297 (Harpers, New York, 1942), and quoted ad, *op. cit.*

greatest single weakness of present-day administration. For every good leader that chance turns up, several poor ones are promoted, meantime plowing under or discouraging by assignments to subordinate positions countless others who are or who could be developed into competent leaders.

An organization is, in the last analysis, just a group of people working together, and people are not going to work together effectively unless they have some incentive for doing a good job. Consequently a very important responsibility of management is to provide leadership, to motivate the organization, to make sure that economic and social incentives are provided, to capture the imagination and the loyalty of the worker and inspire him to do his most effective work and to make sure that employees understand that it is the policy of the organization to encourage its personnel to find some expression self-expression — through their work. Hence there must be communication of ideas, both up and down the line, if the organization is be motivated properly.

Administrative Responsibility for Leadership. There was a time when command could be exercised in a dictatorial manner. Such methods are not only outmoded in our time but usually will not be tolerated a democratic society; the alternative is leadership — leadership in broadest sense. The responsibility of management, particularly of management, for leadership is to set the "tone" of the organization. the long run no organization can be any better or any stronger than the man in the front office. The survival of an organization, in fact depends upon the quality of its leadership. The man at the top should as far as is humanly possible, be a living example of the qualities that are desired in the subordinate administrative personnel within the organization.

If the "chief" is cold, sharp, petty, domineering, there is no reason to expect his office to be cheerful and pleasant and his subordinates generous, helpful, and encouraging in their relations with employees or with the public. He should be a well-poised, well-balanced individual, free from a sense of personal insecurity or a lack of confidence in himself. In an address before the Council of Personnel Administration in Washington in September, 1945, Mr. Tead made some pertinent remarks on this question when he said: [5]

---

[5] "Summary of Council Meeting Devoted to Opportunities Ahead for Improving eral Personnel Management, in Honor of Mr. George J. Schoeneman and Mr. Zimmerman, September 27, 1945," p. 7.

I say without reservation that in whatever setting it may be, from General Marshall and General Eisenhower down, it is a peculiar characteristic — if not "the" characteristic — of people successful as leaders, that they are "other-centered." They are centered on other people, on the task, on their purposes, on activities which are outside themselves. The longer my experience in human relations, the more profound is my conclusion that one of the greatest handicaps to good line supervision is that there are so many people in it who for various reasons, personal, domestic, social, vocational, or educational, feel insecure, lack confidence in themselves, are in some subtle internal way frustrated. Therefore their supervisory work becomes an aggressive, tough, arbitrary compensation for internal difficulties which they have not been able otherwise to adjust. If we are going to get a vast body of lower and higher supervisors in the Federal service who are "other-centered" and who are not taking it out on their subordinates because of internal insecurities of their own, we have to think out a kind of social psychiatry. By understanding people, we advance them out of internal insecurity and frustration. Thus as they deal with people, they can afford to think in terms of the welfare of the agency, the welfare and development of the people rather than how they personally shall register, how they shall be big shots in an autocratic way because of that internal adjustment which has been unsolved.

Marshall E. Dimock, on the basis of extensive experience in responsible administrative positions, had much the same thing in mind when he wrote: [6]

The executive who is reluctant to allow his subordinates full growth for fear they will rival and possibly displace him is unfit to be the head of any organization. The executive leader does an outstanding job only when he nurtures the largest possible crop of individuals qualified for greater responsibilities and for more normal and more satisfied personal experiences.

If what has been said here in general has any validity, it would be foolhardy to attempt to establish a rigid set of requirements for leadership in administration or in any other limited field. No such attempt will be made; but in the paragraphs which follow, some of the more important duties and responsibilities will be suggested. There are perhaps as many ways of discharging these responsibilities as there are types of leadership personalities, but the observance of these standards represents a kind of common denominator of successful leadership in the field of administration.[7]

The Executive in Action, p. 204 (Harpers, New York, 1945).

See Schoenfeld, Benjamin N., "The Psychological Characteristics of Leadership," Social Forces, May, 1948, pp. 391–396. One might attack the problem as Dr. Burleigh B. Gardner, Executive Director of Social Research has done, by analyzing the causes of executive failure resulting in demotion or dismissal, alienation of employees, etc. He listed twelve principal reasons, listed below in briefest possible form:

Inability to see the forest for the trees; "the executive who is lost in a maze of details is doomed to mediocrity"

1. *Selection of Personnel.* The use of the appointing power in any organization is of vital importance. It is no exaggeration to say that this factor alone can easily make or break an organization. An able executive possesses the ability to size up individuals and to evaluate their education, experience, and qualifications in relation to the requirements of a particular job. No one can be infallible in this respect, but a good executive will be able to select personnel with relatively few mistakes. Selection is an art, the practice of which may be greatly strengthened or improved by the use of scientific aids; certainly it cannot be done on the basis of favoritism or hunches. It requires ar intimate knowledge of the requirements of different types of positions and the ability to weigh accurately the qualifications of individuals ir relation thereto.

2. *Delegation of Authority.* The competent executive must have th ability to delegate authority clearly and firmly. It goes without sayin; that the higher-grade executive cannot do all or much of the work o the organization himself, and even if he could, that is not what he wa hired to do. It is his responsibility to see that the work is done, that : is done right and done on time. He cannot hold himself aloof, for th solution of difficult questions and the settlement of disputes requii frequent attention on his part and a high degree of tact and skill i dealing with the members of his staff. But he cannot function as a executive if he is unable or unwilling to delegate authority or if, ha ing gone through the motions of delegation, he later rescinds tl grant of authority or otherwise fails to make the delegation stick. I lets a portion of his responsibility out on loan, as it were; he cann divest himself of it, because his administrative superiors will right hold him accountable. When he delegates authority to a subordina he does so on condition that the subordinate makes proper use of and only for so long as he does so. Authority, like sovereignty, theoretically one and indivisible; it resides in the head and cannot

2. Failure to carry responsibility — unable to make a choice between alternatives ; to plan a proper use of his own time
3. Unconscious desire to do something else, causing disinterest in work
4. Unconscious desire to be something else
5. "A yen for express trains," a tendency to jump to conclusions
6. Inability to make room for other people
7. Resistance to authority, fear of being "pushed around"
8. Arrogance with subordinates
9. Prejudices which interfere with judgment
10. Overemphasis on work, thereby losing the balancing influence of outside inte
11. Gravitation toward self-destruction, due to lack of self-confidence and an i tional belief that they are unfit or unworthy
12. Some actual mental ailment

ransferred or lost. Actually, it is delegated and, through poor man-
gement, may be lost.

. *Loyalty*. This is a two-way attribute. It must be the constant re-
ponsibility of the executive to develop leadership and create loyalty
ɔ himself, not as a person but in his capacity as head of the agency,
ʌhere he stands as a symbol of the agency and of the government as
whole. The other side of the shield is that there must be genuine and
ɪncere loyalty on the part of the executive to his entire personnel —
ɔt merely lip-service loyalty. Each member of the unit must feel
vidly the chief executive's readiness to take a strong stand in support
ː his staff on matters of immediate and genuine concern to them,
ɪch as compensation, promotions, correction of injustices, and dis-
ɪbution of credit for work done. The rank and file must feel that
eir chief is ready to fight their battle not only at great inconven-
ɪce to himself but even at the risk of jeopardizing his own position.[3]

Impartiality. Attainment of genuine impartiality is most difficult.
ː human beings, all of us have prejudices, biases, likes, and dislikes,
ɪt an executive worthy of his position must be constantly striving to
ʌhieve as near a genuine impartiality in dealing with the members of
ɪ staff as can possibly be attained. Nothing is more demoralizing to
organization than the prevalence of a belief — whether or not it is
tified — that certain individuals are "in right" with the boss and
ɪ do no wrong or that he "has it in for" other individuals whom he
ɛs not like.

Personal Interest in Employees. The human relations of the execu-
ː to each member of his organization involve two different con-
ɛrations. His interest in his employees should go beyond office
ɪrs and the walls of the office. Human beings are subject to illness,
ɛavements, domestic and financial difficulties, and little personal
ɪhes between one employee and another, as well as to some of the
ɪsures of life. The impact of these personal factors upon the indi-
ɪal has much to do with his or her value as an employee. The exec-
ʾe may well take a leaf from the experience of the professional
ɪtician who, because he likes people, takes a personal interest in all
ʾ vitally concerns his constituents. Evidence of the executive's
ful consideration of the personal interests of employees is deeply
ɪreciated by them and does much to bolster their morale. It makes
ɪ feel important and pleased that the executive should, in the

---

ɪdensed from a report of an address by Frederick P. Gruenberg on "The Role of
Chief Executive in Personnel Administration," before the Philadelphia Federal
ɪcil of Personnel Administration, September 20, 1944.

midst of his consideration of important problems, find the time and the interest to concern himself with their personal welfare.

6. *Curiosity*. Louis Brownlow has emphasized the fact that a good administrator must have a very broad and catholic interest in people and things — in other words, an insatiable curiosity. This curiosity leads him to inquiries as to what his people are really thinking; this he cannot ascertain either from irate citizens who come to his office to enter complaints or from other citizens who deluge him with flattery because they want something. He must avail himself of opportunities to see and talk with citizens under more normal circumstances if he is to learn what they are actually thinking and talking about.

His curiosity may enable him to render better service to the public at less cost. Mr. Brownlow recites a homely illustration of the man in charge of garbage collection and disposal when he was Commissioner in Washington, D.C., many years ago. This man lifted the lids of garbage cans all over the city in order to find out what was in them. He developed maps of the city, spotting areas in which garbage was high in fats and sugars, trash rich in rags and in valuable papers put out for collection. He reorganized the collection system to give more frequent service without increasing the total cost ($800,000) but at the same time doubling the receipts from salable materials ($200,000 to $400,000). Fats were sold to soap companies, rags and paper to paper manufacturers.[9]

7. *Example*. A chief executive actually has about as much privacy as a goldfish in a bowl. His industry and integrity — whether or not he is a petty cheat of government time, toll calls, and postage, whether he assumes privileges because of his position or power — are all thoroughly known even to the humblest messenger in the organization. A case in point is found in the war agencies, in which unexpected night and Sunday work was frequently necessary. In these situations a real leader will always be the first to assume the extra burdens and not merely tell his subordinates what they must do. He cannot afford to ask others to make sacrifices which he is unwilling to make himself. And in the field of example perhaps there is nothing more important than the constant responsibility of the chief executive so to conduct himself with courtesy, consideration, and good breeding that the relations of his organization with the public will not only add to the effectiveness of the unit's operations but will be a credit to the public service as a whole.[10]

---

[9] From an address before the Graduate Political Science Club, University of Chicago, January 23, 1936.
[10] Gruenberg, *op. cit.*

3. *Ruthlessness and Sympathy.* A good executive is frequently called upon to deal with situations which require at one and the same time a delicate combination of ruthlessness or toughness on the one hand and of sympathy on the other. He cannot condone bungling and inefficiency and maintain an efficient operating organization, and yet he must ever remember that he is dealing with human beings whose senibilities are as delicate as his own. He cannot falter and hesitate in the discharge of his responsibilities, but he can proceed with the utmost fairness, tempering justice with mercy. Mr. Dimock thus comments on this difficult problem: [11]

> From the standpoint of the personal characteristics involved, the executive must be trusting and generous, but also firm and tough when need be. Most executives commonly go too far in one direction or the other. They are either too easygoing and trusting or they are the hardboiled, order-snapping type. In terms of the personal qualifications involved, the successful leader must be ruthless as well as magnanimous. He must be ruthless when need be or he cannot do a proper job.

Theory and Practice. One of the most difficult tasks imposed upon the executive is that of reconciling the requirements of "theory" and "practice" in administration. His responsibility to his organization does not cease at the close of the day's business. He must know the "theory"; he must be informed as to recent thought regarding the problems of administration as set forth in the current literature. He must read extensively, join professional associations, and take an active part in their activities in an effort to increase his knowledge and enhance his value to his agency. This certainly cannot be done on a 9:00 A.M. to 5:30 P.M. basis as many executives seem to think. It is the responsibility of the executive to see that up-to-date methods are adapted to the needs of his organization and its problems whenever and wherever possible. Unless he does so, he cannot expect to have an efficient and progressive organization.

Outstanding Careers in Public Service

For at least a generation there has been a widespread demand for the development of a career service in this country. Teachers in their classrooms, speakers on the public platform, writers in newspapers and magazines, not to mention high public officials, have pleaded for a public service in which able and well-trained individuals might be inducted and promoted to positions of successively greater responsibility on a career basis. Commissioner Flemming echoed this plea in his address at the testimonial dinner given in his honor upon his

---

Dimock, *op. cit.*, p. 199.

retirement, after ten years on the Civil Service Commission, in August 1948. The experiences of war and reconstruction can serve only to raise a serious question, a question as to whether many Americans have not been giving lip service to an ideal that, as a people, they do not really desire or intend to carry out.

In the years immediately following World War II the morale of the public service sank to an exceedingly low level. For this ther was a variety of reasons. When hostilities ceased, reduction-in-force (RIF) and veterans' preference loomed large. The loyalty investiga tions created fear and anxiety in the minds of large numbers of inno cent persons. The economy drive of 1947–1948 kept many employee for months at a time in a state of anxiety as to whether they would hav a job or not. The political campaign of 1948 was responsible for tw additional disturbing factors: one was a widely prevalent idea that th results of the election were going to be different from what the proved to be; the other was loose and irresponsible talk of budg slashes and wholesale dismissals.

The demoralizing effect of these various influences was reflected headlines about large numbers of top jobs in the Federal service goin begging, and the damaging effects upon this or that program of the r luctance of well-qualified people to serve. The truth is that no organiz tion can function at its best without high employee morale, which just as important in the top brackets as in the lower. Like leadership is an intangible thing, a sensitive thing, difficult to define or describe. is likely to express itself in the belief that "this is a good organizati to work for." It is, as Tead has observed, the deliberate product of tw factors: of structural arrangements and of personal elements of eff tive, interpretative leadership. Leadership and morale are inextricat related. There must be a structure and machinery which aid coordi tion, but there must be personal leadership of high quality to facilit the coordinating.[12]

The classification and analysis of a large number of cases involv top-level officials suggest the possibility of setting up four major ca gories of public officials:

Group I: those with long periods of service who retired on age or disab or died in service

Group II: those who after a considerable period of service resigned, usu because of inadequate compensation

Group III: those who, in spite of outstanding qualifications in a special fi were subjected to persecution during or after leaving office

Group IV: those who, in spite of outstanding qualifications and service to public, were demoted or dismissed by higher authority

---

[12] Tead, *op. cit.*, pp. 16, 22.

In the Federal Service. GROUP I. In spite of the difficult problems suggested by this classification, the picture is not all black. Through the years, there has been a remarkable series of public servants at all three levels of government, many of whom have been relatively unknown to the citizenry they served but whose contributions to the welfare of society have later received recognition. The Washington papers report almost daily the names of individuals or groups of individuals who are retiring after a lifetime of service. Thus, on June 7, 1948, for example:

At Agriculture, recent notable retirements include those of Robert B. Mull, forty-three years' service; Bernard J. Cunningham and Arthur H. Stankey, forty-one years' service; Helen Ferguson, thirty-nine years; Joseph E. Fleming and Michael J. Hastings, thirty-seven years; Frank I. Runnels, thirty-six years; Wilbert M. Borchers, Warren S. Fisher, and Joseph H. Kitzhofer, thirty-five years.

Individual stories like these are common; mentioning the names of a few is not intended to minimize in any way the equally significant services of many, many more:

Dr. Oscar E. Meinzer, 70, geologist and authority on ground water hydrology, has retired after more than forty years of service in the Geological Survey, Interior Department (January 10, 1947).

Charles K. Moser, 70, chief of the Far Eastern Division, Department of Commerce, will retire today, ending thirty-five years' service with the Federal Government.

Clarence A. Reed, Takoma Park, Md., nut culture specialist in the Department of Agriculture, has retired after forty years of scientific work for the Government.

The quiet scientific work of many Federal agencies has been universally acclaimed. Early in 1948 Dr. Hugh M. Bennett, 67-year-old chief of the Soil Conservation Service, Department of Agriculture, was awarded the Cullim Medal of the American Geographical Society, being described as "the man who helped lift the United States from the category of the worst despoiler of soil to leader in soil conservation." In the same Department there was Ferdinand A. Silcox, who devoted his life to the Forest Service.[13] Dr. L. O. Howard, perhaps the world's outstanding entomologist, headed for years a bureau in the Department of Agriculture and made contributions to the world's health and economic well-being that were recognized even by hardheaded men of affairs. Then by contrast, there was the young Goldberger, a junior medical officer in the United States Public Health Service, whose devoted studies in the causes of pellagra and hookworm paved the way

See Kotok, E. I., and Hammett, R. F., "Ferdinand Augustus Silcox," *Public Administration Review*, Summer, 1942, pp. 240–253.

for conquering those devastating and once widespread diseases. His career, unlike Dr. Howard's, ended tragically for want of encouragement and recognition, but his service to mankind will endure.

Of the career men in Federal service perhaps none is better known than Alve A. Adee, who served sixty-eight years in the State Department. No man in our time has given years of more distinguished service than the late Joseph B. Eastman, Interstate Commerce Commissioner from 1919 and at the time of his death Federal Coordinator of Transportation.[14] Warner W. Stockberger was for many years personnel officer of the Department of Agriculture, and Harold D. Smith was long Director of the Budget. The latter was truly a career man in government with extensive experience at the municipal, state, and Federal levels, and was regarded as one of the ablest public servants in Washington.[15]

Other career administrators of our time, still in active service, include Jesse M. Donaldson, first career Postmaster General, who entered the service in 1908, and George J. Schoeneman, appointed Commissioner of Internal Revenue in 1947, after exactly thirty-six years of Federal service. Then there are Frederick M. Davenport, distinguished chairman of the Federal Personnel Council since its establishment; Charles A. Piozet, long personnel officer of the Navy Department Oliver S. Short, personnel officer of the Department of Commerce Gordon R. Clapp, Chairman of the Tennessee Valley Authority; and David E. Lilienthal, Chairman of the Atomic Energy Commission.[16]

In State and Local Government. Such records of service are by no means confined to the personnel of the Federal government; the reade will be able to supply local illustrations from states and cities with which he is familiar. In states like California, Minnesota, New Jersey New York, and Wisconsin one finds a definite conviction among employees that there are opportunities for a career in state and local government. One notes too a general tendency, particularly in the South to maintain the same individuals in many local offices over long period

14 See Swisher, Carl B., "Joseph B. Eastman – Public Servant," *Public Administration Review*, Winter, 1945, pp. 34–54.
15 See Appleby, Paul H., "Harold D. Smith – Public Administrator," *Public Administration Review*, Spring, 1947, pp. 77–81; Olson, Herbert A., "Harold D. Smith – What He Meant to State and Local Government," *ibid.*, pp. 82–84; and Johnson, Eldon "The Administrative Career of Dr. W. W. Stockberger," *ibid.*, Autumn, 1941, pp. 50–64.
16 This list has purposely been limited to individuals, for the most part under Civil Service, who have made a career of administrative work. For comment on those with long careers in elective office, see Salter, John T., Ed., *Public Men in and Out of Office* (University of North Carolina Press, 1946), and White, Leonard D., "Franklin Roosevelt and the Public Service," *Public Administration Review*, July, 1945, pp. 139–146.

of time. A few specific cases from the state and local field may well be mentioned.

California Highways and Public Works reported: "George R. Winslow retires after twenty-nine years in state service" (June, 1941); "George B. McDougall retires after twenty-five years as state architect" (November, 1938). The long service of Charles P. Messick of the New Jersey Civil Service Commission is known to all in the personnel field. Henry H. Curran retired in 1947 as a Justice of the Court of Quarter Sessions in New York, thereby bringing to a close a period of fifty years of public service which had included membership in the Board of Aldermen, presidency of Manhattan Borough, Commissioner of Immigration, City Magistrate (six years as Chief Magistrate), and Deputy Mayor. In 1941 in Red Wing, Minnesota, City Clerk Samuel T. Irvine, connected with the clerk's office for thirty-three years, relinquished the post to his deputy, H. E. Nordholm, who had served with him in that capacity since 1923.

Careers for Women. The number of women who have given long and distinguished service is constantly increasing. At the Federal level one recalls Frances Perkins who, after serving for four years as Industrial Commissioner of New York, became Secretary of Labor for twelve years, first woman Cabinet member and later a member of the United States Civil Service Commission for several years; Julia Lathrop, for many years head of the Children's Bureau, and her successor, Katherine F. Lenroot; Mary Anderson of the Women's Bureau and her successor, Frieda S. Miller; Clara M. Beyer, Assistant Director, Bureau of Labor Standards; Dr. Alice Hamilton, renowned authority on industrial diseases; Nellie Tayloe Ross, long Director of the Bureau of the Mint; Jane M. Hoey, Director of the Bureau of Public Assistance, and Ellen S. Woodward, Director of Inter-Agency and International Relations in the Federal Security Agency; and Bess Goodykoontz, long connected with the United States Office of Education.[17] In a number of states women have had long periods of tenure in such offices as secretary of state and in health and welfare agencies. In the latter group Dr. Ellen M. Potter of New Jersey is a conspicuous example.

Obstacles to a Career Service

In order to establish a real career service, the government must be able to attract and hold able men and women. The door at the top or very

---

[17] Nyswander, Rachel F., and Hooks, Janet M., prepared an excellent study, *Employment of Women in the Federal Government, 1923 to 1939* (Women's Bureau, Washington, 1941). Appendix B presents a summary of the activities of women in supervisory and administrative positions, 1925 to 1941.

close to the top must be kept open. The employees of government must be generally respected by the public. These employees, in private conversations with nongovernment people, must be able truthfully and conscientiously to encourage others to enter the service. Rules and regulations must protect the competent rather than the incompetent. Officials who do their tasks well must not be made the victims of character assassination. None of these conditions have as yet been met. Great numbers of citizens still delight in belittling and deriding government employees as bureaucrats, pigs feeding at the public trough, parasites on the body politic. During the war period many well-qualified and able persons were drawn into government employment to assist in the war effort. In the process of reconversion practically all of them were swept out, and, more's the pity, many of them were delighted to go.

Obstacles Arising in the Legislative Branch. GROUP II. There are an enormous number of able and devoted public servants, living and dead, who have after a considerable period of service felt obliged to resign. The usual reason has been the inadequacy of the salaries in top-level positions in the Federal service, although an exactly comparable situation exists in many state and local jurisdictions. This has happened repeatedly with outstanding members of Congress like Robert Ramspeck.[18] Scores and scores of cases have occurred in administrative positions, with the result that the operations of many agencies have been seriously affected by the kaleidoscopic changes in their top-level personnel. The following may be considered as significant illustrations:

John J. Corson, who resigned as Director of the Bureau of Old-Age and Survivors Insurance in the Federal Security Administration, to accept a position with the *Washington Post* at a much higher salary. That he retains an active interest in public administration is demonstrated by his numerous articles and addresses in this field, and his Presidency of the American Society for Public Administration during 1948–1949.

Charles Denny, who finally gave up his position as Chairman of the Federal Communications Commission to accept a more lucrative offer "across the street" with the National Broadcasting Company as Vice-President and general counsel. When he left office at the end of October, 1947, he was the sixth chairman since 1934, and the third in the preceding eight years.

Robert P. Patterson, former Federal judge and Secretary of War, resigned

18 See his article, "I Couldn't Afford to Be a Congressman," *Collier's*, March 9, 19
he left the House to accept a $25,000 a year position as executive secretary of the
Transport Association of America. Clifton A. Woodrum left the House at the sa
time to accept a similar position with the American Plant Food Council. See
James F. Byrnes' comment on the same subject in *American Magazine*, February, 1
Whatever improvement resulted from the provisions of the Legislative Reorganizat
Act has been absorbed in the postwar inflation.

return to New York to engage in the private practice of law. A competent and well-liked administrator, his loss to the Government service was no inconsiderable one.

Augustus Giegengack, Public Printer for thirteen and a half years, resigned to accept a position with a New York graphic arts consulting service at "better than double" the Federal salary. "I take this action because my duty to my family demands that I increase my income substantially above the salary fixed by Congress for the position under a law passed twenty years ago."

James J. Caffrey, last of the career men among the Securities and Exchange Commissioners, resigned as Chairman in December, 1947, to enter the private practice of law in New York City. He joined the SEC in 1935 as a staff attorney, later serving eight years as Regional Director in the Boston and New York offices. He was appointed Commissioner in May, 1945, and became Chairman in July, 1946, when his predecessor, *Ganson Purcell,* resigned for the same reason. Mr. Caffrey wrote in his letter of resignation that he was resigning because of "family responsibilities which I can no longer ignore."

Harold D. Smith, who resigned as Director of the Budget to become Vice-President of the International Bank in 1946, writing to President Truman as he did so: "I feel that I must accept this opportunity, not only because of my keen interest in the international field, but also because it offers greater compensation [more than twice that of his Federal position, tax free]. I must confess that had this opportunity not arisen it would only have been a short time until existing limitations on the salaries of public officials would have forced me out of the Federal Government."

There is probably no point in extending this list further, although it could be extended almost indefinitely with the names of Milo Perkins, John J. McCloy, Wendell Berge, Oscar S. Cox, Howard C. Peterson, Randolph Paul, James Lawrence Fly, and scores of others. Harry T. Kranz, Director of the Twelfth United States Civil Service Region, well stated the situation in an address before a personnel management conference in San Francisco, May 13, 1948:

There are today thousands upon thousands of business and professional people in this country who annually pay in income taxes sums that are far greater than the total annual salaries of all but a very few of the most highly placed Federal administrators. If one works his way to the highest pinnacle of success as an administrator in the Federal government, his salary will be, with rare statutory exceptions, $10,000 per annum. In a Federal civilian army of almost 2,000,000, there were, as of July 31, 1947, 158 persons receiving salaries in excess of $10,000 per annum — a ratio of about one for every 11,500 Federal employees. Excepting the President and Vice-President, and outside of the Department of State, there were 130 positions above $10,000, ranging up to $18,000 — with only two of these positions (two out of about 2,000,000) paying above $15,000 per year.

Almost every one of the cases cited serves to emphasize anew the urgent need for raising the level of salaries in top-grade positions.[19] The

See Pringle, Henry F., and Katherine, "It's Hard to Work for Uncle Sam," *Ladies' Home Journal,* October, 1947, pp. 52–53, 155 ff., and a report prepared by the author,

situation would not be quite so critical, however, if the second-level administrators and scientific personnel were not also affected. Their salaries cannot be raised until top-level salaries are increased. The result is that every year the Government loses many experienced employees in these brackets to private firms at double or treble the salary paid by government.

GROUP III. The necessity for democratic controls over administration has caused the development of what have come to be established patterns of legislative procedure in dealing with the executive branch of government. Among these are the exhaustive public inquiries frequently made prior to the confirmation of executive appointments, the inquiries undertaken by the Appropriations Committee and its subcommittees in reviewing the policies and procedures of departments and agencies whose budget requests are before them for consideration, and other investigations into the conduct of the administration.

In the course of legislative investigations representatives of business are often subjected to searching questions, but the individual who is or who is willing to consider holding an important official position must realize beforehand that he is likely at any time to become the subject of a merciless grilling in which every conceivable aspect of his public and private activity will be called into question. It is not the purpose of this discussion to criticize this procedure. It is, in the first place, a necessary and essential part of our democratic system. It is frequently the means of bringing into the open facts which should be known and publicized. In the past it has not infrequently happened that persons have been kept from important public positions for which they lacked proper qualifications or that as a result of such legislative inquiry serious abuses in the executive branch have been revealed and corrected.

The ever-present possibility that one may become the subject of such an investigation is one of the necessary risks in accepting a responsible public position. Our political mores are such that investigations or control measures instituted as a result of them may react decidedly to the detriment of persons innocent of any wrongdoing. The number of such cases is not large, but even so they are important partly because of the injury that is done to innocent persons, partly because the wide publicity given to them tends to create in the public mind an exaggerated conception of this hazard in the public service. The following specific cases illustrate some of them.

David E. Lilienthal, Chairman of the Atomic Energy Commission. This graduate of the Harvard Law School served as a member of the Wisconsin Pub

Salaries in Top Level Position — in Government, in Industry and in the Profession (Legislative Reference Service, Library of Congress, 1947).

lic Service Commission and then on the Board of the Tennessee Valley Authority from its inception to 1946, during the last five years as Chairman. Although he made a very distinguished record as an administrator, a record acclaimed by students and practitioners alike and by the public, the presentation of his name before the Senate regularly becomes a signal for extensive investigation and bitter controversy.

Edward U. Condon, world renowned physicist who has since 1945 served as Director of the National Bureau of Standards. Although numerous persons of standing who knew him well were willing to vouch for his loyalty, the attacks upon him were so long continued and so bitter that many citizens were deeply concerned. At a time when the Government needed the services of outstanding scientists, many were made extremely hesitant about entering government service lest a similar fate befall them.

John C. Virden, Director of the Office of Industry Cooperation in the Department of Commerce. Mr. Virden had been a successful American businessman and an outspoken opponent of Communism. When his twenty-one year old daughter went to work for the Soviet news agency, Tass, relations between her and her family were broken. In spite of these facts and of the confidence of the President and the Secretary of Commerce, public demands were made that Mr. Virden resign or that he be dismissed. In fact, he decided to resign, reconsidered, and actually resigned a few months later.

In some cases the result is not merely a rough and unsympathetic handling of a witness or the impeachment of the character of an individual of high standing in the community, but an actual attempt at what may be called a legislative ouster. Its significance, so far as this discussion is concerned, is to be found in its demoralizing effect upon members of the service generally. In the interplay of conflicting forces in our government and politics, its use has been thwarted in some instances by the courts, in others by the executive. For instance, after Congress had passed an appropriation rider in March, 1943, forbidding the payment of any Federal salary to Messrs. Watson, Dodd, and Lovett, designating these three individuals by name, the Supreme Court termed the action a bill of attainder and therefore unconstitutional.[20]

Much the same thing was attempted five years later with respect to Messrs. Straus and Boke, two officials in the Bureau of Reclamation. In this instance, however, the officials were not mentioned by name, but qualifications were imposed upon their offices which were obviously designed to exclude them. When this legislation became effective, the Secretary of the Interior permitted them to continue on duty without compensation, on the basis of assurance that it was not unlawful to have an official serving without pay and in the hope that, given an op-

In the Court of Claims, Lovett v. United States, Watson v. Same, Dodd v. Same, F. Supp. 142 (1945) and on appeal to the Supreme Court, United States v. Lovett, United States v. Watson, and United States v. Dodd, 328 U.S. 303 (1946).

portunity to do so, the Congress might reconsider its action and remove the restriction.

Obstacles Arising in the Executive Branch. The problems of salary rates and the use of investigatory powers as a mechanism for control over administration arise largely out of legislative actions; attention is now directed to certain other obstacles to a career service arising in the executive branch. These obstacles are of two sorts, growing out of conflicting philosophies of administration. One of these is responsibility; here the control of top-level officials is involved. The other is the idea of a career service, which cannot under our system include officials of higher rank than bureau chiefs.

Among the obstacles affecting the career service may be mentioned the distortion of the rules, faulty promotion policies, and the demotion or dismissal, by higher authority, of persons of outstanding qualifications and public service. So far as the first of these points is concerned, it may be noted that the elaborate system of rules governing personnel transactions frequently stifles initiative and protects and rewards mediocrity. This, obviously, was not intended. Taken individually, most of the rules seem reasonable enough. They were in most cases designed to correct previous abuses. But taken as a whole and judged by the results of their application, there is only one possible conclusion: that the rules are used, or are permitted to be used, to reward the mediocre and incompetent and to penalize the able and the competent.

A striking illustration is found in the evolution of the reduction-in-force regulations put out by the Civil Service Commission at the end of World War II. The original regulations gave equal weight to efficiency ratings and to length of service. Granting that the efficiency rating system is far from perfect, this was still a reasonable arrangement and one that was in the public interest. But the old-line employees, many of whom feared they might be displaced by abler and better trained war-service employees, insisted that the rules be modified so that seniority counted for everything and the efficiency rating for little or nothing. As a result, agency after agency lost all or nearly all its able war-service employees, some of whom would have remained in government service and many of whom the agencies would gladly have retained.

Faulty promotion policies represent another major barrier to career service, in a proper meaning of that term. Great numbers of war service employees, many of whom left highly responsible positions to do their bit in the war effort, found themselves working under the direction and supervision of persons who had no qualifications for the positions they held. Reasonable men and women are usually willing take instructions from those whose ability and accomplishment are superior or even equal to their own, but nothing is more annoying to a highly qualified person than to have to take orders from some "pipsqueak" administrator. Unfortunately these cases were not rare, and it is no explanation to say that a major war was in progress. These people were in the government service in key positions long before the United States entered the war, and they were promoted time after time under the existing regulations until they arrived in positions six sizes too big for them. Actually these abuses are of long standing and have long been recognized. Because of them, the Tennessee Valley Authority was authorized by law in 1933 to do what many other agencies would like to do — not for the purpose of evading the application of the merit system but rather to attain its more effective operation — namely, to set up and operate its own personnel system.

GROUP IV. This group includes officials who, in spite of outstanding qualifications, were demoted or dismissed by higher authority. The number of cases is not large, but those which do occur have a demoralizing effect upon the remainder of the service and a deterring effect upon individuals who might otherwise be inclined to enter it. This difficulty arises normally, not from the action of the legislative branch of government, but from the executive. In the absence of standards of evaluation, the cases cited here represent the best judgment of informed persons; they are not to be construed as an attack upon the administration during which they occurred nor an implication that similar situations have not occurred in the past or may not occur again in the future.

When, for instance, the European Recovery Administration was being organized, it was reported that the administration was trying to interest Mr. Nathaniel Dyke in a top job. He was a member of the Home Loan Bank Board and according to reports had been promised the chairmanship. The next thing he knew, however, he was fired, and according to the press the very White House assistant who "knifed" him was talking him up for the ERA job.

Francis Biddle's was another case in point; having been definitely assured that the President desired him to remain as Attorney General, he was amazed when his resignation was requested.

James M. Landis had been appointed a full professor in the Harvard Law School before he was thirty and dean before he was forty. In the meantime he had taken time out to serve in a number of responsible positions in the Federal government prior to and during World War II. In 1946 he was appointed chairman of the Civil Aeronautics Administration. But in the words of Harold L. Ickes, himself a public administrator of no mean standing, Mr. Landis suddenly found the rug pulled out from under his feet. The President, said Mr. Ickes, reached out for "good men for Federal office" with one hand while with the other he struck down any good man within reach.

Marriner Eccles had come from Idaho to Washington as Assistant to the

Secretary of the Treasury in 1934. He had served as Governor of the Federal Reserve Board for two years and as Chairman of the Board of Governors of the Federal Reserve System for twelve years from February 1, 1936. His conduct of this important office through this difficult period had merited the respect and confidence with which he was generally regarded. He too had been assured that he would be reappointed as Chairman, but this was not to be. Fortunately Mr. Eccles, who might have been excused had he decided to retire, chose to remain to serve out his full term as a member of the Board.

In periods of emergency, whether of depression or of war, with all the accompanying excitement and confusion, some administrators have risen to the heights of true greatness, yet because of the frequently unpopular nature of the programs for which they are responsible, their tenure has been more than normally insecure. One might, in fact, put it down as an axiom that there is a direct relationship between the degree of public acceptance of a program and the security of tenure of its top job. The occupants of positions in such agencies are obliged to break new ground, for there are few if any precedents available. In the natural course of events they stir up opposition which sooner or later creates a situation in which the administration feels obliged to sacrifice them, regardless of the general excellence of their performance.

Such a case was that of Leon Henderson. What he did in organizing rationing, price control, and rent control not only added immeasurably to the success of the war effort but built a solid foundation upon which a wise statesmanship might have avoided in the postwar era many of the pitfalls that have followed in the wake of both World Wars. But in the end he proved to be a handy scapegoat and was virtually forced out of office.

His successor, Chester Bowles, was a totally different type of public servant who had early in life amassed a fortune in the advertising business. That he was no professor, no brain-truster, but an eminently "practical" businessman made little difference when he continued the basic established policies of the Office of Price Administration and when he proved to be an all too efficient administrator. Although he had the conventional American success-story background, he was actually little less harassed in carrying out his thankless duties than his predecessor had been.

Some Possible Solutions

It would be unfair to say or even to imply that this problem of obtaining and holding competent leadership in government is peculiar to the civilian service, critical as it is in that area. The same problem exists in the armed forces and in many areas of private endeavor as well. General Eisenhower, when he retired as Chief of Staff, stated in his final report to Army Secretary Royall that "despite the largest professional military establishment in our peacetime history," the nation is not adequately defended. He also stated that our position five, ten, and fifteen years hence is being determined right now. So far as the armed service are concerned, this situation is attributable largely to two factors. The appointment system to the training academies is poor, "pull" often weighing heavier than merit, at a time when an uncertain future demands that the best qualified men be groomed for officer roles in the armed services. The other factor here — as in the civilian services — is low pay. A recent investigator reports that graduates of universities and colleges of the same standing as Annapolis and West Point can look forward to a much better situation in civilian life than graduates of Annapolis and West Point can find in the armed services, even if the former start after graduation at less pay than a second lieutenant in the Army or an ensign in the Navy.[21]

The truth is that there is a severe shortage of high-grade leadership material in most walks of life. This fact has been only too deeply impressed upon anyone who has ever done any recruiting work over a long period of time. Under these circumstances small wonder it is that government — laboring under such handicaps as lack of prestige and low pay scales — encounters serious difficulties in securing an adequate supply of the high-grade personnel it must have to meet its urgent requirements.

Continuance of Existing Efforts. In view of this shortage of leadership talent, the inadequacy of our methods in identifying it, and our frequent failure to enlist the services of those leaders known to exist, it is appropriate to inquire into possible solutions of this problem of a career service. The most obvious solution is to continue the conscious effort to develop leadership and morale within the service, and the campaign of education to develop respect for the service on the part of the general public. Mr. Kranz remarks that if those leaders who have access to the public ear and who are molders of public opinion cannot summon the initiative and the sense of responsibility that are required for this job, they can at least be helpful in a negative way by refraining from attacks and criticisms aimed at undermining the people's confidence in and respect for their government and their civil servants. All this, to be sure, is "old stuff," but it is a sound program and there is every reason for continuing the effort. Since it has not yet produced the desired results, however, consideration may well be given to additional and supplementary methods.

The TVA Solution. David E. Lilienthal reports the background relating to the earlier suggestion involving TVA. It appears that Senator Lister Hill, who as a Representative was one of the conference mana-

---

This situation was corrected in part, at least, by the Armed Services Pay Act of 1949.

gers for the original bill, said in a communication to the Senate Judiciary Committee more than a decade later that it was "the intent of the whole TVA statute to create an agency that would be free of some of the government red tape about which we complain, which would have authority commensurate with its responsibilities. We made certain that it could not 'pass the buck' to another bureau or department in the event of failure and that it would not be required to waste time and energy in jurisdictional disputes. It was intended that the Board alone be held responsible for the effective administration of the policies laid down by Congress." [22] That this purpose has been achieved to a notable degree has been testified by a large number of competent and impartial observers. Mr. Lilienthal further quotes from a report of Sir Ernest Simon, a distinguished Manchester businessman who came to Knoxville and made an extensive study of TVA in 1943:

> The TVA Directors . . . have done all they can to delegate responsibility right down through the staff . . . and to cut out Civil Service red tape and the spirit of bureaucracy. The whole staff is encouraged to take responsibility, and not to worry if they make mistakes. The Directors have managed, I think, to get a spirit of constructive initiative throughout the staff as good as anything in the best of private business.

It may well be that a plan which has been so successful in the administration of TVA would work well in other agencies, although it seems unfortunate that it should be necessary to give serious consideration to a device for by-passing the Civil Service Commission in order to achieve that which should be best accomplished under Commission leadership.

Universal Civil Service. For nearly a century the idea has been gaining strength that all able-bodied males have a responsibility to serve in the defense of their country in time of need. This idea found expression in the draft laws of Civil War and World War I days and in the Selective Service Law of World War II. The opposition which expressed itself in draft riots during the Civil War has all but disappeared in the twentieth century. In 1948 the idea was extended, after prolonged debate, in a law which provided for the first peacetime draft in American history.

At a Commencement address at the University of Virginia in June 1948, Mr. Lilienthal came forward with a new idea that seems to have much merit — an idea which may best be stated in his own words: [23]

---

[22] See Lilienthal, David E., "For 'U. P. S.' — Universal Public Service," *New York Times Magazine*, June 27, 1948, pp. 7, 42 ff.
[23] Lilienthal, *op. cit.*

This period will not only call for steadfastness and faith but for great skills in self-government, great judgment and open-mindedness in the development of public policies, and creativeness in all the arts of government. In these circumstances we must summon all of our talents for citizenship, for self-government, for public service, as we chart our course through these dark waters. . . . In the next three decades, I urge that every educated person who is qualified to do so plan definitely to set aside a number of years for the rendering of service in the legislature, or executive branches of his local, State or Federal government, and that as nearly as possible this be full-time service.

This proposal obviously seeks to extend to the requirements of the peacetime public service the precedents established by selective service for the armed forces and by dollar-a-year and war-service appointees in the civilian service of wartime. It recognizes simultaneously the normal difficulties encountered by government in attracting its share of the nation's annual output of trained personnel, and the obligation which devolves upon all citizens to bear their share of the common burden. President Truman doubtless had this situation in mind when in his address at the Princeton Bicentennial Celebration he said, "The success of the Government's effort . . . will depend upon the extent to which our leaders in business, labor, the professions, agriculture, and every other field, appreciate the role of their Government and the greatness of its task."

In operation such a plan might be expected to accomplish at least two desirable results. Presumably it would supplement the supply of high-grade personnel available for the administration of the many functions of government at all levels, but it might also prove to be a very effective recruiting device. There is every probability that some who entered the service on a supposedly temporary basis would find that they liked it and wished to remain. This happened in many cases after World War II, while many of those who left did so with a greatly improved understanding of the problems of governmental administration.

Government Reserve Corps. Early in 1948 nine young men who served their government during World War II in important administrative assignments developed a plan for a Government Reserve Corps at a series of luncheon meetings in New York City.[24] Devised to obtain the best possible personnel for supervisory positions under the Marshall Plan, it was extended to include emergency assignments at home as well as abroad. Briefly, the plan proposes a pool of specially skilled men from which government could borrow individuals for specific emer-

Described in an article by Sigrid Arne, "Government 'Brains Pool' Is New Idea," *Washington Post*, February 22, 1948.

gency jobs. The men would be given a leave of absence from their private positions, the employers — as they did during World War II — piecing out their governmental salaries so that they would not be obliged to suffer a loss in income.

The plan was conceived as a means of aiding government to obtain the services of qualified men for key supervisory positions. In operation, some respected American would be selected to run a very small office which would comb the wartime lists for men who had done special jobs in many fields — taxation, rationing, shipping, foreign trade, public relations, industrial management, labor relations, transportation, and education. These men would receive invitations to put their names on the Reserve Corps list. Those who qualified after the usual government tests for character, integrity, and suitability, would have their names placed on the list; others who were qualified could volunteer for service. All on the list would be subject to call when and if needed. In order to protect the government, it was proposed that the statute authorizing the establishment of the plan should provide that no man on emergency government assignment could work on anything that might benefit his private employer. Since most of the jobs would be administrative in character, this requirement could readily be enforced.

SELECTED REFERENCES

Gantt, Henry L., *Industrial Leadership* (Yale University Press, 1916). A pioneer in scientific management discusses leadership in industry.

Hart, James, and Spicer, George W., "Executive Leadership in Administration," in Haines, Charles G., and Dimock, Marshall E., Eds., *Essays on the Law and Practice of Governmental Administration* (Johns Hopkins Press, 1935); also Merriam, Charles E., "The New Management" in his *The New Democracy and the New Despotism* (McGraw-Hill, New York, 1939). Three well-known political scientists discuss leadership in administration at the top level.

Herring, E. Pendleton, *Presidential Leadership* (Farrar & Rinehart, New York, 1940). Analysis of the new leadership responsibilities of the presidential office.

Stone, Donald C., "Notes on the Governmental Executive: His Role and His Method," in Martin, Roscoe C., *New Horizons in Public Administration* (University of Alabama Press, 1946). An outstanding analysis of the role of the executive, including responsibility for leadership.

Tead, Ordway, *Democratic Administration* (Association Press, New York, 1945) and *The Art of Leadership* (McGraw-Hill, New York, 1935). An established authority on leadership, its characteristics and methods of functioning, presents the result of his study, in the latter volume particularly with regard to administration.

White, Leonard D., and Smith, T. V., *Politics and the Public Service* (Harpers, New York, 1939). An interesting discussion which emphasizes the importance of leadership.

Whitehead, T. N., *Leadership in a Free Society* (Harvard University Press, 1936). A fine philosophical discussion of the place and function of leadership in society.

PART V

EXTERNAL RELATIONS:
THE EXECUTION OF POLICY

29

ADMINISTRATIVE PROCEDURE

THE preceding Part has been concerned with the problems of internal organization and management involved in performing the administrative job assigned to a department or agency. Part V will consider certain phases of the external relations of an agency relating to the execution of policy and discussed here under the general and broadly inclusive heading of administrative procedure. The former had to do with the relations of management to the personnel of the department or agency; the latter deals with the relations of the entire agency with persons and groups ouside and, under normal circumstances, with that portion of the public benefiting from the services or subject to the regulation of the department or agency.

There are many facets to this problem of external relations. A survey of the various forms of control over administration (Chapters 30–32) will, in this discussion, be followed by chapters on administrative adjudication (Chapter 33) and on judicial review (Chapter 34). The two concluding chapters are concerned with the pressures or influences which outside forces exert on the policies and conduct of administrative agencies and with the public relations of an agency — with the things which an agency should and should not do if it is to function in that happy situation which exists when it is said to have "good public relations."

Any governmental unit may employ, as instruments for the execution of its policies, powers delegated to it either by statute or by subdelegation from a higher echelon within the department or agency of which it is a part. Administrative legislation comes into existence through the exercise of the power to promulgate rules and regulations, within limits fixed by the legislature, to implement and particularize the legislative purpose. The Senate Judiciary Committee has defined a rule as any agency statement of general applicability designed to implement, interpret, or prescribe law, policy, organization, procedure, or practice requirements. "When promulgated, an administrative regulation fixes rules of future conduct and action governing all persons subject thereto. The breadth of this power to regulate gives administrative agencies an important legislative role, affecting not only private individuals but entire industries." [1]

Any governmental unit may be authorized to use, within the limits specified in the delegation, any or all of the devices for administrative regulation broadly referred to as sanctions. Landis observes that "sanctions, as the methods that exist for the realization of policy, may be thought of as constituting the armory of government." [2] Somewhat more specifically, the Senate Judiciary Committee defined sanctions as including withholding of relief, or any agency prohibition, penalty, seizure, assessment, requirement, or restriction. The power to invoke sanctions includes the power to police and take affirmative quasi-judicial action in the field under supervision, irrespective of any function to issue or invoke a license or approval.[3]

As an instrument for securing compliance, power to give relief may play an important part. Relief, as defined by the Committee, includes any grant, recognition, or other beneficial action. In other words, the agency may on occasion contribute quite as much to realization of policy by giving awards as by invoking penalties. The rewards are technically known as relief; the penalties, as sanctions.

Types of Sanctions and Enforcement Procedures

It is significant that there is not even a catalog of the devices for enforcement nor any very exact knowledge of the fields in which these devices have been or should be employed. Mr. Landis called attention to this in 1931; it is interesting that he came back to the same recommendation some years later, after he had had extensive administrativ experience with a number of different agencies, when he wrote: [4]

And the weapons themselves (in the armory of government) are many. The criminal penalty, the civil penalty, the resort to the injunctive side of equity, th tripling of damage claims, the informer's share, the usefulness of mere publici

---

[1] Jacobs, Nathan L., and Davis, Nathan, *A Report on the State Administrative Agenc in New Jersey*, pp. 6-31 (Eighth Report of the Judicial Council of New Jersey, Tre ton, 1938). These concepts apply alike at the state as well as at the Federal level: "Th the state Minimum Wage Law for Women and Children, after pronouncing that wage is against public policy when below the reasonable value of the work done a the necessary cost of living, delegates to the Commissioner of Labor the power establish, in terms of dollars, what the minimum wage shall be with respect to all pe sons employed in a particular occupation."

[2] *The Administrative Process*, pp. 89-90.

[3] Jacobs and Davis, *op. cit.*, point out again the applicability of these concepts at t state level: "In many instances, the legislature has vested administrative agencies wi power to make judicial or quasi-judicial determinations affecting persons who are n operating under licenses or approvals to do business. Thus the Department of Agric ture may order the quarantine or destruction of diseased animals; the Department Tenement House Supervision may order the vacation of certain tenement houses a that construction or alteration of certain buildings shall cease, et cetera."

[4] Landis, *op. cit.*, pp. 90-91.

as a means for coercing action, the license as a condition of pursuing certain conduct, the confiscation of offending property — these represent only a few of the many weapons in that armory. Their effectiveness to control conduct in one field, their ineffectiveness to achieve that same control in another field have never been scientifically stated. Why is it, for example, that the informer's share, a method commonly employed in colonial legislation, has generally disappeared from the statute books but nevertheless still survives in the field of customs collection? What leads to a device of permitting a litigant to recover triple damages for certain injuries, and how effective is that claim to bring about enforcement of the law by this effort to stimulate individual initiative? Questions such as these, which can so readily be put, have as yet failed to stir research. Far less have they received even tentative answers.

The aggregate of power delegated to administrative agencies to use these various devices is tremendous. Their determinations vitally affect the personal and property rights of individuals and corporations in their everyday activities. Not all agencies are endowed alike as to either the nature or the extent of the powers delegated to them. Some of the more common devices are listed and briefly described in the paragraphs which follow; most of them will be considered more at length in later chapters.

Licenses and Permits. The term "license" may be defined as any form of required official permission, such as certification, charter, or other form of authorization to engage in the type of activity in question. The delegation of the licensing power permits the agency, within broad limits fixed by legislation, to grant, refuse, review or modify, suspend or revoke a license or approval requisite to the conduct of a designated professional practice, vocation, or business.[5]

When an administrative agency considers an application for license or approval to engage in business subject to government supervision, it must determine the fitness and qualifications of the applicant, and in considering whether license or approval shall be suspended or revoked, it must determine whether proper cause therefor exists. In each instance, there must be an adjudication of fact and a declaration of judgment as to the proper course of action to be taken.

Large numbers of illustrations of this type of regulatory action may be found in any jurisdiction — lawyers, doctors, dentists, architects, and engineers among the professions; barbers, beauticians, plumbers, motion picture projectionists, and others among the vocations. Licenses are required as a condition of engaging in many types of business activity; in other cases, permits may be used; in still others, mere registration suffices as a means of establishing a basis for the enforcement of regulations.

Ibid.

Inspection. Many types of administrative program may be enforced, in whole or in part, through the work of an inspection force. Inspectors are hired to visit individuals, plants, or properties under the supervision of the department or agency to ascertain by examining the records, inspecting the premises, or otherwise that the requirements of the statutes under which the agency operates and its rules and regulations supplementary thereto are being observed. This device is commonly used in the enforcement of regulations governing

> The production and processing of milk
> Cleanliness and sanitation of restaurants and eating places
> Weights and measures
> Building construction and maintenance
> Tenement house regulation
> Safety regulations in factories
> Sale of food and drug products
> And many other purposes

Administrative Adjudication. When an agency undertakes to adjudicate matters resembling private controversies in which the legislature has a particular purpose and in which the administrative agency participates to aid in the effectuation of that purpose, it is said to be exercising powers of administrative adjudication. To quote again from the report of the New Jersey Council:

> The powers delegated to administrative agencies to adjudicate private controversies between individuals are still narrow but ever increasing. The most familiar example is the Workmen's Compensation Bureau where the referee may conduct summary hearings and has power to approve or disapprove settlements and compromises. A further example of recent origin is the Unemployment Compensation Commission, which is empowered to adjudicate upon the claims of individuals for benefits under the Unemployment Compensation Law.

Threat of Prosecution. In most cases all that is required to secure compliance is instruction or persuasion, although publicity and threats of punitive action may sometimes be needed. "Whatever the justice of the adjustments which settle so many more cases than the formal hearing with its safeguards for the respondent, this informal and preparatory sanction can be used with an effect that largely nullifies the respondent's formal safeguards." [6] Mr. Landis, writing of his experience

---

[6] Chamberlain, Dowling, and Hays, *op. cit.*, p. 86. The authors cite an instance of insurance company that settled a $30,000 claim during the depression, rather than face the risk of publicity attending a threatened revocation or withdrawal of their charter by the state in question. Although the company had good defenses, they did not use them. The Chairman of the Appropriations Committee represented the plaintiff, and the appropriation for the Department of Insurance was then pending. The Department could not get what it wanted unless this case was settled, hence the pressure on the insurance company.

as chairman of the Securities and Exchange Commission, gives a striking estimate of the effectiveness of the threat of prosecution and of the value of the protection afforded by the requirement of judicial procedure: [7]

The ability to sell a substantial block of securities depends upon creation of a belief that that issue is, like Calpurnia, above suspicion. . . . The very institution of proceedings is frequently sufficient to destroy . . . [this] quality, for the Commission's allegation that some untruthfulness attends their registration is sufficient to create grave suspicion as to their merit. Administrative adjudication in these cases is, to all intents and purposes, final. But more than this, the threat of initiating a proceeding, because of its tendency to assail the reputation of an issue . . . is sufficient in the normal case to bring about compliance with the desires of the administrative.

The significant power that is exercised by the administrative in these cases is in its capacity as prosecutor rather than as judge. . . . The initiation of a complaint is public. Of itself, it is an attack upon the conduct of the respondent. . . . I advert to this power to prosecute primarily to emphasize the point that the charge of arbitrariness, which is commonly made against administrative action, usually appertains to the exercise of the power to prosecute rather than to the power to adjudicate. It is restraints upon the exercise of that power that in my judgment are of far greater significance than the creation of restraints upon the power to adjudicate.

The same point has been made, in substance, by a number of other writers. In a study of the Federal Trade Commission made a number of years ago by Gerard C. Henderson, it is pointed out that the serious effects of prosecution, regardless of outcome, give the Commission an effective sanction in the mere threat of prosecution: [8]

A complaint frequently heard among businessmen and attorneys who have had to do with the Commission, is directed against the injustice of a formal complaint by a governmental tribunal, publicly charging serious offenses against reputable citizens, and based merely upon a provisional and tentative belief that the charges may be true. The complaint is given to the newspapers and naturally attracts much attention. Many months later, it may be withdrawn or dismissed, but the injury to the respondent's reputation has already been done.

It is as though an individual — possibly the reader of these lines — were arrested on the basis of mistaken identity and charged with disorderly conduct. The name goes on the police blotter and into the newspapers, thereby causing great embarrassment to the individual and injury to his reputation. While publicity may later be given to the fact that an error was made, the exoneration never quite catches up with the accusation. Doubts have been raised in the minds of many persons about the individual's character.

Landis, *op. cit.*, pp. 108–110.
The Federal Trade Commission, pp. 330–331.

Such a situation is pretty serious to an individual or to a business firm. Possible remedies might be found either in withholding formal charges pending the outcome of an investigation or, as is customary in all governmental agencies in the handling of many matters, in regarding the charges as confidential until the agency is in possession of sufficient evidence to indicate that prosecution is a proper and necessary step. Either procedure would prevent the "character assassination" of individuals or firms merely suspected of having violated the law, without at the same time preventing the agency from availing itself of the aid of publicity if the use of that coercive device should become necessary or desirable.

Publicity. As previously indicated, publicity may be a very potent means of securing compliance. Unfavorable publicity is not much more acceptable to the lawbreaker than to the law-abiding individual. In the latter case it is a source of personal embarrassment; in the former it is likely to interfere with business. Of the many instances which might be cited of the effective use of publicity, none is perhaps more suitable than an incident which occurred in the early days of the Federal Trade Commission.

Time was when the secondhand and rebuilt typewriter business was largely concentrated in Chicago. About the time the Federal Trade Commission Act was passed, one of these concerns obtained copy of the list of customers of a competing firm, and to each of the names it addressed a letter stating that the latter was about to retire from business and that it would be advisable to make other arrangements for securing future needs in typewriters and supplies. Now so happened that the injured company had no intention whatever of retiring. The company consulted its attorneys to find out what remedial measures might be taken.

The attorney remembered the new Federal Trade Commission Act and proceeded posthaste to Washington to find out what the new agency could do. He presented his case. The complaint was received and docketed. The offending company was summoned for a hearing. But the company did not want a hearing and the attending publicity. Was there not, they inquired, some way in which the matter could settled quietly? The Commission agreed that there was: that the defendant company might send another letter to all the names to which the first was sent, explaining that the information was in error and apologizing for any inconvenience that might have been caused. The company agreed to send the letter, and the whole matter was cleared up within a month's time — before the business of the injured company had been either seriously or permanently affected.

Another illustration from quite a different field may be drawn from the experience of the new fair employment practice commissions. These bodies in no less than half a dozen states have relied chiefly on education, conference and consultation, and conciliation to secure compliance; up to the end of 1948 not a single case had been taken into the courts. In the few instances where these methods have failed, the threat of publicity has brought speedy compliance. The chairman of the New York State Commission reports an interesting case of an employer who did not want to settle a complaint in the manner suggested by the Commission: [9]

I could see that he was getting embarrassed. His face was red and he looked out of the window. When I assured him that he didn't have to follow this recommendation, that it was in no way compulsory, he asked what the next step would be. I said that I would then recommend it for a hearing, in which case the issue would be reviewed before three commissioners — going over the entire record. He asked whether the public would be at the meeting.

'Yes,' I replied.

To this he said: 'I don't want a hearing.'

Embarrassment, not harassment or punishment, is the chief sanction — embarrassment over being caught not living up in deeds to American principles of fairness we all acknowledge in words.

Classification as to Type. It is possible to classify these various types of functions within broad categories, such as coercive and noncoercive, judicial and nonjudicial, intermediate and final. The judicial sanctions may be either formal or informal. Since these types are not mutually exclusive, perhaps their nature may best be indicated by a simple chart such as the one on page 585. The lists are long enough to be suggestive, but no claim is made for their completeness.

Evolution of the Federal Administrative Procedure Act [10]

It is not surprising that, with the tremendous increase in the use of all these types of administrative procedure, there should have been a good deal of criticism of the procedures. Some of it — as will be evident later — has been well founded, for at some times and in some agencies there have been instances in which the long-recognized legal rights of individuals in English-speaking countries have not been fully or ade-

Ransom, Kings, in *New York Herald-Tribune*, August 6, 1948, and reprinted in the Appendix of the *Congressional Record* of the same date, pp. A5226–A5227.
See Isenbergh, Maxwell S., "Developments in Administrative Law, 1930–1940," *Virginia Law Review*, November, 1940, pp. 29–74 — one of the best summaries of developments in this area.

THE CONGRESS OF THE UNITED STATES OF AMERICA

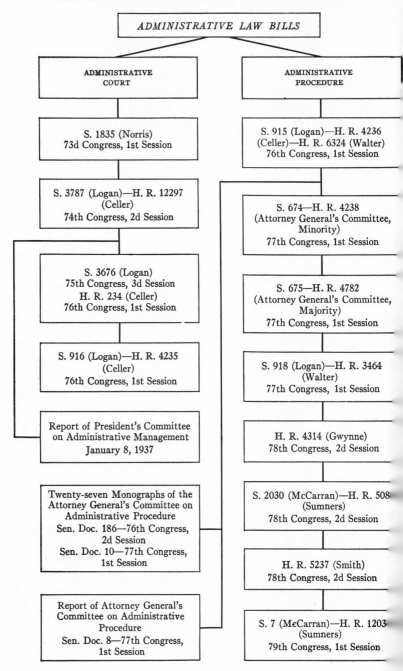

ADMINISTRATIVE LAW BILLS

ADMINISTRATIVE COURT

S. 1835 (Norris)
73d Congress, 1st Session

S. 3787 (Logan)—H. R. 12297 (Celler)
74th Congress, 2d Session

S. 3676 (Logan)
75th Congress, 3d Session
H. R. 234 (Celler)
76th Congress, 1st Session

S. 916 (Logan)—H. R. 4235 (Celler)
76th Congress, 1st Session

Report of President's Committee on Administrative Management
January 8, 1937

Twenty-seven Monographs of the Attorney General's Committee on Administrative Procedure
Sen. Doc. 186—76th Congress, 2d Session
Sen. Doc. 10—77th Congress, 1st Session

Report of Attorney General's Committee on Administrative Procedure
Sen. Doc. 8—77th Congress, 1st Session

ADMINISTRATIVE PROCEDURE

S. 915 (Logan)—H. R. 4236 (Celler)—H. R. 6324 (Walter)
76th Congress, 1st Session

S. 674—H. R. 4238 (Attorney General's Committee, Minority)
77th Congress, 1st Session

S. 675—H. R. 4782 (Attorney General's Committee, Majority)
77th Congress, 1st Session

S. 918 (Logan)—H. R. 3464 (Walter)
77th Congress, 1st Session

H. R. 4314 (Gwynne)
78th Congress, 2d Session

S. 2030 (McCarran)—H. R. 508 (Sumners)
78th Congress, 2d Session

H. R. 5237 (Smith)
78th Congress, 2d Session

S. 7 (McCarran)—H. R. 1203 (Sumners)
79th Congress, 1st Session

Types of Sanctions

	JUDICIAL	NONJUDICIAL
Coercive	Judgments Fines Prison sentences Informer's share Penalties Rewards Injunctions Writs Reparations	Licenses Approvals Investigations Inspections Threat of prosecution Prohibitory orders Fraud orders Triple damages Summary seizure

Noncoercive	Pretrial procedures	Informal settlements
		Declarations of public policy
		  Decisions
		  Rules and Regulations
		Declaration of legal obligation, with no sanction
		  for nonobservance
		Establishment of voluntary commercial standards
		Provision of standards by example: government
		  as model employer
		Educational campaigns
		Demonstrations
		Conferences
		Mediation and conciliation
		Purchase of capacity to act; purchase of consent
		Compliance through publicity
		Yardstick regulation
		Public relations and administrative publicity

nately observed. Lawyers and the bar associations have been particularly prone to object to what they have regarded as short cuts to established judicial procedures.

Particular objection has been raised to the failure to publicize administrative rules and regulations, to the lack of uniformity in administrative proceedings in different agencies, and to the inadequate protection given to personal and property rights of individuals in others. Over the years enough individuals have complained to enough legislatures so that proposals for statutory modification of administrative procedures have been frequent.

The chart on page 584 presents in chronological form the principal bills introduced since the 73rd Congress looking toward the establishment of an administrative court and toward the standardization of administrative procedures.[11] Each of these proposals received widespread notice and consideration both in and out of Congress. Some of the recommendations were good, some bad, but each represented an attempt to grapple with the tremendously difficult and important problems which the rapid rise of this so-called fourth branch of government

Senate Committee on the Judiciary, *Report on S. 7*, p. 2 (79th Cong., 1st Sess., Report No. 752).

presented. Reference is here made to two or three of these proposals, with consideration of the Administrative Procedure Act of 1945 reserved for the concluding section of this chapter.

Report of the President's Committee (1937). Mention has been made from time to time in preceding chapters of the excellent report of the President's Committee on Administrative Management. The problem was clearly stated by the Committee in the following words: [12]

> The executive branch of the Government of the United States has . . . grown up without plan or design. . . . To look at it now, no one would ever recognize the structure which the Founding Fathers erected a century and a half ago. . . . Commissions have been the result of legislative groping rather than the pursuit of a consistent policy. . . . They are in reality miniature independent governments set up to deal with the railroad problem, the banking problem or the radio problem. They constitute a headless "fourth branch" of the government, a haphazard deposit of irresponsible agencies and uncoordinated powers . . . There is a conflict of principle involved in their make-up and functions . . . They are vested with duties of administration . . . and at the same time they are given important judicial work. . . . The evils resulting from this confusion of principles are insidious and far reaching. . . . Pressures and influence properly enough directed toward officers responsible for formulating and administering policy constitute an unwholesome atmosphere in which to adjudicate private rights. But the mixed duties of the commissions render escape from these subversive influences impossible. Furthermore, the same men are obliged to serve both as prosecutors and as judges. This not only undermines judicial fairness; it weakens public confidence in that fairness. Commission decisions affecting private rights and conduct lie under the suspicion of being rationalization of the preliminary findings which the Commission, in the role of prosecutor presented to itself.

To this statement, in transmitting the *Report* to the Congress, the President added: [13]

> I have examined this report carefully and thoughtfully, and am convinced that it is a great document of permanent importance. . . . The practice of creating independent regulatory commissions, who perform administrative work in addition to judicial work, threatens to develop a "fourth branch" of the government for which there is no sanction in the Constitution.

The Committee proposed a very drastic remedy for the situation a complete separation of the investigative-prosecuting functions and personnel from the deciding functions and personnel. This proposal was further developed by Professor Cushman, who wrote this portion of the *Report*, in his volume on *The Independent Regulatory Commission* which was published a few years later.

---

[12] *Report with Special Studies*, pp. 32–33, 39–40 (Washington, 1937).
[13] *Ibid.*, pp. iii–v; for additional comments on this subject, see pp. 41–42, 207–210, 219, 222–223, and 230–239.

The Attorney-General's Committee (1938). Attorney General Murphy, renewing the suggestion he had previously made respecting the need for procedural reform in the wide and growing field of administrative law, recommended the appointment of a commission to make a thorough survey of existing practices and procedures and to point the way to improvements. The President concurred, and the Attorney General appointed a committee composed of government officials, professors of law, judges, and private practitioners. Its staff prepared and in 1940–1941 issued a series of studies of the procedures of the principal administrative agencies and bureaus in the Federal government. The Committee then held public hearings and executive sessions over a long period of time, at which representatives of Federal agencies were heard. It finally issued a voluminous report which represented the most thorough study of Federal administrative practices and procedures ever undertaken.[14]

A bill embodying the more important findings and recommendations of the Committee was introduced in Congress; it included the following provisions:

> A formal grant of power to every agency to delegate to its responsible members power to manage its internal affairs; to dispose informally of complaints and requests, issue orders, and govern matters of preliminary procedure. This section would have included also the power to delegate to one or more members of an agency, subject to internal review by an agency tribunal, the power to decide cases after hearing or on appeal.

> Provision was to be made for the appointment by the President, with the advice and consent of the Senate, of a Director of Federal Administrative Procedure, for a term of seven years at $10,000 per year. There would have been an Office of Federal Administrative Procedure, composed of the Director, a justice of the United States Court of Appeals for the District of Columbia, and the Director of the Administrative Office of the United States Courts.

> An Advisory Committee to the above Office would have been constituted and staffed by representatives of the several administrative agencies.

> Every agency would have been enjoined to make public and keep current information with regard to their organization and structure and all their general policies and interpretations of law. Save by special procedure no regulation

---

See *Administrative Procedure in Government Agencies — Report of the Committee Administrative Procedure, Appointed by the Attorney General, at the Request of President, to Investigate the Need for Procedural Reform in Various Administrative Tribunals and to Suggest Improvements Therein* (S. Doc. No. 8, 77th Cong., 1st), and summarized in Jaffe, Louis J., "The Report of the Attorney General's Committee on Administrative Procedure," *University of Chicago Law Review*, April, 1941, 401–440; see also articles by Dickinson, John, "The Acheson Report: A Novel Approach to Administrative Law," *University of Pennsylvania Law Review*, May, 1942, 757–779, and Hart, James, "The Acheson Report: A Critique," *Iowa Law Review*, 1941, pp. 801–818, and "The Final Report of the Attorney General's Committee Administrative Procedure," *American Political Science Review*, June, 1941, pp. 806.

would take effect until forty-five days after its publication in *The Federal Register*.

5. Every agency entrusted with the duty of deciding cases would be commanded to appoint "Hearing Commissioners" before whom disputes would be heard and decided, subject to final administrative review by an agency tribunal and also judicial review in amenable cases. These commissioners would be empowered to administer oaths, subpoena persons and documents, take testimony, admit and exclude evidence, and render decisions.

6. Power would be given to each agency tribunal, at its discretion, to issue declaratory rulings concerning rights, status, or other legal relations arising under the pertinent statutes or regulations. In the absence of judicial reversal, these rulings would have the same force as a final order of the agency tribunal.

American Bar Association Committees. From 1933 through 1943 the Special Committee on Administrative Law of the American Bar Association put out a series of reports containing a wealth of valuable material.[15] These reports offered three quite different types of statutory proposals for administrative reform. First came the proposal for a Federal Administrative Court, which died an early death (see chart on page 584). Then came the so-called Walter-Logan Bill, presently to be considered in some detail. Finally, the Committee recommended the McCarran-Sumners Bill, enacted during the 79th Congress and now known as the Administrative Procedures Act of 1945.

The Walter-Logan Bill (1940). The Walter-Logan Bill [16] was passed by Congress and vetoed in a stirring message by President Roosevelt. It was typical of a good many bills introduced into Congress at the time — bills more concerned with hamstringing the administrative agencies than with standardizing procedure and correcting actual abuses. contained four basic provisions relating respectively to the promulgation of rules; to the establishment of uniform procedures for reviewing the decisions of subordinates; to the judicial review of rules; and to standardization of procedure and scope of judicial review of the decisions and orders of administrative agencies.

In connection with the first of these provisions, namely, the promulgation of rules, it was provided that all agencies must promulgate their rules and regulations under any future statute within one year from the date of enactment of that statute. Rules should be adopted only after adequate notice to interested parties and after public hearings and should become effective only after publication in the *Federal Register*. Provision was also made for petition to the agency for

---

[15] See Stason, E. Blythe, "Administrative Law: Significant Developments During War Years," *Michigan Law Review*, April, 1946, pp. 797–810, for full list of citations.
[16] H. R. 6324 (1939), 76th Cong., 3rd Sess.

consideration, within a period of one year from the date of enactment of the Walter-Logan Bill, of existing rules which had not been in effect for as long as three years. The second major provision sought to establish uniformity in procedure for reviewing the decisions of subordinates within a given agency; as was pointed out at the time, however, such uniformity is neither possible nor desirable among agencies charged with carrying on widely different functions. In the case of the third provision, the Court of Appeals for the District of Columbia would have been given the jurisdiction to review any rule on petition of any interested person within thirty days of publication of the rule. This was to be in addition to the power of the courts in usual cases to adjudge any rule valid or invalid in any suit or appeal, before such court, involving such rule. The fourth provision, looking toward the standardization of procedure for review of decisions and orders of administrative agencies, was unobjectionable; but that providing for extension of the scope of review was highly objectionable.

As the President pointed out in his veto message, the measure was badly timed, in as much as the whole subject was under survey by the Attorney General's Committee. The effect would have been so to increase the opportunities for court review of rules and for court appeals in decisions of administrative agencies as to prevent the effective operation of the administrative agencies concerned.[17] Furthermore, the courts would probably have been so burdened with the volume of appeals that they would never have been able to carry the load.

Administrative Procedure Act of 1946. After years of controversy the Congress in 1946 enacted the Administrative Procedure Act of 1946, known at the time as the McCarran-Sumners Bill.[18] This act is short and concise, its provisions generally satisfactory — at least by comparison with most of the proposals that preceded it. The chart on page 590 indicates the contents of its several sections. It will be noted that it covers the various aspects of administrative procedure without setting up any new or separate machinery such as the administrative court earlier proposed.

A tremendous amount of literature dealing with this bill was published, as is shown in the bibliography compiled by the Joint Reference Library, Chicago, May 13, 1940, supplement, August 12, 1940. Most of the arguments on both sides were summarized in the *Congressional Digest*, May, 1940; see also Jaretski, Alfred Jr., "The Administrative Law Bill: Unsound and Unworkable," *Louisiana Law Review*, January, , pp. 294–329, and Landis, James M., "Crucial Issues in Administrative Law: The Walter-Logan Bill," *Harvard Law Review*, May, 1940, pp. 1077–1102, and the former's letter to the Editor of the *New York Times*, October 6, 1940.

Public Law No. 404, 79th Congress; for good comments, see Brown, Ray A., "The Federal Administrative Procedure Act," *Wisconsin Law Review*, January, 1947, pp. , and Nathanson, Nathaniel L., "Some Comments on the Administrative Procedure " *Illinois Law Review*, September–October, 1946, pp. 368–422.

FEDERAL ADMINISTRATIVE PROCEDURE ACT OF 1946

*DIAGRAM OF PRINCIPAL SECTIONS**

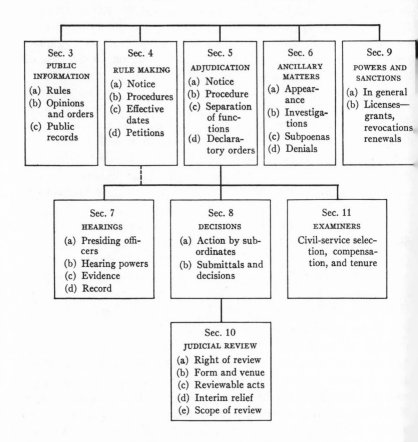

CLASSIFICATION OF SECTIONS ACCORDING TO FUNCTION

General Provisions

Sec. 1 — Title	Sec. 6 — Ancillary Matters
Sec. 2 — Definitions	Sec. 9 — Sanctions and Powers
Sec. 3 — Public Information	Sec. 12 — Construction and Effect

Quasi-Legislative Functions	*Quasi-Judicial Functions*
Sec. 4 — Rule Making	Sec. 5 — Adjudication
Sec. 7 — Hearings	Sec. 11 — Examiners
Sec. 8 — Decisions	

Judicial Review

Sec. 10 — Judicial Review

* From Senate Committee on the Judiciary, *op. cit.*, p. 9.

Section 1 prescribes the title; Section 2, the definitions of terms; and Section 3, the effective dates and rules of construction. In the diagram, the sections shown in the first row (Nos. 3, 4, 5, 6, and 9) set forth the several types of requirements, procedures, and limitations; those in the second row (Nos. 7, 8, and 11) relate to hearing and decision requirements where other statutes require a hearing. Section 10, on judicial review, relates not only to decisions rendered after agency hearing but, in appropriate cases, to the exercise of any other administrative power or authority. The classification of the sections according to function is also shown. The nature of these provisions and their application in practice will be considered in more detail later.

Developments in the States

While these developments were taking place at the Federal level, the states — or at least some of them — were likewise engaged in an effort to establish suitable systems of administrative procedure. The same criticisms directed at Federal procedure prior to the act of 1945, were also voiced in the states, in which somewhat parallel attempts were made to determine through surveys and reports the essential qualities of a desirable procedure. Notable among these was the so-called Benjamin Report in New York in 1942.[19]

Mr. Benjamin was appointed in 1939 as Commissioner under Section 8 of the Executive Law and charged with the duty of studying, examining, and investigating the exercise of the quasi-judicial functions of any board, commission, or department of the State. A sizable staff, employed over a period of three years to conduct the investigation, produced a formidable report of some 369 pages, which also included consideration of the problem of judicial review. Admitting that there is room for improvement in many respects, the Commissioner still believed that the State could "take merited satisfaction in its system of administrative adjudication and legislation and judicial review."

The report, characterized by Dean Stason of the University of Michigan Law School as "by all odds the best available study of state administrative law," sets forth some fourteen general considerations and conclusions. General principles are regarded as valuable primarily as criteria; "they do not solve the essential problems of method, of adjusting the administrative and judicial machinery to the accomplishment of the desired ends." It is regarded as "impossible, if it were desirable, to change too much at once," the development of ideal procedures in any field being a matter of growth. More can be accomplished by voluntary improvement of administrative procedures than

Benjamin, Robert M., *Administrative Adjudication in the State of New York*.

by improvement imposed by legislation. These items, to be sure, in
dicate more about the approach used in the investigation than abou
its specific recommendations.

Surveys of procedure have been undertaken in many other state
often by bar associations, sometimes by official bodies. One of the firs
was the Jacobs and Davis survey in New Jersey, included in the 193
report of the Judicial Council to the Governor. In 1938 and 1939 th
American Bar Association had a Committee on Administrative Ager
cies and Tribunals in its Section on Judicial Administration. The tw
reports of this Committee dealt primarily with state administrative pr
cedure and submitted a recommended bill for its improvement. B
tween 1940 and 1943 the National Conference of Commissioners c
Uniform State Laws had a committee at work on the drafting of
Model State Administrative Procedure Act. Dean Stason, who serv
as chairman of the committee, emphasized the fact that this propos
act "deals primarily with major principles, not with minor matters
procedural detail." The following "basic principles of common sen
justice, and fair play are deemed to be an irreducible minimum, and
such are embodied in the provisions of the measure":

1. Assurance of proper publicity for administrative rules that affect the publi
2. Provisions for advance determinations, or "declaratory judgments," on
   validity of administrative rules, and provision for "declaratory rulings"
   fording advance understanding of the application of administrative rules
   particular cases
3. Guaranties of fundamental fairness in administrative hearings, particularl
   regard to rules of evidence and the giving of official notice in quasi-judi
   proceedings
4. Provisions assuring personal familiarity on the part of the responsible age
   heads, with the evidence in quasi-judicial cases decided by them
5. Assurances of proper scope of judicial review of administrative orders to g
   antee correction of administrative errors

Reactions to this draft vary, as they always do to proposals in this fi
While some authorities regard it favorably, one distinguished c
mentator observed in conversation that he had little enthusiasm fc
and believed its greatest usefulness might prove to be in deterring
states from enacting something worse.

In Illinois in 1944 an Administrative Practice and Review C
mission, after holding public hearings, undertook the drafting of a
providing for a uniform method of judicial review of administr
decisions and orders. Possibly more significant was the survey of
cedure in California, published in 1944 in the biennial report o
State Judicial Council. Both of these surveys resulted in legislatio

may be best, however, to indicate by year and by state the enactments of this character thus far adopted: [20]

State Administrative Procedure Acts

1939 *North Carolina* — Laws 1939, Ch. 218; amended Laws 1943, Sec. 150–1–150–8.

Provides a uniform procedure in the revocation of certain types of licenses, including prior notice, hearing, appearance by counsel, written findings of fact, right to subpoenas, and judicial appeal.

1941 *North Dakota* — Laws 1941, Ch. 240.[21]

Enacted the Administrative Agencies Uniform Practice Act, somewhat along the lines of the Model Act. The first of the general remedial acts, it provides for basic procedures both for rule making and for adjudication.

1943 *Ohio* — Laws 1943, 120 v. 358; amended Laws 1945, 121 v. 578.

The act prescribes procedure for licensing agencies only, although the term "licensing" is broadly defined. Provides for public notice and hearings, with right to appear by counsel and to subpoena witnesses, etc.

Wisconsin — Laws 1943, Ch. 375.[22]

Wisconsin adopted the Model Act.

1944 *Virginia* — Laws 1944, Ch. 160.

This act provides for notice of proposals to change or amend rules, specifies hearing procedures, including notice, evidence, appeals, etc.

1945 *California* — Laws 1945, Ch. 867, 868, 869.[23]

The first of these three related acts provides for the procedure in administrative adjudications and gives the right of judicial review; the second provides procedure for judicial review by mandamus; and the third for a staff of qualified hearing officers, to be assigned to the various boards upon request.

Illinois — Laws 1945, p. 1144.[24]

The Administrative Review Act concerns itself with the judicial review of administrative decisions.

Minnesota — Laws 1945, Ch. 452.

This act deals with the method of procedure in making rules, providing that no new rules are to be promulgated without hearing, and notice

---

Data based on Stason article; Unsigned, "Administrative Procedure in the States," *te Government*, September, 1948, pp. 193–195; and *Book of the States, 1948–1949*, 171–175.

See Hoyt, Ralph M., "North Dakota Leads in Administrative Law Field," *Journal the American Judicature Society*, December, 1941, pp. 114–116.

See Hoyt, Ralph M., "The Wisconsin Administrative Procedure Act," *Wisconsin v Review*, July, 1944, pp. 213–239.

These were as recommended in the survey report; see Kleps, Ralph N., "California's proach to the Improvement of Administrative Procedure," *California Law Review*, ember, 1944, pp. 416–426, and "The Reform of Administrative Procedure in Cali-nia," *State Government*, November, 1945, pp. 200–203, and the Division's *First Bien-Report to the Governor and the Legislature*, January 1, 1947 (Sacramento, 1947). Kleps serves as Chief of the Division.

ee Illinois Administrative Practice and Review Commission, *Report to the Sixty- General Assembly* (Springfield, 1947).

thereof being sent in advance to trade groups and others interested, by the Secretary of State. Interested persons may ask for reconsideration of any rule and in such case a public hearing is to be granted.

Pennsylvania — Laws 1945, P. L. 1388.

This enactment is based largely upon the Model Act, providing for publication of all administrative rules and regulations.

1946   *Missouri* — Laws 1946, S. B. 196.

This enactment is essentially an adaptation of the Model Act.

1947   *Indiana* — Laws 1947, Ch. 365.

This enactment is very similar to the Model Act.

It thus appears that between 1939 and 1947 no less than eleven states adopted laws dealing more or less comprehensively with administrative procedure. Four of these cover substantially all the subjects suggested in the Model Act. Several of them provide for some kind of supervisory or enforcement agency. The Illinois Administrative Practice and Review Commission, as a matter of fact, antedates the law for whose enforcement it is now responsible. The agitation for such legislation began in 1939. In 1943 a bill to provide a uniform method of judicial review of administrative decisions failed, but another to create this Commission to study the problems was approved. Its report, submitted the next year, prompted the passage of the act of 1945.

The Illinois Commission consists of nine members, of whom three are Senators, three Representatives, and three appointees of the Governor. Of the last named, one has been selected from a state administrativ agency, one from a local government agency, one as a representative of the general public. This group is authorized to investigate modes of practice before administrative agencies in the state; to study the various types of procedures for the judicial review of administrative order decisions, and determinations; and to report its findings to the General Assembly. After reviewing the accomplishments of the Commission during the first two years of its existence, Roscoe Pound, at the tim chairman of the ABA Committee on Improving the Administration of Justice, wrote:

It seems to me very well done and to make a real step forward. Nothi could be in worse confusion than the subject of review of administrative ord in most of our states. A consistent system of review, safeguarding the rights individuals and yet not substituting the discretion of the court for that of administrative agency is obviously what is needed, and the Commission see to have hit upon an effective program in that direction.

The California setup is somewhat different. The survey in that st recommended that the existing Department of Professional and Vo tional Standards be converted into a Department of Administrat

Procedure. This recommendation was followed only in part, a Division of Administrative Procedure being set up within the Department, which was otherwise not changed. The responsibility of this agency differs radically from that of the Illinois Commission, being rather to maintain a staff of qualified hearing officers to handle cases arising in those agencies which do not have such officers of their own. During its first year the Division's eighteen hearing officers conducted 1890 hearings, following which only eleven filed mandamus actions in the superior court, as a dissatisfied individual is authorized to do, under the provisions of the law.

The Exercise of Discretion

One of the major problems in this whole area, one which arises in all regulatory agencies, whether administrative departments or boards and commissions, and which presents itself in connection with the use of all types of sanctions and enforcement procedures, is that of the exercise of discretion. The word "discretion" is defined in the dictionary as the liberty or power of acting without other control than one's own judgment. One may well ask: how does it happen that this element of discretion is so important, the area of its exercise so large?

This problem arises because laws never enforce themselves. No matter how specific they are or how carefully the draftsman has attempted to make provision for every possible contingency, somebody — some enforcement officer — has to decide exactly what the language in the statute means, whether or not it is applicable to a given set of facts, and if so, how.

There is an oft-quoted maxim handed down for generations to the effect that the ideal should be a government of laws and not of men. This maxim is little more than the expression of a wish, based upon the parallel assumptions that the law itself is definite and certain while the judgment of men is variable and uncertain. Actually, no such thing as government of laws is possible without men to enforce them. If the law is very specific and very detailed, then obviously the area of discretion is limited, but this type of detailed legislation — once common — tends to defeat itself. It is inelastic. It is difficult to change. And because no man can foretell the future clearly enough to anticipate all possible contingencies, such a law becomes exceedingly difficult to administer. As conditions change, some of the provisions are no longer applicable, while other situations which should be covered elude its provisions completely.

So in the twentieth century detail legislation has gradually given way to outline legislation, to measures in which the lawmaking body has sought to define policies and establish principles, leaving to the appropriate administrative agency the task of rounding out the statute by supplying in the form of rules and regulations supplementary and interpretative material that would be necessary to make the provisions of the law effective. Two important results may be noted. The first has been to change in an important way the role of Congress and the state legislatures in the lawmaking process. Where regulatory work is involved — as it so often is — the lawmaking body has delegated to a department or a commission the task of devising as well as enforcing policies and programs designed to achieve purposes enunciated in legislative acts. The second result has been greatly to enlarge the area of discretion entrusted to administrative officers. Outline legislation is elastic and adaptable to changed circumstances and conditions; the enforcing agency is responsible for formulating and promulgating rules and regulations designed to supply the detail formerly incorporated in the statute itself.

Great as is the element of discretion involved in this process, that which must be exercised in the later stages of enforcement may be even greater. The law, as supplemented by the rules and regulations, sets forth the conditions under which individuals and groups may exercise certain privileges; how, for instance, an individual may establish eligibility for a license in a given profession. In many instances the question of eligibility is clear; in many others it may be clouded by doubts as to the standing of the school from which the candidate was graduated, the adequacy of his apprenticeship training, the extent of his guilt in some alleged irregularity in practice. Decision in all such cases requires the weighing of evidence and the exercise of discretion. The annual renewal of the license provides an opportunity for review of any question regarding the professional standing of the registrant while any serious violation of the ethics or canons of the professional group may call for disciplinary action, possibly even the revocation of the license. The public is entitled to protection from illegal and unauthorized practice. The enforcing agency is responsible for providing that protection and is entitled to powers adequate to permit it to accomplish that result. But the accused registrant also has rights.

This brings one face to face with the fact that the powers of the enforcing agency must be exercised within the limits imposed by basic legal concepts of justice and fair play. In large numbers of agencies, in the past, the procedures in connection with which these broad discretionary powers were exercised were not clearly defined, and in a too many cases they were exercised without due regard to the rights of the defendant. In other words, the discretionary powers were often

sed and in such manner that the defendant — whether guilty or
— was left without the legal protections to which all are entitled
ler the principles of the Anglo-Saxon legal system.

The President's Committee on Administrative Management, in its
ort in 1937, after reviewing this situation felt constrained to say that
Federal "independent regulatory commissions could more accu-
:ly be called the irresponsible regulatory commissions, for they are
is of unaccountability." The same could have been said with equal
priety of the similar agencies in most of the states. It was the wide-
:ad realization that all was not well in this field that prompted the
ipaign carried on over a period of more than a decade at both the
leral and state levels to systematize and regularize such procedures
to make adequate provision for independent review, to the end
: the constitutional and legal rights of all parties at interest in such
ceedings might be fully protected.[25]

ECTED REFERENCES

n, Carlton K., *Law and Order* (Stevens & Sons, Ltd., London, 1945). An outstanding
work discussing basic problems as seen by an English authority.

rney General's Committee on Administrative Procedure, *Administrative Procedure
in Government Agencies* (77 Cong., 1st Sess., Sen. Doc. No. 8). Most significant
survey of the problems involved as they appear at the Federal level.

amin, Robert M., *Administrative Adjudication in the State of New York* (Albany,
1942). By all odds the best of numerous surveys at the state level.

lly, Frederick F., and Oatman, Miriam E., *Federal Regulatory Action and Control*
(Brookings Institution, Washington, 1940). Two recognized authorities discuss various aspects of administrative procedure at the Federal level.

nberlain, Joseph F., Dowling, Noel T., and Hays, Paul R., *The Judicial Function
in the Federal Agencies* (Commonwealth Fund, New York, 1942). Three competent students analyze the exercise of the judicial function by the Federal regulatory agencies.

merce Clearing House, *Federal Administrative Procedure* (Chicago, 1944). An extremely useful handbook.

iman, Robert E., *The Independent Regulatory Commissions* (Oxford University
Press, New York, 1941). The standard treatise on the Federal regulatory commissions; for much the same kind of treatment of the state agencies, see Fesler,
James W., *The Independence of State Regulatory Agencies* (Public Administration Service, Chicago, 1942).

nd, Ernst, *Administrative Powers Over Persons and Property* (University of Chicago Press, 1928; *Cases on Administrative Law*, Second Edition (West Publishing
Company, 1928); and *Legislative Regulation* (Commonwealth Fund, New York,
1936). Three works by a pioneer student in the field of administrative law.

horn, Walter, *Administrative Law: Cases and Comments*, Second Edition (Founda-

n this general subject, see Fuller, Ambrose, "Limits on Administrative Discretion,"
ic Management, August, 1939, pp. 230–235; Leys, Wayne A. R., "Administrative
retion," *Public Administration Review*, Winter, 1943, pp. 10–23; Marx, Fritz M.,
nparative Administrative Law: A Note on Review of Discretion," *University of
sylvania Law Review*, June, 1939, pp. 954–978, Pinney, Harvey, "Administrative
retion and the National Labor Relations Board," *Social Forces*, December, 1939,
75–280.

tion Press, Brooklyn, 1947) and *Federal Administrative Proceedings* (Johns Hopkins Press, 1941). Two very useful works by the staff director of the Attorney General's Committee; the first of these and Katz, Milton, *Cases and Materials on Administrative Law* (West Publishing Company, St. Paul, 1948) are the most recent casebooks in this field.

Harris, Arthur, and Ward, Robert, *Administrative Decision and Judicial Review* (Bureau of Public Administration, University of California, 1941). A useful study of two important aspects of the problem at the state level.

Landis, James M., *The Administrative Process* (Yale University Press, 1938). A brief but valuable treatise on the administrative process. Pound, Roscoe, *Administrative Law, Its Growth, Procedure, and Significance* (University of Pittsburgh Press, 1942) is a similarly useful title.

United States Department of Justice, *Attorney General's Manual on the Administrative Procedure Act* (Washington, 1947). A recent manual prepared by the staff of the Attorney General.

Warren, George, Ed., *Federal Administrative Procedure Act and the Administrative Agencies* (New York University School of Law, 1947). A symposium discussing various aspects of the operation of the Federal act.

30

ADMINISTRATIVE LEGISLATION

Nature and Development of Administrative Rule-Making

THE rule-making power has been defined as the legal authority of administrative officers or agencies of government to prescribe discretionary ·or interpretative rules and regulations of general application and legal effect or to determine the existence of the conditions under which contingent statutes are to become operative.[1] The product of this rule-making power is variously designated as "rules and regulations," "administrative legislation," and "sublegislation." The words "rules" and "regulations" are commonly used interchangeably or in combination, with no differentiation in meaning.

Some distinctions between rules and regulations and such other terms as "legislation," "adjudication," and "administrative orders" must, however, be noted. Legislation is the statutory product of the duly elected representatives of the people in Congress or in the state legislatures. It is not, therefore, to be confused with the supplementary and interpretative pronouncements of the executive branch of the government, which are based on legislative delegation and are often referred to as administrative legislation — the title of this chapter. Adjudication is the process of determining issues raised by individuals or groups affected by either legislation or supplementary rules and regulations. This is to be distinguished from the formulation of policy, within the limits prescribed by the controlling statutes, exercised in connection with the process of rule-making. Administrative orders apply to particular individuals, companies, or groups, whereas rules and regulations are of general application. Thus a regulatory commission may issue the latter to inform all concerned of its policies and procedures, but it will issue orders — such as cease and desist orders — only to individuals who have failed to comply with the regulations or who have been guilty of objectionable practices.

Historically the use of the rule-making power is not new. It is reported that [2]

Hart, in President's Committee on Administrative Management, *Report with Special Studies*, p. 310; see also Comer, Chapters 1 and 2.

Hart, *op. cit.*, p. 322; this same point is emphasized by John F. Dulles in his address, *Administrative Law* (Privately printed, New York, 1939).

As early as 1794, Congress authorized President Washington, during its recess, to lay an embargo "whenever, in his opinion, the public safety shall so require." The act continued: "And the President is hereby fully authorized to give all such orders to the officers of the United States, as may be necessary to carry the same into full effect." This was the broadest of the early delegations; but the fact remains that delegations of one sort or another have been scattered through subsequent history. They are no recent novelty in the Federal government.

Delegations of rule-making powers reached maximums in four periods of emergency. The first was 1789–1815, the period when the United States was trying to defend its neutral trade against British orders in council and Napoleonic decrees. The second was 1861–1875, the period of the Civil War and Reconstruction. The third was 1917–1918, the period of participation in World War I. The fourth period was 1933–1935, the period of the New Deal attack upon the depression.

To this enumeration should, of course, be added the period of World War II, during which under the first and second War Powers Acts and other pieces of war legislation the rule-making powers of the President were suddenly and enormously increased.

Although the use of proclamations and Executive Orders had long been an established practice in the Federal government, the volume of such legislation has shown a steady and consistent increase, particularly since the administration of Theodore Roosevelt — as is shown in the two tables on page 601. Lincoln used it to order the return of deserters to the armed forces; Theodore Roosevelt, to carry out his land program; Wilson, to delegate war powers; Harding, to transfer certain Naval Oil Reserves to his Secretary of the Interior; and Franklin D. Roosevelt used it many times in the emergencies of depression and war.

Hart reports that while proclamations have been numbered from the days of the founding (although Washington issued only six), old-time employees of the State Department claim that the numbering of Executive Orders began in 1862 and so No. 1 in the series is an Executive Order of President Lincoln. In 1905 the State Department made the first effort to centralize their custody, and in 1906 President Theodore Roosevelt wrote to Secretary of State Root specifying that thereafter the originals of Executive Orders should be sent to the Department of State, which should furnish copies to the departments concerned.[3]

Two significant developments occurred during the long tenure of President Franklin D. Roosevelt. The Economy Act of 1933 gave him sweeping powers within designated limits to reduce the salary scale of Federal administrative employees. The far-reaching National In

[3] See *List and Index of the Presidential Executive Orders* (Archives Publishing Company, New York, 1943).

President of the United States
Number of Proclamations for Each Administration, 1861–1949 *

PRESIDENT	PROCLAMATIONS	TOTAL NUMBER	AVERAGE NUMBER PER MONTH
Lincoln	80 to 128	49	1.00
Johnson	129 to 179	51	1.08
Grant	180 to 234	55	.57
Hayes	235 to 249	15	.31
Garfield		0	.00
Arthur	250, 250½ to 265	17	.40
Cleveland	266 to 286	22	.46
Harrison	287 to 354	66	1.38
Cleveland	355 to 405	53	1.10
McKinley	406 to 464	60	1.11
T. Roosevelt	465 to 871	407	4.52
Taft	872 to 1,236	365	7.60
Wilson	1,237 to 1,588	361	3.76
Harding	1,589 to 1,668	80	2.75
Coolidge	1,669 to 1,869	201	3.00
Hoover	1,870 to 2,037	168	3.50
F. D. Roosevelt	2,038 to 2,647	609	4.18
Truman	2,648 to 2,847**		

Number of Executive Orders for Each Administration
Since the Numbering Began in 1862

PRESIDENT	EXECUTIVE ORDERS	TOTAL NUMBER	AVERAGE NUMBER PER MONTH
Lincoln	1 to 2	2	.04
Johnson	3 to 7	5	.10
Grant	8 to 20	13	.13
Hayes		0	.00
Garfield		0	.00
Arthur	21 to 23	3	.07
Cleveland	23A to 27	5	.10
Harrison	27A to 29	3	.06
Cleveland	30 to 96	68	1.41
McKinley	97 to 137	50	.93
Roosevelt	141 to 1,050	1,011	11.23
Taft	1,051 to 1,743	599	14.56
Wilson	1,744 to 3,416	1,770	18.43
Harding	3,417 to 3,885	484	16.68
Coolidge	3,885A to 5,074	1,248	18.63
Hoover	5,075 to 6,070	1,004	20.91
D. Roosevelt	6,071 to 9,537	3,466	23.75
Truman	9,538 to 10,072**		

From Hart, in *Report* of the President's Committee, p. 44.
Up to and including July 29, 1949.

...strial Recovery Act, passed approximately three months later, pro-
...ded that "to effectuate the policy of this title, the President is hereby
...thorized to establish such agencies, to accept and utilize such volun-
...'y and uncompensated services, . . . to appoint such officers and

employees" as should be necessary.[4] He was also authorized "to prescribe such rules and regulations as may be necessary to carry out the purposes" of the act. The codes regulating business, industry, and commerce were given final approval by him, were issued in his name, and had the force of law. As Professor Shoup has observed, "These and many other acts loaded the President with ordinance powers which were thinly disguised legislative powers." The second development of his regime was the issuance of Executive Order No. 7298, setting forth regulations governing the preparation, presentation, filing, and distribution of Executive Orders and proclamations — the provisions of which will be considered later in this chapter. Responsibility for custody of these documents was transferred to the Division of the Federal Register, under the Archivist of the United States.

The grants of rule-making power are usually made in such general terms as the following: *necessary to carry out the purpose of this act; necessary for the administration of this act; for the purpose of carrying out the provisions of this act; necessary or expedient for the carrying out of this chapter; necessary to carry into effect the provisions of this act; for the administration and enforcement of the provisions hereof.* The number of instances in which such phraseology is found in the laws of any given jurisdiction is so great that it becomes difficult to list them all. In the California laws, for instance, they are found in the following codes: Agriculture, Business and Professions, Health and Safety, Military and Veterans, Vehicle, Water, Welfare and Institutions, Revenue and Taxation, as well as in the general administrative code.[5] They relate to some portion of the operation of no less than thirty-seven different administrative departments and agencies. The list for the Department of Agriculture alone includes well over a dozen items.

In individual cases, the authorization takes such forms as the following:

The Director of Agriculture "shall establish regulations and standards as the basis for the certification of pure cottonseed in the State and fix and collect reasonable fees for the certification of pure cottonseed" (Ag. Code, Sec. 931) an "shall make rules and regulations to carry out the provisions of this article, an to make possible careful checking of previous crops, foundation seed, and ne essary field inspections" (Ag. Code, Sec. 933). In enforcing the law in respee to agricultural warehouses, the Director of Agriculture from time to time "m: establish and promulgate standards for products by which their quality or val may be judged or determined" (Ag. Code, Sec. 1248).

---

[4] These illustrations, 48 Stat. 8 (March 20, 1933) and 48 Stat. 195 (June 16, 1933) a cited from Shoup, Earl L., *The Government of the American People*, p. 578 (Gi Boston, 1946).
[5] These data are taken from Assembly Interim Committee on Administrative Regu tion, *Supplement to the Report* (Sacramento, 1947); see also this Committee's *Summc of California Statutory Provisions Conferring Quasi-Legislative Functions upon ministrative Agencies* (Sacramento, 1946).

California Agricultural Code

In some instances the authorizations specify in considerable detail the nature of the grants as, for instance, in the following provisions relating also to the Department of Agriculture:

The Director, by rules and regulations promulgated as provided in Section 917.5, shall:

(a) Adopt germination standards for vegetable seeds

(b) Adopt tolerances to be applied to all enforcement procedures required by this article

(c) Prescribe methods of procedure in the examination of lots of agricultural and vegetable seeds, and in securing samples thereof

(d) Fix the maximum number of samples that may be tested free of charge for any one person in any period of time

(e) Fix a schedule of charges for tests or samples in excess of those tested free of charge

(f) Adopt a procedure for hearings to show cause why complaint should not be filed for alleged violation of any provision of this article

(g) Issue such other orders, schedules, and announcements as will assist in carrying out the purposes of this article (Ag. Code, Sec. 917.3)

In the same state parallel authorizations are found in numerous other codes. The Education Code imposes upon the State Board of Education the duty of adopting "uniform regulations governing the keeping of attendance in all secondary schools" and fixing minimum standards entitling high school or junior college "districts to receive state aid for the support of junior colleges." The Department of Welfare, the Youth Authority, and the various professional examining boards, among others, are invested with rule-making authority appropriate to their major functions.

While in the early years of the nation's history the rule-making

power was known, it was for more or less obvious reasons used ratl
infrequently. In those days, when government was small, when it (
few things and did not do them very well, there was seldom need f
rule-making — certainly not in the normal course of events. The st
utes could and did deal with various problems comprehensively and
some detail. As life — and government — grew more complex in t
process of transition from an agricultural to an industrial society, t
type of legislation became less and less suitable. Many contingenc
arose which were not foreseen by the legislators and were not, thei
fore, covered by the statutes; and obtaining legislative amendmei
took time. Many provisions included in the laws proved useless a
unworkable, and again obtaining legislative modification took tin
Clearly some speedier and more elastic procedure had to be four
Thus it was that the present-day procedures of rule-making develope

General Rule-Making Authority

The use of the rule-making authority may be authorized, unauthorize
or extraordinary or emergency. It may be authorized by the consti(
tion or, more frequently, by statute. Where not authorized, it is n
forbidden; consequently interpretative rules may be and frequently a
issued by agencies not specifically authorized by constitution or `
statute to issue rules. The extraordinary or emergency rule-maki
power attaches chiefly to the office of the chief executive, its use resu
ing in the issuance of Executive Orders and proclamations.

Authorized Rule-Making Authority. The rule-making power exercis
under statutory delegation has been classified by Professor Hart in ;
cordance with the process involved in its exercise, into three class
where the process consists of: (1) discretionary elaboration of ru
and regulations; (2) interpretation of statutory provisions; (3) findi
of the existence of conditions under which a contingent statute p!
vides that its clauses shall become operative.[6] The third of these ite!

---

[6] Hart, *An Introduction to Administrative Law,* pp. 153–154. Olverson, John B.,
"Legislation by Administrative Agencies," *Georgetown Law Journal,* February, 19
pp. 637–645, has a similar classification, the first two items of which are the same,
third being execution of the statute, the fourth, rules governing internal organizat
of administrative departments. At the state level, Stene, Edwin O., *Filing and Publ*
tion of Administrative Regulations, p. ix (Kansas Legislative Council, Topeka, 194
presents the results of a survey of all the rules and regulations existing in Kansas,
the basis of which he concluded that there were ten different groups:

1. Rules filling in details of legislative acts
2. Rules interpreting legislative acts
3. Rules prescribing procedures for public contracts
4. Rules regarding forms and methods of keeping records
5. Rules for the care and management of public property
6. Regulations for management of state institutions

requires some comment. The term "contingent statute," first used by Professor Comer, is applied to those acts which provide that their provisions shall become operative when and if certain conditions shall exist. This means that some administrative department or agency whose responsibility it is to control the subject in question, shall upon inquiry and investigation find that the conditions specified do in fact exist. The agency then issues a "finding," which invokes the provisions of the law as of a specified time. Such provisions, in other words, are not self-executing.

When rules in any of these three classes are issued, a considerable time may elapse before there is any final decision with regard to the legality or even the constitutionality of the regulations. Means for the early determination of such questions are urgently needed. It should not be necessary to wait until someone claims that his rights have been impaired before one can ascertain whether a rule is legal or what the rule means. As Professor Field has said, "It is the sheerest of nonsense that a regulation cannot be read or a statute understood without an official act of injury predicated upon them. The question whether a regulation is within the scope of statutory authority is to be solved by focusing both eyes upon the statute and both eyes upon the regulation." [7]

Extraordinary and Emergency Authority. There are three sources of the President's authority to issue Executive Orders and proclamations: (1) his constitutional powers such as his power as commander in chief; (2) powers delegated to him by the Congress, as by the Flexible Tariff Act, the Economy Act of the depression period, or the War Powers Acts of World War II; (3) the general power of direction which he derives from his position as administrative superior to heads of departments, a relation which is logically implied in his power to remove them at pleasure.[8]

This power has been exercised with increasing frequency over the years. Studies made for the President's Committee on Administrative Management showed that only two Presidents — William Henry Harrison and James A. Garfield — failed to use the power to issue proclamations at all. Rutherford B. Hayes and James A. Garfield issued no Exec-

7. Office regulations affecting only the internal operations of a department or agency
8. Regulations for general administrative management
9. Regulations applicable to particular times or places
10. Miscellaneous resolutions, instructions, and codes
See Field, Oliver P., "Confining Administrative Regulations Within the Law," *An-*, May, 1942, pp. 108–114.
Hart, *op. cit.,* p. 331.

utive Orders. The enormous increase in the use of these procedu
in the last two decades has already been noted. In 1933 President Roo
velt issued an Executive Order which included regulations governi
the preparation, presentation, filing, and distribution of Executi
Orders and proclamations. This was superseded in 1936 by Executi
Order No. 7298, which makes the following provisions with regard
procedure:

> The proposed executive order or proclamation shall first be submitted to
> Director of the Bureau of the Budget. If the Director of the Bureau of
> Budget approves it, he shall submit it to the Attorney General for his conside
> tion as to both form and legality. If the Attorney General approves it, he sl
> transmit it to the Director of the Division of the Federal Register, the Natio
> Archives. If it conforms to the requirements of paragraph one hereof (in fo
> and style), the Director of the Division of the Federal Register shall transmi
> and three copies thereof to the President. If it is disapproved by the Director
> the Budget or the Attorney General, it shall not thereafter be presented to
> President unless it is accompanied by the statement of the reasons for such
> approval.

One may well observe, as President Stoke of Louisiana State U
versity has done, that this description of procedure does not fully rev
the process: [9]

> The term "Bureau of the Budget" is a legal designation of the assistant in
> Bureau who reviews the estimates of the originating agency. The "Attorney G
> eral" really means an Assistant Solicitor or any one of six lawyers working un
> his direction. The Director of the Division of the Federal Register is merely
> officer who approves the work of clerks, experts in style and form, who prep
> the order for the Presidential signature. Thus, the issuance of an Executive Or
> by the President cannot, except in rare cases, be an independent act of judgm
> and direction, but rather a final coordination of the work of many officers a
> agencies.

Preparation of Rules. The provisions with regard to preparation requ
the inclusion of a title, citation of authority, and observance of p
scribed standards of punctuation, spelling, format, etc. The follow
specifications relating to Executive Orders and proclamations of
President, set forth in Executive Order No. 7298, may be taken
illustrative:

1. Proposed Executive Orders and proclamations shall be prepared in accorda
   with the following requirements:
   (a) A suitable title for the order or proclamation shall be provided
   (b) The authority under which the order or proclamation is promulga
       shall be cited in the body thereof
   (c) Punctuation, capitalization, orthography, and other matters of s

[9] See Stoke, Harold W., "Presidential Coordination of Policy," *Annals*, May, 1
pp. 101-107, and Hart, *op. cit.*, pp. 347-352.

shall conform to the most recent edition of the *Style Manual* of the United States Government Printing Office

(d) The spelling of geographic names shall conform to the most recent official decisions made pursuant to Executive Orders No. 27-A, of September 4, 1890, No. 399, of January 23, 1906, and No. 6680, of April 17, 1934

(e) Descriptions of tracts of land shall conform, so far as practicable, with the most recent edition of the *Specifications for Descriptions of Tracts of Land for Use in Executive Orders and Proclamations*, published by the Federal Board of Surveys and Maps

(f) Proposed Executive Orders and proclamations shall be typewritten on paper approximately 8 x 12½ inches, shall have a left-hand margin of approximately 2 inches, and a right-hand margin of approximately 1 inch, and shall be double-spaced, except that quotations, tabulations, or descriptions of land may be single-spaced

Provision is also made for distribution, including publication in the *Federal Register*. This procedure, which will be considered later, represents a distinct advance as compared with previous arrangements.

Form, Content, and Types of Rules. Many bodies of administrative rules have grown gradually over a period of years from small sets into compilations of formidable size. Largely because of this fact, these rules have frequently developed in a somewhat haphazard manner, little effort being made to classify them according to type. In an orderly classification, rules would be sorted into such categories as the following: (1) statements of agency organization; (2) substantive rules including (a) statements of general policy, (b) agency interpretations, and (c) substantive regulations; (3) rules of practice and procedure; (4) forms; and (5) instructions.[10] This process of classification resembles somewhat the procedure followed in the codification of statutes.

Requisites of Valid Delegation. If the rules and regulations issued by an agency are to be valid, obviously the delegation under which they are issued must be valid. What, then, are the requisites of a valid delegation? Professor Hart, on the basis of a careful analysis of such decisions those in the Hot Oil and Schechter cases,[11] among others, suggests the following. Congress, he says, must: [12]

Itself have power in the premises to regulate. This is more or less obvious. If the legislature is without power to act, the legislation making the delegation is unconstitutional. "The legislation making it is *ultra vires*, and the regulations issued in pursuance thereof are void."

Commerce Clearing House, *Administrative Procedure*, p. 46 (Chicago, 1944).

Panama Refining Company v. Ryan, 293 U.S. 388, 1935, and Schechter v. United ites, 295 U.S. 495, 1935.

Hart, *An Introduction to Administrative Law*, pp. 165, 170; also found in his "Some pects of Delegated Rule-Making."

2. Definitely limit the delegation by (a) defining the subject of the delegation and (b) providing a policy in the form of a primary standard or criterion to guide the rule-making authority. "In the Hot Oil case, Congress was found to have defined the subject, but to have provided no standard. In the Schechter case, it was found not even to have defined the subject."

3. Require, in the cast of contingent legislation, a finding.[13]

4. Delegate the power to public officers or authorities, not to private persons or groups.

5. Itself provide — not leave to the enforcing agency to provide — any penal sanction for violation of resulting rules.[14]

Rule-Making Procedures

Attention has been given to the nature and development of administrative rule-making and to various aspects of the general rule-making power. The next major consideration involves the actual formulation of the rules in a typical department or agency, including the initiation of the process; preliminary investigations; public notice of intention to make rules; public participation in the process through conferences, consultations, and hearings; and, after the agency decision with regard to the adoption of the new rules, the final step of putting them into effect. The discussion of these several steps will be followed by the text of the pertinent provisions of the Administrative Procedure Act of 1946.

Preliminary Stages of Rule-Making. Rule-making procedures may be initiated either through action by the agency itself or as a result of out-

---

[13] See *supra*, pp. 604–605, and Hart, *Introduction to Administrative Law.*

[14] Authorities seem to differ on the right of an enforcing agency to create and prescribe punishment for administrative crimes. State of Louisiana v. Maitrejean, 193 La 824 (1939) supports the Hart view. The Louisiana Milk Commission had been established by law, with broad rule-making powers, and supported by the declaration tha "any violation of such regulations shall be a misdemeanor and shall be punishable b fine or imprisonment or both." The Commission by regulation provided that any mil distributor or processor should first post "bond with the Commission in sufficier amount to cover at least fifteen days shipments of milk, to be computed by the Con mission." The defendants were indicted for violating this rule. The court held both th statute and the rule unconstitutional and therefor void, on the ground that all crim in Louisiana are statutory and that there can be no crime which is not so defined. C the contrary view, see Schwenk, Edmund H., "The Administrative Crime, Its Creati and Punishment by Administrative Agencies," *Michigan Law Review*, August, 19 pp. 51–86, and the following quotation from a note in the *Columbia Law Revie* March, 1943, pp. 213–218: "There are two possible methods of establishing penalties f violations of administrative regulations. In one, the legislature fixes, in the statute, t penalty for violating any of the regulations issued pursuant to statutory declaration; the other, along with rule-making power, there is a delegation to the agency to provi by regulation that violations of its rules shall be punished by some statute-designa penalty or by a penalty within the limits fixed by statute or within the discretion of agency."

side pressures. The enactment of a new statute may obviously require the enforcing agency to formulate appropriate rules and regulations. Existing rules may, because of changed conditions, require revision. Private parties may through informal methods request the modification of rules. Individuals or organizations in the exercise of the right of petition may request that consideration be given to the formulation of new rules or the revision of existing ones. Critics of executive rule-making have made much of this right of petition, long recognized in Anglo-Saxon law in connection with the legislature, contending that it should likewise be formally recognized in connection with administrative legislation.

The decision having been made to formulate rules, members of the agency staff may be assigned to assemble data from existing reports and to make special studies in order to secure essential basic facts. Private parties may or may not be asked to assist in the preparation of this material. Where agencies invite or are required to permit public participation in administrative rule-making, some form of public notice must be given. Such notice ordinarily consists of two elements: [15]

. Notice that hearings or other forms of public participation will be permitted, with a specification of the times and places, and

. Notice of the nature of the rule-making to be considered, with as great detail as practicable as to the precise nature of the problems to be considered.

The nature of rule-making is such, however, that sufficiently detailed notice preliminary to public procedures must often be supplemented by further procedures as the proposed rules take on more definite form and the affected public is enabled to study and comment.

Public Participation in Rule-Making. Public participation in rule-making becomes more and more important as the quantity of administrative legislation increases and as the effort is made to realize democratic ideals administrative procedures. Such participation may take any one of number of different forms or combination of forms — conferences, consultations, advisory committees of groups affected, invitations for written views or statements, and hearings, formal and informal, voluntary and mandatory. The Federal Milk Marketing Administration has made extensive use of the referendum in making and amending milk-marketing orders. In all these procedures, of course, public participa-

---

Commerce Clearing House, *op. cit.*, p. 47, and Attorney General's Committee, *Final ort*, p. 108 (Washington, 1942); for procedure in WPB, O'Brien, John L., and schmann, Manley, "The War Production Board: Administrative Policies and Pro- res," *George Washington Law Review*, December, 1944, pp. 1–60, at 37–40.

tion means participation by those individuals or groups interested and affected, not participation by the public as a whole.[16]

Members of the agency staff may consult with members of the public either as individuals or as representatives of groups, for the purpose of obtaining information or their views on questions at issue. In some cases the process of consultation is facilitated by the establishment of advisory committees representing organized groups. While such committees are often voluntary, their use may be required by law, as in the case of the advisory committees serving in the Office of Price Administration during World War II, under the Price Control Administrator. Consultation may take the form of an invitation to receive and a promise to give consideration to written statements, either formal or informal, presenting the views of their authors or of the organizations which they represent. The trade practice submittal conferences, long used by the Federal Trade Commission and the Department of Commerce, represent another form of public participation.

Public hearings, which Professor Hart lists among the "prenatal safeguards, differ from other forms of public participation in that the are normally scheduled well in advance. The following is a typical notice of such a hearing: [17]

The California State Board of Public Health will hold public hearings c Thursday, September 2, 1948, at 10 A.M., in Room 668, Phelan Building, Sa Francisco, on the recision of the regulations governing establishments for hanc capped persons (Sections 860–896, inclusive, Group 10, Subchapter 3, Title 1 Administrative Code) and the adoption of a proposed set of new requiremer for establishments for handicapped persons. Said proposed regulations are to issued pursuant to Sections 1500 to 1517, Chapter 3, Division 2 of the Heal and Safety Code.

Oral presentations are heard, but they may usually be supplement by written submissions. Hearings conducted on an informal basis a not common, conferences and consultations normally being preferre Formal or "adversary" hearing, conducted under the same rules as a used in administrative adjudications, are ordinarily used only when quired by statute. Prior to the adoption of the administrative procedu acts, it may be said that the hearing was not a widely used device rule-making procedures, although it was often urged that hearings some form should be made mandatory.[18]

---

[16] This involves an elementary concept in the field of public opinion. What actu exists is not a single public, but a series of publics — business, professional, frater religious, etc. — in a varying number of which each citizen participates, accordin his background, training, interests, and personal preferences.

[17] From *California's Health*, July 31, 1948, p. 11.

[18] For such an argument by an attorney with a wide experience in practice be administrative boards and commissions, see Duane, Morris, "Mandatory Hearing the Rule Making Process," *Annals*, May, 1943, pp. 115–122, and the provisions of Federal Administrative Procedure Act, presented below.

Procedures following rule-making hearings but preceding agency decision as to the rules differ greatly. The Commerce Clearing House study of Federal administrative procedure thus summarizes the existing situation: [19]

There may be a complete absence of post-hearing procedure, or such procedure may be governed by the type of hearing held or type of rules proposed. Generally speaking, such procedure may or may not involve (1) the submission of briefs or comments; (2) the holding of oral arguments; (3) the submission of tentative report or tentative rules for written or oral comment by the parties, or both, or (4) opportunity for the submission of further evidence or views in written form.

Agency Decision Upon Rules. Eventually, when all the pertinent data have been assembled, all the arguments heard, all the written submissions studied and analyzed, and earlier drafts revised and reworked, a final draft of the rules is considered and adopted by top management of the agency. The procedures involved show the same diversity that characterizes other steps in rule-making. They may include intra-agency discussions, consultation, staff conferences, etc., with an ultimate adoption and promulgation. Once the rules are adopted, parties at interest may still have recourse to further procedures, and the agency itself may make provision for amendment.

Provisions of the Administrative Procedure Act. In November, 1945, the Senate Committee on the Judiciary issued its report on the Administrative Procedure Act, a bill to improve the administration of justice by prescribing fair administrative procedure. This report was the culmination of many years of study in Congress, carried on in cooperation with the American Bar Association and other interested groups. It is, therefore, highly appropriate to consider here the recommendations of this Committee with regard to rule-making, as set forth in Section 4 of the bill and as finally approved by the Congress in the Administrative Procedure Act.[20]

Section 4. RULE–MAKING. The introductory clause exempts from all of the requirements of Section 4 any rule-making so far as there are involved (1) military, naval, or foreign affairs functions or (2) matters relating to agency management or personnel or to public property, loans, grants, benefits, or contracts.

(a) *Notice.* General notice of proposed rule-making must be published in the *Federal Register* and must include (1) time, place, and nature of proceedings, (2) reference to authority under which made, and (3) terms, substance, or rules involved. However, except where notice and hearing are required by some

Commerce Clearing House, *op. cit.*, p. 49.
Senate Committee on the Judiciary, *Report on S.* 7 (79th Cong., 1st Sess., Report 752), and Public Law No. 404, 79th Congress.

other statute, the subsection does not apply to rules other than those of substance or where the agency for good cause finds (and incorporates the finding and reasons therefor in the published rule) that notice and public procedure are impracticable, unnecessary, or contrary to the public interest.

(b) *Procedures*. After such notice, the agency must afford interested person an opportunity to participate in the rule-making at least to the extent of submitting written data, views, or argument; and, after consideration of such presentations, the agency must incorporate in any views adopted a concise general statement of their basis and purpose. However, where other statutes require rules to be made after hearing, the requirements of Sections 7 and 8 (relating to public hearings and decisions thereon) apply in place of the provisions of this subsection.

(c) *Effective Dates*. The required publication or service of any substantive rule must be made not less than thirty days prior to its effective date except (1) as otherwise provided by the agency for good cause found and published or (2) in the case of rules recognizing exemption, or relieving restriction, interpretative rules, and statements of policy.

(d) *Petitions*. Every agency is required to accord any interested person the right to petition for the issuance, amendment, or repeal of a rule.

Putting Rules Into Effect

Numerous problems arise in connection with the initial enforcement of new rules. How and when should they be made effective? Should they be submitted to the legislature for approval before becoming effective? How shall they be published and publicized so that persons affected will have an opportunity to know about them? What provisions shall be made with regard to amendment and revision? These and many similar questions arise, the answers to which may be determined either of two ways — by provisions in the statutes creating the agency and setting forth its powers, or by the legislative enactment of uniform standards applicable to all agencies. The widespread failure to provide for these essential matters under the first procedure has given impetus to the movement for the adoption of the second. To take Alabama as an illustration: the Legislative Reference Service in that state tabulated the requirements of the rule-enacting procedures of twenty laws in 1946. Of this number, only six or seven required notice, hearing, or approval. Nine provided for publication, three others for filing, and only one for both.[21]

Effective Date. It is customary in jurisdictions which prescribe central filing of administrative rules and regulations to provide by law that none of them shall be effective until filed with the designated office. Where systems of publication are established and where provisions

---

[21] *Quasi-Legislative and Quasi-Judicial Functions of Alabama State Administrative Agencies*, p. 16 (Montgomery, 1946).

made for filing with local officers, the legislature often specifies a period which must elapse between filing and the effective date of a new regulation. This additional prenatal safeguard allows time for adequate publicity, gives affected persons time to adjust their affairs, and at the same time recognizes the limitations and insufficiencies of the public rule-making procedures and the difficulties of drafting and application even where such procedures are reasonably satisfactory. In some states, as in Michigan and South Dakota, provision is made for the exercise of emergency powers. Thus the Michigan act of 1943 provides that all regulations must be published before they become effective, unless the governor "shall certify that because of an emergency or other compelling extraordinary circumstances the public interest requires that the rule become effective without the delay required for the prior publication of the rule."

Approval. It is now generally agreed that some form of independent approval or review of proposed rules and regulations should be provided before they become effective. Those who propose approval by the legislature would model American procedure upon that long followed by Great Britain in the system of provisional orders utilized in that country. Orders are drawn up and put in effect by the Government, subject to approval by the Parliament. They are commonly transmitted to the Parliament in large batches and approved in a routine manner without any careful scrutiny.[22] There seems to be some tendency in the states toward legislative review; in 1945 and 1947, such measures were considered in a number of states and adopted in three: Connecticut, Michigan, and Nebraska. These acts not only provide for legislative review of future rules and regulations but reserve the right to disapprove or modify any that have been issued.

For this procedure it may be said that it gives the elected representatives of the people a specific opportunity to disapprove or modify any order which they deem contrary to the public interest. The principal objection would seem to lie in the fact that legislative bodies with limited session time are already overburdened and that the routine approval which might be expected would have very little significance and would provide little protection to the public.

A number of the filing and publication acts confer upon the attorney general considerable powers of review. The uniform-practice of North Dakota provides that "every rule or regulation proposed by any administrative agency, before being adopted shall be submitted

---

See Ogg, Frederic A., *European Governments and Politics*, Second Edition, pp. 112–(Macmillan, New York, 1939).

as to its legality, and the Attorney General shall promptly furnish his opinion as to the legality of any such proposed rule or regulation." The Michigan act grants even more extensive powers to the Attorney General: "No rule hereafter made by any state agency shall be filed with the Secretary of State until it has been approved by the Attorney General as to form and legality and has been subsequently confirmed and formally adopted by the promulgating state agency in accordance with law." There is a question as to how much authority the attorney general should have to pass upon the wisdom of the provisions which come before him. He is already the legal adviser to most if not all agencies of the government; the effect of these two laws is to require that he be consulted in every case and that there be a formal record of such consultation.

Publication. For years one of the principal criticisms of administrative legislation was that it was not properly published and publicized, that citizens were given no opportunity to know what the law was. Among the time-honored maxims of Anglo-Saxon law is the one that ignorance of the law is no excuse. If this be true, then surely the citizen should be told, or should be able to ascertain without difficulty, what the law is. This criticism of laxity in the publication of rules and regulations was entirely justified, but it no longer holds in most jurisdictions.

The Federal Register was established in 1936 under an Act of Congress; [23] it is published daily, Tuesday through Saturday of each week. No rules and regulations of general application may be adopted and enforced by any Federal department or agency without prior publication in this register. The act establishes a permanent administrative committee of three, composed of the Archivist of the United States, an officer of the Department of Justice designated by the Attorney General, and the Public Printer, who shall prescribe, with the approval of the President, regulations for carrying out the provisions of the act. Provision is made that the *Federal Register* shall be judicially noticed and may be cited by volume and page. Publication therein shall be deemed to have given notice to all persons residing within the continental United States (not including Alaska), except in cases where notice by publication is insufficient in law. Furthermore, *The Code of Federal Regulations*, published in 1938, with annual supplements since that date, now comprises more than forty volumes, making all such

---

[23] Public Act No. 220, 74th Congress; see note by Brown, Everett S., "Executive Procedures and Orders — Federal Register," *Michigan Law Review*, November, 1937, 91–93.

regulations in force available in convenient form to any interested person.

Meanwhile the states began to give serious consideration to this problem, and definite progress has been made in approximately half of them. The initial impetus to state action seems to have been stimulated (1) by an article by Edwin E. Witte, published under the challenging title, "A Break for the Citizen," in which he urged that the states should establish more orderly procedures in the making and publication of administrative orders, and (2) by the new Federal requirements, which did not pass unnoticed. The initial action was taken by South Carolina in 1937. In a survey made by the Maryland Legislative Council in 1942 only five states reported that they had a statutory requirement that administrative rules and regulations be published in a single volume. Seven states, however, required such papers to be filed with a designated state official — usually the secretary of state. By 1948, the situation had materially improved, as is shown by the table on page 616. Thirteen states provide for filing and publication, nine for publication only.

The official methods of publication have been classified as four in number: [24] (1) publication of administrative rules and regulations in the same way and under the same cover as the legislative acts; (2) periodic publication of all administrative rules and regulations in a separately bound volume such as the *Wisconsin Red Book;* (3) publication of a central administrative code, supplemented by the publication of new regulations in "administrative registers" issued at such intervals as may be deemed necessary or advisable; and (4) publication of separate bulletins or pamphlets by the different administrative agencies, either under separate requirements of law or on their own initiative. In addition to these systems, many administrative agencies in the states are required to publish new regulations in one or more newspapers. There are, furthermore, informal and largely unofficial methods of distribution through pamphlets and bulletins issued by trade associations for the information of their members, and publication in trade journals and through the use of mailing lists. Sometimes, if the rules and regulations relate to matters of sufficient general interest, a wide coverage may be achieved through the aid of the press and the radio. Determination of what shall be published raises the question of definition. There are, as Stene points out, three general methods of defining what shall be published or filed, namely: (1) general legislative definition, with responsibility placed on the departments to see all regulations falling within that definition are on file; (2) specific

Stene, *op. cit.,* p. ix.

**Filing and Publication of State Administrative
Rules and Regulations — 1948 ***

DATE	FILING AND PUBLICATION	FILING ONLY
1932		Massachusetts General Laws 1932, Ch. 30, Sec. Acts of 1939, Ch. 499, repealed Acts of 1945, Ch. 292
1937	South Carolina Acts of 1937, No. 132	
1939	Wisconsin Acts of 1939, Ch. 428	Kansas Acts of 1939, Ch. 308 Acts of 1947, Ch. 103 Oregon Acts of 1939, Ch. 474 Acts of 1941, Ch. 125 South Dakota Code of 1939, Ch. 65.0106
1941	California Stat. of 1941, Ch. 628, S.B. 742 Ohio Acts of 1941, H.B. 239 Acts of 1943, 120 v. S. 36	North Dakota Acts of 1941, Ch. 241 Tennessee Pub. Acts, 1941, Ch. 111, S.B. 4
1942	Kentucky Acts of 1942, Ch. 178, S.B. 110	
1943	Michigan Acts of 1943, No. 88 Acts of 1947, No. 35	Maryland Acts of 1943, Ch. 872 North Carolina Acts of 1943, Ch. 754
1944	New York Const., Art. IV, Sec. 8 (1938) Acts of 1944, Ch. 618 Virginia Acts of 1944, Ch. 217 & 218	
1945	Connecticut Acts of 1945, Ch. 67 & 307 Gen. Stat., 1945 Supp., Sec. 42h Indiana Acts of 1943, Ch. 213 Acts of 1945, Ch. 120 Nebraska Laws of 1945, Ch. 255 Minnesota Laws of 1945, Ch. 492 & 590 Pennsylvania Acts of 1945, P. L. 1392	
1946		Missouri Acts of 1946, S.B. 196

* Based on data in Mindel, and Moreland in *Book of the States, 1948-1949*, pp. 171-175.

definition in the statutes; and (3) general definition and a grant of
thority to the central agency with which regulations are filed to
termine what matters fall within the scope of the law. As has b
noted, various provisions are found with regard to independent rev
prior to publication.

Amendment and Revision. When new rules are put in effect, a pr
sion may be included permitting the submission of petitions or app

ions for amendment. The agency itself may regard the new rules as
more or less temporary in character. After a trial period during which
here has been an opportunity to study their effect in operation and
to collect data with regard thereto, they may be reissued in revised
form on the agency's own initiative. In the case of established agencies,
however, rule-making calls less for the formulation of new rules than
for the more or less constant revision of existing rules or additions made
necessary by new or supplemental legislation. In these situations, the
procedures are essentially the same as those followed in the initial formulation of the rules.

Interpretation and Effect. Rules are interpreted both by the issuing
agency and by the courts. With regard to such questions as repeal,
retroactive effect, and problems of construction, the principles drawn
from the general law of statutory interpretation apply. Since rules have
the effect of law, they establish the rights of parties under many circumstances, and such parties are entitled to immunity for action taken
in reliance upon them. Agencies, on the other hand, are under obligation that their rules be authorized and reasonable, but they have discretion to waive some types of rules — particularly procedural rules — in
certain cases.

There are two ways in which rules may be presented for official
interpretation. (1) The enforcing agency may conduct a hearing involving either a violation or the rights of an injured party; this involves
the quasi-judicial powers of the agency and is known as administrative
adjudication. (2) An injured party may take his case to the courts; this
involves the exercise of the function of the courts and is known as judicial review. Both of these types will be discussed in later chapters.

Advantages and Disadvantages of Rule-Making

Advantages. Under present-day conditions administrative rule-making
becomes not only desirable but necessary if efficient administration of
the law is to be achieved. The courts, as Mr. Landis has pointed out, are
"remote from the social scene to regulate the technical conduct of
business efficiently and with necessary dispatch. At the same time
regulatory agencies must not be too readily responsive to the influence of interest groups, and they should be to some extent especially
insulated from pleading by special interests; but they must be much
more quickly responsive than are the courts to the tides and movements
of popular sentiment and to changes in conditions. That is the very
reason for their existence." [25] With these proper safeguards delegated

Appleby, Paul H., in USDA's *Lectures on Administrative Regulation*, p. 66.

rule-making has a number of potential advantages over having th
legislature freeze regulatory details into the statutes as well as over per
mitting administrators excessive discretion in applying statutory gen
eralities in particular cases. These advantages are summarized by Profes
sor Hart in the following form: [26]

1. Freed from concern with details, the legislature can concentrate its attentic
   and that of the public upon the enactment of the fundamentals of policy, a
   is thus strengthened as the representative organ of government.
2. The legislature also has additional time in which it may investigate the ma
   ner in which administrative authorities have concretized and enforced
   policies.
3. Since rules are more easily amended than statutes, it becomes easier to c
   rect mistakes and to meet changing conditions, if the difficulty concerns c
   tails rather than basic policy.
4. The administrator is saved from a dilemma that he often faces when
   hands are tied by the red tape of legislative details; he does not have to cho
   between defeating the central purpose of the statute by trying to work
   unworkable, and evading the letter of the law.
5. The administrator is the one who, by constantly rubbing elbows with
   particular problems, can by trial and error work out the specific regulati
   best calculated to attain the statutory objective.
6. In working out the specifics of policy, a bureaucracy is, ideally, subject to
   litical responsibility with respect to discretionary matters, and to professic
   responsibility with respect to technical matters.
7. If discretion in particular cases is untrammeled, it is more liable to abuse t
   if statutory generalities are made more specific and concrete before they
   applied to individual situations.
8. Interpretative regulations are a means of increasing the certainty of the
   especially if the statute provides that no civil or criminal liability shall a
   to any act done or omitted in good faith in conformity with such interp
   tions, notwithstanding that, after such an act or omission, such interpretat
   are held invalid by the courts.
9. Contingent legislation furnishes a means by which a policy can be blocked
   by the legislature, and its coming into operation be made dependent
   unpredictable future contingencies, such as the action of a foreign governm

Long as this list is, it does not include all the advantages of ex
tive rule-making. The availability of expert knowledge in the prep
tion of rules and regulations is a very great advantage, as is the
that this procedure largely eliminates the possibility of party con
over details. The circumstances under which administrative re
tions are prepared are conducive to proper drafting — which ma
may not be true of legislative acts.

---

[26] Hart, *op. cit.*, pp. 154-155; see also his "Exercise of the Rule Making Power
Blachly and Oatman, *Administrative Legislation and Adjudication*, Chapter 3 (I
ings Institution, Washington, 1934).

Disadvantages. As to the disadvantages of administrative legislation, a great deal has been written, much of it by persons who have seemed to lack any clear understanding of the problems involved. Such persons, instead of recognizing the contribution which rules and regulations make to the clarification of the law by making it more precise and more definite, denounce administrative legislation as unnecessary and as excessive in amount; refer to it as an instrument of bureaucracy — which to them is a term of opprobrium — and responsible for endless red tape; and finally, to clinch the argument, call it a threat to "the American way of life." If there are valid objections to administrative legislation, properly formulated and reasonably enforced, these people seldom make use of them.

There are disadvantages relating to this procedure, as to most, which have appeared from time to time and may appear again. An objectionable degree of secrecy may occur in the making of rules. Pressure groups may exercise an undue influence as to their content, and the public good may receive little or no consideration. If some interest groups have a part in the process, the views of other groups may not be adequately considered. In the case of an agency headed by a dominating personality, the rules and regulations may register too strongly his viewpoint rather than the viewpoint of the general good. The legislature may shirk its responsibility, leaving to executive agencies, through delegation, greater powers of policy determination than they should have or should be called upon to exercise.

Most important of all, perhaps, is the possibility of a lack of coordination between departments and agencies dealing with the same subject — a weakness described by Blachly and Oatman in these words: [27]

There may be such a scattering of the sublegislative function that the rules and regulations made independently by various executive and high administrative authorities will not be consistent with one another; that there will be no unity of policy; that there will even be conflicts of policy. The probability that this will happen is particularly great when many independent agencies organized to carry on special functions are endowed with broad powers of sublegislation.

It should be noted that many of these objections to administrative legislation relate quite as much to defects in governmental action generally as to this particular device.

Summary. The arguments pro and con may be summarized in the very simple form in which they were presented in a report of the Kansas Legislative Council a number of years ago:

Blachly and Oatman, *op. cit.,* p. 46.

ADVANTAGES	DISADVANTAGES
Economy of legislative time	Possible inconsistencies in policy
Use of expert knowledge	Inadequate publicity
Absence of partisan conflicts	Surrender of power by the legislature
Elasticity in administration	Improper development of standards
Efficiency in drafting	
Filling in details	

"The most interesting thing about these advantages and disadvantages when thus set forth side by side," Blachly and Oatman comment, "i the fact that the advantages are general, permanent, and inherent in the function of administrative legislation in any government system organized with reasonable care; whereas the disadvantages are almos all dependent upon special conditions and lack of careful organiza tion. This means that due attention to the government structure wil eliminate, or at the least minimize, the disadvantages of administrativ legislation, while all of its advantages will remain."

An overemphasis on the disadvantages may lead one to the belie that a legislative body violates its trust unless it specifies everything i detail — all of which tends, to use again the words of Hart,[28] "to mal modern government unworkable by treating a written constitution as it were a code of civil procedure. The necessary conclusion is to dra a distinction between Congressional abdication or transference of i legislative power and Congressional delegation of rule-making discr tion for the implementation of its policies."

SELECTED REFERENCES

Andrews, John B., *Administrative Labor Legislation* (Harpers, New York, 1936). recognized authority on labor legislation devotes a volume to the discussion of administrative aspects.

Comer, John P., *Legislative Functions of National Administrative Authorities* (Colu bia University Press, 1927). An early study of problems that have since gro greatly in number and significance.

Federal Trade Commission, *Rules, Policy, Organization and Acts* (Washington, 194 A good example of what the rules and regulations of an independent regulat commission look like; for a study of state procedure, see Stene, Edwin O., *Fi and Publication of Administrative Regulations* (Kansas Legislative Council, Top 1943).

Hart, James, *An Introduction to Administrative Law, with Selected Cases* (Crofts, N York, 1940). The standard text on administrative law, covering its various asp including legislation.

Judicial Council of California, *Report on the Administrative Agencies Survey* (T Biennial Report, Sacramento, 1944); Kansas Legislative Council, *Legislative F tions of Administrative Agencies* (Topeka, 1938); and Mindel, Charles, *Filing Publication of Administrative Rules and Regulations* (Maryland Legislative C cil, Baltimore, 1942). Three useful studies of administrative procedure, inclu legislation, in particular states.

Pennock, J. Roland, *Administration and the Rule of Law* (Farrar & Rinehart, York, 1941). A brief but useful treatise, including discussion of administr legislation.

---

[28] "Limits of Legislative Delegation," *Annals*, May, 1942, pp. 87–100, at p. 91.

31

REGISTRATIONS, PERMITS,
AND LICENSES

ᴛʜᴇ administrative process is complicated. One part of it consists in ⌐termining rules of conduct, standards of size or quality, or other re-⌐irements that the public are going to be asked to observe. This ac-ity is primarily legislative in character and is supplemented by the ⌐es and regulations adopted by the administrative agency pursuant ⌐ the authority entrusted to it by statute. The second part of the ⌐ocess is to ascertain how many individuals or organizations are sub-⌐t to these regulations and to establish exactly the identity of those ⌐o are so affected. A third aspect of the process involves the sanctions ⌐ penalties invoked against violators, and the administrative actions ⌐ministrative hearings and later, if necessary, judicial review) which ⌐ose these penalties.

Regulations may be enforced by the use of licenses, registration, ⌐mits, or certificates. The term "license" has been defined as a formal ⌐nission to engage in a business or profession; it is generally granted ⌐ payment of a fee and is subject to annual renewal and other con-⌐ns as set forth by law or regulations.[1] One object of granting li-⌐es is to establish a basis for the enforcement of regulations — either ⌐tory or administrative — relating to a business activity. For instance, ⌐ous types of private health and welfare agencies, such as children's ⌐es, convalescent homes, and private hospitals, are required to pre-⌐ evidence of meeting minimum requirements as to facilities and ⌐pment before a license is granted them, and they must continue ⌐serve minimum standards in the care of patients in order to retain ⌐icense. For comparable reasons, operators of radio stations, sellers ⌐toxicating liquors, pawnbrokers, security salesmen, used-car deal-⌐nd many others are commonly required to obtain a license.[2]

Gill, Norman N., "Administration of Licenses and Permits," *Public Management*, ⌐rch, 1943; II, April, 1943.
⌐ should not overlook the historical and legal significance of the licensing system. ⌐ the breakdown of the gild system there developed under the common law a ⌐, long accepted here as well as in England, that every individual had a right to ⌐ his own calling, subject only to certain regulations for the protection of the pub-

Registration has proved to be both effective and inexpensive as control device. In practice it is a form of census taking in which th responsibility for listing is placed not on enumerators employed b the government but upon the individual, firm, or organization. O dinarily there are no qualifications or requirements which must be me by the registrant; the mere fact of his existence as a member of th group or category described is sufficient. Such forms of registration usually compulsory but sometimes voluntary, find a wide variety c uses. If any fee at all is prescribed, it is nominal. Thus all males specified age groups may be called upon to register under the draft la All births must be registered, all marriages and deaths reported. Phys cians are required to report all cases of various specified diseases. Ch dren of school age must be registered with the school authorities. A citizens eligible to vote are expected to register but are not requir to do so.

In other cases a permit may be used. A permit differs from a licer chiefly in its temporary character. It has been defined as a requireme for the privilege of performing a specific task or activity, generally short duration, the granting of which is usually subject to approval some official under conditions set forth by law or regulations.[3] Thu permit is issued to an applicant while learning to operate a mo vehicle, a license after he has demonstrated his ability to operate c in a safe and proper manner. A property owner or a utility compa or the two together may find it necessary to open a street to make installation or an improvement in service. A permit from the app priate municipal authority provides the city with information whic should have and gives it means of keeping the number of such op ings under control and of seeing that they are properly closed w the work is done. Permits may be required for building construc or repairs, for holding carnivals and fairs, for displays of fireworks, parades, and for many other purposes. At the issuing stage, permits licenses are similar in that the applicant must in either case satisfy sp fied requirements before authorization will be granted.

The value of these devices in affording protection to the publi many areas is very great and often little understood. A recent ar commenting on the aid which a well-administered licensing system provide in the regulation and supervision of business and industry no less than thirteen benefits: [4]

---

lic interest. The establishment and enforcement of standards through the use censing procedures tends to impose severe restrictions on this freedom of choic Beard, William, *Government and Technology*, pp. 492-496 (Macmillan, New 1934).

[3] Gill, *op. cit.*

[4] See Blank, Blanche D., "Licenses Can Be Policemen," *National Municipal R* February, 1948, pp. 45-47.

1. Insure adequate knowledge and skill in particular occupations
2. Raise the standard of services offered to the public
3. Fix moral responsibility on those engaged in occupations affecting the public health and welfare
4. Guarantee financial responsibility in occupations involving the handling of other people's money
5. Protect the public from fraud and dishonesty
6. Provide for the health and safety of workers in certain trades
7. Protect the consumer from goods or services that might prove to be dangerous
8. Eliminate graft and illegitimacy in certain business fields for the benefit of honest enterprisers
9. Encourage citizenship and residency in a particular area
10. Help prevent minor economic crises by precluding overcrowding in certain businesses and trades
11. Aid in general law enforcement and the reduction of criminality
12. Absorb part of the locale's handicapped population by restricting licenses in particular spheres to the blind, maimed, etc.
13. Provide the average citizen of limited time and money with a swift, simple, and inexpensive administrative avenue of redress against petty abuses

The author of this article contends that such a system provides, through complaint procedures and preliminary investigation, an ounce of prevention instead of the usual pound of cure; that its use of administrative adjudication procedures makes available to the citizen a "swift, sure, and simple justice"; and that it provides administrators, especially at the municipal level, with an instrument of unusual economy and efficiency.

Number and Scope of Licensing Laws

In the Federal Government. The application of licensing is by no means peculiar to any one of the three levels of government. Although this fact is not generally recognized, the Congress has been providing in law for the use of licenses and permits — in approximately equal numbers — for the past half century. A tabulation made in 1948 at the close of the 80th Congress showed a total of eighty-two such laws on the statute books;[5] the distribution of these by decades over the last fifty or sixty years is shown on the next page. The authorizations cover a wide range and one after another of the departments and agencies — the Departments of Agriculture, Interior, and Treasury, the Federal Power Commission, the Interstate Commerce Commission, being those occurring most frequently.

In the index files of the American Law Section, Legislative Reference Service, Library of Congress. On this general problem, see Warp, George A., "Licensing as a Device for Federal Regulation," *Tulane Law Review*, December, 1941, pp. 111-121.

Federal Laws Requiring Licenses and Permits

Prior to 1890	5 laws
1890–1899	0
1900–1909	2
1910–1919	6
1920–1929	6
1930–1939	34
1940–1948	29
Total	82

In the State Governments. No complete study of licensing activitie
in the states has ever been made; the need for such a study is great, bi
the size of the undertaking staggering. There is a thorough study c
the work in one state (West Virginia) and a scattering of informatio
about others. A few sampling studies have been conducted by Hug
Wall, by the Marketing Laws Survey, and by the National Educatic
Association. The Wall study, made many years ago, covered eightee
selected states and found some two hundred different professions, o
cupations, and callings licensed in one or more states. The Marketir
Laws Survey covered twenty-four groups for all forty-eight states, r
porting 831 licensing laws out of a possible total of 1152, or an avera
of 17.3 per state. The NEA study was confined to six leading profe
sions. Coverage is complete for numerous important groups, near
complete for others. Some groups, like logging operators, cotton g
operators, or threshermen, are peculiar to the industries of a particu
state or region and cannot be expected to appear elsewhere in suffici
numbers to justify licensing. A few laws are "sports" which are r
duplicated in other jurisdictions at all.

The three following tables will suggest the extent of licensing
tivities in the state governments. The first, on page 625, present
sample of more than one hundred common types of professional, b
ness, or occupational licenses found in varying patterns in the seve
states, usually on an average of two or more dozen per state.[6] The
in each case consists of the group of well-established professions p
a miscellaneous collection of additional occupations. In the sec
table New Jersey is used again to show what a typical state licens
program looks like; some of the data will be useful later in the cha
in another connection. The third table shows the volume of w
performed by the Wisconsin State Board of Health in certain type

---

[6] From the author's article on "Professional and Occupational Restrictions," *Te
University Law Quarterly*, April, 1939, pp. 334–363. North Carolina licenses more
fifty different groups; see Hanft, Frank, and Hamrick, J. Nathaniel, "Haphazard I
tration Under Licensing Statutes," *North Carolina Law Review*, December,
pp. 1–18.

Common Types of Professional, Business, and Occupational Licenses in the States

Accountants	Taxidermists
Apiaries	Teacher certification
Architects	Telegraph operators
Auctioneers and hawkers	Theater owners and ticket brokers
	Title insurance companies
Bakers	Tobacco curers and dealers
Bankers	Truckers
Barkers	
Beauticians and cosmeticians	Undertakers and embalmers
Beer distributors	
Bill collectors	Veterinarians
Bond brokers and salesmen	
Breweries	Waterworks operators
Building and loan association secretaries	Weighmasters
	Well drillers
Chain stores	Wine manufacturers *
Chauffeurs	
Chiropractors	

* A similar list of common types of business licenses and taxes employed in a representative city will be found in "License Fees Charged in 86 Illinois Municipalities," issued by the Illinois League of Municipalities.

State of New Jersey: Licensing Program Before and After Reorganization (1948)

DEPARTMENTAL CONTROL AFTER REORGANIZATION	PROFESSION OR OCCUPATION	LICENSING AGENCY
Banking and Insurance	Banking and Insurance	The Department
	Real Estate	State Real Estate Commission
Health	Barbers	State Board of Barber Examiners
	Beauty Culturists	State Board of Beauty Culture Control
	Embalmers and Funeral Directors	State Board of Embalmers and Funeral Directors
	Health work	The Department
Labor	Factories	The Department
	Mechanical Engineers	The Department
Law	Police work	New Jersey State Police
State	Accountants	State Board of Public Accountants
	Architects	State Board of Architects
	Dentists	State Board of Registration and Examination in Dentistry
	Engineers and Land Surveyors	State Board of Professional Engineers and Land Surveyors
	Nurses	State Board of Nursing
	Optometrists	State Board of Optometrists
	Pharmacists	State Board of Pharmacy
	Physicians	State Board of Medical Examiners
	Shorthand Reporters	State Board of Shorthand Reporting
	Registered Municipal Accountants	State Board of Public Accountants
	Veterinarians	State Board of Veterinary Medical Examiners
Treasury	Racing	State Racing Commission
Apparently Independent	Attorneys	State Board of Bar Examiners
	Pilots	State Board of Commissioners of Pilotage

Wisconsin State Board of Health: Activities in
the Licensing Divisions *

TOTALS OF PLACES LICENSED FOR THE YEARS 1946–1947

HOTELS AND RESTAURANTS

	1946	1947
Large hotels **	266	283
Small hotels	1,082	1,023
Restaurants	13,482	14,055
Tourist rooming houses and cabins	4,085	4,719

BARBERS

Master barbers	4,816	4,770
Shop managers	2,803	2,880
Deaths	76	87

COSMETOLOGY

Managers	3,396	3,479
Operators	4,184	4,494
Beauty parlors	1,872	1,891
Manicurists	58	76
Itinerants	29	24
Student permits	792	499
Apprentice permits	448	282
School certificates	10	10
Instructor certificates	2	10
Electrolysist certificates		3

FUNERAL DIRECTORS AND EMBALMERS

Funeral homes	703	687
Persons licensed	1,708	1,705
Funeral directors	1,538	1,543
Embalmers	1,472	1,471
Apprentices, registered	396	390
Apprentices, active	223	215

PLUMBERS

Master plumbers		
Licenses in force	1,363	1,303
Passed examinations	114	83
Failed examinations	47	74
Journeyman plumbers		
Licenses in force	1,712	1,514
Passed examinations	64	49
Failed examinations	25	55

WELL DRILLERS

Permits issued	371	372

---

* From *Wisconsin State Board of Health Bulletin*, April–June, 1948, p. 295.
** Large hotels are those which offer more than thirty sleeping rooms for transient guests.

licensing during the years 1946 and 1947; it represents, of course, o▪
a portion of the licensing activity carried on by the state.

In the Municipalities. Licensing in cities, like that in the states, ser▪
the twofold purpose of establishing a means of exerting regulat▪
powers and of raising revenue. The first of these is more importan▪

the state level; the second is more important at the municipal level. The scope of the program is quite as broad as in the states, but the powers relating to it are derived entirely from the statutes of the states;[7] while there is some overlapping of the two jurisdictions, the municipal program is for the most part applied to different items. As in the case of the states, the pattern varies from one jurisdiction to another. The urgent need for local revenues in the postwar era has tended greatly to increase both the number of such taxes and the rates applied.[8]

Reasons for Licensing Legislation

There are several reasons for the enormous number and scope of licensing laws at all three levels of government, some emanating from the public, some from those subject to license, and some from government sources. An understanding of this background is essential to any real understanding of the program itself.

Public Demand for Professional Competence. The most significant reason is the public demand for professional competence on the part of those who offer their services as practitioners of law, medicine, dentistry, or other learned professions. When the practice of medicine became something more than bloodletting and the giving of herbs, when it became evident that the required knowledge and skill could be attained only by thorough professional training, obviously some standards had to be established and some means found for enforcing them because the future health — indeed, the very life — of the citizen was at stake. In the practice of the law, personal rights and security of property could scarcely be entrusted to the ignorant and the scheming.

Strange as it may seem, the records of the original adoption of licensing laws in many of the professions are incomplete.[9] There are now approximately a dozen professional groups that are licensed in all forty-eight states[10] and as many more that are licensed in nearly all. The licensing of dentists and pharmacists began at an early date; the former

---

[7] See Mathews, Thomas A., "Municipal Powers to License Businesses," *Illinois Municipal Review*, October, 1943.

[8] See reports on the operation of the Pennsylvania Act of 1947 (P. L. 481), giving all communities practically unrestricted rights to impose any taxes they see fit. Due to the work of the state leagues of municipalities, the material on municipal licenses has been better worked up than is the case in the states. Full information is available from this source for the following states (and probably for others): Alabama, California, Minnesota, Oregon, Virginia, Washington, and Wisconsin.

[9] See the author's article on "Professional and Occupational Restrictions." Some of the professional associations do not know when their own laws were first enacted. The Marketing Laws Survey gives the code citations, but these are of no assistance in determining the dates of original enactment.

[10] Accountants, dentists, insurance men, lawyers, nurses, optometrists, pharmacists, physicians, teachers, undertakers, and veterinarians.

were licensed in all jurisdictions by 1900, the latter by 1910. Some of the laws relating to physicians and lawyers are quite old; coverage was complete for physicians long before it was for lawyers. The Lincoln tradition delayed until a late date the establishment of any real standards for lawyers in some states. The greatest volume of this type of legislation was reached in the decade of the twenties, but it has continued at a fairly high level since that time.

Demand for Licensure from Groups Affected. In spite of all the talk from businessmen about their devotion to the system of free competition and their objection to "government interference," business and semiprofessional groups have been among the most ardent advocates of more and stricter licensing laws. For this there have been two main reasons: as a means of protection from competition, and as a means of enhancing the prestige of their particular group. Neither reason is, from the point of view of the public as a whole, very good.

On the first, Professor McKean has some pertinent observations based on his study of pressure group influences in the New Jersey legislature.[11]

> Businessmen say that they want less government in business, but that is what they say and not what they want. They are always coming to the legislature seeking regulation. They wish to have the state use its licensing power to give them a competitive advantage over other businessmen, especially those outside the state. In the session of 1935, bills were introduced to license bait fishing boats, beauty shops, chain stores, florists, insurance adjustors, photographers, and master painters. The typical bill sets up a commission, authorizes the commission to conduct examinations, provides for a system of licenses — the fees from which are dedicated to the support of the commission — and imposes penalties for violation. Usually the bill authorizes the granting of licenses without examination to persons engaged in the business at the date of the passage of the bill; this provision tends to restrain competition from out-of-state businesses and from new enterprises, and still it does not impose any burden heavier than the cost of the license upon those persons who got into the business early. . . . There is usually no organized opposition to these measures, and some go through every year.

Pursuing the same line of thought, Hanft and Hamrick ask a series of pertinent questions, among them: Did the man on the street put pressure on his representatives in the legislature to protect him from unlicensed chiropodists, tile layers, and photographers? To which they reply: "Many of these laws, it is suspected, are procured by men already in these occupations in order to keep others out." Hugo W? comes to the same conclusion when he states: "The bulk of these law"

---

[11] McKean, Dayton D., *Pressures on the Legislature of New Jersey*, pp. 56–57 (Columbia University Press, 1938).

were passed in the interest of certain economic groups." Hanft and Hamrick continue:

A tart and lucid declaration on this subject was made by the court of the State of Washington as far back as 1906, in connection with a statute licensing plumbers. "We are not permitted to inquire into the motive of the Legislature, and yet, why should a court blindly declare that the public health is involved, when all the rest of mankind know full well that the control of the plumbing business by the board and its licensees is the sole end in view." An article appearing in the *American Mercury* tells how the beauty parlor operators secured the passage of licensing legislation in various states. The official organ of the American Cosmeticians' Society is quoted as follows, " 'These six laws were obtained as a result of much self-sacrifice and hard work on the part of a small group of women in each of these states. They have behind them some fine organization *work*, personal enthusiasm that could not be dampened by setbacks and misunderstandings, meetings without number, countless hours of telephoning, *hundreds of personal interviews with legislators, weeks given over to lobbying* [italics ours] in the state capitals, days of anxiety and disappointment, and a generous amount of that necessary thing — cooperation.' "

These incidents tell the story so well that nothing need be added. The ridiculous character of the second argument, used chiefly by vocational groups seeking to attain the dignity of professional status, is demonstrated in every state in nearly every legislative session. The shoe repairmen in Texas a few years ago, not to be outdone by the professional groups, added a word to the American language when they called themselves "shoetricians." Most extraordinary of all, perhaps, was the barber, speaking for his group before a legislative committee in California, who argued that: [12]

As barbering exists today, there are no mental qualifications whatever. Any man with two arms and two legs can buy a razor and a pair of scissors and, if the public is foolish enough to patronize him, can ply his vocation. That is the thing that we are trying to correct. First of all, he must have a knowledge of the history of the face, of the hair, of the neck, and must have a little better educational qualifications than is today required.

Promotion From Within the Government. Departments and agencies within the government itself have at least two reasons for supporting license laws. One is the fact that licensing provides a mechanism for establishing control; the other, that it produces a considerable amount of revenue. An excellent illustration of both these principles is the industrial registration acts now in force in a few states and proposed from time to time in others.[13]

Commonwealth Club of California, "Occupational Restrictions," p. 235.
Joint Legislative Committee on Finances, *Survey of the Government of Pennsylvania*, 232–233 (Harrisburg, 1934).

Such acts provide for annual registration of industrial establishments, each employer of industrial labor being required to furnish information on the following points:

Name, address, previous address of employer
Character and location of the employment
Description of buildings and equipment, number of floors, elevators, boilers,
  fire escapes, etc.
Number of persons employed, male and female
Scheduled hours of work per week for the ensuing year

Employers engaging in business at any time during the year are required, under penalty, to file this information within ten days after the
opening of their establishment. The department of labor issues a certificate to every employer complying with these provisions; those who
fail to comply are, upon conviction, assessed a small fine and costs of
prosecution.

From the enforcement point of view, such acts are valuable in that
they enable department inspectors to visit *all* manufacturing and industrial establishments within the territory assigned to them, rather than
having to hunt for the factories and being certain to miss some. The
ones that are missed are certain to be the ones which most need inspection and supervision, for they are commonly of the fly-by-night variety
and, owing to lack of any reputable business standing, ignore and defy
all the laws enacted for the protection of labor.

Such acts are not only of great assistance to a department of labor
in the enforcement of the law but may be a source of additional revenue. Employers requiring the services of less than five men may pay
as little as one dollar for their certificate of registration; those with five
or more may pay five dollars. Suppose there are in the state approximately 25,000 manufacturing and industrial establishments; this would
mean some $100,000 a year of additional revenue without imposing any
hardship on anyone and without having to set up any elaborate collection machinery. The extensive use of license laws in cities as a source of
revenue has already been noted.

Continuing Pressure for License Laws. These factors, operating individually or in combination, exert a continuing pressure upon legislative bodies everywhere to enact more and more license laws. Mention
has already been made of the numerous proposals in New Jersey in
1935. A tabulation of the bills introduced in the Pennsylvania legislature in the same year also revealed the magnitude of the problem.
There were 159 bills, wholly or partially of this character, 131 of the

14 Graves, *op. cit.*, p. 338.

in the House, twenty-eight in the Senate, either establishing new licensing provisions or amending existing ones. About one third of the House bills passed the House, and one fifth passed the Senate. Of the Senate bills, approximately one half passed the Senate, and one fourth passed the House. Thirty-four passed both houses, and twenty-eight or one seventh of the total number introduced, became law through the signature of the governor. When one considers that this experience is repeated in every session in every state, it is not surprising that the quantity of license laws reaches such impressive totals.

The Power to License

Licensing and the Police Power. The power to license is an exercise of the police power. Of the various purposes for which the police power may be exercised, protection of the public health and safety is the most important in connection with licensing programs, although some licenses are designed to prevent fraud and the exploitation of the public. A license has been regarded legally as conferring a privilege, not as establishing a contractual relationship protected by the doctrine of the obligation of contract from even a reasonable exercise of the police power.[15]

As has been pointed out, the original thesis was that all citizens would normally have a right to a free choice of the calling they wished to follow. As late as the case of Dent v. West Virginia, which provides the legal basis for much of the modern licensing program, J. Field wrote: [16] "It is undoubtedly the right of every citizen of the United States to follow any calling, business, or profession he may choose, subject only to such restrictions as are imposed upon all persons of like age, sex, and condition." Many years later, in Tyson & Brothers v. Banton, the Court recognized the fact that such privilege might be restricted at such time as the calling becomes affected with a public interest: [17]

The authority to regulate the conduct of a business or to require a license, comes from a branch of the police power which may be quite distinct from the power to fix prices. The latter, ordinarily, does not exist in respect to merely private property or business, but exists only where the business or the property involved has become "affected with a public interest." This phrase, first used by Lord Hale 200 years ago . . . furnishes at best an indefinite standard.

The License Cases, 5 Howard 523, 1847, and Mugler v. Kansas, 123 U.S. 623, 1887. ... is the placing of new restrictions upon existing practitioners to be regarded as a ... ation of the obligation of contract, or a deprivation of property without due process. The article, cited above, is fully annotated.
29 U.S. 114, 1889.
73 U.S. 418, 1927.

In a third phase in the development of judicial thinking on the subject, the Court recognized not merely the fact that restrictions may legitimately be imposed but that there is no right to practice which may not be subject to reasonable restrictions. In Lambert v. Yellowley, the Court said: [18] "There is no right to practice medicine which is not subordinate to the police power . . . , and also to the power of Congress to make laws necessary and proper for carrying into execution the Eighteenth Amendment."

Requirement of Professional Competence. The reasoning of the Court in the Dent case and later in Hawker v. New York,[19] is sufficiently important, not only as it relates to the practice of medicine but because of the basic philosophy, to warrant consideration here. The decision in the former case upheld the power of the state to require professional competence; it arose under a West Virginia statute of 1882, which made it a misdemeanor to practice medicine within the state unless the practitioner first obtained a certificate from the State Board of Health to the effect that he was a graduate of a reputable medical college. Exceptions were made in the case of persons who, upon examination by the Board, were found to be qualified and those who had practiced medicine continuously in the state for ten years prior to March 8 1881.

Dent had practiced in the state continuously since 1876, but he was not a graduate of an acceptable medical college nor had he passed an examination given by the Board. He was convicted of violation of th statute by a Circuit Court, and in 1882 this conviction was sustained b the State Supreme Court. He contended that the statute violate Amendment XIV, depriving him of his right to engage in the practi of his profession, without due process of law. The Court refused to a cept this view and held that the act was not of an arbitrary charact "It applies to all physicians, except those who may be called for special case from another state. It imposes no condition which cann be readily met."

Requirement of Good Moral Character. The doctrine of the Dent c was carried considerably further in the later Hawker case, the decisi of which upheld the power of the state to require good moral charac as a condition of licensure for the practice of medicine. This charac test has since been extensively applied in both law and medicine cause of the confidential nature of these professions. The defendan this case had been convicted of the illegal practice of his professior

---

[18] 272 U.S. 581, 1926.
[19] 170 U.S. 189, 1898.

1873 and sentenced to ten years' imprisonment. While he was serving his term, the legislature passed a law which required all persons engaged in the practice of medicine to be possessed of a good moral character. Hawker was released at the expiration of his term and attempted to re-establish himself in the practice of his profession. The law provided that conviction of a felony should be considered prima facie evidence of the lack of good moral character. Hawker was apprehended, arrested, and brought to trial. He argued that, as applied to him, the statute was ex post facto. For the earlier offense he had been indicted, tried, convicted, sentenced, and had served his time. This act imposed an additional penalty upon him; the practice of medicine was the only kind of work he knew, and to deprive him of the privilege of practicing was not only ex post facto but a taking of his property without due process of law.

In prescribing this test of good moral character it had not been intended to establish a board of censorship; yet the fact of a conviction of a felony could not be regarded as an unreasonable test of character. The Court refused to accept Hawker's contentions, holding that the obligation of the state to protect its citizens from the dangers inherent in improper medical practice was paramount over the property right of any individual to practice his profession. The ex post facto clause could not be interpreted in such a manner as to prevent the state from exercising its police power in the interests of public health and safety. The Court tried to put itself in the position of a man who found himself stranded in a strange city and in need of medical attention. The names of doctors in the telephone book or on the directory of the Medical Arts Building were all strange to him; he had a right to be able to choose any one, with the assurance that, as he did so, he would find an individual worthy of that extreme degree of trust and confidence which necessarily exists between the doctor and his patient.[20]

Administration of the Licensing Program

Few efforts have been made anywhere to see the problem of licensing as a whole. The treatment has been like that of a man who in building a house would lay a few bricks at one time, put in an upright or two at another, put in a door frame or a window frame at another, but never work long enough at any one thing to achieve notable progress.

Similar decisions have not been uncommon. C. J. Rugg in a Massachusetts decision said: "Mere intellectual power and scientific achievement without uprightness of character may be more harmful than ignorance. . . . Highly trained intelligence combined with a disregard of the fundamental virtues is a menace." See note in *Iowa Law Review*, March, 1939, pp. 538–558, on the "Nature of the Professional Relationship Recognized Under Privileged Communication Rule."

Separate Boards v. Central Agencies. Where good administration has been realized, it has usually been in spite of rather than because of the administrative arrangements. The growth of licensing systems, one or two laws at a time, with responsibility scattered all over the organizational map, has tended to create a haphazard system, and the business and professional groups subject to the licensing procedure have exerted all their energy to keep it that way.

Under the original system each licensed group has its own board, with its own officers and employees, supervising the licensing and to some extent the practice of such professions as accountancy, dentistry, law, medicine, or nursing. The terms of the board members range from four to six years. Appointments are usually made by the governor, by and with the advice and consent of the senate. Qualifications of education and experience are often prescribed in the act. Where compensation is paid at all, it is usually on the per diem basis. Expenses incurred by actual attendance at meetings are usually paid by the state. Examinations are given, usually twice a year, at times and places throughout the state that are widely advertised in advance. Most of the licenses are issued for a period of one year, subject to continued renewals. The original fee may be high, but the renewal fees are nominal. Expiration dates are often staggered throughout the calendar year to equalize the work in the office of the issuing agency. In many cases the receipts from licenses are earmarked for the board, which thus becomes independent and self-sufficient.

The boards themselves have a necessary and useful function to perform, but the employees could be — and in some states have been — brought together in a single office which is responsible for performing the administrative and clerical work for all the boards. Pleas for the establishment of such a joint or central secretariat have usually been put solely on the ground of economy. It is true that some economy may result although the staffs are usually small, but the more important consideration is the improved quality of administration that may be expected from such a move. The Detroit Bureau of Governmental Research well stated the advantages of this system: [21]

A consolidated office with centralized records and a joint staff would require a smaller number of employees, less office space and equipment would be needed and travel costs could be reduced. Experience gained by each board could be interchanged with the other boards. Greater technical expertness would be available to the boards; for example, in the preparation of examinations, a staff member versed in "short-answer" or "objective" examining methods and other techniques

[21] *Just a Second*, January 15, 1943; see also Pfiffner, John M., and others, "Coordination of the Permit and License Issuing Functions of the Los Angeles City Government," *Town Hall*, February, 1947, entire issue.

of testing and test analysis could advise all of the boards in the preparation of their examinations.

Another advantage to the general public lies in the fact that the director of this secretarial force would not be a member of the occupational or professional group being supervised. This would permit him to represent the public's interest in these important vocations. This arrangement would also be more convenient to the general public, since all inquiries and problems relating to any occupation or profession would be addressed to one place.

More adequate control over the finances of the boards could be exercised through a central administrative staff. At present some of these boards are limited in their expenditures only by the amount received in fees. In other cases, the board may spend only as much as the legislature appropriates.

Potential savings through consolidation are large in proportion to the amount now being spent for these purposes, although they would be only a small fraction of total state expenditures. Of even more importance than the monetary savings, this consolidation would be a practical demonstration of how the organization of state government can be simplified and made more efficient without impairing services.

What such consolidation may mean in improved service to the public is well illustrated by a proposal for a consolidated permit bureau for Washington, presented by the District Commissioners in 1948 in connection with the budget recommendations for 1949.[22] The organization chart accompanying this proposal is presented on page 636; its advantages were thus summarized in the budget justification:

All except health and recreation permits may be obtained at one office, approximately 60 per cent of them over the counter while the applicant is standing there. Most permits for minor building repairs may be obtained in less than an hour; routine permits for electrical, plumbing, and similar work in approximately one hour.

Permits for most jobs involving "complicated" plans will require only two brief visits to the bureau, one to file the application, the second to pick up the approved permit and pay fees. Persons needing five to ten permits for one job may apply for all at one time, be notified by telephone when they are ready, and pick them all up in one bundle.

All processing will be handled by District employees, and additional information in most cases will be obtained from the applicant by phone or mail instead of in person. To cite an example, a person who wants a permit for building a fence or wall on public space now must wait three days, make two trips to the District Building, and visit a total of seven offices. He will get the same permit in about fifteen minutes with one trip to the new central bureau.

Applicants seeking plumbing permits for house connections to water or sewer systems now spend two hours trudging to seven offices on four separate floors in the District Building. At the proposed central bureau, such permits may be obtained in ten to fifteen minutes — with the applicant waiting comfortably in a chair. About three months and "several" trips to as many as a dozen offices are now required to obtain a permit to construct a new building. Only two trips to the new central office will be necessary.

James Ficken in the *Washington Post*, May 9, 1948.

DISTRICT OF COLUMBIA: PROPOSED PERMIT BUREAU

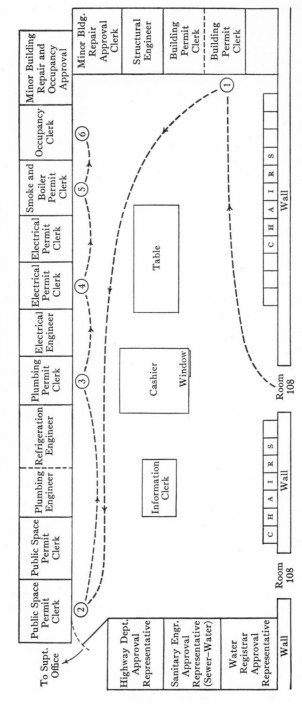

CHART shows proposed layout of streamlined one-stop building permit bureau in the District building. At station No. 1, application would file following permits: razing, excavation, new construction, barricade erection, storage shed and building material; projections beyond building line; retaining wall on private property; fencing, elevator, awnings. Station 2: driveway, parking slip, retaining wall and fence on commercial property. Station 3: gas fitting and plumbing installation; refrigeration. Station 4: electrical fixture installation. Station 5: boiler installation. Station 6: certificate of occupancy. Maximum number of permits necessary for any one job would be 19— for razing a building and replacing it with a new apartment house. All 19 could be filed in one day at the proposed bureau—or about 4 hours if the applicant filled out the blanks in advance.

At this point organized opposition of professional and vocational groups under supervision, as well as of enforcement agencies, presents itself. Each one wants complete autonomy, claiming that it — and only it — is competent to administer the licensing program.[23] It is true that the specialized boards must assume full responsibility for measuring the technical knowledge and proficiency of the applicants in their respective fields, but there is no reason whatever why they should concern themselves with the details of administration. In spite of this opposition, some states have made progress in bringing together in one agency at least part of their licensing operations. From this point of view, they may be classified in several different groups:

1. Those with a completely decentralized system. Formerly all the states were in this category, and the majority of them still are

2. Those with a separate department of licensing, as in California, Illinois, or Washington

3. Those in which licensing functions are grouped in the Department of Education as in New York, or the Department of Public Instruction as in Pennsylvania

4. Those in which licensing functions are grouped in the Department of Health as in Nebraska and, to a certain extent, in New Jersey

5. Those in which licensing functions are grouped in the office of the secretary of state, as in Georgia [24] and New Jersey and, to a certain extent, in New York

Types of Centralized Administration. Attention may first be directed to the New Jersey situation, the details of which are set forth in the table on page 625. New Jersey at the state level licenses twenty-three different groups, and many more, of course, at the municipal level. Prior to the adoption of the new constitution in 1947 (effective January 1, 1948), each examining board functioned as an independent agency. In the process of reorganization these boards were grouped as indicated in the table — eleven of them under the Department of State, four under the Department of Health, the remainder still scattered. There does not, incidentally, appear to be any logical reason for vesting this authority in a health department. The increasing use of the Depart-

Dr. Gill quotes a letter from the Los Angeles City Clerk summarizing this position the following words: "All the departments which issue permits have opposed any ove toward centralization, feeling that all necessary investigations in connection with e issuance of permits would have to be made by the particular department; and that e issuance and collection of the fees for the permits were purely incidental and did t entail a large amount of additional work or require any substantial additional personnel." H. C. Christensen, long Secretary of the National Association of Boards of armacy, has written several articles opposing consolidation at the state level.
See Wilson, John B., "Georgia Coordinates Activities of Examining Boards in the fice of a Joint Secretary," *State Government*, May, 1941, pp. 113, 123.

ment of State may represent an attempt to find some appropriate duties for an old but otherwise relatively unimportant arm of the government.

In 1921 Washington created a separate Department of Licenses, similar to the Department of Registration and Education in Illinois, to collect licenses and fees. One division of the Department collects motor vehicle license fees, while another concerns itself with the various types of professional and miscellaneous licenses. Among the latter are licenses for commercial fishing, operation of game farms, peddling drugs and medicines, and shopkeeping, but not restaurants, milk producers and distributors, hunters, and many other types of persons to whom licenses are necessary. In some cases the nature of the required inspection relates so closely to the work of other departments that, even where a central licensing agency exists, it is not possible for it to do anything like all of the licensing work required by law.

In California there has been since 1929 a separate Department of Professional and Vocational Standards, headed by a director appointed by the governor. Each of the sixteen examining and licensing boards functions in its own field, "setting standards, holding meetings . . . preparing and conducting examinations, passing upon applicants, conducting investigations of violations of laws under its jurisdiction, issuing citations and holding hearings for the revocation of licenses, and the imposing of penalties. . . ." The decisions of each board are not subject to review by the director, but he is in charge of the administrativ and financial affairs of all boards.

New York and Pennsylvania are examples of states in which profes sional registration is organized as part of the Department of Educatior The Director of the Division of Professional Education in New Yor summarizes as follows the practice in that state: [25]

In the case of medicine, dentistry, pharmacy, and nursing, the Boards ha a paid secretary with investigators who have been working under the direction the Secretary. The other professions are under the Director of Professional Ed cation, who has special investigators in optometry and one general investigat for the other professions.

Complaints are received by the Secretaries and the Director and are referr to the investigators if investigation is necessary. Then the reports of the inves gators are referred back to the Secretaries and the Director, who consult wi the Attorney General assigned to the Education Department by the Attorn General's office as to the merits of prosecution in each individual case.

Under this arrangement the central office registers the members eleven professions. A bureau of qualifying certificates and professior examinations conducts examinations for each professional group a

[25] Letter to the author from Charles B. Heisler, Director, and quoted from arti *op. cit.*

issues certificates to the qualified applicants. Examination papers are prepared by the respective boards of examiners and are then forwarded to the central bureau for editing and printing. After the examination the papers are rated by the respective boards. Responsibility for professional conduct rests with an executive secretary for professional conduct. Disciplinary matters and grievances are handled by the several boards.

In Pennsylvania some fourteen or sixteen examining boards operate under the supervision of the Bureau of Professional Licensing in the Department of Public Instruction; yet even here numerous licensing activities are carried on in other departments and agencies of the state government. Motion picture projectionists are licensed by the Department of Labor and Industry, notaries public by the governor's office, milk testers by the Department of Agriculture, mine foremen and mine operators by the Department of Mines, various types of homes and hospitals by the Department of Welfare.

A parallel situation exists in New York, where the Department of State licenses private detectives, auctioneers, steamship ticket agents and theater ticket brokers, billiard and pocket billiard rooms, real estate brokers and salesmen, and notaries public. Other special types of licenses are issued by the departments to whose activities they relate. Even where some degree of centralization has been achieved in the administration of the licensing function, a good deal of confusion still persists.

License procedures in the Federal government are completely decentralized, each department or agency issuing such licenses as may have been authorized relating to its work.

The cities do much better. A survey of twenty-eight cities made a few years ago [26] showed that "nearly all of the larger cities, two of the medium sized cities, and one half of the smaller cities issue licenses directly through a bureau of licenses or a license division. In the larger cities, marriage and dog licenses are granted by some other agency, e.g., the city clerk or health officer, in accordance with state law. Three of the medium sized cities issue licenses through the office of the tax collector or the city treasurer, while in a few of the smaller cities the city clerk is the license officer."

Interstate Relations. In the administration of a licensing program many candidates will present themselves in any state who are already licensed in some one or more other jurisdictions. Such persons are normally capable, at least with some review, of passing the usual type of exami-

---

Gill, *op. cit.*

nation in their chosen profession, but to require them to do so imposes a needless burden upon them. Why should a professional man of established reputation be thus compelled to waste his time in order to conform with a routine procedure that all agree is essential in the case of a new entrant into the profession? The answer is obvious that under normal circumstances he should not.

In dealing with such cases two well-established types of procedure are available. The first of these is reciprocity between the licensing authorities in different states. It is a basic prerequisite of the use of reciprocity that the licensing requirements of the two states for the profession in question shall be the same or essentially the same. No state which imposes rigid requirements of training for a profession can afford to grant a license to an individual as an act of courtesy to him and to another state if the requirements of that state are lower than its own, unless the applicant in question can prove that his training and qualifications are such as to satisfy the higher requirements. To do otherwise would be unfair both to the public and to those practitioners who have been held to the higher requirements.

In practice reciprocity is difficult to administer. It offers the possibility of fraud through forged certificates, although the authenticity of certificates can be easily verified if necessary. Every application, however, presents a problem of checking and evaluating training and experience, which is made even more difficult than normally by the barrier of distance and lack of intimate knowledge of the work of distant institutions or the practices of distant states. The result has been that reciprocal licensing has tended to decline for the well-established professions, its use being confined either to low-standard states or to professions or vocations for which licensing is a relatively recent development.

Obviously what is needed is uniform standards enforced by some impartial central accrediting agency whose certifications are acceptable upon presentation in all the cooperating states. This is exactly what has been done for law, medicine, and other well-established professional groups under the leadership of the appropriate national professional organizations. Thus there are the National Conference of Bar Examiners, developed under the aegis of the American Bar Association; and the National Board of Medical Examiners, under the guidance of the American Medical Association. In each instance agreement has been reached on uniform requirements for professional licensing. Memberships in the national organization are open to those states whose laws meet these requirements. The examinations are prepared, given and rated by the accrediting body, and the results are certified to the boards of the member states. Thus two methods of establishing profe

ional standing are open to the new recruit: he may take the state exam-
nation of the state in which he wishes to practice, or he may take the
examination of his national accrediting agency whose certification en-
itles him to registration in any member state. Administratively this
ystem is comparable to College Board examinations.

One other phase of this development deserves mention. National
rofessional societies, through their committees on education, have
ndertaken to raise their own standards by the rating of professional
chools. Thus the ABA and the AMA, among others, have councils on
ducation which formulate the standards for approved professional
chools and interpret the standards as applied to particular schools by
eriodic inspection or otherwise. Each publishes annually an approved
st. Ordinarily only those persons who graduate from these schools are
igible to license under the law, board ruling, or both. In other words,
ese standards of private origin are accepted and used by public li-
nsing agencies as a basis for their own work.[27]

censing as a Control Device

hinking of licenses now, not in terms of who issues them or why but
ther of their use as control devices, one is confronted by three major
oblems: issuance, enforcement procedures, and suspension and revoca-
n.

uance. The first step on the part of a citizen desiring a license is to
an application. The usual practice at all levels is to provide a sepa-
e form for each type of license issued. Norman Gill thus summarizes
findings, so far as the cities are concerned: [28]

One half of the sixteen cities of more than 75,000 and three fourths of the
ve cities of less than 75,000 use separate forms for the various types of lies. Minneapolis uses one general application form, but each kind of license
ires a supplemental application form. In Detroit several similar activities are
bined on one application blank wherever possible. In Toledo, some licenses
overed by a general application form, and others by a specific form. Miami
ne general form for 90 per cent of the different licenses. Portland uses one
ral form, except for dog licenses. The form used by Berkeley for all types is
ed "Application for Business Permit."

The first step in the licensing agency is to examine the form to as-
in whether the applicant meets the requirements established by
In the case of the professional license the requirements are fairly
rm, but this does not hold true for many of the business and oc-
tion licenses. For a professional license the laws usually require

---

a complete list of these for ten professions, see De Lancy, *op. cit.*, p. 85.
, *op. cit.*

citizenship, good moral character, a minimum age, minimum standard of general education and professional training, the passing of an examination, and the payment of a fee. As Hugo Wall observes, "the requirements for a license set up by the law usually reveal the evils against which the law is directed and the measures taken to check them." [29]

For trade and business licenses, good moral character is required: "in practice, this test is valueless, but our legislators are very fond of it." The bond requirement is perhaps the most important method of establishing reliability. Subsequent failure to render honest and adequate service and to comply with the license law may be followed by suit against the bond. Other requirements may include public notice, as in the case of liquor licenses, thus providing an opportunity to protest issuance of the license. The product of a manufacturer must comply with the minimum standard prescribed either by law or by the rule issued by the licensing authority. Where the public health and safety are involved, the license is issued and held on condition of compliance with established minimum standards.

The actual act of issuance of the certificate or license is performed by the board, if independent, or by the central licensing agency upon recommendation of the board. While in the latter case the details may vary from one jurisdiction to another, the general outlines are pretty well established. The application received by the central agency referred to the department, bureau, or board having jurisdiction over the profession or activity concerned. When approved, it is returned the central agency, which prepares and issues the license or permit. Detroit, whose procedure is regarded by Dr. Gill as typical of the larger cities, this is done in triplicate on electromatic machines. The copies are then taken to the tellers in the same office for collection the fees. The original copy goes to the licensee, the duplicate remains in the license bureau, and the third is sent together with the fees received and an accounting record to the comptroller's office. Almost exactly the same procedure is followed in the District of Columbia the issuance of motor vehicle licenses.

Enforcement Procedure. "Securing compliance" is another way of pressing the idea of enforcement. How is this to be accomplished? One method is inspection, which is the subject of the chapter which follows but there are others. A complaint may be filed, followed by investigation. Mrs. Blank cites the case of the poor housewife who has lost shirts in a laundry through either fraud or carelessness and who is a

[29] See his "The Use of the License Law in the Regulation of Businesses and Professions," *Southwestern Social Science Quarterly*, September, 1931, pp. 1–13.

to seek a cheap and quick redress at the office of the licensing official.[30] "There is no need for counsel, no court expenses, and no legal formalities or time-consuming red tape. The hearing officer delivers an opinion based on evidence, shrewd observation, experience, and common sense — which is generally just what the situation needs. The sanction, loss of the privilege of conducting business, is severe enough to insure immediate compliance." The processes of administrative adjudication and judicial review are considered in later chapters.

The City Collector of Evanston described some years ago the licensing enforcement procedures in his city.[31] The office keeps five separate ledgers on business licenses and accounts due the city, one each for business establishments, chauffeurs and taxicabs, mobile businesses such as peddlers and solicitors, special services provided by the city and damages to city property, and a "black book" or "dead beat" book to which has been affixed the more dignified title of "suspended accounts." The enforcement procedure is based upon periodic surveys:

> The license officer conducts a survey in December for the coming year and billings are made from this survey. Enforcement is begun on February 1. In June a second survey is made. This survey is conducted to add to our file any businesses established since the December check and to prevent these businesses from claiming half-year rates after July 1. Effective July 1, all licenses then delinquent come into the "Final Notice" stage. Merchants are served personally with final notices. The delinquent then has ten days from the service date of the notice to make payment. Failure to comply results in a copy of the final notice being sent to the Municipal Court, where it becomes a Statement of Claim. Summons is served by the bailiff, and court action follows. Failure to pay after judgment results in levy and collection by the city through taking certain commodities and articles used by the city equal in value to the amount of the judgment. At this time the department that receives the commodities is charged with amount of the levy, and the department benefited by the license fee is credited.

An early report on Indiana's hospital licensing program, adopted in 1945, stresses one point that has been consistently emphasized in this volume, namely, the importance of making licensing procedures democratic.[32] This effort begins with a board whose membership contains representatives of all interested groups — the hospital administrators (who predominate), members chosen from the medical and nursing professions, and two ex officio members from the state departments of health and welfare. It is continued by the effort to make the observance

ank, op. cit.
e Sanford, Eugene C., "Enforcing Licenses, Permits and Fees," Municipal Finance, November, 1939, pp. 26–30.
e Burney, L. E., and O'Malley, Martha, "Making Licensure Democratic," Hospital June, 1948, pp. 45–47.

of existing standards and the raising of standards a cooperative enter prise. In connection with the annual inspection of each hospital the surveyor discusses his findings first with the administrator and later at a follow-up meeting with members of the hospital staff and representa tives of the board. The purpose of this procedure is to provide op portunity for democratic discussion of any instances of noncompliance to work out plans for compliance, and, where possible, to raise stand ards above the absolute minimum required.

Suspension and Revocation. In addition to such enforcement feature as disciplinary action or threat of revocation, there is for the mor serious offenses the possibility of suspension or revocation of the licens In most jurisdictions the courts have held that the right to practice legitimately licensed calling is not a property right [33] but a privilege statutory creation only. Under these circumstances it is possible to pr vide either in the statute or in the rules and regulations promulgate by the enforcing agency, sanctions in the form of provisions for rev cation. Hugo Wall examined 1124 license provisions, of which 750 two thirds contained such provisions.[34] The majority of nonrevocal licenses are annual and so are subject to a refusal to renew by the censing authority.

Suspension and revocation operate with the effect of denying individual the pursuit of his accustomed means of earning a livelihoo The rules governing such administrative action therefore become matter of vital concern to the individual affected. Wall found that " majority of the laws, while not expressly denying the right to not and hearing, do not at least provide for it. Such an omission is diffic to justify." With the enactment of present-day administrative proc dure acts, the omission is much less serious than formerly. The grou for revocation are almost uniformly vague; they include incompeter fraud, knowingly deceptive advertising, and dishonest, unprofessio or dishonorable conduct. The details naturally differ from one pro sion to another. The National Education Association in 1938 mad detailed analysis of these provisions for each of six professions – countancy, architecture, law, medicine, nursing, and teaching. In case of lawyers the Association reports: [35]

Causes adjudged sufficient for disbarment of lawyers may be itemized in states, but a tabulation would necessarily be incomplete inasmuch as the not expressly included in statutes. The canons of ethics of the American Association are not rules of law but have been made so by adoption as ru

[33] West Virginia appears to be an exception; see De Lancy, p. 85, and Sloan v. Mi 113 W. Va. 506, 1933.
[34] See Wall article, *op. cit.*
[35] "Statutory Status of Six Professions," *Research Bulletin,* September, 1938, entire

court in several states. Such indefinite statements as in Maine, when a lawyer has become disqualified, indicate that the basis for disbarment is left to the discretion of the court to a large extent. Twenty-three states mention unprofessional conduct as a statutory cause for revoking lawyers' licenses; twelve states mention conviction of a felony; and twenty-four states, misdemeanor involving moral turpitude. Many of the general causes listed for the other professions are mentioned occasionally in the state bar acts of the several states, but such mention is rare.

Of the 750 cases mentioned by Wall, 629 or 84 per cent of those revocable contained such general phrases. Some of the provisions are even more unsatisfactory, making licenses revocable for misconduct, or cause, for just cause, if the public interest demands, at their (the license authority's) pleasure, or at their discretion. Such language is highly unsatisfactory from the point of view of the licensee, who is given very little guidance for his conduct. At the same time it confers upon the licensing agency an undue scope of discretionary authority. The question of appeals from such administrative actions will be dealt with in later chapters. Still another type of provision makes revocation mandatory upon conviction for violation of the law in court; the revocation in this case becomes a ministerial act, and no discretionary authority is involved.

SELECTED REFERENCES

There are few separate studies dealing with the licensing procedure as such, none that deal with it exclusively; surveys of the use of this procedure in particular fields are fairly numerous:

State: California Senate Interim Committee on Governmental Reorganization, *Modernization of Motor Vehicle Registration*, Parts I and II (Sacramento, 1946); Illinois Legislative Council, *Licensing of Funeral Directors and Embalmers* (Springfield, 1940), *Registration of Vital Statistics* (Springfield, 1947), and *State Motor License Plates* (Springfield, 1944); Kansas Legislative Council, *Licensing of Professional Engineers* (Topeka, 1946), *State Registration and Licensing of Architects* (Topeka, 1941), and *The Basic Sciences* (Topeka, 1937).

Municipal: Association of Washington Cities, *Municipal License Fees in Washington* (Seattle, 1938); Bureau of Research and Service, *License Fees and Occupational Taxes in Oregon Cities* (University of Oregon, 1943); Graves, Richard, *Report on Study of Business License Ordinances* (California League of Municipalities, San Francisco, 1936); Industrial Commission of Wisconsin, *Street Trades and Public Exhibition Permits* (Madison, 1944); League of Virginia Municipalities, *License Taxes on Retail Merchants in Virginia Municipalities* (Richmond, 1946); Reid, Ed E., *A Manual on Municipal License Taxes in Alabama* (Alabama League of Municipalities, Montgomery, 1947); and Schenectady Bureau of Municipal Research, *The Administration of Licenses and Permits in Schenectady* (Schenectady, 1943).

Clancy, Frances P., *The Licensing of Professions in West Virginia* (Foundation Press, Chicago, 1938). The only good study available of the operation of the professional licensing system in a particular state; also contains extensive bibliography.

Meeting Laws Survey, *State Occupational Legislation* (Washington, 1942). Best and most recent general survey of licensing procedures in the states, covering twenty selected occupational and professional groups.

National Association of Real Estate Boards, *Real Estate License Laws, Their Development and Results* (Chicago, 1928, and subsequent revisions). Covers thoroughly the requirements of all states for the group specified.

New Jersey State Employment Service, *Directory and Handbook of Occupations and Professions Licensed by New Jersey State Boards and Commissions* (Trenton, 1947). Handbook presenting basic information on the licensing of professional groups in one state. Some state manuals give similar information.

Wall, Hugo, "Occupational Restrictions," *The Commonwealth*, April, 1927, entire issue. The author, who wrote his doctoral dissertation on this subject, covers licensing requirements in eighteen states; he has also written a number of articles on the subject.

32

INSPECTION

INSPECTION work represents an exercise of the government's police power.[1] Its purposes are several: it seeks to protect the honest dealer or producer from the competition of the unscrupulous; to protect the public in its desire to obtain products or services conforming to specified standards of quality and to procure commodities of honest weight or measure; and to protect both producers and public from losses attendant upon the spread of destructive forces such as plant and animal diseases and unfair methods of competition. Inspection is used at all levels of government, but the extent of its use tends to increase inversely with the size of the unit. The Federal government maintains numerous inspection services, the states maintain a large number, and in the cities and counties they are legion.

Although inspection as a form of supervision by public authorities has been known for many centuries, its present extensive use is a relatively modern development, one which has come about gradually. This fact is nowhere better illustrated than in Upson's story of its rise in the city of Detroit: [2]

The city was organized in 1824 and started out inspecting weights and measures and fire hazards. No further inspection was introduced until 1867, when the sanitary patrol was established. Prior to 1900 we find inspection of food and meat (1879), construction of buildings (1885), milk (1887), plumbing (1894), boilers (1896), and electric wiring (1896).

The field of inspection steadily enlarged as Detroit became a greater metropolis and as new problems arose. In 1902, smoke inspection sought to abate the evil of pollution of the air. Safety considerations governed the inspections of elevators and signs (1911) and all inflammables (1915). Other forms of inspection include maternity hospitals (1913), refrigeration (1916), foodhandlers (1918), day nurseries (1922). In 1926 was added inspection of explosives, Negro housing, hairdressers, and cosmeticians. No new subjects of inspection were established during the depression.

An excellent survey of municipal inspection services, made in 1945, covering fourteen different types of inspection in as many major cities,

Marx, Fritz M., "Comparative Administrative Law: Exercise of the Police Power," University of Pennsylvania Law Review, January, 1942, pp. 266–291.
Growth of a City Government, pp. 486–487.

CONSOLIDATED REGULATORY INSPECTIONS IN CERTAIN CITIES 1944–1945

INSPECTIONAL SERVICE	Chicago	Buffalo	Baltimore	Pittsburgh	Milwaukee	Los Angeles	St. Louis	Washington	New York	Cleveland	Detroit	Denver	Cincinnati	Kansas City
Building	X	X	X	X	X	X	X	X	X	X	X	X	X	X
Housing	•	•	X*	•	•	•	•	X*	X	•	X	X	X*	X
Plumbing (Water)	•	X		•	•	X	X	X	X	X	X	X	X	X*
Plumbing (Waste)	X	X		•	•	X	X	X	X	X	X	X	X	X*
Plumbing (Drains)	•	X		•	•	X	X	X	X	X	X	X	X	X
Electrical	•	X	X	X	X	X	•	X	•	X	X	X	U	X
Elevators	X	O	X	O	X	•	X	X	X	X	X	X	X	X
Boilers	•	•	X	X	X	•	X	X	X	X	X	X	O	X
Refrigeration	•	O		X	X	X	O	X	X**	X	X	X	X	X
Ventilation	V	•	O	X*	•	X	O	•	X**	X	•	X	X	X*
Smoke	•	•	X	•	X	O	X	X	X*	X	X	X	X	X
Weights and Measures	•	•	•	O	•	O	X	•	•	•	•	X	•	X
Examining Boards (Crafts)	•					X		*W X	X		X		X	X
Other Inspections					M						F		F	M
Total Consolidated Inspections in City	3V	5	5	6	7	8	8	10	11	11	11	12	13	14

X. Indicates that the function is wholly or in part performed within a consolidated department.

• Indicates assignment to other agency of city.

* Shares responsibility with Department of Health.

** Shares responsibility with Fire Department.

F. Fire Prevention shared in part with Fire Department.

M. Meters on Public Utility Services.

O. City makes no inspections. State, County, or insurance companies sometimes assume duties.

U. Inspection by Fire Underwriters.

V. Ventilation was added to the group in 1945.

W. Shares responsibility with Water, Gas and Elec.

showed Kansas City leading in the number of these services, followed
by Cincinnati and Denver. Cleveland, Detroit, and New York stood
next, each with the same number. The summary is reproduced on page
648.[3] This survey revealed quite as great a diversity in the structural
organization for the performance of inspectional services as in the nature of the services themselves. Similarly, there was no uniformity with
regard to frequency of inspection either for different types within a
given city or for the same type in different cities. In many jurisdictions
the work is farmed out to insurance companies and others because of
inadequate funds and staff.

At the state level one finds a somewhat parallel situation, although
the number of types is somewhat less. The states commonly inspect
steam boilers, elevators, mines, factories, bedding and upholstery, private health and welfare institutions, buildings (sometimes outside of
the largest cities) for observance of fire and panic act provisions, dairy
farms, soft drink manufacturing plants, meat processing plants, refrigeration plants, and numerous others. Nor is there any uniformity in
practice with regard to these. On such a subject as boiler inspection —
a matter of vital concern from the standpoint of the public safety —
some states leave the responsibility to the municipalities, some accept
insurance certificates, and a very few have no provision whatever for
inspection.[4]

At the Federal level the use of inspection has developed mainly
during the present century. Among the types of Federal inspectional
services may be mentioned the following: steam vessels, locomotives,
railway safety appliances, foods, drugs and biological preparations,
meat, airplanes, landing fields, and aeronautical schools.

Organization of Inspectional Services

As inspection services increased in number, the tendency was to operate each separately, even within a given department or agency. There
was complete absence of central supervision and coordination, with the
result that inspection became more costly than necessary. There was
overlapping, not so much in types of work performed as in having a
number of different inspectors covering the same territory, each for a
different purpose. This resulted in waste of public funds and unnecessary costs for all inspection services.

From Chicago Budget Survey Committee, *Report on the Regulatory Inspectional
Services of the City of Chicago*, p. 23.

Some of the treatises on the governments of particular states describe these services,
the report of the Joint Legislative Committee on Finances in Pennsylvania. The
annual or biennial reports of the departments concerned are also useful, as are some of
the state manuals and legislative handbooks. The department of labor or of labor and
industry is responsible for a considerable share of the state inspection work.

The accompanying organization chart of the inspection services and related activities of the San Francisco Department of Public Health is significant for at least two reasons: it shows the enormous scope of this program in a single department in the government of a large city and it presents in graphic form the modern concept of the organization of these services — coordination of the different services, consolidation of inspection forces, and central supervision of personnel.

The achievement of coordination is never easy, for each agency believes that its problems are "different" and fights for the continuance of its independence. But reorganization can be accomplished, as it was in the San Francisco Department of Public Health a few years ago. The inspection divisions of this Department had been divided into four main groups, two of which were subdivided into four separate divisions, each with supervisory personnel. The story of the change made in that reorganization can best be described in the words of the Director: [5]

> Inspectors in these groups crossed and recrossed the same territory daily. In many instances one premises such as a general market would be visited by three or four inspectors in one day, each interested only in his specialty, though were from closely related services in the same department. Obviously such setup was inefficient and could at times prove very annoying to business people.

After the reorganization inspectors were able to spend more actual working hours in the field, and their work was better supervised:

> All inspectors now report to the Central Office at 8:00 A.M. and leave their districts at 8:45 A.M. They return at 4:00 and report off duty at 5:00 P. Each District Supervisor designates certain hours for various inspectors to telephone into the office from the field; thus immediate attention is given to urgent problems. District Supervisors make contact in the field each day with as many inspectors as possible.
>
> The city has been geographically divided into four major districts over each of which is assigned a District Supervisor under the direction of the Chief Food and Sanitary Inspector. The Market and Food-Restaurant Inspectors are consolidated into one group known as Market-Food Inspectors and the Housing Industrial Inspectors into another group designated as Housing-Industrial Inspectors.

After this reduction in the number of inspectors and the consolidation of inspection forces, the Department was able to perform more work with fewer men, at a reduced cost. Several thousand dollars annually were saved on mileage alone, while other savings resulted in the personal service item, through the simplification and standardization forms, and in other ways.

---

[5] See Geiger, J. C., "Inspection Services in San Francisco: Consolidation Reduces Costs," *Tax Digest*, November, 1944, pp. 373–374, 392–393.

Calif. Board of Equalization (Liquor Control)
Calif. Industrial Accident Commission
Calif. Director of Agriculture
Calif. Director of Public Health
State Board of Harbor Commissioners
United States Public Health Service

Business Manager   Emergency Hospitals   Personnel

CHIEF FOOD & SANITARY INSPECTOR

DISTRICT No. 1
District Supervisor
Assistant Supervisor
Inspectors
10 Market-Food
3 Housing-Industrial

1 Clerk-Stenographer
4 City Autos
3 Private Autos

DISTRICT No. 2
District Supervisor
Assistant Supervisor
Inspectors
7 Market-Food
2 Housing-Industrial

1 Clerk-Stenographer
1 City Auto
2 Private Autos

DISTRICT No. 3
District Supervisor
Assistant Supervisor
Inspectors
6 Market-Food
2 Housing-Industrial

1 Clerk-Stenographer
1 City Auto
3 Private Autos

DISTR
District Su
Assistant S
Insp
4 Market-I
3 Housing-

1 Clerk-St
3 City Au
1 Private

MARKET-FOOD INSPECTORS

San Francisco Health Code
San Francisco Building Code
San Francisco Fire Code
San Francisco & California & U.S. Food & Drug Acts
California Agricultural Code (Meats)
California Health & Safety Code
California Penal Code (Nuisances)
Executive Orders

HOUSING-INDUST

San Francisco Health Cc
San Francisco Building (
San Francisco Fire Code
California Health & Safet
California Housing Code
California Industrial Ac
California Penal Code (
Executive Orders

FOOD INSPECTION

Manufacture
Storage
Distribution
  Retail
  Wholesale
Building Construction
Rodent Control
Condemnations
Salvage
Food Poisoning
Complaints
Arrests

RESTAURANT INSP'N

Restaurants
Taverns
Food Venders
Soft Drinks
Caterers
Building Construction
Rodent Control
Condemnations
Salvage
Food Poisoning
Complaints
Arrests

MARKET INSP'N

Meat Processing
Meat Retail
Meat Wholesale
Fish
Poultry
Distribution
Imports
Storage
Rodent Control
Condemnations
Salvage
Complaints
Arrests

INDUSTRIAL

Industrial P
Occupationa
Ventilation-
Building Cc
Laundries—
Stables—Pe
City Water
Private Wa
Swimming
Bathing Be
Sewage Dis
Marine Insp
Fumigation
Poison Wee
Swill Collec
Refuse Col
Refuse Dui
Rodent Co
Noise Abat
Children's
Complaint

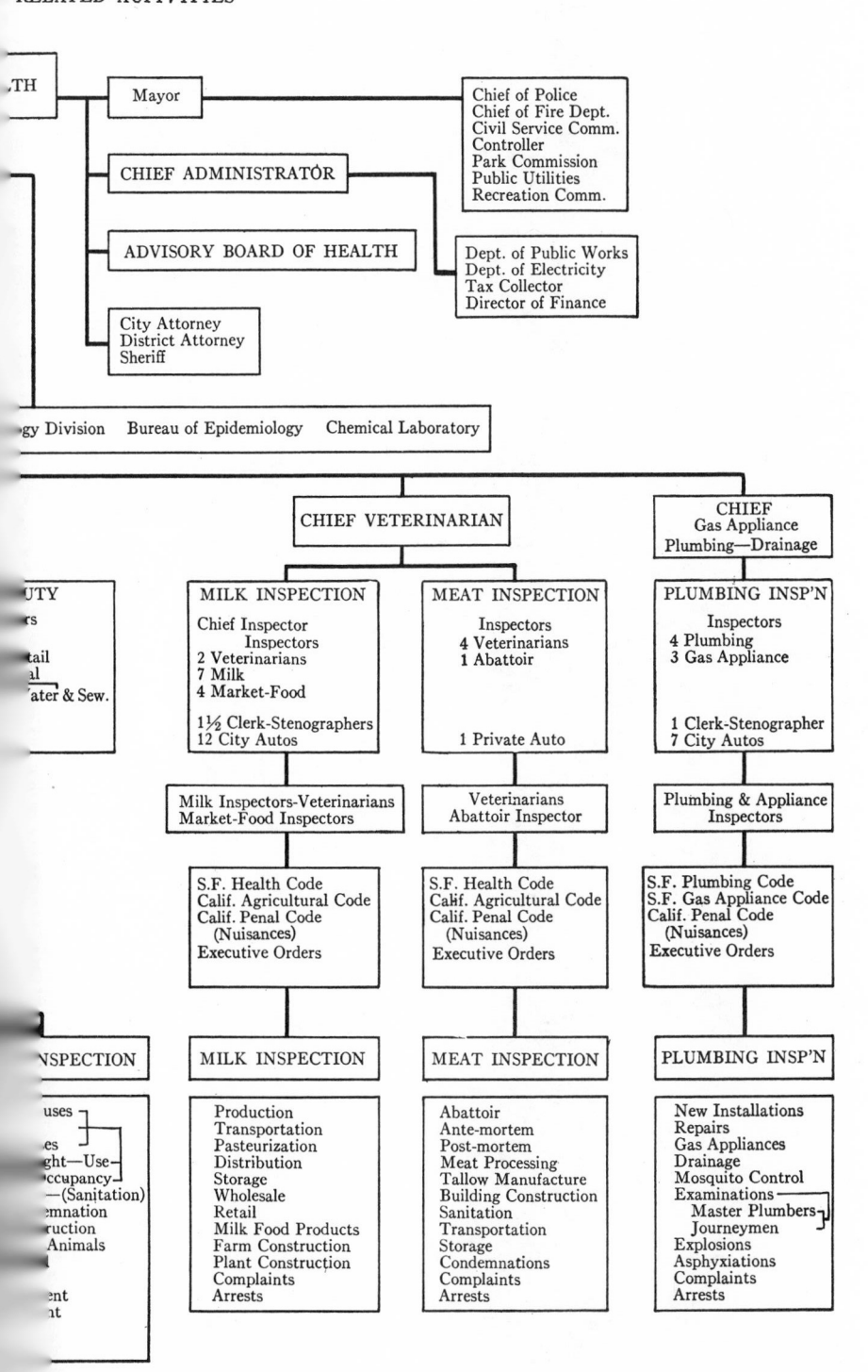

,TH		Mayor			Chief of Police

Mayor

Chief of Police
Chief of Fire Dept.
Civil Service Comm.
Controller
Park Commission
Public Utilities
Recreation Comm.

CHIEF ADMINISTRATOR

ADVISORY BOARD OF HEALTH

Dept. of Public Works
Dept. of Electricity
Tax Collector
Director of Finance

City Attorney
District Attorney
Sheriff

gy Division   Bureau of Epidemiology   Chemical Laboratory

CHIEF VETERINARIAN

CHIEF
Gas Appliance
Plumbing—Drainage

UTY
rs

tail
al
ater & Sew.

MILK INSPECTION

Chief Inspector
Inspectors
2 Veterinarians
7 Milk
4 Market-Food

1½ Clerk-Stenographers
12 City Autos

MEAT INSPECTION

Inspectors
4 Veterinarians
1 Abattoir

1 Private Auto

PLUMBING INSP'N

Inspectors
4 Plumbing
3 Gas Appliance

1 Clerk-Stenographer
7 City Autos

Milk Inspectors-Veterinarians
Market-Food Inspectors

Veterinarians
Abattoir Inspector

Plumbing & Appliance
Inspectors

S.F. Health Code
Calif. Agricultural Code
Calif. Penal Code
   (Nuisances)
Executive Orders

S.F. Health Code
Calif. Agricultural Code
Calif. Penal Code
   (Nuisances)
Executive Orders

S.F. Plumbing Code
S.F. Gas Appliance Code
Calif. Penal Code
   (Nuisances)
Executive Orders

NSPECTION

MILK INSPECTION

MEAT INSPECTION

PLUMBING INSP'N

uses
es
ght—Use
ccupancy
—(Sanitation)
mnation
ruction
Animals

ent
nt

Production
Transportation
Pasteurization
Distribution
Storage
Wholesale
Retail
Milk Food Products
Farm Construction
Plant Construction
Complaints
Arrests

Abattoir
Ante-mortem
Post-mortem
Meat Processing
Tallow Manufacture
Building Construction
Sanitation
Transportation
Storage
Condemnations
Complaints
Arrests

New Installations
Repairs
Gas Appliances
Drainage
Mosquito Control
Examinations
   Master Plumbers
   Journeymen
Explosions
Asphyxiations
Complaints
Arrests

J. C. Geiger, M.D., Director of Public Health
November 15, 1944

llustrative Types of Inspectional Services

'he preceding pages have indicated something of the magnitude of the
ispectional problems at the several levels of government. Obviously
 would be impossible to discuss any considerable number of them in
etail, but a few of the more important may be selected for illustrative
urposes. These have been chosen with a view to obtaining diversity in
ie type of thing inspected and in the level at which the inspectional
ork is done. In some instances two levels, or perhaps all three, may be
ncerned.

otor Vehicle Inspection. The basic purpose of motor vehicle inspec-
n is safety not only for the owner and operator of the vehicle but for
e lives and property of others. Along with standard driver licensing
d examination, accident reporting, competent traffic engineering, and
ety education it has come to be a vital part of the traffic safety pro-
am. Inspection of motor vehicles began in 1927 when Maryland,
issachusetts, and New York included it as a part of their "Save-A-
e" campaigns, which were instituted by proclamation of the gov-
ior of each state for the purpose of requiring all owners of vehicles,
ring a brief stated period, to present them to designated garages for
nplete inspection and repair of all safety equipment.

Motor vehicle safety depends upon seeing, steering, and stopping.
a driver cannot see or if he cannot control his car because the steer-
mechanism is faulty or his brakes will not hold, he may be in for a
y experience. Most such accidents could be prevented by fairly
quent and rigid inspection. It took time, however, to discover how
h inspection should be administered. The earliest technique was to
: garages and service stations what amounted to an opportunity to
stickers at fifty cents or a dollar each. This arrangement was al-
t a total failure except from the point of view of the garages and
ice stations.

The second method was to have inspections made on a state-wide
s by authorized garages designated by the state agency in charge of
or vehicle administration. Such approval is given only to respon-
garages which upon inspection are found to have sufficient space
equipment to enable them to do a decent job. Each approved
n is given some emblem or insignia indicating approval. This
iod was better than the original one but it still left much to be de-
, for not all the authorized stations proved honest and conscien-
in the performance of their duties. Some vehicles were passed
should not have been, while other owners were coerced into pay-
or unnecessary repairs.

The third method of administering the program is for the govern
mental unit to own and operate a series of inspection stations locate
strategically in the various centers of population, so that no owner w
be obliged to travel too far for inspection purposes. This is the mc
satisfactory method of administration; although it is more costly b
cause of buildings, testing equipment, and permanent staff, the resu
are far better. Uniform standards are uniformly applied to all. Su
stations have the most modern testing equipment (which small garag
and service stations could not afford to buy) and are so planned as
permit the handling of a large number of cars per hour by an
sembly line procedure, with a minimum of delay to the motorist. T
instructions mailed to car owners with their license tags provide
a staggering of the workload in such a manner as to assure a reasona
even flow of work.

Weights and Measures Inspection. Weights and measures inspectio
one of the oldest forms of inspection work. There is no single indiv
ual in a community whose interests are not affected by it, for wei
ing and measuring operations to a greater or lesser degree enter i
the distribution of all the necessities of life, particularly food and f
Its purpose is to see that equity prevails in all commercial transact
involving determinations of quantity. All levels of government
concerned with the problem, though in each case in a different n
ner. The National Bureau of Standards provides the standards
by all. The states maintain standards which are exact duplicate
those in Washington, provide supervision of local inspectional serv
and perform some other inspection work themselves. Local unit
most of the actual field inspection. The scope of authority and the
ture of the work performed in this area may best be visualized by
erence to the situation in a particular state.

The Pennsylvania Bureau of Standards was established in 191
an act which provided that: [6]

The establishment of a Bureau of Standards is hereby authorized in th
partment of Internal Affairs of Pennsylvania, for the purpose of regulatin
maintaining a uniform standard of legal weights and measures in this Con
wealth, to conform with the original standards of weights and measu
adopted by Congress, and verified by the National Bureau of Standards;
assist in securing the enforcement of laws relating to sealers of weights and
ures, now in force or that may hereafter be enacted.

The State Administrative Code gives a somewhat more elaborate
ment of the functions of this Bureau. In addition to the duties set

[6] Act of June 23, 1911 (P. L. 1118).

in the statute, it is authorized to have custody of the Commonwealth's standard weights and measures, to test and regulate the standard weights and measures used by all city and borough sealers, to certify to the correctness thereof by affixing the Department's official stamp, and to file annual or other reports received from local sealers of weights and measures. Every conceivable sort of weighing and measuring device is thus subject to their inspection.

Many of the duties performed by this Bureau, as in other agencies of this type, are authorized by special legislative acts. The mention of a number of these items will serve further to indicate both the complexity of the Bureau's assignment and the extent to which its work affects the welfare of individual citizens, very often without their realizing it. One such act defines commodities, regulates the sale thereof, establishes weights per bushel, provides for the marking of the net weight of commodities sold in package form,[7] and gives the Chief of the Bureau authority to make rules and regulations for tolerances of weight. Another provides that bottles or jars of milk or cream are to be measured by the Bureau. It is the duty of sealers of weights and measures to inspect and test instruments used in connection with the weighing of coal at the mines. Two measures prohibit the manufacture and sale of standard Babcock glassware unless it has been tested and approved by this Bureau.

The Bureau, in fact, has broad powers in the regulation and control of the manufacture, sale, and use of weights and measures and of weighing and measuring devices throughout the Commonwealth. In addition every county and city maintains an agency for the inspection and regulation of weights and measures, the size of the unit varying with the population. The Bureau, through its small field force, is obliged to supervise the activities of all the local agencies and to see that the law is enforced. In order to avoid duplication of effort at the local level, the Bureau renders assistance to the local officers and seeks to stimulate their efforts. Those who are familiar with the quality of work frequently done by the local government agencies in this field will fully approve of any effort which may be made to improve the quality of the service. The total number of inspections reported in 1946 was 6,077,346, in which 130,671 seals and measures were condemned. An additional 21,950 were found to be slightly out of order, and were repaired or adjusted.[8]

There are three main phases or divisions of the work of a weights

---

For an interesting case involving a regulation of this character, see Armour & Co. v. North Dakota, 240 U.S. 510, 1916. Lard was the commodity involved.

Joint Legislative Committee on Finances report, pp. 96–97, and various reports in *Bulletin* of the Department of Internal Affairs.

and measures inspector — mechanical, supervisional, and educational. The first has to do with the inspection and testing of equipment; the second, which has to do with the way in which such equipment is used embraces all the so-called supervisional activities of the official; the third covers the education of users of weighing and measuring device and of the public in all matters relating to proper methods to be fol lowed in buying and selling. All three are of extreme importance be cause the official who neglects his inspectional and supervisional ac tivities has little to talk about, and the hard-working official who fail to keep the public informed is doing little to bring about a permaner improvement in the bad conditions continually confronting him.[9]

Agricultural Inspection and Testing Programs. The department agriculture, either Federal or state, is responsible for a multitude inspecting and testing programs. Generally speaking, they fall in two categories: (1) those which are designed to maintain standards quality in the marketing of agricultural products; (2) those which a designed to protect producers in plant industry from losses due to sect pests, and producers in animal industry from losses attributal to infectious or contagious diseases. An examination of the annual biennial report of any active state department of agriculture will rev a wide variety of such programs. The following illustrations invo inspection, surveys, or investigation:

Major Types of Agricultural Inspection Programs

MARKETING OF AGRICULTURAL PRODUCTS	CONTROL OF INSECT PESTS	CONTROL OF ANIMAL DISEASE
Auction markets	Nursery inspection	Bovine tuberculosis
Dairy products marketing	Seed certification	Pullorem disease
Fruit and vegetable marketing	Plant certification	Hog cholera
Poultry products marketing	Gypsy moth counting	Hoof and mouth di
Shipping point inspection	Miscellaneous entomological activities	Bang's disease
Roadside markets		Brucellosis

Limitations of space prevent any adequate treatment of the m inspection activities in this field, only a few of which are listed ab The marketing inspection programs have been developed at the sistence and with the full cooperation of growers and shippers, realized that sound marketing practices were necessary in a highly c petitive field. Thus citrus growers in California, Florida, and T apple growers in Virginia, Washington, and other states; pro

9 Meek, Rollin E., "Weights and Measures Supervision," Indiana State Board of F *Monthly Bulletin*, June, 1945, pp. 145–146.

growers in New Jersey and other states have been instrumental in developing such programs. The rule-making aspect of the programs involves the adoption and promulgation of standards for grading the commodity in question.[10]

A marketing program in any state is a many-sided undertaking, the exact pattern of which depends upon the nature of the chief agricultural products of that state. New Jersey, for instance, is noted for its produce and its poultry industries. Auction places for these products and for livestock are licensed, inspected, and supervised. Since only a portion of the crop is sold at auction, it is necessary to carry on an extensive program of shipping point inspection and inspection and supervision of roadside markets and city farmers' markets. The fruit and vegetable marketing program carries on inspection and certification of these products throughout the state, in accordance with Federal and/or state standards, whether the products are to be used in the fresh form or for processing. "This work is carried on under a three-way agreement between the United States Department of Agriculture, the New Jersey Agricultural Society, and the New Jersey Department of Agriculture. In this agreement the Bureau of Markets is responsible for the proper interpretation and application of grades and standards and for supervision of the service. The Agricultural Society employs inspectors, collects fees for services rendered, and pays salaries and expenses of the inspectors employed." [11] Special certification programs are carried on for apples, peaches, berries, grapes, green corn, and potatoes, both white and sweet. In the white potato program 11,333 inspections were made in 1946, involving 4504 cars plus 336 cars loaded in bulk, totaling 4,077,257 hundredweight. A cannery crops inspection service was maintained for asparagus (more than 30,000 loads of it), for tomatoes (more than 100,000 tons, representing approximately two thirds of the national production), and for other vegetables.

Inspection programs designed to cope with insect pests affecting plants, shrubs, and trees are enormous in scope and variety. Plant certification for significant varieties of commercially valuable species are carried on; certificates indicate freedom from such pests or blight as affect the species in question. Feeds and seeds are likewise certified as to freedom from disease or foreign substances. Most significant, per-

---

These rules are often published by the department in pamphlet form and may be summarized in department reports. As an illustration, see *Connecticut Egg Grades, *s, Regulations and Laws* (Department of Farms and Markets, Hartford, 1948). As many states, the Connecticut grades, standards, and weight classes are the same as United States consumer grades, standards, and weight classes.
New Jersey State Department of Agriculture, *Thirty-Second Annual Report* (1946–), pp. 98–99 (Trenton, 1947); all New Jersey data are from this report.

haps, is the nursery inspection program. In 1948 the Pennsylvania Department was inspecting more than 10,000 acres of trees and plants
grown for sale by more than 1200 nurseries. The New Jersey Department in the preceding year issued certificates of inspection to 467 nurseries. In 181 other nurseries 430 infestations were found; certificates
were issued in these cases only after the infestations were brought
under control.[12]

The animal diseases listed on page 654 are only a few of the most
destructive and, from the point of view of the owners, most costly.
Programs for their control have been under way in most of the states
for many years. One illustration will suffice — the pullorem disease in
poultry, which is often fatal. It is widespread throughout the country, wherever appreciable numbers of poultry are kept. It appears in
chicks during the first two weeks; the death rate in infected broods
runs very high, and those which survive become carriers. The United
States Department of Agriculture reports that satisfactory scientific
methods have been discovered for testing flocks and determining
whether they are infected; for the advancement of this program, the
National Poultry Improvement Plan has been developed, on a cooperative basis between the Department and the industry.

The plan for the control of this disease calls for the designation of
some official state agency to be responsible for the testing of flocks
for the classification of flocks in four categories on the basis of the re
sults of the tests; for the removal of all reactors and infected bird
from the premises, and for their disposition in a manner satisfactory t
the state agency; and for the segregation of the flocks in the classes re
ferred to above. In 1948 an act based upon the National Poultry Im
provement Plan had been adopted in eleven jurisdictions.[13]

Inspection of Food, Drugs, and Public Eating Places. To a certain ex
tent food inspection is related to the inspectional work done by the de
partment of agriculture. The United States Food and Drug Admini

---

[12] The New Jersey Department carried on the following inspectional and entomolo
cal activities in 1947:

White Pine Blister Rust Control-	Domestic Inspections
Area Permits	Foreign Inspections
Dealers' Certificates	Blueberry Plant Inspections
Special Certificates	Gypsy Moth Scouting
Special Instructions on Request	European Corn Borer Survey
Canadian Certificates	White-Fringed Beetle Survey

[13] These were: Alabama, Colorado, Florida, Georgia, Indiana, Minnesota, Monta
North Carolina, North Dakota, Utah, and Vermont. New Jersey, although not inclu
in this list, blood-tested over 500,000 fowls in 1947, not to mention over 7000 truck
of poultry from various states released at the Newark Poultry Terminal. On this
gram, see Nebraska Legislative Council, Sub-Committee Report No. 15, pp. 8–14,
references therein cited (Lincoln, 1948).

tration, formerly in Agriculture, is now in the Federal Security Agency. In most states it is still a phase of the work of the department of agriculture, while in municipalities it is usually entrusted to the department of health. Regardless of the governmental level or of the location in the governmental structure, the purposes are the same: to protect the public from the purchase and consumption of food products (milk and meat inspection are usually carried on by separate agencies functioning under specific legislative authorization) that have been adulterated, misbranded, or produced under unsanitary conditions. Prior to the adoption of the Federal act in 1906 and supporting legislation in the states, the poor quality of the food supply in this country was appalling; nowadays Americans are accustomed to take its purity for granted. Yet abuses still exist; here are some examples of current ones revealed by the inspection work in a large eastern state in 1947:

> Meat spreads containing beef cheeks, pork underlips, pork snouts, or lips and beef lungs
> Cereal labeled as a coffee substitute
> Flood-damaged flour
> Uncolored insecticides likely to get into bakery products
> Use of monochloracetic acid to cover insanitary conditions
> Relabeling of insecticide containers to sell cheese during the can shortage
> Illegal use of saccharin as a sugar substitute
> Improper labeling of soft drinks
> Candy containing weevils and evidence of floor sweepings
> Using horse meat in the manufacture of meat food products

The Federal government and the states have general laws governng the manufacture, sale, and distribution of both food and drug roducts. Both of them maintain inspection forces in the field, the ormer in relation to goods shipped in interstate commerce, the latter ɔ goods manufactured and sold locally. The local units, especially the ties, have inspection forces of their own, but there exists in this field high degree of cooperation between the enforcement officers at all ɪree levels.[14] In addition to the general laws referred to above, the ates have great numbers of individual laws adopted over a period of ears, containing regulations or providing for the promulgation of les and regulations governing a wide variety of food products. Enrcement activity in each field requires inspection, sampling, and alysis. The following list indicates something of the extent of this pe of legislation in one state: [15]

See Conover, Milton, "National, State and Local Cooperation in Food and Drug ntrol," *American Political Science Review*, November, 1928, pp. 910–928, and the hor's *Uniform State Action* (University of North Carolina Press, 1934).
Joint Legislative Committee on Finances report, pp. 17–18; citations to all of these s are given in the report.

Commonwealth of Pennsylvania: Chronological Development of
Food Inspection Functions, State Department of Agriculture

1897	Adulteration and Coloring of Milk and Cream Law	1919	Cold Storage Law
	Vinegar Law		Agricultural Marketing Law
	Cheese Law		Poultry and Egg Marketing Law
1901	Oleomargarine Law		Fresh Eggs Law
	Renovated Butter Law	1920	Butter Law
1905	Fresh Meat Law		Supplement to Oleomargarine Law
	Nonalcoholic Drink Law		Sanitary Bottling Act
	Lard Law	1923	Ice Cream Law
	General Food Law		Filled Milk Law
1911	Sausage Law		Supplement to Filled Milk Law
	Milk and Cream Act	1925	Fruit Syrup Law
1915	Coffee and Chicory Law		Oyster Law
	Meat Inspection Act		Milk Container Law
1917	Apple Marketing Law		Milk Testing Law
			Carbonated Beverage Law
		1929	Grape Marketing Law
		1933	Bakery Licensing and Inspection Act

The provisions of the state food and drug laws are designed to supplement the Federal law. In many instances this is done through the adoption of substantially identical provisions, thus making the coverage complete as regards both interstate and intrastate commerce. In May, 1945, for example, the *Philadelphia Record* made a survey of conditions relating to the manufacture and sale of drugs in Pennsylvania, conditions so serious that the State Board of Pharmacy quickly recognized the need for remedial legislation. The only legal barrier to the indiscriminate manufacture and sale of medicines was that they contain no narcotics or biological products. (If sold outside the state, the products would, of course, have to comply with the more rigid requirements of the Federal act.) The new law, designed to complement the Federal Pure Food and Drug Act, gives residents of the state full protection against false claims and possibly harmful effects from drugs and medicines manufactured under unsanitary conditions or compounded by unqualified personnel. The changes may be clearly seen in the comparison which follows; for present purposes, the significant thing is the setting up of provisions for the inspection of drug manufacturing establishments.

Record Survey Findings. Anyone could establish himself as a drug manufacturer, regardless of the fact that he might have no knowledge of pharmacy or chemistry. No license was required, and the state had no authority to inspect the plant for any purpose. There were no restrictions on the labeling or advertising of the product. The manufacturer, in fact, had only one fear: if his product caused the serious illness or death of many persons, the State Board of Pharmacy could step in and take what was known as "complaint jurisdiction."

Provisions of the Act of 1945. Registration by the manufacturer with the State Board of Pharmacy is now required, the Board issuing certificates of reg tration to those applicants who meet the requirements of the law. The Board is authorized to inspect all such plants, through its field agents, and to purchase samples for tests. The manufacturer is obliged to employ a registered pharmacist, a chemist, or one with at least five years' experience, or one especially approved by the Board after investigation. The label must give an exact description of the curative or therapeutic effects of the product, and all drugs or medical ingredients must be of the professed strength, quality, and purity.

Another phase of this general problem is the inspection of public eating and drinking places. State laws ordinarily provide for the maintenance of minimum sanitary standards in such establishments and for the medical examination of food handlers employed by them. The laws are applicable not only to restaurants, lunch counters, soda fountains, bars, and cocktail lounges, but to eating stands along the public highways, tourists' lodging houses, eating and drinking concessions at country fairs, and kitchen and dining hall service of recreational summer camps, particularly those for children. The characteristic shortcomings of such establishments, unless they are subject to a strict and constant supervision, were clearly revealed in a survey conducted in New Hampshire in 1945: [16]

In carrying out this survey the United States Public Health Service mobile laboratory unit was employed. Each inspection was carried out with a Public Health Service officer in charge accompanied by a local health inspector and a representative of this department. The survey offered the local inspector ample opportunity to see all existing noncompliances, many of which had been overlooked by him on previous visits.

The establishments visited were not chosen with any malice aforethought but picked at random from a hat containing slips with the names of all the establishments in that city or town. Where the city had more than twenty-five such places, a representative number determined from a sliding-scale table were chosen. This method had proved by past experience to give a true picture of the group as a whole.

The survey as conducted showed the major noncompliance items to be as follows:

(1) Failure to provide bactericidal treatment of all eating and cooking utensils following adequate washing

(2) Failure to provide adequate and proper toilet and lavatory facilities for patrons and to keep those now installed in good repair, clean, free from flies, and ventilated to the out-of-doors

(3) Failure to properly store and handle cooking and eating utensils after having been washed and disinfected

(4) Failure to cover cooked food

(5) Failure to provide proper containers for the storage of waste matter and garbage

---

[16] Crowell, Gilman K., "Survey of Eating and Drinking Establishments," *Health News*, February, 1945, pp. 17-19.

(6) Failure to keep counters, meat blocks, hoods, and other equipment used in the preparation of food clean and in good repair

(7) Failure to keep floors, walls, and ceiling in good repair and to have them constructed of material that affords easy cleaning

City health departments are responsible for the enforcement of the provisions of the state laws within their limits, but they frequently supplement these laws by ordinances of their own. Such an ordinance was adopted by the Philadelphia City Council in October, 1945, to enable the city to carry out the requirements of a new and strengthened state law adopted earlier in the same year. Under its terms all eating and drinking establishments are licensed for one year; each is required to be inspected by the city's Department of Public Health at least once every three months. Inspection is made to see that the physical, sanitary, and health provisions of the state law and of the rules and regulations of the state Department of Health are complied with.

Under the ordinance each person, whether proprietor, partner, or employee, who handles any food or drink supplied to the public must obtain on an official blank a certificate from a licensed doctor of medicine, registered in the city Department of Public Health, that he or she is free from specified diseases and is not a carrier of other named diseases. A new certificate must be obtained at intervals of not more than one year. No person without an unexpired and unrevoked health certificate may handle food or drink served to the public; and no proprietor may permit such a person to handle food or drink.

Building Inspection. Building inspection is a matter of major importance in the public safety, yet responsibility for it is divided not only between the states and their municipalities but among a dozen different administrative agencies. Most of the states provide basic laws which are or may be supplemented by municipal ordinances and usually by additional rules and regulations. The laws themselves are, generally speaking, poor, and the enforcement is frequently so bad as to constitute a public disgrace. The laws are bad because their provisions are often lax, sometimes unreasonable, frequently excessively exacting and burdensome in some particulars, and never uniform. The enforcement is bad because it is so often incompetent or dishonest or both.

It is no exaggeration to say that building regulations and their enforcement are one of the conspicuous weak spots in American public administration. There is little excuse for the situation when engineer and construction people know perfectly well what minimum standards are necessary in various types of construction in order to pro tect the public. But all too often this knowledge is not translated into the terms of the law, and even when it is, lax enforcement makes a tragic farce of the whole regulatory effort. The history of the twentieth century abounds in illustrations in point, beginning with the Triangle Waist Company fire in New York in 1911 and followed at intervals by the Ward's Island fire, the Knickerbocker Theater collapse in Washington, the Lansing hotel fire, the dance club fire in Natchez, the Cocoanut Grove night club fire in Boston, the LaSalle Hotel fire in Chicago, with others about the same time in Des Moines and Atlanta, ending with the collapse of the Empire Building in Washington in 1948.

After each disaster there is a little flurry of activity in legislation and a temporary effort at improvement in the administration of the inspection program. The difficulties confronting legislators in this field are great, but they are not insurmountable. Miles L. Colean, an outstanding authority in the housing field, has grouped them in six major categories and has suggested appropriate methods of dealing with them: [17]

1. The problem of what the code should cover
2. The problem of scientific standards
3. The problem of nonuniformity
4. The problem of multiple jurisdiction
5. The problem of legal rigidity
6. The problem of adequate inspection and fair enforcement

The present discussion is primarily concerned with the final problem. The regulation of buildings covers a wide range of subject matter: [18]

Due to the problems presented by the growing complexity of building design and construction, the field of building regulation is becoming more and more broad. In the early colonial days, regulation was limited to the prevention of fire losses due to defective chimneys and to roofs. Today there are some thirteen major classifications under which building is regulated. These include fire resistance and prevention, engineering design, general structural considerations, electrical installations, health regulations, sanitation, including water supply and drainage systems, equipment, including such devices as elevators, heating, natural and artificial lighting, natural and mechanical ventilation, use, planning and zoning.

State building regulations are of two main types. Indiana, Ohio, and Wisconsin have complete codes; other states, like Illinois and Pennsylvania, have legislation relating to many of the individual subjects

---

See his pamphlet, *Your Building Codes.*
Chicago Association of Commerce, *Building Regulations in Chicago,* p. 2. This study, along with the one by Comer on New York, is the best now available.

normally included in a code, enforceable by various state departments and agencies. The Wisconsin code does not consist of a single enactment but rather of a series of 109 orders, numbered consecutively and arranged in ten chapters of related subject matter.[19]

In Illinois and Pennsylvania there is a multiplicity of agencies, each empowered by law to perform some small part in the building inspection program. The situation in the former may best be described by a quotation from the report of the Chicago Association of Commerce: [20]

The state, in granting authority to the cities, however, has not relinquished its power to regulate building. It also regulates building even though the instances of direct state legislation are sporadic and relatively minor in volume and importance. For example, impervious floors are required in establishments where dead animals are prepared for burial, doors on buildings which are places of public assembly are required to open outward, and there are specific requirements for fire escapes and ventilation in hotels.

The state itself licenses architects, structural engineers, and plumbers; it requires the licensing of masonry contractors by cities with a population of more than 150,000; and it permits the licensing of plumbers by cities of 500,000 inhabitants. Although most of the instances of direct legislative control by the state are comparatively narrow in scope, there are ten state agencies charged with responsibility in the field of building regulation. These include the Department of Agriculture, Department of Public Works and Buildings, Department of Labor, the Industrial Commission, Department of Public Safety, Department of Health, Department of Mines and Minerals, Department of Registration and Education, the Commerce Commission, and the Superintendent of Public Instruction.

In all, there are twenty-five specific subjects on which these ten departments of the state have received authority to enforce or develop building regulations. Naturally, these subjects vary considerably in their scope and detail.

Other Types of Enforcement Procedure

Inspection is by far the most important enforcement technique or procedure, but it is not the only one. It has been defined as "a careful viewing and examining to ascertain quality or condition, as the inspection of pork, the inspection of troops." Related forms are examination, investigation, certification, quarantine, and overseeing or viewing. All of these involve "inspection," broadly conceived; but they represent different shades of meaning and are used as enforcement procedures in areas in which inspection in the usual sense is not quite appropriate.

[19] Wisconsin State Building Code, Orders 5,000 to 5,752, summarized in Habermann, Philip S., and Hofeldt, John W., "Wisconsin State Building Code," *Wisconsin Law Review*, May, 1947, pp. 372–393. The ten chapters deal with scope, enforcement procedures, definitions and standards, general requirements, structural requirements, hazardous occupancies, and with special provisions relating to the following types structures: factories, office and mercantile buildings; theaters and assembly halls; schools and other places of instruction; and apartment buildings, hotels, and places of detention.
[20] *Op. cit.*, pp. 28–29.

Examination. By common usage the term "examination" has come to be restricted to the periodic examination of the records of financial institutions — banks and trust companies, building and loan associations, credit unions, loan companies, and the like. This authority is comprehensive; in Pennsylvania, which may be taken as an illustration, the law provides that all corporations "now or hereafter incorporated . . . which have power to receive, or are receiving money on deposit, or for safe-keeping, otherwise than as bailees, including all banks, banking companies, cooperative banking associations, trust, safe deposit, real estate, mortgage, title insurance, guaranty, surety, and indemnity companies, savings institutions, savings banks, provident institutions, national banking associations located within this state, . . . shall be under the supervision of the Department" of Banking.

This supervision is made effective through a group of bank examiners, employed to inspect at frequent but irregular intervals the books and transactions of such institutions. The work is technical and professional, requiring the services of persons of good training, ability, and excellent character. An article by Verne C. Bonesteel, Chief Examiner of the Federal Home Loan Bank Administration, stresses the point that impartial examination has come to be accepted as a necessary procedure from the standpoint of public policy as well as for the internal direction and management of thrift institutions. An understanding of the principles and practices of examination enables the directors and officers to obtain the maximum benefits of the examiner's report. "The examiner's work, like that of any other profession," he continues, "is a science and an art."

The supervisory process begins with regular reports submitted, as required by law, by the institutions under supervision.[21] These are carefully inspected by the Department staff, and any unsatisfactory conditions are noted. The various institutions may be classified into a number of groups on the basis of the soundness of their condition, and the frequency of examination may be determined by the classification. In the larger states a convenient number of districts may be established for administrative purposes, each with a supervising examiner responsible for scheduling examinations. The number of examiners and the length of time required for any particular examination depend upon the size of the bank; an accurate record is kept of both so that the exact cost may be assessed against the bank. The examination covers all

Freund, Ernst, *Legislative Regulation,* pp. 270–271 (Commonwealth Fund, New York, 1932), emphasizes the importance of the power to require information — reports, oral or written, oral testimony, and documentary evidence — along with powers of inspection, as a coordinate phase of the examining powers of administrative agencies.

phases of the bank's activities — assets and liabilities, loans, bonds, mortgages, securities, nonincome-producing investments, etc.

Investigation. Investigation implies something more thorough than either inspection or examination, either of which may normally be completed in a relatively short time. Investigation suggests a thorough inquiry into some complicated or intricate situation, which is likely to consume a good deal of time and effort. It is not a regular or routine procedure but rather one invoked under unusual circumstances to deal with a particular situation. The following are situations in which investigation may be the most appropriate procedure: by the Department of Justice, where there is a suspicion of "a combination in restraint of trade" contrary to the provisions of the Sherman Act; by the Federal Trade Commission, where complaint has been filed regarding the competitive practices of some company; by the Internal Revenue Service or a state or city tax department, on suspicion that a taxpayer has failed to declare all of his earnings; or by the Securities and Exchange Commission, when some organization of dubious integrity makes application for the issue of securities.

Certification. Certification bears some relation to licensing procedures. However, a formal examination is usually required in order to obtain a license, while a certificate is used when inspection reveals that the applicant has met such conditions as may have been specified. Thus it is customary to speak of teacher certification. No special examination is required in any state for certification, as there is for a license to practice medicine or for admission to the bar. The requirements for certification are set forth in the education law or in the department's rules and regulations, indicating minimum educational requirements, number of years of experience, and the like, for each type of certificate. If the credentials are in order and satisfy the requirements, the certificate is issued as a matter of course. Such a certificate is comparable to a position on a civil service register; it shows the type of position to which the holder is entitled. He is not eligible for anything higher, and he does not have to accept anything lower unless he wishes to do so.

There is one special type of certificate in common use — the certificate of convenience and necessity. This is used as a form of authorization for "businesses affected with a public interest." [22] Such certificates have been defined as licenses issued by the public service commission of a state, permitting an individual or corporation to engage in a particular kind of business. Statutes withholding the right to do business without such a certificate first applied to common carriers but not

---

[22] See Hall, *State Control of Business.*

apply to many businesses. The purposes of such certificates are two-fold: to establish a basis for regulation and control, and to prevent duplication of plants and services when such duplication is judged to be not in the public interest.

Overseeing and Viewing. These familiar terms in the realm of local government both involve duties of an inspectional nature. A board of overseers is something akin to a board of supervisors, whose duty it is to exercise a general surveillance or watchfulness over the affairs of the town or village and to look into whatever problems may arise. In the case of roads, actual physical inspection may be necessary. Boards of overseers or viewers were also commonly used for the management and/or inspection of institutions. The term "viewers" was likewise employed as a designation for officials now called assessors, whose duty it was to "view" or inspect properties in connection with assessment for tax purposes.

Quarantine. Several incidental references have been made to quarantine, which may be defined as the isolation of persons, plants, animals, or merchandise afflicted with or suspected of having been exposed to some contagious disease or infection; and the stoppage of the travel of such persons, animals, or commodities into or out of an infected area. Quarantine is used in a wide number of circumstances by Federal, state, and local governments, being enforceable on the part of the latter even though it affects foreign and interstate commerce.

The most frequent users of quarantine are departments of health for the control of contagious and communicable diseases, and departments of agriculture for the control of insect pests and contagious diseases of animals. Its use for health purposes, once common for diphtheria, scarlet fever, whooping cough, measles, typhoid fever, and smallpox, is now less frequent than formerly since vaccination and newer methods of immunization have brought under control most of these diseases. Individuals who become afflicted are still subject to quarantine, but area quarantines have all but disappeared.

The division of epidemiology in the department of health is responsible for enforcing legislation and regulations governing quarantine and the control of contagious diseases, the study of the causes of epidemics of such diseases and their elimination or control, and the furthering of mass immunization looking toward the complete elimination of such preventable infections as smallpox and diphtheria. This work is carried on through the use of toxins, antitoxins, and vaccines, the enforcement of quarantines, and investigation of the causes of epidemics. A state agency must supervise the work of local boards of health, lending the assistance of its field force and central office personnel to local units faced with the handling of serious or perplexing contagious disease problems. Where local agencies are inefficient or incompetent, the state agency may normally render assistance and advice or assume control.

There are literally scores of quarantines throughout the country for the control of insect pests injurious to or destructive of commercially valuable trees, plants, and shrubs. The United States Department of Agriculture has established quarantines for black stem rust, white pine blister rust, and the Japanese beetle, in all areas afflicted by these infections. While the states cooperate in enforcement, they have established a varying number of additional quarantines of their own, depending on the nature of their particular problems. The lists of plant quarantines shown below are illustrative.[23] In addition, quarantines set up for both animal and poultry diseases govern shipments into and out of infected areas.

State Agricultural Quarantines

ARIZONA	CALIFORNIA	
Peach yellows	Citrus canker disease	Colorado potato beetle
European corn borer	Chestnut blight	Vetch weevil
Strawberry root weevil	Filbert blight	Dutch elm disease
Oriental fruit moth	Peach yellows	Citrus white fly
Nut tree insects and nut insects	Nut tree insects	Persimmon root borer
Crown gall	European corn borer	Sweet potato weevil
Citrus insects	Grape phylloxera	
Sweet potato weevil		

It is well to remember that all these procedures are or may be dependent upon the exercise of the rule-making power. Professor Ray gives an interesting illustration.[24] The Texas Live Stock Sanitary Commission was empowered by the Tick Eradication Law to establish quarantine districts and to promulgate rules and regulations controlling the movement of stock out of such districts. He continues:

The statute was attacked on the ground that the Commission had been given the power to legislate, but the court maintained that authorization for such rules ". . . was contained in a law enacted by the Legislature, and no legislative power to enact law was by it vested or sought to be vested in the Sanitary Commission. . . ." Here again the court refused to admit that rule-making legislative. This rule-making power vested in the Live Stock Sanitary Commission has been consistently upheld by the courts. . . . The Pink Bollworm

---

[23] From *Laws, Rules and Regulations Governing the Shipment of Nursery Stock of New Jersey* (State Department of Agriculture, Trenton, 1948), pp. 12–15.
[24] See Ray, Joseph M., "Delegation of Power to State Administrative Agencies in Texas," *Texas Law Review*, December, 1937, pp. 1–27.

provides that under certain conditions the Governor and the Commissioner of Agriculture shall establish quarantine regulations to prevent the exportation or even the growing of cotton in quarantined areas. This act has not been before the courts, but the Attorney General ruled in 1918 that, in view of the decisions on the Tick Eradication Law, the Pink Bollworm Law was valid.

Penalties Resulting from Inspection

A brief word should be added regarding the penalties that may follow inspection work of whatever type when it is found that the law or the rules and regulations have not been complied with. Where a license or permit is involved, renewal may be denied or the existing authorization may be revoked. Such procedure may result in an appeal on the part of the licensee for a hearing (administrative adjudication) or in appeal to the courts (judicial review), both of which will be discussed in later chapters.

Other penalties associated with violations of the conditions of a license are the padlocking of the premises (as in the case of a liquor license) or legal action to close a place of amusement (such as a theater or a dance hall) regarded as a public nuisance. Where a criminal charge is involved, as in the illegal practice of medicine, the licensee may be presented to the grand jury for indictment with a view to prosecution. Criminal prosecution may also result from violation of the criminal clauses of the Sherman Act or other statute making provision with regard to criminal offenses.

Two more types of penalty are associated with the work of administrative agencies. One is the fraud order used by the Post Office Department — an order issued by the Postmaster General which has the effect of withholding all mail service both incoming and outgoing from persons, firms, or organizations against which there is evidence the use of the mails for fraudulent purposes. Any person may file a complaint with the Postmaster General when he has reason to believe that some party or concern is engaged in conducting a scheme for obtaining money or property through the mails by means of false or fraudulent pretenses. If the Postmaster General on the basis of the evidence finds the complaint to be justified, a fraud order barring the offending party from receiving mail will be issued. The law requires that mail returned to the sender in compliance with a fraud order is to have written or stamped on the outside the words: "Fraudulent. Mail to this address returned by order of the Postmaster General." The sender's income may also be cut off through the barring of money orders drawn in his name. From the decision of the Postmaster General with its drastic consequences there is no appeal to the courts with respect to questions of fact. When the objection was raised that giving such power to the Postmaster General was in effect making him a court, the reply of the Supreme Court was: [25]

It is too late to argue that due process of law is denied whenever the disposition of property is affected by the order of an executive department. Many, if not most, of the matters presented to the departments require for their proper solution the judgment or discretion of the head of the department, and in many cases . . . the action of the department is accepted as final by the courts, and even when involving questions of law this action is attended by a strong presumption of its correctness.

Cease and desist orders are another possible result of the discovery of evidence of violation of the rules of the game. The term has been defined as an order issued by an administrative agency to an individual, firm, or corporation requiring that a particular fiscal or business practice be discontinued. It is commonly used by agencies charged with the regulation of business, such as the Federal Trade Commission or a state public service commission. The injured party files his complaint with the appropriate regulatory agency, which thereupon issues notices of hearing to all concerned. If, as a result of the evidence presented, the agency concludes that the charges are well founded and the practice complained of is in reality an "unfair method of competition," it issues a cease and desist order. This is roughly equivalent to saying, "Please stop," for the orders are not self-executing and carry no penalty for violation. The regulatory agency may, when its order are ignored, appeal to the courts for an enforcement decree.

SELECTED REFERENCES

Bauer, John, *The Public Utility Franchise* (Public Administration Service, Chicago 1946). Subtitle: a study of its functions and terms under state regulation.

Campbell, Ernest H., *Meat and Restaurant Inspection* (Bureau of Public Administration, University of Washington, 1947). A case study of inspection procedures in a particular field.

Chicago Association of Commerce, *Building Regulations in Chicago: An Analysis and Recommendations* (Chicago, 1945), and *A Report on the Regulatory Inspection Services of the City of Chicago and a Plan to Simplify Procedures* (Chicago, 1945). Two excellent surveys of inspection services in a major city.

Colean, Miles L., *Your Building Code* (National Committee on Housing, New York 1946). Excellent pamphlet suggesting standards for a building code.

Comer, John P., *New York City Building Control, 1800–1941* (Columbia University Press, 1942). Best study of the performance of a particular type of inspection service in a large city; historical treatment shows evolutionary changes.

Hall, Ford P., *State Control of Business Through Certificates of Convenience and Necessity* (Bureau of Government Research, Indiana University, 1948). A very useful recent study of an important control device at the state level.

---

[25] Public Clearing House v. Coyne, 194 U.S. 497, 1904; for current information on use of this power, see the Annual Reports of the Post Office Department.

Trull, Edna, *The Administration of Regulatory Inspectional Services in American Cities* (Public Administration Service, Chicago, 1932). An old, but still useful survey of regulatory inspectional services at the municipal level.

Upson, Lent D., *The Growth of City Government* (Detroit Bureau of Governmental Research, 1922, 1931, and 1942). Shows historical growth and development of functions of this type in the City of Detroit.

Woellner, Robert C., and Wood, M. Aurilla, *Requirements for Certification of Teachers and Administrators for Elementary Schools, Secondary Schools, and Junior Colleges* (University of Chicago Press, 1947). Deals with a familiar use of certification as a standard setting and control device.

33

ADMINISTRATIVE ADJUDICATION

Problems of Organization

THE doctrine of the separation of powers and the long-established procedural requirements which are a fundamental part of Anglo-Saxon law impose certain inherent difficulties upon the operation of the system of regulation through independent boards and commissions — a system which has developed in the United States mainly during the twentieth century. These agencies find themselves in the normal course of their activities obliged to perform duties which cut across the traditional barriers between the legislative, the executive, and the judicial functions. These regulatory bodies are thought of primarily as executive agencies, but they must in addition not only make rules and regulations supplementing the statutes under which they operate, but apply the law and the rules and regulations to specific individuals and situations. The latter function, of course, involves an exercise of power primarily judicial in character.

It may be — in fact, it has often been suggested — that this separation of powers is ill suited to the governmental needs of the modern age;[1] nevertheless it seems unlikely, in the existing climate of opinion that any radical change will be made in this system in the near future In view of this fact the position of these regulatory agencies in the administrative structure becomes a matter of very great significance. The question is not only an old one but it is a difficult one; and there is yet no generally acceptable answer to it.

It is agreed, however, that the existing arrangements are in many respects unsatisfactory. Each of these agencies proceeds in its own way without any effective supervision on the part of the chief executive any attempt to coordinate the administrative aspects of its activiti with the policies and procedures of the administration as a who Reference has been made earlier to the solution of this problem p

---

[1] See, for instance, Griffith, Ernest S., *The Modern Government in Action* (Colum University Press, 1942), wherein the thesis is presented that, in government as now operates, there are not three but six basic governmental processes, as follows: Value formation and adoption; (2) Leadership; (3) Ways and means of implement popular influence, acceptance, and rejection; (4) Planning of means; (5) Adjustm between groups in accordance with the plan; (6) Research.

sented by the President's Committee on Administrative Management and further developed in Professor Cushman's book on *The Independent Regulatory Commissions*.[2] While there is much to be said for this solution (i.e., bringing these commissions under the appropriate departments, except for the adjudicatory aspects of their work, the complete independence of which was to be preserved), there have also been objections raised to it, chiefly on the ground that it would, in spite of disclaimers of any such intent, give the executive too great an influence over the quasi-judicial functions of these bodies. Regardless of the merits of this proposal, it does not seem, in the period of more than a decade that it has been before the public, to have achieved the wide acceptance which would be necessary to insure its adoption.

This very important problem was discussed at a conference of distinguished political scientists assembled at the University of Michigan in the spring of 1948 as the work of the Hoover Commission was being organized, but no agreement was reached "as to what the solution is or whether there is one."[3] The summary of the proceedings continues:

The primary concern was the problem of over-all coordination of the work of the various regulatory agencies, especially if the trend toward autonomy of operation continues. Among the techniques for bringing about such coordination are closer definition by statute of the functions of each agency, a re-definition of the removal power of the President over members of regulatory commissions, and a granting of power to the President to issue letters of instruction to these agencies.

Some members of the group contended that the maintenance of the absolute neutrality of these commissions was more important than complete consistency of policy among them, that greater control by the President would undermine confidence in their administrative adjudication, and that, therefore, the solution was to be found in convincing Congress in particular instances that remedial action was necessary. While the problems in the economic sphere were considered as "too complicated to permit extensive Presidential control to induce uniformity with the policies of the existing administration," it was not considered inconsistent to provide for executive control over purely administrative matters, even to the extent of establishing such an agency as a Department of Transportation.

Oxford University Press, New York, 1941. See also: Fesler, James W., *The Independence of State Regulatory Agencies* (Public Administration Service, Chicago, 1942); and Carr, Henry C., "A Century of Regulation by Public Utilities Commissions," *Public Utilities Fortnightly*, July 5, 1945, pp. 3-11.

Report of Proceedings of the Conference on the Organization of the Executive Branch of the Government, pp. 8-9 (Published for limited distribution by the Institute of Public Administration of the University of Michigan, 1948).

Nature of Administrative Adjudication

As Blachly and Oatman have pointed out, it is obvious that administrative authorities must make innumerable decisions in carrying out the many and varied functions of government. These decisions are of several different kinds, and it is important at the outset that the distinctions between the different kinds be clearly established. This involves differentiation between such terms as "administration," "adjudication," and "administrative adjudication."

Administration has been defined as the exercise of the constitutional and legal powers of government, the general superintendence of public affairs, and the enforcement of laws, in the process of which many decisions must be made. These decisions relate for the most part to questions of organization and procedure. Adjudication implies the exercise of the judicial function in the determination of a question, as the judgment or decision of a court on a case. But since many decisions of such character are made by administrative agencies, one finds large numbers of cases administratively adjudicated. Thus administrative adjudication means what may reasonably be implied from the meaning of the two words — the determination of questions of a judicial or quasi-judicial nature by an administrative department or agency.

In as much as executive agencies are not, under our legal system, particularly well equipped to perform this function, many questions are raised by this practice — questions involving the protection of the basic constitutional and legal rights of citizens which are protected most automatically by the older procedures of the courts. It is upon these grounds that objections have so frequently been raised to the administrative determination of questions long regarded as justiciable character.

The development of the need for this type of adjudication has been well stated by James M. Landis, who notes that two tendencies in expanding civilization of the nineteenth century seem "to foreshadow the need for methods of government different in kind from that which had prevailed in the past." He continues: [4]

> These are the rise of industrialism and the rise of democracy. Naturally, the two tendencies combined and interacted each upon the other, so that it become difficult to isolate cause and effect. For as a dynamic society does not move vacuo, so an abstract classification of tendencies can have only a relative value. The rise of industrialism and the rise of democracy, however, brought new difficult problems to government. . . .
>
> These forces can be traced by their concrete manifestations in the growth and forms of the administrative process. The high level of transportation charges

---

[4] *The Administrative Process*, pp. 7–10.

and the existence of tariffs that discriminated between communities, commodities, and individuals had made the railroads a political issue. The first attempts at
a direct legislative control of rates and charges proved crude and useless. Such
remedies as the common law and the courts afforded depended upon the initiative of aggrieved shippers. In effect they were more apparent than real because
of the costly and uncertain character of the legal actions that had to be pursued.
The need for nondiscriminatory and reasonable rates, uniformly applicable, could
not be achieved through the intermittent intervention of the judicial process.
. . Some Federal mechanism of necessity had to be invented if the rudiments
of a national railroad policy were to be developed.

One observes here in operation the two forces to which Mr. Landis
referred: the evolution of new means of communication and transpor-
ation and the development of the mechanic arts and, simultaneously,
the popular demand that all citizens — not just a few specially privileged ones — should be permitted to benefit from these developments.
Conditions that developed first in the case of the railroads, resulting in
the passage of the Interstate Commerce Act and the establishment of
the Interstate Commerce Commission, were soon to be repeated in
many other fields of activity, so that the Interstate Commerce Commission became the forerunner of a long list of independent regulatory
agencies (see table on page 675) both in the Federal government and
the states.

The powers of administrative adjudication exercised by these bodies were at first very limited. As time passed, they grew enormously in
scope, partly because of the mounting influence of the two forces that
originally led to their establishment and partly because of an increasing
proficiency in the use of the new mechanism. As in the case of the
courts, their jurisdiction is of two sorts, original and appellate. Blachly
and Oatman show that in the United States the former takes many
separate and fairly distinct forms.[5]

Administrative adjudication is advisory, with the power of final decision vested
in the head of a department or other authority.

Administrative adjudication is sometimes made a condition precedent to the
performance of an administrative act.

Administrative adjudication is often a part of the regular functions of an administrative officer.

Administrative adjudication may be combined with a legislative administrative process.

Regular suits may be brought against administrative decisions.

Administrative adjudication is sometimes exercised in connection with licensing activities.

Administrative adjudication may occur in connection with the settlement of
claims.

Administrative Legislation and Adjudication, Chapter 6.

Appeals from such decisions generally go not to appellate administra
tive agencies but to the courts. There are exceptions, both Federal an
state; in fact, developments of the last few years have tended to in
crease the opportunities for administrative review, preliminary to or i
case a satisfactory settlement is achieved, as a substitute for judicial re
view. The many types of agencies exercising this type of jurisdictio
are shown in the table on page 675.

The Unjudicialized Administrative Process

It has become almost customary since Elihu Root's famous address b
fore the American Bar Association in 1916 to point out how crude ar
how imperfect is the system of administrative law; it was a long tin
before it was able to obtain recognition. These considerations we
emphasized by Frankfurter, Gellhorn, and other writers, Gellhorn u
ing the general title "the unjudicialized administrative process" wi
reference to a variety of information procedures, some of which do a
others of which do not result in formal decisions.[6] Although Chamb
lain, Dowling, and Hays find little uniformity either in subject mat
or in procedure, Gellhorn believes that informal procedures fall mai
into two categories:

> The first group comprises what may be denominated "settlement procedu
> — that is, methods of exploring the facts, reconciling opposed positions, and
> posing of a case prior to a hearing, which, however, is legally available if
> parties desire to resort to it. The second category embraces those informal
> cedures which themselves culminate in a formal decision or order dispositiv
> the matter in issue.

Informal procedures are defined as the disposition of particular c
instituted by complaints, applications, inspections, or what not, with
the conventionalized reception of testimony under oath, subjec
cross-examination and transcribed in a record upon which the deci
is based.

Both of these procedures are in accord with present-day thou
in at least one important respect. While under the basic principle
Anglo-Saxon law there is — at least in theory — a legal remedy
every legal wrong and an appropriate form of court action by w
the remedy may be enforced, it is now recognized that litigation
time-consuming, expensive, and frequently nerve-wracking mear
enforcing one's rights. Every effort is now made, therefore, to s
controversies or at least to provide an opportunity for their settler
before they get into the courts. The more common methods are

---

[6] See his *Federal Administrative Proceedings*, Chapter 2.

pes of Administrative Adjudicating Authorities
the Federal Government *

I. Primarily Independent Administrative Courts
    1. United States Customs Court
    2. Court of Customs and Patent Appeals
    3. Board of Tax Appeals
    4. Court of Claims

I. Special Administrative Tribunals Within Government Departments
    1. Board of Appeals in the Patent Office
    2. Board of Appeals and Insurance Claims Council in the Veterans Administration
    3. The individual deputy commissioners in the Employees' Compensation Commission
    4. Board of Review in the Public Works Administration

. Primarily Regulatory Authorities
    1. Interstate Commerce Commission
    2. Federal Trade Commission
    3. Federal Communications Commission
    4. Federal Power Commission
    5. Federal Reserve Board
    6. Securities and Exchange Commission
    7. United States Shipping Board
    8. Petroleum Administrative Board

Primarily Executive and Administrative Authorities
    1. The President
    2. The heads of the executive departments

Primarily Regular Courts Exercising the Functions of Administrative Tribunals
    1. Supreme Court of the District of Columbia
    2. Court of Appeals of the District of Columbia

Primarily Fact-Finding Authorities
    1. Tariff Commission

Licensing Authorities
    1. Licensing Division in the Bureau of Navigation and Steamboat Inspection
    2. Civil Aeronautics Authority (functions formerly exercised by the Secretary of Commerce)
    3. Federal Reserve Board

The Comptroller General

d on Blachly and Oatman, *op. cit.*, Chapter 7; the authors include a second major category of
line types of tribunals: (1) primarily arbitrating authorities such as function under the supervision
Department of Labor; (2) primarily advisory authorities on questions of administrative adjudi-
which "investigate cases and give reasoned advice on the basis of which an administrative or
ve authority may make the final decision"; (3) primarily personnel authorities, such as the Civil
Commission or the Employees' Compensation Commission.

ces, informal hearings, declaratory rulings,[7] and pre-trial proce-
s of various sorts.

uch proceedings are in the main informal and private. They orig-
either through letters or information furnished by private in-
uals or from the activities of the agency's investigating staff. In
r case the purposes are the same — to establish the facts, to secure
liance with the law and with the regulations and policies of the
y, and ultimately, as has been indicated, to settle controversies
hereby minimize the amount of litigation.

Gellhorn, Walter, "Declaratory Rulings by Federal Agencies," *Annals*, May,
p. 153–159.

Gellhorn suggests a further classification of those cases which cul-
minate in formal decisions, into three groups: complaint cases, applica
tion cases, and private cases.[8] Those falling into the first category are
concerned primarily with securing compliance with statutes and ad
ministrative regulations. Examples may be selected, almost at random
from the work of any of the independent regulatory agencies in eithe
the Federal government or the states. If investigation establishes th
fact of a violation, conferences may be held and a warning issued t
the violator. In more serious cases a public hearing may be schedulec
or, in criminal cases, steps taken toward indictment and prosecu
tion.

The second category arises under legislation in the enforcement c
which the agency has provided that the individual file an applicatio
as for obtaining a professional license, a liquor license, a veteran's pe
sion, a passport, public assistance, or a position under the civil servic
In the application he must supply such information as the agency spec
fies. The agency then makes an investigation; this may be either a casu
examination of the application form itself or an extensive one involvi
field investigation, publication of notice of the filing of the applicati
(to give objectors an opportunity to state their objections), or a care
checking of the files, as may be appropriate. The nature and extent
the investigation varies according to the procedures of the agency a
the purpose of the application. In the absence of derogatory inforn
tion regarding the applicant, the privilege requested is normally cc
ferred, although exceptions exist in those instances where the applic:
must pass an examination or where a hearing is established as a p
requisite.

The decision made by the agency in either of these cases is admir
trative in character; no judicial or quasi-judicial powers are exerci
unless or until a dissatisfied party files an appeal. At that point whate
sort of review procedures the agency has established are set in moti
and simultaneously there arise the confusing questions regarding
executive or judicial character of the agency's powers.

This same type of question is presented in another way in Profe
Gellhorn's third category of cases — those in which an administra
agency serves merely as an arbiter of a dispute between two pri
parties. Even in such cases, where the parallel between agency
court is most apparent, there has been "a discernible tendency . .
perfect the mechanics of information adjudication rather than to e
late their judicial counterparts. The primary administrative effort

---

[8] Gellhorn, op. cit., pp. 47–60. Chamberlain, Dowling, and Hays use a somewhat s
classification covering all types of cases, both formal and informal; op. cit., pp. 2

een to secure expeditious settlements rather than to umpire the litiga-
on of the contenders." [9]

dicialized Administrative Process

s one turns from the informal to the formal administrative processes,
: finds that at least some phases of judicialized processes, such as offi-
al knowledge and notice and the utilization of written evidence not
bject to cross-examination, may function without formalism. These,
)wever, are exceptions, for generally speaking, judicialized processes
e rather strictly formalized. The analysis of these processes may be
oken down under a series of headings, as follows: general require-
:nts, complaint, intervention, trial examiners, evidence, conduct of
arings, findings of fact, and reconsideration and reinstatement. Each
these steps will be considered in the paragraphs which follow.

neral Requirements. The general requirements in formal proceed-
s are derived in part from the basic principles of our legal system
I in part from the constitutional and statutory guarantees of the
its of persons in the jurisdiction concerned; the provisions of the
inistrative procedure act, if such exists; and finally the rules and
ulations of the agency itself. There is probably no better way to
ain a clear idea of the nature of the contents of such rules than to
ent, as is done in the table on page 679, an outline of the rules
)ractice of a well-established agency — the Federal Trade Com-
ion.[10]

t appears that each agency which has been entrusted with quasi-
cial powers, whether Federal or state, is obliged to carry on its
ations within rather definitely prescribed legal limitations. It is
ned that there will be a fair hearing, the minimum conditions of
:h are to be found not only in legislation but in the decisions of
:ourts. Chamberlain, Dowling, and Hays list the following require-
:s, which closely parallel the minimum requirements of due process
fined in relation to state judicial procedure: [11]

he hearing would not be fair unless the issues were sufficiently defined so
he defendant knew what he would be required to meet.
here must have been timely notice and an opportunity to prepare for the
g and to produce evidence.

is certainly true at the Federal level; see Attorney General's Committee on Ad-
ative Procedure, *Final Report*, pp. 64 ff. (Senate Document No. 8, 77th Cong.,
s., 1941).
n *Rules, Policy, Organization, and Acts* (Washington, 1946).
cit., p. 14; see also Dickinson, John, "Judicial Characteristics of Administrative
tion," *New York University Law Quarterly Review*, April, 1948, pp. 239–261.

As a matter of policy the hearing as a rule should be public and certainly t
decision of the agency should be published, so that the parties affected will ha
the protection of publicity against arbitrary action and the agency itself will ha
a safeguard against the charge of using star chamber methods.

These requirements are but the minimum necessary to protect :
dividuals from arbitrary and discriminatory action. Defendants hav
right to know what is expected of them, to know the charges m:
against them, to defend themselves against the charges, to have a de
sion sufficiently definite so that they may understand the basis for
agency's order. The rules may not be changed while the case is in pr
ress. The purpose is not unduly to restrict the agency but rather
provide a system flexible enough to meet the requirements of differ
types of agencies and cases within those broad limits which are ess
tial to the protection of the basic rights of citizens. Whether the
cedures of a given agency are governed by the provisions of an
ministrative procedure act or by its own rules and regulations, t
must be some definition of terms and some indication of the nature
scope of the intended application of the authority to be exercised. (
for instance, those of the Federal Trade Commission on page 679.)

Complaint. The first step in a proceeding of this kind is to form
the complaint in precise and specific terms; the California report r
to this step as the "acquiring of jurisdiction." In the past, many a
cies were often careless about this matter. In order adequately to
guard the rights of respondents, three things are necessary; these
clearly stated in the California report: [12]

1. The charges must be fully communicated to them.
2. They must be advised on how to claim a hearing and protect their
   before the hearing.
3. Jurisdiction must be acquired by the agency in some formal manner.

The same report indicates that, as of 1944, many of the then e
statutes in the state failed to accomplish these purposes. "Alt
some specify that a copy of the complaint is to be served on t
spondent, many others require only that a citation be issued and
specify the contents thereof. Similarly, many of them do not r
that any statement be made to the respondent as to whether an :
is necessary and what he must do to avoid a default. A number
existing statutes omit any provisions as to method of service.
provide that service may be by registered mail but contain no

---

[12] See p. 16; for a good statement of this problem at the Federal level, see (
lain, Dowling, and Hays, *op. cit.,* pp. 16–19.

deral Trade Commission: Rules,
licy, Organization, Acts

on its use to assure that the respondent is reasonably likely to re-
the service." It was to correct such deficiencies that the adminis-
procedure acts were passed in California and other states.

ention. In the proceedings of regulatory bodies it frequently
ns that there are others than the principal parties who have an
st; some provision should be made for their notification and par-

ticipation. For instance, in a rate case other utilities may find themselves in an analogous position with the respondent and may wish to join in presentation of their own cases, even though they may not have been included in the original citation. "For example, whether a license for a radio station shall be granted, or on what terms, depends on the public convenience and necessity and not chiefly on the interest of the applicant. Other license holders, too, will be affected by the grant and under the statute may appeal, so they should have an opportunity to take a part in the hearing." Participation in the hearing does not, however, require that they become parties to the case; the Securities and Exchange Commission and other Federal agencies have been quite liberal in permitting participation by persons who had a special interest whether or not they became formal parties to the action.[13]

Trial Examiners. In the conduct of judicial proceedings in administrative agencies, much of the responsibility rests upon the trial examiner. As Chamberlain, Dowling, and Hays explain,[14] "a formal hearing usually held before a trial examiner, seldom before the head of an agency whether an individual or a commission or a board. The trial examiner is in most cases a member of the staff of the agency, but may be appointed from outside the staff for a particular hearing. It common practice for a trial examiner to conduct the hearing and make his findings of fact and recommendations to the agency, which decide and issues the order. Unless established by statute, his position is created by the agency itself to facilitate the performance of its statutory duties and may be abolished by the agency." Among the more important problems relating to trial examiners are their qualifications, selection, and training, and their place in the administrative structure.

The success of the plan obviously rests upon the caliber of the examiners, which in turn depends initially upon their qualifications and the methods of selection. With regard to the former, there has been a good deal of discussion and debate. Lawyers will always insist that examiners should be members of the bar; legal training would appear to be generally useful in this type of work, essential in some agencies but certainly not in all. The examiners should be mature persons, with a knowledge of and experience in the field in which the agency operates. They should be paid at a sufficiently high rate to attract able men

[13] See Oberst, Paul, "Parties to Administrative Proceedings," *Michigan Law Review*, January, 1942, pp. 378–405.
[14] *Op. cit.*, pp. 35–36; see Godman, Joseph W., "Disqualification for Bias of Judges and Administrative Officers," *New York University Law Quarterly Review*, January, 1948, pp. 109–141.

Their position in the agency should be such that they are relatively free from supervision and control on the part of the regular operating officials. Independence and tenure are both necessary if they are to perform their duties free from outside influences.

Evidence. Although it is an essential requirement of any type of hearing procedure under Anglo-Saxon law that the interested parties shall have ample opportunity to present evidence pertinent to the case, the handling of the question of evidence is by no means a simple matter. As Mr. Benjamin has pointed out, there are three related but distinct questions with regard to evidence in quasi-judicial proceedings.[15]

What kind of evidence is generally admissible in a quasi-judicial proceeding? It is the prevailing view, frequently expressed in statutes, judicial opinions, and critical comment, that "in the conduct of quasi-judicial hearings, administrative agencies are not legally bound by the exclusionary rules of evidence which limit admissibility in judicial proceedings." While some agencies claim that court rules and procedures apply, it is doubtful that they are strictly followed. Hearings are frequently conducted by laymen, very often in cases where neither the respondent nor the agency is represented by counsel. Legally, full observance of judicial procedures is not requisite to a valid determination. As the Judicial Council of California expressed it, "If there is sufficient proper evidence in the record of an administrative proceeding, a decision will be upheld regardless of the fact that evidence such as hearsay was admitted — evidence which would have been improper in a court case." This is the generally accepted view.

What kind of evidence should in practice, as a matter of policy, be admitted? The reasons for the use of relatively informal procedures in administrative proceedings are numerous. The exclusionary safeguards were devised largely to prevent certain types of evidence from reaching an untrained jury; this is less necessary when the decisions are made by experts in a particular field who handle many similar cases and are better able to evaluate testimony than are the members of an ordinary jury. Parties not represented by counsel would be at a disadvantage if court rules were strictly applied, for "the burden of making proper objections cannot reasonably be placed upon laymen, nor can the presiding officer at a hearing rule out evidence without the help of

---

Benjamin report, pp. 170–184, and California Judicial Council report, pp. 21–23; Norwood, John W., "Administrative Evidence in Practice," *George Washington Review*, November, 1941, pp. 15–42; and Stephen, Albert E., "The Extent to Which Fact-Finding Boards Should Be Bound by Rules of Evidence," *Oregon Law Review*, April, 1939, pp. 229–249.

objections." Admission of the existence of such considerations does not, however, warrant the opposite conclusion that the rules are useless or objectionable; on the contrary, it may be said that "the more closely quasi-judicial procedures approach to judicial procedures in formality and in the nature of the issues to be tried, the greater the degree to which the exclusionary rules are applied." Variations in the rules from one agency to another may be justified by differences in the character of the agency operations.

What kind of evidence will support a quasi-judicial determination? It appears that there are two acceptable answers to this question. One has been stated authoritatively in a leading New York case,[16] in which the court said: "There must be in the record some evidence of a sound, competent, and recognizedly probative character to sustain the finding and award made, else the findings and award must in fairness be se aside by the court." This may be interpreted to mean that, although i a given case evidence of an improper character may have been ad mitted, this is not sufficient ground for setting aside the decision *if* i addition other evidence was presented that was adequate to suppo: the decision.

This is known as the "legal residuum" rule or "residuum of leg evidence rule." Mr. Benjamin discusses it at length and comes to th conclusion that the substantive evidence rule "is clearly to be preferre to the legal residuum rule literally applied either to hearsay evidence to evidence violative of other exclusionary rules. I have noted befo that the legal residuum rule is not always literally applied; to the e tent that the courts relax it, they tend to approach the substantive e dence rule." Mr. Benjamin continues:

> My earlier discussion of the reasons why administrative agencies should be legally bound by the exclusionary rules of evidence will have shown, first, t there will be cases where no technically competent evidence is practically av able on some point at issue, and second, that there will be cases where technic incompetent evidence, the only evidence available on a particular point wholly persuasive.

Conduct of Hearings. Attention must now be given to the mechar of hearings, involving such matters as place of hearings, sched whether the hearings will be open or closed, and the like. The plac hearing should be at some point convenient to the majority of th who are to appear. As in the case of judicial proceedings, trave some distant point may impose an undue financial burden upon parties. Mr. Benjamin takes the position that the centralization of h ings can ordinarily be justified only where decentralization is

[16] Matter of Carroll v. Knickerbocker Ice Co., 218 N.Y. 435, 1916.

hibited by a limited hearing personnel or by limitations on the funds available to the agency to defray the expense of hearings. Obviously, too, the hearing should, wherever possible, be held in suitable quarters, with appropriate physical arrangements; this feature is more difficult to realize in decentralized hearings than at the capital.

The schedule of hearings should take account of probable time requirements for different types of cases and should be so arranged as to avoid unnecessarily wasting the time of the parties and of their witnesses and counsel. The hearings themselves should be conducted by a qualified hearing officer and should normally be open to the public, although there are considerations that may justify closed hearings. The procedure for the actual conduct of the hearing is governed by rules making provision for the opening statement, order of proof (the agency, as the accuser, usually presents its case first), extent of control by the hearing officer, testimony under oath or affirmation, methods of expediting hearings, transcript of proceedings, etc.[17] Strict controls have been established by most agencies governing admission to practice.[18]

In the conduct of hearings many points may hinge upon expert testimony. When such instances arise, the agency is likely to have a considerable advantage. Illustrative of the questions which may present themselves, questions upon the answers to which a decision may depend, are those requiring the chemical analysis of a product, an accountant's interpretation of financial records, or the advice of engineers, physicians, attorneys, or members of other professional groups. While the assistance of the technical staff will normally have been obtained in connection with the preparation of the agency's case, additional questions requiring their advice may arise at any time in the course of the proceedings.

Findings of Fact. In judicial procedure the end result is a decision which defines the rights of the parties in the case before the court and states the considerations upon which the decision rests. In quasi-judicial proceedings before an administrative officer or board, a decision must likewise be made at the conclusion of the proceedings, but in this case is technically known as a finding of the facts. This distinction involves more than a mere play on words; it grows out of what is gen-

---

All these matters are discussed in Benjamin, *op. cit.*, pp. 124–147.
See Cragun, John W., "Admission to Practice: Present Regulation by Federal Agencies," American Bar Association *Journal*, February, 1948, pp. 111–116; Morris, George M., "The Nature of Administrative Agencies and Practice Before Them," *Indiana Law Journal*, August, 1939, pp. 479–490; and Pate, James E., "Practice Before Industrial Commission," *Virginia Law Review*, December, 1942, pp. 347–386.

erally believed to be a fundamental differentiation between judicial and administrative determinations.

A court does not ordinarily undertake to investigate the facts; it accepts the facts as they appear on the record and applies the law to them. The basic purpose of administrative proceedings, on the other hand, is to determine the facts; it is usually contended that such an agency is not properly concerned with the interpretation and application of the law. While such a position may be theoretically correct it is often impossible to work it out in practice. It is at this point that administration begins to invade the province of the court and that much of the controversy over the administrative process arises.

Obviously, the process of decision should not begin until all the facts are in. As Mr. Benjamin points out, freedom from control by the legal exclusionary rules imposes a particular obligation on the hearing officer or board; he says that if the administrative judge is permitted consider evidence that would be inadmissible in a judicial proceeding it is his responsibility to exercise considered judgment in appraising the quality of the evidence he admits and the weight properly to be accorded to it. Other aspects of the peculiar position of the administrative officer, such as the limited scope of judicial review on the fact likewise impose an obligation upon him.[19]

In this discussion it has so far been assumed that the pertinent facts would be forthcoming in the course of the proceedings, being more less willingly revealed by the parties involved. Such is not always case. The problems of compelling testimony before administrative agencies are essentially similar to those of compelling testimony before courts; they are, according to the Judicial Council of California, separable into three categories: those affording the parties adequate compulsory process to enable them to present their cases; the protection witnesses from unwarranted demands by the parties; and the enforcement of valid orders.

Thus it is clear that, if the facts essential to a valid determination are to be obtained, the hearing officer or board must be invested law with authority to compel the attendance of witnesses and the production of papers relevant to the case. This is done, as in judicial proceedings, through the use of the power of subpoena. Where the witness is at a distance, a sworn statement or deposition may be obtained. Where the witness ignores a subpoena or is physically present but refuses to testify, such disobedience may constitute a misdemeanor,

---

[19] All these matters are discussed in Benjamin, *op. cit.*, pp. 124–147.

he fact may be reported to a court, which may be authorized then to punish as for contempt of court.[20]

Reconsideration and Reinstatement. Provision is normally made for he correction of errors arising from decisions, in administrative proceedings as well as in the courts. It is important that in such circumstances parties be spared the expense and delay of appeal. In California, a order to prevent an overlapping of jurisdiction between the courts and the agencies, the power of reconsideration is limited to the period before the agency order becomes effective — thirty days unless specifically shortened by the agency. Any party may petition for reconsideration, or the agency may make an order on its own motion. While it contemplated that agencies will consider all petitions for reconsideration, petitions not considered because of late filing or for other reasons are deemed to have been denied.

Reinstatement is a remedial procedure resorted to after the ruling the agency has become effective. The agency may, for instance, wish reduce the penalty. In order to prevent constant applications for instatement or change in penalty, it may be required that a period of east a year must elapse between the effective date of the ruling and application or between successive applications. In the California the Attorney General must be notified of such a filing, in order he or his representative may appear, if it seems desirable, in the insts of the people of the state.

its and Defects of the System

system of administrative adjudication is here, and it is likely to remain for a long time to come. There is little point, therefore, in discussing its advantages and disadvantages, as though one might at will either continue it or abandon it; it is more appropriate to consider its its and defects, with a view to strengthening the one and eliminating the other. In considering either the merits or the defects, distinction well be made between those agencies which are primarily engaged in administering and only incidentally in adjudicating, and those which are primarily concerned with settling disputes and controlling administrative action.

Many advantages or benefits are claimed for the use of administrative adjudication as part of the administrative process. Cases may be decided not only on their merits but with a view to the furthering of avowed public policy. In times of emergency the adjudicative

Schwenk, Edmund H., "The Administrative Crime, Its Creation and Punishment Administrative Agencies," *Michigan Law Review*, August, 1943, pp. 51–86.

process expedites action while permitting a larger degree of freedom and discretion on the part of the administration than might otherwise be possible. In dealing with subject matters which impose new questions and problems, the adjudicative process offers an elasticity not available in more rigidly formalized procedures. Furthermore, there is an advantage in having such new procedures developed and applied in the executive branch which is in sympathy with them and with their purpose.

The courts have often been slow and reluctant to recognize new needs; as Blachly and Oatman have expressed it, they have demonstrated that they are either definitely hostile to new economic, social or legal principles or are so committed to old principles as to be unable to make their decisions conform to new social trends, new policies or new types of social action.[21] Administrative tribunals may aid in supplementing and filling in, in the public law, the deficiencies and inadequacies of the private law. And it has been argued that this process of decision making is so closely integrated with the making of policy and the exercise of discretion as virtually to be inseparable from it.

On the other side, the lack of uniformity in the procedures followed in the different agencies has in the past been severely criticized. This defect was to a large extent inevitable as long as there was no comprehensive administrative, legal, or political philosophy underlying the conduct of this activity; it is now much less apparent with the gradual extension of administrative procedure acts whose purpose is to provide a philosophy and some basic procedural standards. But with such legislation in effect no complete uniformity is to be expected because of the different types of subject matter with which the various agencies must deal.

A second defect that has been the basis for much criticism lies the frequent lack of provision for independent review. The correction of this situation requires not only the establishment of review procedures but such a degree of separation of the reviewing officers from administrative processes and controls as will insure some semblance of impartiality on the part of the reviewing officers. Here again, the developing philosophy of administrative law, as expressed in the administrative procedure acts, is providing standards for independent review.

Administrative law has been — and still is — at a disadvantage compared with other aspects of our legal system, which are subject to some unifying influences from the decisions of the higher appellate

21 *Administrative Legislation and Adjudication*, p. 205.

courts. For administrative law, there is no supreme or final administrative court in this country. As Blachly and Oatman have pointed out, "if the final authority is primarily an authority for the settlement of constitutional law controversies, its decisions will be controlled by this fact rather than by the principles of administration." [22]

SELECTED REFERENCES

Of the numerous surveys of administrative procedure, see Attorney General's Committee on Administrative Procedure, *Final Report* (Washington, 1942), and Benjamin, Robert M., *Administrative Adjudication in the State of New York* (Albany, 1942), which is by all odds the best of the state surveys. See also: California Judicial Council, *Administrative Agencies Survey* (Tenth Biennial Report, Sacramento, 1944), and Jacobs, Nathan L., and Davis, Nathan, *A Report on the State Administrative Agency in New Jersey* (Trenton, 1938).

At the Federal level, several authors have prepared valuable commentaries: Blachly, Frederick F., and Oatman, Miriam E., *Administrative Legislation and Adjudication,* and *Federal Regulatory Action and Control* (both, Brookings Institution, Washington, 1934 and 1940, respectively); Chamberlain, Joseph P., and others, *The Judicial Function in Federal Administrative Agencies* (Commonwealth Fund, New York, 1942); Gellhorn, Walter, *Federal Administrative Proceedings* (Johns Hopkins Press, 1941); and Dr. Blachly's *Working Papers on Administrative Adjudication* (Senate Committee on the Judiciary, 73rd Cong., 3rd Sess., Committee Print).

Among casebooks useful in connection with this subject, see Gellhorn, Walter, *Administrative Law: Cases and Comments,* Second Edition (Foundation Press, 1947); Hart, James, *An Introduction to Administrative Law with Selected Cases* (Crofts, New York, 1940); and Von Bauer, F. Trowbridge, *Federal Administrative Law* (Callaghan, Chicago, 1942).

Freund, Ernst, *Administrative Powers Over Persons and Property* (University of Chicago Press, 1928). Standard work by a pioneer student in the field.

Glaser, Comstock, *Administrative Procedure* (American Council on Public Affairs, Washington, 1941). Subtitle: a practical handbook for the administrative analyst.

Morris, Arthur, and Ward, Robert, *Administrative Decisions and Judicial Review* (Bureau of Public Administration, University of California, 1941). A study of procedures followed in one state.

Harlacker, J. Perry, Ed., "Administrative Regulation of Private Enterprise," *Annals,* May, 1942, entire volume. Symposium dealing with the administrative agency in the governmental structure, some phases of internal organization, and major issues in the formulation of administrative policy, and adjudication.

Landis, James M., *The Administrative Process* (Yale University Press, 1938). Four addresses dealing with the place of the administrative tribunal, the framing of policies, sanctions to enforce policies, and administrative policies and the courts.

Op. cit., p. 229.

34

JUDICIAL REVIEW
OF ADMINISTRATIVE ACTION

WHEN people are confronted by a difficult problem, they are apt to
believe that it is something no one ever had to contend with before.
Usually this is not the case. In late years this situation has existed with
regard to administrative procedure. Many thoughtful persons have
been alarmed at the growth in the number and the powers of the agencies and at the violations or at least the opportunities for violation of
the personal and property rights of citizens. Actually these problems
are nearly three centuries old on American soil, as is clearly shown by
the researches of Albert Smith Faught, a distinguished member of the
Philadelphia bar.

In 1666 Governor Richard Nichols of the Province of New York
found problems in the relations of the English settlers and the Indians
on Long Island for which there was "no remedy in the Ordinary
Courts of Law." When these cases were taken into court, it was discovered that it took "too long a time before a reparacon can be made."
Recognizing these reasons — which have a strangely familiar sound —
justification for the establishment of substitute arrangements, the Governor proceeded to appoint an administrative commission.

Six years later, in 1672, Governor Lovelace found it necessary to
write to "yᵉ Comnrs for yᵉ Indyan Affayres at yᵉ East end of Long
Island," protesting that "yᵉ Indyan Affayres seem to groan under y
heavy Hand" and upbraiding them because they "seem to extrud
Causes properly determinable at yᵉ Sessions, by wᶜʰ means yᵉ Inhabitants will believe themselves debarred from yᵉ Ordinary Establisht w
of Administracion of Justice towards them." [1]

The need for judicial review of administrative determinations arose
in modern times, as Dean Pound has clearly indicated, in part from
the fact that administrative officers are free from certain operating
checks which apply to courts. This is not to say that administrative
officers are not capable people, but merely that their training and con-

[1] Faught, Albert S., "A Preface to a Program as to Judicial Review of Administr
Determinations," *Pennsylvania Bar Association Quarterly*, January, 1940, pp. 71-82

petence often lie in other areas than in the settlement of disputes. The checks which the Dean had in mind were four in number: [2] (1) the judges of a court are, by reason of their training, impelled to conform to settled ideas of judicial conduct; (2) the decisions of courts are subject to criticism by a trained profession to whose opinion the judges, as members of that profession, are keenly sensitive; (3) every decision and the case on which it is based appear in full in public records; (4) every judgment of a single judge is subject to review by a bench of judges, independent of the one whose action is to be scrutinized and constrained by no hierarchical organization or *esprit de corps* to uphold whatever he does.

Owing to the absence of these restraints, the Dean contends, administrative officers are less conscious of the basic requirements of a fair and impartial procedure. They are apt to have the layman's idea that the decision of cases is a rather easy task requiring no special training or qualifications. He points out that outside of the legal profession there are relatively few persons qualified to pass judgment on the conduct of proceedings which are not safeguarded by the detailed and explicit records which hold in check any tendency of a court to act otherwise than impartially and objectively in arriving at its decisions. He contends, furthermore, that review of administrative determinations by an administrative official is a very different thing from review of the action of a judge by an independent bench of judges — which, of course, gives strength to the argument for *judicial* review.

Extent of Judicial Review

The tremendous expansion of governmental services chiefly during the twentieth century has brought with it a corresponding growth in the field of administrative adjudication as well as of administrative legislation. Many of the new services have been regulatory and service functions of a highly complex and technical character. Rules and regulations have been issued by the enforcement agencies and then applied through adjudicatory procedures to the problems of individual citizens, with the result that a vast amount of administrative decisional law has developed. The number of these decisions is so great, as Buchly and Oatman have observed, "so technical is the knowledge required for making them, so intermingled may they be with the administrative process, so important is it that they be made rapidly, that the regular judicial courts are . . . not the proper authorities to make them." [3]

und, Roscoe, "Administrative Law and the Courts," *State Government*, September, pp. 393–397, 410.
ministrative Legislation and Adjudication, p. 2.

Requests for the judicial review of administrative decisions commonly arise from two sources: either from private parties or through enforcement proceedings instituted by the administrative agency charged with responsibility for execution of the law in question. The processes of administrative adjudication have been criticized because, among other things, their use conflicts with the doctrine of the separation of powers, long traditionally accepted. While the patrioteers continue to render lip service to the idea of separation, it no longer exists in fact for the simple reason that a government cannot function under modern conditions under so artificial a concept. The courts have long sanctioned the admixture of executive and legislative powers in the form of quasi-legislative authority and the similar interweaving of executive and judicial powers in the form of quasi-judicial authority. Similarly, the courts have developed doctrines on the finality of administrative decisions and the right of administrative authorities to interpret the law.

In making the extensive use which they do of quasi-legislative and quasi-judicial powers, administrative agencies establish rules and make decisions which at times affect detrimentally the interests of some individuals. The primary purpose of judicial review of these administrative decisions is to insure the legality of the rules and to protect citizens against the invasion of their constitutional rights either through an arbitrary and improper exercise of the rule-making authority or by hearing procedures which provide for the citizen something less than his due under what might be called an administrative due process. Administrative constructions or interpretations are accorded weight by the courts, especially where the administrative construction involves a choice between possible alternatives or where there is a construction of long standing, previously unchallenged. Since no man is punishable except for breach of the law, the problem becomes one of establishing the degree of finality attaching to the findings as to the facts as set forth in the determinations of administrative agencies. Stated in another way, the question becomes one of the limitations of judicial review.

There are two extreme views and a middle ground with regard to this question, all three of which have been clearly stated by Harris and Ward in a study of administrative decisions and judicial review, prepared at the University of California in 1941: [4]

On one hand, it is held that an administrative action involving a constitutional, statutory, or common law right of a citizen should be brought before courts for a trial de novo. This means that the court should completely re-

---

[4] *Administrative Decisions and Judicial Review*, p. 3.

and pass upon the facts of a particular administrative decision and upon the application of the law.

On the other hand, it is held that the court should not pass upon the facts of a decision but only upon whether the action was correct in form and procedure and whether there was a reasonable basis for the decision. There is considerable variation in the extent to which judicial review will go. Court review of fact and law will vary with the subject matter of the administrative decision; with the legislative provisions for appeal procedures; and with the character of the reviewing authority. Thus it is difficult to state specific rules that will stand all tests on the extent of judicial review of administrative decisions. A complete picture of court control over the decisions of administrative agencies would almost necessitate a separate treatment of every individual agency.

Some middle ground must be reached between the two extremes of complete administrative control which might result in bureaucratic government and complete judicial control which might prevent the efficient operation of government's regulatory and service functions. "The courts display a growing tendency . . to refuse to review findings of fact made by administrative tribunals; though they hold firmly to the fundamental principle, expressed in both statutory law and court decisions, that the ordinary courts shall review the decisions of administrative tribunals involving questions of law." [5]

Whatever position one takes with regard to these questions, there are two trends in modern government that now seem indisputable. There has been a definite shift from legislation to administration as the vital element in the process of governing. The Supreme Court has, in view of this development, taken what one author has called "a more modest view of its role in controlling the procedural as well as the substantive aspects of administrative activities," being, no doubt, strengthened in this manner of thought by the decision of Congress and of the state legislatures, to impose the standards of ordinary judicial procedure in administrative actions.[6] The Court has shown "a disposition to recognize the need for reliance on expert administrative bodies and the inapplicability of many of the older ideas drawn from judicial proceedings to the functioning of the administrative process."

Methods of Judicial Review

In normal operations administrative agencies make many decisions. Some of these are reviewed within the agency under procedures for administrative adjudication. When the aggrieved party still believes he has not obtained justice, he may under many circumstances appeal to the courts. The initial question is one of method: how does he go about securing a judicial review of his case? Generally speaking, there are three methods. He may appeal under some one of the com-

---

⁵ Mathly and Oatman, op. cit., p. 185.

⁶ Barnett, Vincent M., Jr., "The Supreme Court and the Capacity to Govern," Political Science Quarterly, September, 1948, pp. 342–367.

mon law writs, under one of the writs in equity, or under some definite appeal procedure established in the statute creating the particular governmental function in connection with which his appeal arises.

Professor Hart has classified the judicial remedies in another way, in two broad categories, public and private. The public remedies call for criminal prosecution of public officers, while the private ones are of half a dozen different types.[7] These include defense to prosecution in the criminal courts and, in the civil courts, suits by or against the government, civil suits against public officers, refusal of the courts to enforce a law or administrative order that can be executed only by resor to civil process, extraordinary remedies (common law writs), declaratory judgment, statutory appeal, and decision against a party who in a purely private suit relies on an administrative regulation or order.

Common Law Writs. Of the many common law writs in common use four (certiorari, mandamus, prohibition, and habeas corpus) are frequently employed in connection with appeals for judicial review of administrative action. Others, used less frequently, are quo warrant or a taxpayer's bill.

Certiorari, the first of the more common writs, has been define as a prerogative writ issued from a superior court, directed to one inferior jurisdiction, commanding the latter to certify and return the former the record in a particular case.[8] This writ, which has be called one of the most valuable and effective remedies derived from the common law, is used in many jurisdictions to review not only t procedure of inferior courts but also the procedure of inferior office boards, and tribunals, in which case the administrative agency is co sidered as a lower tribunal exercising judicial functions. The w widely used for purposes of obtaining review of administrative acti in the states, appears to be rarely used for this purpose in the Fede courts.

Mandamus is an action or judicial proceeding of a civil nature which a writ is issued in the name of the state to an inferior tribui a corporation, a board, or a person, commanding the performance of act which the law specifically enjoins as a duty resulting from office, trust, or station.[9] That is to say, the duty to be performed n be of a purely ministerial character and involve no discretion, altho in some cases the writ will be used to compel the performance of a cretionary duty without specifying the particular method of perfo

---

[7] *Introduction to Administrative Law*, p. 438 ff.
[8] 11 *Corpus Juris* 88.
[9] 38 *Corpus Juris* 541.

e. Thus Blachly and Oatman conclude that "although the writ of
ndamus cannot be used to control the quasi-judicial discretion of
iinistrative tribunals, it can be used to compel them to take juris-
:ion in respect to a statutory duty requiring official decision or
on." [10]

A writ of prohibition is that process by which a superior court pre-
ts inferior courts, tribunals, officers, or persons from usurping or
rcising a jurisdiction with which they have not been vested by law.[11]
udicial functions it is used only to stop illegal jurisdiction and so
s not apply to acts which are administrative in character.

The writ of habeas corpus, one of the most familiar and perhaps the
st important of the common law writs, is directed to the person de-
ing another, commanding him to produce the body of the prisoner
. designated time and place, with the day and cause of his caption
detention, to do, submit to, or receive whatever the court or judge
rding the writ shall consider in that behalf.[12] Some state courts use
writ to determine the legality of detention under quarantine or
lth regulations; in the Federal courts its primary use appears to be in
nection with deportation and exclusion cases arising under the im-
ration laws.

uity Writs. The writ of injunction is an equity proceeding, framed
ording to the circumstances of the case, commanding an act which
court regards as essential to justice or restraining an act which it
ems contrary to equity and good conscience.[13] In practice there
several different types — preliminary, preventive, and mandatory —
used primarily to prevent an action rather than waiting until the
on occurs and then suing for damages. While limitations have been
:ed upon the use of the injunction for review purposes by numerous
rt decisions, it is frequently used in the regulation of business and
ate cases as a means of initiating judicial review of an administrative
er.[14]

utory Appeal Procedures. There are several different types of ar-
gements with regard to the judicial review of administrative deci-
is and orders provided for in the statutes. In the Federal govern-
it the right of appeal is purely statutory.[15] In Pennsylvania, which

---

lachly and Oatman, *op. cit.,* pp. 186–187.
) *Corpus Juris* 654.
ouvier's *Law Dictionary,* and 29 *Corpus Juris* 6.
: *Corpus Juris* 19.
Vhite, Leonard D., *An Introduction to the Study of Public Administration,* Third
ion, p. 579 (Macmillan, New York, 1948).
eike v. United States, 217 U.S. 423, 1909, cited by Blachly and Oatman, *op. cit.,*
)6.

in this respect may be regarded as a typical state, a survey made in 1939 revealed the following types: [16]

> Statutes expressly forbidding appeals
> Statutes making no provision for appeal
> Statutes making specific provision for direct appeal
> Statutes making miscellaneous arrangements regarding appeal

Where no statutory provision for appeal is made, obviously an individual desiring to avail himself of appeal procedure must do so by means of one of the writs. The provisions contained in the statutes which do authorize appeal are anything but uniform. The time allowed for appeal, when prescribed, may be twenty, thirty, or sixty days after the decision of the administrative agency becomes final. While in one statute it is provided that the court may require security "upon the granting of a supercedeas in any case," no provision is made with regard to either security or supercedeas in others.

Nor is there any uniformity with regard either to the prescribed proceedings on appeal or to the finality of the decision when rendered. One statute providing for professional licensure of nurses specifies that "the action of the Court [Dauphin County Court of Common Pleas] on any such appeal shall be final," while another statute of the same type in the same state, applying to dentists, provides that either party may then appeal to the Superior Court within thirty days after entry of the decree.

Facing a perplexing situation such as this and being charged with responsibility for developing some suitable remedy, one is likely to conclude that it is necessary to determine the answers to such questions as the following:

> What should be the scope of the appellate review?
> What are the essential requirements with regard to procedure?
> How much judicial control over administrative findings as to facts?
> How much judicial control over discretionary action?
> How much judicial control over administrative findings as to questions of law?

Albert Smith Faught approaches the solution of this problem by first classifying into six groups the more than half a hundred administrative tribunals in the state, according to the nature of the decision which each is empowered to make: [17]

1. Orders in the nature of permits and licenses, and their revocation

2. Approval of charters and articles of incorporation

3. Mandatory orders

---

4. Orders fixing rates, wages, and quotas, entered by administrative tribunals as agents of the legislature

5. Orders and decisions in the technical field of taxation

6. Orders and decisions in the technical field of mining

Regarding each of these groups as posing a special problem, this author proceeds to write what one might call a prescription for judicial review for each type. In the Harris and Ward survey in California, on the other hand, it is suggested that the problems involved are of two main types: Is the person within the definition of one who may appeal the case? And what weight should be given to the findings of fact and the decisions of the administrative tribunal? All of which leads back to the problem of the extent of judicial review and the degree of finality which will be given to these administrative decisions.

Judicial Review of Federal Administrative Decisions

Existing Methods of Review. Judicial control over administrative action finds its ultimate authority in the law. There provision is made for its exercise upon three different levels — constitutional, statutory, and nonstatutory. The nature of the provisions in each of these cases is well stated by Harris and Ward: [18]

(a) *Constitutional.* The Constitution of the United States is the supreme law of the land, and the courts have established their right to interpret the Constitution and to declare unconstitutional legislation which is contrary to the commandments and prohibitions of that document. Included within this jurisdiction are the actions, orders, rules, and regulations of all Federal administrative agencies. In practice, it has been found that the sections of the Constitution most often invoked against the activities of such agencies are those in the Fifth Amendment relating to due process of law, and the doctrine of the separation of powers, in combination with those portions of Article III vesting the judicial power of the United States in its constitutionally authorized courts. Any person who claims that his constitutional rights have been infringed upon by administrative action may receive redress from the courts if he can establish his contention to their satisfaction. In such a claim, the alleged injury may be either substantive, as in the case of confiscation of property without compensation, or procedural, in which event the plaintiff might assert that no notice was given, a fair hearing was denied, or that substantial evidence was not adduced to support the finding in question.

(b) *Statutory.* Numerous cases arise in which no abridgment of constitutional rights may be alleged and in which no statutory authorization for appeal to the courts either exists or is deemed suitable by the plaintiff. In such an event, a number of recourses are available to the person feeling himself aggrieved by some administrative decision or action. His basic judicial remedy is a private action for damages against the officer or officers enforcing the decision, for while in most cases the government is immune from suit, its officials do not share in this im-

---

Op. cit., pp. 12–14.

munity and are answerable for wrongs committed in the course of their official work. In most cases, though, this remedy is inadequate, and in the United States the equity injunction has become the most common remedy. This may be utilized to prevent the performance or continuance of actions which, unless enjoined, would entitle the plaintiff to maintain an action for damages. A number of other remedies also descend to us from the common law to cope with various instances of administrative abuse or excess. Such would be the writs of habeas corpus, mandamus, prohibition, quo warranto, and certiorari, but, save in exceptional cases, these have tended to fall into disuse as instrumentalities for Federal court control of administrative action. Judicial review of the decisions of Federal administrative agencies through application for a writ of certiorari, for example, is practically unavailable because of the holding that administrative action does not become judicial merely because it requires the use of discretion.[19] A final possibility is afforded by the invocation of a declaratory judgment. Since June, 1934, the Federal courts have been empowered to grant these in "cases of actual controversy." [20] As yet the courts have failed to make extensive use of this power, but its potential utility in this field is indicated by its wide use in other spheres.

(c) *Non-Statutory.* The constituent statutes of most of the new regulatory agencies of the Federal government make provisions for some type of judicial review.[21] This is not true of certain administrative agencies engaged in the older functions of government. Existing statutory provisions are of a widely variant nature. In some cases, the right of appeal lies to the Court of Appeals or Supreme Court of the District of Columbia, in others to Circuit Courts of Appeal, and in still others to a specially constituted three-judge district court.

The Attorney General's Committee on Administrative Procedure after extensive study of the whole problem, arrived at a series of conclusions which it may be well to state as briefly as possible. They were skeptical that a single formula or set of formulae could properly control the various and changing situations in which administrative action is present, yet at the same time they were convinced of the need for generalized consideration of broad procedural questions "studied apart from the concrete situations in which they arise, and also, and perhaps even more importantly, for the extensive examination of aspects of procedure which may be peculiar to particular agencies." The Committee found in the course of its studies, many administrative procedures "which can and should be approved" and they were hopeful that the work might have stimulated agencies in the effort to improve their own procedures. The Committee believed that its work had made a definite contribution in centering attention on the importance of the trial examiner — a device that has come into general use because of the volume of administrative work that must be handled in some agencies. Finally

[19] Degge v. Hitchcock, 299 U.S. 162, 1913.
[20] 48 *Statutes* 955, 1934.
[21] For a survey of these provisions, see McAllister, Breck P., "Statutory Roads to review of Federal Administrative Orders," *California Law Review,* January, pp. 129–167.

the Committee encouraged the use of democratic methods in formulating and revising agency rules.

General Review Procedures. Unless an administrative action falls within an excepted class, it is subject to some form of judicial review if other requisites for judicial action are met. In the first place, however, it is required that all available administrative remedies be first exhausted. Since the statutes do not always specify exactly what acts or orders are reviewable, this question has in practice been very often one for judicial determination. In general, the plaintiff must, in order to establish cause of action, have been subject to some administrative order adversely affecting his interests.

The basic issue on review is the validity of the administrative action complained of, and in all but exceptional cases issues of law or fact upon review must have been presented to and passed on by the administrative agency prior to judicial review. The function of review is not to supersede administrative judgment but rather to ascertain by review proceedings that more or less specific requirements of law have been met. The record upon which review is had is made up administratively in the course of adjudicatory procedures. The scope of judicial review has been developed, partly under legislative requirements, partly under judicial practice. In general, where a pure question of law is involved, the courts will accept jurisdiction. The practical limitations are more significant than those of a legal or constitutional nature. It is difficult for the courts to force administrators to act in the proper administration of the laws; in many instances the expense is prohibitive, while in others the time element may nullify review.

Where a case rests solely upon procedure, the question presented the court is not so much one of administrative procedure as of constitutional law under the due process clause. In other cases involving the interpretation of statutes and the determination of agency jurisdiction, the principal function of the courts in their relation to the agency is to interpret the authority under which the agency acts, including the jurisdiction, standards, definitions, etc., which it exercises or applies. This question, together with the adequacy of the evidence upon which the conclusion was reached, are the two major questions to be determined in any judicial review proceedings.

The statutes relating to administrative bodies are in general subject to the same canons of interpretation as are other statutes, such as the relation of the act in question to other legislation, the intent of the legislature, the reasonableness of the result as measured by what the administrative agency has long been doing, the underlying philosophy of the act, and so on. Review on the administrative record brings before the court for consideration all the questions as to the nature and adequacy of evidence that were considered in the previous chapter, when the subject of the conduct of administrative adjudications was under consideration.

The controlling constitutional provisions of primary importance in this area are the due process clauses of the Fifth and Fourteenth amendments, the former applying to Federal cases, the latter to state cases Other governing considerations revolve around the question of the extent to which private rights may be affected, for the courts are withou general powers to revise or review administrative actions. "The case may be classified from this point of view," says Professor Pennock, "by putting in one group those in which the government is a directly in terested party and is in a favored position; the other group would com prise general 'police power' cases and cases dealing with the regulatio of business." [22] In dealing with the latter, the courts are concerned pri marily with three major questions: the permissible extent of unguide discretion, the review of the scope of valid grants of discretion, an the basic requirements of administrative procedure such as were di cussed in the preceding chapter.

Review Procedures in the States

Large and complicated as it is, the Federal government is simplici itself when compared with the intricacies of dealing with the gover ments of forty-eight states, which not only differ one from another b often lack any semblance of uniform organization and procedu within their individual limits. One illustration will suffice to indic something of the confusion in this field — at least prior to the adopti of administrative procedure acts. Since these have been adopted in or a limited number of states, the confusion still reigns in the remaind

In Pennsylvania in 1937 the General Assembly either enacted amended no less than thirty laws relating to a wide variety of subj matter, each making some provision for judicial review of administ tive decisions. Albert S. Faught, whose long-time interest in this s ject has already been noted, undertook to analyze and classify th statutes from the point of view of the character of the provisions review which they contained. He found thirteen different types procedure specified: [23]

---

[22] *Administration and the Rule of Law*, p. 160; see also Dickinson's volume.
[23] "Multiplication of Administrative Agencies and Problems," *Temple Law Quart* November, 1938, pp. 30–54.

1. Appeal to Court of Common Pleas of proper county   5
2. Appeal to the Court of Common Pleas of Dauphin County   9
3. Appeal to Supreme or Superior Court (no review by Common Pleas)   1
4. Appeal to Superior Court (no review by Common Pleas)   3
5. Review by Court of Common Pleas of proper county   3
6. Review by Court of Common Pleas of Dauphin County   1
7. Exceptions to report or demand for jury trial   2
8. Rule to show cause   1
9. Injunction by Court of Common Pleas of proper county   5
10. Injunction by Court of Common Pleas of Dauphin County   1
11. Certiorari by Court of Common Pleas of proper county   1
12. Hearing *de novo* by Court of Common Pleas of proper county   1
13. Hearing *de novo* by Quarter Sessions Court of proper county   2

The chaos existing in Pennsylvania — and Pennsylvania was no different and no worse in this regard than its sister states — is further illustrated by continuing from other angles the analysis of this same group of thirty statutes. Here were thirteen different requirements with regard to court jurisdiction where appeals were to be taken; when the judicial hearings were held, what effect was the court required to give to the record and to the findings of fact made by the administrative agency? The answers to this question showed a diversity quite as great as that relating to the matter of jurisdiction:

1. Statute silent on the subject   13
2. Hearing *de novo* (no restriction)   7
3. Court may take evidence or refer to referee   1
4. Court may take evidence if there was reasonable ground for failure to produce same   1
5. Remand for taking of after-discovered evidence   1
6. Remand for taking evidence omitted on reasonable grounds   1
7. Finding has weight to report similar to report of referee   2
8. No appeal on question of fact   2
9. Finding if supported by evidence is conclusive   4
10. Accept finding of fact as conclusive   1
11. Court may reverse for lack of evidence to support finding   1
12. No additional testimony to be taken   1

While the requirements of this group of statutes regarding the hearing itself might have been considered in the preceding chapter, it may be noted here that these were no less diverse than the provisions relating to other matters. There were, in fact, eighteen different regulations governing action of administrative agencies, of which the following were typical: hearing to be public, technical rules of evidence to be disregarded, technical rules of procedure to be disregarded, competent evidence to be sufficient, referees appointed by the board to have power to make decisions, board to act by two thirds of all the members, etc.

This same analysis covered one more important point, namely, statutory regulations governing court review of administrative determinations. Here again, a dozen different types of requirements were reported, the variations having little or no relation to the particular problems of the agencies to which they were applied. A bond was required on appeal from the State Milk Control Board but not in connection with appeals from the State Liquor Control Board or the Unemployment Compensation Commission. The appeal would operate as a supercedeas in appeals from three agencies, would not so operate in four, while in six others it was not to be so considered unless ordered by the court. The chart which appears on page 701 attempts to show the various possible degrees of judicial review of administrative decisions; this is quite in contrast to the situation portrayed by Mr. Faught.

After further analysis of these statutes, Mr. Faught concluded that six types of review would appear to be adequate to meet the needs of the agencies covered by the survey. These six were:

1. Appeal with hearing in court *de novo*, following hearing or investigation and order by an administrative agency
2. Rule to show cause, involving a factual hearing in court, following an investigation by the administrative agency
3. Action in equity to abate a nuisance
4. Appeal, with privilege of introducing before the court evidence not reasonably available at the hearing conducted by the administrative agency, the court to examine all the evidence and make its own findings of fact and law
5. Certiorari on a closed record, the court having power to review questions of law and to examine the evidence to see if it supports the findings of fact
6. Certiorari, with power in the court to determine questions at law and the bona fides of the causes assigned for discharge and to decide whether the cause of removal, if true, is a just cause

There are, of course, various other questions in addition to that relating to the type of review. To return to the earlier question of jurisdiction, where ought such appeals to be tried? Obviously in the county court — however it may be designated in any particular state — in the county in which the question arises, except in cases where for special reasons suit might be filed at the state capital or in a higher court. view of the possibility of judicial appeal, administrative boards employing referees with power to make decisions should provide for the preparation of a report which would be accessible to all parties and to which

Chart showing
VARIOUS POSSIBLE DEGREES of JUDICIAL REVIEW of ADMINISTRATIVE DIVISIONS

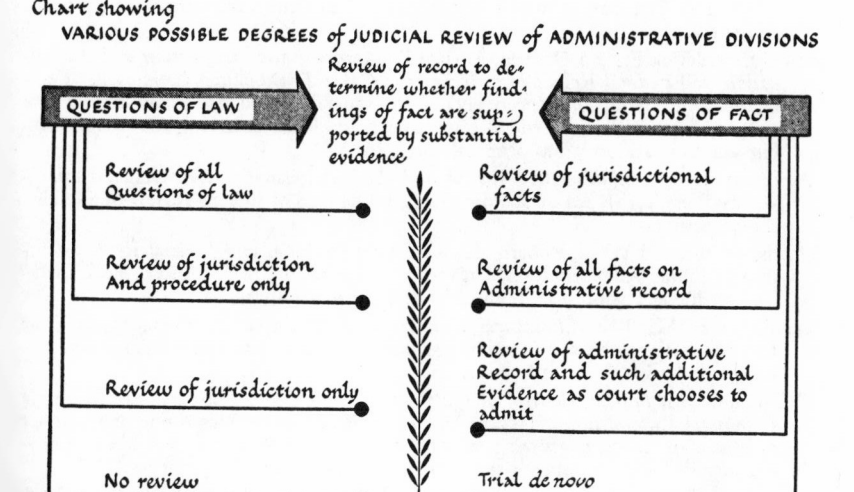

exceptions could be filed. This recommendation would not apply to a
trial examiner empowered only to take testimony but not to make findings or rulings on the evidence.

It is also recommended that, in plural member administrative agencies, the democratic principle of decision by the majority be followed.
In order to prevent unnecessary expense, it it proposed that by rule
of court the original papers and typed notes of testimony should be certified as the record in all cases, subject to the privilege of parties to print
any part thereof, if they so desire, at their own expense. Joint appeals
should, believes Mr. Faught, be encouraged wherever the interests of
two or more parties are substantially similar. Finally, he contends that
rules of court should regulate the filing of formal opinions by administrative agencies whenever such opinions would be helpful upon review
of the proceedings by a court. It has been in the effort to solve some
of these questions, on a basis as nearly uniform as differing conditions
would permit, that the states have been moving toward the adoption of
administrative procedure acts.

SELECTED REFERENCES

Attorney General's Committee on Administrative Procedure, *Report* (Washington,
1940). This is the most extensive study of the subject ever made, including separate
monographs on the procedures used in most of the larger agencies. For general
works of earlier date, see Loughran, Patrick H., *Judicial Review of Federal Executive Action* (Michie Company, Charlottesville, 1930), and Mecham, Floyd B., *A
Treatise on the Law of Administrative Offices and Administrative Officers* (Callaghan, Chicago, 1890).

Benjamin, Robert M., *Administrative Adjudication in the State of New York* (Albany, 1942). This best state study of adjudication gives some attention to the problems of review.

Blachly, Frederick F., and Oatman, Miriam E., *Administrative Legislation and Adjudication*, and *Federal Regulatory Action and Control* (Brookings Institution, Washington, 1934 and 1940, respectively). Two valuable works on administrative law and adjudication in the Federal government, the latter analyzing the present system and evaluating various proposals for reform.

Dickinson, John, *Administrative Justice and the Supremacy of Law* (Harvard University Press, 1927). An outstanding work in the field of judicial review of administrative action.

Harris, Arthur, and Ward, Robert, *Administrative Decisions and Judicial Review* (Bureau of Public Administration, University of California, 1941). An excellent analysis, containing a good deal of material relating to California.

Landis, James M., *The Administrative Process* (Yale University Press, 1938). Four lectures dealing with the functioning of administrative law and administrative tribunals, and with the controversies revolving around them.

McFarland, Carl, *Judicial Control of the Federal Trade Commission and the Interstate Commerce Commission* (Harvard University Press, 1933). This is one of a number of studies of the cases growing out of the work of particular agencies. The Commonwealth Fund published a series of such studies in the early thirties.

Pennock, J. Roland, *Administration and the Rule of Law* (Farrar & Rinehart, New York, 1941). An able and concise treatment of the various problems involved in the relations of the courts to administration.

Stephens, Harold M., *Administrative Tribunals and the Rules of Evidence* (Harvard University Press, 1933). A careful study of the court decisions.

Von Bauer, F. Trowbridge, *Federal Administrative Law* (Callaghan, Chicago, 1941) and Gellhorn, Walter, *Administrative Law — Cases and Comments*, Second Edition (Foundation Press, Brooklyn, 1947). Two casebooks, containing notes and comments.

35

FORMS OF CONTROL
OVER ADMINISTRATION

THERE seems to be a widespread and somewhat naive assumption that the task of the administrator is fairly simple. The legislature enacts a statute creating a new governmental function which may be assigned to an existing agency or to a new one created for the purpose. In either case an administrator is appointed. He is given an office, a desk, a telephone, a secretary, and a staff. What could be simpler? The statute defines his powers and duties, and he now has the necessary tools with which to proceed. He may adopt and issue rules and regulations, establish procedures, and issue orders. In short, he may now "administrate."

This is all true, but it tells only a part — often a very small part — of the story. It is true that he will be held responsible for the impartial and efficient enforcement of the law; that is the thing he was appointed to do. But he is not a free agent in making important decisions as to general policy or even in making decisions as to the application of the law in specific instances. A multitude of outside influences and considerations may enter into the decisions he makes. If he ignores them, he is certain to become involved in difficulties, and he may fail completely as an administrator.

T. V. Smith has frequently emphasized the point that the legislator in a democracy stands as a mediator between conflicting groups, interests, and points of view.[1] What Mr. Smith says of the position of the legislator often applies with equal force to an administrator. He cannot flout public opinion, the wishes of interested pressure groups, the policies of the administration of which he is a part, or the prevailing sentiment in the legislature; he cannot ignore all political considerations and expect to survive himself or to have his program succeed. It is not to be implied that he must always bow to the wishes of some outside influence, but he must certainly take all these factors into consideration when he makes important decisions. His task is not to antagonize individuals and groups but rather to secure as great a degree of cooperation and support

See his "Two Functions of the American State Legislator," *Annals*, January, 1938, 183–188.

as possible from the maximum number of both, in order that the purposes of the agency may be achieved.

Public Opinion and Pressure Group Influences

The field of public opinion, pressure groups, and propaganda is a large one which is likely many times and in many ways to influence the decisions of the administrator. It is, of course, sometimes difficult to know what the public wants, for it is large and unorganized and frequently inarticulate. There are few issues that affect the whole public; most questions concern only a limited portion of it. This portion is likely to be well organized and very articulate. It knows what it wants and how to go about obtaining it. What it wants may or may not be in the interests of the public as a whole.

Influence of Public Opinion. One of the first obligations of an administrator is to keep his finger on the pulse of public opinion on questions pertaining to his program. The most obvious index of opinion in a democratic government is the returns from the last election. "Career officials," says Paul H. Appleby on the basis of many years' experience in Washington,[2] "generally have a profound conviction of their obligation to shift ground in keeping with the shifts of public sentiment as expressed in elections. I have witnessed," he continues, "the effect of that profound conviction. I have seen career officials honestly and ably transfer their loyalties to changing officials, to changing political climates, changing legislative and administrative situations. . . . It is very much as it should be. Knowing that it is this way, citizens generally can have greater confidence in the vitality of the political processes that are necessary in a democratic society."

Another source of information regarding the climate of opinion is to be found in the opinion polls;[3] if an administrator finds that none of the polls have reported on the type of question confronting him, it should not be too difficult to arrange with one of the established polling organizations to sample opinion. The results of this method are not infallible, as the experience during the 1948 Presidential campaign well demonstrates. At the same time one should not jump to the conclusion that this procedure must always be unreliable. If the prevailing sentiment proves to be adverse, the administrator then has the opportunity to modify his procedures or to carry on a campaign of education or

[2] See Appleby, Paul H., *Big Democracy*, p. 93 (Knopf, New York, 1945).
[3] See Bernays, Edward L., "Attitude Polls — Servants or Masters?" *Public Opinion Quarterly*, Fall, 1945, pp. 464-468, and Truman, David R., "Public Opinion Research a Tool of Public Administration," *Public Administration Review*, Winter, 1945, pp. 62-72.

signed to explain to the public the nature and purpose of the program and to win their support.

Failure to do this may lead to serious consequences. When the tuberculin testing of dairy cattle was begun many years ago, the program had to be sold to the farmers, most of whom regarded it as some newfangled nonsense. In state after state this was done, so that the program went steadily forward, the percentage of cattle tested increasing from year to year. Then in the early thirties came the Iowa experience. This state had been backward, up to that time, in its testing program. A new Secretary of Agriculture resolved to correct the situation. He employed a staff of veterinarians and sent them out, with orders to test cattle. The farmers met them at the gate with clubs, pitchforks, and shovels, because they did not understand the program and because the Department had not taken the trouble to explain it to them. Such a bungling performance as this not only undid the work of many years in building up the confidence and cooperation of the farmers of the state but imposed a barrier of ill-will between the Department and the farmers which it would take years of painstaking effort to overcome.

Another case, handled more skillfully, occurred in Pennsylvania. When the State Liquor Control Board was established in anticipation of the repeal of prohibition, it carried on preliminary organization work, including the publication of a price list. There was an immediate reaction from press and public that the prices were too high, whereupon the Board undertook immediately to meet these objections by reductions and by stocking and listing less expensive brands.

Substantial benefits will accrue to the program if the administrator not only listens to public opinion but solicits an expression of opinion and the active cooperation and support of the affected groups. The United States Department of Agriculture learned this many years ago. Public hearings, referenda, and other devices may be used for this purpose. When Agriculture undertakes the administration of a new program, it does not begin by telling the people what to do and when to do it. It knows that the citizens of a free country do not like to be ordered about, and it makes an honest effort to find out what they want. Then that has been done, the subsequent problem of enforcement normally becomes relatively simple.

The Soil Conservation Program may be taken as an example. This service has developed full information as to specific areas where the problems of soil conservation are most urgent. Within the limits of its appropriation and staff it plans its work to continue existing projects and to develop new ones. Its field representatives move into a new area, speak at meetings of farmers, explain the serious effects of erosion and how contour farming will help them to save the irreplaceable top soil. In due time a referendum is held in which the farmers are asked to vote on the question of participation. If the vote is in the affirmative, a new Soil Conservation District is organized, its officers elected, and the program inaugurated.[4]

The effort to build up a supporting public opinion by enlisting the assistance of many members of the public was widely utilized by a number of agencies during World War II. The Office of Price Administration had its citizen boards in each district. Selective Service had similar boards. The Office of Civilian Defense enrolled literally thousands of persons who contributed time and effort to airplane spotting and other defense activities. In many cases the conferring of a title and the use of appropriate insignia transformed a querulous citizen into an enthusiastic supporter of the program.

Opinion research may be used not only by government agencies but by civic groups as a guide in adjusting government programs to the wishes of the public. An interesting innovation of this type was instituted in early 1947 by the Detroit Bureau of Governmental Research. Through a citizen panel which is a representative sample of the adult population, the Bureau attempts to gauge the thinking of the whole community on both current and specific issues. What do citizens think of the operation of the city Water Department? Of the state Liquor Commission? Of the state government in general? Or the city government in general?

An important phase of opinion research, says the Bureau, "is the establishment of bench marks of performance and expectation, level with which to plot trend and change." Normal elections do not provide these guides to policy for they seldom offer a clear-cut choice between alternatives. Opinion research, on the other hand, "provides the sincere and conscientious official with the means to keep in touch with the thinking of his constituents, to keep a scientific ear to the ground." The goal is to make administration responsive to the popular will. Appleby states this ideal admirably when he says [6] that "government shall be so devoted and so considerate that citizens generally need not fear it. This aspect of the freedom from fear I would hold before you as a superior guide to superior public administration."

---

[4] Various publications of the Soil Conservation Service describe their methods procedure. Mark Sullivan, in his column published October 2, 1948, had an excellent statement of the manner in which a similar procedure works in the various milksheds areas in fixing the price of milk.

[5] *Bureau Notes*, April 4, 1947; see also Truman, *op. cit.*

[6] Appleby, *op. cit.*, p. 99.

Pressure Group Influences. There is a popular impression that lobbying and pressure group tactics are confined largely to legislative procedures. Nothing could be farther from the truth. Pressure groups do try to obtain the passage of bills they want, to defeat bills they do not like, and to mold others into a form acceptable to them; but their efforts do not stop there. When they are unsuccessful in their efforts to control the legislative process, they next concentrate on the executive. Here they may, if successful, accomplish by interpretation of a statute what they failed to achieve through influence in formulating its provisions.

Some years ago Pendleton Herring made a significant study of pressure group influences on administration at the national level.[7] He points out that "when a democratic government undertakes to alleviate the maladjustments of the economic system, it stirs up a greed that it may lack power to control. The 'voice of the people' sometimes suggests the squeal of pigs at the trough." But the governmental administration is pledged to adjust its policy in the interests of the public as a whole, not to the advantage of this or that group. This concept of the public interest is a "verbal symbol designed to introduce unity, order, and objectivity into administration." It is to the bureaucracy "what the due process clause is to the judiciary." Continuing, he says:

> Its abstract meaning is vague, but its application has far-reaching effects. The radio commissioners were to execute the law in the "public interest, convenience, and necessity." The trade commissioners are to apply the law when they deem such action "to the interest of the public." Congress has frequently authorized boards and quasi-judicial commissions to determine the public interest.

Much of the difficulty these regulatory bodies experience in discharging their responsibility arises from the fact that every pressure group seeks deliberately to confuse in the public mind and in the minds of the administrative officials their own interests and purposes with those of the public. The relationships between the two are intricate and difficult of adjustment. In some cases the interests of the group may actually conform to the interests of the public, while in others the opposite is true. The official should be familiar, but not too closely identified, with the group; and he should be imbued with an earnest desire to serve the public. His task is then to resolve the issues in fairness both to the group and the public, he representing the latter. He must permit neither the persuasive representatives of the group "to pull his leg" nor pressures from the opposition to induce him to make decisions that are unnecessarily adverse to the desires and interests of the

Public Administration and the Public Interest.

group. The process of settlement thus becomes one of negotiation and adjustment, in the effort to find some common ground, some basis for agreement.

The Herring study shows that at the Federal level these groups are and have been influential in all types of agencies — in those responsible for the administration of such traditional functions as internal revenue, tariff, and foreign affairs and for the administration of regulatory functions relating to business; and in those departments like agriculture, commerce, and labor which were established to serve at least in part the needs of special interest groups. Essentially the same problems are to be found in parallel form at the state level; here the interest groups, dealing with a smaller governmental unit and with officials whom they often know personally, have frequently been even more successful. Before organized labor became strong enough to prevent it, employer organizations were often able to emasculate the labor departments, the public utilities virtually to take over the public service commissions, the private road contractors to take over the highway departments. The influence of these groups at all levels is tremendous; while it is not necessarily contrary to the public interest, administrators who work with representatives of interest groups are constantly obliged to proceed on the basis of what might be called a kind of suspicious cooperation.

An administrator cannot be too careful in the conduct of his relations with representatives of pressure groups functioning within his agency's field of activity. A number of years ago the author knew well a man appointed to an important Federal post. This man was able, had had administrative experience, and was scrupulously honest. Not long after he took office, it developed that he had given desk space in his office to an important representative of a pressure group vitally affected by his agency's program. Knowing the character of the administrator, one might feel wholly confident that this representative had not exerted any improper influence. Nevertheless the action looked bad, very bad, and soon the administrator was on his way home.

Sometimes these pressure group influences arise spontaneously and without warning. In 1945, during the process of demobilization, the War Department announced that in order to maintain a sufficient military force to discharge the nation's responsibilities in foreign lands, it would be necessary to slow down somewhat the process of returning home for discharge the men then awaiting transportation. The announcement may have been poorly timed, and it may have been prepared without proper regard to psychological factors. At any rate it gave rise to a tremendous wave of protest among the men themselves, and subsequently at home, where their mothers, wives, and sweethearts organized "no boat—no vote" demonstrations and besieged the War Department and members of Congress with letters and telegrams demanding the revocation of the order. The demonstrations brought forth a statement by the Chief of Staff to the Congress, which modified the order somewhat and speeded the move to secure necessary replacements. Such incidents are not wholly preventable, but they can be kept at a minimum.

Regulation by Conference. In thus appropriating a phrase used by Commissioner Lowell B. Mason of the Federal Trade Commission, the purpose is twofold. In an address delivered at the University of Kansas in 1947, Mr. Mason calls attention to the fact that the old method of individual prosecution in trade regulatory work was in effect a kind of shotgun method. While one violator was being apprehended and punished, a dozen others were following practices or committing acts equally objectionable. He quotes with approval President Truman's suggestion in his annual message of 1947 that more uniform and effective enforcement might be obtained under present-day conditions by the use of the trade conference method, under which the Antitrust Division of the Department of Justice would concentrate its efforts on major violations of the antitrust laws, and the Commission would "increase its effectiveness by operating on an industry-wide basis rather than through the slower procedure of individual complaints."

The Commission, continued the President, "will also sponsor a larger number of industrial conferences designed to locate and eliminate unfair trade practices through cooperative actions." This proposal has the additional merit of soliciting the cooperation of those subject to regulation, thereby exemplifying the ideals of democratic administration. Such cooperation is incomparably better than the group pressures which so often resulted from the earlier enforcement techniques. In no other way can the opinion of the groups be brought to bear more effectively upon the determination and the execution of public policy.

Governmental Controls

Governmental controls arise from the relations of the executive to the legislative and judicial branches of the government and from the administrator's responsibility to his superior officers. Stated in another way, the administrator in making decisions must be mindful of the possibility of legislative interference with his program, of judicial review of the decisions of his agency, or even of a test case on the constitutionality of the statute under which he operates, and of the possible reactions of his administrative superior to his policies and procedures. Under the American system of government these are all necessary and proper controls or influences on administrative policies.

Legislative Controls. Legislative controls over administration are of several types, affecting policy, organization, finances, and decisions in individual cases. The policy controls have to do with the provisions of the act itself. The powers and duties of the agency, specified by law, were established by the legislature. What the legislature has given, it can modify or revoke. The administrator must have constantly in mind the possibility that, if the agency so conducts its affairs that large numbers of citizens are prompted to complain to their representatives, the legislature may undertake to revise or amend the act, curtail his powers, or even repeal the statute. If the administrator is interested in his agency's program, he certainly will not want to bring about, through sheer administrative ineptitude, its curtailment or abandonment.

Not only the powers of the agency but the general framework of its organization are derived from statutory enactment. If the legislature comes to believe — whether or not the belief is well founded — that the administration is weak, ineffective, or so conducted as to impair the personal and property rights of individuals or corporations, the legislature can and may change the organization. If the agency is independent, it may be combined with another, a commission may be substituted for a single administrator, or some other form of reorganization may be adopted, to ease out the objectionable executive. And of course the administration, in an effort to forestall or appease the legislative wrath, may sacrifice a member of its staff.

Still more important are the legislature's financial controls over administration. In a democratic system the legislature has control of the purse strings. It has a duty to prescribe general policy, and also a duty not to interfere with details of internal administration. If it does not like an agency, a program, or an administrator, it is the easiest thing in the world to cut down on the funds allotted. However unjustified such a cut may be, it can always be urged that the legislature acted solely in the interests of economy, which is always assumed to be a good thing. The public, not well informed and not greatly interested, is likely to accept the decision. The significance is that the administrator must of necessity avoid actions which are likely to antagonize members of the legislature unnecessarily.[8] Several illustrations of legislative interfer

---

[8] That administrative officials do not always take cuts in appropriations without protest is well illustrated from remarks by Representative Norris Cotton before the New Hampshire Federation of Taxpayers Associations in the spring of 1947. He said: "The departments of government do not content themselves with the mere presentation of

ence with administration in the matter of personnel and salaries were presented in Chapter 28.

The legislature is responsible not only for providing funds for the operation of the various departments and agencies but for general surveillance of these departments, to make sure that the money appropriated to them is properly spent and that the services required by law are provided. While it is never an easy matter for the legislature to obtain from the executive the information necessary for making intelligent judgments, the legislature does have at its disposal a number of tools which, if properly employed, are reasonably effective. These are:

1. The members have an opportunity to question department representatives about the activities of their agency at the time of the budget hearings and at such other times as their presence may be requested.

2. They receive regular reports from the auditing of the financial records of the departments and agencies.

3. The executive agencies are required by law to file annually (in most cases) reports with regard to specified phases of their operations. In the Federal government the number of such reports reaches rather formidable proportions.[9]

4. In order that the Congress might be better informed with regard to the operations of the executive agencies, it was provided in the Legislative Reorganization Act of 1946 that a staff of permanent investigators should be employed to analyze and report upon the work of the various agencies, both in their central offices and in the field. The House Appropriations Committee later enlisted the services of some thirty outstanding businessmen to make surveys of the larger Federal agencies and their budget requirements for fiscal 1949.[10]

---

their cause but they sometimes resort to desperate and questionable means to prevent budget reduction. When the general budget bill was before Congress, the War Department notified many Congressmen by telephone that the airfields in his District would be discontinued if their budget was reduced. When the Customs Service appropriation was reduced 10 per cent, the head of the Bureau took no steps to reduce in number the 33,000 employees in Washington but notified the 25,000 operatives in the field that their jobs were in danger and told them to build a fire under their Congressman.

". . . It is obviously impossible and impractical for Congress to attempt to say what employee should be dispensed with and what services should be curtailed. It can only reduce after careful consideration by a reasonable percentage the appropriation of a department, division, or bureau, and rely upon the head of the bureau to apply the necessary economy. *In almost every instance, bureau heads apply the reduction not where it hurts the least but where it hurts the most, so that every benefactor of the department will apply pressure to Congress to restore the reduction.*" (Italics supplied.)

On March 24, 1947, the Director of the Division of Labor Standards sent out a memorandum to the subscribers to the agency's *Legislative Report* – a current report on state legislation – which read as follows: "I regret to inform you that we will be unable to continue our bimonthly *Legislative Report* for the present sessions of the state legislatures. The House Appropriations Committee has made no provision for the continuance of the Division of Labor Standards for the next fiscal year. We have been advised to separate personnel immediately so that terminal leave may be paid out of current appropriations. After these adjustments have been made, if at all possible we will try to complete our annual survey of labor legislation enacted in 1947."

It takes about thirty pages of fine print merely to list them; see *Reports to Be Made Congress* (79th Cong., 2nd Sess., House Document No. 573, 1946).

Reported by John Cramer in *The News* (Washington), January 10, 1948, p. 2.

In still another way the legislature, or rather its individual membe
may influence the decisions of the administrator. It is a common
though perhaps a deplorable practice of Americans to carry any p
sonal problem relating to government to their representative in t
legislature. Thus the legislator becomes a kind of errand boy, a ki
of go-between. If a citizen wants a government job and is declared i
eligible by the Civil Service Commission, he beseeches his represen
tive to take the matter up with the Commission. If he wants a licen
an approval, or a contract with the government, he prevails upon l
representative to see what he can do to "put it over." While most leg
lators are reasonable human beings to whom the agency's action may
explained and justified, there is a natural disposition on the part of a
ministrators "to go along" if at all possible. After all, the legislator ha
vote when the agency's appropriation comes up for consideration.

Judicial and Legal Controls. There are times when an administrat
may welcome judicial clarification of the meaning of the act und
which he operates, or of the limits of his powers. Very often, howev
with a new agency such tests are to be avoided, partly because t
courts are frequently hostile to a new agency, as they were for ma
years to the Interstate Commerce Commission, and overlook no oppc
tunity to limit or circumscribe its powers.[11] Later, after the agency
more firmly established and its powers have been defined and au
mented where necessary by legislative amendments to the original a
relatively few occasions for judicial appeals will arise. In making de
sions, however, the administrator may well bear in mind the possibili
of such an outcome and consider whether or not a court review wou
help or hinder the program of the agency at that particular time.

The courts annually pass upon multitudes of questions involvi
the power of administrative officers to do or not to do some particul
thing,[12] and during World War II an Emergency Court of Appe
was established in Washington to handle the special problems of t
war agencies. Control through judicial review is not, however, by a
means the only type of legal control. In every jurisdiction there is
attorney general or a corporation counsel whose duty is to advise t
administration on legal matters. The opinions of this officer normal
indicate the attitude of the administration with regard to the meani

---

[11] Sharfman, I. L., *The Interstate Commerce Commission*, 5 vols. (Commonwea
Fund, New York, 1931–1937).

[12] For instance, in December, 1946, the Pennsylvania Superior Court ruled that
Commonwealth could not seize an automobile "used to facilitate a gambling operatic
on the ground that the car "is not a gambling device or apparatus in the sense t
roulette wheels, slot machines, etc., are."

of a particular statute or ordinance. Although used as working rules, they have no binding legal effect; they stand as official interpretations of the law unless or until they are challenged in the courts and reversed or modified by judicial opinion.[13]

Administrative Controls. The individual who is a member of an administrative hierarchy is subject to the supervision and control of those whose position is higher than his own, just as those of lower rank within his own organization are subject to his direction. Consequently he has an obligation to make his policies conform to those of the agency, and some administrators are so afraid of incurring the displeasure of the boss by doing something "out of line" that they normally refrain from taking any action at all without approval from the front office. The types of administrative controls and the methods of their exercise are matters of internal management which have been discussed elsewhere. The concern at the moment is with the fact that the approval or disapproval of higher echelons of authority is one more of the factors influencing the decisions of an administrator.

Necessary and desirable as such controls are, they are subject to possible abuse. They can be properly exercised only when the boss is big enough and broad-minded enough to encourage initiative on the part of his staff even though they sometimes make mistakes, and where the staff members have sufficient backbone to do something when necessary without worrying unduly about whether the boss is going to like it.

Political Controls

Political influence and controls may be observed in government administration at all levels, but because of size and distance they tend to become stronger in the smaller units and weaker in the larger. In a great many cities the influence of politics in police administration has been and still is notorious. Lawbreakers purchase immunity if not actual protection by regular payments to the policeman on the beat or to the political organization or to both. Assessments on property are increased or decreased in proportion to the political influence of the property owner rather than in accordance with market values or improvements. Weights and measures inspection is often completely controlled by

---

The opinions of the attorneys general have been for some years collected and digested by the Council of State Governments. Frequently opinions relating to the work a department are featured in its bulletins or other publications. Thus *California's Health* regularly runs a column headed "Opinions of the Attorney General"; in the issue of February 15, 1947, rulings were digested on the power of mosquito abatement districts to borrow, on the formation of hospital districts, and on joint city-county sewerage contracts.

politics. Building permits are granted or withheld on the basis of political influence or the lack of it, and building inspection is often conducted on the same basis.

A striking illustration occurred many years ago when John F. Hylan was Mayor of New York City. The *New York World*, then a force to be reckoned with and still functioning with the crusading zeal of the Pulitzers, made certain charges against him. The charges were perfectly true. Nevertheless Hylan brought a libel suit against the paper. The paper won the case in court, but it was a Pyrrhic victory. Hylan lost the battle, but he won the war. Shortly after the case was concluded, the building inspectors appeared at the Pulitzer Building on Park Row to look over the property. It had recently been inspected and approved, but that made no difference. The inspectors proceeded to condemn every fire escape, fire extinguisher, and fire hose in the entire building, with the result that the company was obliged to spend many thousands of dollars to purchase and install new equipment.

At the state level familiar illustrations of the political control of administrative decisions were formerly found in the selection of state depositories, in the designation of state highways for construction and repair, and in the enforcement of safety regulations in factories and in many other places. Political influence was often combined with pressure group activities in the field of public utility regulation.

At all levels political influence in the making of appointments is or may be strong, even when the administration professes the purest of intentions. A few years ago a new superintendent of public instruction was appointed in a large eastern state. He did not want to take the position unless he would be free to do a high-grade professional job, unless he could be assured that politics would have no part in the administration of his department. He was told that this would be the case, and he was naive enough to accept the assurance at face value. He had not been in office two weeks before the governor sent for him one day and opened the conversation by inquiring when he was going "to get rid of those — — Republican bureau chiefs over there."

The influence of politics on appointments is not always so crude or so obvious, but it is usually present. The administrator who attempts to flout the wishes of the organization is likely to be in for serious trouble — possible removal or impeachment; but so is the administrator who delivers himself body and soul into the hands of the organization. The only safe procedure, from the point of view of good government, is for the executive to insist upon the observance of certain standards of fitness and competence, working with the organization within the its of those standards. Theodore Roosevelt and other outstanding litical executives have done this successfully.[14]

These illustrations suggest that, whether wittingly or unwittingly, e boundary line between politics and administration is often hazy. discussing this problem before the International City Managers Asiation in 1946, Professor Merriam took the position that there could no magic formula — that the answer must be based on common sense d sound judgment. On such a basis the job of responsible policyermining agencies would include laying down general rules, orders, d plans, allocating available resources for public purposes, and genl supervision of the administrative management in the government. e role of administrative management should consist in making the es effective; in exercising responsibility for personnel, budget prepaion, and preliminary planning; and for providing public service as a fied and going concern.[15]

entific and Investigatory Controls

ntrols over administration emanating from scientific research and intigation are relatively recent in most fields, but they are becoming reasingly important. Those relating to matters in the field of natural ence, such as health and safety, are older and better established than se in the field of the social sciences, among which may be mentioned t controls, price fixing, and market stabilization, based upon statisal controls, surveys, and investigations made either by the agency ff or by a special planning staff.

ntrols in the Natural Sciences. Regardless of the strength of conry pressures and influences few administrators today would be fooldy enough to argue with doctors and sanitarians when facing a tical problem in the field of public health. If there is an epidemic of allpox, and wholesale vaccinations are required, arrangements are de to provide them. If an outbreak of infantile paralysis makes it essary to close the schools, the movies, or even the churches, the sing orders are issued. If an epidemic of influenza threatens, approate measures recommended by the medical profession take precede over the desires of those engaged in the amusement business, who uld naturally prefer to remain open as usual. Because the public re-

─────────────

or a full discussion of the relations of the governor to his state party organization, the author's *American State Government,* Third Edition, pp. 379-381 (Heath, ton, 1946).

ee Merriam, Charles E., "Danger Zones Between Politics and Administration," *lic Management,* October, 1946, pp. 290-291.

gards the public health as vital, measures necessary for its protection are given a position of priority.

The strength of the recommendations of scientists is recognized, as it should be, in other fields. Aviation is controlled by Weather Bureau reports of storms and by storm warnings. Merchant shipping is subject to similar controls. Those who are engaged in agricultural administration are accustomed to fashioning their policies to conform to the findings of scientists with regard to the control of plant and animal diseases, methods of cultivating the soil, and methods of controlling flood waters and distributing moisture through irrigation.

Controls in the Social Sciences. Perhaps because they are newer and less well established, the recommendations of social scientists are by no means certain of like consideration. The man in the street thinks he knows just as much about complicated social, political, and economic problems as persons who have devoted their lives to research in the social sciences. He still thinks that all one needs is a little common sense, and that he knows all the answers.

The social scientist knows only too well that he does *not* know all the answers but he does have at his command a vast store of knowledge on social, political, and economic phenomena which, when properly utilized, can save both legislators and administrators from many serious errors. Welfare policies can be adjusted both to the social needs of individual clients and to economic conditions existing at the time. Agricultural policies can be adjusted to market conditions and the existing price structure. Credit policies need to be adjusted to business conditions. Part of these adjustments are controlled by legislation, part by administrative action within the framework of the controlling legislation.

In some areas, where alternative policies are available for choice, the wishes of the public may be consulted. The point is that if choices are to be so determined, the methods employed should be scientifically sound. Since a referendum to obtain the views of the whole public is not always possible, methods of scientific sampling may be employed to ascertain the preferences of the group affected. The United States Department of Agriculture, as noted earlier, has employed this technique in connection with many of its programs.[16]

---

[16] See Howard, L. Vaughn, "The Agricultural Referendum," *Public Administration Review*, Winter, 1942, pp. 9–26. On the use of public opinion research and attitude polls, see Bernays, and Truman, *op. cit.*, and Kriesberg, Martin, "What Congressmen and Administrators Think of the Polls," *Public Opinion Quarterly*, Fall, 1945, pp. 33–337. Afros, John L., "Labor Participation in the O.P.A.," *American Political Science Review*, June, 1946, pp. 458–484 is also pertinent.

The Place of the Expert. All these questions lead to consideration of the basic question of the place of the expert in administration in a democratic society. It is often said that democracy insures the right of the people to decide things for themselves, even though they make mistakes. The people may have a right to make wrong decisions, but there is not much excuse for their doing so frequently. By proper guidance and adequate information regarding the possible alternatives — but not by dictation — they may often be spared the painful consequences of unwise or unjustifiable decisions.

This is where the need for the services of the expert arises. The American people are devoted to education but for some reason are afraid of the person who is educated. Through no fault on his part the learning that a man has, often establishes a barrier between himself and the people. At the same time whatever knowledge he possesses, he holds in trust; it belongs not to him but to all mankind. The people take their guidance, as a rule, not directly from the expert but from their political leadership. The greatest opportunity of the expert, therefore, comes in providing information and guidance for persons in high public office.

The expert must, therefore, under present-day conditions work in the background. He should be willing to shun personal publicity and acclaim, having rather "the passion for anonymity" to which President Roosevelt referred in relation to the administrative assistants to the President in 1937. This is essential in the personal relationship which comes to exist between the expert and the political leader who is responsible for determining administrative policies. The latter "takes the rap" if his policies prove either unsound or unpopular. By the same token he should be permitted to reap whatever benefit may come to him and his party as a result of policies which prove beneficial or popular.

In such a confidential relationship an expert who is a seeker after personal publicity has no place; he can, in fact, do great damage to the cause to which, as a scholar, he should above all be devoted — the cause of the use of accurate information as a guide for public policy.

More and more responsible elected officials, at all levels of government, are turning to experts to help them give citizens more and better public services for their tax dollars. The late Mayor La Guardia, practical politician that he was, asserted that "government administration is science" and that we need "government by specialists"; and he acted on this basis in selecting his administrative aids. In June, 1948, the American Municipal Association reported that local governments, caught between inflation on the one hand and demands for expanded public services on the other, were turning to management experts for assistance. Boosting revenues helps, but there are limits to this type of relief. The best solution lies in increased efficiency of operations. Management specialists, said the Association, "generally conclude each study with a precise plan for administrative reorganization of the city. Often they recommend specific shifts or clarifications of authority and responsibility among top city officials as a further means to greater efficiency." Thus San Francisco plans to spend $100,000 for an efficiency survey of all municipal activities in an effort to eliminate overlapping functions; New York City's fire and police departments have established new research units which will specialize in efficiency studies.[17]

Investigation and Research. Research that may be of value to administrators is carried on by various agencies, some governmental, some quasi-public, some private. As has been shown earlier, there is a growing tendency for government agencies to carry a permanent research staff for assistance in the solution of problems. Of the quasi-public type, the bureaus of public administration in the large universities are important. Among the private agencies one notes the work done by citizen organizations, foundations, privately supported bureaus of research, taxpayers' organizations, and others.[18]

"Investigation" has developed, governmentally, an unfortunate suggestion of punitive measures for some supposed or alleged wrongdoing. Investigation should be regarded merely as inquiry undertaken for the purpose of disclosing the facts regarding some particular problem situation. The common practice is for such inquiries to be conducted by members of the agency staff either on a continuing basis or special assignment. A generally useful method of organization is to be found in the British and Canadian royal commissions of inquiry adopted in American practice by Presidential commissions and by such departments of investigation as have been pioneered in New York State and New York City.[20]

Presidential commissions have frequently been created in recent decades, sometimes by Executive Order or formal proclamation, more often by some more or less informal device such as a letter, a press release, or a telephone conversation. Among the more common purpose

---

17 PACH *News Bulletin*, June 14, 1948.
18 See Anderson, William, and Gaus, John M., *Research in Public Administr* (Public Administration Service, Chicago, 1945), and the Egger and Martin title university bureaus of public administration.
19 See volume by Clokie and Robinson; also Gosnell, Harold F., "British Royal missions of Inquiry," *Political Science Quarterly*, March, 1934, pp. 84–118, and Hod J. E., "Royal Commissions of Inquiry in Canada," *Public Administration Re* Winter, 1949, pp. 22–29.
20 See volumes by Marcy, Missall, and Seidman.

of such bodies, according to the classification used by Marcy, are fact finding and opinion guiding, administration, and inquiry. In order to establish a yardstick by which one may evaluate their effectiveness for the latter purpose, he quotes a list of eight features essential to the successful operation of the British royal commissions: [21]

. Prestige from the royal warrant
. Sense of public duty on the part of the members and the fact that they receive no pay
. Creation only when there is a public demand or clear need for them
. Commissions of a representative character, in some cases impartial, in others, expert, but generally representative of the main interests concerned
. Proper constitution of commissions with terms carefully stated
. Granting of wide powers in connection with committee's own procedures, type of hearings, etc.
Selection of a good chairman
Ability of the commission to crown its efforts by having its recommendations adopted

Marcy suggests a ninth feature, namely, the experience and ability of the secretary upon whom so much depends and to whom credit is rarely given. He concludes that "the only commissions in the United States which can hope to have each of these features — features essential to good fact finding — are those created by the President."

Since 1907 New York State has had on the statute books the Moreland Act, under the terms of which: [22]

The governor is authorized at any time, either in person or by one or more persons appointed by him for the purpose, to examine and investigate the management of the affairs of any department, board, bureau, or commission of the state. The governor and the persons so appointed by him are empowered to subpoena and enforce the attendance of witnesses, to administer oaths and examine witnesses under oath, and to require the production of any books or papers deemed relevant or material. Whenever any person so appointed shall not be regularly in the service of the state his compensation and all necessary expenses of such examinations and investigations shall be paid from the treasury out of any appropriations made for the purpose under the order of the governor and the audit and warrant of the comptroller.

This legislation grew partly out of the insistence of Governor Hughes that sufficient power must be centered in the hands of the governor to insure responsibility, and partly out of his own experience as investigator for the Stevens and the Armstrong committees. The legislation, the principle of which is now accepted and well established

---

Davies, A. Mervyn, "Brains in Government — Commissions to Find the Facts," *——*, May, 1937, pp. 310–315, and Marcy, pp. 102–103.
Laws 1907, Chapter 539, now Section 8 of the Executive Law, as amended by Laws *—* Chapter 131. Quoted here from Missall, pp. 4–5.

in approximately one third of the states, represented a distinct de
ture from what was then the prevailing practice.[23] As Missall says:
granting the governor a general authority to investigate state de
ments, it shared a power with him formerly only delegated by
legislature for specific purposes. The Moreland Act, accordingly
came one of the first contributions to the current development o
executive office. By altering the power relationship between the
ernor and the administrative agencies, it provided the executive o
with an important tool for its growth as the agency responsible fo
ministrative management." [24] In New York the authority grante
this legislation has been repeatedly used and has been highly succe
in operation. The list of Moreland commissioners includes such d
guished names as George Alger, George Gordon Battle, Rober
Benjamin, Archie O. Dawson, Frederick E. Crane, Robert Moses
Lindsay Rogers. The results of some of these investigations have
significant in the history of the state.

In the city of New York the Department of Investigation w
process of development as far back as 1873, when the offices o
Commissioners of Accounts were created. From 1916 to 1924 th
sponsibility was vested in a single Commissioner of Accounts;
1924 to 1938, in the Department of Investigation and Accounts
from 1938 on, in accordance with Sections 801–805 of the present C
ter, in the Department of Investigation. Writing in 1941, Seidman
acterized it as representing "seventy years of trial and error and
cess." In this day of the strengthening of staff services for execu
Seidman takes the position that "if there were no Department o
vestigation in New York City, it would be necessary to create on
With a small budget, a remarkably small staff, and a flexible int
organization, the accomplishments of the Department have been
worthy indeed. Although investigations may originate from no
than half a dozen sources, the office actually functions largely as d
Moreland commissioners at the state level, as an extension of the
of the chief executive, in supplying the latter with facts about the
ernment. Since 1938 the investigation of official irregularities has
the major type of work of the Department, constituting nearly ha

---

[23] It is astonishing that at this late date, in two thirds of the states the governor
without an independent power of investigation. Missall groups the states, as of 1
three groups: fourteen states with no provision for executive inquiry; fifteen state
some legislation on the subject; nineteen states (not including New York) with
tutional or statutory provisions which in varying fashion approximate the Mo
Act. Only four states in the latter group have provisions substantially equival
those of New York: Idaho, Montana, New Jersey, and Wisconsin.
[24] Missall, p. 9; Chapter 2 deals with the origin of the act. One should not los
of the fact that this power may be subject to abuse.

he workload. Specific subjects of inquiry have included administration
of relief, of the election law, of the foreign trade zone, and of public
printing. In one of his annual reports Commissioner Herlands wrote: [25]

This Department is attempting to put into operation the principles of scientific reform. Scientific reform means continuous modernization and reorganiza-
on of the governmental machinery to meet new problems and new situations.
uch inquiry is a necessary part of the regular functions of government. The
roper discharge of that function is the task we have set for ourselves.

tatistical Services. As the Hoover Commission pointed out in its re-
ort on statistical activities, "Americans are a fact-minded people.
'hey want to know the magnitude of every facet of national life. They
ant to measure everything in which they are interested." The result
that literally thousands of employees in the national, state, and local
overnments are engaged in statistical work of various kinds. It is re-
rted that in the Federal government alone, outside of the Depart-
nt of National Defense, 10,500 persons are employed full time for
h work, at an estimated cost of about $43,000,000.

This is no new fancy; on the contrary, vast quantities of statistical
ta have been collected, compiled, and published by government
ncies over the years, on the theory that the information would be of
erest to someone and that it might be of value in developing and en-
cing public policy. The principal faults have been the lack of plan-
g, coordination, and continuity. Lack of planning has been evident
oughout. In the Federal government, prior to 1933, there were no
trols whatever over the statistical activities of the departments and
ncies; the mere listing in a mimeographed directory of the adminis-
ive and supervisory personnel of these agencies, located in Wash-
on, took eighty-five pages. In 1933 the Central Statistical Agency
established "to plan and promote improvement, development, and
rdination of Federal and other statistical services." Since 1939 the
tion has been in the Bureau of the Budget, where a Division of
stical Standards has been set up. Progress has been made, but much
e remains to be done.[26]

t present the work of collecting and publishing statistics is still
ormed by many different agencies. In some cases, as with the Bu-
of the Census or the Bureau of Labor Statistics, it is their primary

---

oted by Seidman, *op. cit.,* p. 150.
the historical background of this problem, see Social Science Research Council,
nment Statistics (New York, 1937); American Statistical Institute, *Statistical
ties of the United States* (Washington, 1941); and such Congressional hearings as
on H. R. 4781 (79th Cong., 2nd Sess., 1946) and on H. R. 1821 (80th Cong., 1st
947). Appendix D of the reports of the Hoover Commission contains the task
report on statistical agencies.

function, while with others like the Social Security Administration or the Securities and Exchange Commission, it is a by-product of their normal activities. Some agencies, like the Council of Economic Advisors, analyze statistical data collected by other agencies, while at least two agencies carry on research on the means of improving statistical techniques. The Hoover Commission found that this system still permitted overlapping and duplication, that many of the statistics gathered were of questionable value, that delays in publication tended to impair the value of others, that the collection process imposed considerable burdens upon private firms and individuals, and that a service charge might be made for much of the material now distributed gratis.

The problem of coordination arises on both an interagency and an intra-agency basis. In the former case the effort must be made to guide the statistical program in such a manner as to provide necessary information for the use of all government agencies — not merely the one collecting the data — and of the public and so far as possible to avoid overlapping and duplication of effort. On the intra-agency basis the problem is largely one of digesting and arranging the data so that they may be presented in meaningful form. There is little or no justification for the expense involved in the publication of vast quantities of undigested data.

Continuity is of vital importance. Ordinarily a single isolated batch of figures is of little value. It is only with the accumulation of data over some appreciable period of time that statistical information reaches its maximum usefulness in making comparisons and in indicating trends. Legislators seem often to forget this. When a set of figures is broken through failure to appropriate the necessary funds, it is rarely possible to repair the damage. The original data may be lost, and even if the project is later restored, time and funds are rarely sufficient to do more than carry the current workload. When so much depends on the continuity of statistical compilations, the need of careful planning becomes even more important, in order to make sure that the data collected are the ones most likely to reveal, on a long-range basis, the type of information desired.

SELECTED REFERENCES

Blaisdell, Donald C., *Economic Power and Political Pressures* (TNEC Monograph No. 26, Washington, 1941), and Herring, E. Pendleton, *Public Administration the Public Interest* (McGraw-Hill, New York, 1936). Excellent studies of the and influence of pressure groups and lobbies at the Federal level — administrative as well as legislatively.

Commission on Organization of the Executive Branch of the Government, *Budget and Accounting*, which contains the report on statistical activities (Washington 1949).

Egger, Rowland, Ed., *A Critical Appraisal of University Bureaus of Public Administration* (Bureau of Public Administration, University of Virginia, 1948), and Martin, Roscoe C., Ed., *The University Bureaus of Public Administration* (Bureau of Public Administration, University of Alabama, 1946). Two symposia on the organization and functioning of these bureaus by carefully selected contributors – those who direct them and those who use their services.

Gill, Norman N., *Municipal Research Bureaus* (American Council of Public Affairs, Washington, 1942), and Seidman, Harold, *Investigating Municipal Administration* (Columbia University Press, 1941). Best studies of fact finding and its influence at the municipal level, the first by private agencies, the second by a public agency.

Graves, W. Brooke, *The Administration of the Lobby Registration Provisions of the Legislative Reorganization Act of 1946* (Legislative Reference Service, Library of Congress, Washington, 1949). A study of experience during the life of the 80th Congress.

Gruening, Ernest, *The Public Pays: A Story of Power Propaganda* (Vanguard Press, New York, 1931). A case study of the influence of the power lobby two decades ago.

Herring, E. Pendleton, *Presidential Leadership* (Farrar & Rinehart, New York, 1940), and Laski, Harold J., *The American President: An Interpretation* (Harpers, New York, 1940). Two studies of the influence of top-level management on both executive and legislative policies.

McCune, Wesley, *The Farm Bloc* (Doubleday, Doran, Garden City, 1943). A student of agricultural problems analyzes the pressure group activities of the farm lobby.

McGeary, M. Nelson, *The Development of Congressional Investigative Power* (Columbia University Press, 1940). Most recent of several good studies of the Congressional powers of investigation; for purposes of comparison, see Clokie, Hugh M., and Robinson, J. William, *Royal Commissions of Inquiry* (Stanford University Press, 1937). On the President's powers of investigation, see Marcy, Carl, *Presidential Commissions* (King's Crown Press, New York, 1945). Missall, J. Ellsworth, *The Moreland Act: Executive Inquiry in the State of New York* (King's Crown Press, New York, 1946) deals with the same problem at the state level.

Tead, Ordway, *Democratic Administration* (Association Press, New York, 1945) and *The Art of Leadership* (McGraw-Hill, New York, 1935). Recognized authority on leadership emphasizes its influence in administration.

White, Leonard D., "Legislative Responsibility for the Public Service," in Martin, Roscoe C., Ed., *New Horizons in Public Administration* (University of Alabama, 1946). Excellent discussion of an important but often neglected influence on administration.

36

PUBLIC RELATION!

ANY organization, no matter how efficient it may be, will experienc
difficulty in carrying out its program unless it develops a favorabl
community opinion. Good public relations are necessary for the cor
tinued success of both public and private organizations, although fc
different reasons. In the case of a private enterprise, they are essenti
to keep business coming in; with a public organization they are a pr
requisite for maximum effectiveness in terms of service to the publi

The purpose of a public relations program in an agency is twofol
first, to inform the public regarding the nature and scope of the ser
ices available; second, to develop in the public mind an attitude of co
fidence in the agency, a general belief that the staff is competent, fa
and devoted to the public interest. In this connection almost no det
is so insignificant as to be unworthy of consideration. Such a progr;
can in fact be carried out only by giving careful and continuous att{
tion to a myriad of details, the neglect of any one of which may off
the effect of months or even years of painstaking attention to oth{

The more unpopular the governmental function may be, the m{
necessary it becomes to develop a favorable community opinion
garding it. Police regulations are never popular; public understand
of the need for them must be established, and public confidence in
ability and integrity of the organization performing them must
created. Other examples might be found in the activities of many of
emergency war agencies and in the operation of inspection services.
agencies – and agencies with police functions in particular – must
terpret their acts in such a way as to gain public support for t
programs and policies.[1]

The public relations program has many aspects, including the ⲉ
tions of the department or agency with other governmental units; ⲉ
lic reporting, both for individual units and for the government
whole, and the use of available media in connection therewith; th
fect of informal contacts; and finally, the difficult problem of enli:

[1] This problem, as related to police administration, is discussed by O. W. Wils
Graham, George A., and Reining, Henry, Jr., *Regulatory Administration*, pp.
(Wiley, New York, 1943).

public assistance and support through the participation of citizens in the administration of the program. Several years ago the Civil Service Assembly published a significant report of its Committee on Public Relations, dealing with the subject from the point of view of the public

General Considerations in Government Public Relations

BASIC ASSUMPTIONS	OBSTACLES
There is not just "the public," but many and varied publics representing a wide range of interests and making a variety of demands.	The complexity of modern government. The usually indifferent attitude of the general public.
Because of the various publics concerned, the public relations program must be broken down into a number of elements. No single report or activity will be sufficient, but rather there must be a comprehensive system which covers each of the publics.	The lack of appreciation on the part of many public officials of the importance of their responsibility in the matter of public relations.
This program must be based upon the presentation of information which flows readily from the records of the agency.	The lack of objective indices to measure the effectiveness of the methods used.
Since considerable competition exists for the attention of the public, the governmental agency must use techniques of presentation that are at least as effective as those of its rivals.	The limited funds available for public relations activities and the consequent necessity of foregoing professional technical assistance.
Public relations is concerned not only with publicity of a more or less formal character but also with personal contacts of every sort between public officials and employees and members of the public. Surprisingly little attention has been paid to this aspect of public relations. Obviously, the most telling impressions gained by the public are in connection with those immediate personal contacts with officials and employees acting in both their official and unofficial capacities.	The difficulty of maintaining impartiality. The difficulty of persuading the public that public relations devices are not necessarily propaganda. The honest fear that "rugged individualists" have of too much government, and their tendency to interpret all governmental publicity as propaganda.
Public relations involves a flow of information and understanding not alone from the agency to the publics, but from the publics to the agency. There must be a "two-way street."	

personnel agency.[2] While primarily concerned with the personnel phase of administration, the summary of general considerations is applicable with slight modification to the general field of public administration. The Committee listed the broad assumptions on which such a program should be based, and the major obstacles to its accomplishment. These are presented in the above table in parallel columns.

Although a good public relations program is essential to the proper conduct of an agency, this is one of the first places where the legisla-

Public Relations of Public Personnel Agencies, pp. 8-9 (Chicago, 1941).

ture feels at liberty to make cuts when a period of budget slashing comes along. This attitude springs from what seems to be the inherent suspicion of many people toward what they fear may become "though control" on the part of government. There seems to be a fear that governmental publicity is being or may be used to build up someone politically or to "put something over" on the legislature or the public, a belief that the executive branch — whether Federal or state — has no moral right to employ experts in "purposeful information." [3] Such an attitude, of course, overlooks the proper responsibility of governmen to provide some leadership for the people and to help them solve prob lems confronting them. The executive is authorized by the constitu tion to make recommendations to the legislature, and there is no goo reason why it should not make them to the people for their informatio and consideration. In either case the people still have the right to mak the final decision.

Effect of Relations with Other Governmental Agencies

The public relations program, broadly conceived, includes not only t direct relations of the agency with individuals and private organizatio but its relations with other governmental agencies at its own level a at other levels. These will be considered under three headings: rel tions with other executive departments and agencies at its own lev relations with the legislature, and relations with agencies at other leve One might contend that the basic problem here was one of coordir tion — or the lack of it — and that this is primarily a matter of inter management. That may be true, but the repercussions of poor coor nation upon public relations may be serious. Conversely, proper ordination of policies and programs as between agencies contribu greatly to the effectiveness of the public relations of all of them, as good employee relations within the agency itself. It is these aspects the problem that are to be considered here.

Relations with Other Executive Agencies. Nothing is more destruc of good public relations on the part of an agency than for the pu to discover that its policies are wholly unrelated to those of some o agency dealing with the same or a related subject. In a large gov mental organization such conflict of jurisdiction and policy is depl ble but to some extent inevitable. The assignment of jurisdiction to ferent agencies is bound to produce a certain amount of overlap and duplication. With proper coordination this need not have

---

[3] This problem is fully discussed in McCamy.

erious consequences on the public relations of either agency; without
t, the effects may be disastrous. Citizens are perplexed and often right-
ully indignant when one agency tells them to do one thing, another
he exact opposite.

The lack of coordination in such situations grows out of a number
f factors. One may be poor supervision and staff work at the top level.
nother is the tendency among government agencies to regard their
wn programs as all-important and to adopt an attitude of contempt
1d/or open hostility toward any other agency whose activities either
verlap or border on their own. A third explanation may be found in
e surprising fact that government officials in different agencies in the
me city are often totally unknown to one another. Since these prob-
ms have been discussed in earlier chapters, only the solutions need be
entioned here. The first two can be solved by proper efforts at coordi-
tion on the part of top management, the third by bringing executives
m different agencies together in such organizations as the Federal
siness Association, personnel councils, and finance councils. Once
e initial contacts have been made, numerous informal contacts are
ely to follow by telephone, at luncheon meetings, and in other ways.

lations with the Legislature. The various aspects of the relations of
nagement with the legislature have been discussed at appropriate
nts in the preceding chapters. Whether these relations are good or
l has definite and direct effects upon the public relations of the
ncy. An agency whose relations with the legislature are poor—
atever the reason—is likely to suffer through inadequate appropria-
s, in which case the staff may be overburdened and its morale de-
yed. Under such circumstances service to the public is likely to be
v or of poor quality or both. Severe cuts in appropriations may ne-
itate the discontinuance of services to which the public has become
stomed, thereby straining still further the public relations of the
ncy.

A situation of this character emphasizes the importance of manage-
t's utilization of every proper means of "keeping in right" with the
lature in general and with the appropriations committees in par-
ar. This can be done in several ways: by tactful but effective pres-
ion of the agency's needs at the hearings of the appropriations
nittees, by prompt and efficient handling of communications from
bers and of complaints from citizens, lest the latter lodge com-
ts with their representatives, and by developing such relations with
gency's clientele that its support will be available if and when
d.

Relations with Other Units of Government. The conditions of modern life in America — social, political, economic — have produced a new type of federalism, under which few if any programs can be administered at one level of government without regard for their impact upon the problems of other levels. This again may involve problems of coordination in the field of interlevel and interjurisdictional relations, but it involves problems in the field of public relations as well. Incompetent and ineffective administration at one level may serve to bring a whole program into question. Illustrations are not difficult to find. WPA suffered all too often, for instance, from partisan and incompetent administration at the local level. Many times a motorist, driving along comfortably over the fine pavement of a state highway, passes a marker noting the city limits, only to find himself bumping over a street on which maintenance work was discontinued during World War II and has never since been resumed.

Coordination between units at different levels of government is difficult to achieve, but probably no more so than coordination between different departments and agencies within the same level. At any rate it is essential not only to good administration but to the operation of federal system of government that such problems be satisfactorily solved.

Public Reporting

Public relations is a broad term encompassing the whole planned program designed to inform the public and enlist its support. Public reporting, which is one of the most important means of carrying out program, includes all the usual devices for informing the public garding the nature and scope of the program. The need for reporti essential at all levels, becomes more pressing in the larger units wh very remoteness from the citizen and whose complexity and size ren them less comprehensible to him. These over-all aspects will be c sidered here, the various media as they relate to the problems of particular departments and agencies in the section which follows.

Actually, there are two types of public reporting: reports design to inform the public on current operations, and reports of an histor nature. While this chapter is concerned primarily with the former t it may be well to note that the latter are often of very great valu students of administration; for example, the published series of rep on such war agencies as the Office of Price Administration, the Production Board, the Petroleum Administration for War, and ot For the preparation of reports of this character, dealing with a agency over a considerable period of time, the quantity of mater o great that the task of examining it, to say nothing of sifting it and organizing it, is monumental. Hoslett lists approximately a dozen different primary sources of information for making such studies.[4]

Mention has been made earlier of the need for clarity in expression, and the avoidance of the type of governmental jargon which Maury Maverick christened "gobbledygook." This admonition applies with particular force to report writing. The development of peculiarities of style and diction are a common failing of business and professional groups; one hears much of "journalese" and of the characteristic dryness and lack of imagination in scholarly monographs, but this is no excuse for the publication of reports that an interested citizen cannot read with either pleasure or profit. During World War II, as a phase of a management improvement program, the United States Civil Service Commission put on a campaign to improve the quality of the writing Federal departments and agencies, of material intended for intra-agency use as well as that designed for general distribution. Standard readability tests which enable an author to get some idea of the effectiveness of his work were devised and are now available for general use.[5]

Federal. Lowell Mellett emphasized in a very interesting manner the need for some central clearinghouse for information on all phases of government's work when he called attention to the tendency of many citizens to write about their problems directly to the chief executive — a procedure usually considered both naive and amusing.[6] "But such stories," he continues, "illustrate in a crude way a fundamental and a fundamental need in our governmental system."

Hoslett, Schuyler D., *Aspects of Army Depot Administration*, pp. 39–42 (American Historical Company, New York, 1945). These sources are: (1) Rules, regulations and instructions contained in printed or mimeographed bulletins, circulars, regulations, instructation letters, etc.; (2) General correspondence files; (3) Files peculiar to an individual office, e.g., "case" files in claims offices; (4) "Reading files" of important papers by individuals or offices for ready reference; (5) Formal historical records; Periodic historical reports; (7) Statistical and operational reports; (8) Personal or confidential files; (9) Report of long-distance telephone calls; (10) Reports of boards, committees, conferences, and meetings; and (11) Conversations with well-informed officials and employees.

Council of Personnel Administration, *How Does Your Writing Read?* (mimeographed, Washington, 1945), and some years later, Masterson, James R., and Phillips, Wendell B., *Federal Prose: How to Write in and/or for Washington* (University of North Carolina Press, 1948); also Maverick, Maury, "The Case Against 'Gobbledy-gook,'" *New York Times Magazine*, May 21, 1944, pp. 11, 35 ff., and Flesch, Rudolph, "A New Readability Yardstick," *Journal of Applied Psychology*, June, 1948, pp. 221–with bibliography, and "More About Gobbledygook," *Public Administration Review*, Summer, 1945, pp. 240–244.

Office of Government Reports," *Public Administration Review*, Winter, 1941, 126–131; see also Williams, Margaret H., "The President's Office of Government Reports," *Public Opinion Quarterly*, Winter, 1941, pp. 549–562.

The fact is that the American citizen wants to be able to deal with a singl responsible center in the Federal administration, a center that can be found on in the Office of the President, and the need for machinery through which th citizen can get information about all departments of the government is one th. has been proved abundantly during recent years.

The first attempt to meet this need dates back to the United Stat Information Service, which functioned under the National Emergenc Council in the early days of the Roosevelt administration. In the yea since, the office has been subject to numerous changes and reorganiz tions, but its basic purposes and functions have remained much the san During World War II, while this program was continued, the task informing citizens regarding questions related to the war effort w carried on by the OWI – Office of War Information.

The purposes and functions of the office were outlined in the orij nal Executive Order creating it, with three operating divisions, as f lows:

1. Division of Field Operations, with thirty-four state and regional offices wh serve as central contact points in the field for citizens and for representati of Federal, state, and local governments
2. Division of Press Intelligence, which maintains for distribution to governm officials the only permanent chronological press record on national affairs
3. United States Information Service, which provides in Washington and N York a central clearing house for inquiries concerning all branches of the ernment

For present purposes the last mentioned is the most important, p viding the public as it did, for the first time, with a central clear house for inquiries concerning all branches of the government, making available to the public, to the Congress, and to the execu departments factual information regarding government departme agencies, and functions. This agency, says Mr. Mellett, "assists the g ernment in serving the public by the direct routing of inquiries general public business. It provides for individuals and organizatio ready means of communicating with the proper Federal offices." service has been carried on for some years as a Division of the Bu of the Budget. Responsibility for publication of the *United States C ernment Manual* has recently been transferred to the National Arch The Foreword to the *Manual* states that "any agency of the ernment which receives inquiries not falling within its jurisdic whether received by mail, telephone, or in person, may refer questions to the Division of Public Inquiries, Government Inform Service, for reply or appropriate referral."

tate. Although state constitutions and laws quite regularly provide
1at executive departments and agencies must submit reports at speci-
ed intervals to the chief executive and/or the legislature,[7] practice
1ows the widest diversity in the degree of conformity with these re-
uirements. Some diversities are the result of provisions of the laws
1emselves; others arise from differing interpretations of the law or
om a complete disregard of what it prescribes. A report of a survey
ade by the Nebraska Legislative Council in 1946 summarized these
versities as follows: (1) Some agencies prepare a brief typewritten
port but do not publish any reports at all. (2) Some agencies publish
me reports but do not adequately comply with the law. (3) There
no uniformity in either the length of time (one year or a biennium)
in the calendar period covered by the reports. (4) "The reports rep-
ent virtually all degrees of adequacy and inadequacy. A few reports
re found which did not even indicate clearly the date of issuance or
 period covered. Some contained great masses of detailed statistical
ormation wholly unrelieved by analysis or explanation. Some others
1tained so little information as to give no clear indication of the
pe, purpose, or activities of the reporting agency."

The Nebraska report concludes that all major agencies should be
uired to submit periodic reports, printed or mimeographed in suffi-
1t quantity to be readily available to the public; that existing reports
examined with a view to eliminating overlapping, duplication, and
ecessary reports; that all reports should be for a uniform length of
 and for a uniform calendar period; and that each should be in-
native but brief, summarizing the duties, the organization, the per-
1el, and the expenditures of the agency, "as well as the activities of
 agency during the period covered by the report, and a summary of
ul information relating to the subject matter with which the
cy is concerned. Finally, it should contain any recommendations
administrative or statutory changes which the reporting agency
 care to present." While striving for comprehensive coverage, they
ld normally avoid lengthy essay material, discourses upon triviali-

---

these provisions, the one in the Nebraska Constitution is typical (Art IV, Sec.
The officers of the executive department and of all the public institutions of the
hall at least ten days preceding each regular session of the Legislature severally
 to the Governor, who shall transmit such reports to the Legislature, together
he reports of the judges of the Supreme Court, of defects in the Constitution and
nd the Governor or either house of the Legislature may at any time require in-
ion, in writing, under oath from the officers of the executive department, all
s, managers of state institutions, upon any subject relating to the condition, man-
nt and expenses of their respective offices." See the two reports of the Nebraska
tive Council on this general subject.

ties, self-praise, partisan observations, etc. In order to insure com
pliance with constitutional and statutory requirements, all report
should be made to the governor, and some one person or office shoul
be made responsible for seeing that reports are made in substantial com
pliance with the requirements.

None of the states has established an information center comparab
to the Federal setup described above, to provide information on a
over-all basis. A number of the states have, however, attempted
bring together in one publication the reports or summaries of the r
ports of the several executive departments and agencies. This has be
done in Illinois, Indiana, and Wisconsin on a biennial basis in the leg
lative manual; in Connecticut and a few other states a separate public
tion has been designed for this purpose.[8] Vermont used to bind all
departmental reports together in one huge volume.

Municipal. In the cities, over-all reporting has during the past deca
made important progress in some jurisdictions, none at all in others.
the more than three thousand municipalities in the United States, or
approximately one hundred, or about one thirty-third of the total (a
tenth of those with over five thousand population), are known to ha
put out an over-all report in 1947. An excellent summary of the sit
tion was prepared by Henry F. Goodnow, who found that most of
reports were published by manager cities.[9] In general, the cities t

---

[8] Unfortunately, there is no study of state government reporting, although cer
portions of the Wilcox volume are valuable. The author has published two article
the subject: "Public Reporting in the American States," *Public Opinion Quart*
April, 1938, pp. 211–228, and "State Government Reporting in Wartime," *State C
ernment*, July, 1943, pp. 159, 166–167. Listed below are a few outstanding report
sued in recent years:
Alabama: *A Report from the Governor to the People of Alabama* (October 1,
     through September 30, 1944)
Indiana: "Public Health Progress, 1946–1948," *Monthly Bulletin* of the Indiana
     Board of Health, October, 1948, entire issue
Kentucky: *Kentucky Government, 1939–1943* (Frankfort, 1943). *Your Kentucky*
     ernment, 1943–1947 (Frankfort, 1947)
Maine: Extension Service, *The Maine Extension Service Reports Progress* (O
     1945)
Pennsylvania: *A Record of Achievement, 1943–1945: A Report to the People* (H
     burg, 1946)
[9] See Goodnow, Henry F., "Trends in Reporting to the Public," *Public Manage*
May, 1948, pp. 126–129; for the best studies of municipal reporting, see Barton,
and Uhl, Raymond, *Local Government Reporting in Maryland* (Maryland State
ning Commission, Baltimore, 1947). For a complete listing of all regularly pub
municipal reports, see Clickner, Louise H., *Checklist of Basic Municipal Docu*
(Bureau of the Census, Division of Governments, 1948).
     Numerous guides have been published for the preparation of good municipal re
the best of these is by Ridley and Simon. Others are:
Bureau of Municipal Research, *A New Kind of City Report* (Philadelphia, 1948
Connecticut Public Expenditure Council, *Modernizing Municipal Reports* (Ha
     1945). [Footnote continued on opposite page]

published reports in 1947 were the same ones that have published them in the past, in most cases for many years. Fifty-eight cities indicated that they had been publishing annual reports for at least ten years. Eight published their first reports in ten years or more. Two thirds of the reports were printed.[10] Mr. Goodwin found that:

The typical report issued in 1947 had 10 percent fewer pages, cost 10 percent more, and came out seven weeks later than its predecessor. It measured 5 x 9 inches, contained 49 printed pages, and cost between $400 and $500. One copy was printed for every 16 citizens and it was distributed a little less than four months after the end of the period covered in the report. It was mailed to a special list of citizens and also made available on request at city hall. Portions of this typical report were summarized in the local papers.

Media in Public Relations

Government agencies have at their disposal practically all the media of publicity, except paid advertising, that are available to private organizations. Some agencies under certain circumstances use even that. The War Assets Administration, for instance, at the close of World War II used it extensively to publicize the merchandise it had for sale. States use it in connection with their campaigns to attract tourists and industrial establishments and in connection with highway safety campaigns. The various types of institutional publicity may be grouped under five major headings. These groupings are not, in every instance, mutually exclusive.

Publications. Use of publications, both governmental and non-governmental, varies according to the major purpose and needs of the agency. No administrative program can be effective unless the public, or that portion of the general public which is affected, is informed of its nature, scope, and purpose. If an agency does not or cannot produce published material, it is hiding its light under a bushel. People are not going to be able to avail themselves of its services because they do not know about them. Yet when an agency does provide such a program, it is immediately accused of propagandizing. The line of demarcation

---

and Sales Company, Inc., *Planning the Modern Municipal Report* (New York, 1948)
New Jersey Taxpayers Association, *Making Municipal Reports Readable* (Trenton, n.d.)
The following are examples of outstanding municipal reports:
Chicago: *Chicago's Report to the People* (1947)
Milwaukee: *Milwaukee Is Ready — Annual Report, 1944-1945*
Rochester: Board of Education, *Building Citizens for a Better City: Budget 1939*
of Mountain Brook, Alabama: *A Report to the Citizens* (October, 1944)
Report of the Village of Wilmette, Illinois, for the Fiscal Year Ending April 21, 1944
Wichita in 1948 put out its report in the form of a tabloid Sunday supplement in the local newspapers, thereby making the city government a topic of general conversation, and reaching a vastly larger audience than would otherwise have been possible.

is not easy to draw. Abuses are possible and have occurred, but a few
abuses should not be seized upon as justification for condemning a program which is basically both sound and necessary.

Among government publications one thinks first of reports, either
annual or biennial, depending upon the appropriations practices of the
jurisdiction. Such reports seek to present through text, pictures, and
statistical compilations a clear picture of the work accomplished by the
agency during the fiscal period covered. Special reports may be issued
on new or important projects, presenting the results of inquiry or investigation or on a daily, weekly, or monthly basis where more frequent and up-to-date information is necessary. The problems involved
in public reporting of a financial nature have been discussed in Chapter
22; of record keeping, in Chapter 25.

Other official publications include compilations of laws, rules and
regulations, or procedural requirements. Many departments, both Federal and state, find it advantageous to issue weekly or monthly bulletins
designed to accomplish the dual purpose of staff instruction and information of the agency's public. Weekly bulletins are especially common in state departments of agriculture and health, monthly bulletins
in departments of labor, public works, and welfare.[11] Leaflets in serial
form are often issued by departments of health, labor, and welfare in
connection with campaigns relating to specific matters such as tuberculosis or venereal disease control, traffic or industrial safety, or social
security.

Specialized agencies issue a wide variety of publications relating to
their particular fields of activity. Thus a library issues catalogues, indices, and bibliographies. Usually, although not always, such items
would be unprofitable for commercial publication, but they fill a very
definite need. Statutes are published by or for the legislative branch of
government, decisions for the courts, official opinions for the attorney
general. Maps may be issued by highway departments, park departments, state publicity agencies, or conservation agencies. Periodic check
lists of publications issued by all departments may be compiled at some
central point, as they are in Massachusetts, New York, and Pennsylvania; and weekly clipsheets of interesting or noteworthy items may
be supplied to the press, as in Illinois and Pennsylvania.

Not much need be said about nongovernmental publications. Newspapers and magazines publish stories and articles, sometimes developed
by their own initiative, sometimes inspired, and reprint or summarize

---

11 See the author's compilation on state departmental reporting in Wilcox, *Manual for
the Use of State Publications*, pp. 9–46; see also the Library of Congress *Monthly
Checklist of State Publications*, and Sullivan, Lawrence, "Government by Mimeograph,"
Atlantic Monthly, March, 1938, pp. 306–315.

portant speeches and reports. They frequently give space to material from clipsheets and press handouts. When opportunity is offered, they gladly publish paid advertising. Generally speaking, the press is very cooperative in giving space to information which governmental agencies desire to have publicized and which may be regarded as of some general interest, such as job opportunities in the civil service, legal notices, or changes in the laws or in the regulations affecting some particular matter.[12]

2. *Public Speeches.* Every important public official is called upon to make speeches; in fact, the number of requests often exceeds the time and energy he can allocate to this purpose. Addresses before conventions, clubs, church groups, and other ready-made audiences provide a convenient opportunity for personal contact with groups that are or should be interested in and informed about the agency's program. Needless to say, care must be exercised in making statements with regard to agency policy. An agency representative, however good he may be as a speaker, can do tremendous harm to his agency if he permits himself to make loose and irresponsible statements regarding policy.

The use of the radio has come to be an essential part of any public relations program. It provides facilities for spot announcements on important matters of general interest, for set speeches, debates, panel discussions, and interviews of agency representatives by news commentators. Most agencies are not in a position to purchase radio time, nor is necessary in most cases that they should be. Ordinarily the requirements of the agency may be met when its material is woven into news reports or utilized in the "public service" features for which all radio chains and stations allocate a certain portion of their time on the air.[13] New York City owns and operates its own radio station.

Visual Aids. Although in the past little attention was given to visual aids, they are recognized today as among the most important and most effective means of getting one's message across to the public. It may that scholars are accustomed to dealing with ideas, with abstractions, but visual aids are far more effective so far as the general public is con-

See Hazelrigg, Hal, "A Newspaper Man Looks at City Hall," *Public Management,* March, 1938, pp. 67–70; Trenholm, Lee, "Press Agents Irritate the Press," *Public Opinion Quarterly,* October, 1938, pp. 671–677; and Wooddy, Carroll H., "Press Relations City Management," *Public Management,* August, 1931, pp. 260–263.
See Tolleris, Bernice K., *Radio — How, When and Why to Use It* (National Public-Council, New York, 1947); Rowlands, David D., "Reporting Municipal Activities Radio," *Public Management,* April, 1941, pp. 102–109; and van Loon, Jan, "Radio Better City Government," *Public Opinion Quarterly,* January, 1938, pp. 100–104.

cerned. Included in this category are charts, graphs, cartoons and photographs,[14] motion pictures, slide series, and various other forms. While some of these devices can be used to brighten up regular reports, many of them may be used in exhibits or as an independent means of presentation.

Movies have been found particularly effective as a means of presentation in agriculture, conservation, education, health and safety programs, both highway and industrial. They may be used, either alone or to accompany speeches, with various types of ready-made audiences. Some agencies have developed extensive libraries of films and slide series, which are available on loan or at nominal cost to any organization desiring to use them.[15]

4. *Miscellaneous Media*. Exhibits rank high among the miscellaneous media, along with guided tours, demonstrations, and other devices that may be used to inform the public regarding an agency's program and services. Although some types of subject matter lend themselves more readily than others to this procedure, nearly all agencies can, with the exercise of a little ingenuity, avail themselves of its benefits. The exhibits at agricultural fairs and farm shows are familiar to all. Few persons who visited the World's Fair in New York City in 1938 and 1939 will forget the "cyclorama" illustrating the "highway of tomorrow." Exhibits normally require considerable space; their use is, therefore, limited largely to fairs, expositions, and large conventions. They are costly but effective.[16]

Tours may often be arranged so that visitors may see with their own eyes exactly what the agency has to offer. This device has been used with good effect by private industrial establishments for many years. Such government agencies as navy yards, arsenals, forts, and depots likewise find it effective (except in time of emergency), as do park services and other agencies whose activities can be better seen than described.

Demonstrations are often valuable. A striking illustration of what can be done with this device was shown in the late summer of 194 when the Soil Conservation Service of the United States Department

[14] See Taylor, James P., "Vermont's Highway Reports Have Gone Graphic," *Dir. Advertising*, April, 1945, pp. 11–13; and Unsigned, "Indiana Health in Graphs," *Month Bulletin* of the Indiana State Board of Health, July, 1946, pp. 148–150, 162.

[15] See Rowland, David D., "Use the Movies in Reporting to Citizens," *Public Manag ment*, March, 1941, pp. 67–71.

[16] See Bratten, Barbara L., "Exhibits as a Medium for Public Reporting and Positi Recruiting," *Public Personnel Review*, April, 1942, pp. 120–124; Hurton, Budd, "C fornia Division of Highways Exhibit at San Bernardino National Orange Show," *C fornia Highways and Public Works*, March–April, 1947, pp. 16–17; and Unsign "State Service Exposition Draws Huge Fair Crowds," *Illinois Public Works*, Win 1946, pp. 24–25.

Agriculture put five hundred men and a huge number of machines to work for a single day on a Maryland farm a few miles out of Washington, to show what modern methods could do in transforming a run-down farm owned by a widow with no resources of her own into an up-to-date model farm. Thousands of people came to witness this demonstration. Newsreel, radio, and press representatives were present — indicating, incidentally, how such a project may be fully utilized for publicity purposes.

5. *Cooperation with Established Organizations.* Established institutions and organizations frequently provide, through their meetings, conventions, and special assemblies, opportunities to cooperate in various ways, such as giving speeches, demonstrations, and exhibits. Schools are a particularly fruitful field for activity, since they provide not only an opportunity for the instruction of an on-coming generation but an indirect means of reaching the parents. This influence is especially strong among foreign populations who are anxious to learn American ways.

Informal Contacts in Public Relations

The formal aspects of a public relations program are handled through carefully planned use of the media just discussed. The success of such a program, however, is greatly influenced by the various types of contact — often entirely informal — between the agency staff and the public. The work contacts, including such matters as interviewing techniques, methods of handling telephone calls, submission of questionnaires and requests for information, composition and appearance of outgoing correspondence, have been discussed in earlier chapters. The adequacy of the record-keeping program of the agency also has a bearing on its public relations. Citizens get an unfavorable impression of an agency and are likely to become irritated when necessary records are found incorrect or cannot be located when needed.

Very often an agency can enlist public cooperation in finding out what people think of its methods of operation. Public agencies may, as hotels and other business establishments have long done, ask their clientele for criticisms or suggestions for the improvement of the service. As noted elsewhere, polling devices may be used to gauge public sentiment on policy matters, so that, within possible limitations, adjustments may be made in conformity to public opinion. Informational material may be supplied to individuals who request it and who thus become a medium for disseminating the agency's message to the public. Such requests are often received from members of discussion groups and study clubs.

The circulation of questionnaires to obtain information is useful and often necessary, but when abused, it may have a destructive effect on good public relations.[17] As a matter of fact, so many Federal agencies sent out questionnaires on so many subjects to so many individuals and firms that Congress in 1942 passed the Federal Reports Act, centralizing authority in the Director of the Budget to review requests from almost all executive agencies for information applying to ten or more concerns or individuals. The act required prior approval by the Director of the Budget before a form could be used, and it instructed him to determine whether or not the form was needed for the proper performance of the functions of the agency or for any other proper purpose. It also instructed the Director to make arrangements among Federal agencies to share information to the maximum extent consistent with the public welfare and, wherever practicable, to designate certain agencies to act for others in the collection of information. The Senate Committee on Small Business, which investigated the operation of the act, found it to be working well. It seemed to be effective in relieving business concerns of unnecessary reporting without at the same time preventing government departments and agencies from securing essential information.

Most important of all, perhaps, in such a program is for the administrator and the members of his staff to remember that they are dealing with human beings whose reactions to various modes of conduct are probably similar to their own. If they can visualize what their reaction would be if they were on the receiving end of their own programs they will spare themselves many a headache resulting from hostile criticism.

Citizen Participation in Public Administration

The proper role of citizens in public administration has long been subject of controversy. The traditional attitude has been to encourage the multiplication of all kinds of citizen boards, partly because of deep-seated distrust of executive power and a consequent unwillingne to concentrate authority in the hands of a single official. The result h been that there have been boards, boards, and more boards at all leve of government.

---

[17] The use of questionnaires for this and other purposes has been a subject of mu controversy; see publications of the Advisory Committee on Government Questio naires, including its periodic reports, and *Reducing Government Questionnaires* (Wa ington, 1944). See also *Issuance of Questionnaires by Governmental Agencies* (Hear on S. Con. Res. 38, before the Joint Committee on Reduction of Nonessential Fede Expenditures, December 1 and 3, 1942), and Senate Small Business Committee, Rep of the Bureau of the Budget, *Two Years of Progress Under the Federal Reports .* (79th Cong., 1st Sess., Senate Report No. 47, Part 2, 1945): and Stringham, Lutl "Government Questionnaires and the Federal Reports Act of 1942," *Public Adminis tion Review,* Spring, 1943, pp. 150–157.

Most familiar have been the school boards in every one of the more than 100,000 school districts in every state in the union. Almost equally familiar are the boards of trustees, directors, supervisors, and the like associated in most jurisdictions with all kinds of public (and private) institutions. The members are selected in various ways — election or appointment by the chief executive or, in some instances, on a self-perpetuating basis. In many cases the membership is composed in part of ex officio members. School administrators, librarians, social workers, public health people all freely express their opposition to administration by such boards; when restricted to an advisory function, they are less objectionable, but still they serve no particularly useful purpose in most instances.

The theory has been that a group of interested citizens are thus enlisted for the discharge of an important civic responsibility in guiding, directing, and exercising a general supervision over the conduct of some public institution or service. However useful this device may once have been, the emergence of a science of management has made these boards in most cases more of an obstacle than an aid to good administrative management. Most members of lay boards lack the background of experience and information that might enable them to make any useful contribution. Many more are not in the least interested in their assignment. Some are political hacks interested only in what they can get out of the job for themselves. The ex officio members are usually too busy with the duties pertaining to their regular assignments to permit them to attend board meetings in person or to make any real contribution on the few occasions when they are able to be present.

About a decade ago the author made an extensive study of the use of unpaid citizen boards in the governments of reorganized states. The investigation led to some quite definite conclusions with regard to their effectiveness at the state level.[18] The theory that the boards are to stand as a buffer between the institutions and the services of government on the one hand and a job-hungry political machine on the other simply does not bear analysis, for the usually political composition of the boards makes it all too obvious that boards so constituted cannot be effective in the accomplishment of this objective.

Nor does it seem more likely that the real purpose of these boards is to secure expert advice of people who would not accept full-time

---

[18] See "Citizen Participation in the Governments of Reorganized States," *Social Forces*, May, 1938, pp. 492–502; for a more friendly view of these boards, see Madeira, Margaret C., "Have Citizen Boards a Real Function Today?" *Public Welfare*, September, 1945, pp. 199–206. Probably the best state law on the subject is one found in New York in relation to visitors at mental hospitals, in *Mental Hygiene Law and Related Statutes*, Art. III, Sec. 30–32, pp. 29–32 (State Hospitals Press, Utica, 1945).

positions. While it is true that many persons of high competence are appointed, it is equally true that these same persons often complain bitterly that their advice on many matters of policy is consistently ignored. Not infrequently they resign in disgust. The idea of providing representation for different points of view in controversial matters is a politically expedient gesture rather than evidence of a desire to get a group together which can actually sit down and agree upon suitable solutions of the problems at hand.

The idea of geographical representation, quite generally employed, is likewise politically expedient. Many of those appointed to such boards know little or nothing of the problems of the department or the needs of the institution on whose board they serve, and hence are quite incapable of either interpreting the department or institution to the public or aiding in any important way in translating the desires of the public into the policy of the department or the institution. In many cases, the provincial attitude of the members of such boards is an actual hindrance to intelligent and effective administration.

The Federal government appears to have been considerably more successful in enlisting the services of citizens. During World War II, thousands gave freely of their time and effort as members of selective service boards, war price and rationing boards,[19] in civilian defense activities, canteen work, and many other ways. Many continue their service as board members in the administration of the nation's first peacetime draft, not to mention boards set up to supervise the administration of numerous programs in the Department of Agriculture and other agencies. The district boards in the soil conservation program constitute an excellent example.

SELECTED REFERENCES

Beyle, Herman C., *Governmental Reporting in Chicago* (University of Chicago Press 1928), and Barton, J. T., *Municipal Public Reporting in Texas* (University o. Texas Bulletin, 1936). Two excellent studies of municipal reporting.

Civil Service Assembly of the United States and Canada, *Public Relations in Publi. Personnel Agencies* (Chicago, 1941). Standard treatise on public relations for specialized type of staff agency.

Irion, Frederick S., *Press Law Handbook* (Division of Research, Department of Gov

[19] See Monsees; and Newman, William H., "Government-Industry Cooperation The Works," *Public Administration Review*, Summer 1946, pp. 240–248, as well as sever: items that have been published dealing with citizen service in OPA: Putnam, Im(gene H., *Volunteers in OPA* (OPA Historical Reports of War Administration, Was! ington, 1947); Aikin, Charles, "Volunteers in Retail Price Control – A Postscript *Public Administration Review*, Autumn, 1948, pp. 300–306; Bowles, Chester, "OP Volunteers: Big Democracy in Action," *ibid.*, Autumn, 1945, pp. 350–359; and Cam; bell, Persia, "Volunteers in Public Administration: A Case Study," *ibid.*, Spring, 194 pp. 108–112.

ernment, University of New Mexico, 1947). A brief treatise designed to give public officials basic information they need for dealing with the press.

McCamy, James L., *Government Publicity* (University of Chicago Press, 1939). Only available study of its practice in Federal departments and agencies.

Masterson, James R., and Phillips, Wendell R., *Federal Prose: How to Write in and/or for Washington* (University of North Carolina Press, 1948), and Council of Personnel Administration, *How Does Your Writing Read?* (Mimeographed, Washington, 1945). Two helpful titles for improving the readability of writing in the Federal service.

Monsees, Carl H., *Industry-Government Cooperation* (Public Affairs Press, Washington, 1944). A study of the participation of advisory committees in public administration.

Nebraska Legislative Council, *Report of Sub-Committee on Reports of State Departments* (Lincoln, 1946), and *State Publications in Nebraska* (Lincoln, 1940). Two reports prepared for the use of legislative committees, on public relations work in a specific state.

Ridley, Clarence E., and Simon, Herbert A., *Specifications for the Annual Municipal Report, Revised Edition* (International City Managers Association, Chicago, 1948). Best handbook for the guidance of municipal officers in the preparation of a good report.

Sanders, Alta G., and Anderson, Chester R., *Business Reports: Investigation and Presentation, Second Edition* (McGraw-Hill, New York, 1940). General treatise on reporting, intended for use by business executives but containing much information of use in any reporting program.

Schmeckebier, Laurence F., *Government Publications and Their Use* (Brookings Institution, Washington, 1936), and Tompkins, Dorothy C., *Materials for the Study of the Federal Government* (Public Administration Service, Chicago, 1948). Standard works on the use of government publications; the first discusses the various types, the second contains classified lists of all important types. See also: Merritt, Leroy C., *The United States Government as Publisher* (University of Chicago Press, 1948).

Wilcox, Jerome K., Ed., *Manual on the Use of State Publications* (American Library Association, Chicago, 1940). Excellent compilation of basic data on state documents. For subsequent information, see Library of Congress, *Monthly Checklist of State Publications*.